Manga's First Century

Manga's First Century

HOW CREATORS AND FANS MADE JAPANESE COMICS, 1905–1989

Andrea Horbinski

UNIVERSITY OF CALIFORNIA PRESS

University of California Press
Oakland, California

Library of Congress Cataloging-in-Publication Data

Names: Horbinski, Andrea, author
Title: Manga's first century : how creators and fans made Japanese comics, 1905–1989 / Andrea Horbinski.
Description: Oakland, California : University of California Press, [2025] | Includes bibliographical references and index.
Identifiers: LCCN 2025008162 | ISBN 9780520403987 cloth | ISBN 9780520403994 paperback | ISBN 9780520404007 ebook
Subjects: LCSH: Manga (Comic books)—20th century—History and criticism | Manga (Comic books)—Japan—History and criticism | Comic books, strips, etc.—Japan—History and criticism | LCGFT: Comics criticism
Classification: LCC PN8291 .H67 2025 | DDC 741.5/952—dc23/eng/20250611
LC record available at https://lccn.loc.gov/2025008162

Manufactured in the United States of America

GPSR Authorized Representative: Easy Access System Europe, Mustamäe tee 50, 10621 Tallinn, Estonia, gpsr.requests@easproject.com

34 33 32 31 30 29 28 27 26 25
10 9 8 7 6 5 4 3 2

publication supported by a grant from
The Community Foundation for Greater New Haven
as part of the *Urban Haven Project*

To Yonezawa Yoshihiro and Meikyū,
Who saw the wave of the future through a crack in the dam—
And grabbed a shovel
And for all of us nasty, rotten women,
Queer people of fandom worldwide—
We built this city.

CONTENTS

List of Illustrations ix
Acknowledgments xi
Note on Names, Styles, and Terms xv

Introduction 1

PART ONE
ORIGINS, 1905–1928

Overview: Manga Against Tradition 13

1 · The Origins of Japanese Comics 16

2 · Arresting the Fleeting Moment: Manga Turns Modern 33

Conclusion: 1928 53

PART TWO
MANGA DURING WARTIME, 1928–1945

Overview: Manga During Wartime 59

3 · Norakuro and Friends 64

4 · The Manga Men 93

Conclusion: Eating Vegetables, Rereading Manga 122

PART THREE
MANGA IN THE POSTWAR ERA, 1945–1963

Overview: Nowhere to Go but Up 127

5 · The Manga Pulps and the God of Manga 131

6 · Manga for Whom? Kashihonya, Gekiga, and the "Ban Bad Books Movement" 158

Conclusion: Postwar Platforms 180

PART FOUR
TV MANGA AND THE AGE OF REVOLUTION, 1963–1975

Overview: Shambling Toward the Postmodern 185

7 · Seeking Alternatives: *Garo*, *COM*, and Manga Fan Culture 190

8 · The Emergence of Seinen Manga and the Shōjo Revolution 218

Conclusion: Tankōbon: The Meaning of a Format 247

PART FIVE
MANGA TURNS POSTMODERN, 1975–1989

Overview: Applauding the DJ 253

9 · Something Postmodern Going On 258

10 · Lost in Wonderland 280

Conclusion: Still Preoccupied with 1989 303

Conclusion: A Distinctive History 307
Note on Sources 317
Glossary 319
Notes 323
Bibliography 373
Index 395

ILLUSTRATIONS

FIGURES

1. Cover of *The Japan Punch* (1865) *18*
2. Cartoon by Honda Kinkichirō from *Marumaru Chinbun* (1880) *21*
3. Manga by Imaizumi Ippyō from *Jiji Shinpō* (1899) *23*
4. Manga manbun by Okamoto Ippei (1916) *34*
5. Norakuro and his fellow recruits in *Norakuro nitōhei* (1933) *75*
6. The Norakuro Harmonica Band (1943) *77*
7. Page from *Shōnen shukō book* (1937) *79*
8. Issues of *Yōnen Kurabu* (1933, 1941, 1944) *91*
9. Eroguro-style manga by Yanase Masamu (1924) *102*
10. Proletarian manga by Yanase Masamu (1928) *105*
11. Cover of *Manga Nihon* by Katō Etsurō (1944) *120*
12. Opening sequence of *Shintakarajima* (1947) *131*
13. Children watching a kamishibai performance (ca. 1948) *138*
14. Cover of *Manga* (1948) *140*
15. Readers in a kashihonya (1948) *159*
16. Cover of *Garo* no. 1 with art by Shirato Sanpei (1964) *197*
17. Cover of *Big Comic* no. 1 (1968) *219*
18. The kiss scene from "In the Sunroom" (1970) *240*
19. Opening pages of *Kaze to ki no uta* (1976) *265*
20. Cover of *Manga Burikko* (1983) *292*

PLATES

Following page 182

1. Cartoon by Kitazawa Rakuten from *Box of Curios* (1896)
2. Cover of *Tokyo Puck*'s first issue (1905)
3. "Desertion of National Army" centerfold in *Tokyo Puck* (1908)
4. Cover of *Jiji Manga* depicting a Modern Girl (1925)
5. Cover of *Jiji Manga* by Ogawa Jihei (1922)
6. Pages from *Shō-chan no bōken*, vol. 2 (1924)
7. Cover of an akahon manga, *Kawaii Betty-san* (1934)
8. *Kanemochi kyōiku* by Yanase Masamu (1930)
9. Cover of *The Manga Man* (1930)
10. Interior pages from *Kaijin skeleton hakushi* (1948)
11. Splash page for *The Rose of Versailles* episode 56 (1973)

ACKNOWLEDGMENTS

This project began in the spring of 2011 as a twinkle in my advisor Andrew Barshay's eye. I was seeking advice on applying for summer funding to study classical Japanese in Kyoto. His response was that it was easier to get funding if one had chosen a dissertation topic: "We still don't have a good history of manga," he told me. "You would be good at that." I had attempted to deny or minimize my interest in popular culture in my graduate school applications (I wasn't lying when I said that I was deeply interested in empire), but a semester and a half of my mentioning scholarship on anime and new media in seminars was more than enough to destroy that pretense. After about five seconds' thought I decided that Barshay was right, and fourteen years later, here we are. I can only hope it was worth the wait.

None of this would have been possible without the efforts of the following people, whom it is a pleasure to thank. Mary Elizabeth Berry has been a bulwark of support and inspiration since I started at Berkeley, particularly since I began writing my dissertation, and she was especially instrumental in pushing me over the finish line during the interminable book proposal stage. Without her fierce conviction, proxy library card, and generous wisdom, I would probably still be wandering in the wilderness and this book would not exist. Her approval remains my great honor. Andrew Barshay took a chance on a prospective graduate student with a suspiciously eclectic background, and staunchly supported my unusual choices. I'm also grateful to the faculty and staff of the Berkeley History Department, especially Mabel Lee.

Also at Berkeley, Abigail De Kosnik gave me a job, a designated emphasis, and a home away from home in the Berkeley Center for New Media. My time on her Fanfiction and Internet Memory research team is one of my treasured Berkeley experiences, and Gail's support and mentorship have been invaluable then and since. The BCNM's financial and material support (I still miss my cubicle) was key to the completion of my studies, and their continued support since has been heartwarming.

Thanks are also due to those who provided assistance in the manuscript phase. Frenchy Lunning has believed in this project since I first mentioned it to her, and in me since we first met twenty years ago, and she has frequently provided another home away from home in Minnesota. Sarah Gold McBride, Bathsheba Demuth, and Marie Brennan generously shared proposal drafts, publishing perspectives, and contracts, respectively. James Welker offered support at many key points. I have presented portions of chapters at lectures, conferences, conventions, and seminars in Asia, North America, and Belgium, and I am grateful for the opportunities to sharpen my findings and conclusions, particularly at the Mechademia conferences, and especially to those who invited me to give talks at their institutions. Patrick W. Galbraith and Ryan Holmberg generously helped with images. Many friends have also been unstintingly supportive, especially Gillian Chisom, Jen and Dan, and the members of my biweekly Zoom craft circle.

The research for this project was supported by a number of funders, principally at the University of California, Berkeley. The History Department, the Center for Japanese Studies, the Center for New Media, the Institute for East Asian Studies, the Graduate Division, and the Visiting Scholar and Postdoc Affairs unit all supported my research directly and indirectly. Andrew Barshay, Mary Elizabeth Berry, and Abigail De Kosnik also provided financial or in-kind support from their own research funding, for which I am extremely grateful. Some research was undertaken during the 2014 Kadokawa/University of Tokyo Summer Program on the Media Mix, and I am grateful for the financial support of the Kadokawa Foundation, which made the program and my participation in it possible. Marc Steinberg served as the program coordinator, and I have appreciated his encouragement in the intervening years. The Summer Program also introduced me to Professor Yoshimi Shun'ya of the University of Tokyo, whose generous invitation allowed me to spend my research year at Tōdai. Fabrice Preyat at the Université libre de Bruxelles offered me a research affiliation and was a supportive interlocutor during my trips to Belgium. Nele Noppe hosted me for my longest Belgium sojourn and was a generative collaborator at cons and conferences on multiple continents, while Emily Chapman's coffee shop conversation enlivened many days in the Diet Library and my brief stay with her in London.

Although I visited many libraries and archives around the world in the service of this project, first mention must go to Watanabe Tomoko and the staff of the research room at the Kyoto International Manga Museum, who have been unstintingly helpful since I first stepped through their doors in 2008 on a Fulbright Fellowship. No manga, no life. I am also grateful for the continued assistance of Toshie Marra, the Japanese subject librarian at Berkeley.

If there is one thing I have learned in taking this project from dissertation to publication, it is that no one does it alone and no author is an island. I am deeply grateful for the assistance of my editor Enrique Ochoa-Kaup, production editor Jessica Moll, and everyone at the University of California Press who have brought my manuscript to print. My sincere gratitude also goes to the three peer reviewers who took time out of their schedules to read my massive manuscript and offer their feedback. The crisis of taking on too much work is real, and I very much appreciate them stepping up.

Reaching back to my undergraduate days, while many beloved faculty at St. Olaf College had a hand in setting me on this path, I would like to specially thank the late and much-missed Robert Entenmann (1949–2024). Bob graded the only paper I wrote on Japanese history in college (evaluating the historicity of the anime *Samurai Champloo* [2004]), and remained deeply encouraging and interested as I pursued first my PhD and this book. I only wish he had lived to see its publication.

It seems traditional to thank one's family last, but in my case they are the opposite of least. My brother Wade has been my friend and my best partner in crime since we discovered our shared interests in anime, sff, video games, and music when we were children, and I am extremely proud to be one of the two Drs. Horbinski, just like we always said we would be. Wade also schlepped to the Portland State University Library in my stead. My father Paul bought me the collected *Star Wars* novelizations in B. Dalton Bookseller when I was seven years old, setting me on the path to writing this book. Both of them have been endlessly supportive through grad school and beyond, and my father still refuses repayment for the fellowship's worth of financial backing that he provided over several junctures when my formal funding was insufficient. They have also entrusted me with our family parrot, Joey Bag of Donuts, who remains my favorite dinosaur. I am also grateful for the support of my stepmother Mary Jo Butera, not least of which is letting me crash in the basement as necessary.

The final word in these acknowledgments goes to dozens if not hundreds of people whom I cannot possibly remember, let alone name—but you know who you are. Since I first set out on this project in 2011, I have been fortunate enough to hear repeatedly from people I talked to about it that "I'd read that book." To everyone who ever expressed such sentiments to me: I really did and do appreciate it. Now, at long last, here's your chance.

LLAP.

Berkeley, California
June 2025

P.S. Em dashes notwithstanding, no generative "AI" was used in the creation of this book.

NOTE ON NAMES, STYLES, AND TERMS

In this book I use a version of the *Mechademia* style guide, originally developed by Christopher Bolton and further refined by Frenchy Lunning, Sandra Annett, and myself. The major break with *Mechademia* style is my rendering English loanwords as English rather than as transliterated Japanese, with the caveat that Japanese English usage is not always the same as other Englishes. Japanese names appear in this book in Japanese order (i.e., family name followed by given name) unless the person in question has published using Western name order, except for the few figures in manga who are referred to by personal names in accordance with artistic practice. Japanese words are italicized only within titles and when discussed as words. I have retained long vowel markers in Japanese words generally; although loanwords such as *shōnen* and *shōjo* have become current in English without the long vowels, I have retained them here for consistency's sake. Periodicals are usually referred to by cover publication dates, although publishing practices often meant that individual issues went on sale up to a month earlier.

Some scholars hold that using Japanese words in an English text is needlessly obfuscatory, if not exoticizing, but I personally take a different view. Words such as *otaku, shōnen,* and *shōjo* have become sufficiently familiar to people interested in manga and anime that translating them into English would be confusing. Moreover, some direct English translations can be misleading. Saying "manga artist" for "mangaka" is literally correct, for example, but is misleading in the general comics context, as artists and writers are almost always two separate people in mainstream American comics, and this is one of manga's distinguishing characteristics as a comics tradition; Franco-Belgian comics are mixed, as are so-called "indie" American comics. Hence, I tend to use *mangaka, manga creators,* or *cartoonists* interchangeably, but in all cases my usage is specific.

Likewise, my use of terms such as *shōjo manga, seinen manga*, and *shōnen manga* reflects how people discuss them in English; translating *seinen manga* as *adult manga*, for example, would be unclear because *adult* has multiple meanings that could apply in this context. Using Japanese labels for manga categories is meant to short-circuit potential confusions and to restore some much-needed precision.

Similarly, I have adopted Japanese fan scene language in many cases. I frequently use *dōjinshi* to refer to nonprofessionally published comics, and sometimes the English terms *zine* and *fanzine*, which are useful synonyms in some manga contexts. I sometimes use *fanworks* as a synonym for *dōjin works* or *dōjin goods*, though not when said works are original (sōsaku) works unrelated to professionally produced media. *Otaku* and *fujoshi* are rendered as-is into English, because they are (or were) specific terms denoting specific groups of fans and fan practices. Although specific stigmas are still attached to these terms in some contexts, *fanboy* and *fangirl* are not any better and may again have misleading connotations.

All of which is to say that some jargon seemed unavoidable, drawing as this book does on all aspects of the manga sphere, not just the professional manga industry, as well as English-language fan cultures. I have done my best to define terms in the text and have included a glossary, but the blame for any remaining unclear points rests with me.

Introduction

SOMETIME IN THE EARLY 1960S, somewhere in provincial Japan—let's say Kumamoto, a city on the west coast of Kyushu, the southernmost of Japan's four main islands—a child is pelting from his school through the back alleys to the local kashihonya (rental bookstore). It is publication day for one of the leading monthly manga magazines, and the kids who get to the store early have their pick of the twelve or so freebies (furoku) included with each issue of the magazine. Luck is with the child this month, and he arrives to the store first. Like most kashihonya, this one is run as a sideline out of another store, most often a stationery store or a candy shop, and its sole staff person is an old lady who sells the freebies for five or ten yen each. The child pays the fees to purchase one of the paperboard tchotchkes and to rent the thick magazine and walks out sublimely happy. Manga is banned in schools, but everyone reads it, including this elementary schooler and his friends.[1] Yonezawa Yoshihiro does not know it yet, but his generation will witness, and he and his friends will help to set off, a profound transformation in Japanese comics, laying the groundwork for manga to become perhaps the best-known and most popular form of comics worldwide in the twenty-first century.

In Tokyo—let's say it's 1963, the year before the high-speed shinkansen train's debut and Japan's triumphant return to the world stage with the 1964 Tokyo Olympics—another fan is working feverishly alongside a studio of animators to transform his best-selling manga *Tetsuwan Atomu* (*Astro Boy*, 1952–68) into "manga in motion," the first television anime series. Tezuka Osamu's first love was animation, but he was unable to enter the industry due to Occupation-era controls after the war. Instead, he turned his college side job drawing manga for akahon (red book) manga publishers into a full-time career, forsaking the medical degree that he obtained in 1951. In the mid-1980s, a "who's who" guide to Japan still identified him as an internist despite the fact that he never practiced medicine, perhaps a sign of lingering distrust of manga on the establishment's part. Over his career, the man who became known as the "God of Manga" did much to eliminate that distrust, but Tezuka and his contemporaries did not invent manga, even if they helped to reinvent it.

Tokyo, 1934. A girl from Saga prefecture has moved to the capital with her sisters and mother after her father's death. Like most children of the era, she is a huge fan of children's (kodomo) manga, which is published in newspapers and in magazines aimed at children, especially the supremely popular *Shōnen Kurabu* (Boys' club, 1914–62). Despite the title, it is read by children of all genders, whether passed around or read aloud at school, or purchased second-hand from used bookstores. While children's manga as a whole has witnessed a huge boom in this decade, despite the disapproval of conservative bureaucrats, politicians, and military oligarchs, the most popular mangaka is undoubtedly Tagawa Suihō, creator of the hit children's manga *Norakuro* (1931–41). When the girl's mother hears of her secret dream to study with Tagawa and become a mangaka herself, she and the girl's older sister exert themselves so that Machiko can ask Tagawa to be his student directly. Tagawa accepts. Hasegawa Machiko made her manga debut in 1935 at the age of fifteen and went on to publish her long-running four-panel manga *Sazae-san* (1946–74) in the *Asahi* newspaper for decades. The anime based on the manga is the longest-running animated TV show on the planet, and the show's Sunday evening broadcast slot has become a symbol for the weekend's end in Japan.

Yokohama, 1899. Kitazawa Rakuten begins working for the *Jiji Shinpō* newspaper, having cut his teeth as a cartoonist at the English-language *Box of Curios* after the departure of his Australian mentor Frank Arthur Nankivell for America and the globally popular magazine *Puck*. At *Jiji Shinpō*, Rakuten adopts the in-house terminology of "manga" for political cartoons, following the example of the newspaper's staff cartoonist, Imaizumi Ippyō. Six years later, Rakuten will launch Japan's first manga magazine, *Tokyo Puck*.

Today, it's a short train ride from Yokohama to Tokyo, but it's a long journey from nineteenth-century newspapers and illustrated journals to the manga that fills bookstores and digital devices worldwide in the present era. This book traces *manga*'s emergence in the late nineteenth century as a term for high-class political cartoons to the medium's current status as global pop culture juggernaut, asking two questions: How has manga evolved over time? And what makes pop culture popular?

How manga has evolved over time forms the meat of this book. For those familiar with existing discourse on manga, "1905–1989" may seem a surprising period to consider. Many popular articles and some scholarly sources insist that there must be a connection between manga and the vibrant print culture of Japan's early modern or Edo period (1600–1867), in which a growing commercial economy engendered surprisingly high rates of literacy for a nonindustrial society. (A small but dedicated minority insist the connection goes back even further, to the illustrated scrolls of the classical Heian period a thousand years ago.) Popular art and printed media flourished in the Edo period, and woodblock prints (ukiyo-e) or the graphic narratives called *kibyōshi* seem particularly likely to be a direct progenitor of manga.[2] After all, they are visual media, created in Japan.

Media theorist Marc Steinberg has dubbed the search for, and the certainty of, this connection "the return to Edo," but it is not borne out by the historical record.[3] There *is* a connection between Edo-period popular print media and manga, but it is not direct, and it is mediated across the divide of the so-called Meiji Restoration, in which a motley alliance of dissatisfied lower-ranking samurai overthrew the tottering Tokugawa shogunate in the name of restoring direct imperial rule. The stage was set for Japan to chart a new, modernizing course as a society and as a nation-state: The new oligarchy renamed Edo to Tokyo in 1868, with the young Meiji emperor permanently moving from Kyoto in 1869, and the Meiji government began instituting a Western-style program of economic and political modernization, including industrialization.

Creating and fueling an industrial economy required creating a mass society, with universal and compulsory basic education of Japanese subjects as the foundation of both economic activity and leisure consumption of printed media. Western-style periodicals in Japan launched even before the Meiji Restoration, but gained a strong foothold in the 1880s with the advent of nationally circulating newspapers. Topical cartoons in this era were pitched to be understood by readers of varying literacy levels, and they incorporated Edo-period visual techniques derived from ukiyo-e to skate past government censorship, a type of image that came to be known as ponchi or ponchi-e. After returning from five years in the United States, artist Imaizumi Ippyō adopted the Edo-period term *manga*, literally "overflowing images," to differentiate his "high-class" political cartoons from the more lowbrow ponchi-e in other newspapers.

Manga thus has had a long home with newspapers, and some of its most illustrious practitioners have been newspaper mangaka. But this book begins not in 1891 with *Jiji Shinpō* but in 1905 with *Tokyo Puck*, the first independent periodical dedicated solely to manga. Under the pen of its founder Kitazawa Rakuten, *Tokyo Puck* was a runaway success, making Rakuten Japan's first professional cartoonist. Rakuten paved the way for other pioneering mangaka such as Okamoto Ippei, whose own newspaper cartoons satirizing social mores became known as "manga manbun," expanding "manga" beyond the strict definition of "political cartoons" that Rakuten favored and eventually making "manga" the default term for comics in Japanese. 1905 it is.[4]

Ippyō and Rakuten, who succeeded him at *Jiji Shinpō*, revived the term *manga* to differentiate their work from the Edo legacy in visual media. For them, manga was not in continuity with older, premodern art forms, but was rather a new, modern form of dissent that arose from their exposure to Euro-American cartoons and cartoonists. Like other innovative and influential manga creators after them, they wanted to expand the range of artistic expression and content in comics. Manga thus began as an upstart, semi-foreign genre category; but as Rakuten and those mangaka who came after him, starting with Ippei at the *Asahi Shinbun*, became increasingly popular, manga became an established medium in its own right, one that these men used to question and mold social mores in an age of rapid social changes. Rakuten, Ippei, and their students became the medium's patriarchs, and by the mid-1920s, a new crew of young upstarts, once again marinated in the latest global artistic and political developments, challenged the conservative consensus in manga, introducing new forms of artistic expression into the medium along with their radical leftist politics and expanding manga's reach to new, previously unconsidered audiences.

This pattern has repeated itself throughout manga's history: Even as established figures have promoted mainstream social values among readers in manga, groups of marginalized or neglected creators and fans have consistently challenged the prevailing artistic and social consensus in the medium, seeking to reach new audiences through new types of stories, innovations in artistic techniques, and changes in publishing formats. By the 1970s, this pattern expanded the reach of manga beyond the official publishing industry, as college-age manga fans cast off their previous hierarchical relationship with professional creators and inaugurated a new age of horizontal communication among fans through dōjinshi (amateur publications), initially consisting of zines, comics, and fan films. Today, publishers and professional creators alike have a symbiotic relationship with the new trends and creators that bubble up through the dōjinshi scene, which provides much of manga's continuing vitality.

1989 may need less explanation, or not. In January the Shōwa emperor Hirohito, who had ruled Japan as regent for his father and then in his own right since 1921, finally died after a lingering illness. His son Akihito assumed the throne as the Heisei emperor, although he was not formally enthroned until November 1990, by which time the high-flying Bubble economy of the 1980s, which saw Japanese real estate and stock prices rapidly balloon in value, was beginning to burst. The Heisei period (1989–2019) became known as an era of economic stagnation and declining population growth, often called the Lost Decades, and it wrought many changes in manga and in other spheres.

The manga world suffered a severe blow with the death of Tezuka Osamu in February 1989 from stomach cancer. At just sixty years old, the God of Manga was cruelly young, with many works presumably still left in him (his last words in the hospital were reportedly demanding the return of his drawing materials). Though Tezuka's later manga had never quite regained the heights of his popularity in the 1950s and 1960s, the impact on the public and on other manga and anime creators was profound. Then, in December 1989, Tagawa Suihō, one of prewar manga's most important creators, died peacefully at the age of ninety. Tagawa and his runaway hit manga *Norakuro* established many of the manga innovations in both form and format that Tezuka and his contemporaries further innovated on; without Norakuro, there could be no Mighty Atom. For all these reasons and more (the fall of the Berlin Wall, for starters), 1989 seemed a logical end point.

My purpose in writing this book has been to tell a single, reasonably coherent story about manga, from its origins to the cusp of its present popularity. Inevitably, some forms of manga have gotten shorter shrift in my narrative than others: Ultimately, this book is *a* history of manga rather than *the* history of manga. But my goal has been to encompass as much of the story of manga as I possibly could, and along the way, I have found myself returning to several related themes.

First and foremost, the tension between established creators and publishing practices on the one hand and upstarts working on the margins seeking to revolutionize the medium's content and audiences on the other has reemerged repeatedly throughout manga's history. Notable (often young) renegades included Ippyō and Rakuten, Tagawa Suihō, proletarian mangaka, and the Shinmangaha group in the 1930s, Tezuka in the 1940s and 1950s, the gekiga boys in the 1950s, and the shōjo revolution creators and dōjinshi fandom pioneers in the 1970s. Establishment figures included Rakuten and Ippei, former members of the Shinmangaha group in the 1940s, Tezuka in the 1950s and 1960s, and gekiga creators in the 1960s and 1970s. Many creators played dual roles as their innovations were absorbed into mainstream publishing and they became the orthodoxy against which newer creators and fans rebelled in turn. Crucially, innovation has tended to drive manga's expansion as a medium, whether artistically or in terms of audience reach, resulting in the situation today in which manga comprises roughly 40 percent of the Japanese publishing market. In turn, manga's capacious grasp, encompassing a huge range of possible audiences, is what has powered its popularity around the world as particular tranches are exported in translation. Manga's key strength as a medium has been its flexibility, as it has evolved over the past century from high-collar political satire to long-form fictional storytelling in weekly anthology magazines, cheap collected volumes, and beyond.

I have repeatedly emphasized the role of audiences and fans in manga's development and burgeoning popularity. Manga's readership has been passionate from the very start, and it has inspired devotees to pursue careers in it from a very young age, as in the case of Hasegawa Machiko. Few books in either English or Japanese have attempted to encompass as much of manga's history as this one, and those that have looked at much shorter slices of manga's history have usually focused on manga as an industry. But regarding manga solely from the perspective of publishers and professional creators means that a huge portion of the manga field is completely absent from the narrative. Tracing the voices and activities of fans and aspiring or nonprofessional creators is more challenging, but it is possible, and vital to understanding how manga came to be what it is today.

Reader letters, roundtable discussions, zines, memoirs—all of these and more have helped me fill in manga fans' perspectives through the decades, presenting a much more complete picture of manga's development and reaching a zenith in the 1970s, when a group of manga fans inaugurated the Comic Market for selling dōjinshi (amateur manga). Now the world's largest fan event, Comiket has fueled an alternative dōjin (amateur) ecosystem that drives innovation across the contents industry (manga, anime, and video games), and established and new creators now move between mainstream publishing and dōjin activities with relative ease. In its open embrace of dōjinshi, despite copyright laws which do not allow for fair use or transformative works (unlike copyright laws in the United States), the manga publishing industry has managed to both maintain its own centrality in the contents industry and forge a mutually respectful relationship with a dynamic space in which the next big thing may bubble up to the surface at any time. Manga's story since 1975 cannot be accurately told without discussing the dōjin sphere that now constitutes a hugely generative site for manga fans and creators of all kinds, and this book gives these developments and the fans who spearheaded them, including Yonezawa Yoshihiro, their due.

I have also emphasized the importance of format, and by extension of format as a platform, throughout manga's development. There are many studies of manga and works of manga theory that examine the unique qualities of its visual expression in great detail, but I am not a visual artist or an art historian, and my concern with format is pragmatic: Specifics of physical (and, these days, digital) media have had as much of an effect on manga's popularity as its content, but most studies of manga pay much more attention to content than to format. In part this focus seems to arise from an axiomatic understanding that popular culture is popular because it offers popular content. To be sure, content is key, and manga's expansion over the decades has been driven in no small part by the broadening of its audiences, appealing to and drawing out interests that were not yet fully appreciated by the publishing industry with new innovations in content, usually driven by young creators who grew up as manga fans. But format is equally key, and the best manga in the world will struggle if it is not available in a format that meets readers where they are.

The other side of this finding is that manga's format is not necessarily what makes manga manga. Even in the preceding discussion, manga has oscillated between newspapers, magazines, four-panel comics, serialized multi-chapter stories, dōjinshi, and ebooks. While manga has been deeply influenced by format, format is not the be-all and end-all of manga as a medium: Manga's visual style can and has changed to suit its formats, with new formats such as webtoons creating new visual styles in recent years even as the magazine format has seen a gradual decrease in popularity.[5] In other words, manga as a medium transcends formats and platforms, but formats and platforms are always the mediator through which readers consume manga, and they influence manga expression in turn. Formats and platforms are the domain of publishers, who perform a gatekeeping function even as they seek to expand manga audiences. The interplay between publishers' inherently conservative, but also acquisitive, profit motive and the desires of fans and creators to expand manga content and expression to new areas and audiences forms a great deal of the subject of this book.

Finally, although the story of manga that I tell here is largely centered on Japan, I have acknowledged the transnational connections that have contributed to manga's development. Manga is obviously a Japanese medium, and it would be silly to deny that its Japaneseness is part of its draw for some audiences outside Japan. But manga's history has not happened in a global void. Why did Ippyō feel the need to resurrect the early modern term *manga* to differentiate his cartoons from other cartoons? Because for him, the then common term *ponchi-e* (*Punch* drawings), derived from the *Japan Punch* periodical published in Yokohama by English cartoonist Charles Wirgman, was too lowbrow. The very fact that cartoons were known in Japanese as "*Punch* drawings" reveals where they came from, and mangaka from Ippyō and Rakuten on down have been keenly aware of developments in art, cartoons, and animation worldwide. But this is not a one-sided process of influence or export; as art historian Chinghsin Wu has noted of modern art movements in Japan generally, these "only became relevant and meaningful . . . if they could be made to serve some significant function within Japanese culture or somehow responded to contemporary issues in Japan."[6] Manga proved popular in Japan because it served the needs of manga creators and audiences. Having taken what was relevant to them from Euro-American comics and media at multiple points, mangaka over the decades evolved manga in their own local, Japanese context, ultimately creating a media ecosystem with global appeal.

Far from making manga suspect or non-Japanese in some way, this process of appropriation and transformation is a normal aspect of the creative process, and attempts to claim that manga is uniquely Japanese despite—or non-Japanese because of—its foreign antecedents are wrongheaded. If my discussing these antecedents comes as a surprise to readers, that is a sign that manga and anime boosters have promulgated a slanted narrative of their uniqueness, not that this narrative is accurate. As manga scholar Jaqueline Berndt summarizes, "manga and anime intertwine Japanese particularities with transnational traits."[7]

On the flip side of manga's transnational characteristics, I occasionally discuss the two other great comics traditions, American comics and Franco-Belgian *bandes dessinées*, or BD, to offer a dash of comparative perspective. In many ways, all three traced similar paths of development through roughly the end of World War II; nor should this be surprising, as Japan, the United States, and European countries were and are all modern nations participating in the modern industrial order, subject to the same global systemic forces and disasters. In the postwar era, however, these three cousins' destinies have diverged, and the differences offer an illuminating look at how and why manga has in recent decades ascended to the kind of prominence, both domestically and globally, that comics and BD can only dream of.

Whole books could be written about manga's fortunes in the Heisei and now Reiwa (2019–) eras. Suffice it to say, for now, that the transformations in manga that granted it much more cultural prominence in Japan than that enjoyed by comics and BD were also what enabled manga to become globally popular in the 1990s and the early years of the twenty-first century (although, in a reversal of the historical relationship between them in Japan, anime usually arrived in numbers outside Japan first).[8] Manga has remained extremely popular in this century even as domestic magazine sales in Japan have slipped, manga books and magazines have become increasingly digital, and online media have become new competitors for readers' attention. Whatever lies in store for manga in coming decades, these factors, which took it from quirky subgenre of painting in the early 1900s to global publishing juggernaut in the 2020s, remain its greatest strength, and perhaps the key to its future as well.

PART ONE

Origins

1905–1928

Overview

MANGA AGAINST TRADITION

THE QUESTION OF ORIGINS is tricky. The notion that everything changes over time is a cardinal tenet of history, and its observational corollary is that there is very little new under the sun. In the case of manga, the question of origins is partly a question of terminology, but it is also a question of politics, and the question itself has a history that is separate from that of manga as a medium.

Any introduction to manga will tell you that manga are Japanese comics. Many texts also state that the word *manga* was first used in the Edo period (1600–1867) by the ukiyo-e (woodblock print) artist Hokusai to describe his "overflowing pictures." Those two facts may be the only things that just about everyone interested in the history of manga can agree on, and the second isn't even true: As scholars such as Shimizu Isao and Adam L. Kern have noted, *manga* (written *mangwa* in classical orthography) was in use a few decades before Hokusai's popular *Hokusai manga* series began publication in 1814. Why Hokusai chose the term remains unclear, but as Kern concludes, by that point in the early modern period *manga* referred "to a doodle or caricature of some sort, but this it did alongside several terms, enjoying no privileged position."[1]

Although comics are not an ancient art form, significant strands of scholarship and popular discourse insist that manga's roots lie in the picture scrolls of classical Japan, or that a direct line of descent can be drawn from Hokusai's ukiyo-e prints to the volumes of *Fullmetal Alchemist* on my bookshelf.[2] Media theorist Marc Steinberg summarized these arguments as a kind of "return to Edo": because Japan's popular culture in the early modern period featured printed media that seem similar to manga, the media of Japanese popular culture in the modern period must have some kind of meaningful link to those precursors.[3] But the notion of a direct inheritance from ukiyo-e and other popular Edo prints to manga is overblown. The first practitioners of "manga" as a separate category of art in the 1890s, in the middle of the Meiji period (1868–1912), wanted to distance themselves from humorous cartoons that preserved the Edo legacy in print media, called ponchi-e or ponchi, which they viewed as crude and lowbrow.

Rather, the pioneers of manga—Imaizumi Ippyō (1865–1904) and his successor Kitazawa Rakuten (1876–1955)—saw manga as a revolt against that legacy, eschewing ponchi's tendency toward obfuscation and vulgarity and directly portraying the political figures that their work satirized. Rakuten insisted that "manga" consisted solely of political satire, rather than the wider range of subject matter that could be lampooned under the ponchi-e category. The first manga magazine, *Tokyo Puck*, launched under his editorship in 1905. Wildly popular, *Tokyo Puck* popularized the term *manga* and promoted Rakuten's vision of manga as different from and a break with ponchi.

Buoyed by the magazine's rapid success, Rakuten became Japan's first professional cartoonist, and his students went from *Tokyo Puck* to staff cartoonist or "manga kisha" (manga reporter) positions at many other newspapers, taking "manga" with them. Manga in these years was understood not as continuing Edo period artistic practices but rather as breaking with them, as can be seen in an anonymous art critic's evaluation of Rakuten and *Tokyo Puck* in the *Yomiuri Shinbun* in 1909: The author wrote that "the concept of manga appears to be not understood at all among the people of Japan" (because it was fundamentally foreign) and compared Rakuten's manga unfavorably to that found in France and Germany, but praised his artistic skill and his eschewing of obscene material (which was a break from Edo tradition as continued by ponchi-e).[4]

"Manga" expanded after Rakuten left *Tokyo Puck* in 1912 through the increasing popularity of the work of Okamoto Ippei, who in his position at the *Asahi Shinbun* expanded manga to include social satire. These topics were particularly germane to urban readers in the Taishō period (1912–26), which saw increasing uptake of the accoutrements of modern life and increased social changes, such as more women beginning to work outside the home and the rise of single-family households. Rakuten, Ippei, and their students became the Tokyo manga establishment; their work mocked radical notions like women wanting rights such as suffrage, upholding the prevailing conservative social values of the day even as Japan's growing consumer society threatened to melt solid social and economic certainties. Ippei's refusal to accept limits on what manga could depict set the medium on its eventual path to the dominant place in Japan's mediascape that it occupies today, the same place whence it exerts such a strong influence on fans worldwide.

Manga's categories continued to expand over the 1920s, ensuring its growing commercial success and putting the art form on firm enough footing that its practitioners began promulgating their own narrative about its origins and artistic legitimacy. By 1928, most manga creators claimed that manga's roots stretched back to ancient art, elevating their own claims to artistic prestige by arguing that their medium was the heir to a long tradition in both Japan and Europe. This discourse required that certain inconvenient facts be ignored completely, most notably that manga is a modern medium: a form of mass media that relies on, and was created by, the mass audiences that exist only in modern society. Formally speaking, as it continued to evolve, manga's means of expression drew heavily on other mass media of the nineteenth and twentieth centuries, particularly film and radio.

Some scholars and fans continue to argue that manga's roots go back to ukiyo-e or even further. But that idea's origin lies in its invention and its enthusiastic promotion by manga creators in this period, which itself saw an "Edo boom," driven by nostalgia and by general dissatisfaction with modernity. Rather than the backwards past that had to be left behind after the Meiji Restoration kicked off Japan's modernization, as the Meiji oligarchy and its proponents had claimed, in the 1920s the Edo period came to be considered a kind of cultural reservoir of distinctive Japanese traditions.[5] Manga was inserted among those traditions via rhetorical sleight-of-hand.

Manga was a modern phenomenon, and it was thoroughly international from its beginnings in the 1890s. Manga in Japan would not have arisen without the example of Euro-American cartoons and cartoonists. But, as can be seen in the fraught relationship between manga and ponchi-e, manga's development was not simply linear influence but instead one of appropriation, contestation, and transformation. Those processes have continued over the course of manga's history, although they were particularly acute in this first phase.[6] By 1928, manga's practitioners had expanded it from an upstart art form that consisted exclusively of "high-collar" political satire to an established field that encompassed a staggering variety of subjects, artistic styles, and forms of expression.

CHAPTER ONE

The Origins of Japanese Comics

THE TANUKI AND THE TRAIN: PONCHI-E AT THE CROSSROADS

The story of manga starts in the port city of Yokohoma. There, in the early 1890s, a young Japanese artist named Kitazawa Rakuten, trained in Japanese and Western art, was tipped to become the cartoonist for the *Box of Curios* newspaper. Rakuten inherited the job from Australian artist Frank Arthur Nankivell (1869–1959) after the latter sailed for the United States, making Rakuten the only Japanese person on staff. An admirer of the great liberal thinker Fukuzawa Yukichi (1835–1901), for whose *Jiji Shinpō* newspaper he began working in 1899, Rakuten adopted the *Jiji* practice of referring to the cartoons he drew by a more high-class (or, in Meiji parlance, "high collar") term: *manga*. By the end of his life, Rakuten would be universally hailed as manga's grandfather. By using the term *manga*, Rakuten, *Jiji*, and Imaizumi Ippyō, Rakuten's predecessor as the *Jiji* staff cartoonist, were trying to differentiate themselves from, and elevate their work above, what they saw as the debased medium of "ponchi-e" or "ponchi." What was ponchi(-e), and why did they want to distance themselves from it?

The history of magazines and newspapers in Japan goes back to the 1860s, in the midst of the bakumatsu period that ended with the fall of the Tokugawa shogunate and the establishment of a reformist, oligarchical government of disaffected samurai in the name of the restoration of imperial rule. The bakumatsu period began in 1853 with the arrival of U.S. Commodore Matthew C. Perry's "black ships," and the new port city of Yokohama, initially one of only two places where foreigners could legally reside, was a key site in the fifteen years of disorder and innovation that followed. Although

Japan had had a vibrant print culture since the early modern Edo period, supported by a highly commercialized economy and high rates of literacy, Euro-American-style periodicals had not been part of it.

That changed beginning in the 1860s, first with the (foreigner-produced) *The Japan Punch* (1862–87) and then with the short-lived *Seiyō zasshi* (Occidental magazine, 1867–69). As the name indicates, *The Japan Punch* was modeled on Britain's satirical magazine *Punch* (1841–2002) and was aimed at Yokohama's resident foreigners, while *Seiyō zasshi*, whose founder Yanagawa Shunsan (1832–70) coined *zasshi*, the Japanese term for magazine, consisted mostly of translated articles from abroad and was aimed at educated Japanese, although the magazine folded after publishing its sixth issue in 1869. *Seiyō zasshi*'s swift demise owed as much to a mismatch between its aspirations and its production technology as it did to Yanagawa's ill health, and the fact that the market for its product had not yet been created: The magazine was printed using the woodblock method, which cost much more time and resources to produce than movable type.[1]

The Japan Punch is visibly part of the British caricature tradition—not surprisingly, as its founder and publisher, Charles Wirgman (1832–91), was British by birth (although he studied art in France)—and satirically exaggerated bodily traits abound in its pages.[2] Its first issue in May 1862 boldly proclaimed that it would "be the official organ for the publication in Japan of Jollyfications emanating from His Ethereal Majesty's Customhouse and Boathouses in this country."[3] Published by a foreign resident in Yokohama, *The Japan Punch* was not subject to the Japanese governments' censorship regimes, and Wirgman used that freedom to lampoon various political figures, although his cartoons mostly focused on daily life in the foreign settlement.[4] *The Japan Punch* was the first outlet in Japan that satirically combined words and pictures, and it was monumentally influential on the Japanese-produced media that came after.[5] Other periodicals adopted *The Japan Punch*'s habit of referring to itself in the third person, *Osaka Puck* most famous among them, and it is casually multilingual in a matter-of-fact nineteenth-century way: English predominates, but French, German, Italian, and even Latin appear occasionally. Wirgman published *The Japan Punch* monthly beginning in 1873 (figure 1).

That was more than enough time to establish *ponchi-e* (literally, *Punch* drawings) or just *ponchi* as the standard Japanese term for satirical cartoons. The term was coined by Yokohama's *Kōko Shinbun* (The public news) in 1868, which defined it as "comical drawings with secret meanings," comparing it

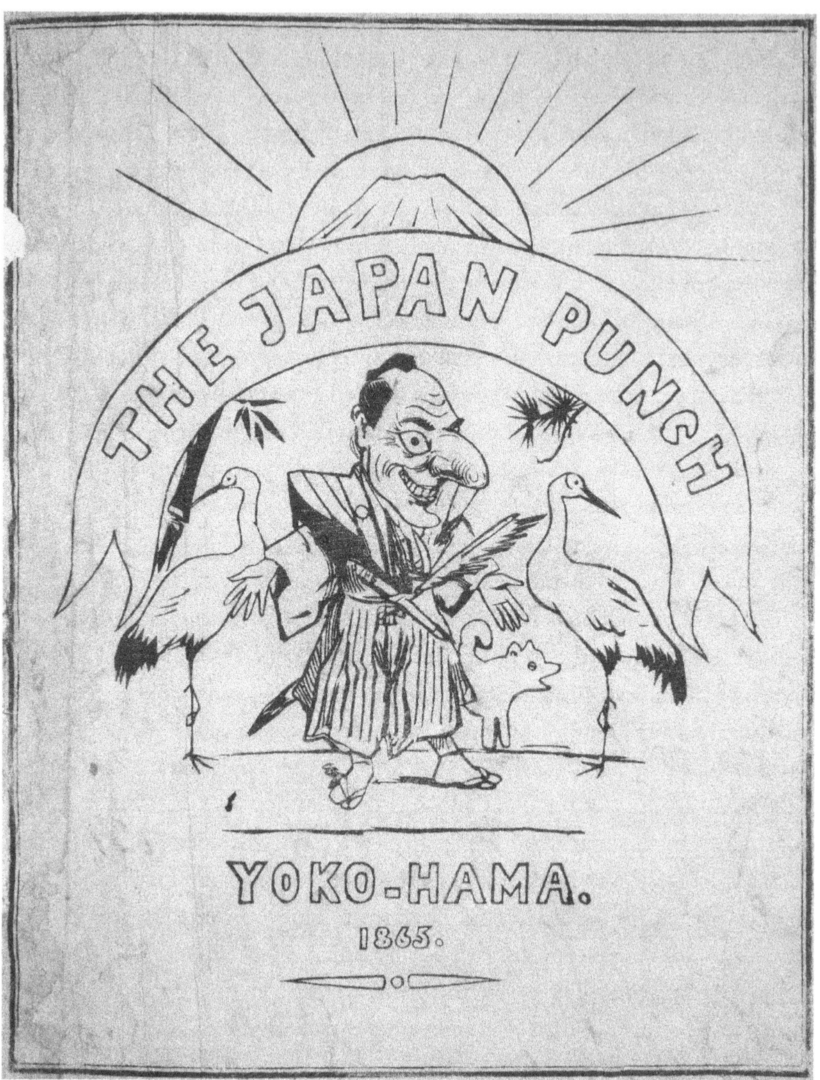

FIGURE 1. Cover of *The Japan Punch* depicting Mr. Punch as a samurai, 1865. Courtesy of Princeton University Library Special Collections.

to puzzle prints and drawings (hanji-e).[6] "Ponchi-e" quickly spread beyond Yokohama, taking Wirgman's use of a pen rather than a brush along with it, and many subsequent periodicals had "Punch" in their titles, further testifying to *The Japan Punch*'s influence.[7]

The country's first newspapers also adopted the ponchi-e trend, particularly the pioneering, liberal *Marumaru Chinbun* (Blue pencil curious news,

1877–1907), named from the contemporary practice of marking words the censors had struck out with two circles (literally OO, "marumaru").[8] *Maruchin*, as it was affectionately nicknamed, was a landmark publication: It was the first Japanese newspaper to use modern publication methods, it was the first to publish national editions throughout the country simultaneously, and it built its circulation to hitherto unseen size by using new postal and road networks to reach readers everywhere. Although its circulation paled compared to what later periodicals would achieve, at the time it was the most massive publication Japan had yet seen.[9] Through its reach, its format, and its liberal politics, it helped create a new public sphere in Japan, popularizing the idea that subjects had a right to know the news and that government leaders and policies could and should be challenged.[10]

The Meiji government instituted compulsory elementary education in 1872, with the result that while high-level literacy was by no means universal, the number of people who could read at a simple level was growing. Accordingly, *Maruchin* and its contemporaries split the difference by publishing a wide variety of pictorial content: landscape illustrations in the styles of traditional Japanese art, hand-drawn illustrations among the articles, and ponchi-e political cartoons. *Maruchin* was also casually bilingual, routinely publishing short articles in English, and its image captions were frequently printed in both English and Japanese. Its founder Nomura Fumio (1836–91) had spent five years in the United Kingdom, and he was certainly familiar with, and inspired by, the British *Punch*. *Maruchin*'s cartoons under its first illustrator, Honda Kinkichirō (1850–1921), adopted a visual language blending Western and Japanese elements, which helped its readership encompass both the intelligentsia and urban residents who were less well educated. *Maruchin*'s latterly famous readers in its heyday included the future renegade journalist Miyatake Gaikotsu (1867–1955) and future radical journalist and socialist Kōtoku Shūsui (1871–1911).[11]

Maruchin's editors defined *ponchi-e* as "an unclassifiable kind of eccentric picture."[12] Although the term implies that ponchi-e was merely copied from *The Japan Punch*, ponchi-e combined the Western concept of satirical cartoons—particularly those of French cartoonist Honoré Daumier (1808–79)—with traditional methods of ukiyo-e satire to produce a new, hybrid form.[13] Ukiyo-e practices visible in *Maruchin* and other periodicals of the time include the placement of (usually hand lettered) explanatory text inside the frame and the use of "humor writing" (gibun) in the captions and "picture puzzle" or "rebus print" (hanji-e) techniques in the images themselves.

Humor writing involved the use of seven- and five-syllable lines and onomatopoeia in order to sound amusing when read aloud. Hanji-e and the related jiguchi-e (pun prints) can be thought of as the visual equivalent of a cryptolect such as Cockney slang or the British gay dialect Polgari: the use of different, coded referents to depict something that was technically forbidden by the authorities, often through the rearrangement of kanji elements.[14] Surveying ponchi-e and its various visual strategies, manga scholar Miyamoto Hirohito concludes that although it adopted modern printing methods, ponchi-e generally retained ukiyo-e's satirical style and methods of expression, thus remaining firmly within the ambit of Edo-period culture.[15]

Some of these visual techniques were potentially confusing to readers, especially those whose education was low or who lacked the requisite in-group knowledge, but rebus and pun prints were quite popular as leisure objects in the late Edo and Meiji periods.[16] The fun in these prints and in ponchi-e was in figuring out what the art depicted, but that took time and required prior knowledge of the "culture of lowbrow literature," which limited the audience.[17] Using these techniques in the popular press was necessary in an era when Japan had no constitution and no guarantee of freedom of the press, and when *Maruchin* in particular was leading the fight for both in print, as part of the Freedom and Popular Rights movement (figure 2). This movement for constitutional representative government and civil rights was effectively crushed by the authorities; *Maruchin*'s popularity declined around the same time, as Honda was dismissed at the government's demand in 1881 and replaced by Kobayashi Kiyochika (1847–1914), muting its political satire.[18] Continuing educational reforms—middle school was made compulsory in 1891—and the expansion of the reading public that they spurred meant that other periodicals came to the fore: Miyamoto has dated the beginning of Japan's magazine age to 1888. Words gradually became less important in ponchi-e during the 1890s, allowing it to reach a wider audience.[19]

The Meiji oligarchs granted the country a constitution from the hand of the emperor in 1889 and a bicameral legislature (the Diet) in 1890; being a constitutional monarchy had become another global benchmark of modernity, and Japan was determined to meet it.[20] However, the Meiji constitution limited the franchise to men who paid a significant amount in property taxes, with the result that only about 5 percent of the adult male population could vote. Civil rights also remained largely nonexistent, as the Meiji constitution framed the relationship between emperor and imperial subjects in

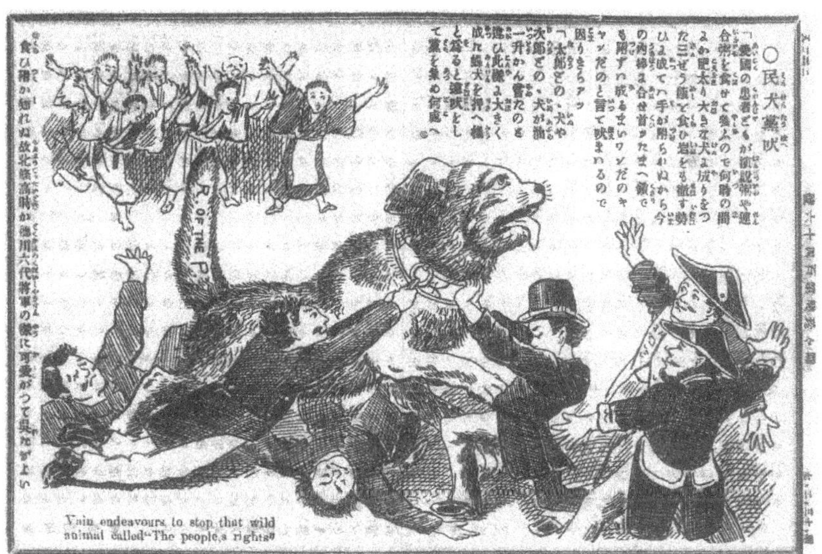

FIGURE 2. Cartoon by Honda Kinkichirō depicting the Freedom and Popular Rights movement as a dog (a pun on *ken*, "dog/rights"), *Marumaru Chinbun*, February 7, 1880. Courtesy of National Diet Library.

terms of subjects' unconditional duties to the sovereign and greatly circumscribed individual rights.

ALL THE NEWS THAT'S FIT TO DRAW: ILLUSTRATED NEWSPAPERS AND *JIJI SHINPŌ*

Newspapers in Japan exploded in popularity during the Meiji period, and by the end of the Freedom and Popular Rights movement they were widespread. *Maruchin*'s popularity derived as much from its politics as from its publication methods, but *Jiji Shinpō* (Current events news, 1882–1955) was founded in 1882 for a different purpose. Fukuzawa Yukichi—statesman, reformer, proponent of "Civilization and Enlightenment" in Japan, called the Japanese Benjamin Franklin—started the newspaper with the explicit idea that it would support the government's efforts to reform the unequal treaties to which Japan was subject and to secure the country's place on the world stage. *Jiji Shinpō* was well placed to take advantage of the reading public's expansion after the nationalist Imperial Rescript on Education was promulgated in 1890: School enrollment rose from 50 percent in that year to 97 percent in

1907, with the result that every Japanese child learned to recite the Rescript and its exhortations to "guard and maintain the prosperity of Our Imperial Throne coeval with heaven and earth."[21]

Impatience was in the air in Japan in the 1890s. Having established a constitution, a legislature, and the imperial monarchical pageantry that went along with them, it was widely felt that the country continuing under the hated unequal treaties was outdated and due for revision: Imposed during the bakumatsu period, these stipulated that foreigners who committed crimes in Japan could not be tried in Japanese courts, among many other unfavorable trade regulations. Japan would shortly start—and win—a successful war with the Qing dynasty, demonstrating both its own military competence and the Qing's increasing weakness.

It was in this atmosphere that one Imaizumi Ippyō, Fukuzawa's nephew by marriage, returned to Japan in 1890 after a five-year sojourn in the United States. Imaizumi was strongly influenced by the latest developments in cartoons abroad, and his innovations at *Jiji Shinpō* were crucial to manga's development. Ippyō first used the term *manga* in print to mean "cartoon" in *Jiji* in February 1890; thereafter, his manga ran alongside Fukuzawa's "Mangen" column.[22] It was Ippyō who took the crucial first steps to differentiate manga from ponchi-e by making it both more timely and easier to grasp: His manga expressed ideas directly, discarding ponchi-e's obfuscatory practices (figure 3). These innovations made Ippyō manga easier to understand, which better suited manga to Japanese newspapers' continuing evolution into a form of mass media.[23] Ippyō, however, wanted to connect manga to fine art; he even showed some of his manga at the renegade Hakubai-kai art society's second exhibition in 1896, under his birth name Hidetarō.[24]

The changes Ippyō made to political cartoons—from ponchi-e to manga—were directly echoed by larger changes in Japanese reading habits and printing technologies at the turn of the twentieth century. Diarist Masamune Hakuchō described reading the magazine *Kokumin no Tomo* (The people's friend, 1887–98) in the 1890s: In an echo of Edo period practices, Masamune read the whole thing cover to cover and word for word multiple times, to the point where he could recite it; he may have also been reading aloud, which would have been congruent with Edo education methods. By the end of the nineteenth century, however, these practices largely ceased as magazines became longer, reading became more visual and piecemeal, and the number of periodicals in print increased dramatically.[25] Ippyō's manga, much easier

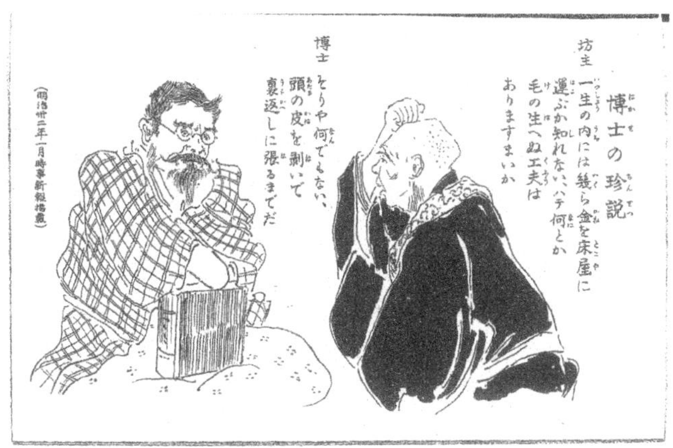

FIGURE 3. Manga by Imaizumi Ippyō, "Hakase no chinsetsu" (The professor's novel idea), *Jiji Shinpō*, January 1899. Courtesy of National Diet Library.

to understand at a glance than ponchi-e, took advantage of and was part of these developments.

Changes in printing technologies were similarly dramatic, and as with much else in modern Japan, they were spurred by the country's wars of imperialism: The ten-year period from 1894 to 1904, which saw the triumphant beginning and end of the Sino-Japanese War (1894–95) and the beginning of the Russo-Japanese War (1904–5), was a boom era for print media. Lithography started to become popular in the second half of the 1880s; the Sino-Japanese War, which was extraordinarily successful for Japan, popularized multicolored lithographic (i.e., planographic) printing and photo printing for the first time. People wanted to see high-quality depictions of far-off battle scenes and victories, and the media business evolved to meet that demand.[26] Political cartoons also became more photorealistic as photography proliferated in print.[27] New publications sprang up every few months, attempting to cash in on the growing readership for these media, including satirical periodicals. The most important of these was *Kokkei Shinbun* (Humorous news, 1901–8), which Miyatake Gaikotsu founded in Osaka in 1901.[28]

The next year, Kitazawa Rakuten made a career choice that proved epochal. Born Kitazawa Yasuji, Rakuten was the son of a family that had supported the wrong side in the Meiji Restoration, with the result that the new government expropriated most of their land and his father was forced to make his living as a used book dealer in Tokyo's Kanda district. He recognized and encouraged Rakuten's artistic talent early, and after Rakuten completed middle school he went to Yokosuka to study ukiyo-e before beginning art school in Yokohama, in which he learned modern, Western-style artistic traditions and techniques.[29] While in Yokohama he met Nankivell, who was working for the English-language satirical paper *Monthly Box of Curios* at the time.[30] In this era Rakuten may also have encountered the Tokyo-based weekly satirical magazine *Tōbaé* (1887–89), produced bilingually in French and Japanese by the French artist Georges Bigot (1860–1927) and notable for its scathing depictions of Japanese modernization.

Nankivell introduced Rakuten to the British tradition of political cartoons of which *The Japan Punch* was a part, and when he finally sailed for the United States in 1894, he tipped Rakuten to take over his job at *Box of Curios*, now a weekly (plate 1). There Rakuten gradually began clashing with his American editor over the content of his cartoons.[31] Rakuten eventually solved this problem by leaving for *Jiji Shinpō* in 1902, when ill health forced Ippyō to retire. Rakuten had already begun working at *Jiji* sporadically from 1899, when he took his pen name meaning 'optimism'; he was introduced to *Jiji* readers in the New Year's Day 1900 issue as a "punch artist" (ponchi gakka), but taking over the *Jiji Manga* Sunday supplement raised his profile.[32]

Although Rakuten left *Weekly Box of Curios* due to disputes with his American editor, his cartoons there and at *Jiji Manga* showed the influence of the American "yellow press," such as *The Katzenjammer Kids* (1897–2006) and The Yellow Kid himself, as well as Japanese and foreign cartoons of various stripes, including the British tradition he had learned from Nankivell.[33] Rakuten himself later wrote that he had been inspired to draw "American manga" (Amerika no manga) after seeing it in *Shōkokumin* (Little imperial subject, 1889–93), a children's periodical, after which he began seeking out foreign periodicals to study it further.[34]

In his politics, Rakuten was an admirer of Fukuzawa, and his views were presumably welcome at Fukuzawa's newspaper. At the time, Japanese elites' nationalism was directed toward a vision of Japan as a modern, upright, civilized member of the international family of nations, which in practice meant the unceremonious jettisoning of many pre-Meiji Japanese cultural practices, from clothing to food to art and leisure. Conveniently and not coincidentally, in this vision, Japan's embrace of (Western) modernity was also what gave it the moral imprimatur to colonize its "backward" Asian cousins, including China and Korea. The Sino-Japanese War had netted Japan its first overseas colony, Taiwan; Japan had helped to suppress the Boxer Rebellion in the Qing Empire alongside the Great Powers in 1900 and 1901; and Japan's colonization of Korea, which it declared a protectorate in 1905, deprived of its internal sovereignty in 1907, and officially annexed in 1910, was well underway.

In this context, Rakuten's noted antipathy toward ponchi-e and the hybrid artistic practices it entailed begins to make more sense: In later writings, he defined manga in opposition to ponchi-e and Edo-period influences, prioritizing art rather than words or wordplay, and argued that mangaka "should endeavor to make the pictures speak." He also complained about ponchi-e's tendency toward what he termed "obscenity" and "meaningless exaggeration." In his view, the "old fashion Edo taste" of ponchi-e did not suit Japan's status as a "first-class country" (ittōkoku), and he continued to use Ippyō's term *manga* to denote his comics, which he regarded as part of a universal, modern visual language that was not uniquely Japanese but rather international. As manga scholar Ronald Stewart writes, it was precisely because "at the time, manga was a rarely used word untainted by Edo-period connotations and therefore available to fill with new meaning," that Rakuten and presumably Ippyō before him adopted it.[35]

By the outbreak of the Russo-Japanese War, *Jiji* was (just barely) not the only newspaper using the term *manga* to refer to political cartoons: *Kokkei Shinbun* had begun using *manga* in 1903, and the antiwar Kyoto newspaper *Jiji manga hibijutsu gahō* (Timely manga unartistic illustrated news, 1904), published by the painter Kanokogi Takeshirō (1874–1941), used "manga" in its three-issue run, but "ponchi-e" was still widespread.[36] For Rakuten, ponchi-e had to be transcended in the name of civilization and enlightenment, and *Kokkei Shinbun*'s success in particular, drawing as it did on the contemporary art nouveau movement rather than the older *Punch* art style, evidently encouraged him to think that he could be the one to do the transcending.[37] He also clashed with his editors at *Jiji* over his desire to publish more explicitly political cartoons, particularly after the outbreak of the Russo-Japanese War.[38]

Rakuten found a publisher for his magazine in the company Yūrakusha, whose head Nakamura Yūjirō was willing to grant him creative control, although they disagreed on the title: The publisher wanted to call it *Tanuki*, after the uncouth animal trickster figure of Japanese folktales. Something so unmodern was abhorrent to Rakuten, and he eventually had his way in calling the magazine *Tokyo Puck* (although he did compromise by drawing the title border in the shape of a tanuki).[39] The name was a reference to the American humor magazine *Puck* (1871–1918), which had become wildly popular worldwide thanks to its satirical content, including cartoons and caricatures. *Tokyo Puck* was meant to signify a new age in Japanese satirical magazines, and it was indeed revolutionary: larger (B4 size), partly printed in color, and all manga.[40]

It was also wildly popular. *Tokyo Puck* became a huge hit almost immediately, and in quick succession it went from monthly to thrice-monthly release to meet demand: At its height, the magazine was selling sixty thousand copies a month. In early twentieth-century Japan, that was enough to earn Rakuten a huge income and make him a star cartoonist, the first person to make his living entirely from drawing manga.[41]

Although *Tokyo Puck* is regarded now as Japan's first manga magazine, and Rakuten as the first professional mangaka, neither of these terms was used consistently in the magazine's early years. The first issue's preface asked readers to submit their own ponchi-e, evidently conceding that *manga* was not necessarily a familiar term. On the other hand, newspaper advertisements for *Tokyo Puck* emphasized that it was a manga magazine, and Rakuten described himself as a *mangashi* (manga master, using an Edo-period term formerly applied to ukiyo-e artists) and ran a manga contest in the magazine's second year; he adopted the term *mangaka* to describe his profession in 1909. On the third hand, the term *ponchi* was used in the magazine to indicate humor for its first three years, which artist and critic Yamamoto Kanae (1882–1946) criticized in an article in 1907—but Yamamoto also praised the magazine's decreasing reliance on material that catered to "the vulgar tastes of yore."[42] Although others used the terms *ponchi* or *ponchi-e* and *manga* interchangeably in these years, *ponchi* vanished from *Tokyo Puck* by about 1912.[43]

HEAVEN IS A PLACE ON EARTH: THE SUCCESS OF *TOKYO PUCK*

To a contemporary eye, the full-color cover of *Tokyo Puck*'s first issue, published during the Russo-Japanese War, appears to show Tsar Nicolas II attempting to fellate himself, but Rakuten was illustrating the phrase "hozo wo kamu" (literally, to bite the bellybutton—an idiom for having bitter regrets).[44] It's difficult to understand what exactly was so revolutionary about this magazine, which described itself in that same first issue as an "illustrated magazine" (kaiga zasshi), at first glance (plate 2).

When contemporary manga critics seek to differentiate manga from mainstream American comics and Franco-Belgian *bandes dessinées*, they often talk about color (manga is monochrome; comics and BD aren't); printed lettering in speech bubbles (comics and BD are hand lettered); and the style of paneling or the use of screentones. Being full-color, comics and BD don't use tones, and while there is much variation in paneling within all three media, manga paneling is often much more freewheeling, frequently using "full bleed"—that is, discarding the gutter (the border at the edge of the page) for visual effect. A lot of manga was colored until approximately the mid-1950s; color printing was a huge draw for early twentieth-century publications worldwide, but it gradually receded as the century wore on. The more important question is paneling: how the page is divided into how many panels and how they relate to each other. The presence or absence of speech bubbles and whether a manga contains captions or dialogue are also important evolutionary markers, as is whether those panels were drawn in a more "theatrical" or a more "cinematic" style (i.e., whether the activity in the panel is oriented as if the viewer is gazing at a stage or more as though the viewer is watching a movie).

In 1905 cinema was only ten years old, but it had been nearly thirty years since the pioneering photographer Eadweard Muybridge had taken a series of precisely timed images of a horse galloping and found that, as some people had wagered, all four of its hooves left the ground while it did so. Muybridge's breakthrough stop-motion studies showed that continuous movement could be broken up into a series of still images and then recombined at speed to furnish the illusion that one was watching that movement take place. These "motion pictures" developed into films by the 1890s in Europe, and the development of film eventually had an epochal impact on the development of comics in general and manga in particular. In 1905, however, all that lay in the future, and Kitazawa Rakuten was still fighting the good fight merely to establish manga—or *puck* (pakku) or *puck art* (pakku-ga), as he began calling it not long after he launched *Tokyo Puck*—as a distinct artistic form that was not ponchi-e.[45]

Tokyo Puck's covers were color, as were its lavish two-page centerfolds and some of its interior pages. Many of its cartoons are one-panel, while its multipanel cartoons sometimes use panel numbering and sometimes don't. In terms of captions and dialogue, *Tokyo Puck* is a very mixed bag: Some of its cartoons feature explanatory text inside the panels, others outside, and some both at once. Dialogue occurs on occasion but is only reported in text blocks inside the panel until November 1908, when speech bubbles with hand lettering appear for the first time.

The placement of text in particular differentiates Rakuten's manga from ponchi-e, which like ukiyo-e used explanatory blocks of text inside the panel: Over *Tokyo Puck*'s first few years, the text gradually became fixed outside the image and direct dialogue became more common inside it. Moreover, that text became increasingly multilingual, until by 1910 each issue routinely ran with editor's notes in three languages: Japanese, Chinese, and English. (Evidently pitched at different audiences, the three editor's notes usually say different things, rather than being translations of the same text.) Most cartoons were captioned in at least two of these three languages as well.

Multilingualism was partly a business strategy. *Tokyo Puck* was the first Japanese magazine that was sold in Taiwan, Korea, and China, and English made it more likely that Westerners would read the magazine, reflecting Rakuten's belief that, in Ronald Stewart's phrase, manga was "an international visual language."[46] They did, although sometimes with pernicious results: The American and German embassies complained to the Foreign Ministry about Rakuten's *Tokyo Puck* cartoons multiple times, and the Home Ministry banned single issues of the magazine on multiple occasions—a fact that Rakuten always joked about in the next issue.[47]

The complaints and embargoes were a consequence of the magazine's popularity, which had two main drivers: First, Rakuten, in the words of manga historian Shimizu Isao, "made political cartoons interesting" by drawing recognizable likenesses of the political figures being satirized—a direct contrast to ponchi-e's obfuscatory visual strategies. Second and most importantly, *Tokyo Puck* copied *Puck*'s centerpiece (pun intended) feature, namely its two-page, full-color centerfolds. Rakuten excelled at these "big screen" manga, and although about half of each *Tokyo Puck* issue was done by the thirty-five assistants under his guidance, he always did the centerfolds personally.[48]

The centerfolds are invariably the most interesting parts of the magazine in terms of paneling and layouts. Although some were a single, large landscape panel, others were laid out like game boards, particularly the traditional illustrated board game sugoroku, which was then enjoying a boom in popularity among children.[49] But Rakuten also excelled at a structure in which the page was divided into four quadrants with a central panel in the middle, often ovoid but sometimes a more unusual shape (hearts, stars) that related to the centerfold's content. Other centerfolds show the influence of other media such as Georges Méliès's short film *La Voyage dans la Lune* (A voyage to the moon, 1902), which was first shown in Japan in 1905.

Even Rakuten's landscape centerfolds creatively play with space: A centerfold from March 1908, "Desertion of National Army," depicts a column of people walking out of the panel into the enlarged gutter (predicting that people will flee the country due to increased taxes like soldiers deserting due to poor treatment), while a November 1908 centerfold satirizing then communications minister Gōtō Shinpei uses the gutter to symbolize dreams and the image itself to depict reality, manipulating the space of the page to depict the interplay between them (plate 3). Rakuten also used space to represent time, dividing the centerfold along a diagonal to depict before-and-after situations. Although other magazines tried to copy Rakuten's centerfolds, hoping to cash in on his success, few succeeded, precisely because Rakuten was the best at it.[50]

Rakuten's *Tokyo Puck* assistants are an important part of manga's story, not just because they inaugurated a labor model that is now standard in the manga industry, but because many became the next generation's leading cartoonists: Rather than dictating slavish adherence to his own style, Rakuten allowed the assistants to develop their own styles. Most of the "Tens"—as homage, many adopted professional pen names containing this element of Rakuten's own pseudonym—did not make a notable mark on manga history, but they were influential at the time, particularly after 1912 when Rakuten himself left the magazine. The assistants also played an important part in making *Tokyo Puck* so international; according to one former assistant, the *Tokyo Puck* break room contained cartoon magazines from the United States, United Kingdom, France, Italy, and Germany, and it was from those magazines that staff got the ideas for speech bubbles and multi-panel comics, as well as (on occasion) subject matter for specific cartoons.[51] Through *Tokyo Puck*'s international practices, speech bubbles and multi-panel comics became important characteristics of manga.

Perhaps Rakuten's most notable student was mangaka and pioneering animator Shimokawa Ōten or Hekoten (1892–1973). As one of the so-called "three pioneers," Shimokawa created one of Japan's first animated films, *Imokawa Mukuzō genkanban no maki* (Story of the concierge Imakawa Mukuzō), which featured his manga character Mukuzō and was released in three parts in 1917. (Mukuzō was thus the first manga character to be adapted for animation.) He made five animated shorts or "manga eiga" for Tenkatsu during 1916–17, but went back to manga because animation was damaging his eyesight.[52] Even as Japanese animation was in its infancy, it was already strongly linked to manga: Mangaka and Rakuten student Kōuchi Jun'ichi (1886–1970) released *Namakura gatana* (The dull sword), another pioneering early animation, in April 1917. Painter Kitayama Seitarō's *Saru to kani* (Battle of a monkey and a crab) followed in May 1917.[53]

"*TOKYO PUCK* HAS CREATED ITS OWN COMPETITORS": INFLUENCE AND ITS DISCONTENTS

Tokyo Puck was influential in many ways: content, artistic practices, labor models, and sheer popularity. Rakuten's magazine inspired many similar periodicals with *Puck* in their titles, of which two are of particular note. *Osaka Puck* was founded in Osaka in 1906 and lasted for forty-three years in print. Like *Tokyo Puck, Osaka Puck* was formed around a Western-style artist, in this case Akamatsu Rinsaku (1878–1953). Like Rakuten, Akamatsu is said to have drafted his students into being his assistants on the magazine, which directly copied *Tokyo Puck*'s format, appearance, and number of issues per month; *Osaka Puck* was two sen cheaper (ten instead of twelve), probably due to varying costs of living in the magazines' respective regions. But whereas *Tokyo Puck* was published in Japan's political center and aimed at the central government and international audiences, *Osaka Puck* was a local outlet less directly concerned with national politics. Befitting its Kansai origins, *Osaka Puck* was also much more plainspoken than *Tokyo Puck*, and it tapped into a local tradition of blunt humor that sustained it and other satirical publications of the day, such as *Kokkei Shinbun*.[54]

Another important spawn of *Tokyo Puck* was the short-lived *Shōnen Puck*, which began publication in 1907 and ceased sometime after 1910. Its editor was Kawabata Ryūshi (1885–1966), a former Rakuten assistant at *Tokyo Puck*, and it styled itself as the first manga magazine for children. Newspaper manga featuring children dated back to "Chame to Dekobō" (the characters' names can be translated, respectively, as Brown Eyes and Beetle-Brow or Playfulness and Mischief), which Rakuten began in *Jiji Manga* in 1902; with these two scamps, he was also the first Japanese cartoonist to create recurring characters.[55] Combining and deepening *Tokyo Puck*'s influence with that of its international fellows, Kawabata's work on *Shōnen Puck* was profoundly influenced by the British weekly *Puck* (1904–40), which published a companion children's paper also called *Puck* featuring comics and stories: Kawabata directly redrew at least one *Puck* comic outright, and frequently copied discrete visual elements wholesale. Like *Tokyo Puck, Shōnen Puck* also featured multi-panel comics, generally about eight panels each, and ten of its twenty-four pages were multicolor printed.[56] Significantly, it popularized the reader participation corner, which featured children's letters to the editor from all over the empire.[57]

At the end of the Meiji period, publishers were making many changes to their printing and distribution models. One important innovation was selling magazines on consignment, which became standard practice across the industry during the Taishō era (1912–26). Inducing distribution outlets to take on more financial risk enabled publishing companies to operate on a more stable footing and to ensure their own profitability. Another important development was the industry's implementation of a fixed price scheme for printed materials nationwide, which brought stability to distributors and bookstores by encouraging cooperation—and enforcing compliance—among industry associations' members. In 1911, the Tokyo Print Workers' Association formed from the merger of the lithographic and typographic printers' unions, enabling printers and publishers to regularize wages and labor costs, respectively.[58]

Meiji's final years also witnessed political changes in the publishing environment. The Newspaper Law of 1909 ended a dozen years of relative press freedom, in which the power to suspend journals from publication rested with the courts, which largely declined to exercise it (twenty-one journals were suspended from 1897 to 1909, whereas 654 journals had been suspended when the bureaucracy held this power during 1890–96). The new law imposed stricter penalties for press violations in most cases and granted the bureaucracy the power to ban particular issues of periodicals and to seize all copies without court proceedings. Empowered bureaucrats repeatedly wielded its provisions to target those deemed beyond the pale of imperial political discourse.[59]

The rising tide of leftism was highlighted by the High Treason Incident of 1910–11. In this infamous case, police in Nagano prefecture found evidence of a leftist assassination plot targeting the emperor in May 1910. The ensuing nationwide roundup eventually resulted in twenty-six people standing trial in a closed court on highly circumstantial evidence, including the famous anarchist Kōtoku Shūsui and his former common-law wife, feminist anarchist Kanno Sugako (1881–1911). Twelve people's death sentences were commuted to life imprisonment by imperial rescript, while the other twelve, including

Kōtoku and Kanno, were executed by hanging on January 24, 1911. While *Tokyo Puck* called the defendants "socialist demons" who had to be exorcised, *Osaka Puck* criticized the "rigorous punishment-ism" of the decision itself.[60]

The High Treason Incident was one of many "incidents" in which security forces used unforeseen contingencies to eliminate people they deemed enemies of the state, either directly through murder or indirectly through the courts. Its impact on larger society was profound. The Japanese press had never been free, but in the two decades since the constitution's promulgation, the press had grown accustomed to a certain amount of room for expression. The High Treason Incident, however, began gradually narrowing that room, starting with political topics, and political manga felt its chilling effects immediately.

By the end of the Meiji period in 1912, while manga was gaining increasing currency, it was still heavily associated with Rakuten, *Tokyo Puck*, and *Jiji Shinpō*, and was by no means universal. Ponchi and ponchi-e still circulated widely; one contemporary dictionary entry used *manga* as a synonym for *ponchi* a few years later.[61] *Tokyo Puck* itself had changed from its initial full-color, image-heavy incarnation: Beginning in 1909, with the introduction of monochrome line illustrations inside issues, the magazine gradually became more text-heavy, and color was rationed. *Tokyo Puck* also changed politically; after the executions, the magazine muted its political satire and thereby its power.[62] These changes cannot have sat well with Rakuten, and Shimizu speculates that they contributed to Rakuten's decision to leave the magazine in 1912 after the publishing rights were sold to a new publisher, who lowered wages for seven people.[63] Rakuten attempted to capitalize on his *Tokyo Puck* fame and started two separate magazines of his own, *Rakuten Puck* and *Katei Puck* (Household Puck), in which he used the term *puck* rather than *manga*, but within two years he was back on staff at *Jiji Shinpō*, where his return was advertised in the New Year's Day 1914 issue of *Rakuten Puck:* "Amusing ponchi: Rakuten's ponchi are easy to understand and amusing."[64] Rakuten's magazines shut down in 1914; he and *Tokyo Puck* were no longer at manga's cutting edge, and *Tokyo Puck* itself shut down in 1915.

CHAPTER TWO

Arresting the Fleeting Moment

MANGA TURNS MODERN

OKAMOTO IPPEI: FACING LIFE

The person who had the greatest influence on manga after Rakuten's departure from *Tokyo Puck* was a young artist named Okamoto Ippei (1886–1948), acclaimed as manga's other grandfather. Born in Hokkaido after its colonization by mainland Japan, Okamoto graduated from art school in Tokyo in 1910 and went to work for the *Asahi Shinbun* as a staff cartoonist in 1912, where he remained until 1933.[1] Though they had broadly similar artistic backgrounds and were only ten years apart in age, Rakuten and Ippei's manga proved very different in very consequential ways, beyond the fact that Rakuten focused on weeklies and magazines while Ippei mainly worked in newspapers.[2]

After *Maruchin*'s decline in the late 1880s, an illustration style called koma-e or komaga evolved in newspapers and magazines. Unlike the political manga of Ippyō and *Jiji*, which Rakuten took over and promoted, komaga was relatively free of narrative content. It consisted of one panel, independent from an accompanying article, but it was timely. Precisely because it did not rely on captions or dialogue within the frame to get its point across, komaga could be somewhat more subversive than Rakuten's manga, which wore its politics on its sleeve and on occasion was banned for it. Shimizu Isao cites the komaga of Kosugi Misei aka Kosugi Hōan (1881–1964), created for the magazine *Senji Gahō* (Wartime illustrated news, 1904) during the Russo-Japanese War, as an example: Though they are ostensibly only reportage, the illustrations are anything but pro-war.[3] Calling Kosugi's work an example of manga, Miyamoto Hirohito praises his ability to condense the front's cruelty into a single image, offering a kind of counterprogramming to wartime jingoism.[4]

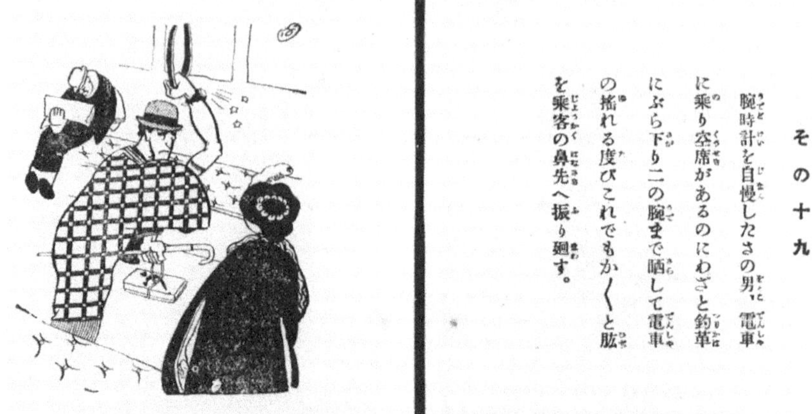

FIGURE 4. Manga manbun by Okamoto Ippei depicting a man ostentatiously showing off his wristwatch while riding public transit. Detail from *Monomiyusan: Manga to bun*, 1916. Courtesy of National Diet Library.

When he started at *Asahi Shinbun*, Okamoto Ippei went in for this kind of realistic art rather than for Rakuten-style satirical political caricature; he had begun contributing komaga to the *Asahi* in 1910 thanks to an introduction from his elementary school classmate, the artist Natori Shunsen (1886–1960). He had also collaborated with Natori and their classmate Nakada Katsunosuke (1886–1945) on the book *Manga to yakubun* (Manga and translations, 1911), in which he and Natori referred to their illustrations depicting daily life as "manga."[5]

From his starting point in *Manga to yakubun*, Ippei developed his own style of manga by 1914, dubbed "manga manbun." Manga manbun combined komaga and Rakuten manga, comprising a one-panel illustration with a long, witty caption attached. But it had several distinctive characteristics: First and most importantly, the butt of Ippei's satire was not the government or politicians, but rather people in general, their habits, foibles, and increasingly nontraditional, modern behaviors and customs.[6] The early Taishō period saw the beginning of what historian Miriam Silverberg aptly dubbed "Japanese modern times," and in this era of accelerating urbanization, consumerism, and social stratification, there was quite a lot to satirize—particularly in Tokyo, the increasingly glitzy center of it all.[7]

Manga manbun fails every kind of manga litmus test other than "Is it called manga?" Although its captions are printed rather than hand lettered, it contains no dialogue, it is only one panel, and it does not use the gutter at all, resembling contemporary avant-garde art rather than cartoon-style illustration. By abandoning color and Rakuten's acid political focus, and appending text to explain the image, Ippei's manga expanded what *manga* meant at the time (figure 4). And in the world of Japanese media after the High Treason Incident, it was much easier to get along if one avoided political commentary altogether.

Novelist Natsume Sōseki famously praised Ippei's ability to unify text and image and draw pictures that were as engaging as the text, writing in 1914 that "it is not an exaggeration to say that there is no other mangaka like you in Japan today."[8] Ippei's work was wildly popular, and from manga manbun he went on to revolutionize manga in several ways. His choice to use the term *manga* to describe his works also most likely saved manga itself: During the Taishō period, *manga* began to displace *ponchi-e* and other terms for cartoons such as *toba-e* or *shiba-e;* and by the early Shōwa period (1926–89), it was used almost exclusively to describe comics, as ponchi had become a category of humorous, educational art for children.[9] Ippei manga's popularity helped *manga* supplant other words to become the term for this general category of sequential art in Japan, rather than fading into obscurity in the early Taishō period with the decline of Rakuten and *Tokyo Puck.*

Manga manbun induced cartoonists to add witty captions to their panels, but Ippei made an equally influential choice on June 4, 1914, when he began bringing cinematic expression into manga with his first "film manga" (eiga manga). By 1916, an Ippei film manga consisted of a story stretched to fifty or a hundred panels with shorter text appended between them, and this form too was hugely popular.[10] It didn't hurt that film, which had been introduced to Japan in 1896 but really began to take off after the Russo-Japanese War, was increasingly popular and was also beginning to be considered "modern."[11] Early films were silent, and film promoters in Japan developed the role of the benshi (orator), who performed, narrated, and interpreted films, including voicing characters. Before and even into the era of talkies, benshi accompanied movies in the theaters for the audience, a role that evolved into shaping the audience's reception of the film from the front of the house before and during projection. Before the rise of "pure film" discourse in Japan created the director-as-auteur and actors-as-stars, benshi were celebrities in their own right.[12]

With this background in mind, it's possible to grasp what it means to say of Ippei's eiga manga that the rhythm of the appended texts in between the panels is that of a benshi performing the action of a movie, with dramatic pauses for emphasis and effect.[13] If Rakuten in his *Tokyo Puck* centerfolds pioneered dramatic and dynamic interactions between panel and gutter, Ippei's eiga manga pioneered dynamic interactions between image and text. The dynamic pacing of Ippei's eiga manga was an important innovation, one that captured readers' attention and that later mangaka took much further.

Ippei set another milestone in manga in 1915, when he, Rakuten, and other leading cartoonists formed Japan's first manga organization, the Tokyo Mangakkai, with the goals of friendship, information exchange, and promoting the job of manga kisha or mangaka to prospective cartoonists. Suzuki Maki notes that the organization was also intended "to improve manga's rank and manga's purpose," since manga had failed to gain respect in the art world.[14] It succeeded; one sign that cartoonists were beginning to regard themselves as creators was that the mangaka who contributed to Ippei's short-lived 1916 magazine *Toba-e* signed their names to their cartoons, unlike the standard anonymous practice in *Tokyo Puck*.[15]

Cartooning is a demanding job, and labor-saving innovations have been just as likely to reduce wages as to make the cartoonist's job easier, with the result that in the long run little if any work is eliminated. Given the job's physical nature, the Tokyo Mangakkai's first stated goal for its existence—to promote friendship among its members—was less a matter of sentiment than of sanity. As sociologist Ian Condry notes of animation production, "A tremendous amount of work is required, with painstaking attention to detail, to create *each frame* of film (or, at least, multiple frames per second). It's a crazy idea."[16] Animation and comics are closely related, and creators of both may easily become isolated in the work; the Tokyo Mangakkai alleviated that isolation for its members. Manga organizations have since played a key role in manga's history, and the Tokyo Mangakkai set another important precedent by creating "Mangasai" (Manga festival), a self-produced magazine, along with group exhibitions, to further its goals. Group members produced one "Mangasai" every summer from 1915 to 1923, when the group reformed as the Nihon Mangakkai.[17]

By 1915, there were quite a few cartoonists in the Tokyo area. *Tokyo Puck*'s meteoric popularity ten years prior had created a generation of would-be cartoonists, and Rakuten had taken many of them on as students and assistants. Happily for their long-term career prospects, by the beginning of the Taishō period the number of people who could read at the newspaper level had grown quite large. The number of newspapers in Japan increased accordingly, and these newspapers increasingly had at least one manga kisha on staff, all men.[18]

Arising out of a different artistic lineage, Ippei manga looked almost nothing like "manga" as it was understood by Rakuten and his followers—but this was evidently not a problem. Despite the popularity of *Tokyo Puck* and its imitators, *manga* was still not the only term for political cartoons or satirical images, regardless of Rakuten's ideas about definitions. Rather than argue endlessly with each other or seek to exclude Ippei and his works, early manga creators simply took Ippei's manga manbun at face value. *Manga* was an elastic term that could and did embrace a wide range of quite different styles and practices under its umbrella. In the 1920s, that umbrella opened even wider.

YES, I CAN SEE NOW: MORE MANGA

Japan entered World War I in 1914 as an ally of Britain. Unlike the empire's previous wars, the Great War created a tough environment for Rakuten-style political manga, causing a manga bust. Patriotism was running high, particularly since the Japanese military had seized Germany's Asian colonies with virtually no fighting. Manga and the Japanese economy went in opposite directions: Japan reaped large profits during the war selling munitions and replacing European-manufactured goods on the world market, but high growth was accompanied by high inflation, which led to social unrest and some political change, and then a postwar slump. Despite the economic uncertainties of the postwar years and the uneven economic outcomes of the following decade, manga's fortunes picked up: *Tokyo Puck* was revived in 1919, and many other manga magazines were founded in the early 1920s.[19]

Tokyo Puck's second incarnation looked very different, and other magazines of this era shared many of its visual features, particularly the retreat of full-color images. Although many magazines retained full-color cover illustrations and initial sections, the bulk of each issue was now published in the much cheaper three-color scheme or entirely in monochrome. The new *Tokyo Puck* had much more interior text, far fewer interior illustrations (and none in color), and far fewer cartoon-style images; realistic, manga manbun-style art predominated. Its increasing number of advertisements also employed different drawing styles than the fine art-style illustrations themselves.[20]

In 1921, Rakuten returned to *Jiji Shinpō* as the editor in chief of *Jiji Manga*, its relaunched Sunday manga supplement. Rakuten had founded his own manga group, the Manga Kōrakkai, in 1918 to find talented students, and though he began *Jiji Manga* drawing all of the key art himself, within nine months his old student Ogawa Jihei (1887–1925) began helping him. By 1922, they were coeditors.[21] *Jiji Manga*, which officially bore the title *Jiji Shinpō* until December 1923, evolved the *Tokyo Puck* concept for an age of increasing newspaper readership: It offered a variety of manga that appealed to everyone in the household, taking its cue from Ippei's more broadly humorous manga.[22] At the beginning, about half of any given issue was photo spreads and collages, indicating that at this point *manga* could and did encompass "images" or "illustrations" as well as "cartoons" or "comics." Covers initially consisted of a main illustration with a four-panel manga superimposed on it, although that inset manga was replaced by inset advertising, and then became a single image. Its interior manga contained numbered panels and direct dialogue within them, but very few speech bubbles (Rakuten seems to have used them mostly to ensure that text could be distinguished in very complicated or dark panels).[23]

After Ogawa officially became coeditor the publication featured more news, and in August 1922 it expanded to eight pages per issue, with manga shrinking to two interior pages plus the cover illustration. That news was distinctly tabloid-ish, with lots of coverage of celebrities such as movie stars and royalty. Manga continued to evolve, and *Jiji* incorporated new forms not seen in Rakuten's first heyday, including vertical panel manga with a filmstrip border (a form that spread to other manga magazines) and, in 1924, a photo manga starring a Kewpie doll that was decidedly creepy but also formally innovative in that it mimicked the principle of film frames, breaking down motion and action into individual, static component images.[24]

The increase in manga magazines was part of Japanese modern times. By 1921, the "big five" Tokyo newspapers had doubled their daily circulation to four hundred thousand copies, and that same voracious readership also read magazines.[25] But the growth was also a response to the labor situation for manga creators in Tokyo: Like Rakuten a decade prior, Ippei had inspired many bright-eyed young men (and at this stage they were apparently all men) to become manga artists. But Rakuten's disciples already occupied most of the jobs, and the Ippei disciples had to either find or create new markets.[26]

Ippei himself pioneered the most important of these new kinds of manga, namely children's (kodomo) manga. Although manga had featured child protagonists as far back as Rakuten's strips in his first stint at *Jiji Manga* in 1903, and children's periodicals had reprinted foreign cartoons such as Winsor McCay's *Little Nemo in Slumberland* for decades, manga specifically created with children in mind was new.[27] Beginning in 1916, Ippei published a number of influential children's manga in the *Asahi* and elsewhere, apparently because there were no good manga for his son Okamoto Tarō (1911–96), later a famous painter and sculptor, to read. The Okamoto family set another manga milestone in 1921 with the publication of "Toshio no mita mono" (What Toshio saw) in the *Asahi;* Ippei did the art while his wife, the feminist writer Okamoto Kanoko (1889–1939), wrote the story, making her the first female manga writer.[28]

Children's manga expanded *manga* far beyond the very limited sense of political satire that Rakuten had initially popularized, and it marked a true turning point in the medium's development. Rakuten picked up children's manga in *Jiji Shinpō* in 1921, and it took off through increasingly popular newspaper manga publications. Ippei took Miyao Shigeo (1902–82) on as a student in 1922; Miyao's first "Manga Tarō" children's manga was published in the *Tokyo Maiyū Shinbun* in that same year. The highly influential children's manga "Shō-chan no bōken" (The adventures of Shō-chan), with art by Kabashima Katsuichi (1888–1965) under the pseudonym Tōfūjin and written by Oda Nobutsune (1889–1967) under the pseudonym Oda Shōsei, ran in the *Asahi Graph* in the first nine months of 1923. It chronicled the exploits of a boy named Shō, accompanied by an alarmingly large talking squirrel, and quickly became a popular book series as well (plate 6). In that same year, the first manga magazine aimed exclusively at children, *Kodomo Puck*, began publication. The illustrator Takehisa Yumeji (1884–1934), whose works and style had a huge influence on girls' culture and early shōjo manga, was involved with *Kodomo Puck*'s production alongside other latterly famous creators, and it achieved a high standard of art not easily equaled by other magazines.[29]

Ippei continued expanding what could be called manga. In 1921 he began serializing what he called shōsetsu (novel) manga in the *Asahi.* Shōsetsu manga could mean different things to different people, but for Ippei it meant a long narrative in which image and text, separated by the panel border, bore equal narrative weight. For other creators, shōsetsu manga were illustrated novels; Ippei, Rakuten, and many others turned their hands to illustrating first-rank literature in this manner before the end of the decade. In shōsetsu manga published in *Joshikai* (Women's world) in 1923–25, Ippei also introduced close-ups and long shots to the vocabulary of manga expression.[30]

Shōsetsu manga was hugely influential; Miyao Shigeo adopted the form for his *Manga Tarō* comics, and it is the format in which Shō-chan and the squirrel had their picture-book adventures. Although by current standards the unrelenting panel/text rhythm is quite boring, at the time it felt—and was—fresh and exciting, particularly since artists were free to choose which moment from the text to depict in each panel, and how to do so. Looking at manga from this era often feels like strolling through a gallery in the modern wing of an art museum, and individual shōsetsu manga panels are often very fine examples of current art trends.

In this era, manga also began to be employed for non-manga purposes, specifically advertising—which Ippei pioneered in 1919 by drawing a manga in which a child drank the newly launched beverage Calpis.[31] Ippei further expanded manga's use in advertising in 1927 by drawing twenty-two manga for a tabi socks company's full-page newspaper advertisement. He later wrote that part of the reason he did it was to extend manga's scope.[32] He succeeded, paving the way for manga characters advertising products unrelated to the manga itself just a few years later, and in the decades since.

THE RESTORATION AND THE GOLDEN AGE

Another important trend in manga after the war was the rise of "nonsense (nansensu) manga." *Nonsense*, along with its counterparts *ero* (erotic) and *guro* (grotesque), was a watchword of the age, particularly after the Great Kanto Earthquake in 1923, which devastated Tokyo, Yokohama, and the surrounding region and marked a decisive acceleration point in the experience of Japanese modern times. *Nonsense* quickly became so ubiquitous as to lose most of its specificity. But as historian Miriam Silverberg argued, in its original usage *nonsense* connoted "a political, ironic humor that took on such themes as the transformations wrought by a modernity dominated by Euro-American mores," and in manga it was the heir to Ippei's manga manbun.[33] Its rise coincided with the expansion of newspaper manga, and in the *Asahi Graph*'s pages in 1923, it found its natural format: the four-panel manga.

The four-panel (yonkoma) comic was a staple of newspaper comics sections worldwide for most of the twentieth century, and it endures today in newspapers and webcomics, but even bread and butter had to be invented at some point. Multi-panel strips in Japan, including those depicting the same recurring characters, dated back to the original *Jiji Manga* supplement, and the revived *Jiji Manga* published quite a few four-panel manga from its launch in 1922. But daily character strips were not a going form in Japan until journalist Suzuki Bunshirō (1890–1951), while attending the first meeting of the International Labour Organization in Washington, D.C., in 1919, observed firsthand newspaper comics' popularity in the United States, where they were published as part of regular editions rather than in separate supplements. Suzuki brought this suggestion back to Japan, and the *Asahi* began publishing George McManus's strip *Bringing Up Father* (1913–2000) in April 1923. Before the earthquake, it appeared in its four-panel format as *Jiggs and Maggie*, then as *Oyaji Kyōiku* (Bringing up the old man) in a weekly one-page format afterward, and was wildly popular.[34]

Newspaper manga's overall popularity irrevocably linked it with the four-panel format, which became standardized across publications.[35] Inspired by McManus, Asō Yukata's four-panel *Nonkina tōsan* (Easygoing dad), launched in May 1923 and became a rapid hit alongside Shō-chan, whose newspaper version first established the now-standard vertical format, and which was directly inspired by the British comic *Pip, Squeak, and Wilfred*.[36] Buoyed by the four-panel strip's popularity, translated Euro-American comics saw their heyday in the era of Japanese modern times. To be sure, they were not an entirely new phenomenon; other translated comics had run in various Japanese periodicals before the earthquake. *Osaka Puck* was reprinting cartoons from the British magazines *Kinema Comic* and *Comic Life* by 1922, and in 1920 the magazine reprinted comics from the British weekly *Comic Cuts* at least once.[37]

The vast majority of these comics' appearances in Japan before the earthquake were wildcat—that is, unauthorized and pirated. The international syndicates that owned the comics caught on eventually and began demanding licensing payments—which is not to say that piracy ceased. Although some comics were legally published in Japan, many others were not; the first run of *Blondie*, for instance, was entirely pirated. The *Tokyo Nichinichi* newspaper was a particularly notable locus of pirated manga, including *Happy Hooligan* (1900–32), which also appeared officially under a bilingual title in *Jiji Manga*.[38]

In the second half of the 1920s, *Jiji Manga* became a reliable source of translated comics; *Happy Hooligan* was replaced in 1925 by *Mr. Dough and Mr. Dubb!*, who resemble two of the Marx Brothers quite strongly. Both comics were created by Frederick Burr Opper (1857–1937), a *Puck* veteran who pioneered American newspaper comics from the beginning of the twentieth century. *Happy Hooligan* was not only the first comic to consistently use speech bubbles, but its hobo protagonist was also most likely an inspiration for Charlie Chaplin's beloved character the Tramp—in the strips published in Japan, the resemblance between the two is uncanny. *Happy* returned to *Jiji* in 1927, by which time the magazine consisted mostly of visuals: Only two pages with column text remained in each issue, changes spurred by *Jiji*'s reformatting to a magazine-style size and binding after the earthquake. Although the line between newspapers and magazines was still blurry, the two formats were steadily diverging by this point in time.

Most translated nonsense manga came from the United States, a fact well known to manga practitioners and readers at the time. The science fiction novelist and mangaka Komatsu Sakyō (1931–2011) recalled recognizing and reading "American manga" as a child in used bookstores, and he noted that the "torrent" of American popular culture that entered Japan beginning in the Taishō era coexisted uneasily with the country's rising militarism in his childhood. In these years, American popular culture became something of an import substitute for European popular culture, whose flow into Japan stopped during World War I and did not regain its former prominence thereafter.[39]

Although the syndicate copyright information in many translated nonsense manga could be difficult to decipher, particularly in pirated versions, that did not confuse Japanese readers as to their origins. Those origins also made no difference to translated nonsense manga's popularity; in some respects, urban mass culture in Japan was casually indistinguishable from urban mass culture in cities such as New York, London, Paris, Rome, and Berlin. By the 1920s, denizens of these metropolises had more in common with each other than they did with those cities' rural peripheries, and manga—comics—were part of that shared experience. Okamoto Ippei confirmed this point in 1927, writing that comparing contemporary Japanese to foreign manga showed that the former was not really inferior to the latter, and that the standard of living in Japan was not unlike that in European countries either—the United States excepted.[40]

Aside from the new four-panel format, American nonsense manga were revolutionary in that they represented a new way of representing nonvisual elements in manga: using speech bubbles, sound effects, and other visual representations of audiovisual and other phenomena to tell a story solely within the panels. These "transdiegetic elements," in Eike Exner's phrase, represent a transition from cartoons to comics, "from picture story to audiovisual comic strip." In his view, these audiovisual comics constitute an entirely new medium, one that developed in the "more advanced" United States before being adopted in Japan.[41] But speech bubbles had been adopted by *Tokyo Puck* staff in 1908, and while audiovisual comics were wildly popular in Japan in the 1920s, both in imported and native form, nonsense manga was only one form of manga that did not displace other types, and these narrative techniques were only one element of nonsense manga's appeal. That appeal was rooted in a shared experience of the modernity that shaped media worldwide, including the spread of film, radio, and other sound reproduction technologies.

This shared modernity did not mean that all things foreign were equally welcome in Japan, however. The Great Kanto Earthquake and the response to it marked an inflection point in imperial Japan's attitude toward the West. The earthquake infamously touched off a xenophobic pogrom, known as the Kanto Massacre, in its immediate aftermath, in which some six thousand resident Korean and Chinese people, as well as Japanese leftists, were murdered by mobs and security forces. In the years that followed, Japanese society slowly but steadily turned away from the West and inward toward Japan and its Asian empire. Manga magazines clearly reflect this gradual narrowing of focus; many shed their bilingual features after the earthquake, beginning with *Osaka Puck*, which axed its English-language editor's notes (though not its image captions) in the second issue after the quake.[42] Similarly, although *Happy Hooligan* returned to *Jiji* in 1927, by 1928 it was no longer printed with any English text—Opper's name was written in katakana.[43]

But while this pattern of withdrawal certainly holds in terms of the upper echelons of politics and high culture, it would be a mistake to equate those elites with the members of the urban crowd, the café waitresses, Modern Girls and Boys, and moviegoers who consumed Japanese popular culture and who were the subject and audience of what Miriam Silverberg and others have called its "vernacular modernism." The florescence of translated comics in manga magazines after the earthquake is ample evidence that appetite for such content had, if anything, only increased at the popular level, and it did not abate. Reflecting this vernacular modernity, many nonsense manga in the 1920s and early 1930s appeared in the Euro-American, left-to-right reading order, rather than the Japanese right-to-left, and some flip-flopped between the two.[44]

In that same 1927 article, Ippei wrote that "it's best to regard now as manga's Meiji Restoration."[45] In his view, manga was being reinvigorated by an influx of foreign ideas after a period of isolation, which accords with the idea that nonsense manga's arrival constituted a break with the earlier manga tradition practiced by Rakuten, Ippei himself, and their students.[46] There is some merit to this view; the likes of four-panel comic strips and newspaper nonsense manga, with their dense use of audiovisual elements, hadn't been seen in Japan before they were imported in this decade. But as with so much else after the Meiji Restoration, Japanese manga creators quickly adopted these forms and made them their own. Mangaka were already adept practitioners of the international visual medium of comics, just as Rakuten envisioned it, and nonsense manga was simply a new style within that familiar medium.

Manga itself was becoming a very big tent, as the huge variation in an August 1926 issue of *Jiji Manga* makes clear: Mr. Dough and Mr. Dubb—speech bubbles and printed lettering and all—are followed by a two-page spread of cartoons produced in Japan, with numbered panels, no speech bubbles, and hand lettering all over the page. Moreover, *Jiji* itself represented only a small portion of manga at this time; Japanese cartoonists in the 1920s understood the term *manga* to encompass a wide variety of subject matter and styles. Ippei claimed that this wide scope was necessary to cater to the tastes of Japanese readers, who thanks to modernization were used to thought and customs transforming every five years: "If you did American-style serial manga in Japan, readers would lose interest after three years." The implication was that, unlike the Euro-American cartoonists who did *Punch* magazine all their lives and became masters of the form, mangaka had to keep on their toes to stay current with evolving fads, art styles, and subject matter.[47] Nonsense manga was just the latest comics trend to incorporate into their repertoire.

In these years, people began talking about the "manga field" (manga no hatake), an indication of its continuing expansion in terms of practitioners and subject matter.[48] Thus, Ippei wrote that the current era was both manga's Meiji Restoration and its "golden age."[49] That golden age was celebrated by the ten-volume anthology *Gendai manga taikan* (Contemporary manga survey, 1928), which sought to simultaneously legitimize manga as an art form, introduce its full scope to as wide a public as possible, and tell a particular story about manga's origins and development. This anthology marks a milestone in prewar manga, and it is worth exploring in depth its claims about what manga had achieved in the twenty-three years since *Tokyo Puck*'s debut.

GENDAI MANGA TAIKAN AND THE MANGA MODERN

The *Gendai manga taikan* (Contemporary manga overview) was published by one Taguchi Kyōjirō, who had worked with the Tokyo Mangakkai cartoonists to produce "Manga 53 Stations of the Tōkaidō Road," a play on the famous Hokusai series of ukiyo-e prints, before the earthquake.[50] Although the *Gendai manga taikan* was Japan's first manga anthology, in this commercially minded age Taguchi was making a shrewd market prediction: In the era of the "enpon" (one-yen book) boom, the anthology was a huge hit, although it did not sell as well as Okamoto Ippei's collected manga, released in several volumes beginning in 1929. The Ippei collection eventually sold fifty thousand sets, inspiring Kitazawa Rakuten to publish his own collected works in a projected twelve volumes—only nine of which were released, due to weak sales.[51]

The anthology's ten volumes were each devoted to a different topic and/or style of manga: contemporary social manga; great works of literature; Meiji and Taishō history; children's manga; humor literature; "Eastern and Western manga"; a tour of Japan; different kinds of jobs; the world of women; and finally, collected contemporary Japanese manga. The anthology is a key site at which to examine manga's history not just because it sold well, but because of its division of content and what individual editors, the leading cartoonists of the day, said about manga in their editor's notes and in their editorial choices. The anthology promoted the idea that manga had ancient roots, but its message differs in important ways from how the "manga as ancient descendant" discourse developed later.

First and foremost, the anthology positions manga as a source of laughter. The 2010 reprint edition also contains a supplement reprinting some of the anthology's original marketing materials: The gist of these advertisements is that modern life is suffocating, but the medicine for modern life is laughter, and the world of manga is that medicine. So, the *Gendai manga taikan*'s publishers were bringing it out to comfort readers.[52]

Laughter appears as the function and justification of manga in many discussions in these years, often with an emphasis on the physical act of laughing itself.[53] Manga is repeatedly described as humorous (kokkei), and being humorous is one of the most important positive qualities any given manga could have. The act of laughter (warau koto) and manga's power to make readers laugh became increasingly important in the 1930s, with popular mangaka insisting that humor was one of manga's most important virtues even as the authorities viewed that very power with increasing suspicion.

Indeed, cartoonists viewed laughter as a salient feature distinguishing manga from other forms of painting and art. Shimokawa Ōten wrote in 1927 that the difference between manga and ponchi was that manga expresses "consciousness" while ponchi merely expresses humor; in manga, humor is the *result* of manga's critical expression, but in ponchi humor is the goal, which is why manga is art and ponchi isn't.[54] Similarly, Ippei declared that ponchi sought to get laughs by being unnatural, which manga was not.[55]

Ippei wrote in 1935 that humor was one of the four important elements of manga (along with nonsense, satire, and realism). According to him, the meaning of *humor* was a bit difficult to express in Japanese. In his view, various words (*kaigyaku, okashimi, odoke*) all missed the mark of "naturally causing people to laugh," for which reason he and everyone else in the field liberally used the Japanicized version of the English word, *yūmoa*.[56] Painter and mangaka Ikebe Hitoshi (1886–1969) took it for granted that fine art and manga were the same. For him, the difference arose from the perspective of results: Unlike fine art, manga "exudes" humor.[57]

Literary critic, writer, and translator Uchida Roan (1869–1929) complained about this aspect of manga in 1927, writing that most contemporary mangaka in both Japan and the West "have insufficient philosophy" (filosofī ga tarinai) but acknowledging that current manga "makes you laugh and be amused against your will." Uchida was not a fan of caricaturized art styles; according to him, these were so distorted in contemporary manga that "people look like Martians."[58] Hosokibara Seiki (1885–1958) had not disavowed humor in his *Nihon mangashi* (History of Japanese manga, 1924), the first full-length history of manga, but he did end the book predicting that the age of manga as folk art was over, and that mangaka, who had used jokes and laughs to pull the masses' strings, were about to wake up, as were those same masses: "Manga that expresses the true meaning of society will certainly be born hereafter."[59]

Thus, there was widespread agreement on the purpose and result of manga (laughter), but it still embraced a plethora of forms and lineages, and for this reason several of the anthology's volumes are worth examining in detail. If the first volume, edited by Shirota Shūichi (1880–1958), is the publishers putting the medium's best foot forward, that foot is rather surprising: Rakuten, Ippei, and Hosokibara supplied most of the contributions, comprising mostly stand-alone illustrations, accompanied by explanatory text of varying quantities. Paging through the book is reminiscent of watching a silent film, with the captions fulfilling the function of intertitles or a benshi's narration.

The *Gendai manga taikan* volumes' order presents an argument about importance and seriousness: It is no coincidence that women are second to last and that the kinds of cartoons that created the medium in the first place were brought out in the final volume. Cartoonists in this era were almost universally graduates of art schools, with fine arts training in both Japanese and Western (or only Western) art, and they were intent on winning recognition of manga's legitimacy as an art form.[60] Shimokawa had made this point explicitly on other grounds in 1927, writing in the art journal *Bijutsu shinron* (New art theory, 1926–40) that "overlooking manga as impure art until now is a mistake" and arguing that "manga is an art that gives form to the abstract" and an art of "exposure" that sought to reveal the truth of things as well as their absurdity.[61]

The irony of attempting to construct manga, a form of mass media, as "art" that was not "commercial" in the age in which mass consumerism emerged in Japan was apparently completely lost on these men, as was the irony of doing so in books like the *Gendai manga taikan* that were unapologetically aimed at the mass of what Silverberg aptly termed "consumer-subjects." Nonetheless, the message that manga was and should be considered art is clear in the second volume, which presents illustrated editions of classic literature, both Japanese and Western: Rakuten adapted Tolstoy, while Ippei chose a short story by his old patron Natsume Sōseki. Ippei didn't even use panels in his illustrations.

The sixth volume, "Eastern and Western manga," is also particularly interesting. In the preface, the aged ukiyo-e artist Shōsai Ikkei wrote: "Regardless of whether the art is good or bad, because manga reads the spirit of the age, it is worthy of being ranked among things that are considered extremely important."[62] Including Western art and calling it "Western manga," the volume presents manga as an art form that transcends national divisions, part of a global artistic tradition going back to seventeenth-century France, with references to earlier Roman and medieval European art. This section is only one-third of the volume, however; the middle third, "Collected Japanese manga," opens with the ancient *Chōjūgiga;* and the final third, "World modern manga," showcases recent works by Euro American artists. Popularly known as the "rabbit and frog scrolls" for their depiction of anthropomorphized rabbits and frogs carrying on in the ridiculous pursuits of humans, the twelfth-century *Chōjūgiga* were first linked with ponchi-e in English-language media beginning in the 1880s, a linkage that was extended to Hokusai manga in the early twentieth century and then to Rakuten manga by the *New York Tribune* in 1921.[63] The scrolls have since become a perennial candidate for manga's "starting point" in popular discussions of manga worldwide.

The anthology obscured manga's actual history by relegating the cartoons that constituted that history's documentary record to the final volume. Thus it presented a certain vision of what manga was and did, one that Hosokibara had expounded in *Nihon mangashi*, but was first articulated in 1918 by artist and critic Ishii Hakutei (1882–1958) in the magazine *Chūō Bijutsu* (Central art). Ishii was apparently the first to suggest in Japanese that manga had roots in Japan that extended beyond the Meiji period, partly because he defined *manga* as "art that is carefree, not regulated by rules, and based on the free observation of mainly human life."[64]

This broad definition contains no information by which change over time or the medium's specific characteristics can be measured. It did, however, make a notable change from previous art-world discourse about manga, which was first articulated by Yamamoto Kanae in 1907: He saw Japanese humorous and satirical art as underdeveloped compared to that of the West and was critical of the popular manga magazines of the day (*Tokyo Puck, Osaka Puck*, and *Jōtō Ponchi* [High-class ponchi]) for their comparative deficits.[65] Precisely *because* Ishii's 1918 definition of manga was nativist, positive, and analytically empty, it was useful: Cartoonists looking to position manga as a dignified, serious art form worthy of critical praise rather than critical scorn used it to suture manga to the existing traditions of Japanese art. By so doing, they ignored manga's doubly hybrid nature as the Japanese version of a global form that willfully and gleefully mixed image and text, image and film, East and West.

Taking up this line of argument, in his book *Shinmanga no kakikata* (How to draw new manga, 1928) Ippei asked whether manga was a strain of contemporary art, or whether it was something that had the special characteristic, "more than thought, more than method of expression," of having no restrictions. His answer: "Manga is art that gets to the heart of contemporary customs and behavior." Furthermore, compared to fine art, which concentrated on beauty, manga concentrated on getting to the heart of reality.[66]

Ippei's remarks on the nature and history of manga in the introduction to the first volume of the *Manga kenkyū shiryō kōza* (1934–35, Manga research materials lectures) in 1934 are worth exploring too. He opens by crediting Hokusai as the first person to use the term *manga*, but although he then discusses the differences between Hokusai's art and modern manga, he undercuts these distinctions by using the concept of "humor" to jump back to the Fujiwara (eighth century?) and Tenmei (1781–89) eras, with their respective traditions of humorous art.[67] Although Ippei concedes that "it's considerably difficult to separate manga from normal drawing," he then tries to do just that, based on both semantic and artistic grounds (but this is difficult; if you say manga is realist, so is normal drawing, but if you say manga is funny, some manga isn't). He then advances an intriguing argument: that another difference between manga and "normal drawing" is that the former is more literary, because "no matter what manga must tell a story about something." Manga is also more explanatory than normal drawing in Ippei's view, for the same reason, just as it's more concerned with time than with space. And though Ippei mentions *Maruchin* in the same breath as *The Japan Punch* and acknowledges the importance of both, *Manga kōza* starts manga's history with ancient Egyptian painting and the aforementioned Fujiwara era.[68]

In other words, Ippei and other leading cartoonists did not readily acknowledge the very elements of manga that had made it, and them, so successful. They also ignored the essence of the mass culture of Japanese modern times that they were currently being personally enriched by, which, as Miriam Silverberg described it, was a hybrid form of Japanese/Western that was being actively created by a montage-like process of cultural code-switching: not one or the other, but consciously incorporating elements of both.[69] The attitude that art has to be serious to be worthwhile, and that *serious/worthwhile* by definition means "not popular" and/or must deal only with certain subjects defined as valuable, is not unique to this particular group of cartoonists; this form of respectability politics has bedeviled the discourse about other forms of comics in other times and places.

Not everyone in manga embraced the idea of premodern origins developed in this era. Rakuten in particular held out against it almost until the end of his life; not until a 1952 essay did he buy into the by-then-established notion of manga's ancient past.[70] By that point it had become the default, unquestioned assumption. But the idea that manga is an ineluctably Japanese art form with roots going back either to the twelfth century or the Edo period, depending on your particular tastes, first took hold in popular consciousness in the *Gendai manga taikan*.

THAT GIRL IS A PROBLEM: MANGA, WOMEN, AND MODERNITY

For a medium whose origins, development, and burgeoning success traced precisely the arc of mass media's growth in Japan, it is somewhat surprising to realize that by 1928 many of manga's leading figures had embraced a vision of its past that emphasized not newness but continuity, updated tradition rather than modern rupture. This vision placed these creators and their manga in a somewhat conservative position with respect to the mass culture of Japanese modern times, a position that is readily comprehensible from the ninth volume of the anthology, "World of women."

None of the cartoonists who participated in the *Gendai manga taikan* were women: None of the professional cartoonists of this era were women. Notwithstanding Okamoto Kanoko, a member of the famous feminist Bluestockings circle and a New Woman in her own right, it was not until the 1930s that women entered the ranks of professional cartoonists in Japan. Indeed, the illustrations for "World of women" are condescending at best and often viciously sexist. But this volume of the anthology is in concert with the tenor of manga overall, which was generally opposed to the rise of the New Woman and her successor the Modern Girl (moga). Shimizu Isao pithily summarized the attitudes of prewar mangaka toward women as "contempt, derision, and scorn."[71]

The slim manga manbun volume *Buta no heso* (The pig's navel, 1928), with art by Kitazawa Rakuten, encapsulates contemporary manga's attitudes and stereotypes about liberated women: Rakuten repeatedly characterizes Modern Girls as sex workers who do intravenous drugs constantly. Urban women not depicted as sex workers outright are depicted as vain, frivolous, lustful, and avaricious, particularly for new Western-style clothing and lifestyle items, and prone to wasting time in cafés, which at the time had an unsavory reputation. Child rearing appears as a particular locus of concern and control, with Modern Girls allegedly shamelessly breastfeeding their infants in cafés or neglecting them in favor of dancing and sex.[72] Rakuten had originally synthesized these themes in *Jiji Manga*, which repeatedly raised the specter of the modern woman as a threat to the established social order (plate 4). Ogawa Jihei did the same, as in the October 1922 cover depicting a modern woman whose household was, according to the description, "on the verge of death" due to her neglect (plate 5).

This opposition to the existence of Modern Girls (i.e., independent New Women who wore Western-style clothing, worked outside the home, and were not necessarily married) went hand in hand with the efflorescence of ero in manga and across mass culture in this era. Short for *erotic*, in practice *ero* often meant simply pornographic—there are a lot of naked women in manga in this era, and many of them are women in pieces: separate, sexualized body parts rather than whole people. These fantastical dismembered women-in-pieces were sometimes connected with guro (grotesque), as in the gory murder novels of Edogawa Ranpo (1894–1965) and others of this era, but the consumption of women in pieces by men is also par for the course under the linkage of capitalism and patriarchy—themselves grotesques. Satires of new social phenomena like the housewife (shufu) and the Modern Girl in manga of this period are decidedly sexist and skeptical—never more so than in manga devoted to mocking the ideas of women's rights and women's suffrage, but misogynist sentiments were widespread throughout the medium.

Japanese mangaka were not the only male cartoonists of this era to be so ambivalent about modernity and its attendant social changes, despite the fact that those very phenomena underlay their careers and their art. American Winsor McCay's pioneering comic strip *Dream of the Rarebit Fiend* (1904–11), for example, was powered by anxieties about the same. As comics scholar Katherine Roeder writes,

> Such anti-urban and antimodern sentiments were rampant in comics and the illustrated press at the turn of the twentieth century, yet the formal operations of the *Rarebit Fiend* contradict its indictment of metropolitan life. The dark humor at the center of McCay's comic strip reveals both a critique of his urban audience and an expression of ambivalence directed at the rapidly changing world at large. Yet, while McCay's comics lampooned the trappings of modernity, his innovative design techniques and groundbreaking use of multiple perspectives all speak to a decidedly modern point of view. The disconnection between the form and content of the comic underscores the paradox of the displaced urban subject.[73]

Nor were McCay (1869–1934) or Japanese cartoonists alone in these sentiments, which were powered not just by overt anxieties about urban traffic violence and anomie, but also by a barely sublimated streak of misogyny, linked to anxiety about the increasing presence of women outside the home. This anxiety was usually expressed in terms of scorn for consumerism, "reflecting," in Roeder's phrase, "societal preoccupations with women as unfettered consumers."[74] The problem with consumption in contemporary post-earthquake Japan was not consumption itself, which had a history stretching back centuries, but the fact that consumption was seen as part of the forces of modernity destabilizing the traditional social order promoted in the Meiji period: Whether as housewives, café waitresses, or Modern Girls, female consumption of nonessential goods was understood as a social problem.[75]

Thus, leading mangaka—while part of the mass culture of Japanese modernity—at times were distinctly uneasy about both modern times and mass culture. In the case of men like Rakuten, as with McKay, their contemporary artistic techniques and their political views as expressed in their art diverged. After 1920, Ippei turned the bulk of his attention to increasingly high-cultural-cachet styles of manga and to literature; Rakuten's political satire was muted after the Home Ministry asked him to design an influenza awareness poster in 1919, and his views became increasingly aligned with the government's—quite a change from his critical beginnings.[76] He and other mangaka thus sought to use their manga to inculcate or promote what they saw as mainstream social values, using satire to criticize new social phenomena.

However, even in their own magazines, the Tokyo Mangakkai elite could not suppress other forms of manga and other mangaka that were much less elitist and much less critical of mass culture, consumerism, and women outside the home. Nonsense manga was inherently allied with the internationally minded, lowbrow vernacular modernism popular among the urban crowd, since it embodied those very characteristics when it was imported as translated comics from abroad and it was a product of the modern times it chronicled everywhere it was produced. Whatever the personal opinions of people like Rakuten, they needed nonsense manga to sell copies of their magazines and newspapers, and in keeping with the need to follow comics trends that Okamoto Ippei had highlighted as a peculiar feature of manga in Japan, Ippei, Rakuten, and others including Miyao Shigeo adopted the audiovisual style of nonsense manga in their own work.[77]

The Tokyo Mangakkai members were also not the only mangaka in the nation; Osaka had been home to a competing lineage of humorous images since at least *Kokkei Shinbun*. By 1928, that tradition was epitomized by *Osaka Puck*, which—unlike virtually every Tokyo manga publication—continued to put out issues immediately after the earthquake, and which was generally more populist (and thus more nonsense-minded) than *Tokyo Puck* and other leading manga publications in the capital.[78] The *Gendai manga taikan* and other Tokyo-produced anthologies did not necessarily speak for all cartoonists around Japan when they argued for manga as the heir to a long tradition of Japanese art. In Osaka they were equally likely to point to other traditional Japanese arts, particularly the comedy forms of rakugo and manzai, and to Edo-period caricatures as important premodern antecedents of manga.

Conclusion

1928

IN 1928, MANGA HAD COME a long way in a short time—thirty-seven years since Imaizumi Ippyō first used the term *manga* in print, twenty-three years since Rakuten's launch of *Tokyo Puck* had increased the term's currency, sixteen years since Ippei joined the *Asahi* and liberated manga from politics, expanding its scope to include social satire. Manga was firmly ensconced in mass culture, both using modern media to articulate socially conservative views (Rakuten, Ippei, the *Gendai manga taikan*) and a product of modern times (nonsense manga, children's manga). Moreover, the mass culture of Japanese modern times was, like manga itself, the product of a global modernity that meant Japanese urbanites had much in common with denizens of other world cities—London, Paris, New York, Berlin.

What did these urbanites share? Advancing industrialization, an increasing number of women working outside the home, the rise of single-family households, and new forms of mass communication, media, and consumption. Jazz Age flappers like Blondie had their Japanese counterparts in the Modern Girl (moga), just as the global figure of the urban dandy was known in Japan as the Modern Boy (mobo). Pointing out these commonalities does not erase important local differences, but broadly speaking, what was happening in Japan in this era was also happening in the other countries that were party to the Peace of Versailles. These countries were modern, and modernity was happening to all of them at approximately the same time and in many of the same ways—at least in this decade.

These countries also shared many of the same media. The Euro-American comics that circulated in Japan had their counterparts in Euro-American movies and movie stars, particularly Charlie Chaplin, a significant figure in Japanese media history and in Japanese modern times. While Japanese comics and movies did not circulate widely outside the Japanese empire (unlike the popular culture of the United States, major European countries, and the Soviet Union), the forms themselves, whether they be newspapers, radio, movies, or comics, were not considered innately national by anyone who practiced them anywhere in the world. Rather, they were *modern* forms that transcended national boundaries and could be put to whatever purpose creators desired. Roeder notes that the American newspaper comic, "both in terms of its form and the mechanics of its production and distribution, embodied the conditions of modernity": Comics publications were made possible by industrialization and urban population growth, as well as advances in printing technology, and powered by urban audiences who read comics widely in syndication.[1] The same conditions made manga possible in Japan.

Many of those American newspaper comics were published in Japan as nonsense manga, the impact of which was significant enough that some critics have sought to portray nonsense manga's introduction in translation as the *real* birth of manga in Japan.[2] This argument ignores the fact that Japanese creators were already steeped in manga, which had already developed independently through manga manbun and other local forms that had no foreign equivalents. For mangaka in 1923 nonsense manga, including its audiovisual elements, were a new, modern evolution of their medium rather than a break from it. It also ignores the fact that nonsense manga was only one strain of manga in Japan; other types that did not rely on audiovisual elements or narrative persisted for decades after 1923. To be sure, translated nonsense manga had a huge impact on manga's development, but the mangaka who adopted nonsense manga as a form created their own takes on it in the Japanese context rather than mindlessly copying American originals. As Chinghsin Wu notes in her discussion of avant-garde art movements in Japan, while ideas from abroad were sometimes catalysts or accelerants, "this effect was intermittent and could only apply when Japanese modernism's internal development allowed space for a new trend or a change in direction, or when Japanese artists had already encountered a similar artistic problem."[3] In retrospect, 1923 was one such moment, as Ippei indicated when he described nonsense manga's impact as having kicked off a "Meiji Restoration" in manga.

The flow of translated comics in this era also contextualizes what is otherwise a curious one-off in manga history, *The Four Immigrants Manga* (Manga yonin shosei, 1931) by the painter Kiyama "Henry" Yoshitaka (1885–1951).

Kiyama emigrated to San Francisco in 1904 and worked as a houseboy, among many other jobs, while studying painting; he drew the manga's fifty-two strips, which chronicled his and his friends' experiences in the United States, beginning around 1924. Although he had hoped to serialize it in a local Japanese-language newspaper, it was too long and too multilingual (English and Cantonese appear as-is), but he exhibited it in San Francisco in 1927 and eventually self-published the collected manga in a book in 1931.[4] The manga's depictions of cash-strapped immigrant life are reminiscent of contemporary proletarian manga, and its social satire angle fits right in with newspaper comics in both Japan and the United States, while Kiyama's fine arts training placed him squarely in the mangaka mainstream even as the manga's multilingualism harked back to an earlier era. Manga was comprehensible in the Japanese diaspora because it circulated through imported Japanese-language media and because comics were familiar from the wider cultures emigrants lived in as well.

The very media and publishing infrastructure that adopted nonsense manga in translation, both pirated and legally syndicated, grew up as part of Japan's modernization and industrialization beginning in the Meiji period. Nonsense manga being called "nonsense manga" in Japan speaks to the impact of Ippyō, Rakuten, Ippei, and their followers, who created manga as a distinct media form that was different from ponchi (which still persisted into this era as humorous drawings for children's education).[5] That form could and did change rapidly as artists took in other art and comics and sought ways to express their consciousness through their manga, as Shimokawa Ōten put it.[6] Translated nonsense manga most directly impacted not only the children's manga that would eventually become the manga mainstream, but also the underappreciated proletarian manga.

While the *Gendai manga taikan* consolidated a particular narrative about manga's past, manga's present contained at least four general strains: (1) elite manga, epitomized by the patriarchs Rakuten and Ippei, which attempted to court the fine arts establishment's approval even as it depended on mass culture for its sales; (2) nonsense manga, which depicted the absurdities of modern life around the world at the popular level; (3) children's manga, generally short-running fictional narratives aimed at children, who had themselves been created as consumers by the rise of mass culture; and (4) proletarian manga, which was worker-centric and thus inherently radical. In terms of format, manga still encompassed a wide variety of publication types, with newspapers and magazines—still not entirely differentiated from one another—equally likely to feature multiple kinds of manga. These same forms were also present in the Kansai region, centered around Osaka, while newspapers across the country published manga in their pages.

Okamoto Ippei wrote in *Bijutsu shinron* in 1927: "Passing through the current Meiji Restoration of manga's golden age, I have the feeling that manga has stagnated a little. And I feel that a second golden age will come. Right now some child is taking their course of study and will awaken as a true genius of manga. That's the presentiment I have. I think a good mangaka will appear from this field [hatake]. They will deeply study economics or something and awaken to seize the zeitgeist [sesō]. That's how I feel."[7] At first glance Ippei appears to prophesy Tezuka Osamu's birth in 1928. But his predictions of a "second golden age" heralded by the arrival of a "true genius of manga" could also be said to have come true in the 1930s.

If manga had stagnated a little by 1928, it had stagnated at a remarkable level of achievement for a form that was only a few decades old. Nor was there necessarily any particular reason to expect any of manga's prominent strands to do radically better than the others in the next decade. But by the formal end of Japan's era of imperial democracy in 1940, all these forms of manga had been winnowed or extinguished—even as manga's popularity only became further entrenched. How manga changed from 1928 to 1945, both through the efforts of a true genius of manga and through external pressures, is the subject of the next chapter.

PART TWO

Manga During Wartime

1928–1945

Overview

MANGA DURING WARTIME

THE CREATOR OF PREWAR MANGA'S best-selling work, Tagawa Suihō, could also be the "true genius of manga" whose coming Ippei boldly foretold: Tagawa's manga debut in 1928 was an event no less epochal for the medium than Tezuka's debut after the war.[1] A former member of the radical left-wing art movement MAVO, through which he was familiar with contemporary art movements including constructivism, futurism, Dada, surrealism, and more, Tagawa popularized the Czech term *robot* in Japanese when he created the first science fiction manga, *Jinzō ningen* (Artificial human, 1929). When he launched the children's manga *Norakuro* (1931–41), his mastery of humorous dialogue, empathy for child readers' interests and concerns, and innovative storytelling produced a bestseller the likes of which had never before been seen. Tagawa's use of humorous dialogue, derived from his background in the traditional Japanese comedy form of rakugo, and the manga's decade-long serialized story radically expanded manga's scope yet again, drawing in new crowds of devoted fans, old and especially young.

Norakuro was a generational smash, and it cemented the love of manga among children across the empire and paved the way for numerous other popular children's manga. Many of these were published in the Kodansha sibling magazines, which were aimed at various tranches of youngsters; the flagship *Shōnen Kurabu* reinvented itself as a home for manga in the early Shōwa period thanks to Norakuro.[2] The little dog and his friends inspired countless imitators across various publications and formats, and manga merchandising began in earnest with Norakuro toys, candy, and tie-in media marketed to children, extending the manga's reach and cementing children as consumers.

But Norakuro's rise took place against the backdrop of increasing fascism and militarism in Japan. Party government ended in practice in 1932 and was formally abolished in 1940, even as the imperial military's adventurism on the Asian continent and then in the Pacific drew the empire into what became known as the Fifteen Years' or Asia-Pacific War. The war drove manga and publishing in general to new heights by 1940, when the empire reached its zenith, but sociopolitical changes in the home islands, driven by Japan's reorganization into a fascist state, profoundly altered manga's trajectory as well.

Scholars have argued for decades about whether it is appropriate to describe the wartime state that emerged in imperial Japan in the 1930s as fascist. But if it looks like a duck and quacks like a duck, we may reasonably conclude that it *is* a duck for the purposes of categorization—and imperial Japan in this period acted like a fascist society. As historian Aaron Herald Skabelund summarizes, "Popular mass antiliberal and antisocialist nationalist movements and regimes that used a common language of unity, purity and violence appeared in a number of modern nations that had previously seemed to be on a path toward expanding democracy in the early twentieth century. Societies displaying these characteristics can be meaningfully grouped under the label 'fascist' as long as we keep in mind that no two societies are the same."[3] Japan is amply comparable to Mussolini's Italy and Nazi Germany, the other major fascist societies of the period.

Historian Kenneth J. Ruoff discusses Japan and its Axis allies as examples of "reactionary modernism": These regimes integrated appeals to ideologies of nativist traditions with the technological and political infrastructure of modernity.[4] Rejecting the painful shocks of unfettered capitalism and the labor movement that had sought to mitigate it, as well as the consumer culture that seemed to be vitiating the traditional social order, bureaucrats and regime supporters alike thought that "communitarian values of the countryside or the distant past could restore a cultural and spiritual purity to a nation that had experienced foreign-influenced decadence of the city and a recent history of modernization and Westernization."[5] Crucially, however, the very apparatus of state power, as well as the mass media and other cultural realms that it sought to control, were themselves products of industrial modernity, and in that respect there could be no going back.

Thus the creation of things like propaganda films and Zero fighter planes to further the war effort, even though "traditional" Japan did not have powered flight or movies. But even outside the war effort, the empire at war became more modern, not less, as civilians' wartime nationalism was expressed primarily through consumerism in the 1930s, even while the imperial government became distrustful of consumerism as it attempted to direct capital toward the war effort. As Ruoff writes, although it is easy to take at face value an exhortation to "unrelenting sacrifice" from government campaigns preaching slogans such as "Luxury Is the Enemy," in fact, "consumption per se was not problematic so long as it could be cast as dutiful." Far from curtailing consumption, wartime economic gains increased it. Many Japanese subjects in the home islands experienced a feeling of material prosperity until as late as mid-1942, when military setbacks against the United States further eroded daily living conditions.[6]

The temptation has been to narrate the story of Japan's experience in the Fifteen Years' War as a descent into a "dark valley" of political repression, but as Ruoff notes, the experience of daily life for most imperial subjects in the home islands was much more mixed, bright and dark together. The best year ever for the Japanese publishing industry to date was 1940, thanks to general wartime prosperity: Increasing disposable income over the 1930s allowed more and more imperial subjects to participate in wartime consumerism.[7] Manga directly benefited from these developments, which enabled the rise of a new group of young mangaka, the Shinmangaha Shūdan (New manga faction group), whose upstart members successfully spread manga to many different kinds of periodicals, including women's media. Predictions of a continuing boom proved premature, however, as manga became a target of state repression and control, just like all other forms of popular media in this era. Increasing repression contributed to the rise of manga groups by the mid-1930s, at which point almost everyone in the profession was affiliated with one or more groups.[8]

The empire and its wars permeated media and society in the 1930s, beginning with the media event that was the Manchurian Incident in 1931, which drove radio-set adoption to new heights as people clamored to keep up with the latest news on the imperial army's invasion of northeast China. Jingoism in media pushed the war, and the continuation of the war encouraged more and more people to consume media about the war, making the mass media ever more mass.[9]

But one form of manga stood alone against this tide, a beacon in a broader arts movement that advocated for workers' rights and criticized capitalism: proletarian manga, born of left-wing thought in the 1920s, which was fast becoming unthinkable in the imperial Japan of the 1930s. The movement's leading manga figure, Yanase Masamu (1900–45), had also incubated in MAVO in the previous decade (he likely coined MAVO's name), and for a time he straddled both bourgeois and proletarian publications before multiple arrests blunted his political activities.[10] Proletarian artists sought to unite contemporary art movements with leftist thought, both of which circulated globally in these years, and proletarian mangaka sought to expand manga beyond its previous realms in terms of publication venues, content, and audiences, encompassing the working classes throughout the empire and in Asia. They succeeded for a time, but the movement was wholly suppressed by 1936–37. Most former proletarian artists converted to the new regime and "returned to Japan" (tenkō), whether voluntarily or through torture and imprisonment.

After proletarian manga's extermination, children's manga became the next target. Although Kodansha's children's manga in particular has incurred heavy postwar criticism for promoting militarism to children (as though manga alone were responsible for pushing the war in society), government bureaucrats under the empire took a very dim view of children's manga, which from their perspective promoted not militarism but consumerism to young readers. Through a variety of censorship maneuvers, by the end of 1941 children's manga was brought to heel and made to serve solely as a vehicle for "education," ranging from science facts to outright propaganda.

Manga for adults was straitened too, with the forcible consolidation of most newspapers and magazines leaving few officially sanctioned outlets in which to publish. Those that survived went all in with the empire as a matter of course—it was not possible to do otherwise and continue to receive the censors' approval. Needless to say, that approval was not extended to the erotic grotesque nonsense that had proved so popular in the 1920s, or to the political manga of previous decades. But reciting the government line did not spare those few manga periodicals that were allowed to continue publication from paper shortages, evacuations, and the draft, and all shut down by June 1945. In these conditions, the end of the empire could very well have spelled the end of manga as well.

It did not, however, and the innovations in manga during the wartime era, epitomized by *Norakuro*'s runaway success, had a significant influence on its future. The 1930s were also the era in which the first people who had grown up as fans of manga became manga professionals, and the decade witnessed the dōjin (amateur) "first wave," in that amateurs began drawing manga without formal arts training en masse and professionals sought to foster amateurs' participation. The 1930s also saw women enter the ranks of professional mangaka, although female creators found it far harder to gain a stable foothold in the profession. Two notable female mangaka who managed to carve out long careers for themselves were Hasegawa Machiko (1920–92) and Ueda Toshiko (1917–2008), while their contemporary Yazaki Takeko (née Katō, 1912–?) walked a more uncertain and, for female professionals of this generation, more typical road. The full force of all these innovations was first felt after the war, but it was the wartime era that made them possible in the first place.

CHAPTER THREE

Norakuro and Friends

THE RISE OF CHILDREN'S MANGA

The story of children's manga in the 1930s is the story of children's magazines, and the story of children's magazines is centered on Kodansha, even today the biggest publishing company in Japan. Kodansha's dominance began in the 1920s, when its flagship family magazine *Kingu* (King, 1924–57) became Japan's first periodical to sell a million copies of a single issue in 1927. To achieve this feat, Kodansha took advantage of mass production's cost efficiencies, coupled with a household-oriented content strategy (the magazine contained something for everyone in the family) and a massive advertising campaign. That three-pronged strategy led to the "enpon" (one-yen book) boom of 1926–29, which was founded on cheap books, advertised copiously.[1]

Kodansha also pioneered the practice of targeting magazines at increasingly narrow market segments, the better to maximize profits from all of them. Its initial lead title *Kōdan Kurabu* (Conversation club, 1911–62) was followed by *Shōnen Kurabu* (Boys' club, 1914–62), *Fujin Kurabu* (Ladies' club, 1920–88), *Shōjo Kurabu* (Girls' club, 1923–62), and finally *Yōnen Kurabu* (Children's club, 1926–58). All told, Kodansha eventually had nine big magazines, but the three "sibling" magazines aimed at children are the most important for manga.[2]

Although *Shōnen Kurabu* and *Shōjo Kurabu* are today best remembered as a forum for the publication of manga and of novels and illustrations, respectively, both magazines, along with their younger sibling *Yōnen Kurabu*, came relatively late to manga. *Shōnen Kurabu*, the longest-running and most popular of the three, featured a mixture of illustrations, serialized novels or short stories, and informational photo spreads about various aspects of

"Japanese" life: usually the imperial military, cultural landmarks from the home islands, or the customs and peoples or landscapes of imperial colonies. Until 1922, the magazine printed two pages of manga per issue at most, often unsigned.[3] *Yōnen Kurabu* was more of the same except pitched at a lower reading level, while *Shōjo Kurabu* leavened its photo features, illustrations, and serialized novels with spreads of girls and women doing various feminine-coded things such as cooking and sewing. *Shōnen Kurabu*'s circulation increased from eighty thousand copies in 1921 to more than seven hundred thousand copies at the end of 1932.[4] By 1936, nearly 80 percent of sixth-year students surveyed by the Ministry of Education read *Shōnen Kurabu* frequently.[5]

Children's magazines began featuring manga from the early 1920s, particularly after 1925, but *manga* meant a wide variety of things, and the most popular children's manga of the 1920s such as Miyao Shigeo's *Manga Tarō* were often serialized in newspapers rather than magazines. The expansion of children's manga in the age of media massification meant that there was a lot of room to experiment, and there was no sense among publishers or mangaka that the age of the audience required any artistic restrictions on the content of children's manga. Miyao was celebrated among professionals for his ability to borrow freely from art theory in his work, and the wide latitude that fine arts-trained creators were given meant that when formal innovations proved popular, they caught on quickly.[6]

Miyao's manga manbun-style children's manga was quite popular, even after the advent of *Shō-chan no bōken*, which was modeled after current British newspaper comics and thus included dialogue inside the panels in addition to narrative text outside it.[7] Dialogue became increasingly important in manga during the 1920s, not only due to audiovisual nonsense manga; science fiction writer Komatsu Sakyō, who recalled that he learned the katakana syllabary by reading the surrealist superhero manga *Tank Tankurō* (1934–36) in *Yōnen Kurabu*, connected the rise of dialogue in manga to the spread of vaudeville alongside rakugo and other forms of performance in modern urban culture in these years.[8]

One of the most important formal innovations that children's manga popularized in the 1920s was *story*. Miyao's *Manga Tarō* pioneered this; before Miyao's debut, discrete narratives were not routinely found in manga, which was rooted in topical satire as popularized by Rakuten and Ippei. Political cartoons are necessarily one-offs in that they are explicitly commenting on discrete events; while public figures may recur, the cartoons added together are just a series of commentaries on things that happened (one damn thing after another), not any kind of larger, overarching narrative. Ippei's social satire was similarly reactive, a series of one-offs. But from the 1920s on, and particularly in children's manga, discrete narratives became a regular feature of manga.

Another important formal innovation of the 1920s was *character*. As stories became an important element in this decade, characters began to populate them: For the first time, visually distinctive recurring characters became increasingly common.[9] Shō-chan is distinguished as much by his trademark yarn cap as he is by his nonchalant attitude, frequently depicted strolling along with his hands in his pockets. Crucially, however, nonchalance is only one facet of Shō-chan's temperament. Previous attempts at characters in manga were characterized by *caricature* (i.e., a given personage was dominated by a single, archetypal trait). Rakuten's strip *Chame to Dekobō*, introduced during his first stint at *Jiji Shinpō* in the early 1900s, is a perfect example: Chame and Dekobō faced every new situation with the same reaction, based on the traits for which they were named (i.e., playfulness and mischief). Rakuten did not bring Chame and Dekobō to *Tokyo Puck*, though he did resurrect them for *Jiji Manga* in this decade.

But the introduction of story—at this point, usually several discrete extended episodes, as in *Shō-chan* and other four-panel manga—allowed characters to become more complex, developing a degree of interiority and reacting to differing situations with different emotions. (Characters' interiority remained hidden from readers; interior monologues would not become widespread in manga for decades.) Visual distinctiveness—the fact that characters tend to wear the same unique outfit and to look the same over the course of the story—helped contribute to the rise of characters, though it arose out of labor-saving impulses. Characters were the mainstay of, and essential condition for, the success of four-panel comics like those serialized in newspapers; characters carrying over between strips allowed creators to focus on setting up and getting the joke across rather than having to introduce new personalities every time.

Yet even the influential *Shō-chan* still has its narration outside the panel frames, as does Miyao's manga from this decade. Miyao's characters are barely there; his *Karutobi Karusuke: Manga monogatari* (Karutobi Karusuke: Manga story, 1927) and *Manga no omatsuri* (Manga festival, 1931) both rely predominantly on the image-plus-text pattern of manga manbun, while the characters in the images often appear to be floating in space.[10] *Shō-chan*, by contrast, placed the character in discrete settings in the images, and had sound effects and dialogue inside the panel as well as narration outside the frame. As manga critic Chūjō Shōhei has pointed out, *Shō-chan* was an evolution beyond Miyao's style, although Miyao kept producing children's manga in his "old" style throughout the 1930s, as it remained quite popular: Miyao's works were a hit with readers because of their stories, while *Shō-chan*'s interest lay primarily in the character himself.[11]

Shō-chan was so popular that his hat was mass produced and sold to children in what was most likely the first manga merchandising, leading Miyamoto Hirohito to describe him as the first case of a character "separating from the story and going on a walkabout."[12] The *Tokyo Asahi* editors responded to fan questions about Shō-chan's parents and other matters in the newspaper manga's margins as though he were a cub reporter for the paper, heightening the sense of Sho-chan as a character separate from the manga (and the grounds for comparison with Hergé's Tintin, another adventurous kid reporter with an animal companion).[13] Shō-chan was also a devoted *Tokyo Asahi* reader, strengthening the bond between character and publication.

In some ways, the *Sho-chan* books anticipated aspects of "emonogatari" (illustrated stories), a new form of narrative with images that *Shōnen Kurabu* introduced in 1932. Emonogatari were invented by kamishibai (paper street theater) creator Yamakawa Sōji (1908–92), who defined them as "kamishibai on paper." Featuring a series of naturalistic one-panel images with narration outside the frame, emonogatari quickly became a popular art form and a competitor to children's manga, which was livelier thanks to its use of dialogue inside the frame, as well as paneling, but slower paced in terms of narrative. Emonogatari remained staples of *Shōnen Kurabu* and children's magazines throughout the 1930s and beyond.

STRAY DOG STRUT: NORAKURO ARRIVES

By the 1930s, the global Depression's effects were readily apparent in Japan, particularly in Tokyo, where the down-and-out tended to gather in the honky-tonk Asakusa district. Charlie Chaplin, already a global star, became even more important to Japanese popular culture as his famous character, the Tramp, came to be called by the same noun, *lumpen* (runpen), as was applied to the Asakusa vagrants. (The word is an abbreviation of the Marxist term *lumpenproletariat*, referring to the unorganized lower echelons of society not interested in revolutionary activities, demonstrating socialist thought's circulation in Japanese society.) The Tramp was a character through which the marginalized gained a representative, and the voiceless were given, not a voice (*The Tramp* is a silent movie, released in 1915 before the advent of talkies), but a means to protest their marginalization all the same: the lumpen as hero. In Miriam Silverberg's phrase, by the 1930s, "Charlie belonged to Japan because he belonged to the world."[14]

Charlie's closest native counterpart in Japan was canine. In January 1931, Kodansha debuted a new children's manga by Tagawa Suihō, *Norakuro*, in *Shōnen Kurabu*. The eponymous title character is a stray dog (norainu) who is black (kuro) and who enlists in the Imperial Japanese Army, which in the manga is entirely staffed by canines. Norakuro, whose real name is Kurokichi ("black fortune"), is prone to pratfalls and, particularly at the manga's beginning, often makes mistakes that cause his superior officers headaches. But he is also loyal, hardworking, and has a good sense of humor. The manga itself was nothing short of revolutionary.

Tagawa Suihō was already a manga veteran; he had debuted three years before with *Medama no chibi-chan* (Big-eyed kid, 1928) in *Shōnen Kurabu*. Starring a human-animal duo à la Shō-chan and the squirrel but more violent and dynamic, the manga was popular enough that the next year Tagawa began publishing *Jinzō ningen* (1929–31) in the adult-oriented magazine *Fuji*, the first manga to feature a robot character, the butler Gamuzē ("Gamu" for short).[15] Tagawa used the Japanese transliteration of the Czech term *robot*, which had been coined only eight years before; trained as a fine artist, Tagawa had been a member of the radical art movement MAVO, which adopted elements from avant-garde art in Central Europe. He still affected the outré dress of the "mobo," or Modern Boy, complete with a bobbed "okappa" hairstyle—MAVO artists consciously used clothing and fashion as part of their personal images. The story goes that when a Kodansha editor went to Tagawa's house—decorated with avant-garde murals—to ask him to start writing manga for the publisher, he initially thought that Tagawa himself was the artist's houseboy.[16]

MAVO's members were roughly divided into two groups, the original core members and a second wave, including Tagawa, who were generally more radical. It was Tagawa who lobbed rocks at and broke the roof of the building hosting the Nika art exhibition during MAVO's infamous August 1923 protest of the same. The second, more radical anarchist faction of MAVO came to dominate the group before it faded by late 1925, in part due to what art historian Gennifer S. Weisenfeld calls "a fundamental tension in the group's work—an increasing incongruity between their leftist idealism and the realities of a rapidly modernizing bourgeois culture." Working for hire in that culture expanded their art's reach, but as Weisenfeld notes, "participation in consumer culture directly contradicted the group's proletarian and revolutionary sympathies."[17]

After MAVO's demise, Tagawa supported himself with a mixture of design and advertising commissions and rakugo scriptwriting and illustrating. Rakugo has been described as "traditional Japanese standup comedy, sitting down," and Tagawa's "new rakugo" scripts and insert art were well received; Tagawa was known for being a prankster himself, always telling jokes and making people laugh.[18] Murayama Tomoyoshi remarked that he never once saw Tagawa sad or angry, and Tagawa's wife, writer Takamizawa Junko, recalled that from his MAVO days he was always doing "manga-like things."[19] His rakugo scripts made the Kodansha editorial team think that he might make a good mangaka, since his scripts and art were both "manga-esque" (mangafū) and he'd already published in all four of their major magazines. Beginning with *Jinzō ningen*, Tagawa published continuously in Kodansha magazines for the next twelve years.[20] His manga were popular enough that Kodansha took the then unprecedented step of publishing a collected volume (tankōbon) of Tagawa's manga in 1930, the first time that children's manga that had been previously published in a magazine were thus republished.[21] The *Manga no kanzume* (Canned manga) and *Manga jōsetsukan* (Manga cinema, 1931) omnibuses made Tagawa a bestseller even before *Norakuro* launched him into the stratosphere.[22]

Tagawa's avant-garde background directly influenced his manga; he later wrote that, "because playing with concepts and logical contradictions are where humor is born, practicing conceptual denial [gainen hitei, a fundamental MAVO concept] with MAVO came in handy when I became a mangaka." Sun Minqiao notes that aside from being the first robot character, Gamu is an adaptation of the avant-garde idea of the "mechanical body" into the mass medium of manga; *Jinzō ningen* is thus where manga and the avant-garde meet. Although avant-garde artists in Japan and Europe were bewitched by the image of the robot as an immortal, ageless superman, Tagawa used conceptual denial to find the idea's contradictions. His popularization of the robot concept in mass culture gave the robot a human identity and a mechanical body, creating a character that had "an exterior that surpasses humans and a human-like interior." Thus, Gamu and his exploits were extremely sympathetic to readers, and Sun argues that Norakuro has some of this dual-sided appeal too.[23]

The two words immediately used to describe Norakuro and his adventures were *kokkei* (humorous) and *pēsos* (having pathos), which gets at some of what made the little dog such a huge and immediate hit. Norakuro and his adventures were *funny*. Although manga and laughter were tightly linked, that laughter was not necessarily derived from witty dialogue; it was usually derived from satire (the jokes in syndicated manga didn't necessarily translate well at the level of wordplay) or from the physical comedy of characters like the Tramp and Felix the Cat, whose movies were serialized in Japan from 1930–32 and were the most popular animation in Japan until Disney films arrived.[24] But the wordplay and verbal jokes in Norakuro were new, and they were a huge hit with readers of all ages.

Tagawa's importing wordplay and witty dialogue from rakugo into manga elevated dialogue's importance and changed manga forever. Partly it cemented the audiovisual turn in children's manga, proving that audiovisual techniques like speech bubbles and music were effective elements in telling a long, fictional story. From this point, and well into the 1950s, manga was competing with serialized juvenile novels and emonogatari in children's magazines, including *Shōnen Kurabu*. Tagawa's differentiating *Norakuro* from these media through witty dialogue helped popularize manga in *Shōnen Kurabu* and among children generally.

Norakuro himself was also consciously designed to tug at readers' heartstrings. Tagawa hit on the idea of doing a children's manga in which a dog joined the imperial military because children already loved dogs and the military; having a dog join the military would amuse them.[25] The connection was anything but natural: Rather, the affinity between children and dogs was deliberately constructed and encouraged through national education textbooks in the 1930s by military and government entities seeking to inculcate support for the military, the empire, and the war in children. These activities were predicated on an already existing linkage between children and dogs in children's media, all of which were part and parcel of Japan's emerging middle class—the very first issue of Kodansha's *Shōnen Kurabu* in 1914 depicts a schoolboy and his dog on the cover. The entanglement of children and dogs with a new middle class placed Japan squarely in the vanguard of other modernizing countries, which had seen such sentiments emerge in the nineteenth century alongside their industrial development. As historian Aaron Herald

Skabelund notes, "cultural discourse about dogs aimed primarily at young people flooded 1930s Japan as never before," and Norakuro himself was probably the most famous canine of them all.[26]

Tagawa drew on memories of a stray dog that he had encountered near his home for Norakuro's design, and on his experiences during his mandatory service in the imperial army (which he had hated) for Norakuro's exploits. He also once admitted to his brother-in-law, the literary critic Kobayashi Hideo, that Norakuro had an autobiographical element; in Kobayashi's phrase, Tagawa had had a difficult childhood in which he was "discarded like a puppy." Kobayashi wrote: "I had felt before that *Norakuro* was a carefree manga with a kind of pathos running through it, but before I heard his words, I couldn't grasp that feeling. Surely that was it. And perhaps those children who were moved by *Norakuro*, who embraced *Norakuro* with feelings of deep affection, were all intuiting that. Perhaps I was the only one who was heedless of it."[27]

Coupled with Tagawa's frequent exhortations to readers to care for the stray dogs they saw around them, Norakuro's pitiable backstory made the little dog easy for people to take into their hearts. (Norakuro initially started out fairly canine, but became more anthropomorphized as the manga went on and the story evolved.)[28] Tagawa later wrote that he had deliberately given Norakuro an even harder life than those of his young readers: Even the worst-off children could look at the little military dog and think they weren't doing so badly because Norakuro had started out so low.[29] Playwright Yashiro Sei'ichi (1927–98) later remarked that Norakuro had "spiritually shaped" him: Growing up poor in the 1930s, when Japan's wealth gap was large, the manga's message that cooperating with poor people was admirable "was a huge emotional support."[30] Finally, Norakuro's character design is reminiscent of Felix the Cat and also of the Tramp, an impression strengthened by the manga's physical comedy. Charlie was a huge hit in Japan, and evoking the Tramp, as well as the incomparable Buster Keaton, was another strategy that made Norakuro popular. Anthropologist Yamaguchi Masao (1931–2013) later remarked that "*Norakuro* was the representative of our times" due to the way it united all of these elements, as well as the artistic background of MAVO, including futurism, Dada, and constructivism.[31]

In the original preface to *Manga no kanzume*, Tagawa wrote that manga was interesting because it was trying to amuse (hohoemaseru) rather than trying to be beautiful.[32] In this respect, Tagawa's apologia for manga in general, and later for *Norakuro* in particular, recall MAVO ideas about the role of art in society, particularly the "art of daily life" (seikatsu no geijutsu), which held that art and the artist had a utilitarian function.[33] In book form, *Norakuro* is not as immediately breathtaking as Winsor McCay's groundbreaking *Little Nemo in Slumberland* (1905–27) or George Herriman's *Krazy Kat* (1913–44), American comics that set a gold standard for comics art that stands even today, and after the war it was dismissed as "static." But *Norakuro* was innovative, not just in its content, but visually as well: Although the panels in the collected volumes are primarily rectilinear, and are oriented "theatrically" toward the viewer (i.e., the point of view of the action is outside the subject, objective rather than subjective), as the manga went on Tagawa became quite visually innovative in his paneling when it served the story to do so.

Manga no kanzume shows that Tagawa could work well in a variety of manga styles: Individual manga are done in the vertical four-panel style, the grid four-panel style, the six-panel style, the manga manbun style, and the three-panel horizontal style that Tagawa invented. Part of what gave *Norakuro* its "unputdownable" quality was Tagawa uniting all of these styles into one manga, changing his page layouts for the collected volumes to match the story in terms of pacing and action.

This was a crucial innovation, one that often goes unacknowledged. The same page that usually held a grid of six panels in *Norakuro*'s magazine chapters was reconfigured in the collected volumes to hold a horizontal three-panel layout; or five horizontally, with one of those same panels divided asymmetrically for emphasis; two horizontal panels, with their width acting as dramatic emphasis in an establishing/close-up relationship directly reminiscent of movies; or much more strikingly, three long vertical panels or even a Tetris-like configuration of L-shaped panels—the latter two often used when Norakuro or his soldiers were providing air support to their fellows, or to show simultaneous action at multiple elevations. Tagawa also changed up the flow with the occasional one-page panel, or even a full two-page spread.[34] Manga critic Natsume Fusanosuke later wrote that "in Tagawa's manga, we can see the genealogy of modern Japan's *modernism*, and the connectivity between fine art and mass culture," and the fluidity of Tagawa's paneling coupled with the manga's striking colors in the collected volumes (Tagawa had studied with a painter who had recently studied with Matisse) is a perfect example.[35]

Uniting the entire arsenal of manga forms in one manga was a big part of what made *Norakuro* so influential for later creators after the war. At the beginning, however, there was no plan for *Norakuro* to be anything other than what had come before, a serialized magazine manga that lasted one year at most. At that time, serialized manga ended to keep things fresh and fast paced, so Tagawa originally planned to end the story after the events of *Norakuro jōtōhei* (Private first-class Norakuro, 1932), in which Norakuro received the first of what became many promotions.[36] Norakuro's young fans, however, prompted a drastic revision to the standard publishing plan.

NORAKURO FEVER

The Kodansha children's magazines shared a consequential editorial practice, namely the "Readers' Corner" or "Readers' Pages" (dokusha no tayori), in which readers' letters to the editors were published with short responses every month. *Shōnen Kurabu* did not invent this practice, but *ShōKu* (as its readers affectionately called it) and its siblings certainly perfected it. Looking at *Shōjo Kurabu* and other prewar girls' magazines, literary scholar Deborah Shamoon has argued that editorial practices such as the readers' corner "helped to form an imagined community of girls by encouraging reader-generated content and interactivity."[37] All three of the sibling magazines had their own imagined communities, or perhaps publics.

But these imagined communities did not arise spontaneously. In the Kodansha sibling magazines, these communities were created through unequal but real collaboration between readers and editors: Readers wrote in every month to profess their love for the magazine and for individual stories and authors, to express their good wishes to the magazine staff and to their fellow super-fans (aidokusha), and to share stories from their lives meant to amuse and/or to demonstrate their status as fans—but it was the editors who carefully selected for publication and replied to individual letters that not only did all these things, but that also represented a very deliberate geographic breadth among the readership. From 1925 to 1937, the readers' corners in *Shōnen Kurabu* and *Yōnen Kurabu* almost always featured a reader letter or telegram from either the colonies or the Japanese diaspora outside the empire, although the number of subscribers in these far-flung territories was quite low. These letters often included photos or postcards which the editors reprinted, educating everyone about life outside of the home islands.

Editorial curation determined what readers saw in the readers' corners, but it was the readers themselves—children and fans—who supplied the content in the first place. In the case of *Norakuro*, the response was immediate:

Children started writing "a mountain of letters" about how much they loved Norakuro, in Tagawa's phrase, and the editors said they couldn't cancel a manga that had so many fans, so Norakuro's story continued for another year.[38] *Norakuro*'s serialization lasted until 1941.

Tagawa was not merely being modest when he laid the credit for *Norakuro*'s enduring serialization at the feet of readers and their "Norakuro fever."[39] The *Shōnen Kurabu* editorial staff stoked readers' passion for the military canine, encouraging participatory practices by which readers could engage with Norakuro and the magazine, and readers responded. The readers' corner published Norakuro-related contributions from readers, including fan-created manga, which staff encouraged by publishing "how to draw Norakuro" guides created by Tagawa; replies from Norakuro himself were appended to reader letters and contributions published in the magazine; guides on how to draw Norakuro's regimental flag, which became a symbol of the readers' club and spread through fanworks, were printed in the readers' corner, as were the lyrics to the Norakuro song.[40] Norakuro illustrated postcards, bookmarks, cards, and pin badges were all prizes for the monthly prize drawings, and editorial staff mailed these items to readers who wrote in with feedback, resorting to sending Norakuro stationery in envelopes if the postcards ran out. Magazine staff kept Norakuro stickers alongside cards with the magazine's information in their pockets and passed them out to children in the street.[41]

By the beginning of 1934 the "Norakuro boom" was in full swing. Kodansha sought to cash in on the manga's popularity first by releasing it in tankōbon format (the first time children's manga was released in such single-story anthologies) and then through successive media tie-ins—probably the first time a manga character had appeared on merchandise and the first time a manga character had jumped artistic media for widespread consumption.[42] Norakuro was a hit in kamishibai, the paper street theater, and was also the star of Japan's first full-length manga eiga ("cartoon films"), also called "manga talkies," five of which were produced from 1933 to 1938, all written or cowritten by Tagawa (figure 5).[43] Norakuro also starred in several color "paper films" (kami firumu), toy animations that people could watch at home using a hand-cranked projector, produced by the Tokyo company REFCY from 1932 to 1938.[44]

Particularly notable among the Norakuro merchandise (much of which was not officially licensed) and media was the predominance of items relating to sound: Norakuro harmonicas and the Norakuro audio dramas ("radio manga," which were also broadcast on the radio), released by then Kodansha subsidiary

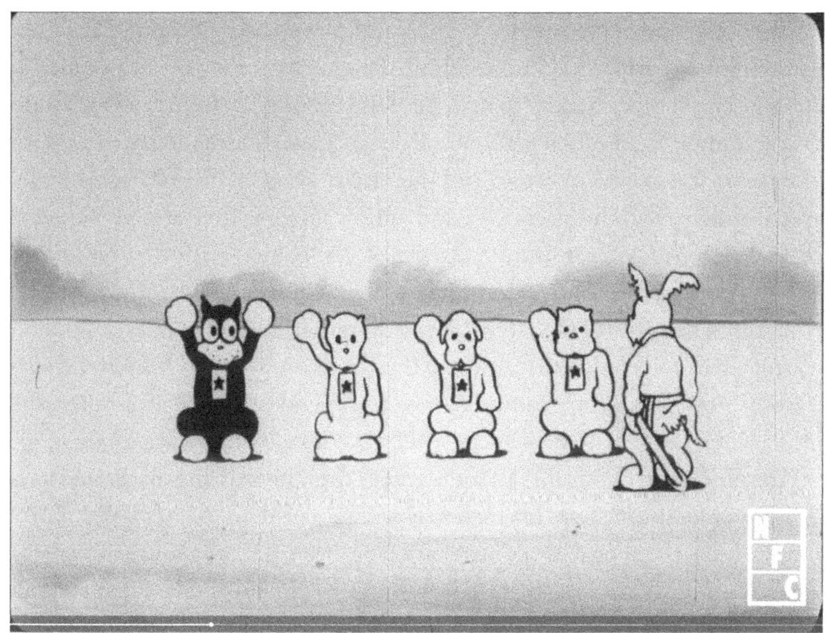

FIGURE 5. Norakuro and his fellow recruits in *Norakuro nitōhei* (Private Norakuro, 1933). Courtesy of National Film Archive of Japan.

King Records, were wildly popular, as was the Norakuro song. Reader letters attest that the song became universally known and was sung at virtually any location where children gathered, especially school; *Shōnen Kurabu* published a photo of children singing the song in 1933. There was no inherent connection between Norakuro and the harmonica that he advertised, but at a certain point it didn't matter: The harmonica tied the manga and commercialism together, and children using the harmonica to play and accompany the Norakuro song reinforced the linkage. Readers' Norakuro musical performances expanded Norakuro's reach, and also advertised the manga.[45]

Marketing properties across multiple media simultaneously, using one form of media to grow the popularity of all of them, is known as the "media mix."[46] Looking at the Norakuro boom as a prewar kind of media mix demonstrates that sound lay at the center, not surprising given radio's predominance at the time: Introduced in 1925, by 1934, approximately 13.4 percent of the population had a radio in the household, after a notable uptick caused by the Manchurian Incident in 1931.[47] Influenced by nonsense manga's use of audiovisual elements, manga in this era began incorporating radio broadcasts, sound, and music, which *Norakuro* readers recreated for themselves.[48]

The sound media through which Norakuro circulated among children were highly participatory: From singing the song to playing the harmonica—often in a harmonica band—to reading aloud to listening to the audio dramas on a record player, Norakuro sound media enabled children to have fun with Norakuro themselves in direct and interactive ways, as Tagawa continually asked readers to do in interviews and author's notes. They also encouraged children's consumer consumption; even if you couldn't afford a Norakuro harmonica or a Norakuro alarm clock, you could probably afford to buy Norakuro candy or see the latest Norakuro talkie in the cheap seats. And no matter what, you could learn and sing the Norakuro song, and you could also learn to draw Norakuro yourself, since the Norakuro books reprinted the music and lyrics for the song and the "how to draw Norakuro" tutorials.[49]

The Norakuro media mix to some extent drew on existing magazine practices; the Norakuro song, for instance, was modeled on the *Shōnen Kurabu* song, which the magazine's super-fans had been learning and singing for years. The Norakuro song had two versions, the second and lasting of which had catchier lyrics and was set to a melody that children already knew, specifically an old naval tune composed for the Sino-Japanese War in 1895.[50] (The song's lyrics did not exaggerate: "Once a vagabond stray dog, / Now part of a regiment of fierce dogs, / He is popular everywhere, / His feats of laughter are uncounted.")[51] But these practices, when combined with the character of Norakuro himself and with Tagawa's pioneering manga storytelling, worked exceedingly well. Judging from readers' letters, they also inaugurated an expansive community: Not only children of all genders but also the entire family routinely read *Norakuro*, and *Shōnen* and *Yōnen Kurabu*. Innumerable letters from fans mention that their whole family loves the magazine, that their older brother likes *Yōnen Kurabu* better than magazines for adults or that their mother only reads *Yōnen Kurabu*, "because it's an interesting magazine," that a certain story made their grandmother cry.[52] Education was at this time compulsory only until the end of middle school, and many of these adults were probably not much above that reading level.

Furthermore, the magazines themselves were avidly shared among children: Letter after letter describes sharing magazines with friends and classmates, usually at school, or at each other's homes, just as letter after letter relates how the writer became a super-fan after a friend introduced them to the magazine. Letters repeatedly mention singing the Norakuro song, listening to Norakuro records, and reading the manga aloud with friends. Postwar writers recalled how, even at schools whose students were so poor that only

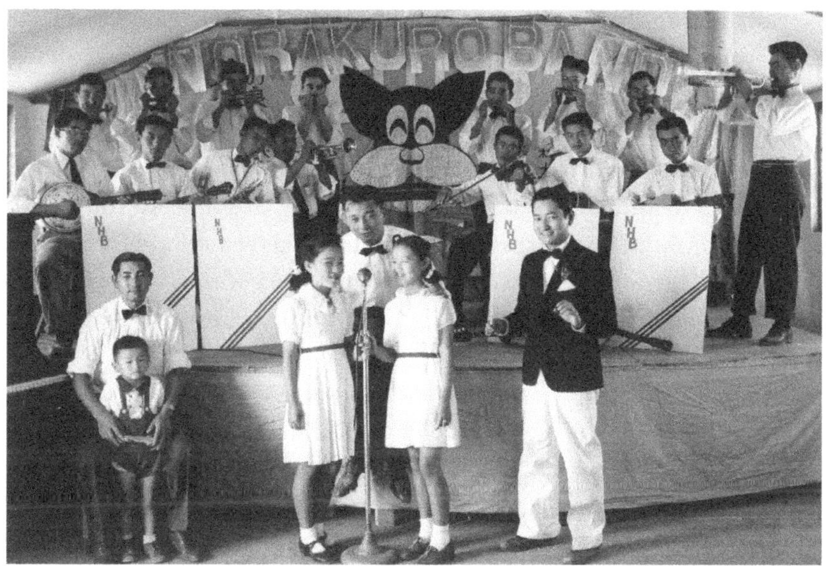

FIGURE 6. The Norakuro Harmonica Band in the Minidoka concentration camp, Idaho, June 1943. U.S. National Archives photo no. 539490.

one or two children could afford the latest issue of *Shōnen Kurabu*, copies of the magazine were handed around or read aloud so that everyone knew what amusing scrapes Norakuro had gotten into that month.[53] *Shōnen Kurabu* and its siblings were also resold in used bookstores, providing another way for readers to access the manga at lower prices.

Norakuro and the sibling magazines also crossed imperial borders: Letters from Manchukuo and the colonies talk about Japanese children sharing manga and the magazine with Chinese and other non-Japanese children, while children regularly wrote in from the worldwide Japanese diaspora attesting that *Yōnen Kurabu* was used as a textbook in their Japanese language class, that the magazine had helped them with their Japanese, that it helped them feel they understood Japan. *Yōnen Kurabu* super-fan lists regularly featured readers from the colonies.[54] Norakuro was popular enough in the diaspora that in 1943 children and adults in the Minidoka concentration camp in Idaho put together a Norakuro Harmonica Band (with as many harmonicas as other instruments) under the baton of one Roy Matsunaga, formerly of Portland, Oregon (figure 6).[55]

If sound was the glue that held the Norakuro media mix together, the Norakuro manga itself was the engine powering the entire assemblage, and

Tagawa rose to the occasion afforded by the manga's popularity, both as a designer and as a manga creator.[56] What we might call the manga's rereadability or high resale value—not in the sense of prices at used bookstores, but the fact that it was still engaging upon rereading and that readers could still enjoy the story even if they bought a pre-owned copy of the magazine, stripped of its furoku (freebies)—was something that Tagawa consciously considered when creating the manga. He designed the magazine versions in such a way that even children too poor to buy *Shōnen Kurabu* outright could enjoy the manga and feel included in the manga experience by singing the song, drawing Norakuro, and so on.[57]

To ensure that the Norakuro tankōbon, comparatively expensive at one yen each, gave children a good value for the money, Tagawa redrew the eight-page magazine chapters, which usually employed a six-panel grid, into the three-panel layout he had invented. He adjusted these layouts to suit the story as necessary, but for ease of reading, he also eliminated panel numbers in the tankōbon versions and used a standard right-to-left, top-to-bottom reading direction.[58] Reading direction had fluctuated during the 1920s under the influence of American nonsense manga, and Tagawa's employing R-L, top-bottom for *Norakuro* helped standardize this Japanese style paradigm once and for all.[59] Eliminating panel numbers was a revolutionary choice: These remained standard in some manga magazines into the 1970s, but abandoning them made the narrative, and future narrative manga, more engrossing. Tagawa's horizontal three-panel page layout had a huge influence on manga in general, immediately becoming a standard layout in akahon manga and remaining so well into the 1950s in kashihon manga. Tagawa also tightened up the content for the tankōbon, altering gags, dialogue, and whole plot elements as he saw fit so that the manga would be enjoyable on every reread.[60]

Additionally, Tagawa personally designed every element of the hardcover *Norakuro* manga tankōbon, from the slipcases to the repeating patterns on the endpapers and the new art created for the tables of contents, author's notes, and covers.[61] This degree of personal control over every aspect of the design process was unusual for a mangaka at the time and remains so today. The book design, in particular, was very pleasing to Norakuro fans: The pages were large, Norakuro's face was on the covers, and the books were all in full color.[62]

Kodansha's own advertisements proclaimed that there had never been a book that sold so well and that even the booksellers were surprised.[63]

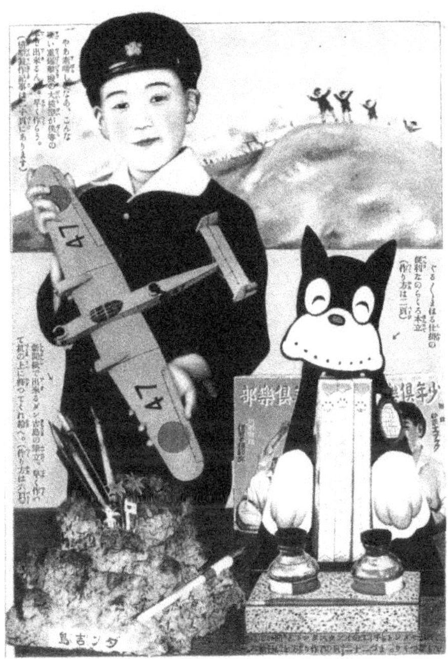

FIGURE 7. This page from *Shōnen shukō book* (Boys' handicrafts book, 1937), a *Shōnen Kurabu* furoku, depicts a schoolboy with a Norakuro magazine holder and a "Dankichi island" pen holder. The booklet contained instructions for assembling both items.

Bookstores also capitalized on the Norakuro craze; Kodansha encouraged them to feature magazine issues with Norakuro freebies in their display cases, and one bookstore in Gifu even used a tent to create a "Norakuro house" devoted exclusively to Norakuro books, magazines, and merchandise. Through these practices, Norakuro came to be associated with *ShōKu* and with Kodansha: He was used to advertise Kodansha itself, and became the readers' mascot.[64] Kodansha even distributed cardboard Norakuro display stands, which booksellers could set up to display the latest Norakuro volume indoors if they weren't willing to set up a tent outside.[65]

The booksellers were doing for profit what Norakuro's readers were doing for fun; cardboard items that could be assembled at home were common *Shōnen Kurabu* freebies, and throughout the 1930s many featured Norakuro (figure 7). Norakuro manga was restricted almost exclusively to *Shōnen Kurabu* until the three-book "Continent Trilogy," which was published directly in tankōbon beginning in 1937. But Norakuro and *Shōnen Kurabu* were heavily advertised in the sibling magazines, and children wrote to *Yōnen Kurabu* about Norakuro as well.[66]

Tagawa's and Norakuro's popularity drove the expansion of children's manga in multiple ways. To start, *Shōnen Kurabu* reoriented itself around manga, marketing itself as the home for children's manga and publishing many other serial titles, including the decade's second most popular manga, *Bōken Dankichi* (Adventure Dankichi, 1933–39).[67] Created by Shimada Keizō (1900–73), a former Rakuten student, the protagonist is a brave Japanese youth whose adventures among various indigenous peoples, mostly in the South Seas and all depicted using the grossest racial stereotypes, sought to uphold the same "Japanese spirit" (Yamato damashii) at the heart of all of Kodansha's children's publications. Tagawa described it in *Norakuro* as being cheerful in duty, deep in feeling, surpassing in wit, and loyal with a strong will, "just the same as you readers."[68] Like Norakuro, Dankichi was also merchandised, principally through dolls and chocolates. Unlike *Norakuro*, Dankichi's adventures were portrayed in a more emonogatari style, which suited the story better.[69]

Along with Tagawa and Shimada, the last of the "three warriors" of *Shōnen Kurabu* in this era was Nakajima Sakuo (1897–1962), whose manga *Hinomaru Hatanosuke* (1935–41) was the magazine's third most popular title.[70] *Shōjo Kurabu* also frequently published manga one-shots, and *Yōnen Kurabu* got in on the serial manga action with titles such as *Tank Tankurō*, a surrealist superhero story. Its creator, Sakamoto Gajō (1895–1973), studied painting for five years before becoming a mangaka on Ippei's advice; he drew children's manga at the *Nihon Keizai Shinbun* from 1932–36, where he got almost no editorial or reader feedback. But the *Yōnen Kurabu* editor liked *Tank Tankurō* immediately, as did child readers: It was wildly popular.[71]

Seeking to capitalize on Norakuro's and manga's popularity, Kodansha and other publishers continued to request more manga from Tagawa, not all for children, and through most of the 1930s he was drawing as many as ten series per month, all by himself, as well as furoku (freebies), and redrawing *Norakuro* for the tankōbon. Most of these manga were not collected in tankōbon at the time, and have never been republished, although some of Tagawa's characters from other series appeared in *Norakuro* in later years, creating a shared "Tagawa universe."[72]

Some of Tagawa's series were published as "bessatsu furoku" (separate manga booklets) for magazines, particularly magazines aimed at adult women. Tagawa's surrealist children's manga about a young male rabbit,

Dekoboko Kurobē (Beetlebrow kid Kurobē, 1933–36), was published as a bessatsu furoku for Kodansha's *Fujin Kurabu* beginning in May 1933. At the time, *Fujin Kurabu* was locked in a fierce competition with its rival magazine *Fujin no Tomo* (Lady's friend, 1903–), and Tagawa's manga was included with *Fujin Kurabu* on the theory that mothers would be more likely to buy the magazine so they could give the freebie booklet to their children. *Dekoboko Kurobē* started as sixteen pages, but from 1935 it increased to twenty-four, and Kurobē himself was quite popular. Another women's magazine, *Shufu no Tomo* (Housewife's friend, 1917–2008), included a manga freebie booklet aimed at children, "Shufu no tomo ehon," which included serialized manga from heavy hitters like Tagawa and Shimada and ran for over seven years, publishing more than fifty manga. Circulation of women's magazines in this era was more than a million copies per month, while *Shōnen Kurabu*'s circulation peaked at about 750,000 copies. In other words, women's magazines rivaled the leading children's magazine in terms of putting children's manga in front of readers.[73] Children's manga had already expanded beyond the bounds of children's publishing.

Bessatsu furoku were introduced in February 1933, when Tagawa released *Norakuro tosshintai* (Norakuro charger squad) as a twenty-four-page, two-color booklet for *Shōnen Kurabu*. His editor had come up with the concept to ward off the so-called February scaries: January and July (when the February and August issues were published, respectively) were the worst months for magazine sales. But the booklet contained six months' worth of manga all at once, and the issue in question saw a 96.8 percent sales increase to 411,000 copies, the best February issue ever.[74] From 1935 on, every New Year's issue of *Shōnen Kurabu* included a Norakuro manga booklet, and New Year's issues of competitor magazines followed suit with their own bessatsu furoku. Bessatsu furoku aimed at children were also published throughout the year, with publisher Shogakukan being particularly gung-ho about them. Bessatsu furoku manga's rapid expansion provided another market for mangaka, and bessatsu furoku tended to be welcoming to newcomers. Even tankōbon books got in on the bessatsu furoku phenomenon: Each volume of the eight-volume nonsense manga anthology *Gendai renzoku manga zenshū* (Collected contemporary serial manga, 1935; to which Tagawa contributed an original work, *Mr. Chanchara*) came with a bessatsu furoku by Miyao Shigeo.[75]

Tagawa and Norakuro also sparked another boom entirely, in akahon manga. *Akahon* means "red book" and seems to have evolved from stores selling back issues of magazines and remaindered books in the Meiji period, but may also refer to the red ink used liberally on the covers to catch children's eyes.[76] Emerging in the 1920s in the entertainment district of Asakusa in Tokyo and the area around Matsuya-chō in Osaka, akahon manga were cheaply published short books aimed at children, sold at open-air stalls, candy shops, and other non-bookstore venues.[77] Most akahon publishers were ramshackle at best, and akahon manga itself was considered disposable, meaning that very little akahon manga has survived, and even less of it from the prewar period.[78]

Akahon manga was published anonymously or under pseudonyms, and the vast majority of its content was derivative: Animation and movie characters and actors such as Norakuro, Mickey Mouse, Charlie Chaplin, Betty Boop, Shirley Temple, and Mito Kōmon were mainstays of the medium (plate 7). The other akahon mainstay was jidaigeki, or historical action, usually featuring ninja, samurai, and other figures from Japan's Edo past, as well as detective stories. Miyao Shigeo's *Manga Tarō* and *Dangokushisuke manyūki* (Record of Dangokushisuke's pleasure trip, 1925) were some of the first manga series to be extended in unauthorized form in akahon at the end of the Taishō period, and manga became a wellspring for akahon. If kids liked it, akahon would copy it. The Norakuro akahon boom deepened that relationship and provided children with even more of what they wanted: manga featuring their beloved Norakuro. Akahon even copied creators' pen names: One popular Norakuro akahon was published under the name "Higawa Suisen," quite close to Tagawa's own pen name.[79]

Akahon manga varied widely in price and page count, but the nicest versions were sold in bookstores and department stores: From 1935 onward, these were in the semi-standard akahon format of a B5 hardcover of thirty-two or sixty-four pages.[80] The Nakamura Manga Library, a series put out by the akahon publisher Nakamura Shoten, were released in this format, and in the sea of derivative, poor-quality akahon manga, they stood out for their originality—eventually. Nakamura published seventy titles from 1933 to 1939, a breakneck pace that meant creators were granted wide latitude in their stories, although many started out copying earlier manga—Ōshiro Noboru (1905–98) published *Yukaina tankentai* (Delightful expedition force) in March 1933, only a few months after Tagawa's *Norakuro jōtōhei* (1932), which it copied in almost every particular except the price. The Kodansha book was one yen, whereas the Nakamura volume sold for 75 sen.[81]

Copying the *Norakuro* tankōbon, as Ōshiro did, further popularized Tagawa's innovations in manga structure and format. Ōshiro eventually contributed thirteen volumes to the Manga Library Series, while Shaka Bontarō (1891–1963) did twenty-seven, almost one-third, and Ni'izeki Seika (1898–1953) did another thirteen. While Ōshiro evolved the most original style, all three contributed stories that enthralled their child readers.[82] Komatsu Sakyō recalled that for children, prewar manga was defined by Kodansha manga and Nakamura Shoten akahon manga. Tezuka was "mad for" Tagawa's works and was an avid reader of *Shōnen Kurabu* and the manga volumes in the Kodansha Ehon series, as well as other prewar publications like *Asashi Graph*.[83] He also owned the entire Nakamura catalog, and after the war he asked the publisher why their books were so reminiscent of Kodansha. The answer: They took *Norakuro* as their exemplar.[84]

Akahon manga was filling a gap in the children's manga market that Kodansha chose to leave open. Aside from *Norakuro*, Kodansha didn't collect most of its popular manga into tankōbon; at most, it published two or three volumes of manga per month, whereas Nakamura published as many as sixteen. Employees at the time said that Kodansha was too nervous about putting out only "beneficial" reading material: Even manga that was deemed morally acceptable for serialization in *Shōnen Kurabu*, like Tagawa's popular *Shinshū Sakuranosuke* (Sakuranosuke from Shinshū) and *Hayabusa kotantei* (Young detective Hayabusa) by Yoshimoto Sanpei (1900–40), a student of Shimokawa Ōten and a member of the Shinmangaha Shūdan, were deemed not worth the effort of redoing for tankōbon.[85] Despite Kodansha's marketing hyping *Shōnen Kurabu* as the home of children's manga, by the numbers it remained a small proportion of each issue, about 10 percent.[86] Other children's publications in this era filled that gap too; the children's newspaper *Mainichi Shōgakusei Shinbun* (Daily elementary schooler news, 1936–), printed four-panel manga in every issue and had a special manga section on Sundays.[87]

Spurred by Tagawa and Norakuro, children's manga overall mushroomed across publications, with talking animals at the forefront of the category. Just as manga in general spilled out of newspapers and specialist publications and into the wider media in these years, manga also began to be featured in advertisements and packaging for commercial goods, particularly those aimed at children. Candy companies Morinaga and Glico used manga characters for ads, and even published actual manga featuring candy-inspired characters such as *Umaimontarō* (Delicious-things-tarō). These omake (gift with purchase) manga were reputedly quite difficult to actually get one's hands on, but the candy was readily obtained, and the ads were ubiquitous. Manga was also frequently an omake in newspapers aimed at children.[88] Through these tactics, children's manga and children's commercialism became tightly linked in popular consciousness.

Kodansha was not wrong to be concerned about its manga's reception: Criticism of children's manga rose along with akahon manga's popularity, with concerned parents and educators focusing particularly on the use of sound effects and onomatopoeia for things like shouts and screams, as well as children generally imitating manga and manga dialogue in their play.[89] The company contested these views through the readers' letters of the sibling magazines, which began routinely printing letters from mothers of child readers praising the magazine's educational content, embodying the well-known slogan depicting the ideal schoolboy holding "textbook in the right hand, *Shōnen Kurabu* in the left."[90] Kodansha also countered them explicitly through the prefaces to the manga volumes of its Kodansha Ehon (Picture Book) series.

This series launched in 1936 under the editorship of Katō Ken'ichi, with the goal of providing appropriate reading material for three-year-old Crown Prince Akihito and every Japanese child. This was the age group below *Yōnen Kurabu*, which the company had not previously targeted.[91] Under the motto "picture books to improve children," the series published four volumes a month until its cancellation in 1942, a quarter of which were manga until March 1941, when the manga volumes ceased. The most popular volumes sold more than four hundred thousand copies, and via the same network effects that helped propel *Shōnen Kurabu* to an audience greater than its circulation numbers, many more children read them even if they didn't buy them—some volumes were even used in schools.[92]

Manga volumes were usually anthologies featuring multiple authors. Present and future manga luminaries, including Shimada, Tagawa, Inoue Kazuo, and Hasegawa Machiko, were frequent contributors, all of whom acted as "leadoff hitters" in one or more volumes.[93] Ehon manga contributor Sugiura Shigeru (1908–2000) and Hasegawa were both Tagawa's students, while Inoue and Hayashida Takashi (?–?), another frequent contributor, had been discovered when they submitted Norakuro fan manga to the *Shōnen Kurabu* readers' letters page. Katō also welcomed leading Nakamura Manga Library creators, including Ni'izeki Seika. Released monthly and featuring at least 108 pages of manga in every volume, the manga installments of the Kodansha Ehon series were in effect the era's most manga-ful children's manga periodical.[94]

The Ehon manga volumes represented a concerted effort by Kodansha to allay parental and especially educational concerns about manga: The manga themselves consisted of broadly didactic, morally educational topics in the series' first years, and then shifted to more blatantly pedagogical stories. The series also marshaled a collection of educators, politicians, and military men to argue for the value of manga in the prefaces, declaring repeatedly that because manga's influence was strong and children's critical thinking skills were weak, the Ehon books contained only good manga that would not be a bad influence on children—in fact, it would be beneficial.[95]

Educator Sasaki Hideichi wrote the preface to volume 22 (May 1937), declaring that "you can't leave it [choosing reading material] to kids, sufficient control is required" and assuring adults that the manga volumes' "ingredients are top quality" and that "we consciously gathered manga that could almost be called education manga" for them. Educators were suspicious of manga; kids were wild for it, and teachers felt that there was "a danger that manga would mislead children," in one educator's phrase. Another, Okamoto Hanako, wrote in her preface that "children cannot be dispossessed of manga. There are people who thoughtlessly reject manga without considering children's reason for this. It goes without saying that manga created thoughtlessly exerts a bad influence on children, but good manga bringing happiness to children's lifestyles is a wonderful thing." The goal of the series, in her words, was "to instruct while making children laugh."[96]

NORAKURO'S FATE

You don't climb all the way to the top without making a few enemies, even if you're a lovable stray dog who enlists in the military and improbably becomes an officer. *Norakuro* sold 1.5 million copies in book form in the 1930s and was prewar manga's indisputable runaway success.[97] But by 1938, the fascist military-bureaucratic clique that had taken over Japanese politics had grown deeply suspicious of Japan's most famous fictional canine, and of children's manga in general. Sakamoto, who pulled *Tank Tankurō* from *Yōnen Kurabu* after an unfriendly, realist-minded editor took over, saw which way the wind was blowing when the prime minister and minister of education, General Hayashi Senjūrō (1876–1943), declared in 1937 that he hated manga and magazines began dropping it. Sakamoto later described these years as "a time where people were made to feel submissive and powerless. Fantasies and dreams were almost considered vices."[98]

By 1938, Norakuro was fighting a war on the continent against the pigs (China, a racially charged equivalence, given the popular stereotype that dogs are smarter than pigs) in the so-called Continent Trilogy, in order to make a new nation, a land where the "five races" (two types of dogs, pigs, goats, and bears) could live in harmony (gozoku kyōwa).[99] No one needed to be told the connection between the war against China, the five types of animals in *Norakuro*, and the five races in the Manchukuo puppet state: Japanese, Russian, Korean, Manchu, and Mongol.[100] Yet military officers found the idea that a dog could serve in the military insulting, notwithstanding the fact that dogs did serve in the Japanese military and police forces throughout the empire.[101]

Norakuro's story largely depicted the military in a positive light, or at least in a child's idealized vision, which formed the linchpin of the postwar charges that *Norakuro* in particular and *Shōnen Kurabu* in general were responsible for promoting wartime militarism to children.[102] These charges are extremely ironic on one level, as Tagawa had hated his mandatory military service—since 1872, two years had been required for all able-bodied men at age twenty. He spent his in colonial Korea, where he cared for messenger pigeons and participated in counterraids against horse thieves in the Jiandao border region, and the military he depicted in *Norakuro* no longer existed: respectful to superiors, kind to subordinates, comradely toward everyone, mutually striving for the good of the country.[103] By the time of the Siberian Intervention in 1918–22, a toxic internal dynamic had already become established in the Japanese military: Impoverished enlisted soldiers exported the abuse they received from their repressive senior officers down the chain, the ultimate result being the numerous war crimes and atrocities committed against civilians and prisoners of war throughout Asia.[104]

Despite Tagawa's personal feelings about the military, it would be fatuous to deny that Norakuro and Dankichi were pro-empire; reading both manga in book format increases this impression, since it removes them from their original magazine context. *Norakuro*'s emphasis shifted toward more military content over time, culminating in the Continent Trilogy, which changed from "war games" with made-up countries to a more realistic retelling of the current war with China.[105] Through it all, Norakuro himself remained a well-meaning bumbler, a hero in spite of himself; he was even wounded in battle and spent a long time recovering in the hospital, injecting more realism into the narrative.[106]

But the *Kurabu* magazines' military and imperial content from the 1920s onward was by no means unusual for the time; rather, it was bog-standard, especially under censorship's steady escalation after 1931. Domestic support for the Japanese empire was overdetermined precisely because so many components of society supported imperialism, often unthinkingly: Imperialism was normal.[107] Children and adults in Japan taking part in large-scale, officially approved war games became common in the 1920s, on the theory that war games prepared children to become soldiers and spiritually united adults with the military; children's play increasingly featured war games, a development that educators officially endorsed in the media after 1931.[108]

Kodansha and its magazines not only reinforced but catered to those base assumptions about empire and militarism, assumptions that children absorbed from everyone around them in society as well as from the magazines, which regularly featured a remarkable number of photo spreads showcasing military parades, military reviews, military hardware, and military personnel. All these combined to create a children's culture of imperialism, as well as a model of what made someone a Japanese child, including dogs. As Skabelund summarizes, "Popular culture, just like official literature, actively fostered affinity for dogs—both real and fictional—in children and at the same time took advantage of that familiarity to encourage an interest in becoming a soldier and to cultivate values that supported militarism and imperialism." Skabelund also grimly notes that the boys of the so-called Norakuro generation, born in 1922 (coincidentally, the year of the dog in the Chinese zodiac) and nineteen years old in 1941, sustained the most war dead out of any Japanese age cohort in the Asia-Pacific Wars.[109]

In scholar Abe Noriko's evaluation, there was initially no "shadow of the war" on the Ehon series manga volumes, but that changed rapidly after the beginning of full-scale war with China in 1937: By December 1938, the manga ehon proudly contained manga "bidan," stories in the media that glorified war heroes. Ehon manga were more direct than *Norakuro* and *Dankichi*, talking about killing Chinese soldiers, "encouraging killing the enemy, while laughing," and publishing war songs and games such as a jan-ken-pon (rock-paper-scissors) variation themed around invading Nanjing. Nakano Seiji's serialized *Chibiwan tokkanhei* (Assault soldier little dog, 1937–40) was extremely realistic, even depicting Japanese soldiers conducting "local procurement" (i.e., pillaging the Chinese peasantry for supplies—a war crime). Essentially, the manga ehon taught children to see the enemy as inhuman, just as the adults did.[110]

No matter how fervently the manga ehon embraced the empire and the war effort, however, it was not enough. The question of what it meant to be a proper Japanese child, a little imperial subject (shōkokumin), eventually brought down Norakuro and Dankichi, and children's manga in general. Beginning in late 1937, the National Spiritual Total Mobilization Movement promulgated by the military-bureaucratic government emboldened bureaucrats at the Home Ministry, the center of media censorship under the wartime government. By mid-1938, they had promulgated long lists of forbidden content in media and placed a new emphasis on morality, including a ban on "introduction of gaudy new fashions fostering ostentation or frivolous tastes contrary to the spirit of frugality."[111] In their eyes, the *Kurabu* magazines were not primarily a site for teaching children about imperialism and loyalty, but rather a site for the formation and transmission of a very different set of values, namely that of mass culture, consumerism, and modernity.

The bureaucrats weren't wrong. Alongside the military photo spreads, the *Kurabu* magazines promoted contemporary mass culture, a child-friendly version of "erotic grotesque nonsense." Children too participated in Japanese modern times, visible in the *Kurabu* magazines in the form of fashion illustrations (particularly in girls' magazines), advertisements for products ranging from candy to harmonicas to record players, and illustrations depicting modern children doing a variety of modern things such as going to the beach. The magazines regularly featured articles about global celebrities such as Charles Lindbergh, Amelia Earhart, Henry Ford, and other notable figures; although less prominent in the *Kurabu* magazines than in other children's periodicals, articles about movies and movie stars were all the rage in the 1930s too. The burgeoning popularity of Santa Claus, who became a fixture in year-end issues of children's magazines in the 1920s, must have been particularly nightmarish for a group who fancied themselves the restorers and exemplars of "Japanese tradition."

Consumerism and modern times became increasingly anathematized in official pronouncements after 1937, along with capitalism itself, although the effect was that consumption was recast as "dutiful" to be acceptable: Tourism to imperial sites throughout the empire, for example, was portrayed as patriotic. By that year, Tagawa was telling his young readers in the foreword to the Continent Trilogy's first tankōbon, *Norakuro sōkōgeki* (Norakuro all-out attack), that the time was coming when they would have to be soldiers of the empire and that they should read the book in preparation for that, as well as henceforth be mentally ready for it.[112]

Ultimately, these efforts were for naught. Akahon manga's overwhelming popularity among children was the impetus behind the Home Ministry's "children's literature purification policy" in 1938: The story was that two bureaucrats walked into a Kansai bookstore, asked the proprietor what was the most popular publication among children, and were shocked to learn it was akahon manga. By that year, akahon publishers were issuing approximately four hundred books per year with an average print run of three thousand copies. In October, the Home Ministry issued the policy, which did not make any distinction between manga and children's ehon and which stipulated that both should be educational, not merely entertaining. Akahon manga was banned outright, so akahon mangaka created the Nihon Jidōmangaka Kyōkai (Japan Children's Mangaka Association) in 1939; to survive, members cooperated with publishers and bureaucrats to draw manga that received censors' approval. Manga became didactic, and much quieter; mangaka stopped using speech balloons, and the use of panel layouts decreased as the emonogatari style of image and narration became more prominent. Mangaka also took to using the term *ebanashi* (illustrated tale) or *emonogatari* rather than *manga*.[113]

The regulations also contained an explicit directive to reduce the number of manga, and "in particular to reduce serial manga"—in other words, *Norakuro, Dankichi*, and *Hatanosuke*. In promulgating this policy, the bureaucrats intended to purify children's manga and to create good little imperial subjects with an eye to the empire's presumably glorious postwar future.[114] The policy also abolished furoku in children's magazines, but it singularly failed to stifle children's manga: Neither *Norakuro, Dankichi*, nor *Hatanosuke* ceased publication, although many of their lesser animal imitators did, and the emphasis on "educational" content led to a short-lived boom in science fiction manga.[115] In 1939, Nakamura Shoten changed the Nakamura Manga Library to the Nakamura Esōsho (Illustrated Publication Series), under the editorship of Oguma Hideo (1901–40), and for a few years Nakamura and other akahon publishers produced propaganda and educational material, including science fiction. By the end of 1942, paper shortages and publisher consolidation extinguished the format.[116]

Children's mangaka cooperated with the government in other ways too. Tagawa traveled to Manchukuo at the invitation of the Colonial Ministry, which ran the Manchukuo hinterlands, three times during 1938–41. These monthlong visits were aimed at bolstering morale among members of the paramilitary Patriotic Youth Brigade, male farmer-colonists aged fourteen to twenty-one who had been recruited to emigrate from the home islands' "overpopulated" rural areas and settle in camps on the Manchukuo periphery near the Soviet border, on land expropriated from Chinese peasants for the purpose.[117] Ueda Toshiko also visited Youth Brigade camps on a Mantetsu whistle-stop tour and did kamishibai for them with a Chinese colleague; Sakamoto Gajō visited and drew manga for them too, as he had taken a public relations job with the Manchukuo government, encouraging outmigration from the home islands.[118]

Sakamoto traveled all over Manchukuo for his work and taught Youth Brigade members how to draw manga; although the so-called Manga Troop was very popular, they had no paper and had to draw on the backs of letters from home.[119] Tagawa later called their conditions "miserable"; as well as entertaining them with old rakugo routines, he taught the boys how to use drafting tools to draw geometric figures on the mud walls of their dwellings, which had no electricity and were very cold.[120] But he wrote up his trip to Manchukuo in *Shōnen Kurabu* in 1939, and illustrated advertisements for the Youth Brigade's recruitment efforts.[121] He also drew manga based on his trips for the Manchuria Immigration Association's magazines *Shinmanshū* (New Manchuria, 1939–40) and *Kaitaku: Tōa ippanshi* (Pioneer: East Asia general magazine, 1941–45). Sakamoto ran into Tagawa in Shinkyō, the Manchukuo capital, on one visit; he later recalled that "we saw each other and laughed, 'ha ha . . .' and there was a deep meaning to the laugh that was beyond words."[122]

At the end of the final published volume in 1939, Norakuro set off with his friend Chameken to "build the continent" (tairiku kensetsu); in May 1940, a decorated captain tipped for promotion, he made an emotional farewell speech to his troops and resigned his commission to return to Manchukuo.[123] Norakuro's resignation was partly inspired by Tagawa's Manchukuo tours and partly by his fears that Norakuro attaining higher rank would incur the military's ire.[124] In the manga's last two years of serialization, battle scenes disappeared, along with Norakuro's clumsiness, and Norakuro became a surveyor prospecting for mineral resources in Manchukuo for the "good of the family state" (kokka).[125] But Tagawa's support for the Youth Brigade and Manchukuo's colonial development held little water with Home Ministry officials: As manga critic Ozaki Hotsuki noted, in their view, "Norakuro was cooperating with the publishers' commercialism, not the military."[126]

Having failed the first time, in 1941 the Home Ministry succeeded by other means. Tagawa was compelled to take a "consultation meeting," where

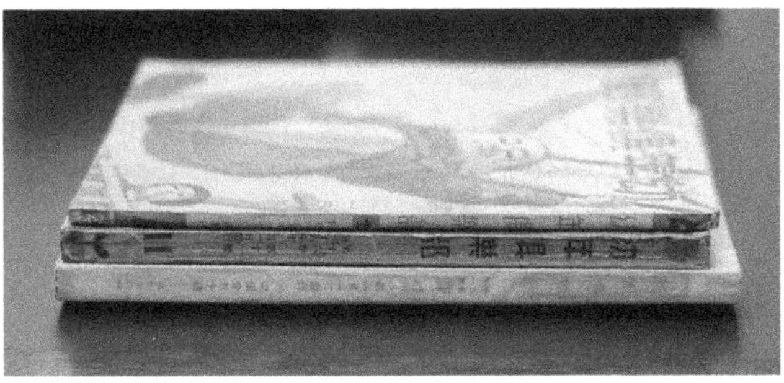

FIGURE 8. Shrinking issues of *Yōnen Kurabu* from (bottom to top) 1933, 1941, and 1944.

bureaucrats told him: "In this time of emergency [hijōji], it's unforgivable to spend precious paper resources on magazines that print frivolous crap like manga.... We want *Shōnen Kurabu* to stop cooperating with commercialism and start cooperating with national policy. So we want *Norakuro* to stop." Tagawa objected that *Norakuro* was cooperating with national policy, and improving youth morale, but to no avail. Norakuro's adventures ended in October 1941. According to regulations at the time, paper rations were allotted on the basis of a periodical's previous month's sales; *Norakuro* was axed to decrease *Shōnen Kurabu*'s circulation.[127] The magazine's formerly teeming manga section was reduced to a few propaganda one-shots per issue; the overall page count shrank from more than five hundred pages per issue in 1937 to just sixty-four in 1945 (figure 8).[128]

Tezuka Osamu later remarked that the end of *Norakuro* came as a shock to everyone.[129] In his memoir, Tagawa remarked: "War sacrifices the people of a country. In wartime, all people make many great sacrifices. My writing *Norakuro* became a sacrifice of war too." He also reflected that if *Norakuro* had continued, he would have been made to actively cooperate with the war against his will and make the manga overtly militaristic—which would have doomed its postwar prospects.[130] Sakamoto Gajō had pulled *Tank Tankurō* over similar demands, such as giving the soldiers in the manga formal ranks and centering the story on the war specifically.[131] The distinction between support and propaganda may seem subtle, but it was real.

For the duration of the war, the manga that was permitted to be published was, in Tezuka's phrase, "in the gutter." So-called "national policy manga" was, as Ōshiro Noboru put it, basically a physical education textbook. The art in wartime manga became very obedient and quiet (otonashii), often at official behest: Ōshiro recounted being told inane things such as not to draw colored insects even in science manga, and no matter what, creators had to take officials' statements as orders. Most manga magazines ceased publication in 1941, while those few that did struggle on halted altogether by June 1945.[132]

Nor was manga unique. Under the wartime press control laws that bureaucrats used to consolidate publications, the number of magazines in print shrank from 16,788 at the end of 1937 to 942 at the end of 1944, while newspapers were reduced from 13,286 to 1,606 in the same period. Children's magazines were slashed from forty-one to six between December 1943 and May 1944.[133] According to Ōshiro, who was summoned to the first of many consultation meetings in 1940 after the promulgation of the agglomeration law, which required all voluntary associations to merge into national associations overseen by the government, by 1943 the official attitude was that in this time of national emergency, manga wasn't necessary for children.[134]

For all intents and purposes, as the Empire of Japan struggled on toward the suicidal and pointless "decisive battle" (kessen) for which its leaders yearned in the first half of 1945, it seemed as though children's manga was already among the war's manifold casualties.

CHAPTER FOUR

The Manga Men

THE MANGA MAN AND THE SHŌWA MANGA BOOM

If the 1930s were a decade of astonishing successes for children's manga, until the cliff, manga for adults weathered more vicissitudes, but it also witnessed notable flowerings in talent and amateur production. The era in which undesirable leftist politics in manga were brutally suppressed also saw the rise of one of Japanese comics' most notable conservative propagandists, Katō Etsurō—who began his career as a proletarian and ended it as a communist. Women entered the manga profession for the first time, but found it even harder than men to maintain careers as censorship squeezed. Yet before manga was slowly constricted by the state along with the rest of mass media, amateur manga saw its first florescence. Ultimately, some mainstream mangaka gained official imprimatur from the New Order's wartime associations, a level of formal governmental approval not enjoyed before or since.

Revived and widely adopted, Sunday supplements became increasingly popular at the end of the 1920s. Collectively, *Jiji Manga* and its competitors shifted the default audience of what came to be called "newspaper manga" (since they were originally the Sunday supplements of newspapers), with the result that newspaper manga came to be aimed at the entire household, its contents pitched at a deliberately broad audience.[1] (The success of *King*'s family reading strategy, under the motto "one copy, one household," also contributed to this shift in scope.)[2] In 1931 *Jiji Manga* changed its name to *Manga to Yomimono* (Manga and reading material) to compete with other Sunday supplements: Aimed at the whole family, these periodicals had more photos, more movies, more sports, and less manga. The former *Jiji Manga* changed its name again less than a year later, this time to *Manga to Shashin* (Manga and photographs), two months before Rakuten left the Jiji company for the final time after three decades. The magazine published its last issue three months later, in October 1932.[3]

In an era of market uncertainty, magazines tried many different tactics to create both guaranteed audiences and a certain supply of cash up front. Perhaps taking a page from children's manga, several magazines for adults in this era tried to start fan clubs among readers, with mixed results. *Tokyo Puck*, which by 1933 was in its so-called fourth era, launched a fan club that year; once the club reached three hundred members (at the membership rate of 1.2 yen for six months and 2.4 yen per year), the magazine would produce a special supplement for them. But although *Tokyo Puck* lasted until 1941 in its penultimate monthly incarnation, ultimately folding as a consequence of the same paper-rationing edict that ended *Norakuro* and *Hatanosuke*, the fan club never reached three hundred members and the supplement was never produced.[4]

Other magazines staked their success on high production values. Two magazines in particular attempted this approach, with mixed results: *Yomiuri Sunday Manga* and *The Manga Man*. The former had a particularly meteoric rise and fall, beginning in the so-called "early Shōwa manga boom" in 1930. Printed at full newspaper size, it was four pages with color offset, seven-pass printing, but even this high quality was not enough to attract readers: At its peak, its circulation was just 220,000 copies, compared with *Jiji Manga*'s 500,000. Created to boost the *Yomiuri* newspaper's circulation, *Yomiuri Sunday Manga* took a deliberately catholic approach to manga: Although nonsense is the most common subject of its manga, the former head of the secret police and current *Yomiuri* editor and owner, Shōriki Matsutarō (1885–1969), wanted it to have something for everyone, with the result that it included children's manga, satire, and political cartoons, with six or seven serialized strips per issue.[5] Shimokawa Ōten's *Otokoyamome no Gan-san* (Bachelor Gan-san, 1932–33) was one of them, and it was popular enough that it transferred from *Yomiuri Sunday Manga* to the *Yomiuri Shinbun* after the former's demise. Gan-san became the first manga character to be adapted to live action film in 1933.[6] Collected volumes of the manga featured images of Gan-san's live-action and manga versions, side by side.

Proletarian mangaka Yanase Masamu (1900–45), a former MAVO comrade of Tagawa, contributed another popular strip, *Kanemochi kyōiku*

(Bringing up moneybags, 1930–31), an obvious play on *Oyaji kyōiku;* Yanase had first joined the paper in 1920 through his patron, the journalist Hasegawa Nyozekan (plate 8).[7] *Yomiuri Sunday Manga* also featured works by mangaka Shishido Sakō (1888–1969), whose *Speed Tarō* used cinematic-style techniques to convey motion and proved quite popular.

The magazine set another milestone when painter Saeki Yoneko (1903–72) drew comics for it for about two months, making her probably the first female mangaka in Japan.[8] She was not, however, the first woman who was interested in drawing manga; a female reader won one of *Jiji Manga*'s readers' submission contests in July 1903 (the prize was a paint set), and ads for aspiring artists in *Tokyo Puck* in 1907 stated that both men and women could apply. Amid the general Shōwa media boom in these years, women began entering the profession in part because media expansion meant more venues for their work.[9]

Manga to Shashin's June 1932 issue, the penultimate issue before Rakuten's retirement, published a spread of eight female mangaka, with Katō Takeko featured among them. Rakuten wrote in his commentary that "it's a joy to see young women entering the world of manga. If career and marriage could be harmonized, we could see the emergence of outstanding female cartoonists. Women with a unique, delicate, and precise sensibility will be able to break new ground as cartoonists separate from men."[10] Rakuten's commentary perceptively hit on the problem that female mangaka faced, namely their expected additional roles as wives and mothers, but he also established a pattern of regarding women's manga as somehow categorically different than men's, a "separate but equal" perception that female mangaka subsequently struggled with for decades. Borrowed from literature, the phrase "joryū [female-style] manga" emerged in these years to designate manga by women, marking it as fundamentally other.

Yomiuri Sunday Manga folded in 1931 after just thirteen months. Its most popular strip, Shishido's *Speed Tarō*, was moved mid-serialization to a specialized children's publication, the *Yomiuri Shōnen Shōjo Shinbun* (Yomiuri boys and girls' newspaper), and the Sunday supplement disbanded in November 1931 when the *Yomiuri* began publishing an evening edition. Most mangaka who continued working at Yomiuri moved to weekly publication of their strips in a morning edition, while Yanase, having joined the Japanese Communist Party the previous month, left to do exclusively political cartoons.[11] Despite its short duration, *Kanemochi kyōiku* proved enormously influential on an artistic level, with leading satirical mangaka such as Kondō Hidezō visibly affected by Yanase's art.[12]

Shimizu Isao called *Yomiuri Sunday Manga* the "most luxurious" of the prewar Sunday supplements, but *Gekkan Manga Man* (*The Manga Man*) gives it a run for its money, in luxurious full color.[13] *The Manga Man* lasted less than two years, from August 1929 to June 1931, and was published monthly in B4 size (plate 9). The January 1930 issue trumpeted its use of color offset printing, the serialized manga it contained, creators' names, and that the issue was "fully loaded" (mansai) with foreign manga. The latter was no idle boast; the issue featured *Gardner* by Scottish artist Arthur Ferrier (1891–1973) and comics by Ernie Bushmiller (1905–82), as well as other strips, which lacked artists' names but were clearly labeled by country of origin (e.g., "English manga").[14] The magazine also published Harold Knerr's *The Katzenjammer Kids* (1914–49) in translation.[15]

Much like *Yomiuri Sunday Manga, The Manga Man* tried to include all current forms of manga. A single issue contained articles with illustrations, full-page colored panels, and the two-page "Japanese art" (Nihonga) style, but the centerpiece was eleven straight pages of full-color, one-page comics. The strips were hand lettered and all had panel numbers. Strips by Japanese creators, including Miyao Shigeo, Nagasaki Batten (1904–81), and Shishidō, as well as Ippei in the first issue, prominently displayed their names. The monthly compiled both multiple episodes of strips (particularly those syndicated from abroad) and long single episodes.[16] It also adopted the syndicated comics' practice of the "topper," a smaller strip that ran above a Sunday comic to fill all the available space. Whereas both the topper and the main strip were usually drawn by the same artist in the syndicates' practice, *The Manga Man*'s toppers, called "obi" in Japanese after the belt for kimono, were usually unrelated and drawn by Japanese artists to accommodate the syndicated comics from abroad.

The Manga Man did not turn to translated comics simply because the staff liked American nonsense manga. The magazine's original manga were produced collaboratively, with staff members assisting in all aspects of production; printing syndicated content meant that less space had to be filled with original comics.[17] All these factors together meant that *The Manga Man* set a high-water mark for production values that would rarely if ever again be met, let alone equaled, in Japanese comics. But its real influence lay not in its actual publication history, but in the connections and community building among mangaka that it enabled.

THE RISE OF MANGAKKAI AND THE CONSTRICTION OF MANGA

Okamoto Ippei pioneered the concept of mangakkai in 1915, and early mangakkai even produced publications put together by the group's members on a semi-regular basis. Ippei's Tokyo Mangakkai released its publication annually from 1915 until 1923, when the group merged with and took the name of the Nihon Mangakkai. Something between a social club and a professional organization, the Nihon Mangakkai was not open to just anyone who wanted to join. Its membership was effectively closed after Miyao Shigeo was inducted, and Miyao himself was forever known as the association's youngest member.[18]

The Nihon Mangakkai played an important part in the publication of the *Gendai manga taikan* anthology; the "Manga 53 Stations of the Tōkaidō Road" its members had produced before the merger formed the anthology's seventh volume, and the membership themselves comprised the Japanese creators featured in the anthology, in both artistic and editorial capacities. They were the most senior and respected figures in manga, and they dominated the "space" of manga in Tokyo. Younger creators coalesced into new groups, such as the Shōwa Mangakkai formed in the late 1930s under Tagawa's auspices, or the Jiji Manga Kenkyūkai, which united cartoonists throughout the Tokyo region in the middle of the decade, meeting once a month. The latter also had a women's chapter, the Kyūkokai, which counted Yazaki Takeko and Kaneko Hisako (1919–?) among its nine pioneering female members.[19]

Young artists coming to manga in the early years of the Shōwa era (1926–89) found that the existing positions were filled: The manga veterans already occupied the prestigious staff positions at newspapers, and the manga these men drew was still dominated by the painterly, caricaturized style requiring long explanations for full comprehension.[20] Thus new and aspiring mangaka founded new publications like *The Manga Man* and looked to expand manga's reach into new markets.

In 1932, the year after *The Manga Man* folded, about twenty people associated with the magazine formed the Shinmangaha Shūdan (New Manga Faction Group). They were self-consciously young, and self-consciously iconoclastic: They rejected the paintbrush in favor of the sharpened pen for drawing, and they drew witty manga with short captions, consciously drawing on contemporary Euro-American art and comics. Their motto was that "manga must be interesting and funny"—in the deteriorating political climate, they moved away from politics and satire to poking more general fun at the human condition.[21] Notably, they were not all men, either; Yazaki Takeko was one of the group's founding members.[22] Having previously published in *The Manga Man*, she was one of the first professional female mangaka in Japanese history, although she initially was so broke that she had to borrow inks and paints from her Shinmangaha cohorts, whom she had originally met through a male cartoonist who introduced her to his friends while they were both working at a department store.[23] She eventually married another Shinmangaha member, Ippei student Yazaki Shigeshi (1907–46), and they had two children.[24]

The Shinmangaha published a book, *Shinmangaha shūdan nenkan* (Shinmangaha group yearbook, 1933), that constituted something of a manifesto and a line in the sand by which they attempted to differentiate themselves from senior members of their profession. Even as they credited Kitazawa Rakuten as the grandfather of modern manga in Japan, group members questioned whether it was acceptable to "place things from the infancy of manga's birth in the category of full-fledged manga" and criticized the idea of drawing a direct line from classical Japanese or medieval European art to contemporary comics. They were even more plainspoken in their critique of manga's present situation and their reasons for forming their group. They argued that the current unity of mangaka was enabled by the plethora of newspaper and publishing jobs, but that this situation couldn't last, and that the impossibility of politics and thought in the present age (i.e., increasing repression by the thought police) would not allow the young men of tomorrow to form a mainstream. They pointed out the current difficulty of young mangaka's international development (due to the aforementioned political repression) and hoped that more than two or three mangaka at a time might become well known, unlike the present situation with magazines (group members didn't consider newspapers worth mentioning).[25]

Despite the phrase "new manga" in the group's name, the manga in their yearbook, although divided into many different genres, are mostly pen-and-ink, contemporary-art-style updates to Ippei's manga manbun: Usually they comprise one image, always with a caption outside, sometimes with dialogue inside but never speech bubbles, and not much paneling overall. The Shinmangaha shūdan's "new manga" constituted, evidently, a revolution not so much in content as in placement.

To achieve their goals, Shinmangaha members took manga outside the venues in which it had previously been concentrated. Members did manga for all the leading periodicals of the day (*Shōnen Kurabu, King, Asahi Graph, Ie no Hikari, Fujin Kurabu, Fujin Kōron*, and *Shinseinen*), thereby spreading manga throughout the mass media in the era of the wartime state. This appeal to the mass market, and getting beyond the stable job of manga kisha and the argumentative content of political manga (which, as they pointed out, was becoming difficult to publish), was in keeping with the group's slogan, "market acquisition" (shijō no kakutoku). Convinced that laughter was the soul of manga, and that the manga pioneered by Rakuten and Ippei was too intellectual, thus limiting its mass appeal, they wanted to create demand for manga in larger spheres.[26]

The three most famous Shinmangaha figures were Kondō Hidezō (1908–79), Sugiura Yukio (1911–2004), and Yokoyama Ryūichi (1909–2001), all of whom had worked on *The Manga Man*. Yokoyama and Sugiura had both been inspired to become mangaka by reading foreign manga.[27] Kondō and Sugiura were Ippei students in the late 1920s, and Kondō eventually married Yokoyama's younger sister. Kondō and Sugiura were especially close friends, although they made an odd pair at first glance: Two years older, Kondō was essentially a hick from rural Nagano prefecture, while Sugiura was Tokyo born and bred and, at the time of their first meeting, very much a "Modern Boy" urban sophisticate. In the 1930s they were both devotees of anarchism, although it was not explicitly reflected in their work and they saw no contradiction between anarchism and their ambition to become best-selling mangaka.[28]

Anarchism was fairly popular in imperial Japan, specifically social anarchism, which entailed amorphous notions of communal property and living in a post-state utopia. In Japan, that vision went hand in hand with the rejection of Soviet-style class-based struggle and centralized organization, which left anarchists especially vulnerable to being co-opted by the wartime state. In the 1930s, as conservative calls for the preservation of the kokutai (national polity) against subversive elements grew louder, the vaguely communitarian ideology that most Japanese anarchists subscribed to in some form or another, which historian Tatiana Linkhoeva characterizes as an "anti-authoritarian quest and continuous striving for communality and totality," was easily identified either with the conservative vision of the local/national community (kyōdōtai) or with the utopian nationalist vision for the kokutai offered by fascist propagandists. The kokutai, literally the "national body," was the animating conception of the imperial body politic under the 1889 constitution, and in the 1930s it became the justification for the "eight corners of the world under one roof" (hakkō ichiu), that of the emperor, providing an expansionist vision of world peace and a justification for the empire's wars of conquest.[29] The case of Tagawa Suihō, himself an adherent of "pure," anti-Soviet anarchism in the 1920s, is instructive: None of his beliefs about the ideal society prevented him from participating in mass consumer culture, or from supporting the empire in *Norakuro*.

Thus, there was very little intellectual contradiction in the story Sugiura told at the Shinmangaha's fiftieth anniversary party in 1982, in which he revealed that he and Kondō had sworn a written oath vowing that the group's formation actually constituted a realization of anarchism. (They also vowed never to reveal this fact, but Sugiura evidently considered that clause void after Kondō's death.)[30] In some ways this secret conviction seems to be a final echo of the optimistic view of mass culture that artists working in Japan, Europe, and the United States in the 1920s adopted: They saw it as an autonomous sphere not created by the state, which meant that they could propagate their ideas through it.[31]

In this respect, the Shinmangaha's stated policy of having sexual content in their manga, in direct opposition to the old guard (all of whom had been born in the nineteenth century), appears both as a sign of the times and as an explicit challenge to received wisdom. Yet, however anarchist they were at heart, their ambitions and their earnings were thoroughly bourgeois: In 1935, for example, Yokoyama, the group's highest earner, made 439 yen in September and 443 yen in October, in an era in which salarymen struggled to achieve an income of 100 yen a month.[32] The nonsense manga boom that the group nurtured was quite good to them financially, and they fared much better politically than their fellow young bloods, the members of the proletarian manga movement.

NO PLACE ANYWHERE: THE PROLETARIANS

Although they both started from similarly dissatisfied positions and were heavily influenced by contemporary comics from abroad, the proletarians' history was on the whole shorter, less successful, and more violent than that of the Shinmangaha. Whereas Shinmangaha members achieved a kind of soft landing by being co-opted into the New Order after they became the manga mainstream, proletarian mangaka faced only escalating state repression. Before that, however, they expanded manga to embrace and express the working classes' perspective and unabashedly left-wing politics, a deeply radical move in an unequal, status-conscious, and conservative society.

The proletarian arts movement's roots reached back to the Taishō period. The short-lived manga periodical *Aka* (Red, 1919), centered on the socialist-leaning Ogawa Jihei, was an important forerunner, one of many new leftist publications that launched in 1919 on the wings of a huge surge in the labor movement. Marxism and socialism had circulated in Japan since the 1890s, but class consciousness became increasingly widespread in the wake of the 1917 Bolshevik Revolution and the movement for imperial democracy, which climaxed in 1918 and drove a wedge between political elites and everyday urbanites. In Linkhoeva's summary, "Inflation and political scandals created a new image of the rich as swindlers, politics as essentially rotten, and the whole system as unfair."[33] Agitation was in the air.

Party government in imperial Japan lasted from 1918–32, and universal adult male suffrage became law in 1925. Empowered by their own political emancipation as well as a lengthy tradition of labor activism and a period of relative government tolerance, workers began asserting their own equality of status, a radical idea.[34] Proletarian manga depicted workers and their families on the same terms as the subjects of elite manga, which was just as radical. Artistically, it was far more documentarian than satirical, which derived from the Ippei manga manbun strain of manga, but it owed much to contemporary art movements and nonsense manga as well as to contemporary politics.

The proletarian arts movement in manga kicked off in earnest in 1926, when Yanase Masamu, Murayama Tomoyoshi (1901–77), Arita Shigeshi (1887–1941), and Shishido Sakō formed the short-lived Nihon Mangaka Renmei, aka Manren or Japan Cartoonists League.[35] Murayama had founded MAVO, and Yanase had been a key early member; he had already had a violent encounter with the security forces, having been held for five days, beaten and bayoneted by soldiers, after the earthquake in 1923 (figure 9). Both Murayama and Yanase turned to proletarian art as MAVO gradually disintegrated.[36]

The next year, before the Nihon Mangaka Renmei's demise, Shimokawa Ōten wrote glowingly of proletarian manga in *Bijutsu Shinron*, naming manga first among other proletarian art forms, including book design and theatrical sets, but declaring that all these "have an existence only as weapons in the class struggle." Shimokawa singled out Yanase as an example of a mangaka's consciousness being expressed in their manga, specifically his proletarian consciousness.[37] Yanase and other mangaka with proletarian consciousness "are

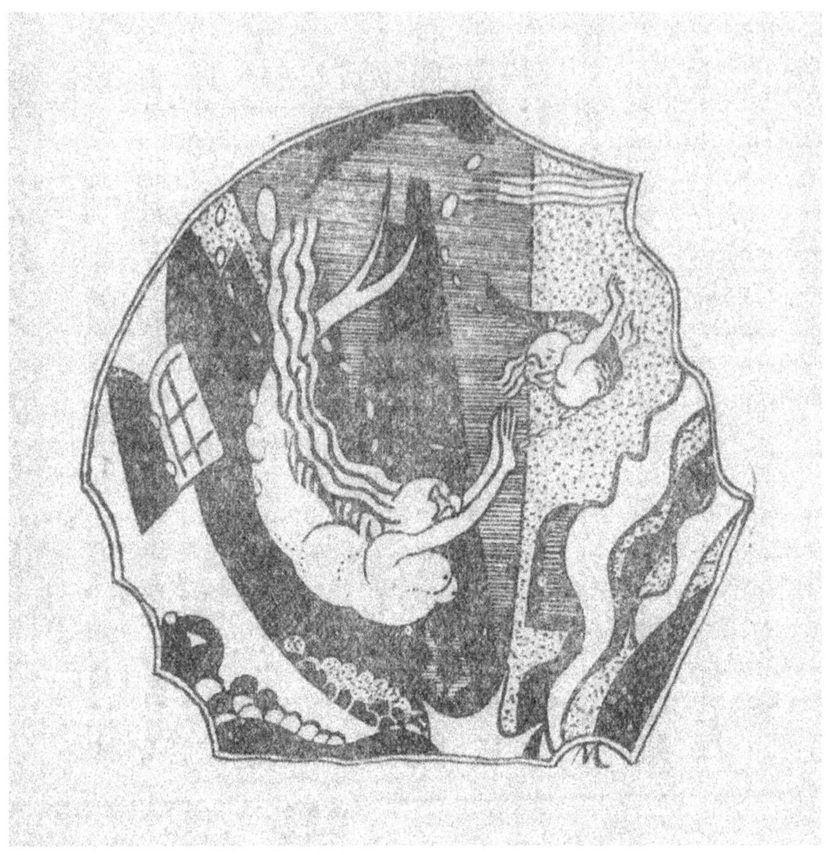

FIGURE 9. Interstitial eroguro-style manga by Yanase Masamu, published in multiple issues of the women's magazine *Josei Nihonjin* (Japanese woman) in 1924. Courtesy of National Diet Library.

now playing an extremely important role, because the thing that is proletarian art must begin to live in proletarian society [tenka]." For Shimokawa, the division in the manga world was no longer between ponchi artists and mangaka but rather between bourgeois and proletarian mangaka, and safeguarding the growth of proletarian manga was the Nihon Mangaka Renmei's most important duty (figure 10).[38]

Manren was not the first proletarian arts group; that seems to have been the Nihon Proletarian Geijutsu Renmei (Japan Proletarian Arts League), which was founded in 1925; in 1926, having expelled its anarchist members after the infamous "ana-Boru (anarchist-Bolshevik) split," it reorganized under the "Pro Gei" name. "Bolshevik" indicates these groups' adherence to communism, specifically the Third International (aka Comintern), which was led and controlled by the Soviet Union. These groups were not limited to mangaka; Yanase was a member of both Pro Gei and Manren, and other proletarian mangaka like Matsuyama Fumio (1902–82) joined Pro Gei subsequently. A year later, Pro Gei joined its sister organization Zen Gei (Zenei Geijutsuka Dōmei, Avant-Garde Artists League) to form the Zen Nihon Musansha Geijutsu Renmei (All-Japan Proletarian Arts League, NAP) after the March 15 Incident.[39] NAP reorganized into the Nihon Proletarian Bijutsuka Dōmei (Japan Proletarian Artists League, YAP) the following year.

The movement's first turning point was in 1928. That year, the death penalty was added to the existing 1925 Peace Preservation Law, and the March 15 Incident had an epochal effect on the arts: The general government crackdown on Marxists and socialists beginning on that date created sharp divisions across the cultural sphere, as those who had no potentially compromising history of leftist thought pulled away from those who did. The crackdown's immediate cause was the outlawed Communist Party's successful showing in the February 1928 general election, the first with universal male suffrage. More than sixteen hundred people were arrested across Japan, leaving those who remained free vulnerable.[40]

The hodgepodge of names and rapid-fire sequence of events speak to the Japanese left's propensity for disunity and infighting. This tendency did leftists no favors in the face of the draconian Peace Preservation Laws, which the state readily wielded in the name of "thought control." Specific regulations in the 1925 Peace Preservation Law aimed at forcing the separation of manga and political newspapers had already taken a toll on manga as a form of political expression.[41] These laws, which went beyond the existing press laws and censorship system, were applied exclusively against the radical left until 1935, "by which time there were few true radicals left to arrest," in historian Gregory J. Kasza's phrase. By that point, the range of acceptable discourse had narrowed considerably, accelerated by the fact that, as Kasza put it, "more conspicuous than revolutionary agitation was the vicious treatment of leftist prisoners."[42] Police torture and being held for months without charge was the norm for people detained under these laws.

In the early years, the young and inexperienced proletarian mangaka were directed by their editors at proletarian periodicals to essentially copy from American left-wing propaganda art; *agitprop* (agipuro) became a term of approbation for movement members. The wholesale copying was particularly noticeable in 1927 during the Sacco & Venzetti affair in the United States;

leftist American artists became a huge influence on the movement, and to some extent this influence led to a degree of homogenization. The proletarian mangaka were also radicalized by their American models, and came to expect a certain amount of drama in their lives in the movement due to that influence.[43] The imperial government satisfied these expectations.

The proletarian arts movement was extraordinarily open to foreign art, and studying proletarian manga in other countries formed a major part of members' activities. Mangaka were hungry for exposure to original materials; the fact that proletarian art used printed matter as its platform meant that it circulated internationally very easily, language barriers notwithstanding. Proletarian mangaka organized a Proletarian Manga Kenkyūkai (Research Group) which looked at proletarian art from the United Kingdom, France, Germany, the United States, Italy, Hungary, Mexico, China, and the Soviet Union over the course of three years. The Japanese proletarian arts movement also exerted a major influence on leftist arts across East Asia, especially inside the Japanese empire and in the Republic of China; Yanase's work in particular was hugely popular and influential on the continent, and he traveled to China and Manchuria several times beginning in 1929 (figure 10).[44] Yanase also played a key role in the introduction of the caricature-style works of contemporary Weimar artist George Grosz (1893–1959) to Japan from 1923, after Murayama brought Grosz's collected works back with him from Germany.[45] The Hungarian-American artist Hugo Gellert (1892–1985), European emigré and avowed socialist, was another major artistic source, specifically his cartoons for the radical magazine *The Liberator* (1918–24).[46]

Yanase's *Kanemochi kyoiku* was a high point in the movement's mass cultural reach and impact, and other proletarian artists criticized him for it. Yanase, however, saw no contradiction between writing a popular manga satirizing the bourgeoisie in the *Yomiuri* and being a proletarian mangaka—the strip enabled him to get the word out about the class struggle, which he saw as manga's role.[47] He also managed the manga division of the *Musansha Shinbun* (Proletarian news, 1925–32) and edited the *Musansha Graph* (Proletarian graph, 1928–29). Proletarian mangaka Okamoto Tōki (1903–86) and Matsuyama Fumio, who wrote a history of the movement in the 1960s, emphasized that there was no money in it, and thus proletarian mangaka had to work in "bourgeois journalism" to put food on the table. They compensated for selling out by practicing very harsh criticism: Proletarian mangaka could reliably be found castigating each other in proletarian magazines for failing to express a sufficiently proletarian or revolutionary spirit in their

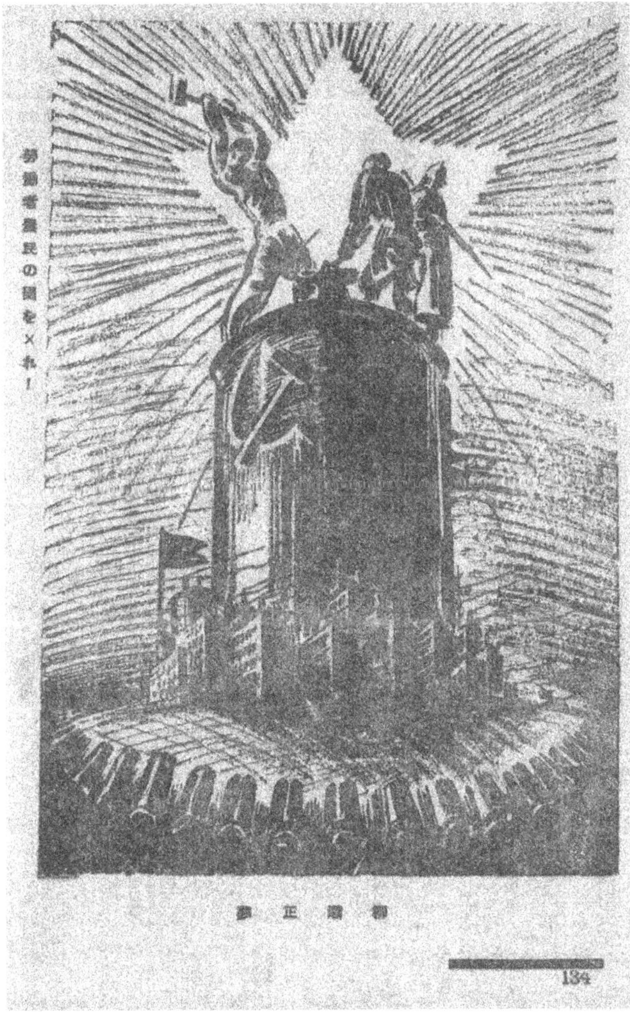

FIGURE 10. Proletarian manga by Yanase Masamu: "Rōnō no kuni o mamore!" (Protect the country of farmers and workers!), *Senki* (Battle flag) magazine, July 1928. "X" replaces the censored character "protect" in the title. Courtesy of National Diet Library.

work.[48] This spirit of criticism extended to their own influences, as when Yanase criticized Grosz in 1929 for being too bourgeois, too capitalist, and not having done enough for the revolution, even though he himself had been heavily influenced by Grosz. Indeed, according to the editor of the proletarian magazine *Mushin*, until his exposure to Grosz's work, Yanase's artistic ambitions were limited to drawing women's genitals, in classic eroguro fashion—a biased characterization of MAVO that indicates how its members' work was viewed after its heyday.[49]

The class struggle and eroguro did not necessarily contradict one another, however. *Tokyo Puck* in its final years became a home for proletarian manga—its editor Shimoda Ken'ichirō (1899–1943) never lost his increasingly dangerous conviction that manga should have something political to say, and he embraced both proletarian and nonsense manga under the motto that *Tokyo Puck* was "a pro [proletarian] and ero manga magazine." Like the proletarians, Shimoda was enamored of contemporary European art, and after he bought the Tokyo Puck company in 1928, its influence on the magazine grew. In this respect, *Tokyo Puck* and the proletarians were a natural fit: The latter were the creators most heavily influenced by modernism (particularly German modernism in Grosz's vein) and by contemporary European comics, and their work handily advanced Shimoda's aim for the magazine to be "manga as art." But Shimoda's stubborn and increasingly old-fashioned belief that "manga" meant something that mocked politics or social mores in a one-page drawing meant that *Tokyo Puck* became increasingly unprofitable as the decade wore on. Although he and the proletarians pushed the bounds of expression in these one-panel manga (Shimizu terms them "tableaux manga"), that kind of manga was fast falling out of the mainstream in the mid-1930s.[50] Shimoda also supported democracy, another increasingly dangerous position, and his providing a platform to proletarian and leftist mangaka in the magazine meant that by the end it was operating at a loss, and mangaka took losses to publish in it.[51]

A major round of repression came in 1933, with dozens of prominent figures arrested for alleged violations of the Peace Preservation Laws. Many proletarian mangaka were targeted, including Yashima Tarō (1908–94) and his wife artist Yashima Mitsu (1908–88), who spent nearly her entire pregnancy in jail but who was never formally charged or brought before a judge. Mangaka Suyama Kei'ichi (1905–75) was arrested and sentenced to five years' hard labor, which was eventually commuted to three, and in 1941 he gave up manga for oil painting for the duration of the war. Okamoto Tōki had been arrested and tortured in 1932, the same year that Matsuyama was arrested for the second time and imprisoned for more than two and a half years. Yanase had been picked up by the security forces for alleged violations of the Peace Preservation Laws in December 1932: After refusing to recant his beliefs under torture, he was held in Tokyo's notorious Ichigaya prison, charged and sentenced to two years' hard labor with a stay of five years; both sentences were commuted in late

1933 after his wife's death. Unlike many members of the proletarian arts movement, however, at the time Yanase's encounters with the state's repression left him only more determined to conduct his political and artistic activities.[52]

The last proletarian organizations were forcibly dissolved in 1935, and the first volume of the *Manga kenkyū shiryō kōza* (Manga research material lectures, 1935) conspicuously declined to list anything related to politics in its manga typology, just as Ippei's introduction ignored the pivotal role that Rakuten's political manga had played in the medium's establishment. The writer Mizushima Niō did, however, argue in the anthology's first article, "Writings on the History of Japanese Manga," that "having more laughter is the most valuable thing in human life."[53] It was still barely possible to publish such sentiments, but not for long.

Early in 1936, the February 26 Incident's attempted coup d'etat sounded satirical manga's death knell. Four-panel manga became the newspaper manga mainstay after the incident, and the proletarian movement's remnants foundered after the First Contemporary Manga Exhibition held that year, which consisted almost entirely of proletarian manga. The following year Yanase and Matsuyama were arrested again, and the planned Second Contemporary Manga Exhibition never materialized; Yanase had already largely abandoned manga for oil painting.[54] In the years after 1937, military-bureaucratic rule fomented what Kasza terms "a fundamental reorganization of many social sectors" in the home islands:

> All labor unions were dissolved and replaced with joint-labor management consultation committees in each firm. Agrarian workers were mobilized into the Agricultural Patriotic Association, the first comprehensive organization in this sector. Similar bodies targeted youth, women, artists, writers, and other groups. Heavy industries were reorganized into oligopolies of large producers linked by monopolistic distribution companies, and each industrial area was supervised by a civil-bureaucratic control organization. Journals and film producers were pressed into a similar format, thousands of small to medium-sized firms being systematically driven out of business. No one familiar with the structure of Japan's media industries in 1937 would have recognized them five years later.[55]

Key to the system of bureaucratic social control formalized under the "New Order" beginning in 1938 was bureaucrats' extralegal use of several censorship tools. "Consultation meetings," in which members of various industries were summoned to (allegedly informal, off-the-record) sessions with Home Ministry bureaucrats and given their marching orders, were one such tool; this was the kind of meeting in which Tagawa Suihō was told that his manga was corrupting Japanese children and that it would not continue in publication in 1941. Although *Norakuro* was banned, Tagawa himself was not blacklisted (another policy that was, in practice, communicated to editors but not to the writers in question themselves). Another, completely extralegal instrument was the policy requiring the consolidation of periodicals in various fields, both to squeeze out people whose speech was undesirable or ideologically suspect and to make the teeming media industries easier for the Home Ministry to censor in advance, as had become the norm via submission of production galleys for administrative review. By November 1941, just before consolidation of publications became legal under new regulations, bureaucrats had reduced periodicals to 10,186, down from 28,268 in circulation in July 1938, and squeezed the number of general daily newspapers from 528 to 202, in line with the official goal of having just one daily newspaper per prefecture, as was the case in sixteen of forty-seven prefectures by December 1941.[56]

Along with the birth of the New Order, 1938 witnessed another round of crackdowns. Suyama and Yashima Tarō were both arrested again, while Katō Etsurō experienced his own tenkō (conversion) and became completely nationalist. Nor was Katō alone in his conversion, although his was more extreme than most; Gennifer Weisenfeld estimates that 95 percent of former proletarian arts figures returned to the kokutai's spiritual fold by the end of the decade.[57] Yashima Tarō and Mitsu were rare exceptions; in February 1939 they fled to the United States, where they eventually produced antifascist propaganda for the U.S. government. Naturalized as U.S. citizens, they returned to Japan after the war only to retrieve their son, who had been left behind with relatives when they fled. In May 1939, proletarians Onozawa Wataru (1909–?) and Kume Kōichi (1917–91) fled Japan for the uncertain haven of China; Onozawa did not return to Japan for fourteen years. *Tokyo Puck* ceased publication in 1941; Shimoda and his wife died after eating bad seafood in 1943, while Yanase died in the May 1945 firebombing of Tokyo.[58]

NATIONAL POLICY MANGA AND THE STRANGE CASE OF KATŌ ETSURŌ

Matsuyama, Yanase, and Katō Etsurō (1899–1959) formed the Fūshiga Kenkyūkai (Caricature Research Group) in 1935, offering themselves and other creators a non-proletarian artistic forum. In 1938, Fūshiga Kenkyūkai members under the leadership of Matsushita Ichio (1910–90), Kume Kōichi, Onozawa Wataru, and Ōta Kōji (1909–98) launched the short-lived magazine *Karikare* (Caricature) as an in-house publication (kikanshi) of the Tokyo Manga Kenkyūsho (Research Institute). Its motto: "with works founded on an attitude of the highest artistry, the deepest life (jinseisei), and the widest humanity as its base, manga will record only true significance, and will be a sincere reflector of the living age together with the times." The magazine continued until April 1941, when Ōta and the others were arrested for thought crimes, but in that span *Karikare* cemented the proletarian manga movement's most far-reaching legacy: the invention of manga criticism. Proletarian manga's expansion went hand-in-hand with theorizing manga as an art form in its own right, and Matsuyama Fumio published the first book-length work of manga criticism in 1937.[59]

Analysis of manga predated the 1930s and the proletarian arts movement; manga had been discussed in arts journals as early as 1907. The manga criticism that grew out of the proletarian arts movement was distinguished from earlier efforts by its approach: Whereas previous generations of art critics and cartoonists had debated manga as, in Rei Okamoto Inouye's phrase, a "marginalized . . . subgenre of painting," the proletarian arts movement members assumed that manga was its own hybrid artform, with its own distinct capabilities.[60] Thus, as one writer argued in 1938, manga criticism ought to communicate the truth of the artist's intention, and a work's value, according to its methods.[61]

The birth of manga criticism is usually dated to 1936, when Suyama published *Gendai sekai mangashū* (Contemporary world manga compilation) and *Manga tōsho no tebiki* (Guide to amateur manga contributions) through the Nihon Manga Kenkyūkai. This organization also published former streetcar trade unionist Nakane Kōnosuke's *Manga kōza* (Manga lectures) series and, also edited by Nakane (1900–87), the monthly *Manga no Kuni* (Manga country, 1935–40), which sought to offer amateurs a path into the profession. Besides readers' amateur manga submissions, *Manga no Kuni* published short profiles on members countrywide, articles on how to become a mangaka and how to use maquettes for drawing references, alongside ads for supplies like pens, models, and paper. Most intriguingly, it offered a monthly evaluation of amateur manga submissions as well as a regular column called "Funny Paper" that profiled foreign comics, written by Ōta, who was known primarily as a printmaker.[62]

Manga no Kuni's emergence was part of manga's expansion in these years, and the emergence of mangaka as a job to which a wider range of people could aspire. Major newspapers, including the *Mainichi Shinbun* and the *Asahi Graph*, began running amateur sections, welcoming manga submissions from anyone and everyone; Shimada Keizō supervised the *Mainichi Shinbun* section.[63] Manga's expansion also welcomed girls and women as creators. In 1932, the *Asahi Shinbun*'s class of about twenty trainee mangaka included women, and Rakuten taught female students at his Rakuten Manga Studio in 1933; at one point the studio had as many as two hundred people. Besides *Manga no Kuni* and related publications, the Nihon Manga Kenkyūkai offered mangaka training correspondence courses, and it ran ads in *Shōjo Kurabu* and other female-oriented magazines encouraging girls and young women to become "jyōryū mangaka (female-style mangaka)." One such ad declared: "There is a great shortage of female-style cartoonists, and nowadays they are in great demand! Come out, female-style cartoonists! Now demand is at its peak!"[64]

Altogether, the flowering of amateur manga in these years was broad enough that it can be considered the "first wave" of dōjin (amateur) manga. But this wave soon crashed; although *Manga no Kuni*'s tone in July 1937 was still optimistic, predicting that the future would be the age of manga because manga was becoming "more entwined with human lifestyles," the magazine's editorials and reader manga became much more militaristic after the formal inauguration of war with China that same month.[65]

The war affected *Karikare* too. An unsigned editor's note in its January 1939 issue implicitly criticized the excesses of modern art in general and eroguro nonsense manga in particular, saying that "mangaka have forgotten to make their works have morals, have forfeited intelligence, and have abandoned the techniques of pictorial expression." On the other hand, the editor asserted that "it is more than enough for [manga] to pull out a smile," and tried to unify these two disparate positions by concluding that "art without life (seikatsu) is like a flower that does not bloom. Even if it's beautiful or interesting, it does not help to raise up humanity. Life and thought must be synonyms."[66] The latter sentiment, including the professed interest in "art that expresses daily life" (seikatsu hyōgen), indicates the magazine's heritage in the defiantly realist proletarian manga movement, and manga historian Ishiko Jun identified *Karikare* as the last manga magazine resisting the state in this period.[67] Former proletarians echoed the state's views on the still popular nonsense manga, however: Ōta called it "silly" and "vulgar" in *Karikare* before his arrest, and Shimokawa Ōten dismissed its practitioners as "amateurs" in his magazine *Manga Ōkoku* (Manga kingdom, 1937).[68]

Ideologically suspect as its ringleaders were, *Karikare* soon found itself playing second fiddle to the magazine *Manga*, which launched in November 1940 after existing manga groups were amalgamated into the Shin Nippon Mangaka Kyōkai (New Japan Mangaka Association). As officials continued to consolidate newspapers and magazines, cooperation with the New Order was the only way to remain in business and to receive sufficient paper rations to enable publication.[69]

Manga and the Shindantai, as it was called, centered around Kondō Hidezō, who did the bulk of the work for each issue of *Manga*.[70] Kondō had himself become fairly nationalist, but next to Katō Etsurō, who had made the very long journey from proletarian manga to fascism in a very short time, he looked like a pacifist. Tenkō (sometimes translated as "apostasy") was normal, as thousands of leftist intellectuals and artists "converted" back to the regime's communitarian views on the nation and the empire, a process that is often euphemistically referred to as a "return to Japan." In many cases, the rapprochement was facilitated by anticapitalism, which the fascist regime and the former leftists shared. Katō went further than most; his book *Shinrinen manga no gihō* (Techniques for the new ideal manga, 1942) included reproductions of his favorable coverage in the Nazi press, complete with swastikas and hideously racist caricatures of Jewish people. He also reiterated his previous critique of his former comrades, namely that the proletarians were too class-conscious when, under the New Order, they should have been "kokutai-conscious."[71]

During the fascist era the kokutai was interpreted in a particularly wide-ranging manner. The figure of the emperor was seen as a mediating and pacifying influence that would, once subjects had accepted total obedience to him, elevate the empire into one unified Japanese nation. The same ideas underlay the Imperial Army's campaigns of conquest in the Pacific War, which were animated by the rallying cry of "hakkō ichiu." In this vision, all differences between imperial subjects, particularly of class and ethnicity, would eventually be flattened and destroyed, although in practice the empire operated on a system of racial discrimination: Without a family register (koseki) attesting that you or your ancestors were born in Japan proper, you were a second-class subject at best.[72]

This, then, was the milieu that Kondō, Katō, and others who committed tenkō happily endorsed, though it's not clear how many mangaka genuinely shared Katō's views, rather than echoing the party line as a means of survival. Katō wrote many screeds arguing that the New Order needed new cartoonists, and when the Shindantai was formed he went so far as to claim that "the young mangaka have stood up, and they have screamed: 'Take back manga's nationality!' And the concrete form of that scream is the Shin Nihon Mangaka Kyōkai!"[73] But reading the discussions in surviving issues of *Manga* produces the distinct sense that Katō was pretty far out on a limb.

A roundtable with Kitazawa Rakuten himself, published in August 1941, is particularly telling in this regard. Kondō, Matsushita Ichio, Sugiura, and Ono Saseo (1905–54) also participated, but the bulk of the discussion consists of Kondō interviewing Rakuten about manga's early days in Japan. Kondō repeatedly tried to associate Rakuten's career with the imperial wars of the Meiji period, a connection that Rakuten repeatedly denied; Kondō brought up the New Order, only to have Rakuten remark pithily that Japan being in a state of timeless stasis was bad for manga—awkward, as fascist propaganda envisioned an idealized national community that existed in timeless stasis and harmony.[74] That Rakuten and Kondō were talking past each other is particularly notable given that Rakuten's politics were always frankly nationalist: There was quite a difference between Rakuten-style patriotism, which saw nothing wrong with criticizing the government in the name of the nation, and the fascism that Kondō espoused, which treated criticizing the government as a betrayal of the nation because it entirely conflated the two.

They were probably still talking past each other even when Rakuten launched into his views on manga's proper role in propaganda. Speaking from his years of experience as a government gadfly, he argued that politicians' understanding, with respect to manga, was limited: "I want them to feel like they should make use of manga. I can't read foreign comics [due to the war], but I think that they are making the war something amusing. But here in Japan we're basically not allowed to draw that. It's very vexing [not to be allowed to draw manga contributing to the war effort]." Compared to the early days of his career, Rakuten argued that "Japan has grown up and so have its responsibilities," but the government still wouldn't let cartoonists "express the spirit of the people in art."[75] The inconvenient truth was that the government still would have preferred that manga be erased from Japanese society.

In the same discussion, Rakuten exhorted contemporary cartoonists to make manga excellent, saying that they all had to walk the way of manga (mangadō) together because they were all the same age. He implicitly criticized children's and nonsense manga with his declaration that he had founded *Tokyo Puck* to provide "high-class laughter," not "mere comedy," but it seems that readers didn't find much excellence or laughter in the Shindantai's officially sanctioned comics.[76] *Manga* did very poorly for its first year; the return rate for the first issue, which had a print run of 140,000 copies, was 50 percent, and the magazine was failing until the February 1942 commemorative Pearl Harbor issue sold 45,000 copies.[77] Rakuten still claimed to believe that manga is "what expresses laughter by conveying the reader's emotions directly," but *Manga* evidently failed to do this anywhere near as effectively as the Kodansha children's magazines and adult-oriented nonsense manga had.[78] Looking back, Komatsu Sakyō described *Manga* as essentially a "national policy magazine," noting that it took a very hard line against enemy leaders such as Roosevelt and Churchill.[79]

In the end, what kept *Manga* alive was continuing government distrust of manga as an art form: Manga was banned from most magazines outside *Manga* and *Manga Nihon*, as *Osaka Puck* rebranded itself in 1943 after English was officially banned from all publications. Newspaper manga fared slightly better; the *Asahi Graph* kept up its manga until the eve of the surrender, but paper and ink shortages meant that the newspaper had long since switched to monochrome printing and cut all but two of its four-panel strips; its long-running translated version of *Jiggs and Maggie* disappeared along with other foreign and nonsense manga in 1940.[80]

Katō quit the Shindantai in 1941 out of disgust at other members' distinct lack of nationalism, perhaps along with lingering suspicions about its leaders' roots in nonsense manga. He had criticized nonsense manga in increasingly strident terms since 1934; he was one of the first to articulate the nationalist view that nonsense manga, ineluctably semi-foreign, unserious, and meaningless, was a corrupted flower that needed to be extirpated.[81] Instead, Katō and several others founded their own group, the Kensetsu Mangakkai (Constructive Manga Organization), whose manga wholeheartedly supported the regime.[82]

In *Shinrinen manga no gihō*, Katō attacked the members of the Shindantai and its predecessors, claiming that the problem with most if not all professional cartoonists in Japan was that they were too liberal and individualistic in their thinking. These faults had made it easy for Euro-American nonsense manga to take over Japanese cartooning in the past decade, aided and abetted by Japanese cartoonists who forgot the "national essence" and who, seduced by proletarianism and communism, produced work that was "nothing but intellectualistic and commercial communist manga." That last may have been a specific dig at his former colleague Yanase, and the proletarians generally; Katō went on to declare that "in a word, manga is an art that must hold the will of the people of the family state (kokka kokumin) and must warn against or proactively attack every unjust, unreasonable, unnatural, or discordant thing in the world."[83] Katō also drew manga for English-language newspaper *The Japan Times* (1897–) during the war, propagandizing the wartime government's actions to the world.[84]

These developments have not received the full attention they deserve in many accounts. Tellingly, editor and critic Minejima Masayuki (1925–2016) wrote in 1984 that "if Kondō is guilty [of inciting militarism], then everyone in mass communications was guilty."[85] That is precisely the point; there was no alternative to espousing militarism and nationalism if one wanted to stay in print, and staying in print was generally the main way for these people to earn a living. Undoubtedly, Kondō and his colleagues can be considered what historian Louise Young called "unofficial propagandists," in that they voluntarily recapitulated the official consensus in their work.[86]

Acknowledging these realities exposes the habit of blaming Norakuro, Dankichi, Tank Tankurō, and children's manga in general for the rise of militarism and the disaster of the Asia-Pacific Wars as, fundamentally, a displacement: Naming Tagawa and other children's manga creators as the primary architects of militarism in children ignores the fact that mainstream Japanese society went all in on militarism and the empire after 1931. Tagawa's former editor Katō Ken'ichi, no stranger to rightist sentiment, also believed that merely "playing war (sensō gokko)" was not enough for *Norakuro* to capture readers' hearts for eleven years; the secret of their passion was the manga's pathos. Tagawa wanted to convey to the boys who read *Norakuro* and played war games that the real thing was terrible and awful; whether he succeeded is another question.[87] But dismissing *Norakuro* and *Tank Tankurō* as "propaganda" neglects their vitality, humor, and innovation: Once you've read official propaganda manga, it's impossible to confuse the two, and it's no wonder that readers preferred the former.

The military and fascism pervaded Japanese society. Children's manga by Tagawa and others reflecting that reality, as critic Natsume Fusanosuke (b. 1950) has acknowledged, is thus unsurprising: "It may be that the militaristic tendency of *Norakuro* does not go beyond what was obvious for the general public and boys at the time," he wrote, in a definitive understatement. Moreover, viewing *Norakuro* as a militaristic manga affirming continual imperial aggression is, in Natsume's view, part of the same "ideology of unconscious progressivism that draws a definite divide between prewar and postwar and that posits the postwar as having progressed."[88] Positing

Norakuro and prewar children's manga as somehow bad or tainted presents postwar children's manga as the sole source of contemporary manga and as simply good and uncorrupted. In reality, important transwar continuities underlay postwar manga developments, and prewar and transwar phenomena played important roles in the postwar mediascape—as did creators and staff who grew up and worked under the wartime state.

Instead of blaming children's manga for the empire, manga critics need to acknowledge the complicity of Japanese society and Japanese subjects generally in the country's fascist history and imperial collapse. Manga editor and critic Ōtsuka Eiji has argued that "an aesthetic unification of Eisenstein and Disney under conditions of fascism is the origins of the Japanese manga and animation that everyone today associates with Japanese traditions or with postmodernism," but in typical polemical fashion he takes a good point too far. Manga did not begin in the postwar era, but Ōtsuka ignores the first three decades of manga's history, going straight from premodern toba-e illustrations to nonsense manga in the 1920s to play up his accusations of Americanism (specifically, Disney and Hollywood) in manga, arguing that "the history of Japanese manga begins in fact with the Disneyification of Japanese manga."[89]

This framing willfully ignores mountains of evidence discussed in these chapters, including the fact that European avant-garde artists, art movements, and films and comics were embraced just as readily as American comics and animation by mangaka including Tagawa in the 1920s and 1930s. The general public felt similarly; as media scholar Hikari Hori points out, European films were widely screened and popular in Japan, as were American films, "right up until the day of the Pearl Harbor attack."[90] German films were shown even after; the first movie Ishinomori Shōtarō (1938–98) saw was the Expressionist *Der Golem, wie er in die Welt kam* (*The Golem: How He Came into the World*, 1920), when he was four or five in backwater Miyagi prefecture.[91] And rather than Tagawa, the prewar children's mangaka most influenced by the deformed style of American animation popularized by Felix and Mickey was Shimada Keizō, particularly in his four-panel manga *Nekonana-sensei* (1939–40), which ran in the *Tokyo Nichinichi Shinbun* (Tokyo daily news, 1872–1943) and was partially collected by Kodansha in 1940. In the uncollected strips, the cat protagonist actually meets Mickey Mouse.[92]

Hori also notes that globally circulating media in this era were "promiscuous," pointing out various instances in which films in one country adopted elements of films made in another country, calling into question the idea of a "national" media.[93] Her point underscores the fact that manga and film in Japan were part of a mutually influential global mediascape, one that Ōtsuka too readily reduces to "Eisenstein and Disney" to tar all of postwar manga and anime with the brush of fascist complicity. It's not necessary to go quite that far to acknowledge that manga was a part of imperial Japan, and—with the proletarians' notable, doomed exception—imperial Japan supported the war effort. Children's manga in general or *Norakuro* and *Dankichi* specifically should not be made scapegoats for an entire society, letting manga for adults and the rest of media off the hook.

THE SAME CATASTROPHE

By the end of 1941, manga as a profession and as an art form was essentially at a standstill. Its pro-war content was so total that Kondō even apologized for it in his editor's note for the April 1942 issue of *Manga*. With almost all former manga venues shut down, no newcomers could enter the profession, and mangaka who retained their jobs worked at the pleasure of the wartime state. It became much more difficult to make a living in manga, as many creators had in the 1930s, which explains why only senior and politically trustworthy creators such as Rakuten participated in the Nihon Manga Hōkōkai (Japan Manga "Public Duty Group," a wartime locution), which was founded in 1943: They didn't have to work and so were able to volunteer.[94] Rakuten served as its president before he evacuated to Miyazaki in January 1945.

It would be a mistake, however, to think that manga did not continue during this era; manga saw both bright and dark spots even after 1941, because the world of manga already extended beyond the manga industry. Although professional publications were straitened, the wartime manga hiatus produced a kind of hothouse effect among manga readers. After the paper-rationing edict effectively ended children's manga, children turned to the personal manga collections they and their peers had already amassed and to used bookstores for secondhand copies of manga books and magazines. As Kajii Jun notes, "compared to the life span of contemporary [paperback] manga, [hardcover] prewar manga books were much, much longer lived."[95] Komatsu Sakyō recalled that he began reading manga for adults in used bookstores in these years, when he was in middle school; he even read the eight-volume *Gendai renzoku manga zenshū* anthology of nonsense manga, which taught him that "there was manga with stories for adults too, which was a huge discovery."[96]

In these practices, children increased their reliance on informal networks of manga sharing that predated the manga restrictions, as *Shōnen Kurabu* readers' letters from the 1930s attested. Komatsu's grandfather had forbade him and his brother reading ponchi-e and manga, saying it would turn them into idiots, but they just bought and read it in secret or at friends' houses.[97] Young Tezuka Osamu had as many as two hundred volumes of manga at his house in Takarazuka; when word got around about it at school, he essentially began running a manga lending library for his classmates. Everyone from the school bullies to the bullied would come over to read manga on Sundays, and some people borrowed books to take home. Eventually Tezuka himself stopped being bullied as a result of the lending library, which he drily called "the blessing of manga."[98] Tezuka, his classmates, and children across the country were normalizing patterns and platforms of manga consumption that would be institutionalized by the postwar manga industry.

The subset of manga readers who felt compelled to try their hands at drawing manga did not vanish during the height of the war either. The *Asahi Graph* kept up its "Readers' Manga" corner, later called "Manga dōjō," as long as it kept printing manga, and amateurs were welcome in this section, which for many kept the dream of creating manga professionally alive—the fact that they had to do pro-war comics to get published notwithstanding.[99] Katō Yoshirō (1925–2006) first submitted manga to *Asahi Graph* in 1939 and won prize money, which shaped his ambitions to become a professional mangaka; he continued racking up acceptances, won a submission prize from *Manga* during the war, and was pointed out as especially promising by Kondō before being drafted.[100] Tezuka spent the war years drawing manga, including a very famous amateur work, "Shōri no hi made" (Until the day of victory), featuring Mickey Mouse piloting a Zero bomber, an incongruous but thoroughly modern juxtaposition.[101] By the summer of 1945, both Tezuka's school and his factory worksite had been destroyed in Allied bombing campaigns, and there was nothing for him to do but stay home and draw manga all day; he later estimated that he completed two thousand pages in manuscript that summer, much of which he published after the war as akahon manga.[102]

Other creators took jobs in the proverbial boondocks, or simply stopped working. Some were drafted; Ono Saseo and Yokoyama Ryūichi joined the military press corps, and Ono even published an art book in Java in 1945 before the surrender made him a prisoner of war. Yokoyama survived the sinking of his troop ship *Sakuramaru* during the Battle of the Sunda Strait in 1942 and was demobilized in March 1945, in time to evacuate his family to Nagano with Kondō Hidezō's help after the Shinmangaha office burned to the ground in the Tokyo firebombing.[103] Although he drew a few non-Norakuro manga under a slightly different pen name before requests dried up, Tagawa mostly spent the war gardening; he and his family eventually evacuated to Nagano.[104] *Shōnen Kurabu* star Nakajima Sakuo had been an elementary school teacher before he became a mangaka; he went back to his old profession after his popular manga was canceled in 1941, teaching his students to draw and self-publishing a school newspaper with them, "Imon Shinbun" (Condolences news), to keep their spirits up as the war worsened.[105] Unable to return to the United States, Kiyama "Henry" Yoshitaka taught art at a high school in his hometown in Tottori and painted.[106]

Hasegawa Machiko, Tagawa's most famous student, moved back to Kyushu with her family and worked as a manga kisha for a provincial paper. Yazaki Takeko saw work gradually dry up from 1937 onward, as publishing's constriction shrank the venues available to her. After her disabled husband developed lung disease, she stopped working to care for him and their sons; although Yazaki Shigeshi did publish in a nationalist anthology, *Yokusan manga susume Yamato ikka* (Government support manga: Advance, Yamato family), in 1942 alongside Hasegawa and others, the family moved in with Shigeshi's parents in the countryside in that same year.[107] Other female mangaka who had made names for themselves in the previous decade, such as Kaneko Hisako, also struggled to maintain their careers as the few remaining publishing venues offered their limited space to more established, male creators.

For others, Manchukuo became something of a bolt hole—until the Red Army rolled in. Ueda Toshiko debuted in the magazine *Shōgaku Rokunensei* (Sixth-year elementary student, 1922–2010) in 1936 and published sporadically thereafter, concentrating on studying art. She then had a fateful meeting with Kondō Hidezō, who told her, "You're hopeless as a mangaka. You were raised as a fine young lady, so you don't know the ways of the world, you must study society. Mangaka pick up society's trash, they are ragpickers, so attend to your workplace." In 1942 she moved back to Manchukuo to gain more life experience. She worked for the South Manchurian Railway Company (Mantetsu), which constituted the half of the Manchukuo government that wasn't the Japanese military, in her native Harbin for two years; her colleagues laughing at her manga-style posters gave her confidence that she could be a mangaka.[108] Ueda then joined the *Manshū Nichinichi* (Daily

Manchuria, 1907–45) newspaper as an illustrator two months before the end of the war. She held that job until a week after the surrender, when the Soviets occupied the city.[109] Sakamoto Gajō had resumed serializing Tankurō's adventures in the *Manshū Shinbun* (Manchuria News, 1938–44); like Ueda and many others, he and his family were interned on the continent for more than a year after the surrender.[110]

There were some qualified exceptions to the strict controls on manga. The authorities let Matsushita Ichio's *Suishin oyaji* (Old man implementation, 1940–44) continue because despite its factory setting it was essentially fascist; along with *Riki-san* by former Shinmangaha member Yokoi Fukutarō (1912–48), it was the last four-panel strip still running in *Asahi Graph* in August 1945.[111] Evidently a politically favored creator, Matsushita also published the era's last serialized children's manga, *Namarin ōjō monogatari* (Royal castle Namarin story, 1943–45) in *Shūkan Shōkokumin* (Weekly young subject, 1942–46).[112]

There was also a brief boom in science manga for children because it was "educational." Although most of these manga were, as Matsumoto Leiji (1938–2023) later remarked, "like eating vegetables," there was one notable exception. *Kasei tanken* (Mars expedition, 1940), a science fiction manga with art by Ōshiro Noboru and story by Asai Tarō (a pen name of Oguma Hideo), was a huge hit that touched off a brief science fiction boom. As Komatsu recalled, it was fun, it had a great story, it was full of up-to-the-minute science, and it was in full, very pretty color. The manga was hugely influential on science fiction and on manga in Japan, as fans of both—they were already closely linked thanks to Tagawa, who published another robot manga about a boy inventor and his robot dog (*Toppio*, 1939–40) in the women's magazine *Ie no hikari*, and others—reread the manga repeatedly during the war years.[113]

But after the Mars expedition, manga rapidly crashed back to earth. Looking at magazines containing manga published during the war years, it's obvious that the medium was slowly being choked off just from the spines' decreasing thickness and the paper's increasing cheapness; advertising shrank too. But the dream of manga as a medium for humor died hard. As *Manga Nihon, Osaka Puck* continued publishing manga until winter 1945; manga stalwart the *Tokyo Shinbun* stopped publishing manga in May, the same month that *Manga* released its final prewar issue.[114] The cover of one of *Manga Nihon*'s final issues before the end of the war depicts a crowd of people under a banner declaring that "the furious 100 million [will] pulverize America and Britain" (figure 11).

FIGURE 11. Cover of *Manga Nihon* by Katō Etsurō, December 1944, depicting "the furious 100 million [ready to] pulverize the United States and Britain." Courtesy of National Diet Library.

And yet, upon opening that issue, the immediate impression is not of overwhelming propaganda but of an art form that was still, despite restrictions, trying to help people laugh amid their present difficulties. Despite Katō's fanatical pronouncements about manga's nationality (belied by his reprinting his own adulatory Nazi press coverage) and the government's efforts to strong-arm the medium into either docility or nonexistence, *Manga Nihon* still contains comics from outside Japan: They are all from Germany, but they are still there, and they are not even (primarily) about the war, but rather depict the difficulties of modern urban life that perturbed consumers and urbanites around the world, even in life during wartime. In the years 1938–45, the wartime state did its level best to take the modern out of manga and out of society—but found, in the end, that it could not take manga, and modern society, out of the modern era.

Conclusion

EATING VEGETABLES, REREADING MANGA

IN SEPTEMBER 1945, less than a month after the surrender on August 15, *Manga Nihon* returned with a new issue that at times seems almost giddy. Just like almost every other publication at the time, it contains a "Japanese/English conversation three-minute study guide" outlining the few key phrases needed to interact with the American GIs who were streaming into the country as part of the Occupation. It also contains a particularly telling aside: a report on the rumor that the Americans would soon be setting up a movie theater, and that therefore "movies will be like movies again." In other words, the dreary propaganda films of the war years weren't really like movies (eigarashii) at all, and now that the war was over, fun was no longer verboten.[1]

Some people experienced the end of the war as a literal return of light and color. Sugiyama Jirō, later a guardian of the netsuke collection chronicled in *The Hare with the Amber Eyes* (2010), recalled that on the day of the surrender he and a friend were taking the afternoon train down from Tokyo to Izu: "It was not easy to get train tickets, and we were chatting on the train when we saw women wearing very colorful clothes. And we couldn't believe it. We hadn't seen color for years and years. And we heard the news that a few hours earlier there had been the declaration of surrender."[2] Tezuka Osamu heard the surrender broadcast but didn't understand it; only when he overheard other people talking later that day did he realize that the war was over, and that they'd lost, which until then had been inconceivable. That night he took the train to Osaka's bombed-out Umeda station: The Hankyū shopping arcade still stood, and its chandelier was lit up without blackout curtains for the first time in years. Looking out at what was left of the city, seeing lights and even some neon signs, Tezuka realized he was glad to be alive, and that he would live—and that now he might be able to become a mangaka.[3]

In Harbin, Ueda Toshiko left the newspaper office early with a colleague and went out to buy sweets, which she and other Japanese nationals had been denying themselves in the spirit of self-restraint—it clearly hadn't worked.[4] Future *Garo* publisher Nagai Katsuichi (1921–96) and his brother started selling "recovered magazines" (back issues of *King, Shōnen Kurabu*, and the like, which had become a staple of used bookstores since 1943 as the publishing situation grew desperate) in Tokyo's Asakusa black market two days after the surrender, and sold out immediately. Despite the lack of streetcar or subway services, it was wildly crowded, and there was a feeling of freedom. Eventually they hit on the idea of selling manga in sixteen-page chunks: as soon as they put it on the table, people would say, "Ah! Manga!" and buy it.[5] To make money while interned in winter 1946, Ueda sold cigarettes and handmade manga featuring popular characters such as Mickey Mouse, Donald Duck, Groucho Marx, and her own characters in the Harbin streets.[6]

Historian Miriam Silverberg discussed (mostly passive) attempts at "hanging onto the modern" in her book *Erotic Grotesque Nonsense*, countering the prevailing interpretation that Japanese modern times were lightly worn and easily discarded by Japanese subjects during the wartime era.[7] Historian Andrew Gordon has discussed how the 1930s were "a time of both mobilizing for war and deepening of modernity," which included the increasing possession of sewing machines and radios, a growing passion for baseball, and the spread of Western clothes and Western-style beauty parlors catering to women.[8] The Japanese film industry's expansion, the new heights that publishing and music reached through 1940, and the rail, air, and communications networks laid throughout the empire for civilian and military purposes all demonstrate modernity's progress in the name of the empire in these years.[9]

Manga fits into this paradigm of "hanging onto wartime modernity" too. Manga was obviously not inherently resistant to co-option by the state, but at the same time that its content was suborned by fascist propaganda, there was something in its form's inalienable hybridity—neither words nor pictures but both at once—and in its undeniable transnational history—neither fully Japanese nor fully foreign—that the wartime state could never completely control and that, consequently, it sought futilely and constantly to deny. The state could and did ban creators, genres, and kinds of manga, but it could not prevent people from remembering and rereading other manga, which seemed more like manga and less like eating vegetables. As soon as the surrender ended the state controls that had artificially suppressed manga creators and fans, they went right back to reading, creating, and enjoying manga. The ways in which manga, as an industry and a medium, was transformed by these newly unleashed energies in the postwar years form the subject of the next chapter.

PART THREE

Manga in the Postwar Era

1945–1963

Overview

NOWHERE TO GO BUT UP

THE END OF THE WAR wiped the Japanese Empire off the map. By the time the surrender was formalized in September 1945, it was clear that the Allied powers envisioned a long occupation to reeducate Japan in the ways of democracy and individualism. The Meiji drive for modernization, industrialization, and normalization of Japan's status on the world stage seemed as ruined as the cities of East Asia.

In the aftermath of defeat, Japan reconstructed itself not as a multiethnic empire but as a monoethnic nation, which became a democracy with universal suffrage after the postwar constitution, written by the Occupation government, took effect in 1947. The Occupation was a jarring but also liberating experience for most Japanese people living in the home islands—despite the deprivation of the first few postwar years, when people turned to the black market to supply what the legal market could not (namely food and amphetamines), the sense of new social freedoms and newly relaxed mores buoyed many people, despite the ubiquitous presence of American GIs.[1] The era was rife with social and labor activism; Japan's first socialist prime minister took office in 1947 after the country's first elections under the new constitution, and labor union membership and actions soared. After reflecting on his own war responsibility and becoming a member of the Japanese Communist Party in 1948, Katō Etsurō began working for its newspaper, then known as *Akahata* (Red flag, 1928–35, 1945–), overseen by former proletarian mangaka Matsuyama Fumio.[2]

The "postwar period," defined as the economic and social recovery from wartime devastation, lasted until 1956. Japan's economic recovery was primed by its status as a staging ground for U.S. armed forces during the Korean War (1951–53), and it continues to outsource most of its defense costs to the United

States under the terms of the U.S.-Japan Security Treaty (Anpo), ratified in 1952 and illegally renewed amid the largest mass protests in Japanese history in 1960. The anti-Anpo protests' defeat presaged a capitulation to the forces of business and bureaucracy that had crucial consequences for manga.

Manga spent the first half of this postwar period regaining its footing. The reconstituted manga industry placed new emphasis on children's manga and on manga magazines, which resumed publication in Tokyo as quickly as possible. But manga's story in this period is also the story of the rise and fall of two intertwined manga publishing and sales phenomena, namely akahon and kashihon manga and kashihonya (rental bookstores). Both are important examples of transwar continuities in manga, as both emerged under the wartime state or earlier, as did kamishibai, the paper street theater that entranced children anew in these years.

Akahon manga flowered again after the Occupation began. Fast, cheap, anonymous, and relying on nontraditional distribution outlets for sales, it was a perfect fit for the black-market era. By the time the Occupation ended in 1952, akahon manga's day had also passed, with its publishers turning to kashihon manga—but while it lasted, as Tezuka said, it was free.[3] Kamishibai, akahon's street theater cousin that employed many mangaka to create its materials, increasingly competed with street-corner and then home television sets, and also largely vanished within the decade. Both media forged important legacies in manga before their eclipse, and both proved extremely fecund.

Akahon's successor kashihon manga and the rental bookstores that nurtured it lasted another fifteen years or so. Widespread before rising standards of living once again made books affordable for most readers, kashihonya put manga and other popular literature within readers' grasp, especially blue-collar readers. Akahon publishers began publishing higher-quality books specifically for the kashihon market, and the format quickly became a kind of counterculture alternative to the Tokyo manga magazines, one that allowed Tezuka to pioneer a new evolution of children's manga, which he dubbed "story manga." Story manga developed narrative and cinematic techniques even further and eschewed humor, a dramatic evolution for a medium that had staked its social value on its ability to provoke laughter.

Tezuka's ambition to expand manga to include tragedy was nothing short of heretical, but it has been overshadowed by the tendentious claim that Tezuka introduced cinematic techniques to manga. To be sure, "cinematic" techniques—specifically, decomposing or breaking down action into individual panels for dramatic effect and depicting action in a more fluid style ultimately derived from animation—did become increasingly common in children's manga after Sakai Shichima (1905–69) and Tezuka employed these and other cinema-derived artistic strategies in their smash hit akahon manga, *Shintakarajima* (New Treasure Island, 1947). But Tezuka alone did not shift children's manga toward adopting these ideas; rather, his techniques were taken up (and, in Tezuka's view, taken too far) by a cadre of former animators who entered the manga industry in these same years. The ex-animators, the most influential of whom was Fukui Ei'ichi (1921–54), adapted their professional experience animating movement to manga, taking Tezuka's notions and running with them. Ultimately they outran Tezuka himself, expanding the scope of story manga to include subjects like sports and leaving behind Tezuka's favored elements such as talking animals and futuristic urban settings, which ultimately derived from the high modernist culture of his childhood home Takarazuka.

All told, these developments shifted the manga vanguard decisively toward children's manga. The vast majority of popular manga today descends from the story manga lineage that Tezuka and others developed from foundations laid by *Norakuro* and other long-form children's manga; Tezuka's innovations were so influential that within just a few years he and his works had become the establishment that young creators sought to rebel against. These young creators had grown up reading manga in the wartime and Occupation years, and they wanted to continue telling long-form fictional narratives in manga, rather than switching to sociopolitical satire, now that they and their readers had graduated middle school and reached young adulthood.[4]

These young Osaka-based kashihon mangaka invented a new form of manga known as *gekiga*—Tatsumi Yoshihiro (1935–2015) coined the term in 1957—to accomplish their goal of expanding manga to include more realism and more psychological stories and depictions (they were particularly fond of noir and detective narratives). Rejecting children's manga as childish and adult satirical manga as boring, encompassing a post-middle school readership, the gekiga boys proclaimed themselves the renegade vanguard of a new wave in Japanese comics culture. Although the Gekiga Workshop group that Tatsumi founded lasted only a year, gekiga steadily made inroads on the Tokyo manga establishment until it too had become the mainstream by the early 1970s.

Before that, however, the rise of gekiga and of story manga, as well as the spread of access to manga via kashihonya, were so challenging that they spawned a movement opposing them, the so-called "ban bad books movement" (akusho tsuihō undō). Parents and educators worried that story manga in general and gekiga in particular would poison children's minds and moral character, but democratic Japan did not have censorship of non-explicit material like the imperial state. Parents and parent-teacher associations instead sought to impose censorship on manga whose content they found objectionable by targeting various nodes in the manga ecosystem. Although they burned books and got some manga creators blacklisted for varying amounts of time, the movement ultimately failed to achieve its goal of ensuring that children's manga contained only "good" content: In postwar society, "good" content was ultimately what readers wanted, not what the state thought they should consume, and publishers and bookstores had little incentive to go against readers' tastes and purchasing power.

Another important transition in this era was less readily apparent. Like Inoue Kazuo, the creator of the hit baseball manga *Bat Kid*, as well as Hasegawa, Tezuka, and virtually every other manga creator thereafter, manga creators who entered the profession after the war were no longer art school graduates with fine arts training, a development augured by the rise of manga correspondence courses and the recruitment of amateurs in the 1930s. Whereas almost every prewar mangaka had trained in fine arts, usually both Western and Japanese, manga creators now acquired the training necessary to create manga first and foremost by avidly consuming manga. Many creators of this era then did individual training with eminent creators of their day; this pattern went as far back as Miyao Shigeo, who had apprenticed with Okamoto Ippei. Hasegawa and Ueda Toshiko had done manga apprenticeships too, but Tezuka broke this mold decisively: His only apprenticeship was to his own prodigious productivity, or perhaps to animated films and American comics, and his collaboration with Sakai.

Postwar creators largely followed the pattern laid down by people like Hasegawa and Tezuka on their route into the profession, with the important difference that, supplemented by a few chance or short meetings with established creators, they drew manga obsessively throughout their childhoods, often in collaboration with friends, and usually received their first publication credits through reader submission contests.[5] After beginning to work in the industry, they would then receive further, informal feedback from editors or older colleagues in the course of creating their first manga. These developments meant that fine arts were no longer among the media that influenced manga expression. Instead, popular media like movies, radio, and (later) television were much more likely sources of manga artists' inspiration.

CHAPTER FIVE

The Manga Pulps and the God of Manga

RESURRECTED MEDIA: AKAHON AND KAMISHIBAI

Those manga publishers that were still standing were remarkably quick to resume publication after Japan's surrender in August 1945. The Kodansha Ehon series relaunched in October 1945, with its initial manga volumes featuring Tagawa's *Chibikuro*, starring Norakuro's hitherto unknown son.[1] In the same month in Osaka, mangaka Ōsaka Tokio self-printed one hundred copies of his book *Nakayoshi Manga* (Good friends manga) in his house using a mimeograph as soon as he was demobilized. Ōsaka hoped to sell just half of them, but the entire print run sold out immediately, and he quickly sold ten thousand copies of other books priced at two yen each. Published in the landscape B6 format at about eighteen pages each, Osaka manga figures began calling these "ehon," and they formed the backbone of akahon manga's initial resurrection in Kansai.[2]

Once again, akahon offered creators a great deal of leeway, and it continued to welcome newcomers. These factors converged in the creation of perhaps the most famous akahon manga of all time, *Shintakarajima*, with story (gensaku) and structure (kōsei) by former *Osaka Puck* mangaka and longtime animator Sakai Shichima and art by Tezuka. Sakai was a veteran mangaka and former animator, who resumed drawing children's manga in 1946; he was the driving force behind Osaka's first postwar children's manga magazine, *Hello! Manga*, whose contributors included Tezuka, Ōsaka Tokio and former *Osaka Puck* mainstay Kotera Kyūho (1889–1962). Ōsaka introduced Tezuka to Sakai in July 1946, and Sakai offered Tezuka the chance to collaborate soon after.[3] Tezuka had made his professional debut in January 1946 with the four panel manga *Ama-chan no nikkichō* (Ama-chan's diary) in the *Shōkokumin Shinbun* newspaper; reportedly, Sakai recruited Tezuka because he did "manga like Disney" and Sakai wanted someone with a fresh style.[4] The plot is a mixture of *Treasure Island, Robinson Crusoe*, and *Tarzan*, with a boy named Pete, who recalls the plucky boy detectives popularized in Edogawa Ranpo's juvenile novels (some of which were serialized in *Shōnen Kurabu* in the 1930s), searching for treasure on a jungle island, accompanied by a stalwart ship's captain and pursued by pirates.[5] Many details in the first half recall Tezuka's amateur work "Oyaji no takarajima" (Old man's treasure island), but Sakai required Tezuka to redo a lot of the art, and he also redrew some of the art and edited Tezuka's dialogue, which he evidently thought too adult for children.[6]

Released in January 1947, *Shintakarajima* became a massive hit and launched Tezuka's career; he published thirty-four works in thirty-six volumes in akahon in Osaka over the next four years, roughly a book a month.[7] His works were so popular from the start that his manga became a huge influence on akahon manga content and expression in only a few years. It perhaps can be difficult today, reading a Tezuka manga that characteristically eschews the use of screentones and occasionally copies a shot from an animated Disney film, to appreciate the fact that Tezuka broke onto the manga scene "like a thunderclap." As Komatsu explained, the cuts in the action of *Shintakarajima*'s initial pages were a huge shock: Rather than a theatrical stage, the manga's opening chase scene looked like a storyboard or a series of key frames in animation. Komatsu recalled that "I thought this might be a revolution in manga expression while I was reading it," and he was right.[8] Future mangaka including Ishinomori Shōtarō, the Fujiko Fujio duo, Akatsuka Fujio (1935–2008), Tatsumi Yoshihiro, and Matsumoto Leiji all read it; future novelist Kida Jun'ichirō (b. 1935) traded a pile of manga magazines to a friend in return for a copy, and stayed up all night rereading it in secret after his family went to bed.[9]

In the years after its publication, as copies became harder to find, *Shintakarajima* became legendary, and the idea that Tezuka's art for it introduced "new cinematic techniques" to manga solidified into common knowledge. Tezuka himself later wrote that he had wanted to introduce techniques from the movies he grew up watching as a kid into manga, and while he freely acknowledged his debt to Disney and "Disney style," people tended to assume that he meant Disney films.[10] But manga had adopted movie techniques since Ippei's first eiga manga in the 1910s, and its cinematic borrowings had continued to evolve along with cinema's development. *Shintakarajima* was strongly influenced rather by the American comic books that were introduced to Japan by American GIs during the Occupation: Tezuka received a mountain of these comics from a Black soldier in spring 1946, apparently including Floyd Gottfredson's Mickey Mouse comics. *Shintakarajima*'s most famous sequence, its opening chase, borrows directly from Gottfredson's "Mickey Mouse Outwits the Phantom Blot" (1939), and other artistic elements, including Sakai's cover illustration, directly echo visuals from other Disney comics and 1930s Disney cartoons.[11] The wordless opening chase scene was almost certainly conceived by Sakai, whose other akahon works contain several similar sequences.[12] Moreover, the overall art is rarely as dynamic as Tezuka achieved in later manga, and the book relies on the three-panel layout Tagawa developed for the *Norakuro* tankōbon.[13]

At heart, *Shintakarajima* was yet another example of akahon's fundamental characteristic: borrowing from other popular works. Yet Disney and other ten-cent American comics were less common in Japan than akahon, and readers perceived *Shintakarajima* as shockingly new. Fujiko F. Fujio (1934–2022), one half of Fujiko Fujio, recalled: "If I think about it now, taking that book in my hand decided my destiny. When I opened to the main text, I felt a shock so great I nearly passed out. . . . I had never seen a manga like this. Two pages with nothing but driving. Why did it make me so excited? I felt a biological feeling of pleasure, as if I myself was riding in that sports car, dashing to the wharf. This was obviously a manga printed on paper, but it felt like the car was racing with stupendous speed. It was like I was watching a movie!"[14] The opening sequence in particular made the manga feel *subjective*, giving readers the sense of being part of the action rather than just witnessing it (figure 12).

Shintakarajima's legend was stoked by the oft-repeated assertion that it sold an incredible four hundred thousand copies, in a year when a picture-book bestseller sold five hundred thousand.[15] But as manga historian Takeuchi Osamu has documented, this claim can ultimately be traced to a 1949 newspaper article, and people in the Osaka manga industry had serious doubts about those figures.[16] *Shintakarajima* and several other of Tezuka's early akahon manga were printed using the cheaper kakihan process, in which a copyist redrew the manuscript in reverse on zinc plates for printing. Transferring the artwork changed the lines, much to Tezuka's displeasure, and he insisted on putting the copyist's name in the table of contents to highlight the change. Eventually he developed the method of submitting a manuscript entirely done in blue pencil, indicating the colors to be used solely by numbers from the printer's key, to save himself the time and labor of inking a manuscript that would be redrawn anyway.[17] But each set of zinc plates was good for only three or four thousand copies before they wore out, and with

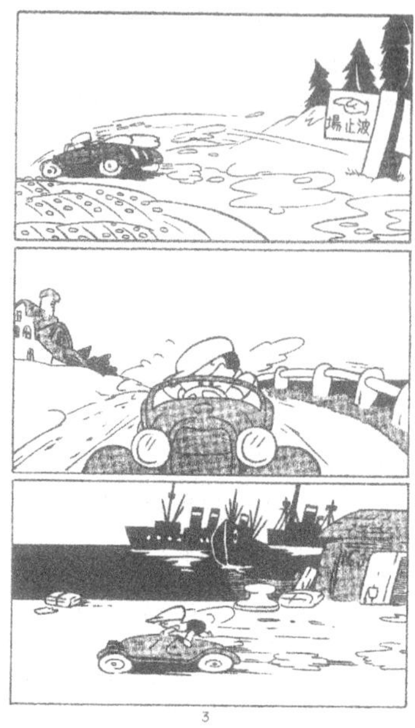

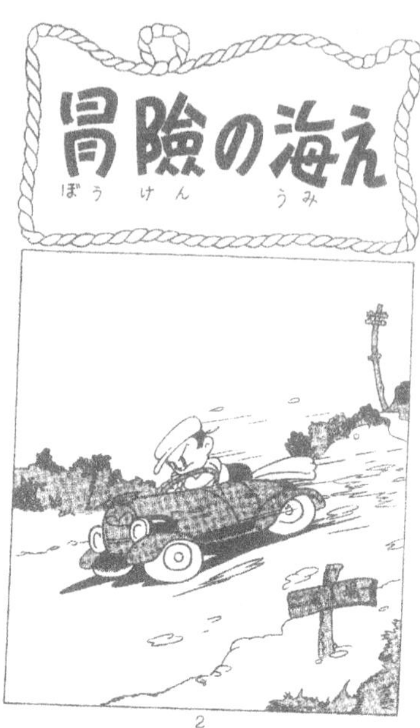

FIGURE 12. Opening sequence of *Shintakarajima*, 1947. The three-panel layout on the second page was originally created by Tagawa Suihō for the *Norakuro* tankōbon. © Tezuka Productions and Sakai Shichima. Used with permission.

just seven print runs documented in 1947 (priced at 25–35 yen), the book's probable sales fall well short of four hundred thousand copies, even with the publisher's later reprints using photographic reproduction.[18]

While most of those seven print runs feature both Sakai's and Tezuka's names on the cover, the first run evidently did not feature Tezuka's name at all; this so incensed Tezuka that, although it was the publisher's decision, he reneged on his agreement to collaborate with Sakai again on a robot manga.[19] Akahon's cheapness bred adaptability; later *Shintakarajima* printings dropped Sakai's name as Tezuka's popularity grew, and replaced Sakai's cover illustration with a more modish image. Indeed, some akahon publishers may have practiced rudimentary A/B testing; according to Tezuka, Osaka publishers would plagiarize manga—usually by cutting it out of a newspaper and gluing it to the front of a book—and see which covers proved more popular, using the winner thereafter.[20]

Shintakarajima also launched an akahon boom.[21] By 1948, akahon publishers were putting out a thousand new books a year. Nagai Katsuichi, for example, started a Tokyo-based akahon publishing company, finding mangaka through a newspaper ad.[22] Priced cheap, at 10–50 yen or 70–90 yen at most, postwar akahon books were normally B6 or B7 hardbacks (sometimes B8), about twenty to forty pages long, printed in monochrome or two-color, and frequently had little information about the creators or the publishers; the format's customary practice of author anonymity may have continued as an attempt to evade censorship, which was reinstituted by the Occupation, though with different goals, after the surrender.[23] Once again, akahon manga bypassed established manga distribution methods and were sold at places such as candy shops, night markets, department stores, and temple and shrine festivals.[24] The main postwar akahon genre was again jidaigeki, notwithstanding Supreme Commander for the Allied Powers (SCAP) regulations that forbade swords in movies and children's magazines.[25]

Above all, akahon manga's cheap production conditions gave creators room to experiment and an opportunity to get paid quickly. Komatsu's first akahon manga (science fiction, naturally), *Kaijin skeleton hakushi* (Mysterious skeleton professor, 1948), was published under his birth name while he was still in high school; he adopted the pen name Komatsu Sakyō to avoid word getting around at school, as akahon was generally considered trash (plate 10). While a college student, he made 3,500 yen per manuscript with Osaka publisher Hinomaru Bunko, in an era when the monthly salary for a new college graduate was 6,000–7,000 yen.[26] As a newcomer, Tezuka was paid 3,000 yen for *Shintakarajima*'s two hundred pages.[27]

The next year, Tezuka published *The Mysterious Underground Men* (*Chiteikoku no kaijin*, 1948) in akahon, which he later described as his first story manga. Like *Shintakarajima*, with which it shares an adventure plot, Tezuka drew on American comics and other Euro-American media for many of its visual elements, and he retained Tagawa's three-panel layout. Unlike *Shintakarajima*, however, *The Mysterious Underground Men* introduced "tragic elements to manga" through the forcibly evolved rabbit Mimio, who shockingly dies at the end in tragic self-sacrifice, in what was probably a first for children's manga. As Ryan Holmberg notes, Tezuka not only moved beyond the use of humor in the manga, he did so specifically by reusing slapstick tragicomic elements from comics and removing their humor, leaving just the tragedy. In American comics and prewar manga, slapstick antics did not fundamentally change characters subjected to them, but for Mimio, they had lasting effects. As Holmberg puts it, "Tragicomedy has been stripped of its comic half, with the result that the story is now part of the character, progressively shaping him along the way."[28]

Above all, *The Mysterious Underground Men* represented a fulfillment of Tezuka's radical vision for manga, which he had articulated in a college publication in 1946: "True manga uses pictures and their expression to make readers cry, excite them, or touch them to the heart. Only then does manga reveal its true value."[29] Tezuka wanting to expand manga beyond humor was nothing short of heretical, given that laughter had been manga's acknowledged raison d'être for decades. But akahon enabled him to demonstrate that readers would buy it, and his vision for the medium eventually won the day, transforming it utterly.

In some respects, akahon's content seems comparable to contemporary pulp novels and comics in the United States, but akahon manga was defiantly, unabashedly derivative and intertextual. As Shimizu notes, "there were no original heroes in akahon manga." Hasegawa Machiko's hit newspaper strip *Sazae-san* was quickly followed by *Tsuruko-san*, written by one "Sugimoto Machiko," and Yokoi Fukutarō's *Bōken Tāzan* (Adventure Tarzan, 1948), itself inspired by a hit Tarzan movie, soon spawned akahon's *Ōja Tāzan* (King Tarzan). Actors remained popular akahon characters; child star Misora Hibari (1937–89) was all the rage in postwar akahon. Akahon manga were thus an excellent barometer for the daily life and quotidian pop culture of their day, and they bear comparison with fanworks of later eras, such as dōjinshi in Japan and fanfiction worldwide.[30]

The akahon practice of adapting stories and characters across media was echoed in the other form of resurrected entertainment whose popularity skyrocketed after the war, namely the street theater called kamishibai (paper theater). Like akahon and kashihonya, kamishibai had its roots in the prewar era but reached new heights of popularity after the surrender: Its format was also well suited to Occupied Japan, and Shimizu Isao recalled that "the greatest pleasure of children immediately after the end of the war was kamishibai."[31]

Kamishibai consisted of a person (usually male in the postwar years) who roamed the streets giving performances at intersections, signaled by the sound of hyōshigi (wooden clappers), which were also used for dramatic emphasis during the performance. Once a sufficient crowd of patrons, mostly children, had gathered, the kamishibai performer charged admission by selling candy for a pittance. (There were always kids who hadn't paid standing around at the back, which was tolerated.)[32] Kamishibai stories were serialized, and each performance ended with some kind of hook or cliffhanger to keep viewers coming back the next time. The performance order was standardized: a slapstick opener, followed by a melodrama aimed at girls, and then an adventure story for boys.[33] Lasting less than an hour, the performance consisted of narration and sound effects provided by the human performer complemented by a set of paper cards (usually printed on durable cardboard) containing illustrations of scenes from the story. The performer cunningly combined moving the cards against one another with vocal tricks to create a narrative that blended planar motion with aural characterization, in which the interval, the space between cards, was key: Media scholar Sharalyn Orbaugh notes that kamishibai was almost hypermodern, as its practitioners and theorists were strongly influenced by Soviet filmmaker Sergei Eisenstein's theory and practice of the montage. In the medium's first florescence in the 1930s, many benshi turned to kamishibai after talkies put them out of a job, cementing vocal effects' importance for the medium.[34] Shimizu Isao recalled that the performer's vocabulary was also more engaging than what children learned in school.[35]

Kamishibai arose around 1929, and by 1933 there were two thousand performers in Tokyo and thirty thousand nationwide, entertaining at least one million children a day. Thus, it was more popular than radio in the 1930s and 1940s, and bigger than manga in the 1950s.[36] During the Occupation it provided a much-needed source of income for returning veterans in particular, who overwhelmingly made up the ranks of itinerant performers, and a much-needed source of entertainment for the children who were its avid fans; at its second peak in 1948–49, it had as many as 1.7 million daily spectators nationwide (figure 13).[37] Like akahon, kamishibai made money by giving children what they wanted regardless of whether it was educational or not, which put a target on the medium's back during the wartime state (like manga and film, kamishibai was purged of leftists and repurposed for propaganda during the war years), but which perfectly suited the anarchic conditions of the early postwar period.[38] Kamishibai was used for education during the Occupation too; Ueda Toshiko drew anti-Soviet kamishibai as part of her job at NHK, the Japanese Broadcasting Corporation, in these years.[39]

On the production side, creating the card sets (which had the narrative's outline printed on the reverse, and which performers rented from the publishers) provided another source of much-needed work for returning and new manga professionals, many of whom switched freely between kamishibai and akahon. Sakai Shichima and Kotera Kyūho worked in kamishibai under other pen names; Mizuki Shigeru (1922–2015), the future creator of *Gegege no Kitarō*, got into kamishibai while living in the same Kobe lodging house

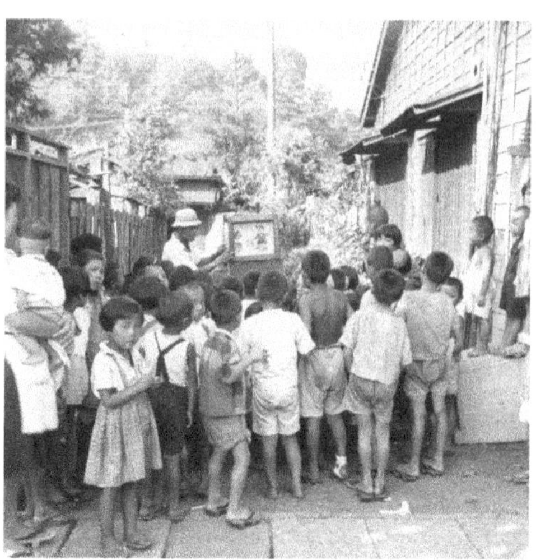

FIGURE 13. Children watching a kamishibai performance, ca. 1948. From the Walter A. Pennino Postwar Japan Photo Collection, courtesy of Center for Japanese Studies, University of Hawai'i at Mānoa.

as one of its luminaries, Suzuki Katsumaru (1904–86).[40] Mizuki's prolific kamishibai output included the first version of his ghost boy hero Kitarō's story, but it was a harsh industry that "kept you on your toes": Deadlines were constant, Mizuki worked every day for twelve hours or more, and finances were unstable for both publishers and creators.[41]

Both akahon and kamishibai borrowed content that had proved popular in other media, a derivative relationship that akahon's successor kashihon manga inherited. Kamishibai's streetcorner performances also directly structured the early paradigm for Japanese television, which thanks to its streetcorner broadcasts was initially known as "electric kamishibai."[42]

MANGA RELAUNCHES: *SAZAE-SAN* AND SATIRE'S SLOW FADE

Manga for adults quickly started anew as well. Shinmangaha Shūdan members refounded the group in October 1945 under the name Manga Shūdan and welcomed new members. "That we had free expression was good," Sugiura recalled in the group's fiftieth anniversary Festschrift, "but we had no paper." (Paper rationing remained an important tool of censorship under SCAP during the Occupation, just as it had been under the Home Ministry in the wartime era.) Ogawa Tetsuo wrote drily: "Not many mangaka died in the war, even though we weren't very strong on the whole. More of us died after the war from drinking bad moonshine."[43] They also died from disease, particularly tuberculosis. In 1946, Yokoyama, Kondō, and many other Manga Shūdan figures joined forces to launch the newspaper *Shinyūkan* (New evening news, 1946–50); Tagawa Suihō and the newly widowed Yazaki Takeko, who had left her children with relatives after her husband's death and returned to Tokyo to find work, were on the manga department staff.[44]

Kondō Hidezō, Sugiura, Yokoyama, and others associated with *Manga* during the war relaunched the magazine in 1946; wartime amateur star Katō Yoshirō debuted there in 1947, and Yazaki Takeko published in it regularly (figure 14). *Manga* lasted until 1951 under the tagline "a magazine of situations to look at" (miru jikyoku zasshi), peddling a mix of sharp-edged political satire (made possible by the new relative freedom of the press under the Occupation) and the same predictable sexism of Japanese modern times: The magazine contained quite a lot of eroticism, and *Tamako-san*, its obligatory answer to *Sazae-san*, is also remarkably sexist.

Sazae-san, a four-panel strip about the trials and tribulations of a young woman who became a housewife, was postwar newspaper manga's breakout hit; the eponymous female protagonist was closely modeled on her creator, Hasegawa Machiko, and Sazae-san's own feminism and indomitable personality came as no surprise to those who knew Hasegawa herself. Hasegawa debuted in 1935 in *Shōjo Kurabu* with a talking animal manga, "Kitsune no men" (The fox's face), then began publishing with Kodansha's Ehon series at sixteen and became a professional mangaka two years later. Her relationship with Kodansha continued during the war; her manga *Nakayoshi techō* (Good friends' notebook, 1940–42) ran in *Shōjo Kurabu*, but she chafed at the restrictions of the censors, who in her recollection rejected all of her good ideas, and she redrew the manga after the war. As the Hasegawa Machiko Museum delicately phrases it, the wartime period was "an age in which people could not draw as they thought." Hasegawa evacuated to Fukuoka with her mother and sisters in 1943, where she worked as a cartoonist for the *Evening Fukunichi*.[45]

Sazae-san ran from 1946 to 1974, for the first few years in the *Fukunichi Shinbun* and for the remainder in the national *Asahi Shinbun*, which recruited Hasegawa to come back to Tokyo, and take Sazae-san with her, in 1949. Hasegawa ultimately drew more than sixty-five hundred strips, and in a canny business maneuver, she kept the rights to the comics and formed a publishing company with her older sister Mariko to publish the collected

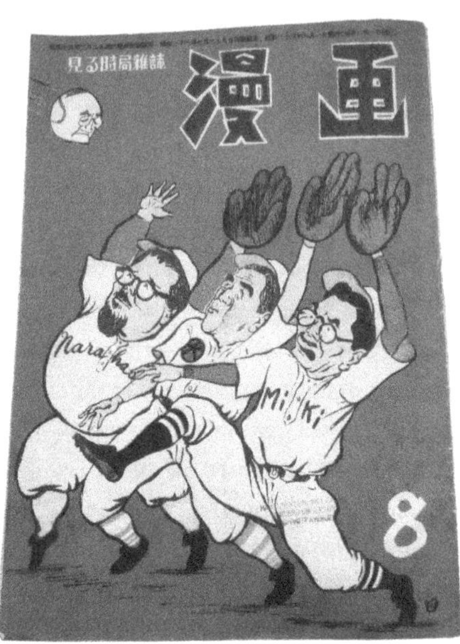

FIGURE 14. Cover of *Manga*, August 1948.

volumes. Although sales of the initial B5 volumes in December 1946 were weak, the books flew off the shelves when they switched to the smaller B6 size in April 1947.[46] The October 1948 issue of the children's manga magazine *Manga Shōnen* featured ads for *Sazae-san*, demonstrating the strip's cross-demographic appeal even before it moved to the *Asahi; Sazae-san* was also serialized in the magazine that year.[47]

Sazae-san has never been unpopular; a February 1956 newspaper survey found that *Sazae-san* and two other newspaper strips were the three most popular manga in Japan.[48] Newspaper manga as a whole, now firmly wedded to the yonkoma format, was wildly popular, with more than seven hundred strips published nationwide.[49] But newspaper manga's success in the postwar years masked an incipient transition in manga that would soon destabilize the prewar paradigms of prestige and economic prowess within the medium. In these years, children's manga became increasingly prominent, and the prewar "family strategy" of marketing publications to an entire household was not revived in the postwar period. It also meant that newspaper manga gradually waned as a site of children's interest; the manga that they were obsessed with increasingly appeared in manga magazines, and children's manga and magazines were producing manga's breakout creative stars. To be sure, four-panel manga and one-panel political cartoons persist today in national newspapers, as well as regional and sports newspapers. Four-panel manga owns the "gag" manga genre, which first cohered with the launch of *Monthly Gagda* in 1981, and has been carried forward by the yonkonma-only *Manga Time* (1981–).[50] Four-panel strips are also still published in general interest as well as manga magazines, and the most popular strips are republished in collected volumes. But none of these are in the manga vanguard, although newspaper manga, and four-panel manga in particular, has inherited manga's original purpose of making people laugh.[51]

The age's changes were embodied by the short-lived *Kodomo Manga Times* (published from around 1949–51), a half-size weekly newspaper aimed at children, priced at six yen, comparable to the cost of renting a book. The outer pages contained vivid full (four)-color manga, while the inner pages contained a mixture of monochrome manga and articles, which were about baseball, baseball, and baseball, leavened with some actual news reports. Cover illustrations varied between reportage and fiction, including *Alice in Wonderland*, a piece about the start of typhoon season, and an image depicting American kids' part-time summer jobs.[52] The "manga times" portion of *Kodomo Manga Times* was written in the katakana syllabary, following the new orthographic practice that equated not using characters for "manga" with a certain au courant attitude.

Kodomo Manga Times seemed to be aiming for the niche that *Tokyo Puck* had once filled, except aimed at children, with uneven results; after shrinking in size in 1951, the newspaper folded not long after publishing its 129th issue, although it managed to outlast the venerable former *Osaka Puck* by at least two years. *Osaka Puck* had relaunched as *Manga to Yomimono* (Manga and Literature) in 1946 with content quite similar to that of *Kodomo Manga Times*, except aimed at adults. Tatsumi Yoshihiro, then a middle school student living twenty minutes away from Tezuka in Osaka, regularly submitted "postcard manga" (four or six panels drawn on a postcard) to its readers' manga contests and won.[53] Despite its storied pedigree, the magazine, at that point bimonthly, ceased publication in March 1950 after more than forty-three years in print. *Tokyo Puck* itself briefly revived in August 1948, but it lasted only three issues before folding again for good. Ultimately, the original manga periodical format, pioneered by *Tokyo Puck* and refined by *Jiji Shinpō* and other publications in the 1920s and 1930s, no longer satisfied audiences.

Satirical manga expanded after the Occupation ended, with *Manga Dokuhon* (Manga reader, 1954–70), *Shūkan Manga Times* (Weekly manga times, 1956–), and *Shūkan Manga Sunday* (Weekly manga Sunday, 1959–

2013) inaugurating a category that became known as "otona manga" or "manga for adults." Mandoku, as it was known, eventually incorporated fictional manga alongside its satirical entries; Tezuka was a contributor.[54] Media studies scholar Fujiki Hideaki notes that these magazines also featured erotic art, "as well as nude gravures [a particular style of photographic soft-core pornography in Japan] and a variety of articles, especially in their early issues."[55] Komatsu Sakyō, who particularly appreciated the American manga that also appeared in *Manga Dokuhon*, recalled that when he first encountered them, "I was happy that adults could also read manga in weekly magazines like this."[56]

Manga overall grew in the 1950s along with the economy, and new and returning female creators found space in the medium again as publication venues increased. Yazaki Takeko published in children's manga magazines regularly; she made enough money to buy land in 1951, then sold it and built her own house about a year later. She worked widely, from the *Asahi* to magazines and government publications, and received increasing media coverage as her popularity grew, boosted by her tragic backstory (her younger son died not long after her husband). Although there were multiple female mangaka in the country, Yazaki was named as one of just two female-type mangaka alongside Hasegawa Machiko in the 1955 edition of Heibonsha's "who's who" biographical dictionary. She even took over *Sazae-san*'s *Asahi* slot with her manga *Ton-chan* for two and a half months when Hasegawa was ill, and her household manga *Osayo-san* did well enough that it was collected in tankōbon and printed on karuta (Japanese playing cards). But by the end of the 1950s, her star was waning, and her last regular gig, the *Yomiuri Shinbun* strip *Haruko-chan*, ended in 1961. Female mangaka often struggled to maintain careers, partly because they didn't have popular works or characters like Sazae-san and Ueda's Fuichin, partly because their patchier publication opportunities didn't give them the chance to develop a breakout hit.[57] They also struggled to balance careers with household labor; not coincidentally, Hasegawa never married, Ueda married and divorced in the 1950s, and Yazaki was a widow.

Declining popularity was not unique to Yazaki and other individual creators, however. Although satirical manga retained its prestige in the postwar era—Kondō Hidezō was more or less the dean of the manga establishment—satirical and newspaper mangaka in the 1950s struggled to retain the hordes of young readers who devoured children's manga as those readers grew older. Instead, the new story manga paradigm diverted readers to fictional, plot-driven stories that did not rely on constant humor, which threatened satirical manga for adults and the established practices of children's manga, and undermined manga's prior claims to social value, as did those creators' refusal to turn to adult-oriented manga. Indeed, kashihon publisher Hinomaru Bunko's 1957 bankruptcy was precipitated by a massive bet on otona manga that didn't pan out: Readers wanted the manga that would soon be called gekiga.[58]

The manga market was changing along with social mores, but many prewar figures adapted for a while, including Tagawa himself. Rumors circulated during the war that Tagawa had died, but as Kobayashi Hideo told people who asked, "The real ones don't die. Norakuro is a real one." After working at *Shinyūkan* for about a year, Tagawa resumed the *Norakuro* manga, first with various small publishers and then back home with Kodansha.[59] Tagawa went on an all-Japan tour of elementary schools in 1950, talking to students and drawing Norakuro at every stop, and *Norakuro* ran again in *Shōnen Club* from 1950 to 1953.[60] In its final episodes, serialized in *Maru* magazine (1948–) from 1961, Norakuro's friends took up a range of occupations that critic Ozaki Hotsuki (1928–99) deemed "symbols of the Shōwa era": stockbroker, pro wrestler, CEO of a small company, municipal representative, and private detective, while Norakuro himself wound up running a coffee house.[61] The Norakuro fan club, founded by fans after the war, outlived his creator.[62]

Norakuro's non-Kodansha adventures began with *Chinpin Norakuro-sō* (Rough draft of Norakuro curios) in March 1948. The manga, which according to the censor's notes had an initial print run of ten thousand copies, opens with Norakuro homeless on the street in Tokyo, saying that no matter how long he thinks about what's been done, it can't be helped ("shikata ga nai"). Readers would have assumed that Norakuro was swept into a prison camp after the fall of Manchukuo, like so many other Japanese soldiers and civilians; written from Norakuro's perspective, the introduction states that he returned to Japan as a repatriate (hikiagesha) without a home and without knowing any of his old friends' current whereabouts. (Happily, he was reunited with his friend Chameken in the next volume, published in December.) In *Chinpin Norakuro-sō*, Norakuro declared that notwithstanding all that, "I, a manga dog," had been greatly cheered by the fact that Japan was building a society in which, with everyone's help, everyone could mutually become happy, and that it was no longer just a country of people who threw their weight around like in the past: Thanks to that, he could once more deeply feel the fun in life, despite his present difficulties.[63]

Tokyo publishers defaulted to wartime models when reviving their operations, but there were notable differences, from technological to artistic. Nagai Katsuichi believed that phototypesetting became popular in manga after the war because it had spread throughout the empire under the wartime state; he had first encountered it in his intelligence work for Mantetsu in Manchukuo.[64] Other changes were subtler. The May 1946 issue of *Shōjo Club* ("club" was now spelled with katakana instead of kanji) looks quite similar to issues of the magazine published before the end of the war—except that there is no content promoting militarism. It also contains an editor's note explicitly stating that Japanese history and culture are *not* for militarism: Readers mustn't think that that history and culture have come to naught (dame ni natta); instead, "now is the time to become good friends with the rest of the world."[65]

The rest of the world was mediated by the United States through the Occupation, which was administered and carried out almost entirely by U.S. forces. Perhaps its most direct impact on manga was its active censorship department, which reviewed every item in Japan prior to publication. Occupation censors perhaps operated somewhat more openly and explicitly than the organs of the fascist imperial government, which had relied just as much on productive ambiguity and "cooperation" with publishers to ensure that published material met the proper standards as on prepublication review. But from late 1945 to mid-1952, when the Occupation ended and Japan regained its sovereignty, every manga publication that reached distribution did so because it passed Occupation inspection. Explicit censorship was sometimes not even necessary when a worldwide postwar paper shortage meant that paper itself was in short supply.

The Occupation authorities also purged publishing figures who had provided material and/or ideological support to the war effort; in late 1945, Kodansha's publisher and senior staff were obliged to resign. Katō Ken'ichi (1896–1975) was among them; he went on to launch the magazine *Manga Shōnen* (Manga Boy, 1947–55), which had a meteoric career as the single most influential publication of the decade after the war, and one of the most influential magazines in manga's history. Katō had previously been on the editorial staff of Kodansha children's magazines including *Shōjo Kurabu* and *Shōnen Kurabu*, where he was head editor from 1921 to 1932, gave the go-ahead for *Norakuro*'s lengthening serialization, and oversaw the Kodansha Ehon series. After separating from Kodansha in 1945, Katō was formally blacklisted from any position of public influence in June 1947.[66]

Although the Occupation purge painted with a broad brush, in Katō's case it was accurate: As a middle school student in Aomori, he had been a member of the Tessetsusha (Steel and Snow Society), an early rightist student society; as a member, Katō edited its newsletter, "Yamato no sakura," having already been on the editorial staff of his school newsletter.[67] When Katō was summarily barred from his livelihood in 1945, as his daughter Katō Misako later recalled, their family comprised ten people, including her parents and her aunt, Ken'ichi's sister; she was the oldest child at seventeen, and her youngest brother was just two. The only thing her father knew how to do was edit magazines, so that's what he did: In 1946 he began working at the new publisher Shōbunkan, which was co-owned by his nephew. Its flagship magazine relaunched as *Yakyū Shōnen* (Baseball Boy) in April 1947, and became one of the top-selling children's publications in Japan by the end of the decade. After his blacklisting, Katō founded the company Gakudōsha with seed money from his nephew and enlisted his family as staff; for added camouflage, they used his wife Masa's sister's address as *Manga Shōnen*'s place of publication, his children delivered business correspondence and publishing materials to contributors and printers by hand to avoid postal censorship, and Masa was listed as the publisher with Misako as the editor. In reality, Ken'ichi was the editor, with Misako as assistant. But with her name on the masthead, it was Misako who brought page proofs to the Occupation's General Headquarters for approval.[68]

Shōnen Kurabu had been founded on the dual premise of enlightenment and entertainment. *Manga Shōnen* was premised on the idea that children liked manga best because it was brightening and fun, and Katō swore to uphold this principle in an editor's note laying out the magazine's philosophy: "*Manga Shōnen* is a book that will brighten and gladden children's hearts, and in *Manga Shōnen* there will be novels and stories that rear children nobly and correctly; all of them will be masterpieces. Children of Japan, read *Manga Shōnen*, and grow up nobly, brightly, and correctly!"[69] Despite the name, however, *Manga Shōnen* did not consist entirely of manga; in addition to emonogatari, the October 1949 issue features articles about celebrities and actual baseball players, including Babe Ruth—and an ad for an all-manga special issue that was special precisely *because* it was all manga.[70]

Gakudōsha arose out of Katō's association with the Gakudō Kaikan, an organization that sought to create a new kind of education for the new Japan; toward the end of his life, Katō told *COM* that he had wanted to create a magazine for that purpose, matching the organization's curricula, as part of his atonement for the war. The first issue, however, didn't sell: At 20 yen, it was too expensive for the inflationary era, and most copies were returned; eventually, the Katō children sold these from the front of their house at a discount.[71] The magazine remained a family affair for the length of its existence. Misako's cousin Kyōko was working as a manga editor at the time; after *Manga Shōnen*, she also worked on Fujiko Fujio's *Manga michi* later in her career. Misako's younger siblings and the family dog served as models for the magazine's cover illustrations, which were done in the same portrait-realism style as the prewar Kodansha magazines—unsurprising, as they were the work of Saitō Ioe (1881–1966), who had done covers for 240 issues of *Shōnen Kurabu*, including the first one, and who created most *Manga Shōnen* covers until 1950.[72]

Katō Misako wrote that her father copied *Shōnen Kurabu*'s editorial methods exactly, starting with the primacy of reader connections; the magazine had a vibrant readers' letters section, just like the Kodansha sibling magazines. *Manga Shōnen* took this feature a step further when Ken'ichi decided to cement the connection between readers and the magazine via "Maruko," in which guise Misako interacted with readers for more than four years, from March 1949 to August 1953. In her view the "Maruko" persona was clearly inspired by *Shōnen Kurabu*, although its editors had always replied to reader letters as an anonymous collective.[73]

Talent was the other important continuity with *Shōnen Kurabu*. *Manga Shōnen* employed many Kodansha creators who had been popular in the 1930s, including perhaps most significantly Shimada Keizō; Shimada also helped new creators, including Fukui Ei'ichi, break into the industry in the early postwar years.[74] Creators working for the magazine were also likely to have been members of the Shōwa Mangakkai, which had formed in the late 1930s under Tagawa's auspices; *Manga Shōnen* surely embodied some of his spirit, as well as publishing Tagawa himself, and a serialized version of Hasegawa's *Sazae-san* in 1948. Indeed, between Tagawa's influence and the fact that many authors and illustrators were well known from their work in the Kodansha sibling magazines, Katō's periodical sometimes felt like a pan-Kodansha reunion tour.[75]

Even its new content had important transwar continuities. Before his dismissal from Kodansha, Katō had been slated to become editor in chief of

Yakyū Zasshi (Baseball magazine), and *Manga Shōnen* was full of the sport. Introduced to Japan in 1872, baseball had become the nation's most popular sport by the end of the 1910s. In the wartime era, Japanese equivalents had simply been substituted for English baseball terminology, effectively nativizing the game. In the postwar years, baseball's popularity was growing again with Occupation encouragement, and *Manga Shōnen*'s first breakout hit was *Bat-kun* (1947–49, *Bat Kid*) by Inoue Kazuo. The story of a kid who played the game, *Bat Kid*'s popularity saved the magazine.[76] It was the first long-running sports manga, laying the foundations for many best-selling manga thereafter, and in the era when girls' softball began in Japan, the manga was read by children of all genders (just as both boys and girls appeared on *Manga Shōnen*'s first cover, literally illustrating its desired audience). In Shimizu's evaluation, *Bat Kid*'s eponymous protagonist was essentially a normal kid, but he didn't always go after lost balls—which would have been unthinkable under the empire.[77] Yonezawa Yoshihiro noted that in addition to being a regular kid with an ordinary life, the protagonist was also depicted realistically, unlike in Tezuka's manga.[78]

Inoue himself was one of the "manga boys," in Miyamoto Hirohito's phrase, who had been nurtured by *Shōnen Kurabu*, where he had been a paid contributor since 1934 after submitting to the readers' corner beginning in the late 1920s, and had published a serial baseball manga in *Yakyū Shōnen*. The back cover of *Manga Shōnen*'s first issue featured an illustration of popular characters playing baseball, including Norakuro, Dankichi, Mickey Mouse, Popeye, and possibly Bugs Bunny, illustrating what was presumed to be popular with children in January 1948—and demonstrating that it was not only akahon that trafficked in non-original characters.[79]

Manga Shōnen continued other *Shōnen Kurabu* elements, including the publication of translated comics, placement of messages from readers in among the manga, and (of course) the readers' corner.[80] But the magazine's most influential feature was its manga contest, open to anyone who wanted to submit. Prewar magazines like *Shōnen Kurabu* had dispensed ranked prizes to readers who wrote in, and had published reader-submitted manga on occasion; although *Manga Shōnen* promised prizes to those whose manga won particular favor from the judges, it took the much more significant step of printing the names of people who'd submitted particularly good manga that month, even if that manga did not run in the magazine alongside the winners'.[81] For example, the October 1948 issue features four pages of readers' manga as well as lists of names under the headings "Especially Well Done" and "Well Done," the latter divided by geography. The magazine even tapped readers to submit continuation chapters of *Bat Kid* after Inoue's death, publishing nine of them, including one by future female kashihon mangaka Takizawa Michiko.[82]

Many future mangaka got their first publication credit in the *Manga Shōnen* reader contests, including Fujiko Fujio, Ishinomori Shōtarō, Matsumoto Leiji, Tatsumi Yoshihiro, who first won a prize in July 1949, and the latter's older (and later semi-estranged) brother Sakurai Shōichi (1933–2003), who had first won a prize three months earlier, in March 1949.[83] Not everyone who submitted manga to the magazine became a professional manga creator; like Yokoo Tadanori (b. 1936), many became graphic designers, illustrators, architects, novelists, poets, and other creative professionals.[84] For these young people, who had their "emotional antenna raised high," in Ishinomori Shōtarō's phrase, manga was a "fascinating new method of expression," and in this respect the *Manga Shōnen* submissions clearly anticipated dōjinshi creators of later eras, many of whom found careers in other creative fields.[85]

For those who did embark on professional manga careers, the magazine was transformative. Sakurai wrote that prior to reading the magazine, he and Tatsumi "didn't know anything about manga": In his view, only *Manga Shōnen* touched the heartstrings of ordinary readers who aimed to be mangaka, and the magazine was "like a lover" (koibito no yōna sonzai de atta). Moreover, the magazine was not just a space for publishing manga, but inasmuch as it offered information on the manga world and tutorials on how to draw manga in Tezuka's monthly *Manga kyōshitsu* (1952–54, Manga classroom), it was a textbook, a gateway to success. Tatsumi used the same romantic language: He wrote that the magazine "was my first love," but hastened to add that "even though I was in love with a boy, it wasn't gay."[86]

Part of what made the love of *Manga Shōnen* so intense was that for children like Sakurai and Tatsumi across the country, the magazine created a centralized, shared experience of manga between readers, as Yonezawa Yoshihiro pointed out: Unlike *Shōnen Kurabu, Manga Shōnen* put manga at the core of this communication between children, collapsing the difference between the media they loved and the periodical that published it.[87] The *Shōnen Kurabu* readers' corner had always emphasized the magazine itself before popular content, even supremely popular content like *Norakuro.*

Tezuka's akahon output made his name in the manga industry, but he was still living in Kansai, and Tokyo was still the center of manga overall. Momentum was shifting back to Tokyo as akahon reached its peak; the akahon publisher Akita Shoten, founded in 1948 by a former Shogakukan editor, used its capital accumulated in akahon to launch the new monthly children's manga magazine *Shōnen Shōjo Bōken Ō* (Boys and girls adventure king, 1949–83), *Bōken Ō* for short. Monthly magazines such as *Manga Shōnen* and *Bōken Ō*, in Tokyo, were where the real action was, and Tezuka frequently traveled up to Tokyo before he began publishing *Jungle Emperor* (*Jungle taitei*, 1950–54) in *Manga Shōnen* in November 1950.

Tezuka later called his meeting with Katō Ken'ichi "epochal" in both their lives: It allowed Tezuka to get out of the Kansai akahon scene and into the Tokyo big time, and to bring his "lifeworks" *Jungle taitei* (Jungle emperor, *Kimba the White Lion*) and *Hi no tori* (*Phoenix*, 1954–55, 1956–57, 1967–73, 1973–81, 1986–88) into the world.[88] At the time, publishing in *Manga Shōnen* was regarded as a real coup for mangaka, burnishing Tezuka's reputation. His work made *Manga Shōnen* a truly popular and consequential publication, and gave Katō a lever to move *Manga Shōnen* out of short humor manga, which he'd been wanting to do for a while.[89]

Jungle emperor came at just the right time, as 1950–51 saw such stiff competition among children's manga magazines that in 1951 all of them published thirteen issues instead of twelve, due to hyping the New Year's issue so far in advance. The competition, however, was set by *Manga Shōnen*, whose features many of its peer publications simply copied outright.[90] These magazines did not yet publish manga exclusively—even *Manga Shōnen* contained a healthy percentage of emonogatari and non-manga content—but they were increasingly *seen* as being popular, to the point where critics and scholars looking back to this decade have claimed that manga "emerged" in the first ten years or so after the war.

That this claim gets made at all speaks to what kind of manga has been regarded as "real" manga, unjustly ignoring akahon and kashihon manga. It also almost certainly indicates some discomfort with the close relationship between prewar and wartime manga and the Japanese empire; in this conception, postwar manga is not ideologically suspect by definition, since the empire was gone. Just as the postwar Japanese identity was constructed partly by means of characterizing colonial returnees (hikiagesha) as others who had come back from "other there" without any explicit mention of the fact that "over there" was Japan's vanished overseas empire, manga in the postwar years came to be characterized as "new" and a "departure" from previous publications and content. But manga's rapid revival after the end of the war was staffed by people who had worked in the industry under the wartime state, and it took decades for an entirely new publication model to displace the established prewar manga paradigm. Tezuka's most famous manga were published well before then.

Jungle emperor and Tezuka's akahon adaptation of Dostoyevsky's *Crime and Punishment* (*Tsumi to batsu*, 1953) were quite influential on other creators within the manga industry, and popular with manga fans.[91] Long enough that Tezuka had originally thought to publish it directly in tankōbon, *Jungle emperor* popularized the "story manga" concept that Tezuka had been trying to enact, shifting children's manga away from short-form humor to long-form narratives portraying a range of emotions, tragedy among them. Tezuka had been dissatisfied with the limits of children's manga since before he became a professional; he wanted to expand the possibilities of composition, strengthen the narrative, and show emotions, and he wanted the freedom to depict characters whose experiences weren't necessarily morally educational.[92]

Above all, Tezuka's decision to include tragedy changed manga irrevocably. Without needing to generate laughs, stories could become much more complex and could have much more varying tones, while protagonists and their character growth acquired much more psychological complexity. Indeed, though some of Tezuka's readers wrote letters complaining about the new protagonist-centric approach of his serial manga, as opposed to his adventure-plot-focused akahon stories, there was no going back.[93] After Tezuka began publishing in the central magazines, long-form, Tezuka-style story manga moved from the avant-garde, in Ishinomori Shōtarō's phrase, to the mainstream in children's manga, and became increasingly popular. In Ishinomori's view, Tezuka's essential innovation was not "cinema-style techniques," which he thought brought nothing more to manga than storyboards and "pseudo-Disney" expression, but tragedy (which for him was epitomized in *Crime and Punishment*), which Disney didn't do and which "liberated" manga from the spirit of funny jokes.[94] Installments in story manga also became longer, sixteen or even thirty-two pages; previously, chapters had been six or eight pages in length.[95]

Tezuka and his innovations faced hostility in Tokyo. Senior mangaka were strongly opposed to them, even saying that Tezuka's manga wasn't manga because it couldn't be laughed at—even though Tezuka's manga from these years still feature quite a lot of slapstick comedy, often amid wild tonal shifts.[96] Sakamoto Gajō complained that story manga subordinated art to narrative, leaving children racing through each chapter for the plot rather than appreciating the artwork.[97] Tokyo mangaka saw the Kansai-born Tezuka as a young, bourgeois upstart (he was practically the only college graduate in the industry for decades) and derisively called him *zeiroku*, a derogatory Edo-era term for money-hungry Osaka merchants, in drinking sessions—and then expected him to pick up the tab.[98] Fukui Ei'ichi, Tezuka's only real competitor, got in his face one night, accusing him of only wanting to make money and not caring about kids: "Yeah, Osaka, I think money's the only reason you make manga!" These accusations got around; at one point a journalist called Tezuka "hankyō" (overseas Osaka-ite), a play on "kakyō" (overseas Chinese), implying that Tezuka had only come to Tokyo to extract money and send it back to Kansai. Tezuka's prodigious output also set a bad example for the rest of the industry (at some point after his debut, he abandoned penciling entirely, going straight to inking to save time), forcing other mangaka onto more rigorous production schedules as magazines increasingly commissioned 60- to 120-page bessatsu furoku manga from creators on top of monthly serials.[99]

Although bessatsu furoku were driven by Akita Shoten, they were inspired by *Manga Shōnen*, which published Tezuka's *Shinpen gessekai shinshi* (New edition: The moony man) as a ninety-six-page furoku in October 1951. The 1930s-era bessatsu furoku practice was revived with this reprint of a Tezuka akahon manga, originally published in Osaka in 1948; republishing it was a coup for *Manga Shōnen*. But it was a coup in the same way that "Blue Monday" was Factory Records' runaway hit and the best-selling twelve-inch single of all time: Since the booklet was oversize, each copy printed actually cost the company money. Competitor magazines then copied the revived bessatsu furoku practice, and poached *Manga Shōnen*'s readers along with it, as these years saw another bessatsu furoku boom. Unwilling to abandon increasingly unpopular old school creators, and no longer directly overseen by Katō Ken'ichi or Katō Misako (he had returned to Kodansha after being rehabilitated in October 1950 under the Occupation's "reverse course"; she left in August 1951 to become a schoolteacher), *Manga Shōnen* went bankrupt in 1955.[100] Even its collapse was generative, however: Ishinomori Shōtarō, then a self-described "second-year high school student from the Tōhoku sticks" who debuted in the magazine in January 1955, would never have been invited to publish a debut manga with no creative restrictions unless the company was in dire straits.[101]

Ishinomori thought that manga would have evolved the new cinema-style techniques eventually one way or another—and he was probably right, given another development in children's manga in the late 1940s, namely the growing exodus of animators from Japan's troubled animation industry.[102] Riven by the Tōhō Labor Disputes at Japan's largest film studio, as the Occupation's reverse course drastically weakened state support for labor unions, animation work became uncertain and many animators sought stable employment in other industries. From April 1949 onward, a number of people who had worked in animation or illustration during the war sought to introduce promising animators to manga publishers including Shogakukan, Kodansha, and Akita Shoten; Seo Mitsuyo (1911–2010), who had directed three Norakuro films in the 1930s and Japan's first full-length animated film, the propaganda movie *Momotarō: Umi no shinpei* (*Momotarō: Sacred Sailors*, 1945), was one of many who took this route, ending his career as a children's book illustrator. Many other animators began working in manga; some of them, like Fukui Ei'ichi, who may have secured his first professional publication credit in *Manga* in 1947, had already worked in akahon to supplement their animation incomes.[103]

These animators-turned-mangaka were already familiar with implementing cinematic techniques from their prior work in the industry, and Tezuka's works provided a model for how to integrate these techniques into manga, as well as for creating more complex, long-form narratives. Ultimately, their adoption of story manga's principles expanded its reach far beyond what even Tezuka could have accomplished.[104] Fukui Ei'ichi in particular shaped story manga alongside Tezuka, having quickly established himself as Tezuka's only real competition, entering children's manga when he was tapped to polish the reader-submitted continuation chapters of *Bat Kid* for *Manga Shōnen* after its creator's sudden death. In his wildly popular judo manga *Igaguri-kun* (1952–54, 1954–60), Fukui laid down the foundations for sports manga and for shōnen manga to come, with a different narrative and artistic style than Tezuka, whom he actually beat out as the top-selling mangaka in 1953. When overwork (specifically the publisher practice of "canning" creators—i.e., shutting them in a room to force them to complete assignments) killed him in 1954, these innovations, particularly his decomposed style of paneling and "exaggerated visual effects," survived him and influenced the development of story manga, kashihon manga, and gekiga overall, especially through Tezuka himself readopting and refining Fukui's innovations on Tezuka's style into his own subsequent works.[105]

Fukui and other children's mangaka enacted their own "return to Japan," eschewing Tezuka's futuristic, high modernism-inflected visions of robots, talking animals, and generally "butter-stinking" (i.e., Western) milieus in favor of subjects that were closer to home. The titular Igaguri-kun is a middle school student competing against other middle school students for Japan's national judo title; the manga was relentlessly grounded in the lived experience of the immediate post-Occupation years, wooden shoes and all, and incorporated elements of the "nekketsu" (hot-blooded) genre found in illustrated fiction and emonogatari aimed at middle schoolers since the 1920s. Judo itself had a long association with nationalism in imperial Japan, and Igaguri himself strove to be an example to his fellow judōka, recasting the moral concerns of the imperial state for the democratic era. People remarked to Tezuka that Fukui had won the future at the latter's funeral, and these observations proved correct: The sports genres and their fusion with nekketsu themes that Fukui pioneered in his works became an important element of children's manga, and were immediately popular in kashihon manga. Shimada Keizō, who had encouraged Fukui's manga career, criticized these developments in 1956, saying that they neglected the "true essence" of children's manga, which according to him should be "filled with dreams and humor, fun to read, and positive."[106] Shōnen manga inherited these legacies after its birth in the 1960s and expanded on them relentlessly. Tezuka became the living God of Manga, but having unleashed the avalanche, he was unable to direct it.

THE END OF CHILDREN'S MANGA

In the wake of Fukui's death, the surviving members of the Tokyo Jidō (Children's) Mangakkai, founded in 1950 by Shimada Keizō, met and agreed to demand a 50 percent increase in pay rates for bessatsu furoku; the publishers acquiesced. As well as a technique for heightening drama, decomposed manga paneling (i.e., breaking down an action scene into individual components) was also a labor-saving device, and other mangaka had copied Fukui's increasing use of it as they all struggled to keep up with growing production demands from publishers. Ultimately, their higher fees went to things like paying assistants, which became common from the mid-1950s on.[107]

Children's manga changed in other ways in this decade too. Manga magazines increasingly eschewed illustrated serial fiction as manga itself scratched the same narrative itch, with faster pacing and more vivid storytelling, thanks to the new story manga paradigm. The late 1950s also saw manga's final triumph over emonogatari, which had almost appeared to be manga's potential replacement at the height of the war. As Yonezawa Yoshihiro recalled, the appeal of emonogatari before the mid-1950s was that you could get the same story in a much faster-paced experience than manga, and that was part of the fun. But by the end of the decade, parts of emonogatari moved closer to manga, while manga took on emonogatari's good points, namely richer, more dramatic narratives and art, and then surpassed them.[108] With emonogatari extinguished, manga dominated children's magazines.

Other elements of manga that are taken for granted today also emerged in these years, such as the use of screentones, which were introduced by Tagawa Suihō student and *Manga Shōnen* contributor Nagata Takemaru (1934–2022) in 1954.[109] Mostly used as art supplies for designers until Nagata began using them for his children's manga, the advantages screentones offered mangaka quickly became apparent.[110] Sheets of thin, tissue-like paper that are cut into the desired shape and pasted onto the manuscript, screentones create a uniform background. Aside from increasing production speed, they are quite useful for evenly coloring blacks, but patterned screentones such as those Nagata first used also leant interest to and created a particular mood in scenes. Screentones spread rapidly throughout manga of all stripes in the 1950s, and they remain a distinctive feature of Japanese comics, just as Tezuka's dogged refusal to adopt screentones increasingly set his manga apart as the years went on.

Nagata was a fellow traveler of the Tokiwa-sō group, comprising mangaka who lived in the Tokiwa-sō apartment building in Toshima; Tezuka moved there in 1953 after finishing his medical training and stayed for a little more than a year. Beginning with Terada Hiroo in 1953, other young mangaka began taking up residence there, and the building began to be called "the manga sō."[111] Fujiko Fujio A and Fujiko F. Fujio, who worked under the shared pen name Fujiko Fujio from 1951 to 1987, shared a single room for the entire seven years they lived in the building, beginning in 1954. Even after Tezuka moved to Namiki House elsewhere in Toshima, Suzuki Shin'ichi

(b. 1933), Moriyasu Naoya, Ishinomori Shōtarō, Fujiko, Mizuno Hideko, Akatsuka Fujio, and Yokota Tokuo continued living in Tokiwa-sō for varying lengths of time until 1961.[112] Tsunoda Jirō (b. 1936) came from Shinjuku to hang out nearly every day.[113]

This list of names is an honor roll of significant manga and anime creators in the postwar decades, and other creators who left marks on the medium were also associated with the Tokiwa-sō group. Members founded the Shinmanga-tō (New Manga Group) in 1954 and reconstituted it in 1955 as a forum not just for talking about manga but for supporting each other in the lifestyle, and to get health insurance; Japan's national health insurance program did not cover everyone in the country until 1961. Some of the Shinmanga-tō's meetings devolved into the legendary gatherings at Tezuka's Namiki House; Matsumoto Leiji and shōjo mangaka Maki Miyako (b. 1935), who married in 1962, met at one of those parties.[114] Even after moving to Namiki House, Tezuka frequently came back to the Tokiwa-sō to check on the mangaka there, to take them to dinner, and to ask for last-minute help on his upcoming deadlines.[115]

Fujiko Fujio A (1933–96) later wrote: "At the Tokiwa-sō, the young manga men of Japan, gathered from hither and yon at the same time, lived in a kind of communal society!" His semi-fictionalized manga memoir depicts the mangaka constantly lending each other a hand with story concepts and on deadlines, as the magazines' bessatsu furoku competition roiled.[116] Ishinomori described Tokiwa-sō, which was actually quite luxurious housing at the time, as a haven from the storms of the manga world outside. In his recollection, everyone behaved maturely and respectfully; they addressed each other as "-shi" rather than "-san," after Tezuka's example, and almost never quarreled or complained about their various worries. They were united in their desire to make good manga for kids, and show the world good, new manga, but they didn't regard each other as rivals, and unlike other manga groups, they didn't engage in mutual criticism—perhaps one of the reasons they all got along so well.[117]

Tokiwa-sō group members were heavily influenced by Tezuka, and irrevocably associated with him; their path through the industry was relatively easy, as they were always in demand because the new paradigm was natural to them. But other mangaka who struggled to adapt had a harder time. Children's humor manga was in what proved to be its last florescence, partly because the media environment that had prevailed since its emergence in the 1920s was rapidly disintegrating: In the late 1950s, kamishibai, radio, and movies all began losing ground to television. While radio manga persisted until the mid-1950s, it faded from the scene thereafter; kamishibai was largely gone by the end of the decade, and movie culture had permanently contracted by the time of the Tokyo Olympics.[118]

The older prewar modes of manga had not yet ceded the stage entirely, however; children's manga, now usually called jidō rather than kodomo, still contained plenty of humor. Akatsuka Fujio started out drawing sad shōjo manga, and was constantly told that "sad manga isn't manga;" his career languished until a Tokiwa-sō brokered introduction brought him to *Manga Ō*, where his one-shot gag manga proved so popular that it relaunched as a serial the very next month, in December 1958.[119] Ueda Toshiko was a leading children's mangaka at this point, excelling in the fading humor paradigm, and in her masterwork *Fuichin-san* (1957–62) she melded humor and story manga to create a funny but moving narrative drawing on her childhood in colonial Harbin. *Fuichin-san* in many ways marked the end of the lineage of children's humor manga: As Ozaki Hotsuki wrote, the manga united the best characteristics of prewar and postwar manga—namely, that Fuichin herself had a charming personality unlike those found in children in the conformist postwar era of "education mamas," though Fuichin's cheerfully anarchic ideas would have been impossible to publish under the wartime state. But for Ozaki, she and the manga's setting also embodied the prewar ideal of "popular exchange based on peaceful friendship" (heiwa shinzen no mizokuteki kōryū) as only Ueda could have done, partly via conveying the reality of Harbin under the Manchukuo puppet state in a way that went beyond mere exoticism.[120]

Ozaki also thought that the manga captured something about living abroad that was echoed in his own experience; born in Taipei, he'd spent more than half his life outside of Japan at that point, and like Ueda and Akatsuka, he was a repatriate—indeed, many of postwar Japan's greatest artistic luminaries across media were repatriates (hikiagesha), Japanese nationals who were expelled from the former colonies after the war, as many scholars have noted. Reading *Fuichin-san* paints an eye-opening picture of life in Manchukuo for rich Chinese people and their Japanese friends under the puppet government: Hypermodern Harbin looks disconcertingly like contemporary Cleveland, but with the simmering threat of bandit (i.e., Chinese resistance) attacks lurking at the edges of the manga's usually sunny events. Like Tezuka, Ueda also declined to adopt screentones, heightening the old-fashioned impression.[121]

Writing in 1969, Ozaki acidly observed that "if Fuichin-san were alive now, she'd be in the Red Guard."[122] Just as Ueda could not have published Fuichin's adventures in the wartime era, the manga could also not have been published later, as it was predicated on a model of cross-gender appeal that became increasingly untenable during the 1960s, when the children's manga paradigm split irrevocably into shōnen and shōjo manga. A female protagonist by definition could not have appealed to young male readers of shōnen magazines by 1970, and Fuichin's humorous exploits would also have made her a tough sell in shōjo magazines, which largely eschewed serial narratives in favor of one-shots. Being neither Japanese nor white Euro-American, and not middle or upper class, would not have helped Fuichin either; all were nearly hegemonic characteristics of shōjo protagonists until the 1970s.

Nor could Fuichin have found a home in the Osaka manga underground or counterculture, namely kashihon manga: Although it welcomed shōjo manga and female mangaka, the format had a strict one-volume limit, whereas Fuichin's adventures were serialized.[123] Ueda was in the fortunate position of not needing to take kashihon manga work thanks to her successful Tokyo publishing career, though kashihon manga was on the whole more welcoming to female creators; a 1951 article in *Himawari* listed just five female mangaka writing for children in Tokyo magazines, Ueda and Yazaki Takeko included.[124] But though they are less discussed today, the kashihon manga format and the kashihonya (rental bookstores) that sold it were just as consequential to manga's development as Tezuka, Fukui, and their followers in the end. Emerging as akahon faded in the early 1950s, kashihon manga and kashihonya expanded manga's reach and scope irrevocably.

CHAPTER SIX

Manga for Whom?

KASHIHONYA, GEKIGA, AND THE "BAN BAD BOOKS MOVEMENT"

KASHIHONYA

The akahon format peaked around 1948 and was virtually gone by 1952, but in that time it became a staple of kashihonya (rental bookstores). These had roots in the Edo period, but they became increasingly common during the war, when publishing's dire straits forced most used bookstores to convert to the *kashihon* lending model, due to difficulties obtaining new stock. Prewar and wartime kashihonya operated on a deposit system, but the new-style kashihonya that mushroomed in the postwar period, when the hunger for entertaining reading material in no way matched people's disposable incomes, operated on a membership system. In 1948, new manga books ranged from 40 to 60 yen, but in 1950 they were priced at 100 yen each; akahon manga typically ranged from 10 to 50 yen.[1] At kashihonya, you could read the same book for not more than 10 yen, and no deposit was required to rent books; all you needed was some form of ID. These cheap prices meant that most kashihonya were not independent businesses—the margins were too low for that—but rather sidelines of other outfits, such as candy or stationery stores or, overwhelmingly, used bookstores: In Kobe in 1958, for example, 60 percent of the national Neo Shobō kashihon chain's outlets were attached to used bookstores.[2]

Neo Shobō and Roman Bunko were both credited with pioneering this type of kashihonya, but manga collector and former kashihonya proprietor Naiki Toshio (1937–2012) was doing the same in Nihonbashi in Tokyo around the same time; he speculated that it was the zeitgeist.[3] Just like akahon before and gekiga afterward, the most prominent kashihonya and kashihon manga started in Kansai and spread to Tokyo. Neo Shobō opened its

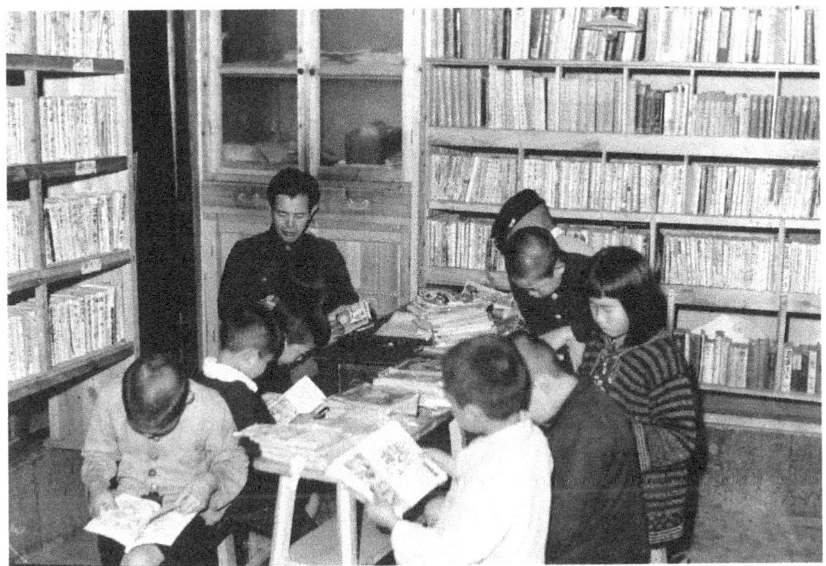

FIGURE 15. Readers perusing books in a kashihonya, 1948. Used with permission of *Yomiuri Shinbun*.

first outlet in Kobe in 1948; by 1952, it had become a regional chain in the Kansai area, and its first Tokyo outlet opened in 1953.[4] Neo Shobō produced a shock of the new when it appeared in the capital: Its branches had neon signs and seemed clearly *different*.[5] At the height of their popularity at the end of the decade, there were officially three thousand kashihonya nationwide, but the true number was probably much higher; kashihonya were popularly called the "town library" (machi no toshokan).[6]

While new materials comprised the majority of loans, kashihonya kept backlist items around to increase profits, which they also sought to maximize by adjusting rental pricing based on the age, size, and popularity of the materials in question and the length of the loan period. To keep a lid on "tachiyomi" (i.e., standing around a used bookstore reading the materials rather than paying for them and leaving), many stores also allowed customers to sit down and read a certain amount of books for a set price (figure 15). Tatsumi and Sakurai paid five yen to read three books at their local stores in Osaka in 1948.[7] Tachiyomi itself was a transwar behavior; a reader letter published in *Manga no Kuni* in 1937 talked about doing it, noting wryly that "the old guys [in the stores] make angry faces" but did nothing to stop it.[8]

Kashihonya quickly became identified with kashihon manga, the next evolution of akahon: Although less derivative, kashihon manga continued the akahon principles of fast and cheap for the era of economic recovery, with improved production values. Most kashihon manga was produced directly for the rental bookstore market; most kashihon creators came from Kansai, but over time most publishers came to be located in the capital.[9] Creators often worked pseudonymously, paid for the right to publish the book first, not the work itself. But like akahon publishers, kashihon publishers were indifferent about returning creators' manuscripts, with the result that the majority of kashihon manga has been lost.[10]

Kashihon manga was tough for creators. After Mizuki Shigeru moved to Tokyo in 1955 with just paper and drawing tools and entered the industry, he worked almost constantly, pawned almost everything he owned except his shoes, pillow, and futon, and nearly starved anyway. On one occasion Mizuki asked his wife, Mura Nunoe, to take his completed manuscript pages to his publisher in Shinjuku (in traditional manga publishing, company staff were dispatched to collect manuscripts in person): She was shocked to see that not only was the publisher himself evidently the only person working in the office, but he looked quite poor; the only couch was also busted. When she asked for the previously agreed-upon payment of 30,000 yen, he refused to hand over more than half because "we can't sell" Mizuki's manga. At the time, salarymen made about 18,000 yen per month; before their arranged marriage in 1961, Mura had believed that Mizuki was a relatively high earner, but the kashihon manga reality was very different.[11] Yet Mura actually came out fairly well on that occasion; some creators walked away with as little as 300–500 yen against a promised payment of 20,000–30,000 yen for an entire volume's work. According to Nagai Katsuichi, in this era Sakurai was drawing two hundred pages a month, but he and his wife still had to leave their apartment at the end of the month and hang out in a park to avoid running up their utility bills: "If publishing was hell, so was drawing."[12]

Nonetheless, kashihon manga offered a creative freedom that the Tokyo magazine-based industry did not. Notably, kashihon manga was strongly associated with comics focusing on and read by young women, particularly those on whom the burden of the postwar economic recovery often fell most heavily in its early years. Kashihon shōjo manga thus contained works that reflected women's postwar experiences quite directly, a notable contrast to kashihon boys' manga, which initially consisted mostly of jidaigeki and action adventure. In this respect, kashihon manga was similar to the Tokyo manga magazines, but kashihon manga were usually marketed by the manga content itself (Westerns, romance, crime, household, etc.).[13] The formation of genres within children's manga began as kashihon manga was taking off, and kashihon manga adhered to the older model in which these labels referred primarily to setting or content.[14] Kashihon manga also offered a much more accepting venue for mangaka, particularly female mangaka, embracing returning prewar creators like Kaneko Hisako as well as new figures like Takizawa Michiko, who had gotten her start in *Manga Shōnen*.

Kashihonya were also notable for organizing *as* kashihonya, which set them apart from other aspects of the publishing world: Although a significant node in manga distribution and consumption networks, they were not necessarily primarily sellers of manga or even primarily bookstores, but they were the main outlet for an entire format and type of manga that embraced multitudes in its audiences and subject matter. In their heyday, they were also a key site for manga fans, for whom trips to the rental bookstores, which now offered unique manga, were part of reading and distribution patterns familiar from the wartime era.

In this era the manga publishing industry was much less consolidated than it is now, when just a handful of large companies located in Tokyo produce the vast majority of titles. In 1957, a kashihonya report identified thirty manga publishers, ranging from those releasing three or four titles a month to those producing anywhere from eighteen to two hundred. Print runs ranged as large as four or five thousand copies, but more commonly averaged around three thousand.[15] Two years later, the National Manga Publishers Association reported twenty-seven member companies, with many more smaller, mom-and-pop or fly-by-night companies not part of the association. Many major publishers of the era were based in Osaka, and many famous creators came from Kansai or western Japan and came up through the Osaka ranks before moving to Tokyo, including Tezuka, Tatsumi and Sakurai, and many others.[16]

Despite their outsize influence on manga's history, kashihon manga never constituted a huge market. The monthly anthology *Kage* (Shadow) sold nine thousand copies at the height of its popularity in 1957–58, while the popular monthly anthology *Machi*, published in Nagoya, sold six to seven thousand, and the first volume of the hit *Ninja bugeichō* (Book of ninja fighting arts, 1959–62) by Shirato Sanpei (1932–2021) sold eight thousand, but most kashihon titles sold between twenty-five hundred and three thousand copies, and four thousand was considered a big hit.[17] With margins this thin, any change in the media environment could be fatal. Thin margins also partly explain kashihon manga's continued reliance on other media, particularly movies:

Kashihon manga copied popular films to capitalize on their demonstrated success, as when there was a brief boom in "Taiyōzoku manga" after the movie *Taiyō no kisetsu* (*Season of the sun*, 1956) became a hit.[18]

The years 1959–62, dominated by Shirato's hit ninja manga, were the format's zenith, but even then stores were closing rapidly and publishers were following them, as the lived environment of Japan also changed rapidly and the so-called Economic Miracle began to take hold. Nagai recounts that he first met Shirato by chance on the street at the end of summer 1957: Shirato's last publisher had just gone under without paying him, and he was wandering around with fresh manuscript pages under his arm, thinking that he might quit manga if he didn't sell them.[19] When Mizuki's main publisher Togetsu Shobō collapsed in 1962, Mizuki alone held 200,000 yen in unpaid promissory notes from the company.[20] Kashihonya were dependent on the economic conditions of the initial postwar period, in which books were priced cheaply to appeal to consumers without much spare money, but once the growth years arrived and consumer spending increased, publishers had no incentive to throttle their own potential profits to coddle kashihonya: They could and did sell their product elsewhere (i.e., in first-run bookstores). Inasmuch as kashihonya allowed multiple readers to peruse just one copy of a book, publishers may have seen kashihonya as depressing book sales. They needed publishers, rather than the other way around.

Thus the kashihonya newspaper *Zenkoku Kashihon Shinbun* (National kashihon news, 1957–72) in 1962 was full of calls for individual proprietors to protest to publishers about proposed increases in book prices, and for kashihonya to form a stronger national association so that they could lobby publishers more effectively. While bestseller lists demonstrate that kashihonya rented more than just manga—Nabokov's controversial novel *Lolita* (1955) was a bestseller in October 1962, for example—they also make it clear that manga was the heart of the business model. By that year, the vast majority of the kashihon newspaper's ads were for manga; one reason kashihonya stridently protested proposed price increases was the fact that kashihonya and the manga publishers' association had informally cooperated on pricing in the past. Overall, the national market was fairly homogeneous: Although books on average were five yen cheaper to rent in Kansai, there was little difference in what books were most popular each month across prefectures.[21]

At the same time as they were becoming targets of the emerging "ban bad books movement," kashihonya were also under pressure from first-run booksellers to commit to contracts maintaining the retail price of books, although the use of such contracts gradually decreased. It was partly to resist such pressures, and repeated calls for a ban on children entering kashihonya (which would have hurt too many businesses and was generally opposed by shopowners), that the National United Kashihon Association (Zenkoku Kashihon Kumiai Rengōkai) formed in August 1957. Its associated newspaper first appeared one month later, bearing the slogan "People in the kashihon industry nationwide, unite!" Tokyo shops formed the association's core, and the newspaper's first editor was one Nakayama Sōjirō, the proprietor of a kashihonya in Shinagawa and a leader on the Tokyo kashihon scene.[22]

An article entitled "Manga Research" in the first issue confirms that manga was, in the proprietors' own words, fundamental to the kashihonya model. According to the Neo company's statistics, manga accounted for 33 percent of the chain's stock and 20 percent of its revenues; those rates were even higher in Osaka, where manga comprised 38 percent of stock and 26 percent of revenues, with growth in both areas. The chain's overall best-selling authors that month were Hasegawa Machiko and Tezuka Osamu, and the most popular single volumes were manga tankōbon: *Igaguri-kun* volume 8 and *Sazae-san* volume 7. The article went on to explain that "according to the manga publishers, having good creators is the most important thing," above and beyond the quality of any single book. Good creators, moreover, were a reliable long-term investment, unlike ephemeral properties such as movie tie-ins, which sold well only while the movie was still in theaters—although in this era that could be as long as a year.[23]

GEKIGA 1: THE GEKIGA BOYS

Nurtured by kashihonya and kashihon manga, one heir to akahon and story manga came to be known as *gekiga*. Tatsumi Yoshihiro devised the term in 1957 (although kamishibai had occasionally been called gekiga in the 1930s): Meaning "dramatic pictures," it was meant to denote a more "adult," "serious" alternative to kashihon and mainstream children's manga.[24] The oldest *Manga Shōnen* readers were now young adults, and they wanted to create and to read manga that was more in line with their lives and interests, however much they may still have loved Tezuka. The gekiga boys—for they were all men—wound up at the forefront of a revolution that was, like so many revolutions in comics, poorly paid and for many years largely ignored. But gekiga proved quite fecund, and the innovations that the gekigaka pioneered were extremely influential in manga's development.

Tatsumi regularly submitted to and won reader manga contests in newspapers and magazines as a middle and high school student; he debuted with Tokyo publisher Tsuru Shobō in 1954, followed by works from Osaka publishers. He and other Hinomaru Bunko creators, including Saitō Takao (1936–2021) and Matsumoto Masahiko (1934–2005), increasingly came to feel hemmed in by the formal and narrative conventions of children's manga, although Hinomaru in particular rarely had any critiques of its authors' manga. The trio grew dissatisfied with the caricaturized character styles, humor, and rigorous pacing that "manga" required and instead sought to create "manga that wasn't manga," wanting to break the age barrier that restricted narrative manga to children and to include more mature content. Like Tezuka and many other mangaka of their generation, Tatsumi and the other gekiga creators went to the movies constantly, and they sought to incorporate cinematic techniques such as elongated pacing and psychological elements depicting a character's interiority into their work.[25] By 1956, they were talking among themselves about the "new manga" they wanted to popularize.[26]

When Hinomaru launched the monthly anthology *Kage* (Shadow, 1956–66) in April 1956, Tatsumi requested that the cover not say the word *manga;* it was subtitled "a detective book" (tantei bukku). *Kage* lasted just ten issues before Hinomaru's bankruptcy forced it into hiatus, but it had a huge influence on kashihon manga. Freed by the bankruptcy from de facto exclusivity agreements, Matsumoto, Tatsumi, Saitō, and other popular *Kage* creators published in other companies' monthly anthologies.[27] Over time, nearly every kashihon publisher copied *Kage*'s successful B5 one-shot anthology format, and kashihon manga thereafter witnessed a long "one-shot boom" that lasted until the list price for kashihon manga rose in the early 1960s.[28]

Later that year, Matsumoto started referring to his work as *komaga*, a word that had been used in the early 1900s in reference to one-panel manga or illustrations. His usage referred to film frames, because for him the most important aspect of a manga was the story, and the composition of the panels was the most important ingredient for an interesting story. Like Tezuka, Matsumoto eschewed laughter, and in his manga he tried to use panels to express genuine emotion through the juxtaposition of images: "I got the idea from movies. In order to pull readers into the story's atmosphere and into the protagonist's emotions, it is necessary to make them feel like they have jumped over inside the story and become the characters themselves." Matsumoto later claimed that his using the term *komaga* inspired Tatsumi to create *gekiga*.[29] While Tatsumi's mature artistic style surpassed Matsumoto's in some respects, Matsumoto's work had a profound influence on Tatsumi during these years. When Sakurai, in typical niggling fashion, later wrote that "one could say that Matsumoto Masahiko was the true innovator of gekiga and today's manga," this deep influence was what he was talking about.[30] Matsumoto published his first komaga in September 1956, two months before Tatsumi's "Kuro fubuki" (Black blizzard), considered the "locus classicus of gekiga style."[31]

Three years later, Tatsumi sought to launch gekiga through a group he called Gekiga Kōbō (Gekiga Workshop) in January 1959; he announced its formation by sending 150 postcards to "newspapers, publishers, and manga artists, including the great Osamu Tezuka":[32]

> The world is changing constantly. The world of manga, created by Toba Sōjō in the twelfth century, is no exception. Manga is a fast-evolving field, and in the Shōwa period, it has been bifurcated into manga for adults, and manga for children. Today, manga for adults alone comprises various genres such as political manga, realist manga, family manga, and story manga [seiji manga, fūzoku manga, katei manga, stōrī manga].
>
> Children's manga has also become diversified and it now includes different genres for different readerships. In the postwar period, the story manga rapidly rose to prominence, principally due to Tezuka Osamu's efforts. With this new prominence, children's manga also improved its social status and continued to develop steadily.
>
> More recently, the story manga has been vitalized through the influence exerted by the supersonic development of other media such as film, television, and radio. This vitalization has given birth to a new genre, which we have named "gekiga."
>
> Manga and "gekiga" differ in methodology, but perhaps more importantly, in their readerships. The demand for manga, written for adolescents, i.e. those readers between childhood and adulthood, has never been answered, because there has never been a forum for such works. This hitherto neglected reader segment is "gekiga's" intended target. It was, in fact, the rental book market [kashihonya] that contributed significantly to the development of "gekiga."
>
> "GEKIGA": THE NEW FRONTIER
>
> Gekiga has a great future. It will also, doubtless, face some difficulties. Success will require unanimous cooperation from all gekiga writers.

> In light of the above, the former TS Workshop and Kansai Manga Artists Group have been consolidated into Gekiga Workshop. Gekiga writers [gekiga raitā] have united to establish a new system under the banner of "Gekiga Workshop."
>
> It is our sincere hope to have your support and understanding for the future endeavors of the Gekiga Workshop.[33]

Notably, Tatsumi and the other seven signatories, the Workshop's original members, paid lip service to the idea that manga traced its origins back to classical Japan, an idea that was only thirty years old. But the real meat of this statement is what it says about the relationship between story manga and gekiga: Although gekiga has been called "anti-Tezuka" or "non-Tezuka," at heart it originated from Tezuka manga.[34] Specifically, in Natsume Fusanosuke's summary, "it came about by taking Tezuka's manga to extremes." Tezuka-style story manga had become the system people had to rebel against, and in Osaka they were quick to rebel against the central hegemony.[35] In an age of chaos and disorder, in Ishinomori's phrase, Tezuka's enemies and even his champions were all against him.[36]

Natsume argues that gekiga was notable for being the first time that people drew manga because they wanted to, not because it would appeal to kids. While there are certainly individual exceptions to this statement, the general point about creators writing to the target audience with editorial input stands, and it points to an important aspect of gekiga's rebellion: People were supposed to abandon manga by the time they reached high school, and reading it even in middle school was considered unusual.[37] But the gekigaka created the manga they wanted to read, and the kashihon readership went with them. Only about 55 percent of male middle school graduates and 47 percent of female middle school graduates continued on to high school in 1955, rates that had risen only about 5 percent each by 1960, and these new members of society were the core of the kashihon and then the gekiga audience.[38] Those secondary education rates also explain why such "mature" topics as those routinely covered in gekiga were aimed at teenagers—although not just "the young blue-collar class" but also actual children read gekiga, as manga activist Nagayama Kaoru pointed out: "In any age, children are insatiable."[39]

A roundtable discussion in the first volume of the Gekiga Kōbō anthology *Matenrō* (Skyscraper, 1959–60) is revealing as to how the Workshop members regarded themselves: Sakurai said, with a laugh, that "gekigaka are men of good taste," while Ishikawa Fumiyasu (1937–2014) declared that "Our fathers and older brothers like *Sazae-san;* our aim is fundamentally different from that." K. Motomitsu (1936–96) remarked that "gekiga is a new branch of the stream called manga, but I wonder whether in future it might become the main branch."[40] His speculation proved prophetic.

Hyperbolic declarations about the gekiga readership and claims about the nature of gekiga are generally borne out by the documentary record. The art style of everyone involved in *Matenrō* is remarkably Tezuka-esque in terms of character designs, but other artistic strategies, in particular the use of cross-hatching and shading in backgrounds (there were definitely no screentones in gekiga) derived from alternate influences. *Matenrō*'s first volume is remarkable for how clearly all the participants blended Tezuka-style character design with other artistic influences, particularly illustrated Westerns and jidaigeki stories. They also strove to adopt movie techniques; in K. Motomitsu's view, whereas manga before had been theatrical, gekiga made free use of cinematic techniques. Motomitsu's claim is hyperbolic (story manga had already adopted the cinematic breakdown of action into component bits), but he was right to point out that gekiga specifically borrowed cinematic techniques to make manga more photorealistic and to mimic photography and movie camera effects, changing manga expression.[41]

The cinematic-style breakdown or decomposition in story manga broke down action into component parts (panels), but gekiga took it much further, and completely subordinated the plot to the action. If Tezuka's manga was rich in its thematic concerns, by the early 1960s ten-year-olds just wanted cool action, and gekiga always prioritized depicting whatever was cool.[42] Above all, gekiga reveled in content that Tokyo magazine creators would never have published, which was the point: The gekiga boys were aiming to produce something that hadn't existed in manga before. Years later, Saitō remarked that he had wanted to draw drama, but you couldn't draw "real drama" in the Tezuka style.[43] The *geki* in *gekiga* meant not just "drama" but also "hageshii" (fierce or violent), a fitting descriptor for the action it depicted.[44]

Of course, mangaka had been incorporating cinematic visual techniques into their work for decades; the gekigaka meant certain kinds of movies, namely contemporary noir and Western genre films from both Hollywood and Japanese studios. Sakurai and Motomitsu both made analogies between gekiga and music: For Sakurai, the new thing about gekiga was that "our method is rockabilly," while Motomitsu likened it to modern jazz. Satō Masa'aki (1937–2004) simply declared that gekiga "has movement," while Ishikawa viewed its defining characteristic more abstractly, saying that "the expression is free (jiyū jizai)." Sakurai agreed, saying "that's what's new about it."[45]

Gekiga and mainstream manga differed not just in subject matter, but also in how that subject matter was treated. Satō claimed that gekiga mixed in "profoundly human psychological depictions," whereas "goggle-eyed manga doesn't depict psychological worries at all." For Yamamori Susumu (b. 1935), the difference was that gekiga depicted things that could possibly happen in reality; thus, "realism" was gekiga's method. These concerns blended into the question of who gekiga was for: In Satō's view, manga and gekiga were "two different schools" and "that contrast is present in the readership as well." Motomitsu put a value judgment on that split when he added that "gekiga readers have better understanding (rikai ryoku) than manga readers," but Ishikawa brought it back to age, pointing out that until now there had been nothing to read in the gap from middle through high school (i.e., roughly fourteen to eighteen). "We're aiming at the gap between children and adults," Satō summarized, and Ishikawa agreed: "That's gekiga."[46]

Motomitsu concluded by declaring that it was fine if only the people with whom gekiga resonated read it: "because the philosophy is woven throughout, the readers are limited." Such ambitions for a small, devoted group of in-the-know readers notwithstanding, the gekigaka mentioned things like "expanding the readership" and "be read by children and adults" when questioned about their hopes for the future. Satō pithily summed up those ideas, commenting that gekiga should or could be "cheaper than novels, more economical than a TV," while Yamamori placed his hopes in "the development of the unexplored territory of gekiga hereafter." The roundtable concluded with the observation that "lately the world of manga has been undergoing huge changes" and that "the foundation of the new world [sekai] of gekiga is one part of those phenomena. . . . [M]anga has at this point become a thing of the past. The world of manga must be born into a new world hereafter."[47]

GEKIGA 2: REBELS WITH A CAUSE

The anthology series *Musō* (Peerless, 1959–60), assembled by the group's members and published by Ugatsu Shobō, is a good example of the gekiga phenomenon. Gekiga was physically indistinguishable from kashihon: It was the same price, the same size, and had the same illustrated endpapers, the same full-color table of contents illustrations, and the same first quire of twelve pages; the only appreciable difference was that the *Musō* series was issued in softcover rather than hardcover editions. Moreover, the visual style of gekiga manga itself evokes a cross between the limited akahon style and postwar jidaigeki manga; it was more realistic than children's manga, but nowhere near as naturalistic as emonogatari.

Tezuka and *Manga Shōnen*'s influence was obvious in other elements. Reader engagement was a key strategy for the gekiga boys, who consciously marketed themselves as individuals, and moreover as cool individuals, to readers via their publications. The fourth volume of *Musō* contains a "readers' letter room" page, which invited readers to submit letters to the editors, "no matter how small the matter" and gives the group's address, saying that "this is the bridge between the readers and the editors."[48] Gekigaka also maintained their brand by strictly policing potential contributions: The call for submissions at the back of the anthology specified not only genre but also page length, page size, and ink color and type.[49]

Musō continued the *Manga Shōnen* strategy of encouraging amateur cartoonists among its readers. A five-page "Kimi nara dō egaku" ("How you would draw it") section reprinted examples of an image from an earlier volume that readers redrew and submitted; Tatsumi himself selected the winners, three of whom received prizes, and many received honorable mentions.[50] There were also efforts to develop the kind of associations around gekiga that had supported manga in prior decades: The second issue of *Matenrō* contained a solicitation for members for the "All Japan Gekiga Kenkyūkai (Research Group)," which met in Osaka and published a zine entitled *Gekigakkai* (Gekiga world).[51]

An interview with Tatsumi in *Matenrō*'s second volume echoed the earlier roundtable's statements about the readership's age range; for him, gekiga was aiming between middle school and the first year of high school (roughly, twelve to sixteen), relying on those readers' increased comprehension. The most important thing in this formulation became the creators' "thought."[52] Readers evidently agreed with Tatsumi's assessment: By *Matenrō*'s fourth issue, one Nakatani Yoshiyasu of Osaka (who also wrote in to the second issue, making him a very early adopter) wrote that "until now, speaking of manga, there was nothing but story manga for middle and elementary school students, but now the name of the new hope for a new age of new reading material that those of us from middle to high school may read is called gekiga." Gekiga raised the age for narrative manga; previously, adults only had satirical or nonsense four-panel manga.[53]

For a time, gekiga became a locus of amateur manga production after the demise of *Manga Shōnen*, specifically via *Kage, Machi* (City, 1957–58), and other short-story anthologies, which featured newcomer competitions directly inspired by *Manga Shōnen*.[54] This gekiga amateur manga phenomenon powered a miniature amateur gekiga boom into the 1960s and, via the *Gekigakkai* zine, created a fan club atmosphere and the same kind of imagined community that had previously developed around *Manga Shōnen*.[55] At the height of their popularity, Gekiga Workshop members also portrayed themselves as quasi-celebrities—they talked about living in the (then extremely peripheral) Kokubunji area of Tokyo, they congratulated each other on marriages and other significant events in the issues' back matter, and features such as the "Gekiga nikki" (Gekiga diary) in *Matenrō* 4 explicitly invited readers along on their daily lives, including their gekiga work.

The gekiga boys also consciously played up the fact that they were men. Gekiga publications are rife with self-consciously masculinist posturing by everyone involved, from the creators (who talked about getting into fights as kids, and posed for photographs variously playing Russian roulette, riding motorcycles, and wearing trenchcoats and berets, as was the style), to the readers, who frequently opened letters with the masculine greeting "Ossu!" Their ostentatious alienation from the vanished imperial social order's moral certainties and their youthful nihilism placed them squarely in the mainstream of disaffected Japanese youth. Yet the gekiga crowd came by their views honestly: Children during the war, many of them had survived the firebombings of Osaka and Kobe, and their traumatic experiences marked them deeply. Tezuka's worldview was also forged by his brush with death toward the end of the war, but his outlook was instead famously sentimental and humanistic.[56]

One amateur creator who spent years drawing gekiga and kashihon manga for potential publication, and failed utterly, was the young Miyazaki Hayao (b. 1941), whose time studying for college entrance exams coincided with gekiga's first efflorescence. Decades later, Miyazaki remarked that "gekiga were filled with their [creators'] grudges and spite, so there were no happy endings," and dismissed the gekigaka as "manga artists who had suffered through misfortune, in particular those who hung out around Osaka." As a mature adult, Miyazaki ultimately found gekiga nihilistic and characterized his infatuation with gekiga as a form of rebellion against his own childhood self, exacerbated by exam despair. But he was a definite minority in this respect; most readers couldn't get enough of gekiga, and even he conceded that they "were interesting and easily accessible to me as a reader."[57]

Given the unrestrained egoism on display in the group's official publications, it is not terribly surprising that interpersonal difficulties arose among

Workshop members. There were frequent disagreements and complaints about who got how many pages or color pages in a given publication. Although group members presented themselves as living in Tokyo, not all of them did, and Tatsumi was left to act as editor in chief by default, since his residing in the capital meant that publishers put pressure on him when deadlines bore down. Chasing after the other members for manuscripts and overseeing the reader contests took up a huge amount of Tatsumi's time, which meant that his membership in the group depressed his own creative output—the opposite of his goal. Publishers were also leery of the group's union-like characteristics; Gekiga Workshop members charged very high rates while it lasted. Lastly, the gekigaka themselves could not agree on fundamental questions such as whether gekiga was part of or separate from manga. Tatsumi quit the group in summer 1959, and the other members gradually followed suit until the group finally folded in January 1960.[58]

Although the Gekiga Workshop lasted only a year, K. Motomitsu was right that gekiga ultimately became the manga mainstream. Gekiga and kashihon creators were well positioned to create manga for the new older readers who began appearing in the 1960s, and kashihon manga gradually became synonymous with gekiga, which eventually merged with story manga by the end of the decade.[59] By the 1970s, the distinction between manga and gekiga became largely meaningless, and by the 1980s, gekiga's foundations underlay a large portion of popular culture in Japan.[60] But as Saitō Takao later told Ishinomori Shōtarō, unlike the Tokiwa-sō crowd, "an elite group who never knew obscurity," for the gekigaka, "our time in obscurity was long."[61] Gekiga creators kept creating gekiga, but they were not welcomed into the lucrative Tokyo magazines until the mid- to late 1960s, a long time to toil in precarity.

Ultimately, the gekiga revolution succeeded, but the Workshop's collapse meant that gekiga-as-separate no longer had any institutional advocates: Kashihon manga publishers had no reason to buy into gekiga as a separate kind of comics, even if readers continued to entertain the distinction. An April 1962 issue of the kashihon newspaper, for example, classifies manga into A and B divisions based on popularity; A titles were "principally shōnen and adult," while B titles were "principally shōjo." Tezuka and Hasegawa topped the list of popular creators, for "science/other" and "*Sazae-san*," respectively, while Tatsumi himself appeared mid-list with "action" as his specialty. When Tatsumi participated in the kashihonya newspaper's "Roundtable encircling manga creators" in October 1963, he answered questions such as "Do you play baseball?" (No) and "Do your ideas come from you or from the publisher?"[62]

DEMOCRACY'S DISCONTENTS: THE BAN BAD BOOKS MOVEMENT

Kashihonya organizing themselves as the National United Kashihon Association was partly a response to one of the least discussed postwar phenomena in manga, namely the akusho tsuihō undō ("ban bad books movement"). It is no coincidence that in the same years that American comics publishers voluntarily instituted a self-censorship regime known as the Comics Code Authority, manga also came under attack from parents and educators.[63] In both countries, the postwar socioeconomic order hinged on notions of meritocracy and of education as a required credential to achieve a stable middle-class lifestyle. In Japan, this resulted in the rise of "education mamas and PTAs" (parent-teacher associations) as mothers sought to provide their children with every possible educational advantage to ensure their long-term success. In their estimation, children reading manga that contained age-inappropriate content, or reading manga at all, was a threat to their healthy development and acquisition of the aforementioned educational credentials. After initially targeting erotic magazines for adults, the ban bad books movement sought to prevent either or both under the rubric of "protecting the youth" from "harsh depictions" and "sexually explicit material."

Criticisms of expression in manga, especially in akahon and kashihon, had emerged among educators as those formats grew in popularity during the Occupation; in the case of akahon manga, these criticisms were often substantively the same and made by the same people as those issued under the wartime state.[64] Criticism of akahon resumed in the press in 1949; manga scholar Takeuchi Osamu points to the "vulgar" portrayals occurring in children's magazines, especially manga, including a great number of violent scenes in those same manga magazines and garish visual expression that recalled prewar eroguro, as a proximate cause for that criticism's reemergence. Manga was banned at schools under a national policy and confiscated on sight.[65] In the early 1950s, national organizations and local PTAs took up the cause of protesting lurid content in manga, which became more visible in 1953 when most children's magazines switched from A5 to B5 size and started publishing more manga in each issue.[66] Their analyses were eventually picked up and sensationalized in the mass media; the "akusho tsuihō undō" phrase was coined by *Yomiuri Shinbun* in April 1955. From there, the movement widened and radicalized.[67]

Manga *was* lurid, violent, and vulgar: It was the first time since the invention of popular media in the Edo period that Japan had neither de facto nor de jure censorship mechanisms for mainstream (i.e., non-pornographic) publications, and publishers and creators were free to put out whatever they wanted. The market, not official morality, was king. Equally importantly, the dislocations of the postwar era had engendered nihilism among youth, as well as nationally publicized incidents of adolescent violence, and parents and educators were confronting these trends across a great divide in values: The older generations had been educated under the imperial state and still retained much of its worldview, in which children were meant to be obedient and virtuous, while the youths had come to maturity in the new democratic Japan and did not share the same mindset. As manga historian Takeuchi Osamu summarizes, changes in political and legal structures, postwar chaos, rapid changes in morals and sexual mores, "new mothers feeling at sea," the "strange existence" of story manga in the new democratic society—all of these together fed the movement.[68]

On one level, the ban bad books movement was the natural end point of the debate about children's manga that had been nurtured by Home Ministry censors and bureaucrats under fascism. Tagawa Suihō had weighed in on this question in his preface to *Chameken to Norakuro* (Chameken and Norakuro, 1948), in which he wrote that it wasn't an educational book: There were others for that purpose, and manga books at least ought to be separate from "learning, homework, and such." In his view, "even if it's illustrated manga-style, if it doesn't have interesting and funny things, it doesn't have the value [neuchi] of manga," and it was important that manga books be interesting, funny things that gave everyone a smile and let them rest their tired bodies.[69]

Tagawa's former *Shōnen Kurabu* editor Katō Ken'ichi felt similarly. Katō repeatedly defended manga in *Manga Shōnen*, insisting that manga was necessary for children and that banning them from reading it wouldn't work because of the spirit that manga contained: "Manga looks like something that anybody with just the inclination to draw can do roughly, so there aren't many people who will apologize to [i.e. acknowledge] manga," he wrote, but he argued that the opposite was in fact the case, and moreover, that the best manga was not only humorous but painful (kurushii), in the sense of having pathos. America loomed large in Katō's defense of manga as a country with a similar marketplace of comics consumption, both "good" and "bad," but also as a place where readers by 1949 had banded together via various organizations such as research meetings and clubs.[70] Ironically, those same U.S. reader organizations that Katō admired were powerless to stop the Comics Code Authority, while Japanese comics largely escaped such measures.[71]

This was not for lack of trying. The ban bad books movement cast a wide net, initially aiming at semi-pornographic "third-rate magazines" but expanding its focus to children's manga, criticizing not only popular manga and creators but newcomers as well.[72] Ban bad books activists complained about all of the following in children's manga: There were too few words, too many guns, too much use of red impaired children's sense of aesthetics, and kids were imitating manga protagonists in their play. Activists got one of Tezuka's manga banned from sale in a department store because it featured a scene in which a female character changed clothes; a PTA in Okayama burned both porn magazines and manga books, in Tezuka's recollection, "like in a witch trial."[73]

Those manga books included kashihon manga and gekiga; there was a strong animus against kashihon manga and its associates among thought leaders in print media in the 1950s.[74] Kashihon manga were easily scapegoated by the ban bad books movement, but it was only natural that people who weren't highly educated were drawn to kashihon's vulgarity—and there was nothing wrong with that.[75] Gekiga became another target alongside kashihon manga, as is made clear from an episode in Tatsumi's memoir *Gekiga hyōryū* (*A Drifting Life*, 1998–2006) detailing an incident in Yamanashi prefecture in September 1959. Declaring that "any book with pages, two-thirds or more of which are without text, is immoral," ban bad books activists in Yamanashi—which seems to have been a hotbed of the movement—specifically cited gekiga works by Satō Masa'aki, which in their description sounded extremely questionable indeed: "The protagonist is a juvenile delinquent. In 124 panels, on 24 pages, there are 25 scenes featuring guns, 20 showing fights, and 61 without any text. Almost all scenes depict juvenile crime. This story is immoral and lacks any sense of justice." Although Tatsumi depicts himself as laughing off the activists' claims, the unfortunate Satō could not get any work for six months: As Tatsumi put it, he was "hung out to dry by every publisher out of fear of the boycott" and resumed work only by attaching himself to a new manga publisher that had no prior knowledge of his "infamy." Satō reportedly later described his forced hiatus as "days of hell."[76]

As the home of kashihon manga and gekiga, kashihonya became activists' perennial targets; the latest movement developments were a constant topic in the *Zenkoku Kashihon Shinbun*. Partly this was a question of access: Kashihonya had little capital, either fiscal or cultural, and it was much easier for local groups, often housewives doing activism in their limited spare time, to bring pressure to bear on their neighborhood rental bookstore than on the predominantly Osaka- and Tokyo-based publishers that created the books available in those bookstores. Although Shogakukan editor Sashikata Ryūji convened a children's manga editors' organization in response to the movement in 1955, consisting of representatives from eight publishers and thirty magazines, they did not ultimately make many substantive changes to their publications.[77] Similarly, roundtables between publishers, kashihonya proprietors, and ban bad books activists went around in circles for two reasons: Activists struggled to define what constituted a "bad book," while publishers continually and successfully evaded being pinned down on what kind of content they would publish.

Ban bad books activists fell back on the 1930s-era canard that "commercialism" automatically meant that content was bad for children, but in democratic Japan commercialism was not ipso facto a bad thing, as a representative from Kobunsha, part of the Kodansha group, made clear in his remarks at a meeting of the "Warui Manga wo Nakusukai" (Committee to Abolish Bad Manga) attended by representatives of ten publishers: "Commercialism surely comes into the choice to publish good or bad manga, but that comes second; what comes first is readers. Since creators and editors both have a direct relationship with readers, you would say what will sell is commercialism, but it's not commercialism to think first of what will make children happy. In conclusion, what makes children happy is not bad manga."[78] For publishers, manga's popularity was now a badge of honor, as opposed to grounds for suspicion; in the moral universe of postwar Japan, it was no longer tenable, even at the formerly morally minded Kodansha, to successfully argue that child readers were moral blank slates or that manga per se was by definition immoral.

Manga critic Kajii Jun called the ban bad books movement going after kashihonya a "frame-up." One locus of the animus against kashihonya was an April 1955 article in the evening *Asahi Shinbun*, which condemned a book of pornography, *Issei teire*, and implicated kashihonya in its being sold to "youth." Pornography at the time, however, was generally considered a "one-time use" item and would not have been available at the rental bookstores for that reason. As Kajii points out, such materials were generally sold at night market shops and street stalls.[79] Kashihonya proprietors and their advocates then and now repeatedly argued that the groups' assumption that kashihon readers were children was false: The Kashihon Manga Kenkyūkai bluntly describes members of the ban bad books movement as "parents who were out of touch with reality."[80]

Looking from the top down, as Takeuchi does, the ban bad books movement peaked in 1955, when conservative prime minister Hatoyama Ichirō (1883–1959) made remarks advocating the extermination of "bad publications" (furyo shuppanmono) including manga, comparing them to chemical stimulants like the amphetamines that had been widely used during the Occupation but by then were rapidly falling out of acceptability.[81] Activists also pushed for the growing adoption of regional ordinances that did not directly regulate manga but instead addressed the behavior of minors in the name of the "healthy development of youth" (seishōnen hogo jyōrei). Just three prefectures had passed these ordinances by 1952, but they spread to an additional twenty-one of forty-seven prefectures between 1955 and 1967. All defined "youths" as under eighteen and generally both provided for the designation of "harmful literature" and directed bookstores to segregate it in some way.[82]

Looking from the bottom up, however, shows that the movement continued to plague kashihonya and manga creators into the 1960s. Mangaka were criticized by both parents and children: When publishers did put out "good manga" that garnered parent and teacher approval, it sold terribly because kids didn't like it. Some mangaka held meetings about what to do in response, with the Nanokakai manga group being founded in the movement's wake, but even if they could have all agreed to only draw "good manga," what was "good manga" and who decided that?[83] In a sign of the movement's continued vitality, October 1963 saw two separate book burnings in Saitama and Yamanashi prefectures organized by local bookseller associations, in which some forty-six hundred books and magazines from sixteen companies were doused with gasoline and incinerated.[84]

In Tezuka's recollection, 1960 was particularly hard for manga creators: Many comrades disappeared, not long before the critics themselves began to vanish like summer soldiers. By 1961, the mood among parents began slowly shifting to bargaining and acceptance; recognizing that they couldn't stop kids from reading manga or liking what they liked, parents began adopting the attitude that "as long as they do their homework, it's fine."[85] Parents' changing attitudes were a sign that mainstream manga was rapidly adapting itself to Japan's emerging social and corporate order, leaving the remaining ban bad books activists out in the cold along with the kashihonya and manga they attacked. That adaptation was mediated by a new development: television.

PROXY WARS: TELEVISION'S EARLY YEARS IN JAPAN

In Japan, both television itself and the new visual medium it supported were extremely disruptive to the media environment after television began broadcasting locally in Tokyo in 1953. Until then, mutatis mutandis, the Japanese mediascape was broadly similar to the one that had existed twenty years earlier in 1933; after 1953, that was no longer the case, and indeed, the transwar continuities between 1933 and 1953 mask substantial differences. Most critically, radio had been commercialized in 1951, the better to serve democratization, and the NHK lost its broadcast monopoly in 1952 after a successful pressure campaign on the government instigated by media mogul and former class A war criminal Shōriki Matsutarō, who launched a competing private television network, Nippon Television (NTV), six months after the NHK began broadcasting in February 1953.[86] Radio sets, which had first become common in the 1930s, became a "standard household appliance" in the 1950s, and radio soon hit on serialized dramas as a profitable and popular evolution of the medium. By the mid-1960s, however, television displaced radio as a source of household entertainment.[87]

Television was the object of an incipient moral panic even before it began broadcasting in Japan. Media historian Jayson Makoto Chun summarizes the view of critics, based in part on the experiences of Japanese who had encountered television abroad, primarily in the United States: "television would need to be regulated. Failure to do so would mean the penetration of commercialism into the middle-class family, children glued to the tube, and neglect of household duties by domestic housewives." Chun quotes an article published in the *Sunday Mainichi* in 1953, just before the advent of television in Japan, which laid out the danger to children in specific terms: "The effect on families is a double-edged sword. The reason is that the sponsors broadcast the most attention-grabbing programs and so the children watch westerns and gangster movies on the screen. They cannot separate themselves from the front of the set, then imitate these programs when they play in front of the TV, and so they fall into lack of exercise and lack of studying."[88]

The genres of programs the *Mainichi* cited were also exceedingly popular in kashihon manga, and the article cites a concern shared by the ban bad books movement, namely children imitating the media they consumed in their play, which went back to the 1930s and criticism of prewar akahon manga. After TV debuted in Japan, it boosted kashihon and children's manga by creating whole new types of content for them to poach, especially pro wrestling.

Early TV in Japan faced barriers to adoption, namely that the cost of a set was extremely high and the picture quality quite low; only the richest early adopters could afford a household television set, or would want one. To circumvent these problems, Shōriki embarked on a strategy that, in Chun's phrase, created "early TV as a mass event": Viewers congregated around street-corner sets for baseball games and other events, especially the matches of Korean-born pro wrestler Rikidōzan (1924–63), who routinely trounced Americans and other foreigners in the ring.[89] NTV installed 220 TVs in fifty-five locations even *before* it started broadcasting; this grew to 278 locations by 1957. Shōriki received daily reports on the street TVs' performance and moved those that weren't doing well—staff scouted prospective TV locations from trains and were repeatedly mistaken for land brokers. In media historian Yoshimi Shun'ya's evaluation, street TVs "demonstrate the inherent connection between television and the mass imagination in the postwar period"; he estimates that up to one million people watched street TVs nationwide in the mid-1950s.[90]

This street-corner practice goes back to the advent of radio in Japan in the 1920s, when crowds would gather in front of radio shops during the day to listen to baseball games because most households had electricity only at night, due to fixed utility contracts.[91] Early TV adopted the performance practices of kamishibai, and like kamishibai its successes were predicated on a vision of television, in Chun's phrase, as "a way to entertain viewers and sell them goods in the process," not "as a public service dedicated to uplifting the cultural level of the nation."[92] Entertainment versus uplift is the same debate that bedeviled early Japanese cinema and placed all forms of popular media in the crosshairs of bureaucratic censorship under the wartime state. It is also the debate about manga that raged from the emergence of children's manga as a popular genre within the medium through to 1959, when the Yamanashi ban bad books activists indicted Satō's manga partly by calculating the ratio of text to images. In their simplistic paradigm, text was good and images were bad; manga that was not sufficiently textual was thus bad prima facie.

The cost of sets gradually came down during the 1950s, and TVs moved off the street into commercial establishments, and finally into individual homes.[93] Although the programming mix changed accordingly and pro wrestling simultaneously began losing its luster, earlier group viewing conditions were recreated on a domestic scale: Since television sets were still a luxury item, "people gathered at houses in the neighborhood that had TVs when it was time for popular programs."[94] TV as a medium also linked the family and the state via "Micchie," the future Heisei empress, and her celebrated royal marriage in 1959; the wedding became a national media event because the number of televisions sets had already reached a tipping point.[95] As it matured and programming practices solidified, TV also structured the lives of Japanese households around a synchronized and gendered national schedule, with morning, afternoon, and "golden time" (evening) programming blocs dominated by particular members of the household: the housewife/mother, the children, and the salaryman/father, respectively.[96] Thus, in Yoshimi's summary, "television functioned to create a uniform sense of national time all over the country," inheriting and deepening this function from radio.[97]

Concerns about the stultifying power of the "boob tube" over children echoed those that ban bad books activists had previously articulated about manga. While parents could exert control over children's television consumption simply by turning off the set or changing the channel once TVs moved into the home (a power that was undermined in practice by the fact that children were often much better TV operators than adults), the comparatively free-wheeling kashihonya were not so easily brought to heel—thus the need to agitate against "bad books" *tout court*, through which concerned parents sought to exercise a similar level of control over children's access to manga. Indeed, Yonezawa Yoshihiro and his comrade Shikijō Kyōtarō later recalled of their childhoods in this era that "unlike TV, which still had the feeling of being watched as a family, manga published in bulk in shōnen magazines was ours alone, a pleasure that furthermore we could read anywhere, any time."[98]

Conclusion

POSTWAR PLATFORMS

IN MANY WAYS THE STORY of the Occupation and the postwar period in manga is the story of Kansai manga's long-delayed revenge. Creators and trends from Kansai revolutionized the medium as innovations in Osaka, manga's countercultural hub of akahon and kashihon manga, filtered into the mainstream Tokyo magazine industry from the bottom up.[1] Story manga, pioneered by Tezuka in akahon and then pushed forward by him and other creators in mainstream magazines, became the dominant paradigm in children's manga by the end of the decade, with the old humorous children's manga fading fast. At the same time, the gekiga crowd took story manga's innovations to their logical extremes, producing manga that was full of action and that sought to use even more cinematic techniques, to be even more "realistic" than story manga. Together, these developments expanded the scope and the audiences for narrative manga beyond its previous limits, when it had been confined to appealing to children.

Akahon and kashihon manga were entwined with kashihonya, which were a prominent node in manga distribution networks in this era, but can also be considered through the framework of platforms, companies whose product allows their customers to connect with others. In the "mediation-type platform" model developed by Japanese platform theorists by the early 2000s, a platform is the intermediary agent in the encounter between multiple groups (i.e., of people or companies). Mediation-type platforms thus create multisided markets where users, money, and contents meet. The video game company Nintendo is a paradigmatic example of a "platform business" (i.e., one that provides a base for other companies to offer products and services, thus allowing transactions between third parties).[2] In Nintendo's case, it sells the console and some games, but also allows authorized third-party developers to make games for the console. Turning this lens back on the postwar era, it is possible to see that kashihonya supported the rise of kashihon manga publishers, which converted from akahon publishing partly to take advantage of a more stable marketplace with higher profit margins.

Thinking of kashihonya themselves as a "platform business" in the years discussed in this chapter illuminates both their success and their failure. Kashihonya fostered a multisided market in which manga readers, kashihonya proprietors, and kashihon and mainstream manga publishers participated in transactions with each other via the kashihonya "platform." A key element of Nintendo's success is that it has created and maintained trust in its platform by ensuring a certain baseline quality in third-party games; kashihonya, by contrast, fell into a unique dilemma when the ban bad books movement systematically began undermining readers' trust in them. The kashihonya response to ban bad books activists alienated the actual people who were giving kashihonya money: manga readers, who wanted the questionable content to which activists objected. At the same time, changing economic and media conditions fatally disrupted another aspect of this multisided market, which was predicated on the lower standard of living before Japan's so-called economic miracle took off beginning in 1956.

The Nintendo example also points to the insoluble problem that kashihonya faced: They did not have a monopoly on manga, and they could not control the kashihon manga publishers who supplied their exclusive kashihon manga. Most kashihon publishers ran on a shoestring budget, and even at the height of the format's popularity kashihon publishing was unstable. Kashihonya had little means by which to influence kashihon manga publishers, just as the ban bad books movement had very few effective levers to influence mainstream publishers. In Steinberg's summation, "the ability to sell and the business model behind it—not simply the code—are what make a platform such," and these aspects of the kashihon business model meant that they were unable to create a true "walled garden" in which they could enforce controls on content and monetize that content effectively.[3] Instead, the boundaries of kashihonya remained porous, as they rented multiple kinds of media and even sold things like freebies from manga magazines.[4] As a platform, they ultimately failed.

This postwar period is often regarded as the era of manga's birth, although the mediascape in many ways had more in common with the years of the wartime state than with that of democratic Japan's later economic heyday. While story manga was synthesized in these years after Tezuka's debut, focusing on either story manga or Tezuka and ignoring other developments in the manga world in this period does that world a grave disservice. Professional manga now has more in common with manga as it stood in the late 1960s or early 1970s than with the era of akahon, kamishibai, kashihonya, and street TV. Contemporary manga became contemporary largely by overturning the remaining foundations, laid in the wartime era, on which the 1950s world of manga was still based.

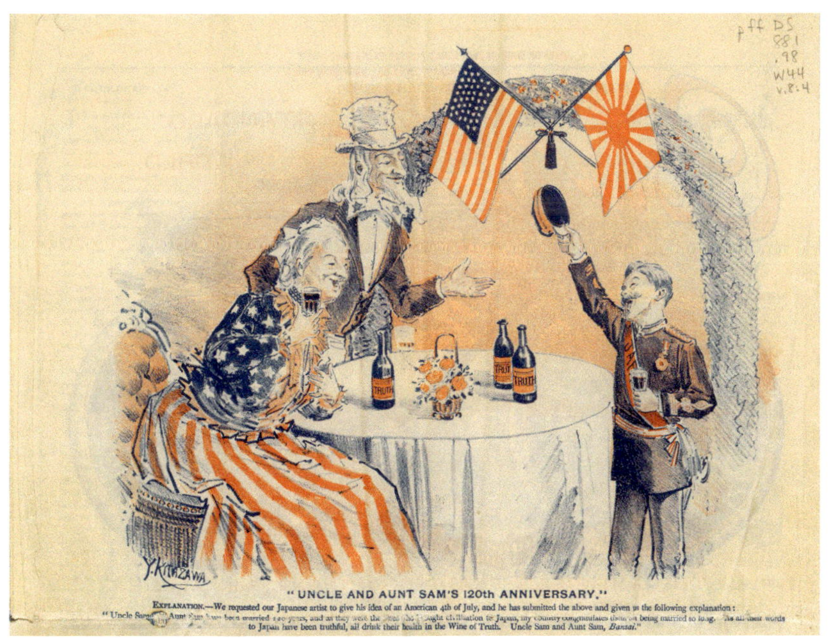

PLATE 1. Cartoon by Kitazawa Rakuten from the July 4, 1896, edition of *Box of Curios*, signed with his birth name, "Y. Kitazawa." Courtesy of Bancroft Library, University of California, Berkeley.

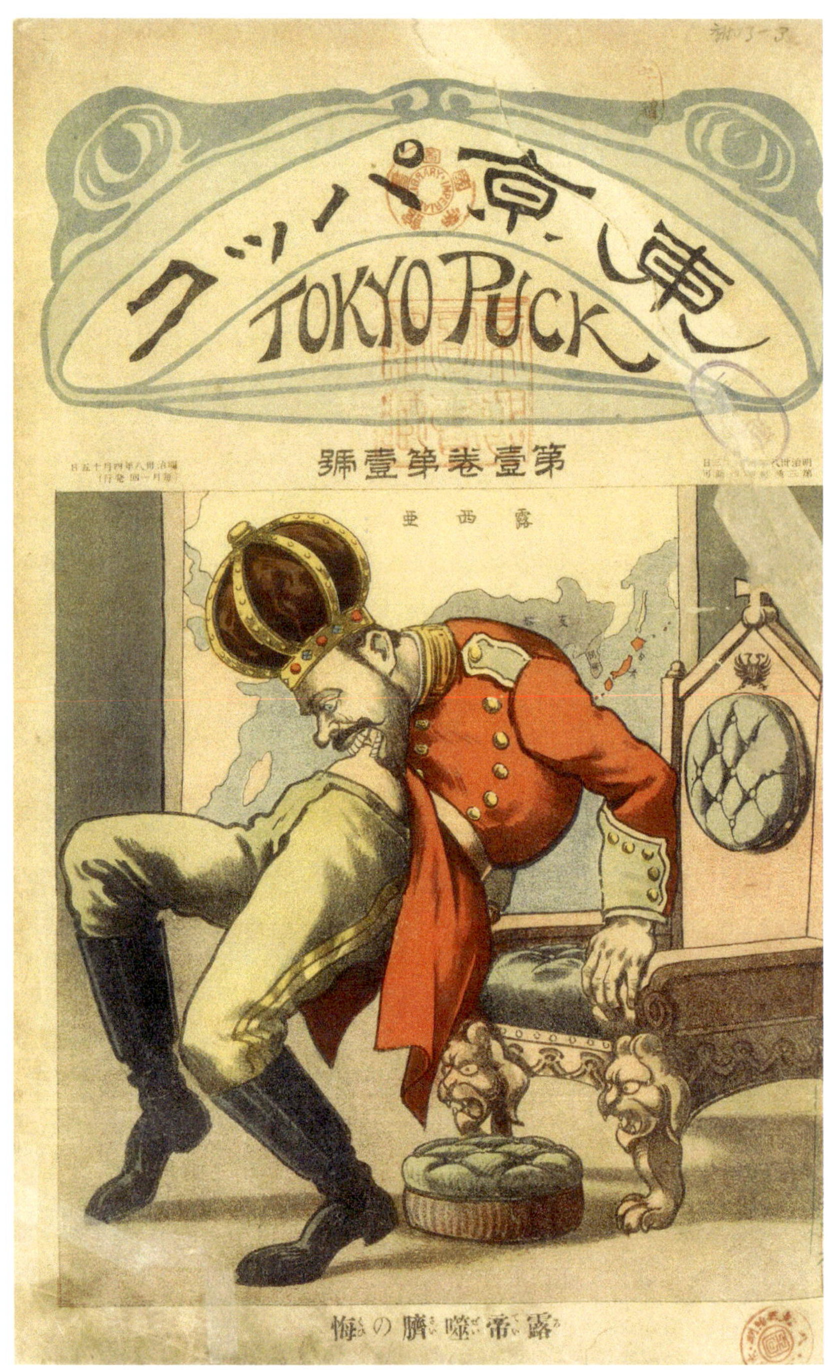

PLATE 2. Cover of *Tokyo Puck*'s first issue: "The Tsar's bitter regrets" (Rotei zeisai [*sic*] no kui), April 15, 1905. Courtesy of National Diet Library.

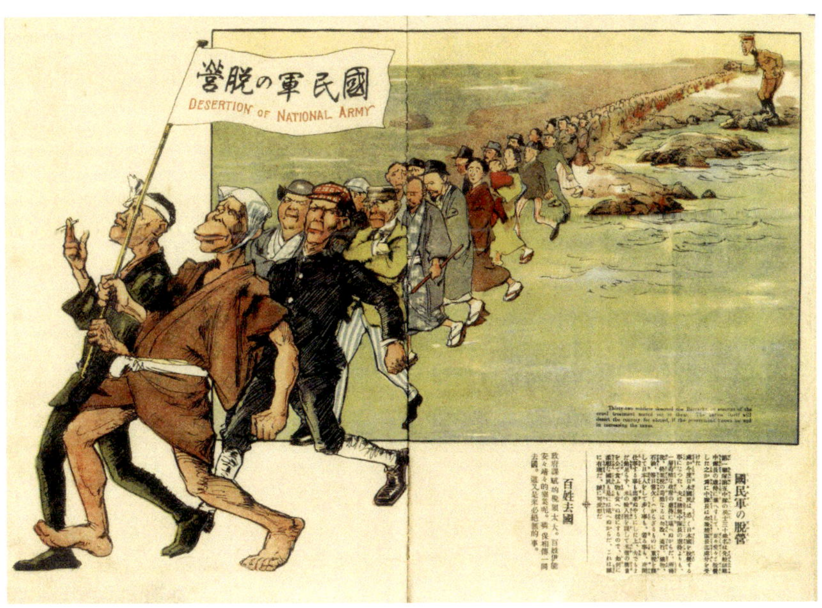

PLATE 3. "Desertion of National Army" (Kokumingun no datsuei) centerfold, *Tokyo Puck* 4, no. 9 (March 1908). Courtesy of National Diet Library.

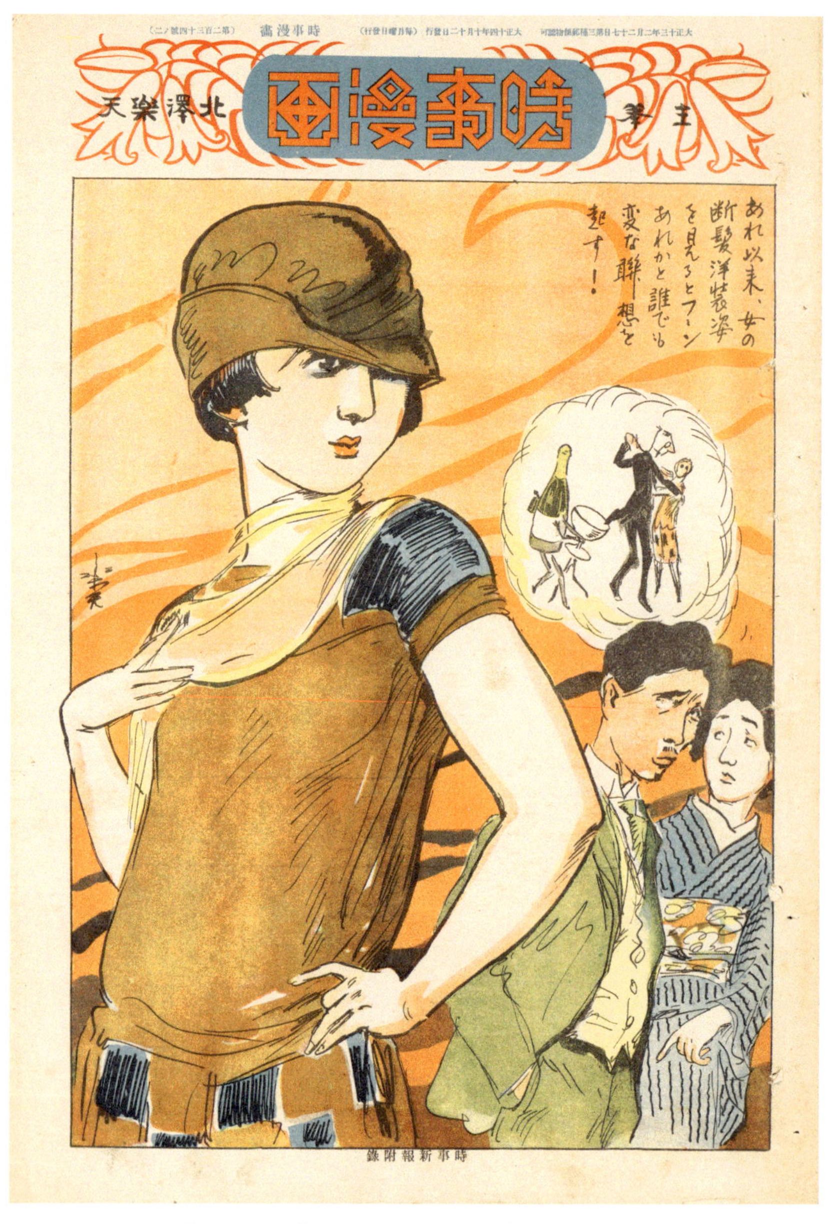

PLATE 4. Cover of *Jiji Manga* by Kitazawa Rakuten depicting a Modern Girl turning a husband's head while his dismayed wife looks on, October 12, 1925. Courtesy of The Ohio State University Billy Ireland Cartoon Library & Museum.

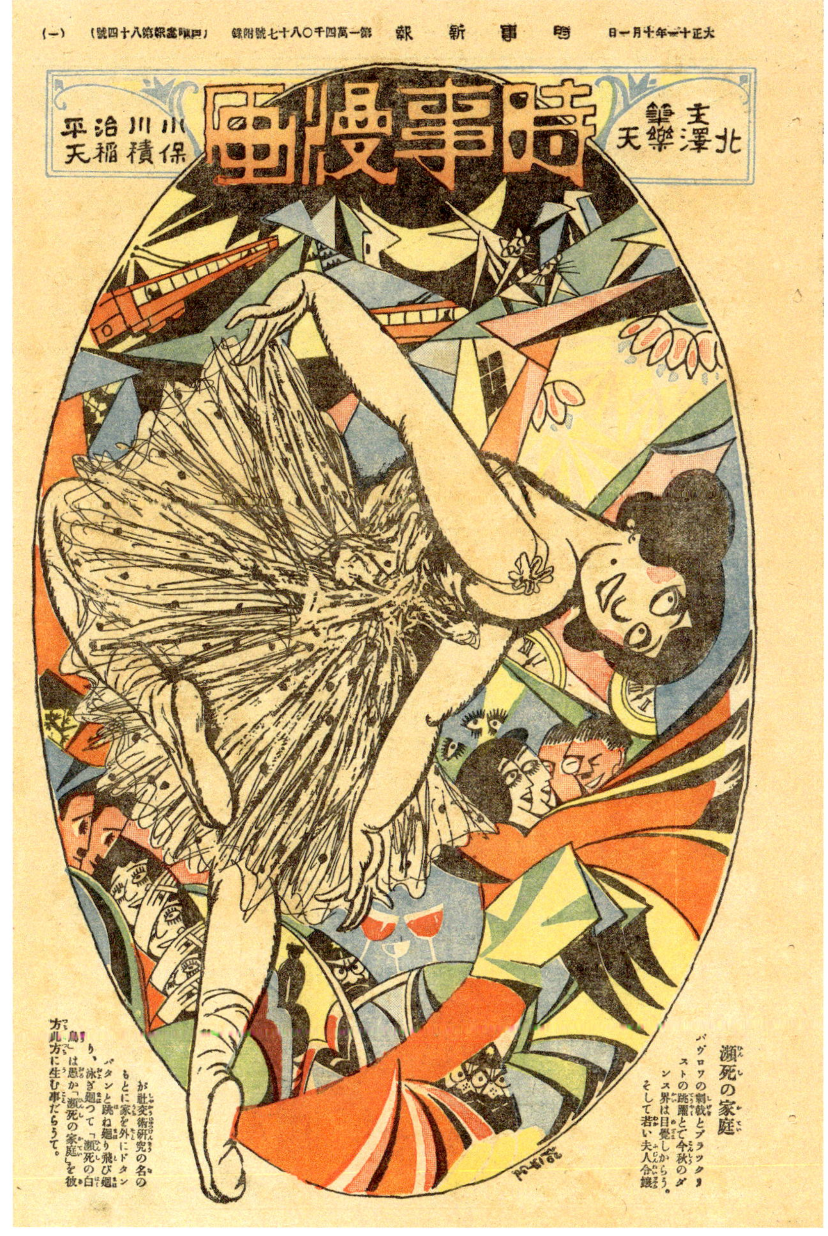

PLATE 5. Cover of *Jiji Manga* ("Hinshi no katei") by Ogawa Jihei, October 1, 1922. Courtesy of The Ohio State University Billy Ireland Cartoon Library & Museum.

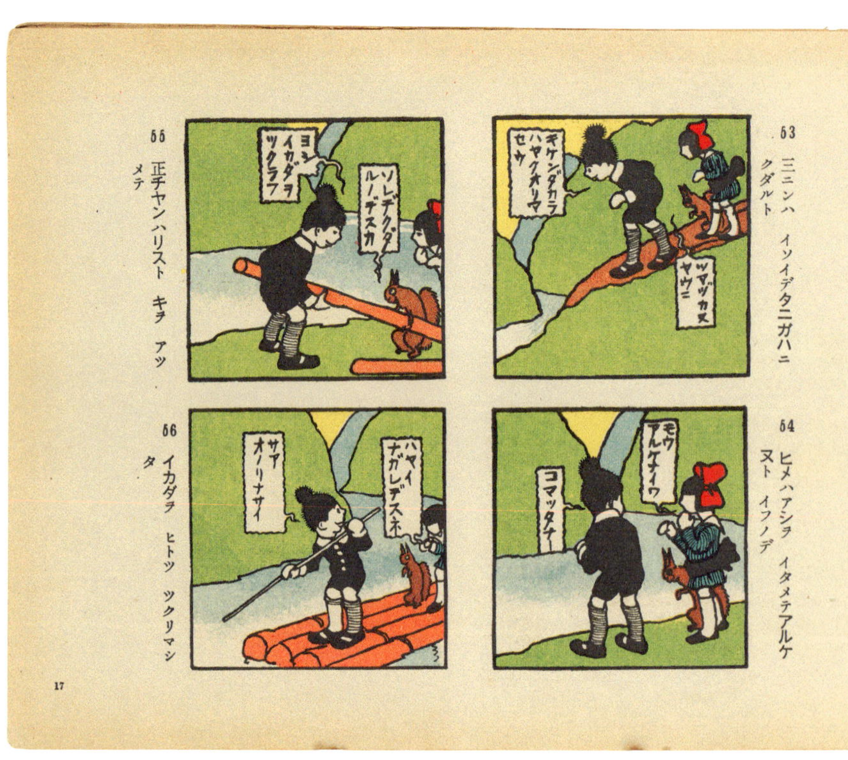

PLATE 6. Pages from *Shō-chan no bōken*, vol. 2 (1924). Their cow steed having been felled by a bandit's rock, Shō-chan and the squirrel build a log raft on which to escape with the princess. Courtesy of New York Public Library.

49 リスハ　オコッテカタキヲ　トルト　リキムノヲ

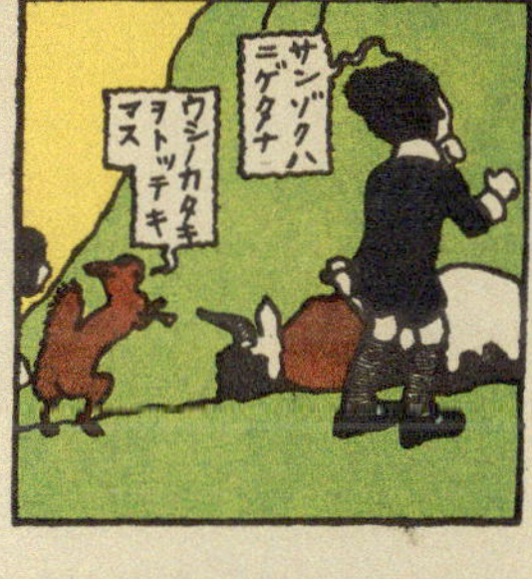

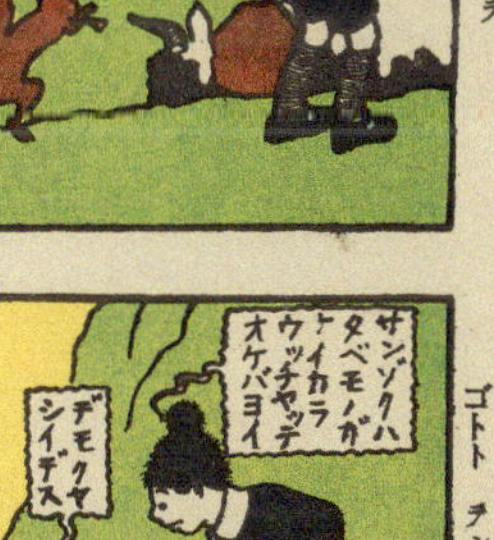

50 ヒメヲ　マモルガ　ダイジノシゴトト　ヲシヘテ

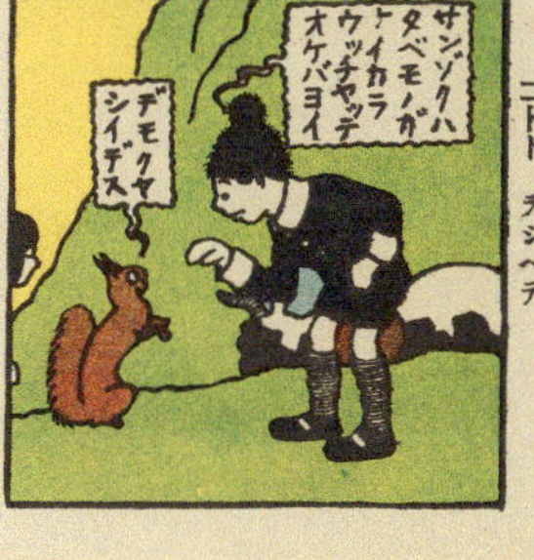

51 ミチニ　サイテルハナヲワシニソナヘ

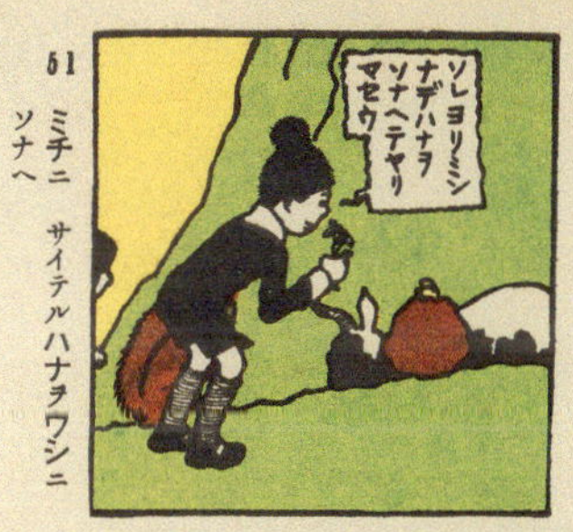

52 三ニン　ヒザマヅイテトムラツテヤリマシタ

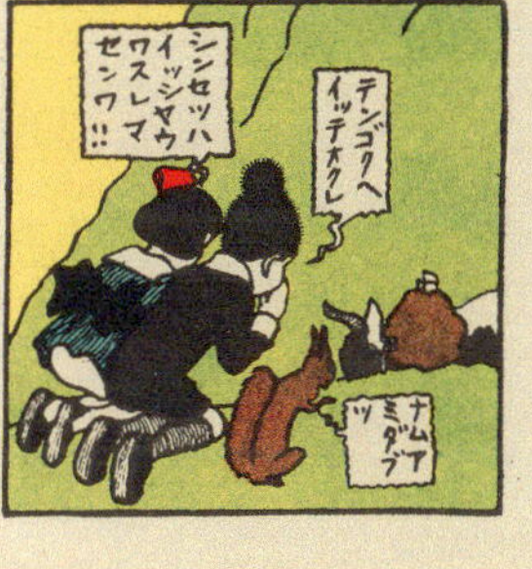

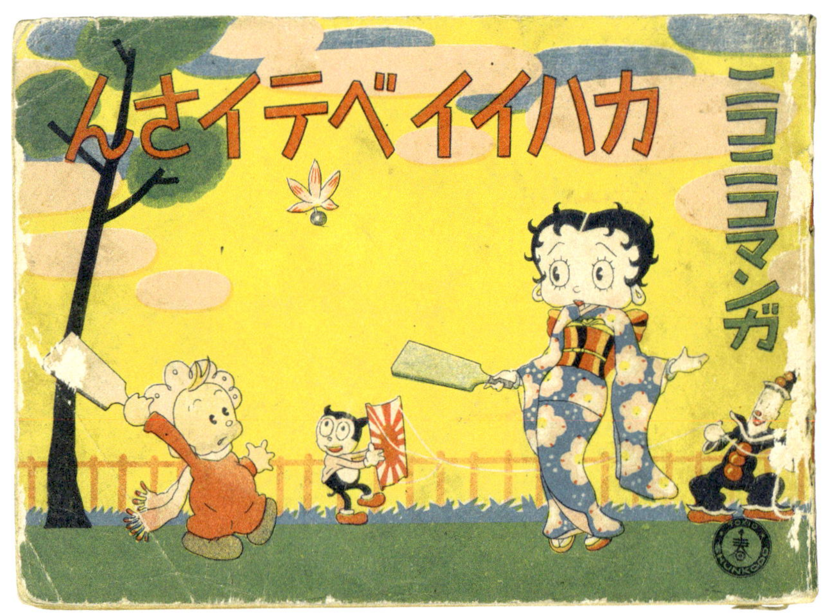

PLATE 7. Cover of an akahon manga, *Kawaii Betty-san* (Cute Ms. Betty, 1934), depicting Betty Boop playing hanetsuki (similar to badminton).

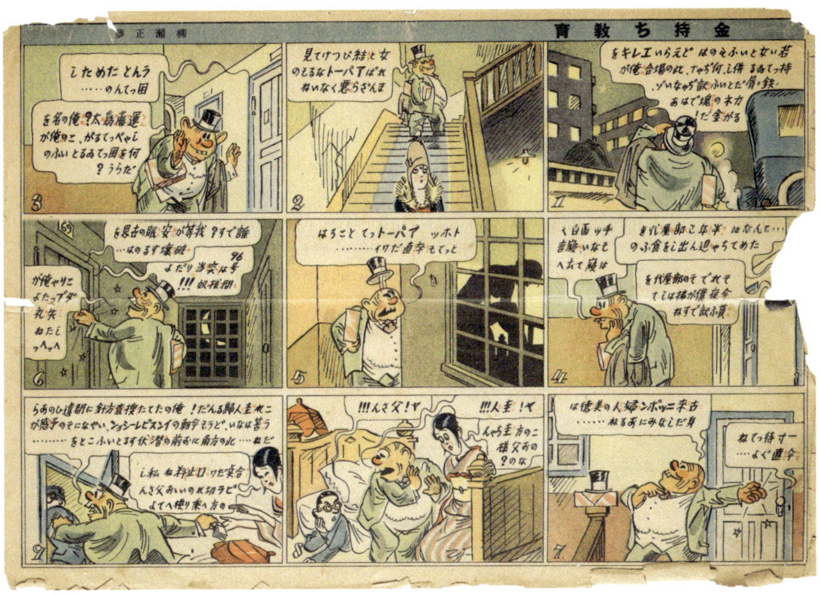

PLATE 8. Yanase Masamu, *Kanemochi kyōiku*, 1930. A rich man goes to visit his mistress and finds his son hiding under her bed. Courtesy of The Ohio State University Billy Ireland Cartoon Library & Museum.

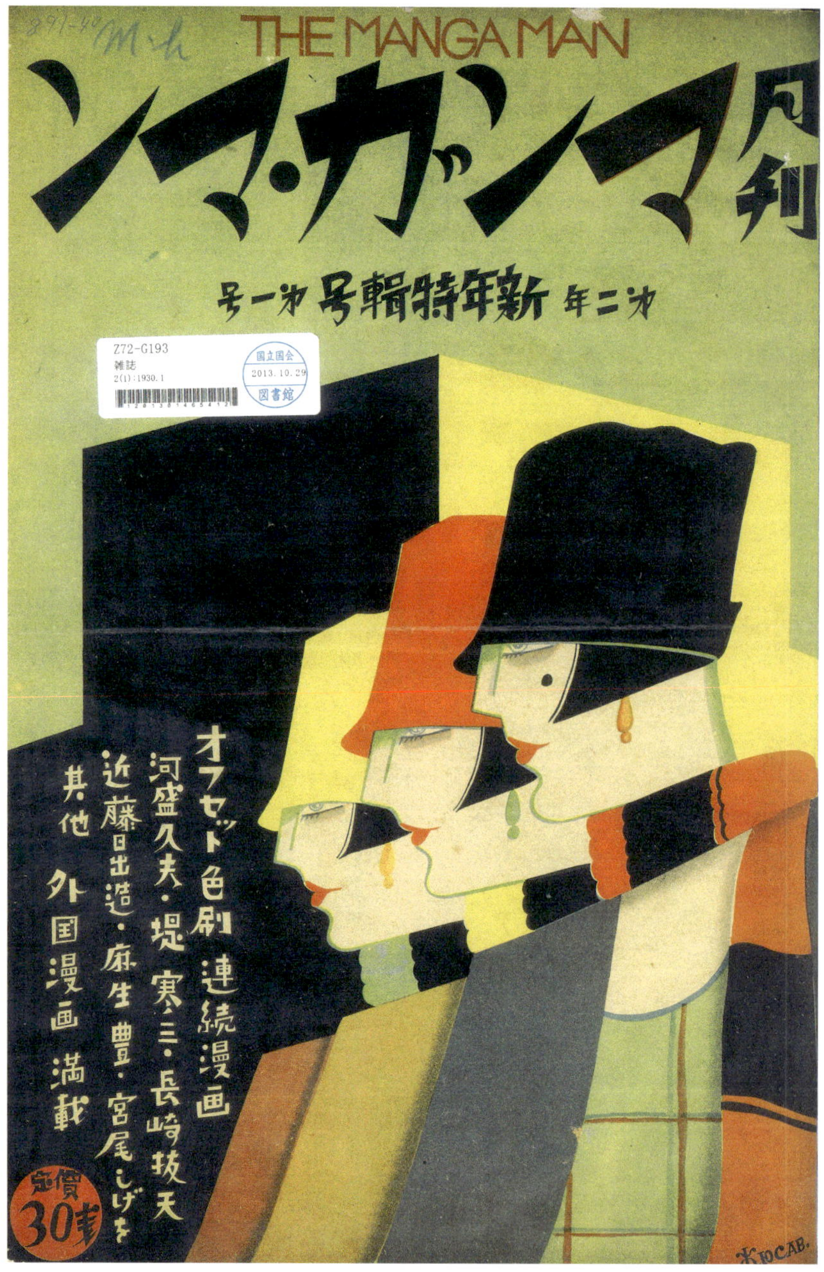

PLATE 9. Cover of *The Manga Man*, January 1930. Nagasaki Batten, Kondō Hidezō, and Miyao Shigeo are among those advertised on the cover, along with offset color printing, serialized manga, and foreign manga. Courtesy of National Diet Library.

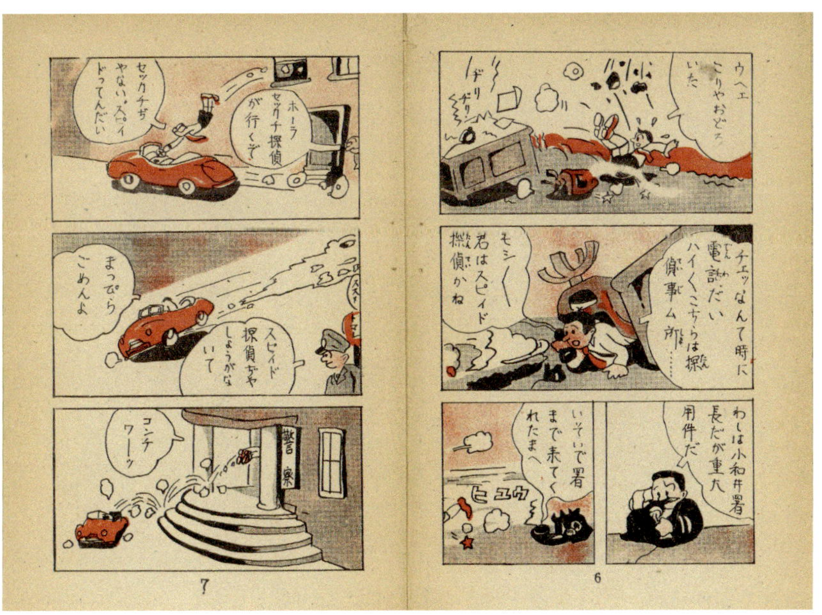

PLATE 10. Two interior pages from *Kaijin skeleton hakushi* (1948) by Komatsu Sakyō. Compare the speeding car with the one in *Shintakarajima* (figure 12). Courtesy of Gordon W. Prange Collection, University of Maryland. © Komatsu Sakyō. Used with permission.

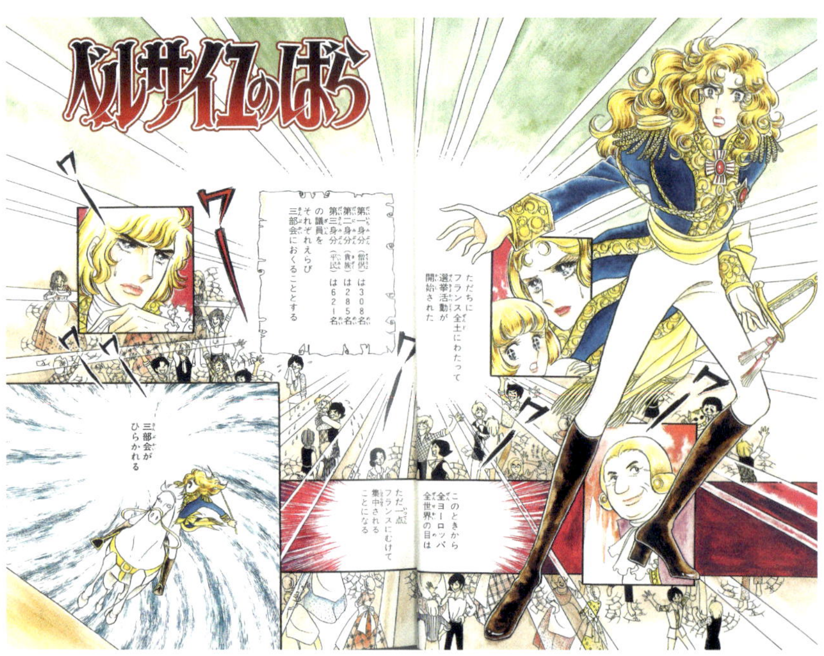

PLATE 11. Splash page for *The Rose of Versailles*, episode 56 (1973), depicting (clockwise from top right) Oscar, Marie Antoinette and the Dauphin Louis Joseph, Louis XVI, and Robespierre at the opening of the Estates General in May 1789. Oscar's full-body pose is a dramatic evolution of the "style picture."

PART FOUR

TV Manga and the Age of Revolution

1963–1975

Overview

SHAMBLING TOWARD THE POSTMODERN

WITH THE POSTWAR ECONOMIC RECOVERY completed in 1956, what some historians have termed Japan's "long postwar" period began. Economic growth only increased, inaugurating the country's "economic miracle," an unprecedented forty-year period of overall positive economic growth that ended only in 1991 and remade Japan into the world's number two economy. Beginning in the early 1960s, Japanese society reconstructed itself, in Andrew Gordon's phrase, around "a broad array of institutions, social policies, and laws, supported and bolstered by a set of 'common-sense' ideas about the natural virtue of meritocratic competition and divided gender roles" that was centered around the corporate hegemony of big business.[1] These gender roles consisted of the salaryman who worked outside the home and the housewife who worked inside it, caring for their children and her spouse. Television reinforced these gender roles by orienting programming schedules around gendered divisions of time and labor inside the home; it also created a weekly rhythm of television viewing that threatened monthly magazines' long-standing primacy in the manga industry.

Manga successfully navigated this transition by realigning itself with the emerging gendered corporatocratic social order. This transition is the process by which the children's manga category was split into the gendered categories of shōnen and shōjo manga, which took place over about a decade from 1957 to 1968, when *Weekly Shōnen Jump* (Shūkan Shōnen Janpu), now Japan's leading manga magazine, made its debut, and the last old-style monthly magazine still standing, *Shōnen* (1946–68), folded.[2] Having embraced a weekly format to compete with television, and having internalized the gendered division of labor endorsed by the corporate hegemony, manga now filled a new social role: Namely, in anthropologist Anne Allison's phrase, manga made "escape from the habits of labor seem possible through everyday practices of consumptive pleasure."[3] In other words, by attaching itself to the new socioeconomic order manga took up the socially licensed role of escapist reading material, a role it continues to fulfill in Japanese society today. Indeed, by 1966 the kashihon newspaper was reporting that mothers now worried that their children *not* reading manga would make them seem weird and abnormal, a strong concern in conformist-minded Japan.[4] Notably, manga's new social role had nothing to do with humor or provoking laughter, its former raison d'être and north star.

Manga dealt with the threat of television not only by creating the new weekly magazine format and reorganizing its genre categories along gender lines, but also through the creation of "TV manga" (terebi manga), which since the mid-1970s has been known by the more familiar term *anime*.[5] The first TV anime was *Tetsuwan Atomu* (1963–66, *Astro Boy*), adapted by Tezuka and his Mushi Productions studio from Tezuka's popular 1950s manga (a live-action TV adaptation had already been broadcast in 1959–60). *Tetsuwan Atomu* was a runaway hit that spawned what came to be known in Japan as the anime media mix, opening up a new TV animation industry to manga creators and publishers and creating vast new merchandising and profit opportunities.

Video may have killed the radio star, but anime ultimately gave manga a new lease on life. The popularity of the *Tetsuwan Atomu* anime adaptation reinvented the role of manga in the age of television precisely because Tezuka and his collaborators wanted to break away from the full animation of Japanese movie studios such as Tōei, which aspired to be the "Disney of the East." Instead, Tezuka and his staff created something that was both "electric kamishibai" and "TV manga." The effect was to enthrone manga as the source of anime, which affirmed its relevance and its primacy in the relationship between the two media even as television proliferated. "With *Tetsuwan Atomu*," Marc Steinberg summarizes, "manga became more than a reservoir of thematic elements of characters (as comics had occasionally been previously); it provided the source of a new visual logic and a new relationship between motion and stillness."[6] The limited animation style that Tezuka and company developed as a unification of manga and kamishibai in motion created new, generative relationships in the pop culture (contents) industries, between fans and creators, between fans and fans, and between companies.

Tetsuwan Atomu generated significant profits for Tezuka and Mushi Productions, which Tezuka plowed back into a series of unprofitable but extremely consequential ventures.[7] Chief among these was the magazine

COM, which, along with the so-called "alternative manga" magazine *Garo*, touched off a wholesale reorganization of the ways that manga fans related to each other and to professional creators and publications. During the "united front years" in which both were in print (1967–71), true manga enthusiasts who read these magazines discovered new creators and radically different manga than those found in mainstream publications. Both magazines welcomed amateur creators, and *COM* sought to organize manga fans nationwide into a system of clubs, a development that gave a huge boost to burgeoning manga fan scenes across the country. Expanding manga to include "alternative" creators and manga, as both *COM* and *Garo* did, gave manga new scope to be experimental, strange, noncommercial, and even antinarrative, though these developments were not always welcomed by established creators such as Tezuka. Expanding the manga sphere to include manga fans' amateur production proved epochal.

At the same time that fan cultures in Japan began growing rapidly, the shōjo manga genre experienced an extremely fecund period of transformation in the early 1970s, spurred by the so-called Shōwa 24 Group and other young female creators entering the industry. Ikeda Riyoko, Hagio Moto, and Takemiya Keiko, among many others, revolutionized shōjo manga, pushing the bounds of comics expression farther than any other comics tradition worldwide had yet done. Young creators born in and around 1949, they sought to expand shōjo manga to tell more adult, complex narratives that reflected the shōjo audience's actual interests and preoccupations, including sexuality. Their collective creativity transformed manga expression in every category and placed the previously roundly despised shōjo category at the medium's vanguard. Their dizzying successes also established a gendered paradigm of manga labor and consumption that reified young women as shōjo manga's ideal creators because they were themselves former shōjo.

Simultaneously, manga publishers adopted many marketing strategies familiar to manga magazine readers today: In these years, manga magazines became advertisements for the industry's product (i.e., tankōbon, the compilation volumes of single series) rather than the product themselves. At the same time, partly spurred by the success of *Garo* and *COM* among college students—and, in particular, among college-age men—the manga industry expanded its reach to encompass these emerging readerships through the invention of seinen (young men's) manga.

From the beginning, seinen was characterized by a much more open depiction of sexuality and eroticism, and it was around this same era that explicit pornography began to proliferate in Japanese comics, giving rise to the new form known as "eromanga," put out by so-called third-rate publishers. Eromanga's existence enabled the proliferation of sex and violence in seinen, which quickly spilled over into shōnen, as creators could now say with some justification that what they were creating was clearly not actually pornographic. The manga-fication of porn that eromanga constituted, moreover, was part and parcel of the burgeoning transformation of creative fields in Japan generally, as ex-mangaka who couldn't endure the punishing pace of weekly magazine publication and the endless popularity competitions of magazines' reader surveys sought careers in other fields. Spurred by the visual innovations of *COM*, *Garo*, and the shōjo revolution, advertising, design, and illustration became increasingly manga-esque from this period on.

All of these changes took place against the backdrop of the late 1960s and early 1970s, the "season of politics" (seiji no kisetsu) in which Japanese society was riven by mass protests from a variety of groups, including the New Left, antiwar protestors, and a renewed, militant student movement. The collision between the young adults born in the postwar era and their conformity-minded elders was global, and globally destabilizing; in Japan, protests coalesced around the second renewal of the Anpo treaty in 1970, the continued U.S. retention of the Okinawan islands (which formally reverted to Japan in 1972 after being ruled in "trusteeship" since 1945), urban destruction in Tokyo, and environmental degradation nationwide; the 1970 Anpo protests even reached manga, with Kondō Hidezō publishing manga supporting the renewal and Ishinomori Shōtarō publishing manga arguing against it.[8] Japan's indirect involvement in the Vietnam War as a staging ground for the U.S. military was also a major focus of protest.

The student protest movement, notoriously marred by sexism, petered out after the second Anpo failure. In Japan the "ūman ribu" or simply "ribu" (women's liberation) movement emerged in 1971, reaching a crescendo in the middle of the decade before it dissipated into more diffuse activism.[9] Unlike previous feminist movements in Japan, ribu emphasized sex and sexuality, a concern it shared with the readers and creators of the shōjo manga revolution.[10] Ultimately, these readers were not just women and girls. In Nagayama Kaoru's judgment, "Just as defeat in the Second World War gave birth to a postwar generation of cynics and nihilists, so too did the two-time defeat of the protest movement."[11] The cynics and nihilists of the previous generation created and read gekiga; in the "clump" (dankai) or baby boomer generation, these young men became some of queer shōjo manga's most ardent fans.

The early 1970s mark a boundary in history too, the boundary between the modern and the postmodern. The transition was symbolized by the Osaka Expo in 1970, which peddled a glorious Space Age vision of the interplanetary future but instead spurred the adoption of decidedly Earth-bound technologies including canned coffee and closed-circuit television surveillance.[12] In the world's advanced industrial economies of the Global North, the postmodern era after 1970 witnessed new politics, including the rise of neoliberalism; new, more intensive forms of capitalism that sought to hook consumers emotionally even as many countries successfully unwound worker protections; and new social justice movements, including feminism and queer liberation, that advocated the dissolution of patriarchal power. Their legacies remain in manga, in Japan, and worldwide.

CHAPTER SEVEN

Seeking Alternatives

GARO, *COM*, AND MANGA FAN CULTURE

MANGA IN MOTION: *TETSUWAN ATOMU* AND ANIME

The question of how to understand or think about anime has attracted a great deal of debate among English-language scholars, who have described it variously as a technology of perception or a force of distribution, as a set of social relations founded on collaborative creativity, or as a medium of communication, while cautioning that defining anime via national boundaries is difficult.[1] As manga scholar Jaqueline Berndt drily notes, "Anime is a matter of perspective."[2] Moreover, all of these perspectives are in some sense correct. Anime, from its very beginning, was not one thing: It sprang into existence in relation to manga and kamishibai, and upon broadcast was enmeshed in capitalist merchandising and distribution networks and in social networks among children and professionals. Animation already had a half-century-long theatrical history in Japan, and it had previously appeared on TV: *Tetsuwan Atomu* must have been something quite different from these previous examples, given its outsize impact.[3] It was.

Tezuka loved animation. He had wanted to make an animated film since elementary school, and he had worked so hard on manga in the 1950s partly to acquire the capital necessary to set up an animation studio.[4] He was well known for repeatedly joking that "if manga was his wife, animation was his mistress"; for Tezuka, not making animation was no choice at all.[5] Tezuka founded Mushi Productions in 1961, the year after he learned the ropes of animation by doing storyboards for Tōei's *Saiyūki* (Journey to the West, 1960), an adaptation of his manga *Boku no Son Gokū* (My Son Gokū, 1952–59).[6] He soon had twenty or thirty people, "a tenth of the staff roster of Tōei, quite literally," in anime historian Jonathan Clements's phrase, because he poached animators from Tōei and other studios. Tezuka paid more than twice what disaffected animators had made at those studios, and even threw in a 100-yen lunch stipend. But the animators paid in other ways, picking up the slack for Tezuka's late deadlines while he got the credit, both then and now.[7]

In *Tetsuwan Atomu*, Tezuka and the Mushi Productions staff broke definitively with the "full animation" style that was ascendant in Japan at the time, derived ultimately from Disney Studios via Tōei Animation, with important influences from the wartime *Momotarō* films.[8] *Full animation* refers to animating at twenty-four frames per second (also known as animating "on ones"), and since each frame is produced by hand, it is expensive—too expensive for an *Atomu* movie. Even slashing the frame rate to limited animation done "on threes"—eight frames per second instead of twenty-four—would cost six million yen per thirty-minute episode, still a prohibitive amount of money no TV station would pay.[9]

Tezuka attacked the problem from both ends. On the production side, the budget was slashed to approximately 2.5 million yen per episode, necessitating that the staff employ a suite of money-saving animation techniques to produce an episode's worth of animation every week. Mushi Pro staff bringing these techniques together and refining them on one production gave birth to what they initially regarded as a style, and which has evolved into anime's visual conventions as a medium.[10] These measures meant that anime looked a lot like manga and kamishibai, and it sounded a lot like kamishibai too: Voice acting and sound effects influenced by kamishibai (and ancestrally from former silent film orators) were employed to generate interest during otherwise static shots. On the distribution side, Tezuka made another fateful choice: accepting much less than half the cost of the production budget in fees from Fuji TV, which picked up the show for broadcast beginning on New Year's Day 1963. The broadcast was sponsored by candy company Meiji Seika.[11]

The officially repeated figure of 550,000 yen per episode became the industry standard rate that studios charged per anime episode.[12] That was roughly 20 percent of the actual costs, necessitating further cost-cutting measures on the production side and finding other external funding sources: initially advertising, and then licensing deals for co-branded goods, led by the epochal Meiji marble chocolates, which included Atom stickers as freebies, and followed by actual Astro Boy merchandise, officially branded by Mushi Pro.[13] "With this decision," animation historian Yamaguchi Yasuo summarizes, "Tezuka became the pioneer of TV animation."[14]

Tezuka's decision, in Yamaguchi's phrase, "made the impossible possible and turned dreams into reality."[15] Radically underselling each episode of *Tetsuwan Atomu* established a pattern in the anime industry that endures to this day, and its infamously depressing effect on studio production budgets—and, by extension, animation staff wages—has earned it the sobriquet "Tezuka's curse" in some quarters. But the "curse" was a *necessary condition:* The only way to make anime was to make it as limited animation and to undersell it, and the fact that it is limited animation that is undersold, requiring the kind of merchandising deals that are now standard for every anime and necessitating the visual and technical constraints inherent to limited animation, even in the digital age, is what makes anime *anime* and not some other kind of animation. In particular, the merchandising deals that anime came to rely on have reconfigured the way that audiences relate to anime series and characters, and to each other.

Through its ubiquity, the *Atomu* merchandising changed the way children related to television, manga, and their lived environments. Children at the time, Yonezawa and Shikijō later wrote that the stickers "awakened an extraordinary excitement among us. The popularity of *Atom* on TV goes without saying, but the pride or something like it that we took in the stickers' coolness and the quantity of our collections had us running wild to collect them."[16] With the stickers in particular, everything in a child's environment could be "Atomized," made into an extension or appendage of *Tetsuwan Atomu* and extending anime's reach into daily life.[17] These developments paved the way for the anime media mix, which relies on characters and character merchandise to connect audiences with media and the narrative worlds that characters inhabit.

The success of *Tetsuwan Atomu*'s TV manga kicked off a veritable gold rush, with manga creators entering the animation industry, and publishers increasingly considering possible anime adaptations when deciding what manga to publish in magazines. With manga now seen as the wellspring of anime adaptations, its primacy over anime was assured.

EXIT KASHIHONYA, PURSUED BY PTAS

Anime married manga and television's distinctive features, and so represented one way of resolving the conflict between the two media. But anime only deepened the threat to kashihonya and kashihon manga, which were bound up with the old monthly manga magazine paradigm and the one-volume story format. As TV ownership reached 30 percent by the end of the 1950s and kept climbing thereafter, combined with the fact that watching TV was now a private, domestic activity, kashihonya foot traffic decreased markedly. During the 1964 Tokyo Olympics, kashihonya proprietors simply closed up shop because everyone was inside watching the broadcast.[18]

Proprietors' research indicated that kashihonya saw a three-year dropoff in manga readership after 1960, exacerbated by the decision to stop stocking "manga with bad content" (naiyō no warui manga) after an early 1963 increase in book prices.[19] The Japan National Publishing Retailers Federation instituted a ban on members selling "harmful magazines" to minors in late 1963, but the committee that was empaneled to define "harmful magazines" couldn't come to a decision before its mandate expired. In the end, the association distributed posters declaring that "this store doesn't sell harmful magazines to minors" to each store, but left enforcement up to them.[20] Having rebuffed such extreme propositions as prohibiting children from entering kashihonya entirely, the remaining kashihonya eventually settled on a de facto strategy of low prices and "clean" content for their rental manga.[21] By that point, local ban bad books groups mostly focused on attempting to enforce age segregation in kashihon rentals.[22] As a result, kashihonya alienated their remaining customer base, who now had sufficient disposable income to obtain manga elsewhere and wanted the questionable content that parents' groups wanted to suppress.

A front-page article in the kashihon newspaper's February 1965 issue, voicing opposition to a volume of manga's price increasing to 330 yen, declared that it would hurt kashihonya and thus manga sales, but this claim was not borne out by reality.[23] Kashihonya proprietors were increasingly at odds with manga publishers, who responded to the TV threat by consolidating and moving to a publishing model in which manga magazines were published weekly, contained little or no non-manga content, and were not intended as durable consumer goods. Instead, they essentially became advertisements for the publishers' actually profitable product: tankōbon volumes of individual series. Magazines' increasing cheapness and tankōbon volumes' increasing prices harmed kashihonya in both ways; an April 1965 kashihonya newspaper analysis concluded that growing manga magazine sales actually hurt their business model because the manga in said magazines were being turned into TV, where kashihonya could not follow. Nonetheless, by the end of the year, the newspaper was publishing lists of books being adapted to TV and encouraging individual proprietors to put such titles on display in their stores.[24]

The air of desperation becomes increasingly palpable in 1966, which seems to have been a turning point for the industry as a whole; the January issue carried a column by the association's president going on at length about how "those without unity will be destroyed," a classic sign of an impending crack-up. Although manga publishers paid kashihonya's concerns a remarkable amount of lip service in these years—the National Manga Publisher Association's president and secretary signed an open letter about price increases of the "we're sorry you feel bad" variety that was printed on the kashihonya newspaper's front page in April 1965, and August 1966 carried a report from yet another roundtable between representatives of the kashihonya association and seven manga publishers—the kashihonya's insistence that manga publishers needed them was clearly no longer accurate.[25]

The remaining anti-manga activists had changed too. The "bad content" ban enabled kashihonya to make a kind of separate peace with many such local groups after 1963, and the kashihon newspaper began reprinting anti-manga articles from local newspapers—for example, an October 1964 *Asahi* article concluded that story manga was too influential, that too much action was dangerous for children, and that "cinematic-type" (eigatekina) motion was bad. The kashihon newspaper had previously published an article in April 1963, "Naiaku manga de jimetsu" (Self-destruction via bad content manga), which blamed the demise of yōnen (elementary schooler) magazines on population change, television and its emphasis on fast action, the rise of weekly magazines, and young mothers focusing on their children's education in the post-postwar era. Manga had evidently moved so firmly into the "fun" category that it could no longer be marketed to elementary school students as educational. The next issue contained a report from a subcommittee established by the national kashihon association to devise strategies for attracting "fujin" (women) customers, listing sixteen in all.[26]

Although kashihonya ultimately did themselves no favors, manga fan cultures were changing rapidly in this period, which also impacted kashihonya's bottom lines, and there was some attempt to keep abreast of the latest manga publishing developments, however difficult that may have been to square with the emphasis on "good" content. There was most likely a generational component to these changes; Yonezawa and Shikijō, both born in 1953, relied on kashihonya for their beloved shōnen magazines and the freebies that came with each issue, but for them, kashihon manga was something they read "if we had time after reading the monthly shōnen magazines."[27] Such concerns notwithstanding, ads for the alternative manga magazine *Garo* appeared in the kashihon newspaper from October 1964, reminding proprietors that the magazine's fourth issue would go on sale in November, along with more from its publisher, Seirindō. *Garo* both encapsulated and created many of the changes among manga fans that the dozen years after *Tetsuwan Atomu*'s debut witnessed, as reports about meetups between fans and creators organized by various bodies from the mid-1960s onward make clear.

One of the first meetup reports mentioning fans in the kashihonya newspaper is from an event organized by a women's group in January 1965, which more than one hundred people attended, including children and such notable creators as Tatsumi. The meetup was successful enough that another was planned for May. Almost two years later, in November 1966, it was reported that too many fans had attended another meetup, where it was only possible to get things signed but not to ask questions. Very few of the fans who attended were children, a clear sign of changing times.[28]

In another sign that mainstream manga was no longer wholly identified with the manga marketed to children, in a question-and-answer promoting the *Jungle emperor (Kimba the White Lion)* anime in autumn 1965, Tezuka bluntly criticized adults in Japan for being "too arbitrary" in that they read pornographic comics (eromanga) and "political manga" themselves but worried about children reading manga at all. Tezuka contrasted the situation in Japan with that in the United States, where according to him more than 90 percent of audiences reported liking *Astro Boy* and both adults and children read comics. He asked retailers not just to give kids manga but to read it themselves, in the belief that if adults actually understood manga's content, they would see that there was no harm in it.[29]

Increasing tensions between manga readers, manga creators, kashihonya proprietors, and education mothers were a recurring feature in the final seven years of the kashihon newspaper's publication. In July 1967 it contained a report on shōjo manga's increasingly mature content, which was a problem for kashihonya because they had counted on it not to be like increasingly violent shōnen manga. (A publisher's representative quoted in the article reiterated that shōnen manga was bought mostly by people high school age and older.) The article concluded by requesting regulations for manga content, which no one in the manga industry had any incentive to support.[30]

Mothers' groups, meanwhile, were softening their stance; by September 1967, the message from ban bad books types was that "manga is not bad, but we want to be careful about how kids read manga." Buoyed by publisher and reader support, however, creators responded along the lines of "well, if kids don't read manga at your house, they'll just read it at a friend's house," while mothers' groups were still asking kashihonya not to rent stuff that was too wild. They had also begun expressing concern about the increasingly common tankōbon of popular shōnen series running in mainstream magazines. Even temporary upticks in kashihon manga readership such as the 1968 yōkai boom were reported in the gloomiest manner possible—in that case yōkai manga, epitomized by Mizuki Shigeru's *Hakaba no Kitarō* (Graveyard Kitarō, 1965–69, renamed *Gegege no Kitarō* ahead of the anime adaptation's 1968 debut), were said to be not good for children and not pleasing to the education mama crowd.[31]

A different article from December 1966, reprinted from the *Nishinippon Shinbun*, sheds more light on why the ban bad books movement softened its stance. That article noted that banning all manga would be bad because nowadays children who didn't read manga were weird, as TV's advent had caused a manga boom and now everyone from pre-K to college read manga. Waving the white flag, the article argued that "the most important thing is to have a household that reads," even if children weren't reading literature. Rather than total proscription, mothers were advised to make sure their children weren't reading too much manga and encouraged them to talk to teachers, other parents, and kashihonya proprietors about content.[32] Manga had won through critics' opposition to begin taking its place as the pillar of popular culture in Japan that it remains today.

Movies took a hit from television's increasing popularity too, but movies ultimately survived TV, albeit in a much-diminished role.[33] Kashihonya did not, although the National United Kashihon Association continued publishing its newsletter until 1972. That was long enough for it to bear witness to kamishibai's final degradation as a going media form, when the few remaining kashihonya latched onto wild schemes of "increasing earnings with kamishibai" by hosting performances in stores. Articles promoting this strategy are illustrated with depressing photos of children watching kamishibai while sitting in chairs in kashihonya, a far cry from the riveting street performances of the medium's heydays in the 1930s and 1950s. Why kamishibai could save kashihonya when selling textbooks, playing cards, candy, *Playboy* magazine, and plushies hadn't was never clear, particularly since kamishibai was concurrently being used in schools for education.[34] In terms of social relations, visual techniques, and verbal storytelling style, kamishibai's true posterity could be seen on TV nightly in the form of anime.

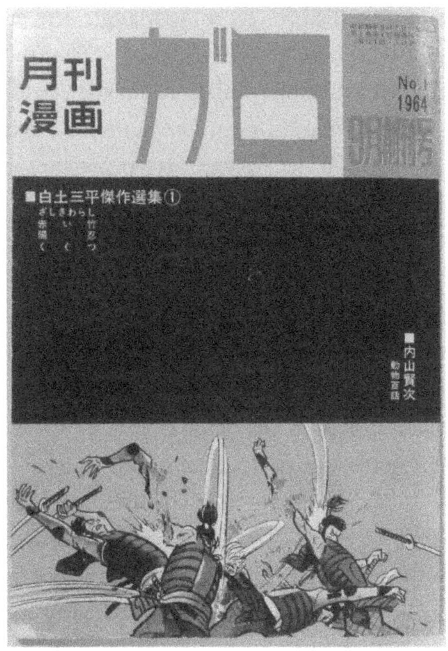

FIGURE 16. Cover of *Garo* no. 1 with art by Shirato Sanpei, September 1964.

GARO: THE WOODEN-MORTARED KINGDOM

One of the most famous magazines in manga history emerged from kashihonya's decline: the monthly magazine *Garo*, the first non-kashihon publication from Seirindō, launched in 1964 (figure 16). Editor Nagai Katsuichi had branched into kashihon publishing in 1956 with Nihon Mangasha, which published Shirato Sanpei's first ninja manga. Nagai and Shirato had the idea for a kashihon magazine in which manga creators could do what they pleased, and in 1962 they founded Seirindō together to do just that.[35] In its submissions guidelines, Shirato exhorted readers in 1965 to submit boldly: "One person's experiments inspire the experiments of others. Only in such experimentation and inspiration can there be growth. Think of *Garo* thus as a place, one without precedent in any other magazine, where you can boldly experiment however you wish."[36] *Garo* welcomed established creators, newcomers, and amateurs equally. But seeing kashihonya disappear from the back alleys and corners they had formerly occupied left Nagai extremely uneasy about their future, and he decided to publish *Garo* in the mainstream market.[37]

Garo was named for a character in one of Shirato's ninja manga, and its biggest hit was Shirato's masterpiece *Kamuyden* (*The Legend of Kamui*, 1964–71), which united his trademark ninja themes with the Marxist worldview he inherited from his father, the proletarian painter Okamoto Tōki (1903–86), who had even drawn a cover for *Tokyo Puck* in 1930 before being arrested and tortured by the thought police in 1932. In the 1960s, Shirato's star was in the ascendant, and his new manga was conceived as the draw for *Garo*. He also served as coeditor for the first few years, and took upon himself the equally thankless role of financial benefactor: He helped pay for the surgery to treat Nagai's chronic tuberculosis, saving Nagai's life; he worked for *Garo* for free until 1967; and he also waived the royalties earned on his other reprints published by Seirindō, keeping *Garo* and the company afloat.[38]

The issue in which *Kamuyden* debuted also contained an interesting foreword on "the appeal of the anti [nega]," written by the head of the Contemporary Children's Center's research office. The article was clearly a response to lingering anti-manga concerns, but it took the developmentalist tack of arguing, not that manga was not "bad," but that it was impossible for children to learn to appreciate life solely by looking on the bright (poji) side. Rather, the dark (nega) side was also necessary for children to develop a rational worldview. Conveniently, Shirato's manga helped with that process by exposing readers to a morally variegated world within its panels.[39] Ryan Holmberg has noted that Shirato explicitly intended *Kamuyden* to be used pedagogically; Shirato's leftist politics suffused the magazine and *Kamuyden*, with the result that, as Holmberg writes, "for the first year or so of its publication, *Garo* can be understood as an antiwar, pro-democracy political magazine for elementary and middle school children, intended as a corrective to their enclosure by conservative education policies."[40]

This was all quite far from ninja action, the reason that readers were ostensibly picking up *Garo* in the first place, and in the event, the magazine never found a readership with elementary and middle school children. For the first year, it hardly sold at all; Nagai and his wife were gradually hemmed in by returned magazines piling up in their house. Their first clue that *Garo* in general and *Kamuyden* in particular were becoming popular with college students (who were not the original kashihon audience) was when those same students started sending in criticism.[41] Even so, *Garo* was in the red until 1967, with many of its eight thousand copies returned each month. (Well into the 1970s, new issues of the magazine advertised back copies of earlier issues obtainable by writing directly to the publisher.) *Kamuyden* gradually lost the pedagogical angle, and the magazine eventually started turning a profit as its content changed to match its actual readership.[42] The magazine's page count and its cover price also increased, from 130 pages at first publication to 202 in April 1966, and from 130 yen to 150 yen, respectively.[43]

Nagai was unusual in the manga world in that he published only works that he actually liked and exercised discernment in his tastes: Almost everyone else operated by a philosophy of "whatever, as long as it sells."[44] *Garo* never lost its deliberate lack of polish; the editors didn't care about a creator's drawing skills or lack thereof (those could be learned by doing), as they were more interested in a distinctive art style and a story to match. Nagai viewed the magazine as a vehicle with two axles; one was *Kamuyden* and the other varied, but for a while it was Mizuki Shigeru, who first appeared in Nagai's kashihon ninja magazine in 1963, and who published frequently in *Garo* in the mid-1960s. Over time, newcomers who debuted in the magazine and other creators came to fill that role, including Tsuge Yoshiharu (b. 1937).[45]

Looking back, former *COM* deputy editor Akiyama Mitsuru wrote of *Garo* that "the atmosphere of anarchy was part of its charm."[46] Some people saw Tezuka's hand weighing heavily on *COM*, whereas at *Garo* everyone did their own thing, as Nagai acknowledged: "*Garo* was a professional magazine, but it had the semi-contradictory character of dōjinshi." But Seirindō couldn't pay pro magazine rates, and Nagai himself was too soft an editor: Because he couldn't pay well, he wasn't harsh enough on submissions.[47] Mizuki earned only 500 yen per page on *Garo* (he'd made 300 yen per page on the ninja magazine; one of Nagai's virtues as a publisher was that he tried to always pay cash, in full, in advance), which in his poverty at the time seemed like a princely sum, but Shirato's Seirindō page rate was 1,500 yen. Kodansha paid ten times as much as *Garo*, 5,000 yen per page, when Mizuki debuted there in the 1965 summer special issue of *Bessatsu Shōnen Magazine*.[48] Consequently, many *Garo* contributors took first or second jobs to get by. Tsuge was a longtime assistant at Mizuki Shigeru's Mizuki Pro, where Tsurita Kuniko (1947–85), the first woman published in *Garo* and one of its two regular female contributors in this period, worked for a month in 1968 before quitting.[49] She had already worked for a year as a freelance in-betweener at Tōei Animation, where *Garo* contributor Hayashi Sei'ichi (b. 1945) worked full-time until leaving to cofound an animation studio in 1967.[50]

Garo quickly became famous as a haven for "alternative" manga, where creators could give their inspiration free rein. Consequently, the magazine was often described in retrospect as having what critic Ueno Kōshi called a "free dōjinshi atmosphere . . . but this was also half-bakedness and indifference."[51] Significantly, *Garo* offered a new publication venue for gekiga creators like Tatsumi, who regularly published in the magazine during its first decade. It also provided a haven for kashihon manga creators who were unable or unwilling to shift to mainstream magazines as the kashihon manga market fell out from under them. By this time, kashihon manga had essentially fused with gekiga, and *Garo* giving kashihon refugees a platform gradually popularized gekiga among manga's burgeoning college readership; the magazine was also beloved in the "angura" (underground) theater movement in Tokyo and in the anime industry in these years.[52] "Comics were firmly part of mass culture and the counterculture both," Holmberg summarizes, "and were a presence in important sectors of the contemporary art world and cultural theory too."[53] Although *COM* and *Garo* remained "enthusiast" (mania) magazines, in Takeuchi Osamu's phrase, *Garo* and other magazines like *Shōnen Magazine* facilitated gekiga being absorbed by the mainstream magazines through creators like Mizuki, and thus the gekiga boom that reached its apex after this assimilation.[54]

Because it placed no limits on creative expression, the alternative manga that *Garo* published was alternative in terms of both story (or lack thereof) and art styles. It quickly established a reputation as a publication for "art" manga, and *Garo*, along with *COM* after 1967, popularized a changing style of panels and images, one that employed panel layouts more like montages. Mangaka Kusunoki Shōhei (1944–74), Shirato's assistant, stated of this visual style: "There is a relation of space and time in the space between the panels, and the expression (hyōgen) [of panels and images] is what separates them from sashie (illustrations) and kamishibai." In other words, the visual style these magazines promoted was that of contemporary manga, and its growing popularity spelled the end of the line for the older, more cartoonish children's manga style.[55] Not coincidentally, this popularization was enabled by *Garo*'s audience of mostly college-age young men: Older and more affluent than child readers, their tastes increasingly constituted the manga vanguard.

That being said, as critic Ono Kōsei points out, positing a straightforward comparison between *Garo* and the "underground comix" movement in the United States around this time is misleading; *Garo* was not "Japanese underground comics," because it was professionally published and had an established position within the Japanese manga industry, as can be seen by how readily creators like Shirato and Mizuki moved between *Garo* and the mainstream magazines.[56] (However, Mizuki did consciously try to adapt more rounded lines as he moved away from kashihon manga and toward the mainstream magazines, to fit in better with their prevailing art style.)[57] For Ono, the son of mangaka Ono Saseo, *Garo* manga's true impact was in its extremely personal viewpoint, a characteristic that explains the frequent invocations of dōjinshi. That viewpoint could be expressed in a variety of ways, as when Ono first read avant-garde manga by Sasaki Maki (b. 1946) in *Garo* and "felt like I was listening to jazz."[58]

The jazz/manga comparison had been made before, during gekiga's first bloom. The fact that *Garo* became a byword for alternative manga in Japan undersells the degree to which its politics were *alternative*, not so much in the sense of "progressive" but in the sense of "anti" and of nostalgia: Although *Garo* manga has sometimes been characterized as avant-garde, its creators' politics were much more likely to be nostalgic and populist, rooted in the 1950s atmosphere that many of *Garo*'s former kashihon creators had come up in. In a word, in Holmberg's summary, "Modernism and progressivism was the exception in Garo. Populism, revivalism, and nostalgia was the rule."[59] With the notable exception of Tsurita, *Garo* creators and staff were also deeply anti-intellectual, a trait they shared with the manga mainstream: Creators ranging from Kondō Hidezō to Tezuka Osamu dismissed experimental manga in print, for reasons ranging from the art being bad and meaningless (Kondō) to Sasaki Maki's work appealing too much to art critics and intellectuals (Tezuka)—unlike other manga, which was part of mass culture and not a waste of regular people's time.[60] Mangaka across the industry saw themselves not as fine artists (geijutsuka) but as working craftspeople who had to produce regularly to eat, a transformation that was also occurring in animation.[61] Ironically, while *Garo* manga obtained the art world and elite culture approval that mangaka in the prewar era had craved, by the time it did so, the manga world had moved on.

One thing that many *Garo* manga and American comix shared was a deep and unquestioned vein of misogyny. Ueno compares *Garo*'s innovations in manga expression to Pop art and the Beatles, which speaks volumes, given how women fared in Andy Warhol's Factory and how Yoko Ono was roundly blamed for breaking up the Beatles even as her artistic career was repeatedly sidelined in favor of John Lennon's.[62] Eromanga scholar Nagayama Kaoru noted that gekiga creators couldn't draw women attractively, a telling sign.[63] Works by popular creators such as Tsuge Yoshiharu routinely featured gender-based violence directed at female characters; in this respect, *Garo* was thoroughly conventional, as that same violence against female characters spread to manga aimed at boys and men after seinen manga's emergence.

Significantly, however, *Garo* and *COM* did not gender their readerships, which left room for female readers and creators looking for alternatives.[64] Although she faced sexism from Seirindō staff and other contributors, the works of Tsurita Kuniko, who debuted in *Garo* in 1965 when she was still a high schooler in Hyōgo prefecture and who also published kashihon manga before its demise, were later described in glowing terms as not being within "the frame of future shōjo manga" because her manga pioneered a new combination of SF and nonsense.[65] She had submitted gekiga shorts multiple times to the kashihon anthology *Machi*'s contests while still in middle school, and had even written a letter to the editors asking why she had never ranked above fourth; the published reply, presumably written by Tatsumi, advised her to draw manga about girls instead.[66] Naka Keiko (1945–2010), *Garo*'s other regular female contributor in these years, won the magazine's newcomer prize in 1968.[67] Yamada Murasaki (1948–2009), a pioneering female mangaka who avoided most mainstream publications, debuted in *COM* in 1969 and published in *Garo* in 1971; Nagai later praised her work as a forerunner of josei (women's) manga, showing what women really wanted outside the prevailing genre norms of the time.[68]

But these women were the exception that proved the rule, and even if the editors would accept female contributors, the magazine's overall vibe in this era remained sexist and male dominated. Invited to comment on the magazine's impact for its twentieth anniversary, Hagio Moto wrote that she didn't know anything about *Garo:* She had once picked up a few issues in a used bookstore and tried to read *Kamuyden*, but found it was too difficult, which was the answer she got when she asked her friends about *Garo*, too. Takemiya Keiko was more tactful; she affirmed that the magazine had an impact on both artists and readers, and wrote that she read it in that spirit, though when she joined the other side—that is, became a professional mangaka—she gradually stopped.[69] Yamada was a fan of Shirato's ninja manga, but she later admitted that she submitted first to *COM* rather than *Garo* for a reason: "[*Garo*] was filled with men, most of whom were older than me." Compared to *COM*'s "openness and foresight," in Holmberg's phrase, *Garo* remained mired in the sexism that pervaded the Japanese counterculture and student movement in this era.[70]

"Honestly," Nagai wrote in 1987, "I've thought of quitting *Garo* many times."[71] But like the surviving ex-Beatles, *Garo* lasted into the twenty-first century: Its final issue was published in 2002, more than eleven years after Nagai sold Seirindō to a games company and nearly six years after his death. The magazine had nearly folded after *Kamuyden* ended; its circulation reached eighty thousand copies in 1968 but fell off rapidly thereafter. Books, not *Garo*, kept Seirindō in business from then on: *Garo* kept the alternative comics flame burning, and gradually shed its sexist atmosphere by the 1980s, but it never again reached the same height of popularity. Many of its creators moved into such varied careers as illustration, picture books, folk music, and even founding the secondhand subculture goods chain Mandarake—Furukawa Masuzō (b. 1950) had debuted in *Garo* in 1969 after garnering praise in a *COM* feature the year before.[72]

COM: LIKE A PHOENIX

Although *Garo* has been retroactively enshrined as a magazine read by those in the know, it was *COM* that bore a cover tagline declaring it "a specialist manga magazine for the manga elite" when it debuted in January 1967. Then a high schooler, Natsume Fusanosuke bought *COM* because he thought "a stimulating magazine has appeared," but he admitted that it was unclear whom *COM* was for, and he wondered what "manga elite" meant and where they were.[73]

In his inaugural editor's note, Tezuka linked the name with three separate concepts: *com*ics, *com*panion, and *com*munication, declaring that *COM* was "a new comic magazine that would communicate mangaka's true heart to those companions who love manga." He continued:

> We are told that this is now a golden age of manga, but were that the case, wouldn't we expect that many qualitatively great works are being published? Isn't it actually the case that most mangaka are being worked to death while compromising, complying with, and yielding before the requirements of strict commercialism?
>
> I want to prove through this magazine what sort of thing the real kind of story manga is. At the same time, like the old *Manga Shōnen*, *COM*, which we're thinking will play the part of welcoming newcomers, will be a magazine for companions who love manga.[74]

Mentioning *Manga Shōnen*, long gone but evidently not forgotten, was significant. Masaki Mori (b. 1941), *COM*'s amateur submissions editor, later pointed out that the only other venues besides *Manga Shōnen* to accept amateur submissions in the postwar years until *COM* and *Garo* were kashihon anthologies like *Machi*. For Tezuka, the amateur submissions were connected to the interrupted serialization of his masterwork *Hi no tori*, which had first been published in *Manga Shōnen*, and he explicitly wanted to bring back the amateur submissions along with restarting the manga's serialization.[75]

Critics (many of whom came of age in this period) have deemed the four years that *Garo* and *COM* were both in print the "united front years," and the two magazines had a lot in common: *Garo*'s influence is clear from *COM*'s first pages. Some of the visual similarities with *Garo* are explained by the fact that the amateur submissions Masaki selected were in line with Tatsumi's picks while he was working on *Machi* and others, which at the time were unusual and different.[76] By the late 1960s, they were also distinctly retro and in line with *Garo*'s nostalgia; as kashihon manga circled the drain, both magazines provided an important new forum for amateurs who had previously submitted to contests in kashihon anthologies like *Machi*.[77] Natsume later wrote that reading *COM* and *Garo* together felt like a revolutionary age had come to manga: A new expression was being born, and manga could really do anything.[78] For Ueno, what made the united front years "so great as to seem like a lie looking back" was that everyone working in the magazines was developing their own style individually, interpreting the age through the medium of themselves.[79]

In the same roundtable, *COM*'s first editor Noguchi Isao (b. 1944) volunteered that the explicit idea was for *COM* to be like *Garo* but cheaper, because Mushi Productions couldn't afford multiple freebies like the monthly shōnen magazines. Nor was it a coincidence that *COM* debuted the year that the *Tetsuwan Atomu* anime ended: Mushi Pro was no longer occupied with producing the Astro Boy fan club magazine. According to Akiyama, *COM* went from planning to production in only two months, which was way too fast, and from the start Tezuka overpromised and underdelivered (as usual), which fostered dissent among the editorial department.[80] For his part, Tezuka called the first issue "dirty" (kitanai) and told Noguchi to fix it—he wanted "pure manga" like the old *Manga Shōnen*.[81] His conservative views on avant-garde manga continued to cause problems; at one point Ishinomori pulled his dreamlike, impressionistic *Jun* (1967–71) after hearing from a fan that Tezuka had said it "wasn't manga," to the editors' despair. Ishinomori relented only after Tezuka came to his house and apologized personally.[82]

Ultimately *COM* mimicked the titular phoenix of Tezuka's manga, as Masaki acknowledged when he recounted that, although the magazine's editorial philosophy was to be adventurous rather than commercial, they may have gotten a bit more adventure than they bargained for. Hagiwara Daisuke echoed the general judgment that while Tezuka was a genius creator, he was a failure as a businessperson, and that essential problem was at the heart of *COM*'s flatlining fortunes. Along with visionary ideas for the future of manga, the magazine was marked by a total inability to judge market conditions. Aimed at a high school readership, the initial print run of one hundred thousand copies was the same as those of *Shōnen Magazine* and other big monthlies, which was wildly optimistic; even at its most popular, *Garo* never sold more than eighty thousand copies per month, which was also *COM*'s peak circulation.[83] Ironically, it wasn't Tezuka's *Phoenix* that made its name; instead, Ishinomori's *Jun*, which won the Shogakukan Manga Prize in its debut year, was the primary draw, along with Nagashima Shinji's series of one-shots *Seishun zankoku monogatari* (Harsh story of youth, 1967–68), a follow-up to his earlier kashihon hit *Mangaka zankoku monogatari* (Harsh story of a mangaka, 1961–64), and the amateurs' section, called "Gura-Com."[84] Amid general dysfunction, short staffing and overwork, and staff upheavals, *COM* folded at the end of 1971.[85]

The magazine was meant to change, or at least counter, anti-manga attitudes that had prevailed in the 1950s and were still current in the 1960s: In the face of anti-manga activism, manga book burnings, and the national school policy to throw away any manga that kids brought to school on sight, *COM* was partly founded with the idea of making an affirmative statement about manga, and enabling people who liked manga to connect with one another.[86] The other way to interpret *COM* as populist is to consider that Tezuka's ambitions for the magazine included not only creating a forum for amateurs, but also building a nationwide organization for dōjinshi—broadly, amateur manga—based on *COM* and running said organization out of the editorial department.

This fan club ambition proved epochal, although not in the way that Tezuka originally envisioned. In the late 1960s, local fan networks were rudimentary at best and were largely created via exchanging postcards and letters through the mail, as phone calls were still quite expensive.[87] But amateur manga production had been stoked outside kashihon anthologies by fan club newsletters, starting with the *Tetsuwan Atomu* fan club in 1963, and continued by fan clubs centered on individual creators such as Akatsuka Fujio, Kaizuka Hiroshi (1938–2023), Tatsumi, and others. By making the nationwide presence of manga fans and amateur creators visible to everyone who read the magazine, *COM* provided a crucial impetus and mechanism by which local fans could connect with each other and organize local and regional groups and meet-ups.[88] But this success also laid the groundwork for the magazine's own failure: The number of places people could share their work increased rapidly thanks to *COM*, as manga fans began forming "circles" (groups of amateur creators) and creating mechanisms to distribute their dōjinshi—essentially, manga zines—among interested parties.[89] As these groups and mechanisms mushroomed, their increasing numbers decreased the need for *COM* to act as either an organizational or publishing clearinghouse, and they surpassed *COM* in their ambitions.[90]

Another aspect of the magazine's "successful failure" was that it came to feel more and more like a dōjinshi itself as time went on, and even professional creators felt like they were writing their own dōjinshi with their contributions.[91] This also made the magazine approachable. "Because everyone's work was published as-is," Yamada recalled, "I think it was easy for readers to relate to the magazine."[92] The amateur submissions contests were also seen, in retrospect, to have effectively been dōjinshi contests; unlike *Manga Shōnen* or *Machi*, the *COM* contests happened in a context where fan networks and groups were becoming increasingly widespread. It was now possible for winning creators to share their work with other manga fans through other means than attempting to turn pro. To be sure, fans' geographic reach was still limited, but *COM* was unquestionably trending toward presenting manga that was seen as different from mainstream, professionally published manga in meaningful ways.

COM was more welcoming to women than *Garo;* significant female creators such as Takemiya, Yamada, and Okada Fumiko (1949–2005) debuted there, and the magazine published dozens of other women. *Garo* rejected Okada before *COM* accepted her work, which inspired both Hagio and Yamada to submit to *COM* themselves; Okada's work also inspired Yamada to pursue manga rather than prose in the first place. Though the two-volume anthology *Garo and COM: The United Front Years* features only three women total—Tsurita, Okada, and Yashiro Masako (b. 1947), who had started in kashihon a few years earlier and became *COM*'s second most frequent contributor after Tezuka—*COM*'s readership was estimated to be 20–30 percent female. Tezuka Productions launched the short-lived magazine *Funny* (1969–70, 1973) to expand on this female readership and provide a forum for women artists, including Takemiya and Yamada; although categorized as shōjo at the time, it is sometimes regarded as a precursor to josei manga. Yamada later recalled that *COM* was "filled with all sorts of amateurs. At a glance, it just seemed easier to slide into that scene."[93] If, as Noguchi asserted in 2009, "*COM* and *Garo* were a bridge to a new era in an age of darkness," *COM* better fulfilled its ambition of "welcoming newcomers."[94]

But the *COM* slush pile was not immune to the reality of publishing the world over, which is that most of it was crap with terrible art and bad stories. The magazine published almost all of the decent submissions it received, because genuinely quality material was scarce. At a rate of two to three hundred per month, the amateur submissions required a punitive amount of labor, as the editorial staff had to look at all of them, divide them by genre, assign prizes, and provide feedback, among other tasks.[95] Yamada found that *COM* editors didn't really provide much feedback after people graduated from the amateur contests to actual contributors, likely partly due to the editors' huge workload. This deficit drove Yamada to eventually submit to *Garo* in 1971, though she waited more than a year out of loyalty to *COM* and her editor Akiyama, and kept it secret from him, as he and the other editors generally pleaded with contributors not to "feed the competition" (i.e., *Garo*).[96]

Thus, the real challenge that *COM* threw down to the established manga industry was, as Yonezawa Yoshihiro later wrote, to touch off what he termed the dōjin third wave (the first was in the 1930s with *Manga no Kuni* and the embrace of amateurs, the second in the 1950s with kashihon gekiga anthologies): By the time *COM* folded, the fan networks it had nurtured were strong enough that they didn't need another magazine to foster them.[97] That third wave is still going strong.

GRAND COMPANIONS

The "Gura-Com" section was the locus of these events. Although it comprised a very small percentage of each issue, it was in many ways the primary driver of *COM*'s enduring interest. (That Akiyama mentions the section only to complain about the workload it imposed is symptomatic of the disconnect between Tezuka's, the editorial staff's, and the fans' visions of the magazine.) The Kitakyushu manga group AS explained the name thusly in their 2016 anniversary volume: *Gura-Com* was derived from the Japanese transliteration of *Grand Companion*, which dated back to the Tokiwa-sō and the Japan

Children's Manga Research Group, and referred to an interregional network of amateur groups with the grand ambition to join everyone into one common enterprise.[98]

COM first promoted fan organization via the letters section in the second issue, when a middle schooler from Kobe put out a call to form a research club (kenkyūkai) via mail, giving his contact information.[99] The "Gura-Com" section debuted in the third issue, at which point the readers' letters section was renamed the "Gura Com Lobby"; in its initial appearance, "Gura-Com" outlined the skeleton of a national organization of fan groups for those who "love manga," "live manga," "weep at manga," and so on. The explicit call was to gather "kindred spirits" (dōshi) into a group with a new structure joining publishers, readers, mangaka, critics, and would-be mangaka, because, the editors reasoned, if everyone in those categories were individual and separate, they were weak, but uniting them would change that: It would strengthen manga and would make those individuals manga masters (mangashi). Significantly, the term *manga* (now written with hiragana rather than characters) explicitly included otona manga, gekiga, jidō (children's) manga, and animation, a fairly large tent and a far cry from the atomized understanding of manga promoted by the gekiga crowd just a decade previously.[100]

The *COM* editorial department acted as a clearinghouse for fan groups in the eight regions into which they divided the country. *COM* appointed a regional head for each group, giving them explicit mandates to create newsletters or dōjinshi about their groups' activities and to organize exhibitions of members' works and other such events, including film screenings.[101] While these regional heads had local control, the overall organization's management was centralized; each section chief (or perhaps "cell leader") was supposed to make contact with the *COM* headquarters in Tokyo once a month and to send their group's publications to Tokyo at least four times per year. They were also obliged to send lists of their members to headquarters and to choose officers for their group, who served for two-year terms. Finally, they were also supposed to forward the works of promising creators in their groups to Tokyo. In contrast to earlier magazine fan clubs or manga groups, there was explicitly no membership fee to join any of these groups, whose contact information was published in the magazine.[102]

The ways in which *COM* directly and indirectly fostered the growth of circles and manga groups in the rest of the country are illustrated by the experience of AS, now the second oldest such group in Japan, which was founded in Kitakyushu in 1966. The group began in a middle school art club, and all of its founders explicitly wanted to get better at drawing together, though not all of them had thoughts of turning pro. (Indeed, in 2016 the group placed particular emphasis on the fact that its members' explicit goal has never been about becoming professionals.) The two founders, both second-year middle school students (giving new meaning to the term *chūnibyō*), found the art club intimidating, so they decided to start a group that focused purely on manga, where lack of formal art knowledge and/or training wouldn't be an issue. They rounded up four classmates who also wanted to draw and liked manga: As the group put it fifty years later, that emotion was all they needed.[103]

AS (the name was a Japanese transliteration of the English word, meant to convey the senses of "alike," "equal," and "with") started modestly, with a wall newspaper (kabe shinbun, an oversize one-sheet format) consisting of one- and four-panel comics. By chance, the first issue of *COM* came out just as AS's kabe shinbun did, and by their own admission, thereafter their publications blatantly imitated the magazine. Nor was this simply admiration: The 1960s were a decade of real information poverty generally. There were only three "how to draw manga" books in print at that time, and the methods illustrated therein hadn't changed at all since the 1950s, if not earlier. In these circumstances, everyone learned by copying manga they liked, but then and now, it was far easier to sustain fannish enthusiasm when it was shared among like-minded individuals than it was to do so on one's own—hence the impetus to start the group in the first place. Thus, copying *COM*'s publication style in their own materials was not only a standard practice but also a tribute to the freshness of the magazine's content.[104] *COM*'s habit of publishing essays on various aspects of how to draw manga was also quite helpful.

COM played a direct role in sustaining AS in 1970, by which time the group's founding members had all gone to different high schools and it was in danger of folding. Just when all seemed lost, however, *COM*'s October issue featured AS's dōjinshi in the "Gura-Com" section, which published not only approving comments and constructive criticism of the dōjinshi in question but also the group's contact information. AS received a sudden influx of new members after being featured in *COM*, increasing the group to fifteen people, only one of whom was an original member. This influx of people who were not bound by a contingent connection (as the founders had been by attending the same middle school) enabled the group to survive and to flourish to 2025 and beyond.[105]

The fan groups that *COM* fostered were not just "circles," in the sense of groups focused on creating and distributing amateur manga. Instead, as Yonezawa and his fellows repeatedly emphasized, *COM* "brought forth a new age" and also inspired a number of "research groups" (kenkyūkai) focused on manga criticism. Neither circles nor research groups were new in manga history; their origins stretched back more than half a century to 1915, when leading Tokyo mangaka had founded an industry group of their own. But the difference in 1971 when *COM* folded was that these groups no longer consisted solely or even primarily of professional creators, as the short-lived "gekigakkai" groups of the 1950s or even the Japan Children's Manga Research Group had. With the advent of Xerox machines, it was now much easier for groups to maintain their cohesion at the local level, and the community found a new structure after *COM*'s demise.[106]

After *COM* folded, the short-lived *COM Comics* attempted to continue *COM*'s manga content without the laborious "Gura-Com" section. This decision only heightened discontent among fan groups: AS bluntly recounts that the decision to create their own manga show and zine, "Hachi no ki," was taken out of dissatisfaction with *COM Comics'* lack of the "Gura-Com" section.[107] The last head of the Gura-Com Kansai group, Nakashima Takashi, recalled that group members saw "Gura-Com" being axed as a great insult, and when faced with a choice between endorsing their own destruction or prolonging its existence, he and some of his comrades chose the latter, first through producing a manga book called *Mangajuman* (1972), which Nakashima called a place for the diehards, and then *Apple Core* (1972–75), "a Gura-Com book," which was more of a dōjinshi and which declared in its first issue, "We can't think that Gura-Com's existence was meaningless." Although Nakashima was from Kansai, he spent most of his time in Tokyo during *Apple Core*'s run (four issues were produced by spring 1975). Its more than forty volunteers operating under the name "Gura-Com Nihon" came from throughout the country, and it featured both amateurs and professional creators such as Yamada Murasaki in its pages.[108]

Apple Core has been called the "missing link" between "Gura-Com" and Comiket, preserving the will for the existence of "Gura-Com" or something like it until the Comiket iconoclasts came along and transformed the manga fandom scene, leaving the last traces of *COM* behind. As one of Nakashima's acquaintances who was involved with Comiket's foundation put it, they were "bidding farewell to *COM* and Gura-Com and creating a new field for manga and fans."[109] National gatherings like Comiket and its predecessor the Nihon

Manga Taikai, inevitably held in Tokyo, were the most prominent fan events after *COM*'s demise, but the infrastructure nationwide was such that groups could now operate independently, as AS did with its local exhibitions and zine activities and still does: Local and regional manga events were also part of *COM*'s legacy.[110]

Where were the manga elite? Everywhere.

THE LIKE-MINDED: DŌJINSHI, KIKANSHI, ZINES

For those familiar with zine and fan cultures elsewhere, the concept of dōjinshi is not too much of a leap. The term itself stretches back to the 1910s and 1920s in Japan, when it is generally translated as "coterie magazine(s)," referring to privately printed material that literary circles created and circulated among themselves. There is some evidence that this concept bled into manga in the 1930s, which had some overlap with those same literary circles; the magazine *Manga no Kuni* is sometimes described as a dōjinshi for its focus on amateur production and converting would-be manga artists into manga professionals.[111] *Manga no Kuni* was particularly notable for publishing amateur manga submissions, along with a recurring feature that evaluated each of the submissions published in that issue, and there are hints in surviving copies that it was part of a larger movement; a January 1938 article described "dōjin magazines" (dōjin zasshi) for readers. Like *Manga no Kuni*, these were presumably wiped out by the war's escalation. By the time the editorial department at Mushi Productions was press-ganged into running a nationwide manga fan organization out of their understaffed offices in 1967, the terms of the discourse had shifted. Although *COM* eventually used the term *dōjinshi* almost exclusively to denote these sorts of amateur publications, it was initially used interchangeably with "kikanshi" (bulletins).

The dōjinshi feature, in which the editors highlighted a dōjinshi that they liked each month, is a fascinating window into how standards evolved and spread among Japanese manga fans via the magazine. Headlined "Dōjin," the feature explicitly described the contents, size, and production values of each dōjinshi before offering constructive criticism. In one example, the editors wrote that "for manga, having the spirit of fun is necessary," and admonished the leadership of the circle in question not to let only the best or most active members in the group dominate the contents of its kikanshi.[112] No justification was offered for how the editorial staff of *COM* knew what made the best dōjinshi, or whether anyone involved with the magazine had any previous involvement in manga circles or other relevant activities, although Masaki, the section editor, had previously submitted to the kashihon anthology *Machi*.[113] Nonetheless, AS members' testimony makes clear that these pronouncements from Ikebukuro were taken very seriously by *COM*'s readers.

On one level, it was almost overdetermined that the term *dōjinshi* would be resurrected from its prewar heyday and used to discuss fan publications in this era, as the self-focus that marked literary production in the era of the shishōsetsu—the "I-novel," a mode of Japanese literature that is ineluctably linked to modern, and particularly Taishō, Japan—recurred in the manga world in the 1960s. One recurring description of *Garo* manga is that it was "practically like an I-novel," denoting an intensely personal approach to storytelling that was new in manga at the time. *Garo* creators did not precisely invent this mode; it had important antecedents in the gekiga crowd's self-promotion, but the transition away from the (melo)dramatic noir narratives common in kashihon manga was accompanied by a distinct turn to introspection in those mangaka who moved from kashihon manga to *Garo* and the alternative comics it promoted. The works of Tatsumi Yoshihiro, whose manga grew steadily more personal over time, are an apt indication of this evolution. Tsuge Yoshiharu, Nagashima Shinji (1937–2005, a former Tezuka assistant), Takita Yū (1931–90, a former Tagawa assistant who debuted in *Manga Shōnen*), and other creators mastered both self-expression and "I-expression" in their work, with the result that magazines that published their "I-manga" in this era became essentially "dōjinshi literature," in Natsume's phrase.[114]

The use of the term *dōjinshi* speaks to the general validation of highly individualized perspectives which is characteristic of the I-novel, both in literature and in manga, and provides some context for the rise of the term *circle* (sākuru) to denote the groups that produce them in manga fan cultures. A circle, after all, is a nonhierarchical organization (think of King Arthur's Round Table), and the circles that produced dōjinshi were intended to be exactly that, which was why the *COM* editors chastised a featured dōjinshi for focusing too much on quality standards to the detriment of general participation. By *COM*'s twelfth issue, the slogan of the "Gura-Com" section was to "gather friends who love and live manga," without regard to the quality of one's fannish output.[115]

Valuing individual perspectives in dōjinshi went hand in hand with valuing egalitarian participation: If the most important thing was not quality per se, but expressing the self, expanding participation to all of a circle's members meant a greater quantity of self-expression. Literary scholar Edward Fowler's description of the dōjin magazines of the Taishō era matches the dōjinshi scene of the 1960s and 1970s almost eerily well: These "coterie magazines," as he translates them, "catered to a small and homogeneous audience. Unlike contemporary [literary] coterie magazines, which often have a nationwide membership, the Taishō magazines were very exclusive and their memberships defined by mutual acquaintance and common purpose, a fact that resulted both in fast friendships and bitter infighting."[116] These features and pitfalls characterize fandom and fan production across language and culture, from dōjinshi to fanfiction and beyond.

Significantly, *COM* matched gekiga's self-promotion by treating professional mangaka as celebrities. These breathless gossip reports about leading creators' lives—Tezuka-sensei is vacationing at Shirahama! Akatsuka-sensei went to Arima onsen!—seem somewhat anomalous from the vantage of the present day, when most manga creators are notoriously reticent about their personal lives and even their images being made public. At the time, however, they served a different purpose: Along with other information that appeared in the magazine, such as publication schedules for manga tankōbon and broadcast schedules for TV anime (and giddy reports about what anime had been licensed where abroad), *COM* was trying to create a community, a feeling that all who considered themselves part of the "manga elite" to which the magazine was pitched were part of this world and, as such, were entitled to be in the know about these things and these people.[117]

The validation of people who were "just" fans and the fannish production that *COM* provided gave a renewed push to fan creation nationwide and encouraged manga fans everywhere to publish their own dōjinshi, regardless of considerations such as quality or originality: The *COM* editors' repeated declaration that excluding people and their work on the basis of those criteria was contrary to the spirit of manga was a direct invitation to continue, full speed ahead. Manga groups and dōjinshi circles' proliferation also decoupled the goal of becoming a professional creator from these practices of amateur production; as AS repeatedly insisted, their activities were about their love of manga (and, implicitly, their own personal satisfaction) rather than about trying to convert that love into a paying career, as had been the focus of manga groups in the 1930s, for example. By the time of *COM*'s demise, making and exchanging dōjinshi—usually for money, to defray production costs if not to make a profit—had become increasingly understood in the manga world as a valid activity in and of itself. Equally significantly (and unlike many fan activities in English-language settings) it was understood by almost everyone as constituting not a threat, but rather a complement, to professional production.

SUBCULTURE MASUKOMII BLUES

With this upwelling of activity in the manga world in the late 1960s, it is striking to read publications from the time frequently and explicitly wondering whether manga was over. To be sure, manga was now a mature professional field: The first manga prizes were founded in this era, starting with the Shogakukan Manga Prize in 1955. The Japan Cartoonists Association formed in 1964 with the explicit goal of providing a mechanism for mangaka of all stripes to deal with problems they all faced: Additional health insurance, life insurance, and other mundane but important concerns were easier to handle if they were unified. Now a nonprofit organization, the group began awarding its own manga prize in 1972.[118]

Despite these developments, the years that saw the birth of seinen and the first stirrings of the shōjo and the fan revolutions were marked by the recurring lament, as one letter to *COM* put it in May 1967, that many current manga had "yielded to commercialism, closing the door on artistry and thoughtfulness." *COM* letters were a reliable source for these anxieties; another connected manga whose only concern was sales with the burgeoning popularity of manga in mass media and with "manga eiga (manga movies) that cannot be said to move" on TV (i.e., anime), and wondered explicitly whether this was the end of manga—only to conclude that the answer was no, because there was still at least one magazine for people who loved manga (i.e., *COM*). Another letter from May 1967 invited comparisons with the student movement at the time by opining that the most important thing for manga as a genre was the spirit of comparing and criticizing reality and justice; and wasn't that the spirit of rebellion?[119]

This was neither the first nor the last moment in manga's history when people thought it was finished; just a few years earlier, the kashihonya newspaper had been downright gloomy about manga's long-term prospects: An article in October 1963 fretted that "recently there have been no masterpieces from the front-rank manga publishers, and it really seems that the manga world is in a discouraging place in terms of its future."[120] For manga fans at the end of the decade, the harbinger of these fears was anime.

Tetsuwan Atomu's wild success—as the fan club magazine proudly trumpeted, it had even been syndicated in the United States—inspired imitation, and many popular manga creators followed Tezuka's lead into the animation industry, either founding studios themselves or working with established companies to create animation based on their works. Perhaps the most successful was Tezuka's protege Ishinomori Shōtarō, who became the father of the tokusatsu superhero genre in the 1970s. (Ironically, Ishinomori had worked for a month as an animator at Tōei in 1959, but quit because he couldn't hack the salaryman lifestyle and hated drawing the same thing over and over.)[121] There was a general stampede to license popular manga for "TV manga," and these TV shows swiftly led to upticks in sales of the associated manga and merchandise based on the anime. Like Mizuki Shigeru, most creators presumably thought only of the increased income that a weekly TV show would bring, and did not even dream of greater success.[122] But like Ishinomori and Mizuki, many undoubtedly found it.

But there were only so many proven hit manga to adapt, and the costs associated with anime production were still high and fixed. Consequently, mainstream manga (which is to say, shōnen; shōjo manga was still largely locked into the short-story paradigm, which took nearly a decade to fully slough off) published in the latter half of the decade were increasingly consciously aimed toward TV adaptation, with the result that they were not very innovative in terms of either visuals or storytelling. Compounding the problem, toy companies—again following in the wake of *Astro Boy*, whose licensing into character toys had almost single-handedly reinvented the domestic market for buriki (metal) toys beginning in 1963—were increasingly likely to be major subsidizers of anime shows, and they wanted to bankroll anime whose toy-selling power could be banked upon, meaning that they tended to fund new shows that were similar to prior shows that had already done well. The number of anime produced each year grew from three in 1963 (all science fiction) to forty-five in 1981 and kept climbing thereafter.[123]

Another way that people characterized manga's current problems was simply as "masukomii" (mass communications), a very Sixties description. This simplistic formulation was a common response in the "Monthly Manga Roundtable" in *COM*'s fourth issue, which tackled the problem with manga in the age of its greatest social reach theretofore; as convener Ozaki Hotsuki remarked, "it's not at all mysterious today that college students read 'manga' along with Marx and Sartre."[124] These college students were part of the "clump" (dankai) or baby boomer generation, and two factors specific to their generation enabled them to keep consuming manga past high school: The new construction of adolescence in society as a separate phase of life, and the fact that an increasing number of people put off joining the workforce by going to college.[125]

The mixture of (male) experts and college students that Ozaki convened harped on familiar themes: The manga boom of the mid-1960s has raised manga's social profile but vitiated its literary value, children's manga is dead, and manga today is just stupid. Specifically, as participants remarked, compared to the manga they had read in elementary school—before the collapse of children's manga had created the rigid, gendered categories of shōnen and shōjo—when each creator used to create their own original world, there was now much more herding, and originality was decreasing. Ozaki observed that the complaints about mass communications and its concomitant lack of originality were partly an implicit protest against the pervasiveness of assistants, who were necessary to meet contemporary publication schedules. In response to his observation that the new distributed production system of lead creators and assistants pushed manga closer to being a composite art form like movies, the students on the panel all worried that individual creators' personalities would be lost in such a system.[126]

These concerns were not unwarranted. In the assistant labor model, the mangaka became the director, but the editor became a producer, thus taking some decisions out of the mangaka's hands.[127] The herding that roundtable participants complained about was partly the result of editorial intervention; editors could be distant and harsh, and they were focused on reader rankings of manga in the magazines as determined by reader surveys. Even established creators could be dropped with little or no warning if their current work wasn't popular enough, with the result that publishers weren't willing to pay for manuscript pages more than a month in advance of publication.[128] But these attitudes were not precisely new; Fujiko Fujio A wrote in his memoir of the Tokiwa-sō era fifteen years before that "the manga world is survival of the fittest!"[129] Even Tezuka lived and died by sales figures then, and that had not changed.

The new assistant model in some ways also merely formalized and institutionalized long-standing labor practices: The *Manga Man* staff worked collaboratively in the 1930s, when editors at other publications were also known to assist creators with page layouts.[130] The Tokiwa-sō creators routinely helped each other out with artistic labor when deadlines loomed, and Mura Nunoe had been drafted into helping Mizuki with his manga after they were married, despite the fact that she had no artistic training, before Mizuki began making enough money to hire assistants.[131] Even Rakuten had worked with assistants on *Tokyo Puck* almost from the beginning, and the increased workload since the 1950s only made them more necessary.[132] Manga, in other words, had relied on joint labor for a very long time, and the era of assistants only formalized that reality, making it an expected practice across the industry.

Shōjo manga, still locked in the older one-shot story paradigm, tended to attract the lion's share of complaints about being stereotypical, dull, and predictable. But shōnen was subject to many of the same editorial approaches, although male editorial staff sometimes dealt less peremptorily with male creators. Moreover, while former kashihon creators could write for mainstream magazines, they were not given the same free rein as before, particularly on the shōjo side. Mizuki, for example, was asked to write an SF manga for Kodansha's flagship *Weekly Shōnen Magazine* before his eventual debut; he declined on the grounds that he didn't think he was good at it. Only when editorial standards were relaxed was he able to publish *Terebi-kun* (TV kid) in 1965, which proved such a hit with readers that he got the go-ahead to serialize *Hakaba no Kitarō*.[133]

In their editorial freedom, *COM* and *Garo* were the exceptions that proved the rule. But strict subject-matter restrictions could still seem like freedom from certain vantage points: Mangaka Murakami Motoka (b. 1951) commented in a 2016 discussion with Takemiya Keiko that as a child he had initially wanted to be a shōjo mangaka, since it was possible to draw a larger variety of things there than in shōnen manga. When Murakami first read Ueda's *Fuichin-san* after Tezuka's manga, it gave him a shock because the world of daily life it portrayed was so different from the fantastical adventures in the latter's work. Shōjo, in his estimation, was the only kind of manga that portrayed that kind of individualized world.[134] In the next decade, that individualized world became the stage for some of the most consequential innovations in manga's history.

CHAPTER EIGHT

The Emergence of Seinen Manga and the Shōjo Revolution

BIG COMIC AND THE BIRTH OF SEINEN

Even as shōnen manga evolved into a defined category in the 1960s, many creators publishing in it wanted to create more explicit narratives that could satisfy an increasingly older readership. Before the decade's end, this continuing expansion of manga was recognized as a new category, seinen, which solidified with the foundation of the third of the so-called big three magazines, *Big Comic*.[1]

Big Comic did not start seinen (youth) manga. *Comic Magazine*, published by Hōbunsha, led off the new category in 1966, and five other seinen magazines launched in 1967 and 1968. Thus, Tezuka justifiably proclaimed that 1967 had witnessed the birth of seinen manga in *COM*'s one-year anniversary message.[2] But *Big Comic*, which was first published in April 1968, set the standard for the category by uniting the big names of the age: the *Garo* faction (Shirato, Mizuki), the *COM* faction (Tezuka, Ishinomori), and gekiga in the person of Saitō Takao, famed for his "luxurious action," in Natsume Fusanosuke's phrase.[3] Nagai Katsuichi observed that only Shogakukan could have gathered all those big names into one magazine—but it wouldn't have been what it was without kashihon manga, which nurtured three of the five.[4] The magazine's concept was essentially "seinen gekiga" (i.e., gekiga that adults could stand to read), but calling it "comic" rather than "manga" or "gekiga" was prophetic: The idea that adults will read any kind of fictional narrative manga, a key plank of manga's dominance in Japan today, is at least partly *Big Comic*'s achievement.[5]

In 1968, however, seinen was still very much an upstart category for young men. *Big Comic* proudly took advantage of recent innovations across the

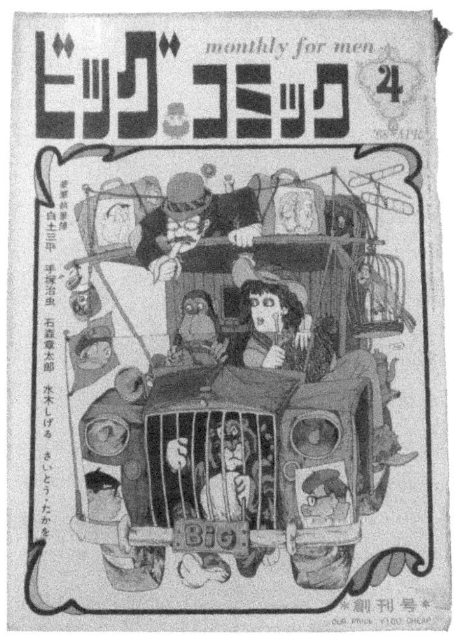

FIGURE 17. Cover of *Big Comic* no. 1, April 1968.

manga industry: Emblazoned on the cover, "Our Price ¥160 CHEAP" was a sign that the magazine was definitely part of the new magazines-as-advertising model (figure 17). Its cover also proclaimed it a "monthly for men," and it was tits out from the very first interior page, which featured an advertisement containing a topless woman that equated female nudity with novelty. *Swallowing the Earth* (*Chikyū o nomu*, 1968–69), the Tezuka series that was serialized from the magazine's first issue, has a lot of nudity, a sign that *Big Comic*'s manga were definitely not to be confused with the children's manga of the earlier age, no matter who wrote them.[6] While *Big Comic* did not quite yet contain solely manga—the first issue featured a translated excerpt from Vin Packer's mystery novel *The Hare in March* (1967), part of the contemporary lesbian sexploitation boom in men's media—even its non-manga content was in line with these themes, as in Komatsu Sakyō's article in the same issue, "SF Erochika" (SF Eroticism).[7]

Like the gekiga boys before them, the men involved in *Big Comic* were not shy about proclaiming their own innovation. The first issue's back page featured messages from the various mangaka congratulating themselves for being so cutting-edge. Ishinomori wrote: "There's no doubt that *Big Comic* is pioneering a new audience. For that purpose . . . I want to show that you can go this far even in comics. In my work for *Big Comic* . . . I want to make a world that has never existed in comics before." Saitō wrote: "I think that *Big Comic* is a magazine that happened because it had to happen at this moment, when comics have completely transformed in order to appeal to young men." Tezuka, meanwhile, asked, "What kind of touch is right for the kind of shōnen manga *Big* will pioneer? It's not the same as children's manga, and it's also different from nonsense manga. That was my first challenge." Mizuki declared: "Through *Big*'s publication shōnen manga—in other words, the new comics—genre has been established. In my work . . . I want to satirize humans and sexual mores."[8]

Manga had appealed to "young men" before April 1968. The reference to nonsense manga is telling, as the last time that such unabashed eroticism had featured in professionally produced manga was the era of eroguro nonsense manga in the 1920s and 1930s, which sold sex in the form of women in pieces in order to sell magazines. In the 1960s, the rise of actual pornography in eromanga placed marketplace pressures on the appeal to the growing demographic of "young men"—who were increasingly college students with disposable income. Thus (female) nudity and eroticism in mainstream manga seemed both necessary for sales and also, in comparison to actual eromanga, comparatively tame. Inasmuch as manga was rapidly becoming a socially licensed outlet for fantasy, the inclusion of sexuality in mainstream manga was, as Saitō implied, necessary if not inevitable: Fulfilling that role *required* that manga incorporate sex and sexuality, particularly in a country that still remained predominantly gender-separated in education, society, and the workforce.

Big Comic incorporated other cutting-edge manga practices from the start, particularly its decision to eschew panel numbers: After more than six decades, readers of Japanese comics could finally be trusted to intuit the reading order of panels on their own, although this change took more than a decade to propagate across all manga magazines. Though *Big Comic* still featured some cheap three-color pages in some manga, its first issue also contained one full-color page insert; one series per issue receiving color pages, with the rest monochrome, became the standard practice across manga magazines over the next decade or so.

An interview with Tezuka in the third issue, using entirely reader-submitted questions, offered more insight into current ideas about seinen. In his answers, Tezuka stated that he had drawn stuff for adults for years, but that *Swallowing the Earth* was his first seinen work. Answering a question about the difference between "ero" and "eroticism art" (erochishizumu geijutsu), he replied that "it's like oden in that it's entirely a matter of personal taste," but in art, some degree of non-realism might be necessary for the purposes of eros, for "if it's like a photograph, it's ugly." As befitted an interview published in 1968, another question asked Tezuka's opinion of underground art, of "saike" [psychedelic art], and "what's a happening you want to do?" Asked about the nature of seinen manga, Tezuka replied that "strangely enough, it's not about fighting spirit or artistic consciousness. It's okay to take the provisions of life from outside the manga."[9]

Reader responses were enthusiastic from the beginning, as evidenced by those published in the inaugural comments section in May 1968. One twenty-year-old wrote: "I thought when I saw *Big*'s contents that finally here was a real comics magazine." Another offered his congratulations on the magazine's publication: "At any rate, I was surprised; this is exactly the comics magazine I've been holding out hope for." Another reader wrote: "I don't need any articles or nudes outside of manga. I just want manga that makes me think. I want you to expand the possibilities of manga." That letter garnered a published response from the editors, who replied, "That is exactly *Big*'s mission."[10]

SHŌNEN WITHOUT SHŌJO

The development of shōjo manga has tended to steal the spotlight in discussions of manga's history, perhaps due to an unthinking assumption that comics for boys are natural while the existence of comics for girls requires explanation. Girls and women began reading manga in the early 1900s, and they entered the profession as creators in the 1930s.[11] The first children's comics in Japan in the 1920s did not make any particular assumptions about the gender of their readership, and children of all genders read manga in magazines without regard to whether those magazines were differentiated by gender through the mid-1960s. Only at that point did the now familiar, rigidly age- and gender-segregated manga marketing categories come into place, deliberately constructed to maximize publishers' profits and to uphold the social ideologies of gender that structured Japanese society (salaryman in the workplace, housewife at home). Looking at magazines from the late 1950s through the 1960s demonstrates that shōnen manga underwent a definite evolution in this period, as both shōnen and shōjo magazines diverged from children's manga.

Weekly Shōnen Magazine (1959–), the leading shōnen manga magazine of the era and still a major player today, went through a typical progression: The December 1959 issue, which billed itself as "a shōnen magazine for dreams and hope," still used the old, cheap, three-color scheme for some series, while the lead manga received one four-color cover page. By October 1968, the magazine had adopted the now standard scheme for differentiating chapters of each series by color: *Shōnen Magazine* used a different color of ink for each series, while nowadays other magazines such as *Shōnen Jump* use different colors of paper stock. Even at this relatively late date, however, *Shōnen Magazine* still retained some articles containing content that could be summed up as "what boys like"—in this case, baseball players and nuclear-powered naval vessels. The magazine no longer bore a slogan, however. *Shōnen Magazine* did away with panel numbers only in 1975, the same year that non-manga content also vanished from the magazine's pages—though the year-end issue still featured a "Movie Times" guide.

By the end of the 1960s, *Shōnen Magazine* had cemented itself as a cutting-edge publication, to the extent that anime producer Okada Toshio (b. 1958) looked back and declared "it was surely the spring of our age."[12] Indeed, in 1969 the Waseda student newspaper updated the old *Shōnen Kurabu* catchphrase for the new era as "*Asahi Journal* in one hand and *Shōnen Magazine* in the other," which was corrected in 1970 to "*Journal* in the hand, *Magazine* in the heart."[13] Okada notes that this "spring" came about through the editors' producer power, as they poached former kashihon creators and debuted new talent.[14] The "gekiga and newcomers" strategy was originally formulated to compete with *Magazine*'s contemporary, the gag-focused *Shōnen Sunday* (1959–), and it succeeded: *Shōnen Magazine*'s circulation reached one million copies in 1967, and then an unprecedented 1.5 million copies by early 1970.[15] *Shōnen Magazine* proved to be an important gateway to gekiga for many readers who were previously unfamiliar with it and with kashihon manga, further increasing gekiga's popularity.[16]

The college-age participants in a *COM*-sponsored roundtable on gekiga in June 1967 agreed that there was no longer much of a distinction between manga and gekiga; one student astutely pointed to gekiga star Saitō Takao currently being published in *Shōnen Magazine* as emblematic of that very fact.[17] Gekiga's emphasis on realism was a key reason behind its appeal; seinen mangaka Murakami Motoka once remarked that as the manga magazines changed in the 1960s and emonogatari (illustrated stories) disappeared, he was unsure what to do for a future career, but by the time he was in high school, manga had become sufficiently realistic that he thought he could try it.[18] Okada succinctly noted that "bright and fun children's manga" couldn't survive the student movement, but gekiga's depiction of the everyday, along with its focus on the self and self-expression, suited the mood of the times.[19]

Seinen manga's emergence had a profound effect on other manga categories, particularly shōnen. *Weekly Shōnen Jump* and its cohort *Weekly Shōnen Champion* (1969–) inaugurated a new kind of shōnen magazine, one that "blur[red] the boundary between shōnen and seinen" in Fujiki Hideaki's phrase.[20] Freed from the need to appeal to female readers, shōnen manga began brimming over with violence and sexual content. Nagai Gō's *Kekkō kamen* (Lovely Mask, 1974–78), in which a female superhero who is naked except for boots, gloves, and mask appears at Sparta Academy to save (mostly female) students who are about to be subjected to sexually humiliating S&M punishments by the (mostly male) teachers, can be taken as representative of shōnen manga in these years: Kekkō Kamen's signature fighting move is landing crotch-first on her (male) opponent's face. Nagai's works "pushed the limits of violence and eroticism," in Nagayama's phrase, starting with *Harenchi gakuen* (Scandalous school, 1968–72), one of *Shōnen Jump*'s debut series. At the same time, Nagai's manga were very deliberately sexy but did not show explicit sex, keeping him safe within the category's bounds, and that general strategy spread to shōnen manga overall.[21] Nagai later remarked that he wanted to create a "safe" space for boys to become familiar with eroticism and nurture their own burgeoning sexuality.[22] Once *Jump* and *Champion* paved the way, the manga in *Shōnen Magazine* got more seinen-esque and explicit too.[23]

The rise of seinen, coupled with the student movement's failures, put an end to the legacy category of otona manga, which were known as the "vulgar weeklies" for their combining manga, true stories, and gravure (soft-core photographs of nude models). The rise of television in the 1960s and the failure of the "season of politics" by 1970 permanently reduced political satire's appeal; *Manga* relaunched in 1968 but couldn't last a year.[24] Political cartoons as a separate category largely failed with *Manga Dokuhon*'s end in 1970, leaving them the sole province of newspapers; as Shimizu Isao noted, there was no longer any career path for aspiring political cartoonists to follow into the professional manga industry.[25] Although late-blooming female mangaka Tamura Hisako (1919–2023) found success with her satirical manga, even winning the Japan Cartoonists Association's Grand Prize in 1978, she was the exception that proved the rule (perhaps because her political manga had a distinctly female perspective), and her work has been forgotten.[26] As Ishiko Jun observed, moreover, the media's focus on newer female mangaka like Tamura obscured living veteran female mangaka who had already faded from view, like Yazaki Takeko.[27]

While some otona manga magazines folded outright, others, like *Weekly Manga Times* and *Weekly Manga Sunday*, converted to seinen or gekiga manga (which were rapidly becoming the same thing), taking advantage of the gekiga boom that had yet to peak.[28] The evolution of *Weekly Manga Times*, one of the first weekly manga magazines when it began publishing in 1956, is telling. The tagline for its first few issues was "a weekly magazine of topics and manga stories"; it initially included a notable proportion of articles along with manga. It converted swiftly to selling sex, with its first cover depicting a beautiful woman being published in May 1957, with the tagline "sex in movies and literature." Ten years later, the amount of sexually charged content in each issue had only increased and now included full-color gravure features.

In 1967, however, the manga in *Weekly Manga Times* still looked stylistically much more like the 1950s than the 1970s: Paneling was still fairly regular and panels were still numbered, while dialogue was still hand lettered. Just three years later, however, in 1970, everything changed with its conversion to seinen, and the magazine now appeared much more contemporary: While old-style manga persisted, there were many new-style manga, readily distinguished by their use of screentones, printed lettering for dialogue, and lack of panel numbers. By 1975, the magazine's transition into the mainstream (and still contemporary) mode was complete, with its final abandonment of articles and its adoption of the three-color scheme for the initial splash pages of some manga series in each issue.

"That feverish season which has already passed into history," the heady years of the late 1960s and the very early 1970s, cut short by the oil shock, encapsulated the first peak of creativity in the seinen category and was bookended by the manga categories aimed at male readers lapsing back into what manga critic Murakami Tomohiko (b. 1951) described in 1978 as a formulaic and mannerist era, a "retrograde age."[29] The 1970s were known as the "Me Decade" in the United States; although the comparable sociopolitical forces in question manifested in Japan as a longing for the furusato, the (vanishing) rural hometown, the ideological shift that Murakami criticized, from societal to personal concerns, was similar.

In the same article, Murakami acknowledged that while "this wasn't the case just a few years ago, now you can't talk about manga on the whole without talking about shōjo manga. The same cannot be said of shōnen manga or seinen manga now; without a doubt, shōjo occupies the mainstream position within manga overall."[30] In the decade between *Big Comic*'s debut and Murakami's writing, the torch of innovation in manga passed to shōnen and seinen's despised younger sister: shōjo, manga for girls.

THE EMERGENCE OF SHŌJO MANGA

The conventional narrative of shōjo manga in Japan is that it "emerged" in the 1950s at the hands of male creators like Tezuka and Ishinomori Shōtarō, who dominated the field until the rise of female creators such as Mizuno Hideko in the late 1960s and the members of the Shōwa 24 group in the 1970s. This is a story of girl power, in which shōjo manga came into its own once it was drawn by creators who were themselves former shōjo, but it is highly misleading in some ways; for one, it ignores the existence of kashihon shōjo, some of which was drawn by female mangaka who had worked in satire and children's manga in the wartime era.

Girls read manga in the prewar and wartime eras, overwhelmingly in magazines such as *Shōnen Kurabu*, since that was where the manga was: Girls wrote letters to the magazine and were featured in photographic spreads of *Shōnen Kurabu* super-fans (aidokusha). Its sibling magazine *Shōjo Kurabu* occasionally featured images of Norakuro or other popular Kodansha manga stars, and published some manga, such as Hasegawa Machiko's debut short in 1935. Presumably, this was partly meant to drive readers toward *Shōnen Kurabu*, which had staked its reputation on being full of manga, but the girls' culture featured in girls' magazines was also aesthetically and culturally distinctive, relying heavily on illustrated novels and frequently depicting "S relationships," passionate friendships between schoolgirls.[31] Although girls would and did read boys' magazines, most boys presumably had no interest in tales of spiritual love between female students at boarding schools.

Aside from their content, the art styles of the illustrations in boys' and girls' magazines were also quite distinct; illustrators such as Takehisa Yumeji (1884–1934) and mangaka Matsumoto Katsuji (1904–86) honed their art, known as jojōga (lyrical illustrations), in prewar girls' magazines, and the aesthetic they pioneered was revived and refined by artists such as Nakahara Jun'ichi (1913–83) in the postwar period along with girls' magazines. Nakahara's visual style eventually came to dominate shōjo manga aesthetics in the 1960s, salted with important innovations by Takahashi Macoto (b. 1934), who also worked in kashihon manga and was responsible for the introduction of characters' wide, sparkling eyes and "style pictures" (sutairuga), full-body character portraits set outside panels that both convey mood and illustrate a character's outfit in detail.[32]

Competing with both kashihon manga and teen movies, girls' magazines in the 1950s began publishing serialized manga for the first time. The first serial shōjo manga is conventionally said to have been Tezuka's *Ribon no kishi* (*Princess Knight*, 1953–56), published in *Shōjo Club,* which brought story manga into comics aimed at girls. The tale of Princess Sapphire, who has both a boy's and a girl's heart and who must live as a boy to inherit her kingdom, drew on Tezuka's childhood experience with the all-female Takarazuka Revue in his hometown in Kansai and has remained influential.[33]

The connection between (shōjo) manga and the Takarazuka Revue almost seems fated. The Revue was founded in 1913 by railway entrepreneur Kobayashi Ichizō (1873–1957) to attract guests to the eponymous onsen town of Takarazuka outside Osaka, which Kobayashi's company, now the Hankyū Railway, was redeveloping, and which became a mecca of foreign, high-collar culture and a center of Keihanshin (Kyoto, Osaka, and Kobe) modernism.[34] The Revue was from the beginning an all-female venture, and the company performs a mixture of Japanese and Western productions, training its own performers, who specialize in male roles (otokoyaku), or female roles (musumeyaku), via an affiliated application-only drama school.[35]

Takarazuka was Tezuka's hometown, and his mother frequently took him to Revue performances as a child; he was thus exposed from a young age to the "gender gymnastics" (in Leonie R. Stickland's phrase) of a theatrical spectacle in which female actors played both male and female roles. The influences went beyond the acknowledged *Ribon no kishi* connection; when Natsume Fusanosuke visited the Revue museum in the 1980s, he saw exhibits of sets from productions in the early Shōwa period that directly recalled backgrounds in Tezuka's manga, until his lines changed under gekiga's influence in the 1960s.[36] Nakano Haruyuki has argued that Takarazuka influences extended to Tezuka's "star system" of characters, whom he divided into troupes à la the Revue, and his famously "stinking of butter" (batā-kusai, i.e., foreign) character designs, which Tezuka himself mused might have come from Takarazuka actors' makeup.[37] Despite Tezuka's early exposure to the Revue, which in Hikari Hori's summary "foregrounds the constructedness of gender norms wherein actors act out imagined and idealized gender roles, which the audience fully understands as a performance," *Ribon no kishi* ultimately ends conventionally, with Sapphire's heterosexual marriage.[38]

After finishing *Ribon no kishi*, Tezuka next published chapters of his episodic masterwork *Hi no tori* in *Shōjo Club*, though it is anything but shōjo manga as such. In this era, girls read not only shōjo manga in magazines but also kashihon manga and mainstream manga such as *Tetsuwan Atomu*, which ran in *Shōnen Magazine*. Despite its name, the magazine was consumed by children generally, and it proved unable to navigate the transition to the gendered weekly manga-magazine paradigm.

Leading prewar girls magazines like *Shōjo no Tomo* (Girls' friend, 1908–55) could not recapture their former popularity, and reader enthusiasm shifted to a new crop of magazines (some of whose target audiences now included upper elementary schoolers as prewar yōnen magazines also faded), such as *Nakayoshi* (Good friends, 1954–) and *Ribon* (Ribbon, 1955–). *Shōjo Club* folded in 1962 and relaunched as *Shōjo Friend* (1963–96); its companion magazine *Bessatsu Friend* (Special edition Friend, 1965–) is still in print. Through these magazines, the implicit construction of masculinity in *Shōnen Magazine* and its fellows was matched by an explicit construction of feminine behavior and mores in shōjo manga.

When anthropologist Jennifer Prough conducted ethnographic research in the shōjo manga industry in the first decade of the twenty-first century, the notion that female mangaka were best suited to be shōjo creators, "under the rubric that those who are recent graduates from girlhood can better intuit the fushigi (mysterious) things that girls like," had long since become axiomatic. Conveniently, this focus on affect elides the gendered division of labor in shōjo manga—young female creators, older male editors—and the pay gap between those two sides of the workforce (comics creators are generally speaking overworked and underpaid worldwide, and women are even more likely to be so). This division is based on the historical fact of the 1970s shōjo manga boom, when shōjo came to be equated with "what girls like," used, in Prough's analysis, "as a descriptor of shōjo manga and the essence of both its content and economic variables."[39]

One of the most notable shōjo magazines then and now is *Nakayoshi*, which has held the record for longest-running comics periodical in Japan since April 1997, when it surpassed *Osaka Puck*. Its content started out as a transposition of the content mix found in children's manga magazines in 1955 (emonogatari, manga, photo spreads, and bound-in freebies of different sizes), under the slogan "a magazine [for] pleasant and fun good friends." By the next issue, the slogan now specified that it was a "magazine for pleasant and fun young female friends." Five years later, the slogan had disappeared and the magazine's content was now at least half manga, with the two leading titles receiving full color cover pages and three-color printing for their interior pages. The *Nakayoshi* editorial staff also transmuted the readers' corner, which took a catholic view of the magazine's contents, into fan pages for particular series. *Ribon no kishi*'s super-fan (aidokusha) pages featured drawings of its characters by fans, fan letters, and instructions on sending in for a giveaway. The fan page for another hit manga featured more of the same, including a photo of a fan dressed up as one of the characters—one of the earliest recorded instances of cosplay.[40]

Freebies were a key shōjo magazine strategy even in the 1960s, as when *Ribon*, which at the time played a distinct second fiddle to *Nakayoshi* due to its publishing fewer marquee mangaka, made freebies a key part of its competition with its rivals from 1961 onward, going so far as to advertise the fact that all of its freebies were long-form bessatsu furoku manga. Creators and editors' testimony about the goals of freebies applied just as well in the 1960s as it did in the 1990s: One editor told Prough bluntly that freebies "are included to deter people from passing the magazines around; this way you want your own. You buy your own magazine because you want the supplements."[41]

Freebies were quickly supplemented by formalized reader surveys, in which readers could fill out and return postcards to express their opinions about what they liked best in the magazine and thereby influence editorial decisions. Reader surveys were the ultimate arbiter of magazine content, and they remain extremely influential; in the mid-1970s, the surveys were so important and codified that Shogakukan allowed only manga ranked fifth or higher in the surveys to receive color pages in its magazines.[42] Prough found that readers' opinions were taken into account even at the granular level of "character prominence and romance; often a side character becomes a main heartthrob or sidekick due to readers' response, and likewise characters and plotlines can be demoted or dropped altogether if unpopular."[43] Takemiya Keiko wrote that when she started paying attention to the reader surveys was when she became a real creator, and her friends in the field became her rivals.[44]

The somewhat self-explanatory practice of survey prizes, which offered readers who returned the surveys the opportunity to win exclusive goods, began in this era, as did the practice of mail-order goods: In a further bid to incentivize readers buying their own individual copies of the magazines, publishers began offering exclusive merchandise that was available only by filling out an application form cut out (not photocopied) from the magazine and returned with a nominal amount of money and postage for shipping costs.[45] By the late 1990s, these items were almost always goods featuring characters from a magazine's popular manga, but this practice solidified only after about 1990; before that, mail-order goods were equally likely to be simply popular merchandise, not necessarily directly related to the manga in the magazine in question.[46]

By the mid-1960s, the impact of kashihonya and kashihon manga's impending demise was being felt across the manga world. Female kashihon mangaka—many of whom had only recently broken into the profession—overwhelmingly tended to switch to the mainstream manga industry's shōjo magazines. Many of these women were children of the postwar era who had grown up reading manga and who were not content to continue the hitherto default paradigm of shōjo manga, which manga scholar Rachel Thorn summarized as comprising "passive, pre-adolescent heroines in melodramatic situations, often involving separation from a mother."[47] Romance was not in the cards; mangaka Imamura Yōko (b. 1935), who started in kashihon manga, got letters of protests from readers when she tried to do a dating plotline in a mainstream shōjo magazine in the late 1950s.[48] While important conventions did evolve in this period, in some ways shōjo manga until the mid-1960s could be characterized as the last refuge of the previous children's manga paradigm, recast with girl-child protagonists. At that point, romance plotlines starring teenage protagonists became more common, but these changes did not improve shōjo manga's reputation.

YOU SAY YOU WANT A REVOLUTION: THE STATE OF SHŌJO MANGA IN 1969

Rather than format, what obsessed everyone concerned with shōjo in the late 1960s were questions of content. Nor was this concern limited to the young women who were starting their careers in shōjo, or even to the people who read it. When *COM* convened a roundtable in August 1967 dedicated to exploring the state of shōjo, Ozaki began the conversation by opining that while shōnen manga had made a lot of progress as conflict and criticism moved to the center of the genre, shōjo manga was in shadow and becalmed. There was widespread agreement among the mixed-gender group of participants, aged thirteen to nineteen, that shōjo manga was boring, predictable, and lacking in the individuality of shōnen manga, which was universally agreed to be better. Some participants noted that girls read shōnen manga, and would read shōjo if it was good, but that boys didn't read shōjo manga.[49]

Opinions differed as to where to place the blame for this state of affairs: One girl stated flatly that shōjo was bad because all the creators were men, while another participant defended shōjo's stereotypical stories and unrealistic depiction of the girl's devoted love as presenting what female readers, especially middle schoolers, wanted and yearned for. Another noted that shōnen was unrealistic or hyperrealistic, but that shōjo actually reflected everyday life and feelings. Many participants complained about the "culturally odorless" (mukokuseki), usually European-ish settings and stereotypical narratives that predominated in shōjo at the time. Participants called for a number of changes: less predictable stories, deepening of creators' individual themes, a shift to talking about shōjo manga as one form of manga expression rather than merely appealing to girls' sentiments, and finally, to have shōjo manga that boys would want to read and would think was interesting.[50] Those wishes came true just a few years later.

Takemiya Keiko echoed the roundtable's perceptions in her memoir, *Shōnen no na wa Gilbert*. "Shōjo manga was full of nothing but things that couldn't be done," she remarked, blaming that squarely on editorial: Besides the storylines being exceedingly stereotyped and predictable, even art and character designs were very similar due to editors' directives. Above all, she found shōjo's depiction of love and romance almost offensively inaccurate: There would be one kiss, a character saying "I'm glad" or a similar phrase, and perhaps a baby appearing at the end. The implication was that a woman's life ended with a kiss, but the members of the Shōwa 24 group wanted to ask, "What happens after the happy ending?"[51]

Yamada Murasaki summed up many of these points in an essay in the Mushi Pro publication *Manga Communication* in May 1971, writing derisively: "It'd be more honest to call shōjo manga 'love play manga.' All that head-over-heels and bent-out-of-shape falling in love stuff, over and over again, never tiring of the same romantic subject. One series ends and the next begins, but the only things that change are the characters' names and the circumstances of their romance and who they're in love with. Be it with someone poor or rich, a prince or a playboy, the romance never transcends Cinderella's world. Only the characters' eyes are drawn with any dedication. The rest just feels slapped together." In her view, readers couldn't identify with the characters, who lacked psychological realism, and the creators were only playing a "foreign love game" among themselves.[52]

Takemiya notes that the depiction of love in pre-Shōwa 24 group manga was almost exclusively spiritual, which in her mind meant that it was practically a different thing than real love, because actual love necessarily changes when the physical component is included. The editorial prohibition on depicting physical relationships was derived from the general idea that girls didn't like bodies' physicality, and that creators would be criticized if their depiction of bodies was too "rough." Thus, character designs for girls in shōjo had a peculiarly weightless quality, while the few boy characters didn't look like real boys. As Takemiya drily observes, all of this was just the opposite for seinen creators of the day.[53]

The paradigm of gender relations that prevailed in shōjo manga at this point was aptly termed the "love trap" by manga scholar Fujimoto Yukari, in that the idea of love that these manga promoted consisted of a girl sacrificing her own hopes and dreams for the boy she loved, and then creating a household with him, endlessly trying to prove her love and win his love in return through self-abnegation.[54] Trading agency for love (and equating love with self-sacrifice) was exactly the bargain that the gendered social ideology of the housewife and the salaryman required, but shōjo manga at this point was failing in its socially sanctioned role of persuading girls to accept this paradigm. Although routinely dismissed as that crap that girls liked, as the *COM* roundtable shows, girls did not actually like it.

Even these dissatisfying romance stories, however, were an evolution from the prior shōjo manga paradigm featuring preadolescent girls and almost no boys, a distinct contrast to contemporaneous girls' magazines in America.[55] The work of female Tokiwa-sō member and former Tezuka assistant Mizuno Hideko (b. 1939) in this respect was a key bridge from the older paradigm to the newer one: Her masterwork *Fire!* (1969–71) encapsulated some of shōjo manga's older tendencies (e.g., setting stories abroad, with half- or non-Japanese characters as protagonists) even while it broke new ground as one of the first manga by a female creator to feature a male protagonist, American musician Aaron, and relatively sexually explicit scenes.[56] Aaron, something of a Bob Dylan figure, was a rock star who wore his hair long, which was part of the manga's distinct youth appeal in the era of the Summer of Love; his being a male protagonist in a shōjo manga looked forward to the 1970s.

Mizuno herself had a grand piano and a full drum kit in her basement as part of her research for *Fire!* She went to great lengths to obtain a degree of verisimilitude, in terms of action and setting, that had not previously been a concern in shōjo. Mizuno's example inspired Takemiya to take research for her own manga more seriously, and other Shōwa 24 group creators followed her lead; she, Masuyama Norie (1950–2021), Hagio Moto, and Yamagishi Ryōko (b. 1947) took a research trip to Europe for forty days in September 1972, documenting details of everyday life ranging from door knobs to street scenes to boys.[57] By the next decade, this physical and emotional realism had become one of shōjo's hallmarks and one of its distinct advantages over shōnen manga of the time.

A MANGA OF THEIR OWN: THE FABULOUS 49ERS

So who were these women? They were children of the postwar, born into Japan's era of de jure (but not de facto) gender equality in or around 1949, for which reason Takemiya dubbed them "the Fabulous Shōwa 24 Group" (hana no 24-nen gumi, usually rendered in English as the "Magnificent" or "Fabulous" 49ers); they were also known as "New Wave shōjo mangaka."[58] Although Takemiya Keiko and Hagio Moto are most familiar, the Shōwa 24 Group included many women whose impact and works were significant to manga's development. Together, they inspired others to follow in their footsteps, many of whom are often categorized as members of the "Post-24 Group." While the 49ers are often associated with the 1970s, when they came to prominence almost overnight, most had careers stretching back to the mid-1960s, when many made their professional debuts while still teenagers.

One thread connecting many of them was kashihonya, and kashihon manga. In interviews with Yonezawa Yoshihiro, Ichijō Yukari (b. 1949), Satonaka Machiko (b. 1948), and Maki Miyako all affirmed the platform's importance to their origins in manga: Ichijō, a self-professed weirdo, recalled spending all her time in kashihonya reading kashihon manga and gekiga as opposed to talking to people, while Satonaka read so much kashihon manga that she was told it was weird for a girl. Yamato Waki (b. 1948) also read a lot of manga as a child, specifically the manga that her older brother bought, while Maki Miyako's family owned a bookstore, with the result that she submitted her first manuscript directly to a kashihon publisher in their Osaka neighborhood and made her magazine debut after her first kashihon manga's publication.[59]

Another important factor in the Shōwa 24 generation's rise was the fact that shōjo magazines, specifically *Shōjo Friend* in 1964, started directly converting amateur manga creators into professionals: Previously, magazines gave prize money without any promise of jobs or helping amateurs break into the industry. The manga contests in *Shōjo Friend* and later *Ribon* found top talent: Ichijō, Satonaka, Morita Jun (b. 1948), Yamato Waki, and Yuzuki Hikaru (b. 1949) were all discovered via the contests.[60] Ichijō won *Ribon*'s inaugural amateur manga prize at eighteen, making her professional debut in the magazine in 1968. Yamato had been told to give up manga in middle school, but in her penultimate year of high school she saw that Satonaka Machiko had been published in *Shōjo Friend:* Realizing that she and Satonaka were both sixteen years old, she resolved to try to become a mangaka herself. Mizuno Hideko noticed the work of Aoike Yasuko (b. 1948) in a *Ribon* contest and told the editors to publish one of Aoike's short comics.[61]

Three central figures in the Shōwa 24 and post–Shōwa 24 groups, Takemiya, Hagio, and Masuyama, created a social group that became an ad hoc support mechanism for the young women involved in it. Takemiya and Hagio first met in the spring of 1970; Takemiya was being "canned" on a deadline when her editor suggested that Hagio, visiting Tokyo on a break from art school in Fukuoka and making the rounds of manga publishers, assist Takemiya.[62] Takemiya wrote that the meeting "changed my destiny for the rest of my life." Through Hagio, she met Hagio's pen pal Masuyama, who had written Hagio an enthusiastic fan letter after *Nakayoshi* published Hagio's first manga in 1969.[63] (Hagio had submitted to *COM* before that, but the magazine didn't publish her submission until January 1971.)[64] Takemiya wrote that her meeting with Masuyama "changed her destiny still further," calling the fact that the three of them—all around twenty years old in 1970—met when they did "miraculous."[65] Masuyama wrote that for her, who believed firmly in manga's infinite capacity for expression, meeting Takemiya, a new mangaka who could give birth to a work with spirit was "a blessing."[66]

Masuyama's role in the shōjo revolution has often been obscured; a fan translator once wondered whether it was going too far to describe her, somewhat tongue-in-cheek, as the "dark lord of shōjo manga."[67] As Takemiya's memoir of the shōjo revolution makes clear, this obscurity was to some extent self-willed: From 1972, Masuyama acted as her manager and creative partner, helping break the plots for Takemiya's manga after Takemiya came up with the initial ideas. At the time, one person writing a manga script and another doing the art was still somewhat stigmatized, so they kept their collaboration quiet. But Masuyama contributed both material and emotional support to the women of the shōjo revolution, and much of the movement's intellectual fire: She was far more passionate about the need to change shōjo manga than either Takemiya or Hagio when they first met.[68] Masuyama agreed, writing that she was the one with vaulting ambition, while Takemiya only cared about creating better work, and she put her all into it. Takemiya joked that she needed Masuyama to motivate her, since Masuyama had that part she lacked; in Masuyama's phrase, "I felt that we had a common destiny."[69]

A movie fanatic and an accomplished classical pianist, Masuyama had originally held an ambition, parentally thwarted, to be a mangaka. Her self-immersion in manga, combined with her impressive knowledge of literature and film, led her to take what was then an uncommon approach to shōjo manga—namely, treating it seriously as an art form worthy of criticism, and thus capable of improvement, in its own right. She also proposed the initial idea for what later became known as the Ōizumi Salon on the explicit model of the Tokiwa-sō, with the idea that its existence would be a good idea for shōjo manga as a whole, not just for the three of them. The house that Masuyama had in mind was a small two-story building just across the street from her own residence in Nerima ward; it was a dump in a cabbage patch, but it was extremely cheap, and Hagio and Takemiya moved in together in late 1970, Hagio coming directly from her parents' house in Fukuoka prefecture and Takemiya moving across town from her previous apartment. The bathroom was so small that they both went to Masuyama's house to take baths.[70]

Living and working side by side, Takemiya and Hagio spent their time in the Salon creating and talking about manga; Masuyama came over every day and was both women's harshest critic, subjecting their works to serious critical evaluation. Masuyama also handled their fan letters, and it was she who instigated the practice of inviting letter writers who seemed like promising talents to come stay at the Salon. The first were Sakata Yasuko (b. 1953) and Kai Yukiko (1954–80), who were already doing dōjinshi and who visited from Tottori on their summer vacation in 1971. Future professionals Sasaya Nanaeko (1950–2024, née Nanae), Itō Aiko (b. 1952), Tarasawa Michi (b. 1954), Satō Shio (1950–2010), Yamada Mineko (b. 1949), and Jō Akiko, who later became Hagio's manager, were also among the guests, and the Salon became a place where they could hang out and talk about manga and the industry among themselves before and after they broke into it. Takemiya and Hagio covered the expenses, and other Salon members who weren't on the lease paid them back by working as their assistants: "I'll pay you back with my body" became their standard way of promising to help with each other's manga.[71]

The Salon members' influence on each other was profound and wide-ranging, and many of them forged lifelong friendships. Satō Shio, for example, encouraged the Salon members' turn toward science fiction; on her deathbed, she called her time in the Salon the best years of her life.[72] The group also operated under the loose principle of, in Masuyama's words, "strength in numbers": Even at the time, Takemiya and the others thought that it was better to have "many comrades." In her judgment, the shōjo revolution was able to succeed because all of them were pushing against the restrictions simultaneously and at multiple publications.[73]

The Ōizumi Salon also provided emotional support for the women who participated in it, as women-only groups often do in male-dominated settings like shōjo manga publishing was at the time (and in many ways still is). Masuyama observed at one point that the Salon resembled nothing so much as a sad story of factory girls from Japan's modernization in terms of their labor conditions: They were paid less per page than male creators; they were hampered by discriminatory regulations for manga expression, such as the fact that the only expectation for shōjo characters was that they possess a "naive simplicity"; they were all subject to exclusivity contracts, which were standard in shōjo at the time despite the fact that all mangaka were ostensibly freelancers; and they also faced simple employment discrimination: Because there were almost no female employees at the publishers, their editors were very detached from the thoughts and feelings of their readership and of the female manga creators.[74]

The Salon helped members push back against many of these practices. Talking among themselves, the Salon mangaka realized that they were all getting paid just 2,500 yen per page while first-rank male creators like Chiba Tetsuya (b. 1939) received 50,000 yen *per page* on *Ashita no Joe* (Tomorrow's Joe, 1968–73) in an era when salarymen cleared 320,000 yen a month—and Chiba was only doing the art. Discussion among Salon members, and between members and other people at industry parties, enabled Salon members to learn things like pay rates, and also to share tips on how to ask for pay increases—which Takemiya's editor Yamamoto Jun'ya (1938–2015) granted, once she did ask.[75]

INNER REVOLUTION: *THE ROSE OF VERSAILLES*

Born slightly earlier, in 1947, Ikeda Riyoko is not always named among the Shōwa 24 group, and there seems to have been little connection between her and the Ōizumi Salon. Unlike many of them, Ikeda attended some amount of college, where she majored in philosophy and joined the student movement, specifically the Democratic Party of Japan (the Japanese Communist Party's youth league) before dropping out; most Shōwa 24 and post–Shōwa 24 members went directly from high school into the industry, and many among the latter got their start acting as assistants to the former.[76] Ikeda began doing kashihon gekiga manga to pay her school fees, and moved to mainstream magazines only after kashihonya entered their final decline. When she worked as a gekigaka, the editors said that she could do whatever she wanted (although a manga about anti-burakumin discrimination was rejected), but her editors in mainstream shōjo publications opposed her creating a historical manga, on the grounds that girls wouldn't read it. She was forced to promise that she'd drop her new series *Berusaiyu no bara* (*The Rose of Versailles*, 1972–74) immediately if it proved unpopular.[77]

But *The Rose of Versailles*, whose Japanese title is often shortened to *BeruBara*, was an epochal manga. It ran in *Margaret* (1966–) and was hugely popular with female middle and high school students, who avidly read the new issue among themselves each week, recalling the old *Norakuro* fever in schools in the 1930s: At the manga's tragic climax, in Deborah Shamoon's summary, "teachers reportedly were forced to suspend classes because all the girl students were in tears, and one distraught fan mailed a letter containing a razor" to Ikeda.[78]

The Rose of Versailles evolved many elements established by *Ribon no kishi*, combining them into a richer, historically grounded narrative. In the waning days of the ancien régime, a French aristocrat raises his daughter Oscar de Jarjeyes as a boy so that she may inherit his position in the French military. Oscar becomes the captain of Marie Antoinette's personal guard; against the backdrop of the burgeoning French Revolution, she nurses an infatuation with Marie Antoinette's lover Count Ferzen, rejects marriage with a man who wants to force her back into female clothing and roles, and eventually finds love with her childhood friend, the household servant André. Her simultaneous political awakening leads her to resign from her royal guard position and eventually to support the revolution (plate 11). She and André consummate their love just before André is killed in a skirmish; Oscar herself dies during the storming of the Bastille, and the manga ends with Marie Antoinette's execution and then Ferzen's death at the hands of a mob some years later.

With little editorial feedback, Ikeda relied on reader responses to shape the story, which she had originally intended as a biography of Marie Antoinette:

Buoyed by readers' adoration, Oscar quickly rose to co-protagonist status, allowing Ikeda to unite her left-wing critiques of economic inequality and the patriarchy in a single glamorous figure.[79] She later acknowledged that the manga was influenced by the ūman ribu movement, which emphasized the liberation of women's sexuality from the gendered family system of salary-man and housewife.[80] Ikeda had intended the manga to express, via the French Revolution, the "inner revolution of the Japanese women," whose own social position was still as low as the Third Estate in the ancien régime.[81] In that she succeeded: Oscar's choices are orthogonal to contemporary gender roles, although the manga's emphasis on France's economic problems and the peasantry's travails was not taken up in later adaptations.

Fujimoto Yukari identified two reasons why teenagers initially and then, after the Takarazuka adaptation's debut, adult women as well fell so hard for Oscar and her story: she was beautiful, cool, and dressed like a man; and, over the course of the manga, she suffered and matured both personally and politically. By 1974, the ūman ribu movement was increasingly visible in society, and Ikeda herself as a postwar writer was "groping for the possibility of a new image of women, of a new society."[82] Hagio, who later became good friends with Ikeda, wrote that "Oscar-sama was the symbol of all girls' desire for love and admiration and transformation, and she had an effect beyond the world of shōjo manga. That was the spirit of liberty and self-reliance."[83]

The image of women and of romance presented in *The Rose of Versailles* also drew on an older lineage of girls' media stretching back to magazines in the Taishō and early Shōwa periods, which promulgated an ideal of platonic "dōseiai" (literally, same-sex love; the word now refers to homosexuality) relationships between schoolgirls. The Oscar/André relationship is a successful romance in that Oscar does not have to compromise her identity to be with André, but the relationship is still predicated on the inequality that structured the love trap. In actual Japan that inequality was gendered, but the inequality between Oscar and André is class based: She is an aristocrat and he is a commoner. André also loses sight in one eye before he and Oscar declare their love, which implies that the man in the partnership must be diminished for him to be believable as a woman's equal.[84]

Furthermore, their gender equality is based on Oscar's taking a man's role in society, and their romance boils down to an androgynous partnership between two characters who resemble one another in dress, hairstyle, and body type. But this was also part of Oscar's appeal; she inspired many letters from girls who didn't fit into traditional gender roles.[85] Visual studies theorist

Akiko Mizoguchi (b. 1962) later wrote that Oscar formed the basis for her own incipient lesbian identity, and deemed Oscar's relationship with André "practically like homosexuality."[86] The fact that the manga ends romantically, with death and heartbreak, is unquestionably part of its popularity, but the stark ending is also a bleak commentary on the impossibility of challenging Japan's gender binary. Ikeda and her readers could not escape it or the hegemonic framework that endorsed it.

The other reason that *BeruBara* struck such a chord among Japanese women and girls, according to Fujimoto, was not just the manga featuring dresses, palaces, doom, and high romance, but also that the manga was contrary to everything that was said at the time about being a woman or about overcoming women. Ikeda herself later agreed, stating her own belief that the reason Oscar was so popular among adult women at that particular moment was because she embodied their heart's desire: to work and to live while being treated as an equal human being—a fantasy in 1970s Japan, and today.[87] In this sense, *The Rose of Versailles* was certainly revolutionary, and it helped touch off an ongoing revolution in Japanese pop culture whose impact reverberates to this day. Understanding that impact requires turning to the other half of the 1970s shōjo revolution: shōnen'ai.

THE INVENTION OF BOYS' LOVE

If *The Rose of Versailles* attempted to depict a heterosexual romance between equals, the Ōizumi Salon members' invention of shōnen'ai, now generally known as boys' love (or BL), represented another attempt to depict equal romances in shōjo manga. While *BeruBara*'s endgame romance depicted its male and female partners androgynously and emphasized their sameness, the shōnen'ai subgenre rejected the figure of the shōjo entirely by depicting same-gender romances between boys.

To some extent, both Takemiya and Hagio were inspired by Masuyama, who introduced them to books and films containing male-male romance themes during the two years they lived together. In her memoir, however, Takemiya noted that both she and Masuyama had been drawn to the potential for emotional entanglements among groups of boys since middle school; that they were both into that kind of thing cemented their friendship almost as soon as they met. Nor was their interest entirely *sui generis:* Takemiya had long been inspired by the Vienna Boys' Choir, which toured Japan in 1964 and received breathless coverage in shōjo magazines, and both she and Masuyama were inspired by a volume of criticism by novelist Inagaki Taruho (1900–77), *Shōnen'ai no bigaku* (The beautiful study of boys' love, 1968), which offered a more analytical take on "aesthetic eroticism" and the potentialities of erotic and romantic relationships among beautiful adolescent boys. Soon after they met, they were delighted to find that they had both already read it.[88]

The Ōizumi Salon was solidly responsible for the development of shōnen'ai in manga, beginning in December 1970 when Takemiya published the short "Yuki to hoshi to tenshi to" ("Snow and stars and angels and . . ."), later republished as "In the Sunroom" ("Sanrūmu nite"), which featured the first same-sex kiss in manga (figure 18).[89] Takemiya had come to Tokyo at her publishers' behest in spring 1970, after debuting in *COM* in 1967 and taking a year off to attend college in 1968. Within the first week of her arrival, she chose to work principally with the up-and-coming publisher Shogakukan: Kodansha's monthly publications were full of established creators she couldn't compete against, but her new editor at Shogakukan, Yamamoto Jun'ya, encouraged her, and as she deemed it the age of weeklies, she wanted to create for weeklies.[90] Kodansha, by contrast, had been slow to adopt the new weekly paradigm and remained reliant on monthlies, extremely profit-conscious, and conservative.[91]

The editorial departments of the era's shōjo magazines had rigid notions about what girls would and wouldn't like, and routinely shot down ideas that didn't fit those constraints without giving creators the chance to prove their popularity via publication. Takemiya related a comment from Masuyama describing the situation: Her work was a ball she was trying to throw to readers, who she was certain would, by reading and "throwing it back," prove that they liked what she was doing and do their part in creating the work collaboratively—but the editorial department did nothing but put up a wall between creators and audiences.[92]

The metaphor highlights the somewhat ambivalent role played by Yamamoto Jun'ya, the editor of *Shōjo Comic* (1968–) at the time. Yamamoto has been hailed as a visionary, largely because he agreed to publish all of Hagio Moto's manga that Kodansha editors had rejected after Takemiya arranged an introduction. He later wrote that Hagio's works weren't normal shōjo manga of the time; rather, they were self-expression, which convinced even him, a man.[93] Yamamoto made up for exercising relatively little editorial control over Hagio with his general opposition to Takemiya's radical ideas in

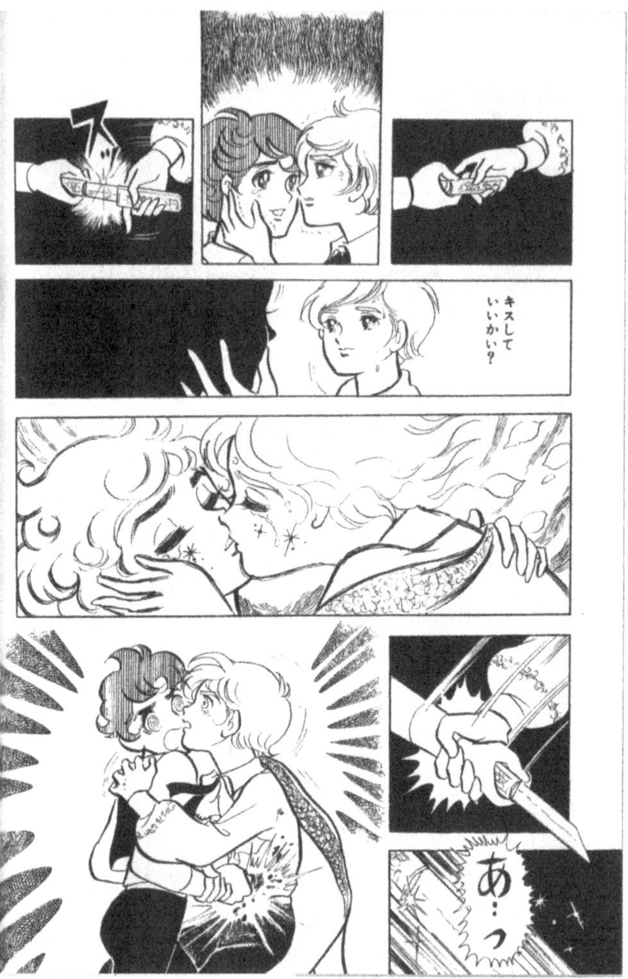

FIGURE 18. The kiss scene from "In the Sunroom," 1970. © Takemiya Keiko. Used with permission.

particular and the idea of the Ōizumi Salon on the whole. Takemiya's one and only coup over him was the publication of "In the Sunroom," which she effected by a fait accompli with deadlines. Yamamoto was opposed to the story's concept and had already rejected it once, because the protagonist was a boy and, rather than being about a boy and a girl, it was about two boys.[94]

Although Takemiya's predictions that readers would love it were vindicated, Yamamoto did not change his general attitude toward her and her work. The real legacy of "In the Sunroom" may be its impact on other creators. Some joined the Ōizumi Salon because of it, starting with Yamagishi Ryōko and Morita Jun: Yamagishi said that she'd been interested in shōnen'ai for a while and was shocked to find she wasn't the only shōjo mangaka who felt that way. At the time, Yamagishi was working with Shueisha, where publishing that kind of work was impossible.[95]

Yamagishi did publish "Shiroi heya no futari" (The couple of the white room) in Shueisha's *Ribon* in February 1971, which is now recognized as one of the first yuri (lesbian or sapphic) or GL (girls' love) manga—although in her original conception the story featured boys, she changed it to girls "as a last resort" since she could not get permission for the boys version.[96] Yashiro Masako had published "Secret Love," another manga that can be taken as the origin of GL, in *Deluxe Margaret* in December 1970; Matsuo Mihoko's two-part lesbian manga *Kamen no koi* (Masked love) appeared in *Funny* in spring 1970. Both manga draw on the tropes of "S-relationships" which circulated in prewar girls' magazines as a paradigm of intimate female friendships, couched through the prism of contemporary homophobic discourse about lesbianism, and both end unhappily with lesbian panic, as does "Shiroi heya no futari." Thus, as James Welker points out, these early examples established a pattern by which lesbian narratives in manga "have often served to perpetuate the dominant patriarchal discourse."[97] These works are what people mean when they say that the 1970s saw the origin of yuri manga, but shōnen'ai manga remained vastly more popular with shōjo readers and creators.[98]

Hagio has since disavowed any interest in or understanding of shōnen'ai, but she did sketch out the general plot of *Tōma no shinzō* (*The Heart of Thomas*, 1974–75) after viewing the French film *Les amitiés particulières* (*This Special Friendship*, 1964) with Takemiya and Masuyama in March 1971. Her 1971 manga "The November Gymnasium (Jūichigatsu no gymnasium)" originated as a what-if "spin-off" of *Thomas*, in which the protagonists were twins.[99] She wrote two versions of the story, one with girls and one with boys, but rejected the girls version because it was "disgusting" (iyarashii); she found the sapphic kiss scene "as sticky as nattō." Hagio stuck to drawing boys in her works for a long time thereafter: She could idealize them, whereas she found drawing girls too true to life.[100] Drawing the girls version also brought home to her the confining nature of culture and society's expectations for girls, along with the pressures on women, whereas writing boys meant that they could move freely without societal constraints.[101] That decision became a path to sidestepping heteronormative social norms and patriarchal gender expectations, depicting alternative communities and relationships in her work.[102]

Yamamoto was willing to accept any manga from Hagio, due to her popularity with readers and her ability to turn pages in on deadline with clockwork regularity; this permissiveness set him apart from other shōjo manga editors.[103] Thus, he published Hagio's early classic *Pō no ichizoku* (*The Poe Clan*, 1972–76, 2016–), an unconventional, interrelated series of short stories about the fourteen-year-old vampire companions Edgar and Alan across time.[104] This manga introduced Hagio's signature innovation of diagonal lines to a wider audience, an element so visually distinctive that it was possible to tell immediately when a creator had read Hagio's work, starting with Ichijō Yukari. In Takemiya's words, "manga is open source," so it wasn't that creators couldn't or didn't ruthlessly pilfer others' visual innovations, but everyone immediately adopted Hagio's style of diagonal lines, and her art remained the standard for this kind of visual approach.[105]

Hagio's popularity also meant that she was the first to introduce movie-style expression into shōjo, and she and other Shōwa 24 creators together expanded movie-style expression into a much more personal and psychological affair. "Utilizing overlapping and cascading panels, fade-outs, close-ups, and panels that fall off the page edge, the pictures in shōjo manga often flow from one to another," writes Jennifer Prough. "These artists took Tezuka's initial cinematic innovations a step further by adding interspersed layers and views to his use of close-ups and cutaways organized neatly in rows. . . . Finally, in order to express inner thoughts and memories along with the main dialogue, different styles of font and text were experimented with, moving beyond word bubbles, to express a wider range of thoughts and feelings."[106]

In the wake of *The Rose of Versailles*, which proved the feasibility of story manga's serial narratives in shōjo, Hagio's editor asked for a weekly serial; she proposed *Thomas*. Set in West Germany, *Thomas* revolves around same-sex relationships between boys at an all-boys school, focusing on the eponymous Thomas and the older Juli, who spurns Thomas's affections, due to his own traumatic backstory. Initial reader responses were dismal. The manga was saved from cancellation only because the *Pō no ichizoku* tankōbon began flying off the shelves (the first printing of thirty thousand copies sold out in three days) as word spread and manga fans who didn't read shōjo magazines picked up the books.[107] *Poe* fans began reading *Thomas*, giving Hagio time to finish her story.[108]

The manga opens with Thomas already having died by suicide, opening up a richer narrative than the simple plot of homophobia and death in *Les amitiés particulières*.[109] Erich, a transfer student who bears an uncanny resemblance to Thomas, arrives at the school and quickly becomes friends with Juli's friend Oskar even as his feelings toward Juli mutually cycle between antipathy and interest. Besides romantic friendships and relationships between the students, the narrative also involves relationships between parents and children. The manga ends when Juli, finally able to reconcile his traumatic past with his love for Thomas and Thomas's love for him thanks to Erich's and Oskar's support and affection, leaves the school and enters a seminary. Although Hagio saw the story as being about boys' friendship and youthful freedom, it was immediately embraced and interpreted as a landmark of shōnen'ai.[110]

The Heart of Thomas blazed a trail, but as scholars of the media mix have noted, it is the second work that is more important than the first, because it is the second work that establishes the pattern.[111] Thus, it was Hagio's former Ōizumi Salon comrades who established shōnen'ai as a new manga category in the second half of the 1970s, led by Takemiya Keiko.

REVOLUTIONARY ROMANCE: THE BERUBARA BOOM AND THE MEDIA MIX

Although *The Rose of Versailles* was extremely popular, with intense engagement among its first readership of middle and high school girls, the so-called BeruBara boom really kicked off in 1974, after the manga's serialization ended, changing the Japanese mediascape forever.[112] The boom was spurred by the Takarazuka musical adaptation of the manga: Its popularity was so sudden and immediate that Ikeda, who had been traveling in Europe when the musical premiered, first learned of the boom when she landed at Haneda Airport and saw a reporter talking about it on TV in the terminal.[113]

Takarazuka was then weathering a slump in its popularity, which scholar Leonie Stickland explains is "usually attributed to overwhelming competition from television, cinema and the 'underground (angura)' theatres of the time."[114] The Revue seemed somewhat stodgy and old-fashioned, but the first *Rose of Versailles* musical was a runaway success that completely changed the company's image and converted many, many girls and women into lifelong Takarazuka fans. At the height of the boom in 1975, the lines for the same-day ticket booth were routinely over one kilometer long, and Takarazuka did over 30 million yen in sales in one day: Fans often traveled to Kansai without having purchased tickets.[115] It was the biggest hit in the company's history, and it remains a milestone in media.[116]

Old-school Takarazuka fans were embarrassed that the company was adapting a manga, and director Ueda Shinji himself later admitted finding the idea absurd until he read it, but the musical's success was undeniable.[117] Moreover, the girls and young women who made pilgrimages to the theater from as far away as Okinawa and Hokkaido, and who cried when they couldn't get same-day tickets and had to watch on the overflow CCTV setup established in the lobby specifically for that purpose, became the company's enduring fan base for the next forty years. The Takarazuka fan magazine's print run was increased from forty thousand to two hundred thousand copies and every show of the musicals' traveling productions sold out, making Takarazuka a household name nationwide.[118] By the time the last *Rose of Versailles* musical closed in 1976, all four Takarazuka troupes had played the productions to a total of 1.5 million attendees. Applications to join the company also spiked.[119]

The *BeruBara* musical was the first time a manga had ever been adapted into this medium. Intriguingly, much as anime was energized by kamishibai, the musical got a shot in the arm from the traditional Japanese theatrical form of kabuki: Kabuki and film actor Hasegawa Kazuo (1908–84) directed the production and taught the actors kabuki-derived practices such as traditional stances and sculptural poses, used to highlight dramatic moments and give the production a stylized atmosphere.[120] Its runaway success not only revived Takarazuka's fortunes, but also profoundly affected the way that manga was adapted across media and the media mix thereafter. There is a direct line between the Takarazuka *BeruBara* musical and every anime musical and stage adaptation ever produced; without the success of Takarazuka's *The Rose of Versailles*, this aspect of the media mix would simply not exist.

The *Rose of Versailles* musical also inaugurated another aspect of the developing anime media mix: the importance of *synergy*. In his landmark study *Anime's Media Mix*, Marc Steinberg focuses on the importance of Kadokawa Books to the anime media mix's maturation in the 1980s, and situates the origins of Kadokawa's winning marketing strategies with Kadokawa Haruki's creation of a film production unit within Kadokawa Books in 1976. But the fact that Kadokawa bet big on a media mix strategy characterized by what Steinberg describes as "the continuous, serial consumption across media texts that characterizes the anime media mix" had a crucial precursor in *BeruBara*'s success.[121]

Specifically, the Revue created multiple versions of the musical, which in Stickland's summary "told the same basic story but focused upon different aspects of the relationships among the main characters, [and] proved to be a flexible vehicle in subsequent years to highlight the talents of various performers."[122] This character-driven media strategy inaugurated a key shift in how audiences consumed and interacted with the media itself. Takarazuka staff noticed immediately that, in the words of the head of the company's publishing division, "what was different about the performances [of the *BeruBara* musical] was that the fans were screaming the names of the characters, not the names or nicknames of the actors, probably because so many of them were fans of the manga."[123]

The *BeruBara* fans who made the pilgrimage to Takarazuka weren't doing it as fans of the Revue; they were doing it because the musical was a new way to consume the characters and story they loved. Takarazuka also played up the manga details; stage backgrounds featured character images from the manga, and Haruna Yuri, the otokoyaku who originated the role of Oscar, studied the manga closely and did her makeup to look as much like the manga as possible.[124] As a form of live theater, the *BeruBara* musical allowed fans to consume their beloved characters not just visually and imaginatively, but in person and face to face. (Some impassioned fans even "tore at stars' hair and clothing to obtain a 'souvenir,'" according to actors in the productions.)[125]

Takarazuka pioneered this character-driven strategy of media adaptations with *The Rose of Versailles;* its next hit, 1977's *Gone with the Wind*, also used dual versions of the same story (specifically, "Butler" and "Scarlett" adaptations) to attract large audiences, totaling nearly 1.34 million people.[126] These developments in the late 1970s took place in a media environment in which adult men had already been captured by new developments in manga, namely the shōjo revolution and seinen before that.[127] Takarazuka and *The Rose of Versailles* together brought the previously underserved demographic of adult women into contact with manga as well, amplified by the *Rose of Versailles* anime (1979–80), preparing the ground for Kadokawa's blockbuster expansion of the anime media mix to encompass still more forms of media in the 1980s.

BeruBara's success as manga, musical, and anime put shōjo manga on the larger cultural map: The number of shōjo magazines jumped from ten in 1973 to twenty-eight in 1978, with nearly two billion copies in print.[128] Manga fans of all ages and genders continued to avidly consume the works that Shōwa 24 group members produced, often with a science fiction emphasis, such as Takemiya's *Tera e . . .* (*To Terra . . .*, 1977–80) and Hagio's *A, A'* (1981–84). Some of these series ran in seinen magazines, beginning with *Tera e . . .* in the short-lived monthly magazine *Manga Shōnen* (1976–81), which featured many former *COM* creators, including Tezuka. Takemiya herself summed up the reasons for this movement out of shōjo when she commented, "There are things seinen can do that shōjo can't, I thought, so I had to go to a place where I could do them."[129]

As both 49ers creators and their initial young female audiences continued to age, shōjo manga became the victim of its own success: Editors fomented a new orthodoxy, and the category's cutting-edge appeal faded. Older readers increasingly wanted manga that spoke to their daily lives and quotidian concerns in addition to their science fiction fixes. The stage was set for the development, in the early 1980s, of another major postmodern manga category: that of josei or women's comics.

Conclusion

TANKŌBON: THE MEANING OF A FORMAT

ANOTHER WAY TO THINK ABOUT the shōjo revolution is as the process by which shōjo manga transitioned from stories written by (mostly) men to socialize girls into their future (unpaid) jobs as wives and mothers to stories written by (mostly) women to provide more directly escapist and less overtly didactic narratives of gender relations. The revolution in shōjo manga in the 1970s assaulted the recently emerged gender paradigm on multiple fronts, trying to use the space for fantasy that manga now constituted to imagine alternatives. On one level, this revolution succeeded; by 1979, all of manga was different than it had been a decade prior, thanks to the work created by these women. On another, it failed dramatically, as even this extremely innovative group of creators could not work out a way to fully spring the love trap. Japan did not become a gender-equal society, and although more women entered the workforce in the 1970s and 1980s, they remained locked into lower-paying jobs without sustained career development through legal and fiscal policies and social norms. Ultimately, the love trap is a consequence of Japanese socioeconomic and political institutions working in concert to enforce an unequal, gendered hierarchy, and those institutions are far upstream of manga, which cannot directly affect them.

The shōjo manga revolution also drove changes in manga formats. The current norm that manga published in a magazine is almost invariably republished in single-series tankōbon editions became the default only in the 1970s. Before that, editors had assumed that series that weren't popular in magazines would not be popular in tankōbon, with the result that they focused maniacally on the reader surveys in the magazines and frequently hesitated to republish even middlingly popular series in tankōbon format. But manga publishers reeling from the oil shock began publishing cheap paperback manga tankōbon, especially in B6 size, and these quickly became a profit center.[1] Shōjo revolution tankōbon paperbacks sold particularly well: As Mizuno Hideko once commented to Murakami Motoka, the 1970s was the first time that shōjo manga tankōbon were more popular than shōnen magazines.[2] Putting manga in paperback allowed it to go places, physically and socially, that it had never been able to reach before.

Japanese manga magazines of the weekly era are massive, unwieldy, and cheap. With spines routinely measuring two to two and a half inches (and, for monthlies, routinely three inches or more), these phonebook-sized volumes are physically awkward to read and printed on the lowest-quality paper possible. With freebies bound in, they bulge even more at the fore-edge, and they are sold tied up to keep the freebies in place. The magazines are so disposable that people once routinely left copies on train platforms rather than carry them home; at the height of its popularity in the 1980s and '90s, the piles of magazines on *Weekly Shōnen Jump*'s publication date were known to reach several feet high at the busiest stations. It is impossible to prevent people from knowing that you are reading a manga magazine in public in Japan: They are visually distinctive and can't be camouflaged, a somewhat unfortunate fact in a society in which bookstore clerks routinely offer to wrap your purchases in anonymous paper covers to obscure what you are reading as you sit or stand on the train.

Social stigma against manga per se has now faded, but it was still quite strong in the 1970s. Tankōbon paperbacks allowed people who wouldn't consider reading the magazines—whether it was male manga fans who had formerly disregarded shōjo or adult women who had put their manga days behind them or had never really read manga in the first place—to read manga in a format that was affordable, disguisable, and portable. Tankōbon paperbacks thus reached different audiences, as when *Pō no ichizoku*'s tankōbon success demonstrated Hagio's massive readership and saved *The Heart of Thomas*'s serialization. They also allowed series to escape the confines of failing magazines, as in the case of Matsumoto Leiji's *Galaxy Express 999* (1977–81), which ran in the doomed *Shōnen King* from 1977 to 1981: The magazine sold dismally while the tankōbon flew off the shelves, particularly after the anime was broadcast in 1978–81.[3] Tankōbon had become just as if not more important than the magazines, and they have remained so even as magazine sales have slipped in recent years, although both are now threatened by ebooks and digital comics.[4]

The shōjo revolution has been described as a revolution in *content*, bringing new subjects and new stories to shōjo manga and thence to Japanese manga in general and, decades later, to the world; in *manga expression*, in that the members of the Shōwa 24 and post–Shōwa 24 groups pushed the bounds of comics expression in terms of psychology and paneling by obviating any difference between the two; and in *creator demographics*, in that the people who made the revolution as manga creators were almost exclusively young and female. But it was a revolution in *audiences and formats*, too, and it was these aspects that turned the tide. If we take Masuyama's metaphor of Takemiya's manga constituting a ball thrown over the editorial fence to the audiences on the other side who helped create the manga by reading it and throwing it back to her, publication formats are the baseball glove by which audiences caught that ball initially. As anyone who has played pickup softball can attest, the glove makes the difference in your ability to catch a ball in play.

Communications scholar Jonathan Sterne argued in his work on the MP3 that scholars should focus not just on media alone but "on the stuff beneath, beyond, and behind the boxes our media come in," including understanding formats in their full social context.[5] In the case of manga, what lies beneath, beyond, and behind the twin formats of this era, the weekly magazine and the tankōbon paperback, is on the one hand television, whose weekly broadcasting schedule produced a powerful imperative for manga to evolve. On the other, it is audiences, who were willing to read across the narrow demographic categories created by manga publishers if the manga itself was good and the format was convenient, some of whose interests (and burgeoning spending power) were not yet fully captured by existing manga categories. Over the next fifteen years, manga evolved to meet the latter challenge—but it was not solely, or even principally, manga professionals and publishers who led the medium into this new era.

PART FIVE

Manga Turns Postmodern

1975–1989

Overview

APPLAUDING THE DJ

TOWARD THE END of the indispensable movie *24 Hour Party People* (dir. Michael Winterbottom, 2002), Steve Coogan, playing Factory Records impresario and local Manchester TV personality Tony Wilson (1950–2007), turns to the camera on the floor of the Haçienda, Factory Records' legendary doomed nightclub. Wilson tells the audience that now, circa 1987, we are witnessing the birth of rave culture: "And tonight, something equally epoch-making is taking place," he says, as the clubgoers around him break into applause. "See? They're applauding the DJ. Not the music, not the musician, not the creator, but the medium. *This is it.*"

"Applauding the DJ" is an effective shorthand for the rise of an entirely new cultural paradigm in which the arrangement, remixing, and juxtaposition of preexisting (and sometimes also new) elements came to be seen as worthy, creative work in its own right. This cultural paradigm is that of postmodernism, and its rise worldwide from the 1970s onward proved epochal in popular culture, elevating new art forms such as hip-hop and transforming others irrevocably. If the era of the DJ marks the advent of postmodernity in music, in manga this transition was marked by fan creators' rise to prominence *as fan-producers* in an industry that had previously marked a clear distinction between fans and professionals. These changes were both symbolized and catalyzed by the creation of Comiket in 1975. Now the world's largest fan event, with more than seven hundred fifty thousand people attending over four days in 2019, the Comic Market's animating principle—that there would be no difference between fans and creators at the event—was a gauntlet defiantly thrown in the face of existing norms in Japanese fan culture.

Comiket's emergence was indirectly related to larger macroeconomic developments. In 1973 the OPEC oil embargo severely impacted the global economy, leading to a great deal of inconvenience, if not misery, in the daily lives of people in those countries subject to the initial embargo (Canada, Japan, the Netherlands, the United Kingdom, and the United States). The economic and social effects of the oil embargo and high inflation rates had a large and long-term systemic effect on the overall direction of the Japanese economy, spurring a shift away from oil-intensive industries to high-technology products such as electronics.[1] Demand for fuel-efficient Japanese cars and other high-value items soared abroad, contributing to the high-flying Bubble economy of the 1980s.

In the short term, the first oil shock spurred a period of retrenchment in the manga industry. Magazine sales shrank and page counts followed, and mangaka's materials costs increased while their pay rates remained the same.[2] With sales down, magazines reverted to a fairly trite content mix, and action and sports manga became the mainstream in shōnen manga magazines in particular. As Comiket 30's anniversary publication put it, "Experimental manga and innovative expression disappeared from the face of magazines."[3] The shōjo revolution creators were a notable exception, but their works were not enough to single-handedly turn an entire commercial tide. Hard-core manga fans turned to the manga fan scene for their fix, not only of critical discussion about manga generally, but also of zines and fan films (made in the Super 8 or Dynavision formats) devoted to manga by Hagio, Takemiya, and other popular creators, as well as amateur manga.

Although Comiket's first few years were dominated by fanworks devoted to shōjo manga, the impact of *Star Wars* and the *Space Battleship Yamato* movies in 1978, the "year of science fiction," swiftly followed by the first *Gundam* anime in 1979–80, proved decisive. Science fiction fans became increasingly prominent on the fandom scene. At the same time, many male fans who had read shōnen'ai and other shōjo manga in the 1970s became fans of what came to be known as lolicon manga, which emerged out of Comiket around the turn of the decade in the fanzine *Cybele* (1979–81) by Azuma Hideo (1950–2019). Lolicon manga centered around cute girl (bishōjo) characters, giving rise to, in anthropologist Patrick W. Galbraith's summary, "a form of eroticism based on manga-like, cartoony, or cute characters."[4] Male fans of lolicon manga came to characterize this fiction-oriented form of affect, both sexual and otherwise, as "moe" (which can be defined as "cute" as a verb), and was succeeded by bishōjo manga, with an art style that more closely resembled anime, after the lolicon boom ended.[5] The male shōjo manga fans who created and read these manga were expanding manga once again, creating a new kind of manga that alienated some people but proved influential nonetheless.

Excessive male fans of anime and manga were contemptuously labeled "otaku" in a niche magazine column in 1983, specifically to delineate fans and fannish behavior that were, as Galbraith puts it, "different, strange, weird, problematic, bad, wrong, and/or abnormal," namely these male fans of bishōjo manga and characters.[6] What made these male fans of anime and manga "abnormal" was fundamentally their orientation of desire toward two-dimensional (nijigen) characters, rather than toward three-dimensional, flesh-and-blood women. This orientation was part of what the editors of *The Book of Otaku* meant when they declared, hyperbolically, that "otaku themselves are the key to deciphering postindustrial society."[7] Between their eschewing 3D reality and their supposed mastery of information technologies like the VCR, in this view otaku represented a "new breed" of human (shinjinrui).

The "otaku" discourse was relentlessly gendered, but female fans of manga and anime were no less active in these years; women too were huge fans of *Yamato* and *Star Wars*, a fact that was immediately visible from Shōwa 24 creators' science fiction turn in the second half of the 1970s. As their careers evolved, many shōjo revolution creators found shōjo constraining: As they and their readers grew older, they increasingly wanted to tell stories that shōjo, for all that they had radically expanded its horizons, simply could not encompass. Many moved to seinen manga, which despite the name was becoming less gender segregated (thanks in part to the shōjo revolution having proved that male readers would read manga by women).

Others moved into the newly created category of "ladies' comics," later rebranded as jōsci (women's) manga. After emerging at the end of the 1970s, the category was received rapturously by its target audience of young women, and by the late 1980s—at the height of the "LC boom"—there were more than a hundred dedicated ladies' comics magazines. Finally, other shōjo revolution creators and newcomers continued creating shōnen'ai manga, both in shōjo magazines and in the subculture magazines *Juné* and *Allan*, which published both professional creators and amateurs' content that would not have flown in shōjo. Shōnen'ai and josei are the last and newest of the major manga categories, and manga's expansion into these realms, driven again by former shōjo revolution readers and creators, showed that it still had new readerships to conquer. With the invention of shōnen'ai and ladies' comics as separate categories, manga truly did offer something to everyone.

Mainstream manga, meanwhile, decisively moved into the cultural mainstream in these years. *Shōnen Jump* became a juggernaut, publishing a string of hit manga series whose names are globally familiar today and cementing the mainstream manga move toward line work and character designs that were increasingly "anime-style," turning away from the older, realistic gekiga art style.[8] A rump faction of niche creators, centered on *Garo* and other low-circulation magazines, continued to publish alternative manga that upheld the experimental/gekiga legacy, to enthusiastic reception from their small audience; in the decades since, global comics tastemakers have embraced these men and their work, making them far more popular abroad than in Japan.[9] Although *COM* ran a regular column on foreign manga, interest in comics from abroad broadly waned in the 1970s, marking manga's maturation as a medium.[10] By the 1980s, Ōtomo Katsuhiro (b. 1954) stood almost alone in being openly influenced by foreign comics, particularly *bandes dessinées* artist Mœbius (1938–2012) in his masterpiece *Akira* (1982–90).[11]

As mainstream manga became increasingly culturally prominent, the dōjin scene continued to grow. Shōnen'ai merged with "aniparo" (anime parody, i.e., fanfiction) dōjinshi to create a new category in the dōjinshi scene by the mid-1980s, which depicted the male characters from popular shōnen manga series published in *Jump* and other magazines in same-sex relationships and which came to be known as "yaoi." Meanwhile, dōjin fans who wanted to focus on original works founded several complementary fan events, the most significant of which is Comitia, which bars dōjin works based on preexisting media and which became a career launching pad for manga creators and creative professionals. The dōjin sphere as a whole increasingly drove trends in manga publishing and became the place to scout new talent, essentially becoming the manga industry's shadow half.

All of these developments took place against the dizzying background of the Bubble, the boom years when Japan was flush with cash and success, when the rest of the world worried about "turning Japanese" and it seemed that Japan would shortly displace the United States as the world's number one economy. Cultural critic Azuma Hiroki (b. 1971) once famously observed that "Japan in the 1980s was entirely a fiction. Yet this fiction, *while it lasted*, was comfortable to dwell in."[12] While Azuma's observation referred to a complicated discourse about the 1980s fad of postmodernity in the Japanese public sphere, it is equally accurate on a purely material level—as long as one was happy paying 10,000 yen for a t-shirt.[13] But the material luxury of the 1980s enabled structural developments in manga that would not have happened otherwise, just as the erosion of that material luxury thereafter has shaped manga's development in the decades since.

CHAPTER NINE

Something Postmodern Going On

THE WORK THAT SHALL BECOME A NEW GENRE ITSELF: COMIKET

Despite—or even because of—*COM*'s untimely demise, the manga fan scene in Japan was thriving by the early 1970s. Osaka, Tokyo, and other major cities boasted several regional groups and events, and local and regional manga fandom scenes were vibrant, but by 1975 there was only one comprehensive national manga fandom event: the Nihon Manga Taikai, held annually in Tokyo since 1972. ManTai, as it was known, was based on science fiction conventions, with the result that it was a poor fit for a scene in which (unlike science fiction) amateur production for its own sake had been given unofficial official imprimatur at the highest levels of the medium.[1]

Yonezawa Yoshihiro, the fan scholar and critic who became one of Comiket's leading organizers, later wrote that its critics had three main problems with ManTai. First, the organizers asserted their right to bar certain people from participating on the nebulous and arbitrary grounds that they thought those people made the event not fun. Second, ManTai restricted "manga" solely to that produced by professional creators and, as such, was too focused on professional media. Finally, the organizers didn't create enough structure in the event itself: Though it was the only national event for manga fandom, it didn't do anything but gather fans together and charge them for the privilege. As Yonezawa sarcastically remarked twenty years later, ManTai participants didn't want to schlep all the way to Tokyo just to discuss *Cyborg 009*.[2]

The fourth ManTai was held in summer 1975, and its decision to bar certain people from participating spurred the members of the circle Meikyū to begin organizing their own counter-event. They named it Comic Market, or

Comiket (sometimes Comike) for short. It was no coincidence that Meikyū raised the banner of opposition to ManTai, just as it was no coincidence that female members of Meikyū were barred by ManTai in the first place. Meikyū (Labyrinth) was, in Yonezawa's phrase, opposed to "commercial magazines' manga stuck in the rut of sports or school love comedies, old-school manga criticism, manga fandom which had fallen into the socially isolated games of BNFs [big name fans], and fans who were under the delusion of *COM:* it was a young generation that was rising, critical of everything. More than just demolishing everything, they were creating a new manga state of affairs within the confused state of affairs. Their intention to separate from manga fests aimed at collectors and ManTai was part of that."[3]

Meikyū was formally established in April 1975, composed of Yonezawa and others including Shimotsuki Takanaka (b. 1951); both had been AS members. Shimotsuki went on to serve as the first "representative" (roughly equivalent to president) of Comiket until he resigned in 1979; Yonezawa took over in 1980.[4] Shimotsuki's discovery that he was not the only male fan of shōjo manga at the first ManTai, in 1972, proved animating; he and other fans founded a national Hagio Moto fan club, Moto no Tomo, and Shimotsuki began producing Hagio dōjinshi. By 1974, he had joined forces with the Wakō University manga club to produce an early fan film, an animated version of Hagio's "November Gymnasium," which comprised about four hundred drawings with a runtime of forty-five minutes.[5] Fan films, somewhat comparable to the early fanvids being produced in anglophone science fiction fandom in this same era, remained a small but important part of the manga fandom scene during this decade.[6]

Meikyū's arguments with and about ManTai occurred concurrently with approximately six months of work in setting up the first Comic Market, and the ManTai controversy dragged on into 1976. Yonezawa later wrote that "it's not inaccurate to say that [the meeting to complain about ManTai] in the summer of '75 was the start of Comiket, but it was only one cause." Despite their simmering opposition to ManTai and the old-school approach it embodied, the Meikyū members piggybacked on ManTai and other popular fannish forums to get word about their plans out, and they started work on their event in earnest in August 1975.[7] Notably, they advertised the event in just one manga magazine: *Bessatsu Shōjo Comic* (1970–), one of Hagio's mainstay publication venues and one of Shimotsuki's favorites.[8]

The Meikyū members had certain goals for their event, some of which were articulated in direct opposition to ManTai's policies: Because ManTai charged a participation fee and barred people from participating, they decided that their event would be free and open to everyone. That way, the participants themselves would be the draw, as opposed to conventional fandom events where the star power of industry guests was (and is) generally the draw for people to attend. In opposition to ManTai defining "manga" as just professionally produced media and in the distinct hope of creating an event that was more fun than ManTai, they decided that their event would welcome people and circles selling their manga dōjinshi at individual tables. Most radically, they also explicitly hoped to revolutionize manga fans' consciousness: They wanted Comiket to be a place that would produce more powerful works, more fan communication, more circles.[9] In an era in which professional manga was—with the exception of shōjo—stale, boring, and predictable, this ambition amounted to displacing professional manga as the key site of innovation in manga overall. The cutting edge of manga, in other words, would move out of publishers' offices in Jinbōchō and into event halls around Tokyo.

This ambition's flip side was that Meikyū members envisioned Comic Market as an event that put fans at the center: Thus, they also made the radical decision to stipulate that those professional creators who did attend would not be addressed as "sensei," the standard industry term of respectful address for professional mangaka. Instead, Comiket "was an event for fans, by fans." Putting their money where their mouths were, Meikyū members each chipped in an initial 3,000 yen to defray costs for printing and other expenses. The Comiket organizing committee continued to borrow money from Meikyū until 1977, when the remaining debt was forgiven in exchange for the circle being guaranteed space at the event in perpetuity. Not coincidentally, this development coincided with the Comiket organizing committee, which had previously been an independent entity only on paper, formally breaking off from Meikyū: Until the end of that year, the event was run entirely by Shimotsuki and Aniwa Jun (1950–2011), with Yonezawa shadowing them and five to ten helpers assisting as needed.[10]

The event did not start out with any particularly auspicious auguries. The first Comic Market, held in December 1975, had about six hundred attendees and just thirty-two participant circles—up from twenty in November, when Meikyū members made a desperate appeal to everyone they knew to exhibit at the event.[11] By Comiket 7, held on two floors of the Ōta-ku Sangyō Kaikan in December 1977 (still a venue for dōjin events now), there were 131 circles officially registered.[12] Although Comiket eventually settled on a policy of covering costs by selling event catalogs in lieu of tickets, later supplemented by sales of official Comiket publications, cosplay fees, and exhibitor fees, its initial years were somewhat touch-and-go financially; the organizing committee was still operating in the red through at least Comiket 15 in September 1980, made possible by deferring printing costs.[13]

The report from Comiket 7 describes what is still a typical pattern for smaller dōjin events in Japan: The venue opened at 9 a.m. for participants to set up, with attendees held outside the venue, lined up and down the stairs, until doors officially opened at 11 a.m.[14] Comiket 7 had the most attendees in the event's history until that point, with organizers estimating that at least twenty-five hundred people attended; 7 was also notable for including a special meeting of animation circles, with a showing of amateur films, including an 8mm *Lupin the Third* fan film by members of the Wako University manga club. The circles mentioned in the official report were mainly focused on animation and shōjo manga, where the greatest energies in both professional and fan circles were concentrated at the time.[15]

Comiket's trials and tribulations sound familiar to anyone who has been involved with similar fan events worldwide. The report describing Comiket 15, held in September 1980 at the Kawasaki Shimin Plaza, recorded 340 circles participating and six to eight thousand attendees. By this time, certain aspects of the event were relatively set, including the general schedule: arrival at 9 a.m. to set up until 11; event opening at 11 a.m. and closing at 5 p.m.; breakdown and cleanup from 5 until 7; followed by the after-party, during which a fan film would be screened. The usual problems were also relatively stable: The report reminded everyone to read the event rules in advance, to dispose of their trash properly and help with cleanup, and that no alcohol was allowed in the event. Other reminders indicate some of the fandom scene's challenges at that point in time, such as reminders that only sales of "original" items were permitted (i.e., items that the sellers made themselves) and that no resale or piracy was permitted, possibly a reference to the practice, later legitimized, of animators selling production artwork from shows they had worked on for extra cash.[16]

Comiket 15 was an inflection point; the report details communication problems between participant circles and the organizing committee, a clear sign of Comiket's increasingly obvious organizational problems. Other complaints were about growing pains. Some felt that Comiket had grown too big and was now more like a rummage sale than a festival: The organizers replied that the shape of Comiket was created within the participants themselves, so it was inevitably going to change as time went on and the participants changed. They also reminded attendees that Comiket's primary purpose was to facilitate communication among manga fans. That communication *took the form* of a dōjinshi marketplace, so Comiket's other animating principle was to offer a place where people who wanted to participate in that marketplace could do so. "Moreover," the report continued, "Comiket will not have the same form more than once. As participants, manga, and manga fans keep changing, Comiket will continue to change. If it doesn't, Comiket won't succeed."[17] These disagreements drove Shimotsuki to resign after Comiket 12 in July 1979, as Comiket had become something other than what he had envisioned.[18]

Comiket 16 in December 1980 saw a decrease in the number of circles; more and more circles refused to participate in Comiket 16, 17, and 18 because the organization was becoming increasingly vexed, and vexing. The problems came down to the fact that running the event three times per year was a brutal pace for any organization, compounded by the fact that the organizing committee's leaders seem to have operated on concentrated bursts of intense activity shortly before the event itself, which conflicted with circles and participants' need for better long-range guidance in advance and made communication between circles, participants, and the organizers difficult.[19]

Tensions came to a head at Comiket 18, held in Yokohama in the summer of 1981, which had 512 participating circles and more than eight thousand attendees but was universally agreed to have been a fiasco. The debacle spurred a coup d'etat on the organizing committee, which was thoroughly reconstructed by means of bringing in new staff and telling old staff not to come back. Yonezawa Yoshihiro's faction on the committee, which saw no reason for Comiket not to expand in perpetuity, prevailed: His vision for Comiket was a festival that accepted everyone. The new leadership put out an emergency appeal to circles and participants for Comiket 19, vowing that they would work toward the next event every day, a pattern that held thereafter. Comiket 19 was an immediate success, with approximately six hundred circles and over nine thousand attendees, and Comiket began selling event catalogs to attendees, including paid advertising, from 1982.[20] In 1984, the event switched to its current biannual schedule, held during the summer and winter school holidays, which significantly alleviated the pressure on the organizing committee.[21]

What were the fans who participated in the first years of Comiket specifically fans of in manga? Overwhelmingly, they were girls and women, but above all they were fans of shōjo: Although women outnumbered men on the Comiket scene, the men were among shōjo manga's most hard-core fans.[22] According to writer and manga editor Takekuma Kentarō (b. 1960), "One of the things that you cannot overlook when talking about manga at this time is that *men started reading shōjo manga*. The 1970s were more than anything the era of shōjo manga. Back then, a man who identified as a manga fan, but didn't read shōjo manga, was basically considered to be unqualified." Reading Hagio and Takemiya was absolutely par for the course.[23] Their works were an important spur to dōjin circles in their own right; fan clubs devoted to Hagio's work frequently evolved into manga circles.[24]

Takemiya's landmark *Kaze to ki no uta* (Song of the wind and trees, 1976–84) laid the groundwork for what is now known as BL ("boys' love") as a separate genre within manga. Takemiya had worked out the manga's general story in 1970, with input from her muse Masuyama, just after she had first come up to Tokyo; six years later, she finally received approval from her new editor at Shogakukan to begin serializing the story.[25] Like *Thomas, KazeKi* is also set in Europe, specifically late nineteenth-century France. The protagonist Gilbert has been banished to an all-male boarding school by his parents; there he allays his spiritual malaise—the result of his uncle's sexual abuse—by taking money for sex with other boys. The central drama revolves around whether Gilbert can escape his incestuous love for his abusive uncle (actually his biological father) Auguste and accept the affections of his boarding-school roommate, the aristocratic Serge.[26]

Takemiya felt that the manga was her greatest contribution to the shōjo revolution.[27] The fact that she and her fellow creators persevered and finally defeated editors' objections and got *KazeKi* and other boundary-pushing manga into print was the mark of its success: To characterize this shift extremely roughly, by 1975–76 shōjo manga had moved from being "manga for girls" to being "manga *by* girls." As critic Ōgi Fusami wrote, "From the 1960s to the 1970s, as 'girls' themselves became creators, the meaning of the 'shōjo' who appeared in 'shōjo manga' began to change. 'Shōjo manga' changed from a genre that represented 'shōjo' to one which was strongly connected with the independence represented by 'girls,' and when 'girls' drew it anything could be 'shōjo manga'—it was that kind of age. In the 1970s works that didn't fit the label of 'shōjo' appeared in great numbers."[28] Virtually all the most popular manga of the Shōwa 24 group "didn't fit the label" of shōjo, as they were about boys.

But *KazeKi*'s publication—and the fact that its last two years ran in a ladies' comics magazine because they were simply too sexually explicit for shōjo—marked the beginning of a shift. Landmarks of shōnen'ai were still published in shōjo magazines, such as Shōwa 24 group member Aoike Yasuko's *From Eroica with Love* (*Eroica yori ai o komete*, 1979–2012), Yamagishi Ryōko's *Hi izuru tokoro no tenshi* (Prince of the land of the rising sun, 1980–84), and Akimi Yoshida's *Banana Fish* (1985–94). But some creators were no longer willing to be bound by shōjo's limits, on sexual expression in particular. Meanwhile, the editors who were left behind adapted their definition of shōjo to become "what girls like," a formulation that was perhaps first endorsed by Mōri Kazuo, Takemiya's editor on *KazeKi*, and one that endures today.[29] Yamada Murasaki complained of shōjo magazines in the mid-1980s that "once editors have made up their minds that that's what girls want, there's no convincing them otherwise." Yamada cited "meaningless flowers," "pretty outfits and glittering eyes," and panels that were "bolder, and split with diagonals" as requirements of this artistic hegemony, which she found "very boring."[30]

KazeKi was a landmark in multiple respects, first and foremost for its relatively explicit depiction of sexuality and sexual relationships, a milestone for shōjo manga in general and for the first magazine of its serialization, *Shōjo Comic*, in particular: The manga opens with Gilbert and another student embracing naked in bed (figure 19).[31] Although the sex scenes appear quite tame by present standards (and were quite tame compared to eromanga at the time), they were nonetheless a significant advance in terms of what sexual expression could be published professionally in manga. Ichijō Yukari had published the first "bed scene" in shōjo manga in 1971, and the groundbreaking and controversial sex scene in *The Rose of Versailles* had blazed a trail thereafter, but sex scenes in shōjo manga were still very abstract or symbolic when *KazeKi* began publication.[32] As sex scenes became more common and less abstract in shōjo and shōnen'ai manga, they normalized and familiarized sexual expression in manga for female readers, a development that eventually led to BL emerging as a commercial juggernaut in the 1990s, and to women drawing eromanga for men.[33]

The first commercial shōnen'ai magazine was the monthly *Comic Jun* (1978–79, 1981–95), which launched in October 1978 from Sun Publishing;

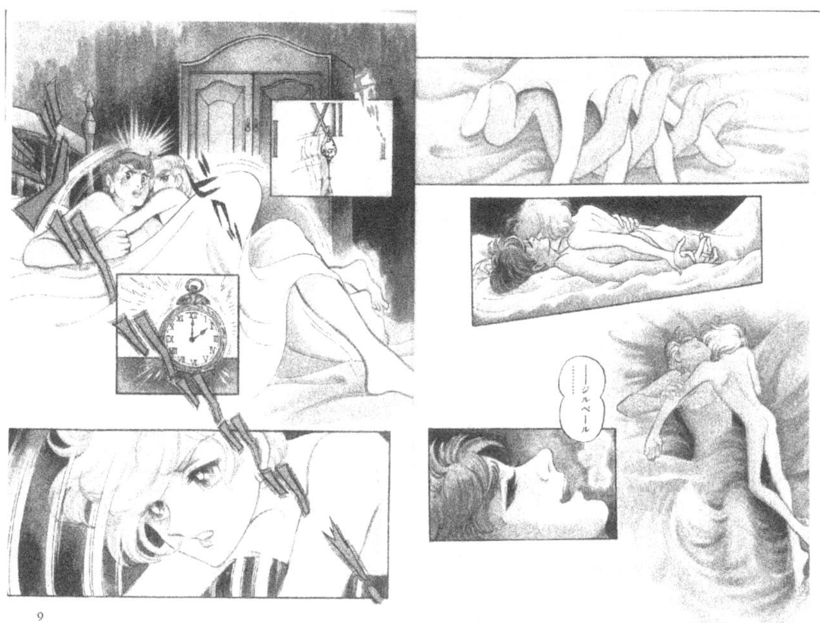

FIGURE 19. Gilbert (blond) in bed with another boy in the opening pages of *Kaze to ki no uta*, 1976. © Takemiya Keiko. Used with permission.

its name changed to *Juné* in the third issue. Its tagline was "Now, awaken a dangerous love," and it was obviously targeted toward a female gaze, with beefcake ads depicting men on the inside front cover of the first issue. Sagawa Toshihiko (b. 1954), who eventually married mangaka Sasaya Nanaeko, was a male manga fan and devoted shōjo manga reader; then a part-time employee at Sun, he proposed the magazine's concept, "a mildly pornographic magazine for women," after seeing the support for and interest in the shōnen'ai manga of the Ōizumi creators and bishōnen (beautiful boys) content in dōjinshi. Founding editor Sakuragi Tetsurō had previously worked on Sun's *Sabu* (Sub), a gay men's magazine. Sagawa later said that *Juné* "was designed to have a cultish, guerrilla-style aura about it, to be something the more established, major publishers wouldn't be able to imitate."[34]

In keeping with these aims, *Juné* mainly operated on a reader submissions model, but its first few years were notable for containing manga by Shōwa 24 group creators and Ōizumi Salon alumnae, most prominently Takemiya and novelist and composer Kurimoto Kaoru (1953–2009), under her other pseudonym Nakajima Azusa. Takemiya and Kurimoto both wrote "how-to" columns about fiction and manga and critiqued reader submissions, and their influence shaped *Juné* and its aesthetics.[35] These overlapped with the aesthetic of David Bowie (1947–2016) in this same period: the post-Thin White Duke "Berlin era" in which his masculine but still distinctly androgynous presentation incorporated aspects of his earlier Ziggy Stardust and *The Man Who Fell to Earth* (dir. Nicolas Roeg, 1976) personas. Bowie had lived briefly in Kyoto earlier in the decade and he was everywhere in *Juné*, both in magazine content focusing on the star himself (the Bowie poster freebies are missing from the Diet Library copies of the magazines) and in reader submissions. These ranged from manga in which distinctly Bowie-looking characters were often the older, more experienced partner in homosexual relationships to fan art depicting Bowie directly as himself or indirectly as readers' "ideal beautiful man (bishōnen)." Bowie also routinely topped or placed highly in reader polls of "favorite stars" and "favorite musicians."[36] Known as "tanbi" (aestheticism), this aesthetic became a prominent style of BL in the 1980s, usually applied to prose and denoting, in James Welker's phrase, "beauty, romance, and eroticism, along with at least a dash of decadence."[37]

The Bowie connection highlights the importance of the global music scene to manga in this era, and especially the rapidly evolving shōnen'ai category. Those characters who don't look like Bowie in early issues of *Juné* look like they could have stepped out of Led Zeppelin, Queen, or other androgynous rock bands of the era; a dōjinshi creator at the time later told critic Itō Gō that she and others focused on foreign musicians in their work (which in the mid-1970s did not yet contain obviously queer elements) because Japanese musicians of the era "weren't cool."[38] Music was now a clear source of inspiration for readers' fantasies, a development that can ultimately be traced back to Mizuno Hideko's *Fire!*

The world of '70s rock was evidently very popular among women who were interested in queer topics, as fan letters to the magazine indicate: Aside from such bands' exceedingly camp aesthetics, female letter writers cited *The Rose of Versailles* and women who took the man's part (dansei-gata josei) as inspiration. Letter writers also routinely evoked the history of same-sex sexualities in ancient Greece and Japan's own Edo period as justifications for their interest in male-male relationships. Reader invocations of past historical milieus in which same-sex sexualities were socially acknowledged were matched by magazine features on gay writers of Europe and America in the nineteenth and twentieth centuries, on gay writers in Japan, and on queer practices in Japanese history.

Juné encouraged a degree of frankness about sexuality that would have been unthinkable just a decade before, starting with the letters from the editor page, titled the "Editors' Restroom," in which, in the first issue, Sakuragi discussed his work on *Sabu* and another editor admitted being a "huge" fan of lolicon manga. The readers' corner was called the "Readers', Writers', and Editors' Bedroom." This candor was matched by the reader-submitted art, which generally fell into two categories: the ideal bishōnen (beautiful boy) and sex scenes, which did not let the magazine's prohibition on depicting penises get in the way of depicting explicit sex acts. That restriction created a clear opening for dōjinshi, which were not bound by the same commercial strictures on explicit images.

SOMETHING QUEER GOING ON

Juné's publication marked a significant milestone in manga history, in that at least one publisher was now willing to not only acknowledge but provide content for the shōnen'ai readership. As a reader submissions magazine, *Juné* had one foot in the dōjin sphere for the length of its publication; both it and *Allan* ran ads from readers seeking manga circle participants, or promoting their dōjinshi.[39] *Juné*'s success established a beachhead for what came to be known as the BL category, which other publishers have served with commercial magazines since the 1990s. Ironically, *Juné* itself could not compete with its latter-day descendants, appearing as it did "before the dawn of BL," in Sagawa's phrase.[40] But inasmuch as the BL category was originally created by manga creators and fans, a commercial shōnen'ai magazine like *Juné* and its later BL magazine posterity represented a fulfillment of Meikyū's ambition for Comiket, and it was a landmark for the industry.

The women who made the shōjo revolution themselves found interactions between boys to be fruitful sites of eroticism and fantasy from a young age. Kurimoto, author of the 130-volume *Guin Saga* science fiction series and a pioneer of shōnen'ai in literature, admitted in an interview in *Juné*'s first issue that the first thing she ever found erotic was not nudity itself but a scene in a certain shōnen manga in which a male character was tied up. In the same interview, Sasaya Nanaeko reminisced about an incident in the first year of middle school when one of her male classmates grabbed another from behind to avoid an accident in science class as a key point in her own erotic maturation. Takemiya Keiko described her affinity for boys of the same age *in groups* as sites of eroticism: thus her enduring obsession with the Vienna Boys' Choir.[41] Later arguments about boys' love posited that the genre's attraction for female readers lay entirely in imaginative erotic transference, enabling readers to imagine themselves as male to avoid the vicissitudes of being female in unequal heterosexual relationships. But the category's pioneers were unequivocal about their interest in actual male-male interactions as well as fictional ones in their own right, not just as a way to avoid thinking about being female or to explore their sexuality in the imaginative sphere.

At the same time, it would be a gross misrepresentation of the social strictures of postmodern Japan to ignore the ways in which the emergence of shōnen'ai was about power and control: specifically, the power of social expectations over girls and women, who surrendered control and agency in their own lives upon marriage, when they were expected to take on the socially licensed and self-abnegating roles of wife and mother. Kurimoto made this clear when she commented frankly that shōnen'ai was related to sadomasochism: In contemporary society it was obvious that women were the ones who would be overcome and that men were the conquerors, and sooner or later, boys grew up to be men. But shōnen'ai perpetrated a pleasurable erotic reversal by exploring the sexual possibilities of boys when immaturity stranded them temporarily on the young and weak side, with the ages of twenty-three to twenty-five, in Kurimoto's view, being especially ripe with dramatic potential for reversals both ways. In the same interview, other people asserted that they had no interest in boys past the age of twenty, a common refrain in early discussions of shōnen'ai in *Juné* and elsewhere.[42]

Depicting male characters also allowed female creators more freedom than they would have had in depicting stories in which the relationships were primarily heterosexual. Male protagonists were a natural reaction to the restrictions on female characters that had stifled shōjo manga no less than girls and women themselves: Takemiya commented in her memoir that she could make boy protagonists do what she couldn't because of society, including going to the places she wanted to go and wearing the clothes she wanted to wear, all of which were closed to her as a woman.[43] In the early 1970s, young women even taking overnight trips in Japan was still faintly scandalous.[44] On the more specific level of eroticism, depicting sexual relationships between two male characters granted creators greater freedom to depict sexuality along with, in some senses, a certain liberatory degree of distance: "Because the characters are boys," Deborah Shamoon wrote in summary of this angle, "they are not only distanced from girl readers' own bodies, but also from the possibilities [one might also say, the depressing reality] of marriage and childbirth. Moreover, in the 1970s, it was easier for readers to imagine sexually active boys than girls."[45] This appeal endures; looking at contemporary BL in Thailand and other Asian countries, anthropologist Thomas Baudinette has found that female BL fans are attracted to the category partly because it allows them space to explore their sexual desires within a socially restrictive society.[46] But again, alongside these considerations, the Ōizumi Salon members were interested in homosexuality for its own sake too.

Many discussions of BL in Japan have ignored the existence of comparable fan cultures elsewhere: Their existence indicates that the consumption of male-male eroticism in media by female fans is not unique to Japan but is inherent in, or related to, the postmodern condition. Notably, English-language m/m or slash fiction—the depiction of male characters from established media properties in sexual relationships with one another—arose in English-language fandom at very nearly the same time as the first shōnen'ai manga. Some female fans of *Star Trek* (1966–69) immediately sensed and began exploring the erotic potentials of the Kirk/Spock relationship, although it was initially spoken of in coded terms such as "the premise" within the larger, hostile Star Trek fandom. What appears to have been the first slash story ever printed, an ambiguous and controversial Kirk/Spock story, was published in 1974, with the first dedicated Kirk/Spock zine published in 1978.[47] Today, much like BL media in Japan and other Asian countries, m/m fiction in particular and fanfiction in general is a thriving—if not overwhelming—part of media consumption online.

The emergence of both slash fiction and shōnen'ai had sociopolitical dimensions: As new media scholar Abigail De Kosnik writes of fanfiction, "female fan authorship [is] a response by women and girls to a media culture in which they rarely see their own narrative priorities and preferences play out, and so feel compelled to create their own versions and extensions of film, television, music, game, and comic culture. It is the very exclusion of female narrative desires from the archives of culture, in other words, that motivates women and girls to write fanfiction."[48] In media in which female characters were either absent or stereotyped and underwritten, it was far easier for female fans to imagine male characters in meaningful relationships, sexual or otherwise, with other male characters, who did not suffer from the stereotypical and shallow writing that plagued female characters. This dynamic was replicated in dōjinshi fandom in the 1980s as female fans began consuming shōnen properties with an eye to creating boys' love dōjinshi about them, but it was also at play in the work of the Shōwa 24 creators when they conceived and created shōjo manga with male protagonists.

This dynamic in female readers' consumption of popular shōnen manga in the 1980s gave rise to yaoi, a "parody" category of dōjinshi depicting sexual relationships between male characters. *Parody*, or *paro* in Japanese, is often translated without remark, but as used in dōjinshi circles it has its own separate meaning and nuance, more like "transformative."[49] Slashing male characters from TV shows to create m/m fanworks appeared in print in 1974; dōjinshi doing the same thing for anime and manga characters did not become widespread in dōjinshi fandom until 1985, when Takahashi Yōichi's manga *Captain Tsubasa* (1981–88), which had been adopted into a popular anime, exploded in popularity.[50] The eponymous Tsubasa is captain of a soccer team; the manga was published in *Weekly Shōnen Jump*. Female fans watched the anime, read the manga, and then created dōjinshi about sexual pairings between the male characters; the sports context, which necessarily entailed a large cast of characters and thus many potential pairings, was key to its popularity as a "genre" (the Comiket term for dōjinshi source texts), which lasted for several years.[51]

CHASING THE NIGHT: QUEERNESS IN SHŌNEN'AI AND MANGA FAN CULTURES

The other reason that girls and women were interested in queer manga is that some of them were queer themselves. Until relatively recently, the default assumption about female fans of slash/BL fanworks both in Japan and in English-language fandom spaces was that they were and are heterosexual, which played into the tendency in some scholarly texts to pathologize fans' interests. But there is compelling evidence that many fans in English-language internet fandom spaces are in fact queer (one fan's meta-analysis of fannish surveys found that approximately 60 percent of online fans identified as queer), and it is reasonable to assume that, although the numbers may vary, similar dynamics are at play among fans in the Japanese-language boys' love sphere.[52]

Despite later portrayals of early BL manga fans as shy cisgender heterosexuals, queer BL manga readers existed from its earliest days. Akiko Mizoguchi was one of them; as a child in the 1970s, she recalled that the Shōwa 24 group's shōnen'ai manga was "the only 'homosexual' representation I had access to."

She read Hagio's *Pō no ichizoku* in middle school, and liked its young vampire protagonists not only for their androgynous beauty "but also because they were the only people (albeit fictional ones) who demonstrated that the 'other' had the right to live in the world." Moreover, their otherness was what allowed the reader to identify with them, affirming readers' differences too. Future lesbian activist Ōe Chizuka (b. 1961) took a page from the manga to the salon so that she could get the vampire Allan's haircut; she interpreted the manga as saying that the grotesque was sublime.[53] For young queer girl readers, then, these manga offered existential comfort, even if they lacked actual lesbian representation. BL narratives still appeal to queer readers who want to consume queer narratives in fiction, both in Japan and outside it.[54]

Queer readers of *Juné* and *Allan* (1980–84), another magazine that targeted the same readership when *Juné*'s publication was suspended in 1979, and that also published mostly reader-submitted content, were not shy in expressing their interest in queer, lesbian, and other nonnormative sexualities in the readers' letters pages. James Welker notes that every issue of *Juné*'s first year printed at least one reader letter calling for more lesbian representation or complaining about BL fans misunderstanding lesbians. *Allan*, which was more textually oriented than *Juné*, went so far as to publish a monthly "Yuri tsūshin" (Lily communication) column, providing a space for queer fans of the magazine to connect with each other through personal ads. Japan's largest lesbian organization at the time even ran a recruitment ad in *Allan*'s June 1983 issue. Looking at the two magazines, Welker concludes that "young Japanese women-loving and transgender women carved out a space for themselves literally and figuratively on the margins of a community of female fans of beautiful young men."[55] For these fans then and for fans now, BL fandom provided a space to explore and cultivate their own nascent queer sexualities and identities.[56]

These fans putting pen to paper was all the more remarkable given the compulsory heterosexuality and homophobia that predominated in Japanese society at the time, just as in the United States and the other countries of the Global North that today are the mainstays of English-language fandom online. In 2025, Japan is an outlier among these countries in not permitting same-sex marriage (although polls show a majority of the public supports the idea), but that outcome was by no means foreseeable in the early 1980s. For this reason, many queer BL fans or creators may have felt unable to be safely out in any capacity, even in the relatively cloistered community of the *Juné* and *Allan* readers' letters.

Furthermore, aspects of fandom activity are inherently queer regardless of fans' actual sexualities. In addition to queering male characters whose heterosexuality is usually the unmarked default assumption, De Kosnik writes, "female fans *queer themselves* when they identify with male characters in heterosexual narratives."[57] Mizoguchi calls fans of yaoi "virtual lesbians" who engage in "virtual lesbian sex" with each other, regardless of their "actual" sexuality, through their activities in BL fandom.[58] De Kosnik agrees: "Female fans *engage in queer relations* by writing sexual or romantic fiction specifically for fellow female fans, for the purpose of intentionally turning other women on, or at the least, fulfilling those women's desires to be temporarily transported into an imaginary that is highly charged with libidinal energies. Whichever of these acts women and girls perform when they make and consume fanfiction, they are *all acts of queering*."[59] Ultimately, BL and media fans are queer not just in the specific sense of some of them being not straight, but in the more expansive sense of "queer" as nonnormative: In queer theorist David M. Halperin's phrase, "queer is by definition *whatever* is at odds with the normal, the legitimate, the dominant."[60]

As part of its queer alignment with the non-normal and the illegitimate, the perception that girls and women are interested in BL/slash in particular or fannish activities in general may have real social consequences; the figure of the fujoshi, the obsessive female fan of BL media, still attracts some stigma in contemporary Japanese society. The fujoshi transgresses in two ways: First, by creating and consuming pornography; and second, by liking m/m romance even though she is a woman.[61] Basic fan etiquette among contemporary fujoshi dictates that they display the signs by which fellow fans can read them as such (ita bags, cosplay, official merchandise, etc.) only in certain designated times and places, such as on the weekends in Ikebukuro or at cosplay meetups or dōjin events. In transit to and from such locations, one changes one's clothes and meticulously hides these signs. "If your ability to conduct your personal life is directly affected by people's perceptions of your fantasy life, because of things they read in relation to your identity and desire, then that is a kind of queerness," media scholar Henry Jenkins once remarked; because of the homophobia inherent in modernity worldwide, that holds true even across national boundaries.[62]

The flip side of this effort to conceal one's interests among those who do not understand them is the payoff of friendship and *community*. It is fairly common for female fans in English to describe their discovery of fandom as something beyond their own personal emotions as a moment of recognition; in realizing that they are not alone, that there are other people like them out there, in De Kosnik's phrase, "the experience described by fans is that of learning that a community exists to which one instinctively feels she is already a member."[63] Work on the experiences of contemporary fujoshi has highlighted the ways in which fans' engagement with BL media enables their engagement with each other: As Galbraith says specifically of nonprofessional BL media, "its pleasures are nevertheless meant to be shared. . . . When someone stops at a table [at a dōjin event], picks up a fanzine, and flips through it, there is palpable tension; the creator waits in nervous anticipation of a response. Only if the prospective reader decides to buy the fanzine do the two women begin to engage in conversation, first confirming what the work is about and then discussing their shared interest."[64]

Galbraith has also documented the deployment of the attraction to characters known as moe, specifically "moe talk" (moe-banashi) among fujoshi, arguing that "in pursuit of moe, the fujoshi interacts with fiction, other people, and the world differently." The examples he documents among his informants, in which they playfully discuss the potential of roads, their boyfriends, and classic artworks as parties in BL scenarios and tropes, and then create those scenarios in conversation, would not be unfamiliar as examples of what used to be known as "slash goggles" among female media fans on the 1990s and early 2000s anglophone internet. Fujoshi, according to Galbraith's informants, differ from normal people and from normal fans of anime and manga in that they "seek alternatives."[65]

Dōjinshi are on one level ways to make those alternatives real, or at least tangible and non-ephemeral. They are used to form connections between strangers through personal interactions at events and through the contact information printed in the dōjinshi themselves, and to deepen one's connections with one's preexisting fannish friends. Indeed, a selling point of many conventions and fan groups in the pre-Internet era in the English- and Japanese-language fan spheres was the chance to meet up with like-minded people; this went double for slash fans in English, who were a distinct minority within a larger subculture. A huge and important factor in the growth of shōnen'ai and of Shōwa 24 dōjinshi was the fact that both the creators and the fans themselves experienced such moments of recognition with each other, forging in some cases lifelong relationships, such as those between Takemiya and Masuyama or Hagio and Kurimoto. Shōwa 24 creators encouraged this feeling of community through fan clubs; Takemiya, for example, routinely sent her fan club members ephemera from her annual trips to Europe through the club's contests and newsletters.[66]

Aside from the fact of queerness, there is also a postmodern aspect to media fandom, which is not unique to Japan or to anglophone countries and online spaces. The impulse to consume more content about one's favorite characters is not new; witness the Norakuro boom in akahon manga in the 1930s, as children turned to akahon manga to get more Norakuro content than Tagawa Suihō could provide. In the 1930s, the only way those children could share their Norakuro fan manga with other fans was to submit it to *Shōnen Kurabu*. But by the late 1960s, fans could channel that same impulse into creating and sharing their dōjinshi with one another.

At the most obvious level—collective emotional and creative response to a mass media text—fandom relies on the modern fact of mechanical reproduction: Everyone everywhere is, mutatis mutandis, consuming the same media objects. But it is the liberatory, fragmenting energies of the postmodern period that really enable and fuel fandom, which is centered as much on *sharing* one's personal emotional and creative response to a given text with fellow fans as it is about anything else. It is in the postmodern era when, in philosopher Azuma Hiroki's summary, "the coexistence of countless smaller standards replace the loss of the singular and vast social standard."[67] These "countless smaller standards" apply among subcultures such as media fandom and BL fandom, allowing members to resist or ignore standards and narratives that dominate larger society and to celebrate minority perspectives.

The idea of dōjinshi as "coterie magazines," small publications aimed at an exceedingly narrow and like-minded tranche of people, is key: In their proliferation, dōjinshi signal the rise of individual viewpoints on media in the wake of, as Azuma puts it, the breakdown of the singular social standard. Just as *Garo* manga was drawn via the medium of the self, characters in fanworks are interpreted via individual fans' own perspective. Because a given fan or circle's interpretation of or interest in a given character or relationship was by definition both different from and as valid as another fan or circle's, fandom was powered by and enabled the rise of dōjin culture, the consumption and production of those individual, smaller viewpoints. Fandom activities valorize the individual perspective, and emphasize the pleasure of remix and repetition rather than originality. No matter how many times you've read dōjinshi or fanfiction about your two favorite characters getting together, there's always room to read one more, an individual creator's individual take on the scenario, and enjoy it just as much as the first version.

Early dōjinshi fandom was powered by dōjinshi based on the works of Shōwa 24 creators. The fans who produced and consumed these dōjinshi were in some respects picking up what Shōwa 24 creators were putting down in their manga: Takemiya deliberately inculcated works that were not explicitly BL with BL subtext, which like-minded readers could and did pick up on.[68] While the earliest dōjinshi of the *COM* era were usually original works, produced either for their own sake or with an eye toward turning professional, the female dōjin fans who dominated Comiket's early years were inaugurating a strain of Japanese fan culture which has now come to play a major role: transformative works, often known (somewhat dismissively) as "derivative works" (niji sōsaku) in Japanese. But as Nagayama Kaoru remarks, "the pleasure of producing a derivative work—in other words, the excitement of reading into and out of the original text, intentionally misreading and dismantling it—is also important."[69] Like many fannish pleasures, this one grows when it is shared.

JOSEI MANGA: THE FINAL FRONTIER

Shōjo manga's rapid changes were also a sign of incipient social changes in Japanese society, whose impact was fully felt in the 1980s with the rise of the "OL" (office lady) and the beginning of birth and marriage rates' continuing collapse. Women worked outside the home in increasing numbers, and though various strategies to try to force them back in emerged, such as the "joke" that women were like Christmas cakes—no good after the 25th—that phenomenon has never really slowed in the decades since. (By the current Reiwa era, the "joke" became that women are like New Year's cuisine, which is prepared to be eaten on the 31st.) Ikeda Riyoko herself reflected on this fact in a retrospective about *The Rose of Versailles*'s impact: She commented that at the time of the *BeruBara* boom, shōjo manga's low position was the same as women's, who were expected to look young and pretty, to get married and have kids, and that was it.[70] Economically, working outside the home gave more women in the 1980s time and money to devote to consumption, and manga publishers followed the money.

Shōjo manga in the latter half of the 1970s was dominated by the magazine *Ribon*, which published manga from leading Shōwa 24 creators Yamagishi Ryōko, Ichijō Yukari, and others, whose styles and content came to be known as "otomechikku" (girly), winning a loyal readership among its middle and high school girl and college-age men readers. At the height of its popularity, the University of Tokyo had a club called Ribonist, devoted entirely to the magazine and with an all-male membership.[71] *Ribon* achieved this popularity through its manga content, but also through its innovations in freebies. By 1975, *Ribon* freebies had changed from paper products to useful items for school and daily life such as letter sets, tissues, clothes hangers, little boxes, and so on, all illustrated by the mangaka publishing in the magazine. The previous era's paper freebies were mostly manga supplements and idol goods such as posters, bromides (a kind of commercial portrait featuring stars and celebrities), stickers, and the like. The new-style, higher-quality freebies played a big part in retaining older female readers, who became the OLs of the 1980s and the first readers of ladies' comics. They loved the freebies; when Ōtsuka Eiji put out a call for *Ribon* freebies from this era in the early 1990s, he got responses from more than three thousand people, who could still recall their favorites more than a decade later.[72] *Ribon*'s making the (largely female) mangaka the draw for its freebies rather than unrelated pop culture figures heightened their profile, pointing toward the 1980s when many of these creators moved into seinen and ladies' comics and took their readers with them.[73]

The time was ripe for a new category of manga aimed at adult women, initially known as "ladies' comics" when Kodansha's *Be Love* debuted in September 1980 as *Be in Love* (the name changed in 1982). Aimed at housewives and working women, the manga in *Be Love* tackled topics including sex, relationships, marriage, and domestic violence—all things that definitely wouldn't have been published in shōjo.[74] Although the category was new, it had important precursors in the work of Maki Miyako, who switched to seinen and gekiga in the late 1960s because she wanted to depict relationships between adults, and ladies' comics didn't exist yet. Similarly, Watanabe Masako (b. 1929), who had started as an illustrator, debuted in akahon in 1952, and worked in shōjo thereafter, quickly switched to ladies' comics, pioneering the category's explicit sexuality.[75]

Be Love's initial reception was rapturous, with multiple letter writers confirming that there had been a lot of pent-up demand. One woman wrote in saying that, as someone who had lost interest in shōjo manga, she was very excited about the magazine's birth: "I'm certainly not the only one who wished for a volume like this." Another wrote that, as a woman over thirty who just couldn't quit manga, it was a magazine whose publication she'd been awaiting anxiously for a long time.[76] Josei really was where no manga had gone before: It took adult women seriously as consumers with their own money to spend for their own sake. Josei also depicted women as the subjects of stories that grappled with various facets of their experience from their perspective.

This is not to say that this final frontier was any kind of utopia divorced from society; indeed, society was all too *with* josei readers and creators. You can tell that *Be Love* was aimed at women who were deemed socially normal from the weight loss ads featured prominently in each issue.[77] But the josei category itself was a direct answer to Shōwa 24 group members' complaints about shōjo manga a decade earlier: Whereas prerevolutionary shōjo told the same highly constrained story about (heterosexual) love over and over, the variety of heterosexual relationships and the problems with them that the magazine portrayed neatly illustrated the assertion that "love could take various shapes."

Much as in *Juné*, the overtly sexual edge to the readers' letters in *Be Love* was further proof of a sea change in manga aimed at female readers in terms of acknowledging sex and relationships in their lives. One woman whose letter was published in December 1982 signed her name "I want to get married" and openly admitted to living with her boyfriend before detailing an incident in which the magazine caused a couple's fight when the boyfriend didn't bring home the new issue because it was already sold out at bookshops. Another letter writer admitted in the next issue that the magazine was a better "friend at night" than her fiancé and wrote that she would keep buying *Be Love* even if she and her future husband got divorced.[78] While these women were probably at the *Be Love* readership's extreme edge in terms of their devotion to the magazine, their willingness to put manga at the same level or higher than their actual male significant others is a telling rebuke to the current notion that only degenerate fujoshi put their personal pleasure in media ahead of their socially dictated reproductive labor.

There is a further irony in the fact that the magazine was published by Kodansha, which had been stodgy to the point of forcing Hagio Moto to decamp for Shogakukan just ten years earlier. The company had evidently learned its lesson; when the magazine debuted in November 1980 it had Ōizumi Salon alumna Satonaka Machiko's name displayed prominently on the cover along with Takeda Kyōko (b. 1940) and Tachihara Ayumi (b. 1946), both of whom soon left shōjo manga for good. The magazine's slogan was "A new comics magazine for adult tastes." In case its intended audience was unclear despite all of this, "young ladies" was written in katakana under the *Be in Love* title, and the magazine's mascot was a fluffy white pussy cat.

Ladies' comics exploded in popularity during the 1980s; *Big Comic* got in on the action in 1981 with *Big Comic for Lady* (1981–90), and Shogakukan followed with *Judy* (1985–2008) a few years later. These were just two of the nearly one hundred magazines published at the height of the ladies' comics boom; the genre developed a reputation for tawdry sex scenes over the course of the 1980s, particularly after the launch of the magazine *May* (1984–2005, 2006 as *may familiar*). *May* was the first magazine that acquired the somewhat déclassé reputation of being "porno for women," with its creators referred to as "women H cartoonists" (onna no ko H mangaka), where the H stands for "hentai," in this case meaning raunchy or lewd.[79] Sometimes known as "fūzoku (sex service) ladies' comics," more and more such magazines launched from 1985 on and did well, cementing the ladies' comics image as "the manga version of Harlequin romances" at best, or just outright porn. Many women H mangaka recruited for these magazines were paid as part-timers, and thus there was not much difference between them and the readership: Unlike creators in other categories, these women didn't have a path to forge a long-term manga career. Similarly, although readers (particularly girls and women) circulate freely between the other manga categories (shōnen, shōjo, seinen), the readership of ladies' comics tends to be closed off, with little overlap.[80] To escape this reputation, the category as a whole later rebranded under the more highbrow "josei manga" moniker.

There was, however, vigorous disagreement among readers about sex scenes in *Be Love*'s initial issues. One letter writer said that she wanted to see "harsher" material depicted such as masturbation and menstruation, to which a male editor responded, in an obvious dodge, that such things were up to the creators themselves. Other letters complained that there were too many sex scenes, while still others said that the sex scenes were boring because they were ubiquitous throughout the magazine. Another woman wrote that, as someone who had only experienced "C" sex so far, the sex scenes were embarrassing because they reminded her too much of her own life.[81]

The sex scenes debate continued for several issues, a clear sign that the magazine had found a sensitive spot among its readership. Intriguingly, the debate recapitulated in a more explicit register many critiques of pre-Shōwa 24 shōjo manga, as when one letter writer claimed that talking about love without sex was a lie, and that people who said it was okay to remove sex scenes from a manga depicting love had no "reading qualifications." Another letter writer requested both more sex scenes and that *Be in Love* be a magazine "like current ones," excising the non-manga content it initially contained (mostly poems and illustrations). Another letter writer asked that the magazine be more "adult-esque" (otonappoi) and "explicit" (echhi). Other letters asked for manga that weren't all happy endings, because portraying love that always ended happily was not reflective of the different "shapes of love" (ai no katachi), while others commended the magazine for one series' depiction of childbirth, another topic closely related to many women's lives that was infrequently portrayed in manga.[82]

The fact that the *Be Love* readership recapitulated some of these debates, and that readers from high school students to young housewives consistently wrote in saying that the manga it published resembled their actual lives, further corroborated letters published in the magazine's third issue in which several writers talked about how they had used to read shōjo, but that the genre no longer satisfied them now that they were older and mothers and/or working women.[83] The girls who had breathlessly read *The Rose of Versailles* and sighed over Oscar and André's romantic first time, or cried over Juli's tragedy in *The Heart of Thomas*, were now young women. Their interests and what they wanted from manga had evolved accordingly.

CHAPTER TEN

Lost in Wonderland

SUNDAY, JUMP, MAGAZINE, CHAMPION: CONVERGENT EVOLUTION

Although mainstream manga were derided for falling into the doldrums after the oil shock, even in the age of high inflation these publications, particularly shōnen magazines, were not idle. Prices on things like pens and ink shot up as well, but the oil shock's biggest effect on manga was a paper shortage: People were panic-buying toilet paper at grocery and department stores, costs skyrocketed, manga magazines went into the red and cut their page numbers, and sales slumped too.[1] Locked in fierce competition with each other and with the gekiga boom, which was fueled by "small, medium, and micro publishers" and which peaked around 1975, the magazines competed on manga and on other types of content for scarce reader yen.[2] *Shōnen Sunday* even instituted a "Dōjinshi Grand Prix" to find newcomers, demonstrating the new reach of manga fan cultures.[3]

Ostensibly aimed at middle schoolers, *Shōnen Magazine* had expanded its reach to high school and college-age readers with the baseball manga *Kyojin no hoshi* (Star of the Giants, 1966–71) and the legendary boxing manga *Ashita no Joe* (Tomorrow's Joe, 1968–73); *Magazine* also expanded into gravure photos to stand out in comparison to *Jump* and *Sunday*, and to compete with the erotic "third-rate gekiga" magazines that became increasingly popular by the late 1970s.[4] But out of all the leading shōnen magazines, *Magazine* suffered the most after the oil shock: Adults cut manga out of their budgets, and if kids only bought one magazine, they bought *Sunday*.[5] *Shōnen Jump* thus overtook *Magazine* after the oil shock with large-scale stories that also appealed to girls; it launched an "older brother" seinen magazine, *Young*

Jump, in 1979, and by the 1980s all the other major shōnen publishers had a "young" title as well, composed of seinen manga and aimed at college students.[6] *Young Jump* was influenced by *Garo* and *COM* in that it had a much more permissive editorial style (particularly compared with *Shōnen Jump*'s, which has been called "dictatorial"); it was where the pioneering *Garo* mangaka Tsurita Kuniko made her professional debut in 1980, having won its manga competition under a pseudonym (although the editor, a fan of Tsurita's early *Garo* work, suspected her true identity).[7]

Under the influence of and in response to shōjo manga's "psychological depiction" of romance, a love comedy boom broke out in the shōnen category beginning in 1978.[8] Although *Magazine* first launched the love comedy boom, it was *Sunday* that really capitalized on it with *Urusei Yatsura* (Those annoying aliens, 1978–87) by Takahashi Rumiko (b. 1957), who was then just twenty-one years old.[9] The manga's plot revolves around the alien princess Lum moving in with the feckless human Ataru, insisting that the two are married; she eventually enrolls in Ataru's high school to spend more time with him. Lum was an instant icon, and the series became a hit for its mixture of slapstick, sci-fi, folklore, and—above all—cute girls (bishōjo), led by Lum herself, who habitually wore a tiger-print bikini and boots.

Psychologist and manga critic Saitō Tamaki (b. 1961) recalled that when he first saw Lum on the magazine's cover at a friend's house, it produced a real shock: Though it was still 1978, he immediately thought that "the 1980s have begun."[10] Manga critic Itō Gō (b. 1967) also experienced *Urusei Yatsura* as a psychological shock in sixth grade.[11] They were both reacting to Lum's character design, particularly her huge eyes that looked like glass marbles, and the manga's overall "anime style." Although the manga's art begins with some realistic gekiga influence, it became thoroughly anime-style with flat lines by about volume 10 (of 34) of the tankobon; and by volume 20, the anime adaptation (1981–86) began influencing Takahashi's art: In particular, Lum's eyes began looking like spheres.[12] Overall, the anime style in manga involved using lots of screentones, and it put much more emphasis on the character silhouette, with flatter lines. That style's popularity spelled the death knell for more realistic, gekiga-style manga art, which retreated from mainstream and eromanga into the niche alternative comics world.[13] Both mainstream and eromanga readers, whose tastes shifted to bishōjo eromanga during these same years as the anime generation matured, wanted to rebel against the 1960s and 1970s, which in manga meant gekiga.[14]

As shōnen manga changed from depicting "a man's way of life" to more everyday stories, it became more open to female characters along with love comedies—most likely another influence from shōjo manga, which had been lauded for its greater openness to realism at the hands of the Shōwa 24 group.[15] But love comedies became more or less the exclusive province of *Sunday*, which eventually stood alone as *the* love comedy magazine and which entered a second golden age from 1982 to 1985. Although *Magazine* tried to imitate *Sunday*'s success in this category, its "producer-style" editorial process weighed against mangaka putting their whole heart into whatever they were creating, in Okada Toshio's view; thus, all its love comedies were "stinking of old man" with upskirt shots, boob grabbing, and other light sexual harassment, for which otaku readers mocked these series. From 1984 to 1986, *Magazine* launched thirty-six series and canceled thirty-four of them.[16]

Shōnen Jump couldn't really do love comedies either, but it didn't need to. *Jump*'s name had arisen from the idea of impressing a sense of urgency on everyone, and the founding editor in chief and his colleagues deliberately sought out newcomer mangaka who were young, scrappy, and hungry to give the magazine that same feeling. Its initial tagline was "all manga, a new manga shinkansen."[17] *Jump* grew its popularity by ruthlessly instrumentalizing the reader surveys, cutting whatever manga ranked last for three weeks straight, and making editors compete among themselves as well. This strategy paid off; the "*Jump* miracle" began in 1984 with a string of immortal hits, many of whose names remain familiar to fans worldwide today: *Fist of the North Star* (Hokuto no ken, 1983–88), *Kinnikuman* (*Ultimate Muscle*, 1979–87), *Saint Seiya* (1985–90), *Captain Tsubasa*, and *Dragon Ball* (1984–85). In the mid-1980s, the circulation of all four major shōnen magazines together exceeded ten million copies weekly, a striking testament to manga's increasing popularity.[18] *Sunday*, however, went into a minor slump after *Urusei Yatsura* ended, launching thirty-seven series during 1987–89 and canceling thirty-two of them: The magazine's editorial philosophy let the creators drive, which meant that a lack of visionary creators directly impacted its fortunes.[19]

Notably, Takahashi Rumiko was a female mangaka publishing shōnen manga, and her success was part of a general 1980s trend in which female mangaka found increasing visibility outside the shōjo and ladies' manga categories. That visibility finally put paid to the hoary notion that women could draw only shōjo manga, as well as the older idea of "joryū [female-style] manga"—that women's manga or female mangaka were somehow inherently different.[20] The frank eroticism with which Lum and other female characters were drawn also had an epochal impact on male manga and anime fans at the time. Takahashi's works set the standard for love comedies as a genre, both with Lum as a character and in the basic story pattern, in mainstream manga and in explicit eromanga.[21]

Takahashi also drew readers of all genders to her series and to *Sunday*, part of the general trend of shōnen expanding to appeal to female readers in this era, which contributed to the magazines' dizzyingly high sales numbers. BL mangaka Kumota Haruko wrote that, inspired by *Urusei Yatsura*, she bought so many tankōbon of Shogakukan series that appeared in *Sunday* that she still gets excited when she sees the logo on books.[22] This phenomenon was eventually deemed the "new shōnen": As the number of children began shrinking, shōnen publishers sought to attract female readers and increasingly toned down the sexism and sexual violence that had been standard in the genre since seinen's emergence.

Manga had become more like anime in another respect as well, namely, its volume, thanks to the profusion of mimetic words (used for sound effects) on the page, which reached a tipping point in the 1970s. Introduced in the 1920s, mimetic words were used only sparingly in the era of *Norakuro*, but their presence gradually became denser by the 1970s, and they began to be used not just for sound but for everything from characters' mannerisms to emotions. By the 1980s, the mimetic words themselves began to be composed as part of the action, increasingly dominating individual panels for dramatic effect.[23]

Ultimately, the convergence of manga and anime artistic styles, and the increasing importance of character design in manga, contributed to the rise of the anime media mix: Characters having one stable design from their debut in manga to the anime adaptation and beyond contributed to the ease of their transfer between media, to merchandise, dōjinshi, and beyond. Characters thus became the animating force that holds the media mix together, even as various adaptations may tell radically different versions of the story, and individual media where they appear become less important than consuming the story and characters themselves.[24]

NOT SO LONG AGO, IN A GALAXY NOT VERY FAR AWAY AT ALL

The science fiction elements of *Urusei Yatsura* and other hit shōnen manga were a draw for female readers; science fiction had been popular among female manga fans since the 1960s, when the sci-fi elements of *COM*'s leading series *Phoenix* and *Jun* contributed to the magazine's sizable female readership.[25] Science fiction became an increasingly prominent subgenre within manga and anime from the end of the 1970s and early 1980s, when new hits and new fans transformed the fandom scenes.

It was science fiction, specifically a military science fiction anime, that brought male fans into the dōjin sphere in increasing numbers. This was *Yamato the Movie* (1977), a compilation of several *Space Battleship Yamato* (*Uchū senkan Yamato,* 1974–75) episodes from the show's original broadcast run. Unlike the original series, the movie did extremely well, and a sequel film, *Farewell Space Battleship Yamato* (*Saraba uchū senkan Yamato: Ai no senshitachi*, 1978) was successful enough that a sequel series, *Space Battleship Yamato II* (*Uchū senkan Yamato 2*, 1978–79), was greenlit for the same year. All three were directed by Matsumoto Leiji, who began his career as a shōjo mangaka. After the July release of *Star Wars* cemented the genre's box office popularity, 1978 became known as the "year of science fiction"; the movie's antiestablishment politics may also have appealed to youth movement veterans.

By contrast, *Yamato*'s basic plot—in 2199, humans resurrect the World War II–era warship *Yamato* as a space-capable starship to fight the alien conquerors—appealed to a generation that knew war only in their parents' stories; the youngest among them were the children of people who had been children during the war, not adults. But the story also reflected an increasingly technologically oriented age: To mitigate the impacts of the oil shocks, Japan moved away from low-value industrial products to high-value, high-technology goods like cars and consumer electronics. The emphasis on hardware and materiel in media that became popular with otaku was partly an effect of this development.

Manga and science fiction had intersected since Tagawa Suihō created the first robot manga in 1929. But although *Kasei tanken* (1940) was beloved by everyone who read it, until the shōjo revolution, manga was not taken seriously by "pure" (read: literary) science fiction fans as an arena for serious science fiction storytelling. Although Komatsu Sakyō began selling science fiction stories in 1961, and published his first classic novel *Nihon Apache zoku* (*The Japanese Apache*) in 1964, Komatsu's prior career in akahon manga, all featuring sci-fi narratives, was largely forgotten for fifty years until one volume was rediscovered in Mandarake and several were reissued in facsimile in honor of Komatsu's seventieth birthday, the first time that Komatsu had publicly acknowledged his own manga background.[26] Prior to the rapprochement between science fiction and manga that occurred by the mid-1970s, doing so could have damaged his standing in the field.

Manga became accepted as a vehicle for "serious" science fiction partly through the shōjo revolution creators, who in the late 1970s spearheaded a number of developments that had crucial effects on manga, sci-fi, and fandom. In 1977, publisher Hayakawa's Science Fiction Bunko book series began commissioning Hagio Moto as a cover illustrator in a ploy to bring some of Hagio's female readers to the books, which worked.[27] In that same year, Hagio began adapting the classic science fiction novel *Ten Billion Days and One Hundred Billion Nights* (*Hyakuoku no hiru to sen'oku no yoru*, 1968) by Mitsuse Ryū (1928–99) as a manga (1977–78) for *Shōnen Champion*. Mitsuse later collaborated with Takemiya on the space opera manga *Andromeda Stories* (1980–82), after Takemiya won the 1978 Seiun Award for her science fiction epic *Tera e*. . . .

The people who became known as "otaku" and the science fiction media they consumed were both conditioned by the failures and triumphs of the 1960s and early 1970s. By the oil shock era, the fire had gone out of the protest movements, which ultimately foundered in the face of the complacency and complicity of the alleged political opposition parties, although environmental protection did secure notable victories. At the extreme end, some former movement participants became members of international and domestic terrorist and guerrilla organizations; others became proto-otaku, the men who were so into shōjo manga in the mid-1970s.[28] Disillusion with political utopias was certainly a factor that manga critic Murakami Tomohiko identified in shōjo manga's appeal to seinen readers in 1978: "We may have been too impatient to follow our dreams," he reflected. "To discover the path connected to dreams within the mere everyday, it may have been necessary only to refine our sensitivity." For him, part of shōjo manga's appeal was that it could express the spirit of this "difficult age" within its depiction of the everyday, as opposed to explicitly discussing political subject matter.[29]

Science fiction's rise on the manga and anime fandom scene slowly but surely changed Comiket. Anime circles began increasing from Comiket 7 in December 1977, with cosplayers first appearing in notable numbers at the next event in April 1978; 1977 marked the beginning of the anime boom, which lasted until 1985.[30] By Comiket 12 in July 1979, the organizers began spatially dividing anime and manga circles for ease of navigation. Although the next Comiket in December 1979 witnessed a spontaneous *Gundam* corner, Yonezawa dated the sharp jump in the number of military cosplayers and anime-related participants from Comiket 17 in April 1981.[31] That was just after the famous "declaration of the new anime century" at the February 1981 premiere of the first *Mobile Suit Gundam* movie, which nearly turned into a riot and was retroactively seen to have marked the moment at which anime had definitively arrived, with a new cadre of shows that appealed to adults giving rise to anime fandom as a distinct group.[32] General attendees at Comiket reached rough gender parity in this year, although there was still a large gender gap in circle participants, with vastly more women than men.[33]

The increase in male participation at Comiket was driven not just by *Yamato* and *Gundam* but also by a new kind of manga oriented toward a new kind of male reader. The eromanga that had held sway during the prior decade was known as "ero gekiga" due to its adopting the gekiga conventions of psychological and artistic realism, with professionally published ero gekiga magazines peaking at about a hundred titles per month in 1977. Their collapse was swift, however, and by 1980 the eromanga trend had reversed away from gekiga-style realism and toward a more deformed character style familiar from anime, which first appeared as "lolicon" and then evolved into "bishōjo comics," their protagonists drawn as "cute" or "anime-style."[34]

The readers who consumed these comics were members of the incipient otaku generation, who disliked the ero gekiga style that had appealed to the postwar generation; Takekuma Kentarō later wrote that lolicon manga started out as a way to differentiate its fans from adults.[35] Many came to Comiket through shōjo manga fandom, beginning with the most popular creators like Hagio and Takemiya and moving on to mangaka such as Ōshima Yumiko, Okada Fumiko, and others. These "lolicon" fans (from the Japanese abbreviation for "Lolita complex," after the Nabokov novel) flocked to the bishōjo comics dōjinshi of pioneering creator Azuma Hideo (1950–2019) in particular. Azuma first participated in Comiket in 1979, a decade after he had made his professional debut in the magazine *Manga Ō* (Manga King, 1952–71).[36]

Few words have generated as much interest and opprobrium as *otaku*, which was banned on-air at NHK, the Japanese Broadcasting Corporation, until 2008. People active in manga fandom at the time recall that the term became familiar at conventions (it is a polite second-person pronoun literally meaning "your house"); in Ōtsuka Eiji's recollection, after it was coined as a derogatory label in 1983, "we actively adopted the name for ourselves."[37] Although the term *otaku* has been applied to a wide range of people since, sometimes with little or no overlap between the groups so designated, the stereotypical traits of the "otaku," particularly his excessive fandom, have remained stable. As Ian Condry writes: "In some ways, the image of the Japanese otaku as a geeky, obsessive, socially inept, technologically fluent nerd represents the polar opposite of the image of the gregarious, socializing breadwinner, the salaryman. If the salaryman is measured by his productivity, then the loner otaku, with his comic book collections, expensive figurines, and encyclopedic knowledge of trivia, can be viewed as a puzzle of rampant, asocial consumerism."[38]

The first use of the term *otaku* in professional publication was apparently in the magazine *Manga Burikko* (Comic fake girl, 1982–85), beginning in the "'Otaku' Research" ("Otaku" no kenkyū) column by Nakamori Akio with Eji Sonta, in 1983. Although the first column took a swipe at everyone who attended Comiket as bizarre weirdos, among many other groups of enthusiasts, calling all of them "otaku," Nakamori reserved special scorn for male manga and anime fans who were attracted to cute girl characters and who thus had what Eji termed a "reality problem" (genjitsu mondai). Over four installments, Nakamori and Eji took an outsider's perspective on the otaku phenomenon, concluding in the final column, written by Eji in December 1983, that "the essence of manga maniacs and anime fans . . . insisting on 'lolicon' is the feeling of not wanting to mature and wanting instead to maintain a state of moratorium." In other words, otaku refuse to grow up and put aside childish things, namely cute girl characters; instead, they masturbate to images of cute girl characters, which is abnormal and weird (bukimi na mon). As Galbraith summarizes, in these articles, this preference for characters rather than real women is a real problem in that it enables the "refusal to face reality and grow up, which means taking on roles and responsibilities that make one an adult member of society in Japan. In insisting on fictional alternatives, the 'otaku' becomes a failed man, adult, and member of society."[39]

In creating *otaku* as a derogatory term, Nakamori was attempting to draw a distinction between "good" and "bad" fans, with himself as an example of the former, an attempt that culminated in 1985 when he was identified as one of the front-runners of the so-called shinjinrui ("newtype," a *Gundam* reference), anime and video fans who supposedly excelled at deciphering signs and manipulating information but who were otherwise socially normal. (Nakamori proudly declared that he had a girlfriend in one of his columns.) The "'Otaku' Research" columns led to a fierce debate among *Manga Burikko* readers and editors, some of whom protested the use of *otaku* as discriminatory, ultimately raising the profile of "otaku."[40] The word began circulating outside fandom by 1989; editors of *The Book of Otaku* (Otaku no hon, 1989) declared that "the characteristic preference of 'otaku' called lolicon is actually a manifestation of the desire of 'not wanting to become men.' By obtaining the 'platform' of shared fantasy called the fictional bishōjo, it was no longer necessary for boys to force themselves to date flesh-and-blood women. And so, the magnetic force of this 'platform' which makes maturity unnecessary is itself the living body of 'otaku'!" In other words, using both media and personal technology to connect with one another via the bishōjo character obviates the need to obtain what is called "maturity" in the larger society; instead, otaku mutually create and inhabit their own shared reality, populated by themselves and by characters.[41] As Galbraith points out, this is definitely not heterosexual, and thus the otaku social orientation is queered with respect to larger society—just like that of fujoshi, fudanshi, and female m/m fans then and now.[42]

Against the rising image of otaku as weird loners, the *Manga Burikko* editors also insisted that otaku were not solitary. While it was easier for individuals to develop and live an alternative lifestyle in the high-growth economy of the 1980s, those material conditions also enabled fans to seek out and connect with one another, albeit not always in face-to-face, three-dimensional spaces. Nonetheless, such spaces proved crucial to creating and maintaining the new social realities of fan culture, whether those "spaces" or "platforms" were Comiket, fanzines, or niche publications such as *Manga Burikko* and other magazines aimed at hard-core manga and anime fans.[43] Writing in *Otaku no hon*, Yonezawa Yoshihiro perceptively and presciently commented that Comiket was "a space that is consolidated from a sense of oneness, passion, and freedom, while being chaotic. If anything is scary, it might be that such spaces exist," spaces where alternatives to social norms can develop and grow.[44]

AM I AWAKE OR DO I DREAM? THE RISE OF BISHŌJO MANGA

Expanding shōjo manga to depict shōnen'ai was partly an expression of dissatisfaction with the gendered sociopolitical order for the women who undertook it, and it remains so for people who continue to consume and produce BL media today. Similarly, lolicon and bishōjo manga fandom was also partly a form of resistance against the gendered sociopolitical order for the men who participated in it. The postmodern sociopolitical order in Japan figured women as housewives and mothers of children; the gender role for men was the salaryman, the vaunted corporate samurai who sublimated his entire identity to one company for the four-decade span of his career before his retirement. Companies in Japan demanded long hours in the office and regular socialization sessions outside it in order to suture male employees' sense of identity and self-worth to the workplace, partly through paid office outings to "hostess bars" where women were employed to make men feel manly through flirting, drinking, and conversation.[45] In the 1980s the phenomenon known as karōshi (death by overwork) became increasingly publicized, making the ultimate potential cost of this form of white-collar employment painfully clear. All this time spent at work took men away from their families whether they wanted to spend time with said families or not; animation historian Yamaguchi Yasuo notes that 1972 saw both the introduction of the remote control and the beginning of dads' disappearance from the home as the economy improved. Together, these developments meant that anime no longer had to appeal to families, who were no longer watching together in the evening. Instead, anime could appeal to more specialized demographics, who quickly learned how to operate the remote control.[46]

The otaku retreat into consumption was on one level a choice to drop out of this paradigm rather than prop it up through one's own existence within it; the late-night broadcast slot that most anime popular with hard-core anime fans occupied handily symbolized this difference, as they were literally living on a different kind of national/TV time than the rest of society. Thus, Galbraith describes otaku as "reluctant insiders of the hegemony of masculinity seeking alternatives."[47] If the relations between men and women that society endorsed were fundamentally false anyway—on the one hand, supporting a wife and children who were essentially strangers with one's paycheck, while spending all of one's "free" time socializing with sex trade professionals who were being paid to give one their attention, on the other—then being enraptured with nonexistent characters was a no less authentic affective relationship.

Despite the name, lolicon fans were not proclaiming their attraction to actual, physical children but rather to "cuteness" (kawai-rashisa) and "girlness" (shōjo-sei) in the worlds of manga and anime; having grown up in the era of Tezuka's domination, television anime, and the transition to weekly manga magazines, they were predisposed to like "cute things" and characters that were "manga-like" (mangappoi) and "anime-like"(animeppoi), and most of all two-dimensional (nijigen) rather than actual flesh and blood. As Patrick Galbraith summarizes, "the orientation of the cute movement, of lolicon, was not toward the girl per se, but rather the shōjo, or girl character, and the bishōjo, or cute girl character, specifically."[48] Realism didn't do it for these fans; instead, they were drawn to fictional girl characters as objects of desire, since characters contain both the icon and the ideal.[49]

Galbraith documents many lolicon fans looking back on their experiences in which reading shōjo manga in this era, including boys' love manga, led them to question their own sense of gender and gender roles, as well as their own social positions. Shōjo manga fan Itō Kimio (b. 1951), who went on to pioneer men's studies in Japan, wrote: "In the last phase of the countercultural wave, when I was feeling a kind of alienation from the so-called male culture, shōjo manga offered me the opportunity to reconsider masculinity and to critically review the present situation of gender."[50] Lolicon manga pioneer Nakajima Fumio (b. 1950), who started out drawing gekiga-style manga, was living in a Tokyo apartment during this era and would pick his upstairs neighbor's shōjo manga magazines out of her trash and pore over them. One day she showed up at his door and gave them to him directly: It was Yamagishi Ryōko.[51] Having followed shōjo manga to Comiket, these interests next led fans like Nakajima and Itō to begin producing their own manga featuring cute girl characters.

Although "lolicon" became well known in the manga fandom scene at the tail end of the 1970s, Yonezawa Yoshihiro documented the term's first use in the June 1974 issue of *Bessatsu Margaret*, in a manga by male shōjo mangaka Wada Shinji (1950–2011), specifically by a male character to describe Lewis Carroll. Galbraith speculates that this may have been an "in-joke" aimed at the magazine's male readers, who officially were unacknowledged but whom Wada would have been well aware of as another male fan of shōjo manga.[52] By 1979, with the publication of the first issue of the *Cybele* dōjinshi series, anchored by Azuma Hideo (working under a pseudonym), lolicon comics were becoming increasingly popular. People "wanted to read erotic manga featuring manga-anime-like drawing" (i.e., cute); lolicon was partly born of distaste for the graphic sexual expression in third-rate gekiga, and can be understood as a movement to bring back "Tezuka-style drawing" in eromanga.[53]

Azuma later wrote that both shōjo manga and his bishōjo manga shared a "lack of reality" (riaritī no nasa), explicitly rejecting gekiga and realism for a style that fused Tezuka-style character designs with the emotional character expressions of shōjo manga, a style he termed "cute eroticism" (kawaii ero). Much like the male shōjo fans who founded Comiket, his dōjinshi were an attempt to find others like him among the Comiket crowds, who at that time were still predominantly female and who were frequently, if not overwhelmingly, oriented toward boys' love manga: "I wanted friends."[54] For Azuma and his collaborators, lolicon dōjinshi were the male equivalent of those BL zines and comics: Shimotsuki, himself a BL fan, later wrote that lolicon dōjinshi were, like BL, "a pure apparatus for the pursuit of pleasure *that can only exist as manga*."[55] Just as BL allowed female readers space to play with gender and sexuality, expanding manga to include cute girl comics carved out a similar space for male readers.

At the same time, other creators' works and characters also began attracting lolicon fans' interest, including Lum in *Urusei Yatsura* and Clarisse, the female protagonist of *Lupin III: The Castle of Cagliostro* (1979), Miyazaki Hayao's first animated film. At the end of the decade, male readers and aspiring mangaka also flocked to *Ribon*, which had raised its target reading level in 1974–75 and was now known for the quality of its manga along with its coveted freebies. By 1978, even the *Ribon* editors were giving shoutouts to the "University of Tokyo students" who were picking up the magazine alongside "elementary school children." The *Ribon* aesthetic filtered into cute girl comics both directly through creators who published, or sought to publish, in the professional magazine, and indirectly through creators and fans who read the magazine and made its aesthetic popular. Notably, those creators included both female and male mangaka.[56] All of these developments combined, and the years 1980–84 came to be known as the era of the "lolicon boom."

Just as with shōnen'ai, in the years of the lolicon boom, publishers began creating professionally produced magazines catering to the lolicon market, frequently run on the same semi-open submissions model as *Juné* and *Allan*. The most notable of these was *Manga Burikko*, edited by Ōtsuka Eiji (b. 1958), who was a huge *Ribon* fan in the late 1970s. *Manga Burikko* launched in November 1982 as an adult gekiga magazine, but as sales slipped Ōtsuka and Ogata Katsuhiro were tapped to take over, and Ōtsuka soon became the de facto editor in chief. *Manga Burikko* transformed into an eromanga magazine focused on "shōjo manga for boys": The subtitle on the May 1983 cover was "Bishōjo Comic Magazine for Dreaming Boys," and the issue sold out (figure 20). Over the course of 1983, the subtitle became "Two-Dimensional Idol Comic Magazine for Boys," and then "Totally Bishōjo Manga," part of a "double move away from reality" in Galbraith's phrase, eschewing the realistic art style and the gravure photographs of "real women" that had become

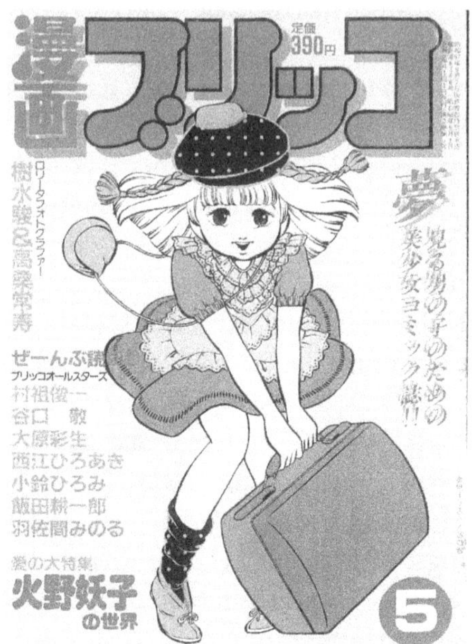

FIGURE 20. Cover of *Manga Burikko*, May 1983.

standard in male-oriented manga magazines since the rise of seinen, and forgoing explicit depictions of sex.[57] Lolicon and bishōjo manga, which supplanted lolicon as the fad for the former waned, were not *not* about sex; *Manga Burikko* was an erotic manga magazine, but it was also definitely *not* about real, physical, 3D women and girls. As hentai manga researcher Kimi Rito summarizes: "The main factor in defining bishōjo comics at this time was that cute girls appear, and the prevailing opinion at the time was that sex was not entirely necessary. In the majority of cases, an anime-style or cute heroine appears in somewhat erotic scenes that contained panty shots and nudity."[58] As the lolicon boom died out, bishōjo-style eromanga took its place, with the readership happily riding the next wave of eromanga fashion.[59]

Moreover, these manga were not created or influenced solely by male manga fans. Shōwa 24 group member Ōshima Yumiko was beloved by lolicon and bishōjo readers at least partly because she invented the latterly notorious "cat ears" (nekomimi) manga trope in the 1970s, which later evolved into the character type known as the cat girl, and thence to bunny girls and beyond. Reader surveys indicated that 15 percent of *Manga Burikko*'s readers were women, and female creators published in the magazine, as did creators who worked under genderless as well as both male and female pseudonyms. Galbraith concludes that "the bishōjo characters in *Manga Burikko* were not fetish objects drawn solely by and for men, but rather were the culmination of movement across gender/genre lines—of men consuming and then producing shōjo manga, women drawing for men, and the emergence of a space of fluid and hybrid expression."[60] Eromanga has remained a space of fluid and hybrid visual and sexual expression, which has allowed it to become a source of new tropes for manga, "and because of that," in Nagayama Kaoru's judgment, "it helped the gene pool of manga overall become rich and plentiful. The influence is mutual and reciprocal."[61]

GOLDEN YEARS: MANGA, VIDEO GAMES, AND THE MEDIA MIX

Video games were adopted into the anime media mix just a few years after the introduction of Nintendo's first home gaming console, offering another medium into which stories and characters could be adapted and thus merchandised. All three media are related to one another: Manga imparted crucial narrative DNA into the structure of video games as reinvented and then popularized globally by Nintendo. The global gaming market, which in 2024 generated an estimated $455 billion across platforms from consoles to mobile phones to computers worldwide, thus has at least some of its roots in manga—a remarkable legacy.[62]

Home video game consoles were largely pioneered in Japan after the infamous 1983 video game crash left the U.S. market wide open to Kyoto-based Nintendo, which was founded in 1889 as a manufacturer of hanafuda playing cards. Nintendo's first major success was the arcade game *Donkey Kong* (1980), the first game in which the story and characters were created before the gameplay, and to include noninteractive, cinematic cut scenes to develop the story before and between levels. Unlike previous arcade games, *Donkey Kong* subordinated earning a high score to completing the simple story, in which Mario (known initially as "Jump-Man," because he could jump) must rescue his girlfriend Pauline from the obstreperous ape Donkey Kong. Players had to clear each level in a single playthrough before moving on to the next: This type of game became known as a "platformer," and the model remains central to video games as a whole. The concept of "levels" was a revolutionary development in video games, and it was drawn directly from manga.[63]

Speaking to games writer Chris Kohler, *Donkey Kong* designer Miyamoto Shigeru (b. 1952) reflected on designing the four "levels" (at the time, single screens) of the game: "Thinking back, I would say that although it wasn't done consciously, I ended up designing *Donkey Kong* like a traditional Japanese four-panel manga. . . . That way of telling a story in four distinct parts seemed natural to me, so I created four separate screens from the opening to the conclusion." Miyamoto had been a huge manga fan from middle school, even starting a manga club at his high school; he went into industrial design after deciding against becoming a professional mangaka.[64] The four-panel structure of *Donkey Kong* then evolved into the eight four-level worlds of *Super Mario Bros.* (1985). Manga thus contributed to transforming video games at a crucial moment, giving rise to a new narrative structure that eventually flowered into much more complex stories. Adding story to video games ultimately made playing the games more enticing, as players, especially children, consistently reported that they enjoyed video games because it gave them control over the story: Unlike in anime, by controlling the player characters, they could participate directly in the narrative.[65]

Conspicuous consumption transformed Japanese society in the 1980s; home video game consoles made sense in an era of increasing discretionary spending. Publishing, too, benefited from the money sloshing around the country, and the annual publishing databooks tell a particularly interesting story about manga in the 1980s. It was not until 1986 that these yearbooks included commentary on the year in manga as a separate category; before that, manga categories were sliced and diced into other magazine publishing categories, ranging from girls' to boys' to women's to sports. In part, this reflected a new acknowledgment by the industry overall that manga was a legitimate form of media, spurred by the fact that manga grew to constitute an increasingly large portion of things published in Japan: Manga comprised 40.4 percent of the country's publishing market in 2021, a figure that has held steady for years.[66]

Manga's success in the Bubble economy years—and its problems—are encapsulated by *Weekly Shōnen Jump*. Its circulation numbers ballooned from 2.55 million copies per week in 1982 to 6.53 million copies per week in 1995, an increase so large that the magazine, which like all postmodern manga magazines was designed as a loss-leading advertisement for the real moneymakers (manga tankōbon and sales related to anime media mixes of hit series), turned a profit in these years despite Shueisha's best efforts.[67]

Readers liked *Jump*'s hit manga series, but in the age of the anime media mix a hit manga is by definition only part of the story. Publishers noted that manga sales were increasingly synergized with (i.e., spurred by) TV and media mix adaptations.[68] Sales of *Jump* in particular boomed, with the 1988 New Year issue selling five million copies and the December 19, 1990, issue selling six million, an increase that the 1991 yearbook deemed "astounding." Publishers speculated that one probable cause of the magazine's success was adults buying it too, which was certainly part of the story; the publishing yearbook also shrewdly noted that "the generation that was raised with comics" was now reaching their forties, in the prime of their consumption habits and possessing unprecedented material wealth.[69] Much of the history of manga throughout this book has been this generation's history; the problem publishers confronted after 1989 was how to maintain profits when mere demographics no longer buoyed their sales.

In this respect the media mix's cross-category marketing potential became increasingly important: The anime media mix made potential audiences aware of content in other media that might appeal to them. As Marc Steinberg writes, "Since each media-commodity is also an advertisement for further products in the same franchise, this is a consumption that produces more consumption."[70] Thus, the media mix (specifically, anime adaptations of *Jump* manga) propelled female readers' consumption of *Jump* manga, a trend that began with *Captain Tsubasa* and gained strength as the dōjin sphere increasingly turned to creating dōjinshi directly based on existing media. A yaoi fan might read a *Captain Tsubasa* dōjinshi, and decide to watch the anime; she might watch the anime, detect pairing potential between two characters, and then go looking for dōjinshi about that pairing. And at any point she might decide to pick up the manga too.

Even as *Jump* made money, however, video games exerted increasing influence on popular culture in general, and became an increasingly important part of media consumption and the anime media mix. Though the *Dragon Quest* media mix was still in its infancy in 1990, that year the publishing yearbook remarked frankly that they wanted the game to be made into a manga so that manga publishers could be included in its "explosive popularity."[71] Publishers observed almost immediately that the existence of video games related to a given manga had a visible effect on manga sales, and video games became an increasingly important part of the annual reports on comics from 1986 onward. The rise of video games also represented a passing of the torch: Children of the manga generation got hooked first and hardest on the new home consoles, and video games as a form of new media decisively shifted the terms of the discourse about children's media consumption. The moral panics of the years after 1986 were directed toward video games, anime, and/or specific forms of eromanga, but the manga medium overall was no longer attacked as deleterious across the board.

As its logic took over what became known as the "contents industry" (anime, manga, video games), the anime media mix increasingly effaced and undercut manga's historical status as the progenitor of anime and the unidirectional source of successful franchises. This shift was partly due to the rise of the production committee system in the anime industry, in which stakeholders across media come together to fund the production of an anime that will power an anime media mix.[72] This new production logic, which is now the model across most pop culture media production in Japan, increasingly subjugated manga to anime as another component of the anime media mix. In concrete terms, in the 1980s, the mature form of the anime media mix meant that an increasing number of manga were produced as manga versions of anime or video games which had not started as comics. Between these properties and anime adaptations increasingly driving manga sales, manga became another way of consuming a popular story, rather that that story's origin.

By the end of the 1980s, many observers were beginning to bemoan manga's current circumstances as creative doldrums. But there was more going on than was apparent from observing only the professional manga industry, rather than the manga field as a whole.

EMERGING PARADIGMS: COMITIA AND THE IMPORTANCE OF AMATEURS

Looking at the manga field as a whole that comprises both the dōjin sphere and the professional industry is crucial to accurately understanding manga's situation since the mid-1980s. Although Comiket has acquired a reputation as an important venue in which emerging creators are now scouted into the professional ranks of the content industry, this image is in some respects not wholly accurate, and it was even less the case in 1983 than in 2025. But Comiket has, over its fifty years of history, changed the face of the contents industry and how it relates to itself and its audiences, and by 1985 the event had clearly succeeded in its original organizers' ambitions of restructuring the manga field.

Proof of this success lies not just in Comiket itself but in the foundation of other dōjinshi events in the late 1970s and 1980s, when "almost every month a dōjinshi-related event started somewhere in Japan."[73] The early 1980s were also years in which dōjinshi publishing made rapid strides, becoming comparable to commercial magazines in production quality; the rise in quality increased competition among dōjinshi circles, which kept prices down. While early dōjinshi were aimed at a niche, in-group audience, the emphasis changed to "sellable products" in these years, which also drove sales higher.[74] By the end of the 1980s, the quarterly Tokyo event Comitia in particular became a crucial node in the altered relations between dōjinshi and professional publishing.

Comitia emerged, indirectly, out of the same debates within dōjinshi fandom that had spurred Shimotsuki to quit as Comiket's first representative in 1979: Whether or not to allow cosplay and "aniparo" (anime parody) works became a key dividing line between events. Now generally known as "fanfiction" or "nijisōsaku" (derivative works) dōjinshi, circles began producing these in greater numbers after 1977 and *Yamato*. Another key Meikyū member, Aniwa Jun, founded a different dōjin event, Manga Mini Market, in August 1980 because he didn't like Comiket allowing aniparo works. Manga Mini Market, which changed its name to Manga Gallery and Market (MGM) the following year, had a "sōsaku [original works] only" policy along with a gallery show; it lasted until its one hundredth occurrence in 2013, and its successor MGM2 has continued through 2025. The concept was a small version of Comiket where readers and creators could communicate with each other. Aniwa wrote in 1983 that, unlike Comiket, "MGM clearly places original works on top. That is MGM's choice. . . . Between 'a wide-open place' or 'we don't want to become Comiket,' MGM chooses 'we don't want to become Comiket' without hesitation."[75]

Similar sentiments were expressed by Comitia cofounder Tsuchiya Shinji, who wrote in the Comiket 26 catalog in 1984 that "I totally don't understand the meaning of anime zines and fan clubs. I don't precisely reject cosplay, but it's unsightly, and I don't think it's necessary at a dōjin event (sokubaikai)." Both Tsuchiya and the other Comitia cofounder, Kumada Masahiro, were involved with dōjinshi circles in Tokyo; they met in April 1984 when Tsuchiya interviewed Kumada for the manga fan magazine *Puff* (1974–) and decided to create a new dōjinshi event, one that showcased circles from all over Japan and allowed them to sell their books on consignment, enabling greater exchange between them. Tsuchiya and Kumada asked Nakamura

Kimihiko (b. 1961), then in charge of *Puff*'s dōjinshi corner, for his help and that of the magazine, which was quite bold since dōjinshi events were then strongly opposed on principle to commercial magazines, even a niche manga fan magazine like *Puff*.[76]

Nakamura and his editor agreed, and a staff of about thirty people put on the first Comitia in November 1984 with about one hundred circles and four hundred attendees; in 2023, its events ranged from three thousand to four thousand circles participating, with fifteen thousand to twenty-five thousand attendees.[77] Nakamura was too young for *COM*, but he was a huge manga fan, and he first heard about dōjinshi from the *Puff* (then known as *Dachs*) "dōjinshi introduction" page when he bought a special issue focused on Ōshima Yumiko in 1978; his first Comiket was 11, in April 1979.[78] After Tsuchiya and Kumada graduated college, Nakamura became the Comitia representative in 1985 to keep the event alive from its third occurrence, despite the fact that he saw himself as more of a helper than a leader; he retired from the position in 2022. The executive committee jointly received the Tezuka Osamu Cultural Award's Special Prize in 2024, recognizing Comitia's importance to the development of manga culture overall.[79]

Tsuchiya and Kumada chose the name Comitia, from the Latin *comitium* (gathering place), because they wanted to create a place where dōjinshi circles throughout Japan could gather. To differentiate Comitia from MGM, which was stagnating, they established three principles: First, they wanted to create an event where dōjinshi fans from around Tokyo could not only hold regional circles' books in their hands, but also buy them in a calm atmosphere. Second, they wanted to make that a reality in the biggest possible place in Japan they could, namely Tokyo, to respond to the demand for and appeal of regional circles and their dōjinshi. Third, in light of dōjinshi's recent flourishing throughout Japan, they wanted to create the possibility of connections between circles in Tokyo and regional circles. Regional circles lay at the heart of these ideas; the cofounders wanted to demonstrate and show off the quality of regional circles' dōjinshi to the Tokyo dōjin world.[80]

Besides these principles, Comitia's essence was that anyone could participate at all skill levels and that it would (unlike, by this point in time, Comiket) feature all genres mixed together, forming a truly chaotic "assembly of expression." The cardinal rule that separated it from Comiket, however, was also its organizing principle: that original works would be the only genre.[81] Unlike Comiket and the "anything goes" culture of mixed transformative and original dōjin works that it encouraged, where professional creators were held at something of a distance, Comitia treated pros and amateurs the same: Whereas Comiket was originally founded as a means of communication among manga fans, with that communication taking the form of a dōjinshi marketplace, Comitia was founded as a "place" where readers and creators could interact directly. And because Comitia has acquired a reputation as a good event to become popular at, regardless of one's current status in or vis à vis the professional industry, it has become the origin point for many professional creators' careers, not only in manga but in related creative fields such as design, illustration, advertising, and anime production.[82]

Some creators such as the mangaka BELNE (b. 1955), who made her professional debut in a shōjo manga magazine in 1976, have moved freely between professional publishing and releasing dōjinshi at Comitia. BELNE, who became an important advisor to Nakamura on the creators' viewpoint, noted: "If MGM or Comiket are places where you draw works that can't be drawn in commercial magazines, Comitia has no relationship to whether something can or can't be drawn there. Comitia is a place where you can publish your own works. That precisely showed the editors' raw spirit at Comitia from the start, since it's an event created by editors. That's why creators set out with seriousness there."[83]

Those developments, however, took time. Nakamura dated the era when Comitia began to be a place where popular creators were emerging from Comitita 13 in 1989, the first of those being Nightow Yasuhiro (b. 1967), best known for *Trigun* (1995–97). Comitia implemented a franchise system in 1991, starting with Niigata; franchisee events have the same name and same "original works only" policy, but everything else is run independently. In 2025, these events were held in six other cities nationwide, including on Hokkaido and Kyushu. Over its first ten years of existence, in addition to creating franchise events, Comitia itself grew to about a thousand participating circles on average.[84]

For a while in the late 1980s and early 1990s, people ceasing activity in the dōjin world to turn pro was also a fairly normal occurrence, though that is less the case now simply because turning pro is no longer seen as the ideal career path through the manga world, and established creators regularly sell dōjinshi based on their own works at Comiket. All of these developments are a sign of the manga market's increasing maturity: Although some may see the creators of transformative dōjin works who exhibit at Comiket and other events as having lesser skill than those who exhibit original works at Comitia or who turn pro, in practice this hierarchy breaks down completely and it is just as normal for creators of original dōjin works who exhibit at Comiket, particularly anime and video games, to turn pro directly from there as from Comitia. Editorial departments of manga magazines also set up booths at Comiket and Comitia to meet with promising creators.[85]

While dōjinshi in the age of *COM* were rudimentary fare, that is no longer the case; instead, dōjinshi today are essentially "independently produced books," and the dōjin sphere constitutes an alternative publishing ecosystem without the restrictions of the commercial press. Popularity in this world is a good sign of commercial potential, and the dōjinshi sphere is "both upstream and downstream" of mainstream publishing in that it both reacts to professionally published media and produces trends, media, and creators that make their way into professional publication.[86]

Manga's extreme variety today, particularly in the seinen category—which has by now been thoroughly "de-gendered" and comprises manga for adults that does not fit into the josei or BL categories—is also a consequence of the dōjin sphere and its influence on manga.[87] Seinen featured a steadily increasing variety of content from the late 1970s onward, as people like Takemiya entered the category and flourished. Although the 1990 publishing yearbook noted that this increasing variety "could be said to be a response to population growth," this explanation seems inadequate thirty years later, when population shrink has had little effect on the variety of manga available in the professional and dōjin spheres: It has only grown.[88] Even by 1990, there was so much manga being produced that being able to tell what was or wasn't "adult-oriented" (i.e., sexually explicit) had become a problem for libraries, which some solved by putting a "seijin [adult] mark" on books that were deemed "inappropriate to boys and girls' healthy development": shades of the ban bad books movement.[89] Publishers later began adopting the "adult manga" label voluntarily.[90]

By the 1990s, some seinen publishing figures thought that the dōjin sphere's existence had vitiated creativity among both professional and dōjin creators. It would be equally accurate to say that these editors were alienated from manga fan cultures and that their preconceptions hindered them from monetizing these fan cultures' products under the existing publishing paradigm.[91] Yamada Murasaki was highly unimpressed with their general ilk and their lack of vision: "Among the editors at big companies are men who hardly deserve that job title," she wrote in 1991. "They show up to meetings with artists as the money-wielding representatives of their companies, ordering artists to draw in accordance with the company's wishes. When you don't draw as they say, they rub salt in your wounds while chuckling and claiming they're just being friendly. Many of them did not become editors because they like manga. They only see manga superficially as a fad."[92] It is hardly surprising that this caliber of manga professional was unable or unwilling to embrace the creativity and possibility that the dōjin sphere encompassed, but as Yamada mentions, they did not initially aim to work with manga: instead, they had aspired to work in other categories like fashion magazines or educational books, depending on the publisher.[93]

But it is equally true that the dōjin sphere did not need the validation of turning pro, and its participants similarly did not necessarily need or want to turn pro. Dōjinshi are not "a substrate" of professional manga, in Nagayama Kaoru's phrase: "Rather, it is another, alternative manga world."[94] The essential point of seinen, boys' love manga, Comiket, and Comitia was that the existence of the dōjin sphere, and works and types of content gaining popularity within it, provided a structural alternative to professional manga publishing that worked in several ways: Most importantly, it demonstrated that works that would once have been considered too weird or too niche would, if published professionally, do well in that world as well. Today's extreme diversity of manga subject matter was the eventual result of this development, but that diversity took more than a decade for editors and publishers to embrace.

In the meantime, publishers attempted to use seinen's flexibility as a vehicle for new manga subgenres with pedagogical and didactic aims: This was the result of a new editorial paradigm that began in 1986 with Ishinomori Shōtarō's *Japan Inc.*, a hagiographic handbook to the Japanese economy in manga form that became the origin point for so-called gakushū (education) manga.[95] Over the next ten years, editors stretched the seinen category to its limits by instigating "new genres of political and economic adult [seinen] manga."[96] The publication of the *Manga History of Japan* (*Manga Nihonshi*, 1989) was an early landmark in this movement, and its eventual approval for use as a school textbook marked a total and telling reversal from the 1950s and 1960s, when national policy dictated that manga in school be confiscated on sight, although it did recall manga's didactic mobilization under the wartime state in the 1940s. By 1989, in other words, manga had arrived; newer media, specifically anime and video games, made manga seem positively traditional.

The prestige manga gained in Japan in the 1990s was partly a function of mere demographics: The "manga generation" born in the postwar years was now of an age to command socioeconomic and cultural prestige and power, and as members of that generation increasingly took key roles in political and cultural institutions, those institutions naturally shifted to accommodate their views. This prestige was a far cry from the art world bona fides that Kitazawa Rakuten, Okamoto Ippei, and their contemporaries had struggled to acquire for their upstart medium in the 1910s and 1920s: Manga had changed irrevocably in the intervening seventy-five years, and in the 1990s it was recognized on its own terms, as a hybrid art form with its own unique means of expression. Indeed, the bulk of manga criticism in Japan thenceforth set itself the task of theorizing manga's uniqueness as a form of sequential art, a notable turnaround from the art journal arguments nearly a century earlier. The stage was set for manga to reach new heights in Japan and worldwide, and to begin slow but irrevocable transformations in the paradigm described here over the next three decades.

Conclusion

STILL PREOCCUPIED WITH 1989

THE YEAR 1989 was a watershed for Japan, for manga, and for the world. On January 7, the Shōwa emperor finally died, after a lingering illness that paralyzed the country's social life until its resolution. Barely a month later, the anime and manga world was shocked by Tezuka Osamu's death from stomach cancer at the cruelly young age of sixty. Miyazaki Hayao wrote in May of that year: "When I heard that Tezuka had passed away, I finally felt that it was the end of the Shōwa era, even more so than when I heard that the Shōwa emperor himself had passed away."[1] Beloved singer and actor Misora Hibari (1937–89), who inspired countless akahon in her youth and embodied the Shōwa period in her career, died in June. In November, the end of the Cold War began with the fall of the Berlin Wall, and in December, Tagawa Suihō passed away peacefully at ninety years old. It was, in every possible sense, the end of an era.

The summer of 1989 also witnessed the gruesome Miyazaki incident, in which a young man named Miyazaki Tsutomu (1962–2008) was arrested for, and eventually found guilty of, the murder and postmortem sexual molestation of four elementary schoolgirls. Anime, manga, and other media found in his apartment engendered a discourse linking those media with his crimes; Miyazaki's putative excessive media habits and lack of social skills led to him being labeled an "otaku" and the "otaku murderer."[2] Being seen as a fan of anime in particular became a mark of deep social stigma—notwithstanding the fact that according to some journalists who were there, Miyazaki owned only a few volumes of adult manga, which members of the press staged in the foreground of their pictures. The reality problem became not "otaku" turning away from reality but "otaku" being assumed to be pedophiles and potential predators.[3] Manga and anime fan cultures were deeply affected by this development, making the 1990s and early 2000s a very different atmosphere in which to participate in either.[4]

Before 1989, however, manga had come a long way in a remarkably short time. As a medium, it entered the cultural mainstream in Japan in the 1980s, a decade after adults began openly reading manga on trains—which, Natsume Fusanosuke noted, had greatly surprised Euro-Americans.[5] That rising tide lifted all boats, with most forms of manga acquiring new prestige, even those outside the mainstream like the alternative creators associated with *Garo* and other niche magazines. Manga criticism also gained a foothold in the Japanese academy.

In manga itself, the dōjin sphere expanded to encompass manga altogether, securing a position that was both "upstream and downstream" of traditional publishing as the dōjin world both drove trends that were adapted into manga and anime and reflected popular manga and anime.[6] The foundation of Comitia, and its evolution into a space that nurtured new professional creators, symbolized the dōjin sphere's maturation. On the professional industry side, the expansion of shōnen and the de-gendering of seinen gathered even more readers to these manga categories, while the continuing boom in ladies' comics and BL dōjinshi continued to prove that women very much did read manga catering to their specific tastes.

Manga also contributed to the rise of video games, granting them a new way to evolve and to secure players' interest by grafting a flexible narrative structure into the new medium's early foundations. Although manga became an equal pillar of the contents industry alongside anime and video games, both anime and video games owed their ultimate existence to manga. The anime media mix, as it evolved into its mature form in this decade, ultimately made manga one form of media among many, but its origins also lay in manga, and in manga characters.

Yonezawa Yoshihiro's place in manga's history would be secure if he had done nothing else in his life other than cofounding Comiket, but his vantage point in the dōjin world and his abiding love of manga gave him an incisive perspective on the medium's history and future that few have matched. In Yonezawa's meditation on the evolution of manga in the post-postwar era, he remarked of its development that "in other words, there was always a back-alley group of enthusiast manga within the age, different from mainstream because it was B or C grade, half-professional. And even though it was scorned and looked down upon, through that energy and newness it became the popular manga of the next age."[7] That formulation held true for kashihon and gekiga, for the newcomers of *COM* and *Garo*, and for BL and bishōjo manga. From the 1980s onward, the back-alley group of enthusiast manga was the dōjin sphere, and its new products continue to breathe new life into the contents industry, the media mix, and manga.

Conclusion

A DISTINCTIVE HISTORY

THE HISTORY OF MANGA is a story of influence and innovation, but also of inspiration and rupture. Manga arose as a break with the hybrid medium of ponchi-e at the end of the nineteenth century, seeking to repudiate what its pioneers saw as the uncouth legacy of the Tokugawa era that had blended with Euro-American cartooning. By rejecting this legacy within a media environment dominated by ponchi-e and other forms of illustrated media, and drawing on Euro-American comics, Imaizumi Ippyō and Kitazawa Rakuten sought to create a new cartooning art form that could rank Japan among other advanced, industrializing nations. Rakuten's artistic and satirical innovations, focused on political subjects, made *Tokyo Puck* Japan's first manga magazine and him its first professional mangaka—although those terms would not be fixed for at least another decade. Okamoto Ippei's cartoons took Rakuten's ideas and expanded them beyond the world of politics, expanding the targets of satire to wider society and thus expanding the concept of "manga."

The rush of Euro-American comics into Japan in the 1920s, particularly after the 1923 Great Kantō earthquake, has sometimes been called the real beginning of manga. But the very fact that these foreign comics were universally known as "nonsense manga" in Japan points to the problems with that idea: Unlike in the 1860s, when Charles Wirgman began publishing *The Japan Punch*, Japan already had a rich media environment rife with newspapers, magazines, and comics in the 1920s when nonsense manga arrived. Nonsense manga was thus not a new foreign thing, but an evolution of a shared artistic medium. Moreover, foreign comics had not been hitherto unknown in Japan; *Tokyo Puck* assistants read foreign comics in the office and immediately adopted innovations they liked into the magazine. Rather,

Ippei described nonsense manga's arrival as a kind of "Meiji Restoration": Mangaka adopted and adapted its practices and brought manga into line with wider, global trends in comics. Whether produced domestically or abroad, nonsense manga was part of the global modern times in the 1920s, and mangaka understood its ability to produce laughter as one of manga's unique features. Although audiovisual nonsense manga were popular, expanding manga's audience in newspapers, they did not eradicate other forms of manga, then or now.

Manga's development changed with the debut of Tagawa Suihō, who had trained as a painter and marinated in contemporary avant-garde art through his participation in the radical MAVO movement. It was his rakugo scripts—a traditional Japanese comedy art form—that initially brought him to Kodansha editors' attention, and it was partly that rakugo heritage, blended with his artistic influences (including movies like *Felix the Cat* and *The Tramp*) and mastery of manga paneling in the collected volumes, that made *Norakuro* so irresistible because it was so funny. Expanding manga to include serialized narrative and humorous dialogue meant that it now encompassed new potentialities. Norakuro's popularity explosively expanded children's manga and akahon manga, bringing the former to new readers and magazines and driving it to new heights of popularity as akahon publishers sought to satisfy children's thirst for more manga about their favorite characters. *Norakuro*, children's manga, and the akahon Nakamura Manga Library, not nonsense (or proletarian or satirical) manga, were the foundations of Tezuka Osamu's postwar rupture in manga, in which he blended his manga, comics, literature, and movie influences and came up with the long-form narrative of story manga, which rejected manga's former emphasis on humor and instead expanded manga to embrace tragedy.

Many commenters have wanted to begin the story of manga with Tezuka, for many reasons, but none of them hold up to scrutiny. To say that Tezuka was not sui generis is not to downplay his genius, or the degree to which his bold innovations led children's manga permanently into the mainstream and reinvented the category, but rather to acknowledge that his work was part of a preexisting mediascape, some parts of which, like four-panel newspaper manga, have continued nearly unchanged down to the present day.[1] To the extent that Tezuka pioneered a more "cinematic" style in manga, its success was dependent on a group of former animators entering the manga industry at virtually the same time. These men had the background and training to take Tezuka's ideas and run with them, ultimately taking manga to places that Tezuka did not want it to go.

Focusing on Tezuka obscures the degree to which his story manga paradigm had become the establishment in children's manga by the end of the decade, with humorous short-form manga for children in the older style and humor itself rapidly dying out. Understanding story manga as the establishment helps in understanding the revolt of the gekigaka, who took Tezuka as their point of departure and went even further, expanding manga to include more action, more cinematic expression, and more psychological realism. Although they defined gekiga as a separate medium from manga, their work ultimately seeped into mainstream manga over the course of the 1960s, as the kashihon manga format that gave them their initial home slowly collapsed.

The preexisting media frameworks in which these innovations occurred cannot be ignored; attempting to cut off manga's history at 1945 or 1923 denies essential context, without which the story of manga after these years doesn't make sense. Moreover, as chasing down many of manga's lesser-known strands shows, the medium as a whole did not necessarily develop in a linear fashion. It took two prior occurrences before the dōjinshi phenomenon finally took off in the late 1960s, made possible by the Xerox machine, for example. The manga research groups of the 1930s and 1950s did not found Comiket because Comiket was not an inevitable development in manga history; instead, it was made by manga fans, and the dōjin sphere continues to shape and be shaped by manga fandom today.

The role that manga's fans have played in its development from a very early era is an essential point. Understanding manga as being propelled by people who love manga explains the *Norakuro* boom, the dizzying ascent of children's manga, and the entrance into the industry of people like Tezuka and Hasegawa Machiko, who grew up reading manga as children and aspired to become mangaka at a young age. The pathway from child manga fan to manga creator shifted manga away from its previous roots in painting, and most creators no longer went to art school to become mangaka.

Manga fans also played a pivotal role in what may well be manga's most consequential expansion, namely its encompassing middle school graduates through gekiga beginning in the late 1950s. Gekiga creators knew that fans would follow them, because they were those same manga fans, except stationed at the desk in a dumpy apartment over a restaurant, drawing the manga.[2] Offering this demographic a form of narrative fiction in manga, rather than the satirical and newspaper manga that were previously the sole forms of manga for adults, forever altered manga's trajectory, setting it on the path to becoming the domestic and global juggernaut that it is today. Gekiga eventually gave rise to seinen manga, which was formulated as "gekiga for adults" (i.e., college age and above) only a decade later when mainstream creators made the same move to expand manga's demographic reach yet again. Seinen was initially laser-focused on male readers, with a concomitant increase in violence and sex, which had a spillover effect on shōnen manga as well. But within a few years, seinen began to welcome female creators and different kinds of stories, auguring its eventual "de-gendering" into a miscellaneous category for adults, heavily influenced by the dōjin sphere.

Fans made more consequential moves in the late 1960s and 1970s, creating dōjin circles nationwide under *COM*'s aegis, embracing the manga of the shōjo revolution creators, and organizing national manga fan events such as the Manga Taikai and then, epochally, Comiket. (Tezuka's role in unleashing this revolution in manga fandom via *COM* is, if anything, underappreciated.) Without the publishing industry getting between them, fans connected with one another through manga, fan films, and beyond, expanding over time to "a level which no longer allows one to characterize [dōjinshi] as small-scale, amateurish, or entirely non-commercial," as Jaqueline Berndt puts it.[3] Perceptively, she notes that dōjinshi are the true "alternative manga" in the twenty-first century, as they operate on a scale that dwarfs the official publishing industry—much the same way that anglophone fanfiction dwarfs the output of the U.S. publishing industry.[4]

Manga fans' unmet appetite for shōnen'ai led to the creation of the semiprofessional magazines *Juné* and *Allan*, which proved an audience existed for what became known as BL and paved the way for its emergence as a professional manga genre in the 1990s. Similarly, shōjo mangaka and fans embraced the new category of ladies' comics in the early 1980s, expanding manga's reach to include adult women and their interests that weren't covered by queer manga. Driven by fans' desires, by the 1990s, manga as an industry offered something for almost everyone.

Manga also spawned its eventual peers in the contents industry: anime, in the form of Tezuka's animated TV series *Tetsuwan Atomu;* and video games, by imparting a narrative structure into the DNA of Nintendo games that gradually expanded to propel an entire medium into the homes and hands of people around the world. In the 1980s, all three became partners in the anime media mix, by which elements of a given property, especially characters, are adapted across as many media as possible to capture as much money from audiences as possible.

Although manga remained an important source of stories to adapt for the anime media mix, the rise of video games, anime OVAs, and above all the dōjin sphere, which has increasingly become the source of properties to adapt into anime and beyond in the twenty-first century, tended to displace manga from its previous position as the surefire source of proven hit stories. The dōjin sphere and anime and manga fandom worldwide have also combined to displace manga from another direction, as Jaqueline Berndt notes: "For many dedicated fans, a single manga's intrinsic quality as a narrative work is less important than its potential as a text to invite participation, facilitate relationships, and mediate taste communities."[5] In other words, manga is no longer an end in and of itself; instead, it is a beginning, a gateway from which to launch into a new fandom, to make new friends and reconnect with old ones, and to share in critical appreciation or condemnation across the wider fan community.[6] In this respect, manga itself has become a kind of platform, a multisided marketplace or a literal medium that connects people.

On that note, this story would be incomplete without a final reconsideration of the questions of platform and format. In particular, comparing the story of manga with comics in the United States and *bandes dessinées* (BD) in France and Belgium makes clear that what makes the medium so popular in Japan is not (solely) its content; adults in Japan read manga because manga contains things they want to read, not limited to fiction. But what enabled manga to emerge from a very low social position—comparable to that of American comics and BD in, say, 1937—to its 40 percent share of the publishing market overall in Japan in 2025 are the more prosaic, but ultimately more consequential, facts of *format*.

The question of format comes into focus readily if manga is compared to BD. When manga critics in Japan discuss francophone comics, one of the standard facile differences used to set manga apart is inevitably BD's beautiful full-color printing on high-quality glossy paper. The standard BD format is known as the album: roughly A4 standard size, about thirty by twenty-three centimeters (fifteen by eleven inches), often hardcover. Comparable to picture books in the United States, the format has been adapted for other European comics traditions.

The social position of comics in the francophone sphere is, if anything, even higher than that of manga in Japan, with comics acclaimed as the "ninth art" and comics scholarship respected in the francophone academy for more than half a century. But just as a classic is, according to Mark Twain, a book that is praised but not read, BD manifestly do not have the same social currency as manga. With the exception of beloved characters such as Tintin, Asterix, and the Smurfs, whose fame has even reached Japan and the United States, BD are popular, but nowhere near as popular as manga. I have never seen adults reading BD albums on mass transit in Brussels, for example, though I have seen adults reading manga and manga tankōbon openly on mass transit—sometimes even without a cover on the books, and increasingly on digital devices—almost every time I have taken public transportation in Tokyo.

Again, this is not a question of content; BD's storylines, roughly speaking, tend to be as driven by adventure and science fiction as indie comics in the States or seinen manga. It is, unequivocally, a question of *format:* People read manga on the train in Japan because the paperback manga tankōbon or smaller paperback bunkōbon (compact A6 paperback) is convenient to carry with them on their very long commutes, tucked into a briefcase or a bag or a purse. Manga on one's personal digital device is even more so, and digital comics' popularity continues to grow. Weekly magazines remain important in the francophone comics sphere, but they are also awkwardly sized for portable reading, and a BD album is no better, particularly in the close quarters of mass transit. Although mainstream U.S. comics, whether the single-issue "floppies" or collected trade paperbacks, are smaller than a BD album, that is not much better. Manga's permeation of Japanese society is partly attributable to the paperback format's portability and affordability as well as to the wide range of content it offers—both are necessary.

The flip side of this coin is that the manga industry has been oriented around the sales of paperback (and now digital) tankōbon and the profits from media mixes, including manga series, rather than magazine sales, which have mostly been a loss leader for decades. Although tankōbon are losing market share to digital comics, the visual style of manga is still composed with print books in mind, as it has been since tankōbon publication became standard in the 1970s.[7]

The exact opposite is true in the case of "mainstream" U.S. comics, with detrimental effects on the industry: Only in the past fifteen years or so, partly through the rise of digital comics and partly through the increasingly undeniable presence of female comics fans and creators, have Marvel and DC Comics begun to adjust their business models to factor in sales of trade collections of comics, which are overwhelmingly consumed by "nontraditional" comics fans (i.e., women and younger readers). Both companies and their independent competitors remain oriented toward the weekly publication of single-issue magazine-style installments of single comics series, which generally release new chapters on a monthly basis. Since approximately the early 1980s, both Marvel and DC pursued a strategy of simultaneously publishing many different series, many featuring the same casts of characters in different permutations with bewildering connections to the so-called "main continuity" of each universe.[8] The overall effect was to make mainstream U.S. comics much harder for the average person to discover and begin reading, the exact opposite of what happened with manga in Japan.

Single issues are everything that a manga magazine is not: Manga magazines are fundamentally anthologies designed to get as many series in front of readers' eyeballs as possible at once. Magazines do not even have tables of contents, the better to force readers to flip through them. The manga magazine publishing model, in other words, is extensive rather than intensive, and the magazines are not the only way that potential audiences can consume the publishers' product: Though manga magazines are generally bought either casually and occasionally, or regularly by hard-core fans, or even more frequently read while standing in a store and not purchased at all, manga tankōbon are the publishers' real source of income, and readers can come to a given series' tankōbon through multiple ways, including via the anime media mix.[9] Even as physical book sales have fallen in recent years, the overall publishing market has grown slightly since 2019 thanks to rising digital sales, with digital magazines also becoming more common.[10]

The other reason that manga enjoys its current position in the Japanese mediascape is that manga has not sought to limit its audiences by gender. While mainstream U.S. comics companies largely abandoned the idea of female readers from the late 1970s to early 1980s (although female readers emphatically did not abandon comics), in those same years manga publishers were expanding their audiences to encompass not only middle and high school girls but also adult women, a demographic whose consumption has become increasingly central to the profits of the contents industry generally since *The Rose of Versailles* first appeared on the Takarazuka stage in 1974. Manga and anime formats are also not gendered, unlike U.S. comics, where single issues, trade paperbacks, collected editions, and digital formats are thought to appeal to very different demographics.

The history of kashihonya in the postwar years reminds us that platforms are an important element of manga and comics history too. In Japan, manga magazines and tankōbon were ubiquitous in convenience stores, bookstores, and transit platform kiosks for decades; by contrast, comics disappeared from newsstands in America after the 1970s and retreated almost entirely to specialty comics shops as white flight vitiated urban landscapes and energized the entropic suburban sprawl. Mainstream comics audiences shrank along with the move to comics shops, and the anime and manga-led growth in American animation, comics, and graphic novels over the past two decades initially benefited the trade book market and general bookstores more than specialized comics shops, which were slower to catch on to the new development.[11]

Manga's history was remarkably comparable to that of American and Franco-Belgian comics until roughly 1963. All three sequential art lineages began at the turn of the twentieth century and navigated a rocky wartime history of collaboration and social censure through the early postwar years, but their histories diverged sharply thereafter.[12] Despite the efforts of mothers in the ban bad books movement, manga sutured itself to the postwar social order in Japan, partly through its rapprochement with television in the form of anime. In the United States, meanwhile, the self-imposed Comics Code Authority stifled comics expression in the crucial decade of the 1950s, and movies and TV came to provide the socially sanctioned forms of escapist media: Comics failed to obtain the same social position as manga did. Although manga censorship efforts flared up again in the early 1990s in the wake of the Miyazaki incident, and a landmark set of Tokyo metropolitan regulations passed in 2010 has also put vague constraints on depictions of underage characters in manga, manga as a whole has survived these attacks relatively unscathed.[13] Indeed, since the turn of the third millennium, manga, anime, and video games have increasingly been marketed as sources of national prestige and potential tourism revenue by various entities in Japan, initially as part of the government's "Cool Japan" campaign.

The other key feature differentiating manga from its fellow forms of comics is the existence of the dōjin sphere and its vibrancy and prominence within the Japanese mediascape overall. Comiket remains one of the largest fan events in the world, and it is only the pinnacle of a nationwide network of similar events that draw millions of participants annually. There are of course many zine fests, comic cons, and other events in other countries, to say nothing of the internet and social media. But the dōjin sphere provides a more regularized, structured playing field in which successful creators have found a range of successful outcomes since the 1970s, from professional careers to fame and popularity as dōjin creators, to an enjoyable hobby, to the increasingly common hybrid model incorporating elements of all three. The dōjin sphere is now both upstream and downstream of the professional manga industry, whose output it dwarfs and whose trends it increasingly drives (although rights holders have cooled on transformative dōjinshi somewhat in the last few years and the long-standing copyright détente may be endangered).[14] Yet without the dōjin sphere and its participants, manga would not be the global juggernaut that it is today.

Since 1970, Japan's experience under postmodernity has repeatedly been positioned as a global outlier, perhaps most famously in the 1980s when the fear of "turning Japanese" animated hit pop songs and entire cottage industries of racial-economic paranoia and techno-Orientalism worldwide. What has repeatedly proved true, however, is that Japan has simply experienced aspects of the postmodern earlier than other capitalist societies; it is only a matter of time, generally speaking, before phenomena that are initially Othered as uniquely and weirdly Japanese have come to the rest of the world. Bearing that insight in mind, it may well be that the dōjin sphere in Japan is a model for or a forerunner of what the mediascape will look like around the world in a few decades. BL in particular has expanded throughout East and Southeast Asia, seeded in Hong Kong, China, South Korea, Taiwan, Thailand, and the Philippines by bootleg and fan translations of Japanese BL dōjinshi and manga in the 1980s and 1990s, and now constituting thriving, globally consumed media in their own right, encompassing K-pop, TV series, comics, Chinese danmei novels, and more, including dōjinshi.[15]

Whatever does transpire, the history of manga in the twentieth century makes it clear that the question of how and why pop culture becomes popular is intimately connected with the work that pop culture does in society and the formats it takes, and that manga's work, both in Japan and worldwide, is not yet done.

NOTE ON SOURCES

The bulk of the research for this book was conducted at the National Diet Library in Tokyo during 2014–15. The collections of the National Diet Library and the International Library of Children's Literature are second to none overall, and I consulted many periodicals discussed in this book in the original, but many are available only in digitized format. Others are available in reprinted volumes, either of original editions or collected scholarly efforts. I looked at others in museum exhibits and exhibition catalogs. Still other sources came via anniversary editions of various manga.

In the course of research, I consulted archival collections around the world. The research collections of the Kyoto International Manga Museum come first in this list, but I also examined holdings at the Yokohama City Archives, the Bancroft Library at the University of California, the Cotsen Children's Collection at the Princeton University Library in my native land of New Jersey, the Nihon Kindai Bungakukan in Tokyo, the Harvard-Yenching East Asia Library in Cambridge, Massachusetts, and the Kodansha company library in Tokyo. I also visited the research library and display collections of the Centre Belge de la Bande Dessinée in Brussels and the Yonezawa Yoshihiro Memorial Library in Tokyo, the latter is the most complete archive of Japanese manga fan materials, primarily dōjinshi, in existence. I also visited comics museums, including the Musee Hergé in Louvain-la-Neuve, Belgium; the Cartoon Museum in London; and the Billy Ireland Cartoon Library and Museum in Columbus, Ohio; as well as museums and ward hall displays dedicated to Kitazawa Rakuten, Tagawa Suihō, and Hasegawa Machiko in Kantō. The Berkeley, Oakland, and San Francisco public libraries came in clutch in the project's final phase, as did the Stanford libraries.

In attempting to wrap my brain around more than a century's worth of material, I have relied on other scholars' work to fill out my picture of the Japanese publishing industry at large beyond the narrow confines of manga, particularly at the beginning of the twentieth century. I would like to specially acknowledge manga scholar Shimizu Isao (1939–2021), whose tireless archival legwork and wide-ranging publications on manga's early history in Japan blazed a trail for me and every other manga researcher, particularly his *Manga zasshi hakubutsukan* series. Hail and farewell, sensei.

GLOSSARY

AKAHON MANGA Cheap, rapidly produced manga that flourished in the 1930s and during the Occupation. Frequently anonymous, it featured unauthorized appearances by popular characters and celebrities. Distributed through alternative outlets such as shrine fairs, open-air stalls, candy shops, and department stores, rather than solely through bookstores.

DŌJINSHI "Amateur publications," ranging from amateur manga and zines to dōjin media and goods such as video games, figures, and more. Dōjinshi production took off in the late 1960s and has grown increasingly popular, with regular local and regional events nationwide and national events like Comitia and Comiket.

EDO PERIOD The early modern period from 1600 to 1867, when the Tokugawa shogunate ruled Japan. The so-called Pax Tokugawa saw growing economic and commercial activity, rising rates of literacy, and a vibrant popular culture including print media like ukiyo-e.

EHON Picture books. Kōdansha's famous Kodansha Ehon book series was launched to provide beneficial reading material for young children in 1936, and contained nearly one-quarter manga volumes until 1941. After the war, the first akahon manga printed in Osaka were known as "ehon" since they were B6, landscape volumes.

EMONOGATARI "Illustrated stories," conceived as "kamishibai on paper," which became a staple of children's magazines from 1932 until the end of the 1950s, when manga finally surpassed them.

EROMANGA Erotic manga, aka pornography. Taking off in the 1960s and initially published solely by so-called "third-rate publishers," it is now also a significant portion of the dōjinshi sphere, and continues to influence manga expression generally.

FUJOSHI Literally "rotten women," a semi-pejorative term for female fans of BL media. They are "rotten" in that they marinate in these media rather than doing their societal duty (i.e., marrying a man and having children). "Fudanshi" (rotten men) are their more recent counterparts.

FUROKU "Supplements" or "freebies," included with magazines as a purchase bonus for more than a century. In earlier decades' children's magazines these were largely paper goods or extremely cheap toys, but in 1970s manga magazines they became increasingly luxe objects for daily life, often depicting popular manga from the magazine in question. "Bessatsu furoku" are separate manga booklets, launched in 1933 to stoke sales.

GEKIGA "Dramatic pictures." The term was coined by Tatsumi Yoshihiro to describe the new-style, realist and psychological manga he sought to create that would appeal to middle school graduates in the late 1950s. Gekiga gradually fused with the manga mainstream, but its realistic art style was largely abandoned by mainstream manga in the 1980s in favor of a more stylized, anime-derived look.

HEISEI PERIOD The years 1989–2019, sometimes called the Lost Decades, in that postmodern Japan's post-Bubble economy largely stagnated as the population began aging rapidly. Infamously marked by a series of calamities, including the Hanshin earthquake and the Aum Shinrikyō sarin gas attacks in 1995 and the "Triple Disaster" (Tōhoku earthquake and tsunami, Fukushima nuclear meltdown) of March 2011, along with increasing precarity.

IMPERIAL JAPAN The years 1895–1945, when Japan held external colonies throughout Asia (a development prefigured by its "internal colonization" of Hokkaido and Okinawa in the 1870s). The end of World War II summarily ended the Japanese Empire.

JOSEI MANGA A major manga category that emerged in the 1980s, aimed at adult women. Initially known as "ladies' comics"; rebranded as "josei [women's] manga" after ladies' comics acquired a tawdry reputation.

KAMISHIBAI "Paper theater," a form of street performance that emerged at the end of the 1920s, became wildly popular, and was then suborned for propaganda by the wartime state. Kamishibai consisted of a storytelling performance, accompanied by vocal sound effects and percussion, while the performer manipulated illustrated cards to depict the action. Audiences paid a pittance for candy to hear a roughly one-hour program in three parts. Kamishibai reemerged during the Occupation and enthralled children (and employed mangaka) until the end of the 1950s, when it was supplanted by TV.

KASHIHONYA Rental bookstores, which emerged during the wartime era and mushroomed during the Occupation. Customers paid a small fee to read books on site or to rent them to read at home; they could also buy magazine freebies outright. Kashihonya, the last of which shuttered in the early 1970s, were famous as the sole outlet for KASHIHON MANGA, akahon's higher-quality successor, which offered creators greater freedom in one-volume stories than mainstream magazines.

KODOMO MANGA AKA JIDŌ MANGA Children's manga, which emerged during the 1920s and remained a coherent category until the mid-1960s, when it split along gendered lines into shōnen and shōjo manga (along with yōnen manga, aimed at younger readers). Although magazines that published children's manga had gendered titles, children read manga across these divisions.

KOMAGA "Panel image" (written with a different "koma" than that used for film cuts), originally used to describe a kind of wordless, one-panel realist illustration in the 1900s. Matsumoto Masahiko hit upon this term to describe his proto-gekiga in 1956, since he regarded panel arrangement as the heart of a comics story.

MANGA KISHA "Manga reporter," the job title most staff cartoonists held at newspapers and magazines from the 1910s onward.

MANGA MANBUN Okamoto Ippei's signature manga innovation, consisting of a single illustration accompanied by a witty, discursive caption.

MANGAKA "Cartoonist." Unlike mainstream U.S. comics, most mangaka both write and illustrate their own stories, with the help of uncredited assistants.

MEIJI PERIOD The beginning of modern Japan, 1868–1912. Under a new government headed by an oligarchy of disaffected low-ranking samurai, Japan embarked on a drive to comprehensively modernize and industrialize its society so that it could compete on the world stage as an equal.

OTAKU Literally "your house," a term for male super-fans of anime, manga, and video games since the mid-1980s, often with a derogatory valence. The word *otaku* was banned on air by NHK, Japan's national broadcaster, until 2008, after the 1989 Miyazaki incident associated otaku with social deviance in popular consciousness.

OTONA MANGA Manga for adults, in the sense of "not for children." The term emerged in the 1950s as children's manga became increasingly prominent in the medium, encompassing satirical, newspaper, and other forms of manga.

PONCHI-E AKA PONCHI "*Punch* drawings." The first Japanese term for satirical cartoons, from 1863 until roughly the late 1920s, when it was supplanted by *manga*.

SEINEN Literally "young men," this manga category sought to capture male college student readers beginning in the late 1960s. Seinen has now been de-gendered and is a catchall category for narrative manga aimed at adults that is not josei or BL.

SHŌJO "Girls' manga," aimed at middle school girls but frequently read by older readers as well.

SHŌNEN "Boys' manga," notionally aimed at middle schoolers but nowadays read widely worldwide by fans of all genders and ages.

SHŌNEN'AI AKA YAOI AKA BL A new genre of manga that emerged within shōjo manga in the 1970s depicting same-sex romances between male characters. In the 1980s, *shōnen'ai* was supplanted by the dōjinshi term *yaoi*, and both have now been replaced by *BL* or *boys' love*. BL manga emerged as a semiprofessional manga category in the late 1970s and became a professional category in the 1990s.

Yuri or *GL* ("girls' love") has emerged as the equivalent term for manga depicting sapphic relationships between female characters.

SHŌWA PERIOD The years 1926–89, dominated by the emergence of the fascist wartime state until 1945 and by the Occupation, transition to democracy, and Japan's economic miracle thereafter.

TAISHŌ PERIOD The years 1912–26, a time when Japan's modernization seemed to accelerate, particularly after the 1923 Great Kantō earthquake, and urbanites began adopting more modern ("Western") practices in daily life.

TANKŌBON Collected volumes of manga, which first appeared in the 1920s in hardcover and are now a publishing mainstay in paperback and ebook.

UKIYO-E Woodblock prints, a popular art form in the Edo period. After the Meiji government banned pornography, ukiyo-e's mainstay, it rebranded as "nishiki-e" (brocade pictures) and was frequently used for news illustrations until photographic reproduction technology replaced it in the 1900s, after which ukiyo-e transformed again, into fine art.

NOTES

INTRODUCTION

1. Yonezawa Yoshihiro and Shikijō Kyōtarō, *2Bdan gindama sensō no hibi: Shōwa 30-nendai—yume no shōnen ōkoku* (Tokyo: Shinpyosha, 1982), 77–85.

2. See Jaqueline Berndt, "Premodern Roots of Story-Manga?," in *The Cambridge Companion to Manga and Anime*, ed. Jaqueline Berndt (Cambridge: Cambridge University Press, 2024), for a formal analysis of these contenders' claims to manga's lineage.

3. Marc Steinberg, "Otaku Consumption, Superflat Art and the Return to Edo," *Japan Forum* 16, no. 3 (2004), 449.

4. Shige (CJ) Suzuki and Ronald Stewart begin their historical overview of manga in the 1890s in *Manga: A Critical Guide* (London: Bloomsbury Academic, 2023).

5. See Dalma Kálovics, "Manga Across Media: Style Adapting to Form in the 1950s and 1960s and in the Digital Age," *Mechademia* 12, no. 2 (2020): 102–23.

6. Chinghsin Wu, *Parallel Modernism: Koga Harue and Avant-Garde Art in Modern Japan* (Oakland: University of California Press, 2019), 3.

7. Jaqueline Berndt, "Introduction: Two Media Forms in Correlation," in Berndt, *Cambridge Companion to Manga and Anime*, 5.

8. See Kathryn Hemmann, *Manga Cultures and the Female Gaze* (Cham, Switzerland: Palgrave Macmillan, 2020).

PART ONE OVERVIEW: MANGA AGAINST TRADITION

1. Adam L. Kern, *Manga from the Floating World: Comicbook Culture and the Kibyōshi of Edo Japan*, 2nd ed. (Cambridge, MA: Harvard University Press, 2019), 140–42. The word *manga* originally referred to a spoonbill in Sino-Japanese; some speculate that Hokusai chose the word to analogize his free-ranging selection of topics and the bird's foraging behaviors. Gekigaka Matsumoto Masahiko defined the *man* in *manga* as "to travel without any aim." Matsumoto Masahiko, "What

Was Komaga?," in *The Man Next Door*, trans. Ryan Holmberg (London: Breakdown Press, 2014), n.p.

2. For a recent version of this argument, see Shuichiro Takeda, *The Beginner's Guide to Anime and Manga* (New York: Scholastic, 2024).

3. Marc Steinberg, "Otaku Consumption, Superflat Art and the Return to Edo," *Japan Forum* 16, no. 3 (2004), 449.

4. Quoted in Ronald Stewart, "Manga as Schism: Kitazawa Rakuten's Resistance to 'Old-Fashioned' Japan," in *Manga's Cultural Crossroads*, ed. Jaqueline Berndt and Bettina Kümmerling-Meibauer (London: Routledge, 2013), 27, 43.

5. Steinberg, "Otaku Consumption," 449–50.

6. Discussing a similar movement of adoption and adaptation to local conditions among groups of women in the 1970s, James Welker uses the concept "transfiguration," which he defines as "*a change in form in the process of crossing from one culture to another*" and uses to draw attention to relations of power in, as well as subjects and results of, this process. James Welker, *Transfiguring Women in Late Twentieth-Century Japan: Feminists, Lesbians, and Girls' Comics Artists and Fans* (Honolulu: University of Hawai'i Press, 2024), 11–13.

CHAPTER ONE: THE ORIGINS OF JAPANESE COMICS

1. Shinozawa Misako, "The Birth of a Million Seller: Magazines as Media in the Meiji-Taishō Era," in *Million seller tanjō e! Meiji, Taishō no zasshi media*, ed. Insatsubutsukan (Tokyo: Tokyo Shoseki, 2008), 179.

2. Futagami Hirokazu, "Manga to zasshi," in *Mangagaku nyūmon*, ed. Natsume Fusanosuke and Takeuchi Osamu (Kyoto: Minerva Shobō, 2009), 56.

3. *The Japan Punch*, May 1862, 3.

4. Peter Duus, "'Punch Pictures'—Localising Punch in Meiji Japan," in *Asian Punches: A Transcultural Affair*, ed. Hans Harder and Barbara Mittler (Berlin: Springer, 2013), 313.

5. Miyamoto Hirohito, "'Ponchi' kara 'manga' e: Journalism to 'bijutsu' no aida de hyōgen o migaku," in *Visual wide Meiji jidaikan*, ed. Masato Miyachi (Tokyo: Shogakukan, 2005), 390.

6. Duus, "Punch," 307.

7. Miyamoto, "'Ponchi' kara 'manga' e," 390.

8. Duus, "Punch," 328.

9. Shimizu Isao, *Manga zasshi hakubutsukan* (Tokyo: National Diet Library, 1986–87; 12 vols.), vol. 1, 1; Nagamine Shigetoshi, "Magazines in Modern Japan and Their Readers," in Insatsubutsukan, *Million seller tanjō e!*, 189–90.

10. Duus, "Punch," 334.

11. Duus, 326–27.

12. Quoted in Duus, 328.

13. Shimizu Isao, *Manga tanjō: Taishō democracy kara no shuppatsu* (Tokyo: Yoshikawa, 1999), 165.

14. Miyamoto Hirohito, "'Ponchi-e' to 'manga,' sono shinbun no kakawari," in *Shinbun manga no me: Hito seiji sekai*, ed. Nihon Shinbun Hakubutsukan (Yokohama: Newspark, 2003), 106–9.

15. Miyamoto, "'Ponchi' kara 'manga' e," 390–91.

16. Rebecca Salter, *Japanese Popular Prints: From Votive Slips to Playing Cards* (Honolulu: University of Hawai'i Press, 2006), 146–48.

17. Miyamoto, "'Ponchi' kara 'manga' e," 391.

18. Duus, "Punch," 332.

19. Miyamoto, "'Ponchi' kara 'manga' e," 391.

20. See Takashi Fujitani, *Splendid Monarchy: Power and Pageantry in Modern Japan* (Berkeley: University of California Press, 1996).

21. Shinozawa, "Million Seller," 180.

22. Miyamoto Hirohito, "Is This the First Manga?," Google Arts and Culture, https://artsandculture.google.com/story/is-this-the-first-manga/fQUBrahtn-RoFKw (accessed November 2, 2023); Jaqueline Berndt, "Manga, Which Manga? Publication Formats, Genres, Users," in *Japanese Civilization in the 21st Century*, ed. Andrew Targowski, Juri Abe, and Hisanori Kato (New York: Nova Science Publishers, 2016), 123.

23. Miyamoto, "'Ponchi-e' to 'manga,'" 106.

24. Miyamoto, "'Ponchi' kara 'manga' e," 391.

25. Nagamine, "Magazines," 189–90.

26. Shinozawa, "Million Seller," 181–82.

27. Haruhara Akihiko, "Introduction," in *Shinbun manga no me*, ed. Nihon Shinbun Hakubutsukan (Yokohama: Newspark, 2003), 5.

28. Sonja Hotwagner, "'*Punch*'s Heirs' Between the (Battle) Lines: Satirical Journalism in the Age of the Russo-Japanese War of 1904–05," in Harder and Mittler, *Asian Punches*, 351.

29. Omiya-shi, ed., *Kitazawa Rakuten, Founder of the Modern Japanese Cartoon* (Omiya, Japan: Omiya City Planning Department International Culture Division, 1991), n.p.

30. Shimizu, *Manga zasshi hakubutsukan*, vol. 5, 157.

31. Shimizu, 157.

32. Ronald Stewart, "Manga as Schism: Kitazawa Rakuten's Resistance to 'Old-Fashioned' Japan," in *Manga's Cultural Crossroads*, ed. Jaqueline Berndt and Bettina Kümmerling-Meibauer (London: Routledge, 2013), 27–28, 36.

33. Shimizu, *Manga zasshi hakubutsukan*, vol. 6, 157; Miyamoto, "First Manga?"

34. Stewart, "Schism," 34.

35. Quoted in Stewart, 34, 35, 42–43.

36. Hotwagner, "Heirs," 360; Haruhara, "Introduction," 7.

37. Hotwagner, "Heirs," 351.

38. Stewart, "Schism," 39.

39. Stewart, 35, 39.

40. Shimizu, *Manga zasshi hakubutsukan*, vol. 5, 158.

41. Shimizu, 158, n.p.

42. Stewart, "Schism," 39–40; Yamamoto Kanae, "Gendai no kokkeiga oyobi fūshiga nitsuite," *Hōsun*, February 1907, 3.

43. Stewart, "Schism," 28.

44. Many thanks to Fred Schodt for this point.

45. Stewart, "Schism," 40.

46. Stewart, 34; Hotwagner, "Heirs," 356.

47. Omiya-shi, ed., *Rakuten*, 14, 22.

48. Shimizu, *Manga zasshi hakubutsukan*, vol. 5, n.p., 158.

49. Salter, *Prints*, 181. *Tokyo Puck* may have started the prewar manga magazine practice of publishing sugoroku game boards in the New Year's issue for the family to play over the holidays.

50. Shimizu, *Manga zasshi hakubutsukan*, vol. 5, n.p., 158.

51. Shimizu, n.p., 158.

52. Jonathan Clements, *Anime: A History*, 2nd ed. (London: Bloomsbury and the British Film Institute, 2023), 42–43. Shimokawa's pen name is often read *Ōten* in connection with animation and *Hekoten* in connection with manga, although there is evidence he used *Ōten* for manga too. For clarity, I use *Ōten* throughout.

53. Almost all of these films are lost, but *Namakura gatana*'s two halves were separately rediscovered in 2008 and in 2014, with more footage found in 2017. It is now available online: https://animation.filmarchives.jp/en/works/view/100183.

54. Shimizu, *Manga zasshi hakubutsukan*, vol. 8, n.p., 169.

55. Stewart, "Schism," 28.

56. Shimizu, *Manga tanjō*, 96, 100–04, 107–10; "Puck 898 (UK Comic Books)," October 8, 1921, Comic Book Plus, https://comicbookplus.com/?dlid = 28592 (accessed December 2, 2023).

57. Readers' letters first appear in children's magazines in the April 1891 issue of *Yōnen Zasshi*, which was also an early adopter of freebies (furoku), in the February issue.

58. Shinozawa, "Million Seller," 182.

59. Gregory J. Kasza, *The State and the Mass Media in Japan, 1918–1945* (Berkeley: University of California Press, 1988), 14–18.

60. Shimizu, *Manga zasshi hakubutsukan*, vol. 8, 169.

61. Miyake Okiko and Kōsokabe Hideyuki, eds., *Taishōki no ehon, ezasshi no kenkyū: Ichi shōnen no collection o tōshite* (Tokyo: Kanrin Shobō, 2009), 220.

62. Shimizu, *Manga tanjō*, 31.

63. Stewart, "Schism," 41.

64. Shimizu, *Manga zasshi hakubutsukan*, vol. 5, 159; quoted in Stewart, "Schism," 41, 42.

CHAPTER TWO: ARRESTING THE FLEETING MOMENT

1. Shimizu Isao, *Manga tanjō: Taishō democracy kara no shuppatsu* (Tokyo: Yoshikawa, 1999), 74; Ishiko Jun, *Nihon mangashi* (Tokyo: Shakai Shisōsha, 1988), 85.

2. Ishiko, *Nihon mangashi*, 85.

3. Shimizu, *Manga tanjō*, 68–69, 19, 23.

4. Miyamoto Hirohito, "'Ponchi' kara 'manga' e: Journalism to 'bijutsu' no aida de hyōgen o migaku," in *Visual wide Meiji jidaikan*, ed. Masato Miyachi (Tokyo: Shogakukan, 2005), 391.

5. Sunohara Fumihiro, "Mangaka e no shuppatsuten toshite no '*Manga to yakubun*' to Okamoto Ippei no sengo no hyōka," in Okamoto Ippei, Natori Shunsen, and Nakada Katsunosuke, *Manga to yakubun* (Tokyo: Kabushiki Kaisha Kokusho Kankōkai, 2019), 223. These illustrations accompanied Nakada's translations of Baudelaire.

6. Shimizu, *Manga tanjō*, 82–83.

7. Miriam Silverberg, *Erotic Grotesque Nonsense: The Mass Culture of Japanese Modern Times* (Berkeley: University of California Press, 2006).

8. Natsume Sōseki, "Okamoto Ippei no manga," in Okamoto, Natori, and Nakada, *Manga to yakubun*, 203.

9. Shimizu, *Manga tanjō*, 4; Miyake Okiko and Kōsokabe Hideyuki, eds., *Taishōki no ehon, ezasshi no kenkyū: Ichi shōnen no collection o tōshite* (Tokyo: Kanrin Shobō, 2009), 231.

10. Shimizu, *Manga tanjō*, 84–86.

11. Aaron Gerow, *Visions of Japanese Modernity: Articulations of Cinema, Nation, and Spectatorship, 1895–1925* (Berkeley: University of California Press, 2010), 59–64.

12. Gerow, 156, 160, 140–47, 209–12.

13. Shimizu, *Manga tanjō*, 86.

14. Suzuki Maki, "'Manga-teki image no kakusan': 'Manga' to 'kōkoku' no kaikō o megutte," in *Dōin no media mix: "Sōsaku suru taishū" no senjika, sengo*, ed. Ōtsuka Eiji (Kyoto: Shibunkaku Shuppan, 2017), 109–10.

15. Shimizu, *Manga tanjō*, 95; Hosokibara Seiki, *Nihon mangashi* (Tokyo: Yūzankaku, 1924), 232.

16. Ian Condry, *The Soul of Anime: Collaborative Creativity and Japan's Media Success Story* (Durham, NC: Duke University Press, 2013), 8. Emphasis in original.

17. Shimizu, *Manga tanjō*, 90–92.

18. Shimizu Isao, *Manga zasshi hakubutsukan* (Tokyo: National Diet Library, 1986–87; 12 vols.), vol. 6, n.p.

19. Shimizu, *Manga zasshi hakubutsukan*, vol. 7, n.p.

20. See Shimizu, *Manga zasshi hakubutsukan*, vol. 7.

21. Shimizu, *Manga zasshi hakubutsukan*, vol. 6, 157–58.

22. Haruhara Akihiko, "Introduction," in *Shinbun manga no me*, ed. Nihon Shinbun Hakubutsukan (Yokohama: Newspark, 2003), 3.

23. *Jiji Manga*, February 11, 1921; November 12, 1922.

24. *Jiji Manga*, April 24, 1921; March 30, 1924.

25. Shimizu, *Manga tanjō*, 124.

26. Kozawa Jō, "Shinmangaha Shūdan no hitotachi," *Gendaishi Konwakai* 108 (2002): 14.

27. Ni'imi Takuma, ed., *Norakuro de arimasu! Tagawa Suihō to kodomo manga no wonderland* (Kawasaki, Japan: Kawasaki City Museum, 2019), 13–17.

28. Shimizu, *Manga tanjō*, 114.

29. Shimizu, 105.

30. Shimizu, 87–89.

31. Sunohara, "Mangaka e no shuppatsuten," 216.

32. The socks company then employed Miyao Shigeo for more manga ads. Suzuki, "Manga-teki image," 107, 110–12.

33. Silverberg, *Nonsense*, 30.

34. Ozaki Hotsuki, "Norakuro no hanseiki," in Tagawa Suihō, *Bokura no Norakuro: Norakuro 50-nen kinen album* (Tokyo: Kodansha, 1984), 43; Shimizu, *Manga tanjō*, 182; Ono Kōsei, "Ōbei no shinbun manga wa Nihon de dono yō ni ukeireraretaka," in Nihon Shinbun Hakubutsukan, ed., *Shinbun manga no me: Hito seiji sekai* (Yokohama: Newspark, 2003), 119. Bilingual collected editions of *Oyaji Kyōiku* were published beginning in 1924, with an appreciative note from McManus.

35. Haruhara, "Introduction," 3.

36. Ronald Stewart, "Newspaper Comic Strips: Laughs in Four Panels," in Jaqueline Berndt, ed., *The Cambridge Companion to Manga and Anime* (Cambridge: Cambridge University Press, 2024), 34.

37. *Osaka Puck*, February 1920 and August 1921.

38. Ono, "Ōbei," 118–21.

39. Komatsu Sakyō, "Taiken toshite no mangashi," in *Maboroshi no Komatsu Sakyō = Mori Minoru manga zenshū, vol. 4: Kaisetsuhen* (Tokyo: Shogakukan, 2002), 9.

40. Okamoto Ippei, "Manga zassō," *Bijutsu Shinron* 2, no. 8 (August 1927): 45.

41. Eike Exner, *Comics and the Origins of Manga: A Revisionist History* (New Brunswick, NJ: Rutgers University Press, 2021), 3, 9–10.

42. *Osaka Puck* 18, no. 8 (September 15, 1923).

43. *Jiji Manga*, January 15, 1928.

44. Exner, *Comics*, 146. *Jiji Manga* was one notable flip-flopper.

45. Okamoto, "Manga zassō," 44.

46. Komatsu, "Taiken," 9.

47. Okamoto, "Manga zassō," 44.

48. Hosokibara, *Nihon mangashi*, 232.

49. Okamoto, "Manga zassō," 46.

50. Shimizu Isao, "*Gendai manga taikan* zen 10-hen no motsu imi," in Ōkūsha, ed., *Gendai manga taikan bessatsu* (Tokyo: Ōzorasha, 2010), 12.

51. Shimizu, "*Gendai manga taikan*," 10; Shimizu, *Manga tanjō*, 178.

52. Ōkūsha, *Gendai manga taikan bessatsu*, n.p.

53. This emphasis on laughing as a bodily practice recalls Miriam Silverberg's highlighting the gesture as an important, if difficult to trace, site of politics in Japanese modern times. Silverberg, *Nonsense*, 20.

54. Shimokawa Ōten, "Shinmanga, shinmangaka," *Bijutsu Shinron* 2, no. 8 (August 1927), 52.

55. Okamoto Ippei, *Shinmanga no kakikata* (Tokyo: Chūō Bijutsusha, 1928), 26.

56. Okamoto Ippei, "Introduction," in *Manga kenkyū shiryō kōza*, ed. Ōhira Akira and Nihon Manga Kenkyūkai (Tokyo: Nihon Manga Kenkyūkai, 1935), vol. 1, 9.

57. Ikebe Hitoshi, *Sugu dekiru manga no kakikata* (Tokyo: Sūbundō Shoten, 1931), 1.

58. Uchida Roan, "Manga mandan," *Bijutsu Shinron* 2, no. 8 (August 1927): 38, 40.

59. Hosokibara, *Nihon mangashi*, 234–35, 235.

60. Rei Okamoto Inouye, "Theorizing Manga: Nationalism and Discourse on the Role of Wartime Manga," *Mechademia* 4 (2009), 20.

61. Shimokawa, "Shinmanga," 52–53.

62. Shirota Shūichi, ed., *Gendai manga taikan* (Tokyo: Chūō Bijutsusha, 1928), vol. 6, n.p. Shōsai's first work was published in 1870, putting him at least in his mid-seventies in 1928.

63. Ronald Stewart, "Manga as Schism: Kitazawa Rakuten's Resistance to 'Old-Fashioned' Japan," in *Manga's Cultural Crossroads*, ed. Jaqueline Berndt and Bettina Kümmerling-Meibauer, 39–61 (London: Routledge, 2013), 29. In *Nihon mangashi*, Hosokibara mentions the Genji picture scrolls in his history of manga, but then jumps almost immediately to the Kamakura period (9–10).

64. Ishii Hakutei, "Honchō mangashi," *Chūō Bijutsu* 4, no. 1 (January 1918): 139–42.

65. Yamamoto Kanae, "Gendai no kokkeiga oyobi fūshiga nitsuite," *Hōsun*, February 1907, 3–4.

66. Okamoto, *Shinmanga*, 5–6.

67. In *Nihon mangashi*, Hosokibara defines the "Fujiwara era" as the Tempyō era, which encompassed five sequential eras from 729 to 67, in the Nara period (9).

68. Okamoto, "Introduction," 6–8; Ōhira Akira and Nihon Manga Kenkyūkai, *Manga kenkyū shiryō kōza*, vol. 1, 16–20.

69. Silverberg, *Nonsense*, 32–34.

70. Stewart, "Schism," 36. Jaqueline Berndt points out that the particular premodern antecedent claimed is related to manga's dominant paradigms at the time; in the 1960s, with the rise of story manga, Edo period kibyōshi (graphic fiction) began being claimed as the origin of manga. Jaqueline Berndt, "Premodern Roots of Story-Manga?," in Berndt, *Cambridge Companion to Manga and Anime*, 20.

71. Shimizu, *Manga tanjō*, 164.

72. Kobayashi Kiyoshi and Kitazawa Rakuten, *Buta no heso: Manbun, manga* (Tokyo: Kōbunsha, 1928), n.p.

73. Katherine Roeder, *Wide Awake in Slumberland: Fantasy, Mass Culture, and Modernism in the Art of Winsor McCay* (Jackson: University of Mississippi Press, 2014), 158.

74. Roeder, 147.

75. See Silverberg, *Nonsense*, esp. 20–28. The flapper invited similar scorn in the United States.

76. Shimizu, *Manga tanjō*, 123.
77. Exner, *Comics*, 163–65.
78. Shimizu, *Manga zasshi hakubutsukan*, vol. 5, 158.

PART ONE CONCLUSION: 1928

1. Katherine Roeder, *Wide Awake in Slumberland: Fantasy, Mass Culture, and Modernism in the Art of Winsor McCay* (Jackson: University Press of Mississippi, 2014), 180–81.

2. See Eike Exner, *Comics and the Origins of Manga: A Revisionist History* (New Brunswick, NJ: Rutgers University Press, 2021); Ōtsuka Eiji, "An Unholy Alliance of Eisenstein and Disney: The Fascist Origins of Otaku Culture," trans. Thomas Lamarre, *Mechademia* 8 (2013). No stranger to polemics, Ōtsuka goes so far as to say that Tagawa Suihō in *Norakuro* was just pirating Mickey Mouse—an assertion that doesn't hold up to an actual reading of *Norakuro* (255).

3. Chinghsin Wu, *Parallel Modernism: Koga Harue and Avant-Garde Art in Modern Japan* (Oakland: University of California Press, 2019), 7. Wu's concept of "parallel modernisms" describes manga's relation to Euro-American comics in these years extremely well.

4. Kiyama Henry Yoshitaka, *Manga yonin shosei* (San Francisco: Kiyama Yoshitaka Gashitsu, 1931); Frederik L. Schodt, "Henry (Yoshitaka) Kiyama," Stone Bridge Press, https://www.stonebridge.com/authors/henry-(yoshitaka)-kiyama (accessed March 29, 2025).

5. Miyake Okiko and Hideyuki Kōsokabe, eds., *Taishōki no ehon, ezasshi no kenkyū: Ichi shōnen no collection o tōshite* (Tokyo: Kanrin Shobō, 2009), 237, 242–43.

6. Shimokawa Ōten, "Shinmanga, shinmangaka," *Bijutsu Shinron* 2, no. 8 (August 1927), 53.

7. Okamoto Ippei, "Manga zassō," *Bijutsu Shinron* 2, no. 8 (August 1927), 46.

PART TWO OVERVIEW: MANGA DURING WARTIME

1. Komatsu Sakyō, "Taiken toshite no mangashi," in *Maboroshi no Komatsu Sakyō = Mori Minoru manga zenshū, vol. 4: Kaisetsuhen* (Tokyo: Shogakukan, 2002), 9.

2. Suzuki Maki, "'Manga-teki image no kakusan': 'Manga' to 'kōkoku' no kaikō o megutte," in *Dōin no media mix: "Sōsaku suru taishū" no senjika, sengo*, ed. Ōtsuka Eiji, 105–31 (Kyoto: Shibunkaku Shuppan, 2017), 115–16.

3. Aaron Herald Skabelund, *Empire of Dogs: Canines, Japan, and the Making of the Modern Imperial World* (Ithaca, NY: Cornell University Press, 2012), 90.

4. Kenneth J. Ruoff, *Imperial Japan at Its Zenith: The Wartime Celebration of the Empire's 2,600th Anniversary* (Ithaca, NY: Cornell University Press, 2010), 78.

5. Skabelund, *Dogs*, 91.

6. Ruoff, *Zenith*, 4, 80, 7.

7. Ruoff, 18, 33–34.

8. Ishiko Jun, *Nihon mangashi* (Tokyo: Shakai Shisōsha, 1988), 181.

9. Louise Young, *Japan's Total Empire: Manchuria and the Culture of Wartime Imperialism* (Berkeley: University of California Press, 1998), 57.

10. Gennifer S. Weisenfeld, *MAVO: Japanese Artists and the Avant-Garde, 1905–1931* (Berkeley: University of California Press, 2002), 63.

CHAPTER THREE: NORAKURO AND FRIENDS

1. Shinozawa Misako, "The Birth of a Million Seller: Magazines as Media in the Meiji-Taishō Era," in *Million seller tanjō e! Meiji, Taishō no zasshi media*, ed. Insatsubutsukan (Tokyo: Tokyo Shoseki, 2008), 182–83.

2. Ni'imi Takuma, ed., *Norakuro de arimasu! Tagawa Suihō to kodomo manga no wonderland* (Kawasaki, Japan: Kawasaki City Museum, 2019), 56. Although the pronunciation of *Club* did not change, I have directly transcribed *Kurabu* to indicate that the prewar titles were written with kanji.

3. Suzuki Maki, "'Manga-teki image no kakusan': 'Manga' to 'kōkoku' no kaikō o megutte," in *Dōin no media mix: "Sōsaku suru taishū" no senjika, sengo*, ed. Ōtsuka Eiji (Kyoto: Shibunkaku Shuppan, 2017), 115.

4. Ryan Holmberg, "*Manga Shōnen:* Katō Ken'ichi and the Manga Boys," *Mechademia* 8 (2013), 177.

5. Aaron Herald Skabelund, *Empire of Dogs: Canines, Japan, and the Making of the Modern Imperial World* (Ithaca, NY: Cornell University Press, 2012), 152.

6. Ippei Seishiki, "Foreword," in Miyao Shigeo, *Miyao Shigeo no hon, vol. 11: Shigeo manga zukan 1* (Tokyo: Kanō Shobō, 1984), 1.

7. Takeuchi Osamu, "Mangashi ni okeru *Shō-chan no boken*," in Oda Shōsei and Kabashima Katsuichi, *Shō-chan no bōken* (Tokyo: Shogakukan Creative, 2003), 136.

8. Komatsu Sakyō, "Taiken toshite no mangashi," in *Maboroshi no Komatsu Sakyō = Mori Minoru manga zenshū, vol. 4: Kaisetsuhen* (Tokyo: Shogakukan, 2002), 6–7.

9. Suzuki, "Manga-teki image," 112.

10. Miyao Shigeo, *Manga no omatsuri* (Tokyo: Kodansha, 1931).

11. Chūjō Shōhei, "Gendai manga to Shō-chan," in Oda and Kabashima, *Shō-chan*, 132; Takeuchi, "*Shō-chan*," 136–37.

12. Quoted in Suzuki, "Manga-teki image," 112. Shō-chan can also be regarded as an early media mix, as he appeared in both books and newspapers simultaneously and was merchandised; so was Aso's Tō-san (toys and animation).

13. Chūjō, "Shō-chan," 132–34.

14. Miriam Silverberg, *Erotic Grotesque Nonsense: The Mass Culture of Japanese Modern Times* (Berkeley: University of California Press, 2006), 213.

15. Sun Minqiao, "'*Jinzō ningen*' wa naze naku ka? Tagawa Suihō *Jinzō ningen* ni miru manga to avant-garde geijutsu no setten," in *Undō toshite no taishū bunka: Kyōdō, fan, bunka kōsaku*, ed. Ōtsuka Eiji (Tokyo: Suiseisha, 2021), 131, 140–41; Tagawa Suihō, *Manga no kanzume* (Tokyo: Kodansha, 1930), 3–53.

16. Takamizawa Junko, "Tagawa Suihō no kioku," in *Tsuitō Tagawa Suihō-ten: Norakuro to ayunda 90-nen*, ed. Machida Shiritsu Kokusai Hanga Bijutsukan (Machida, Tokyo: Machida Shiritsu Kokusai Hanga Bijutsukan, 1990), 11; Gennifer S. Weisenfeld, *MAVO: Japanese Artists and the Avant-Garde, 1905–1931* (Berkeley: University of California Press, 2002), 175, 178.

17. Weisenfeld, *MAVO*, 76–77, 154, 170.

18. Weisenfeld, 60.

19. Tagawa Suihō and Takamizawa Junko, *Norakuro ichidaiki: Tagawa Suihō jijoden* (Tokyo: Kodansha, 1991), 105, 110.

20. Weisenfeld, *MAVO*, 10–11; Tagawa Suihō, *Norakuro tosshintai: Manga book* (Tokyo: Kodansha, 1933), 26.

21. Tagawa, *Manga no kanzume*, preface.

22. Ni'imi, *Norakuro de arimasu!*, 24.

23. Sun, "*Jinzō ningen*," 132–33, 144–47. Atom, Tezuka's famous boy robot hero, also shares these characteristics. Tezuka once wrote that all his gags came from Tagawa.

24. Ono Kōsei, "Ōbei no shinbun manga wa Nihon de dono yō ni ukeireraretaka," in Nihon Shinbun Hakubutsukan, ed., *Shinbun manga no me: Hito seiji sekai* (Yokohama: Newspark, 2003), 120.

25. Tagawa Suihō, "Norakuro tanjōki," in *Manga kenkyū 2* (Tokyo: Nihon Jidō Manga Kenkyūkai, n.d./ca. 1950s), 46–47.

26. Skabelund, *Dogs*, 144–46.

27. Kobayashi Hideo, "Manga," in *Shintei Kobayashi Hideo zenshū, vol. 12: Kangaeru hinto*, ed. Ōoka Shōhei, Nakamura Mitsuo, and Etō Jun (Tokyo: Shinchōsha, 1978), 50–52. Kobayashi praises Tagawa's channeling his autobiographical narrative into Norakuro as a way to escape the confines of the I-novel (shishōsetsu) and direct discussion of the self.

28. Tagawa Suihō, *Norakuro sōchō* (Tokyo: Kodansha, 1935), n.p.

29. Tagawa, "Norakuro tanjōki," 46.

30. Tagawa and Takamizawa, *Norakuro ichidaiki*, 150.

31. Quoted in Natsume Fusanosuke, "*Norakuro* to aratana mangashi," in *Kokkei to pathos: Tagawa Suihō "Norakuro" ichidaiki-ten*, ed. Machida Shimin Bunka Gakkan Kotobarando (Machida, Tokyo: Machida Shimin Bunka Gakkan Kotobarando, 2013), 5.

32. Tagawa, *Manga no kanzume*, 1.

33. Weisenfeld, *MAVO*, 103.

34. See Tagawa Suihō, *Norakuro jōtōhei* (Tokyo: Kodansha, 1932).

35. Natsume, "*Norakuro* to aratana mangashi," 5; Weisenfeld, *MAVO*, 60.

36. Tagawa Suihō, *Bokura no Norakuro: Norakuro 50-nen kinen album* (Tokyo: Kodansha, 1984), 16.

37. Deborah Shamoon, *Passionate Friendship: The Aesthetics of Girls' Culture in Japan* (Honolulu: University of Hawai'i Press, 2012), 48.

38. Tagawa, *Bokura*, 16.

39. Tagawa, 16.

40. Suzuki, "Manga-teki image," 116–20.

41. Katō Ken'ichi, *Shōnen Kurabu jidai: Henshūchō no kaisō* (Tokyo: Kodansha, 1968), 103–4.

42. Tagawa, *Bokura*, 16; Machida Shiritsu Kokusai Hanga Bijutsukan, *Tagawa*, 22. Comics characters were used in ads across media and for unrelated products in the United States starting in the late nineteenth century. Suzuki, "Manga-teki image," 106.

43. Suzuki, 125.

44. Eric Faden, email message to the author, June 19, 2024; Tamamura Yuka, Nemoto Hikaru, and Sato Yō, "Kami no kogeru nioi no naka ni: REFCY kami film no digital-ka to animation eiga no ikōki," *Kyōritsu Review* 51 (2023): 41–42.

45. Suzuki, "Manga-teki image," 122–23.

46. See Marc Steinberg, *Anime's Media Mix: Franchising Toys and Characters in Japan* (Minneapolis: University of Minnesota Press, 2012).

47. Louise Young, *Japan's Total Empire: Manchuria and the Culture of Wartime Imperialism* (Berkeley: University of California Press, 1998), 64.

48. Eike Exner, *Comics and the Origins of Manga: A Revisionist History* (New Brunswick, NJ: Rutgers University Press, 2021), 150–52.

49. Tagawa, *Norakuro jōtōhei*, 30–33, 110.

50. Suzuki, "Manga-teki image," 119–20.

51. Chakuwiki, "Yūkannaru suihei no kaeuta." https://chakuwiki.org/wiki/勇敢なる水兵の替え歌 (accessed 25 June 2022). Laughter is mentioned in all three verses.

52. *Yōnen Kurabu*, September 1927, 164; March 1928, 166; April 1928, 146.

53. Kajii Jun, *Tore, yōchō no jū to pen: Senjika mangashi nōto* (Tokyo: Wise Shuppan, 1999), 99.

54. *Yōnen Kurabu*, March 1930, 143; May 1934, n.p.; September 1933, 136; October 1934, 139; July 1932, 164; August 1932, 162; September 1932, foldout.

55. "National Archives Photo No. 539490, 'Minidoka Relocation Center, Hunt, Idaho. Norakuro Band.,'" August 20, 1943, Records of the War Relocation Authority, Records Group 210, Central Photographic File of the War Relocation Authority, U.S. National Archives at College Park—Still Pictures, College Park, Maryland, https://catalog.archives.gov/id/539490 (accessed November 27, 2015).

56. Thomas Lamarre, "Manga Empire: Comics and Companion Species," lecture at Sophia University, Tokyo, Japan, April 27, 2015.

57. Tagawa, "Norakuro tanjōki," 46.

58. Ni'imi, *Norakuro de arimasu!*, 28.

59. Exner, *Comics*, 141–49. Previously the standard was top-bottom, right-left.

60. Ni'imi, *Norakuro de arimasu!*, 29.

61. Tagawa's designs for the Norakuro hardcovers directly echo Yanase Masamu's "total book design" philosophy, which integrated images on the book boards with slipcase art. Weisenfeld, *MAVO*, 195.

62. Ozaki Hotsuki, "Norakuro no hanseiki," in Tagawa Suihō, *Bokura no Norakuro: Norakuro 50-nen kinen album* (Tokyo: Kodansha, 1984), 42–45.

63. *Yōnen Kurabu*, March 1933, B4.

64. Suzuki, "Manga-teki image," 124–25.

65. On display in the manga library of the Taito ward office adjacent to the Tagawa Suihō memorial hall in February 2015.

66. For Norakuro ads, see *Yōnen Kurabu*, July 1933, B2–3; February 1934, B7.

67. Suzuki, "Manga-teki image," 115–16.

68. Tagawa Suihō, *Norakuro gunsō* (Tokyo: Kodansha, 1934), preface.

69. Shimada Keizō, *Bōken Dankichi manga zenshū*, ed. Katō Ken'ichi (Tokyo: Kodansha, 1967), 674–76.

70. Ni'imi, *Norakuro de arimasu!*, 92.

71. Gajō Sakamoto, "How I Created Tank Tankuro," in *Tank Tankuro: Prewar Works, 1934–1935*, trans. Maki Hakui and Shunsuke Nakazawa (Tokyo: Presspop, 2011), ii–iii; Naoki Sakamoto, "Memories of My Father, Sakamoto Gajō," in Sakamoto, *Tank Tankuro*, vii.

72. Ni'imi, *Norakuro de arimasu!*, 36, 43. These crossover appearances may have inspired Tezuka's "star system" for his characters.

73. Ni'imi, 46, 78; *Yōnen Kurabu*, November 1935, A1.

74. Katō, *Shōnen Kurabu jidai*, 106. To ward off the August scaries, ShōKu published "summer manga festival" issues featuring extra manga.

75. Ni'imi, *Norakuro de arimasu!*, 44, 75, 79.

76. Miyamoto Hirohito, "Akahon manga," in *Mangagaku nyūmon*, ed. Natsume Fusanosuke and Takeuchi Osamu (Kyoto: Minerva Shobō, 2009), 22–23; Ni'imi, *Norakuro de arimasu!*, 19.

77. Ni'imi, 19.

78. Tezuka Osamu, Ōshiro Noboru, and Matsumoto Leiji, "'Oh! Manga' 2: Sensō made" [1972], in Asai Tarō and Ōshiro Noboru, *Kasei tanken* (Tokyo: Tōdosha, 2003), 200; Miyamoto, "Akahon," 23–24.

79. Ni'imi, *Norakuro de arimasu!*, 17, 52, 48.

80. Ni'imi, 48; Miyamoto, "Akahon," 23–24.

81. Ni'imi, *Norakuro de arimasu!*, 47–50.

82. Ni'imi, 48, 50.

83. Abe Noriko, *"Kodomo ga yoku naru Kōdansha no ehon" no kenkyū: Kaisetsu to saimoku database* (Tokyo: Kazama Shobō, 2011), 97; Tezuka Osamu, "Norakuro no miryoku," in Tagawa Suihō, *Norakuro zenshū* (Tokyo: Kodansha, 1967), 802.

84. Komatsu Sakyō, "Manga to bungaku ni akekureta seishun," in *Maboroshi no Komatsu Sakyō = Mori Minoru manga zenshū, vol. 4: Kaisetsuhen* (Tokyo: Shogakukan, 2002), 72; Abe, *"Kodomo,"* 97; Tezuka, Ōshiro, and Matsumoto, "'Oh! Manga' 2," 200.

85. Ni'imi, *Norakuro de arimasu!*, 53.

86. Miyamoto Hirohito, "'Kōdansha no ehon' ni okeru 'kodomo ga yoku naru' manga no senren katei," *Manga Kenkyū* 10 (March 2007), 56.

87. Ni'imi, *Norakuro de arimasu!*, 80.

88. Ni'imi, 77, 47.

89. Ni'imi, 52.

90. Skabelund, *Dogs*, 153.

91. Ni'imi, *Norakuro de arimasu!*, 56.

92. Ryan Holmberg, "Bat Kid: Inoue Kazuo and the Origins of Baseball Manga," in Inoue Kazuo, *Bat Kid*, trans. Ryan Holmberg (Richmond, VA: Bubbles Zine Publications, 2021), xi; Abe, *"Kodomo,"* i–ii.

93. Abe, 90–91.

94. Ni'imi, *Norakuro de arimasu!*, 37, 60, 56.

95. Miyamoto, "Kōdansha no ehon," 57–58.

96. Quoted in Abe, *"Kodomo,"* 90–91, 97.

97. Shimizu Isao, *Manga zasshi hakubutsukan* (Tokyo: National Diet Library, 1986–87; 12 vols.), vol. 12, 35.

98. Sakamoto, "How I Created Tank Tankuro," iii–iv. The manga's noticeable Buddhist elements may also have put it in bad odor with the imperial government, which regarded Buddhism with suspicion. Sakamoto eventually quit manga to practice Buddhist art.

99. Tagawa Suihō, *Norakuro tankentai* (Tokyo: Kodansha, 1939), preface.

100. Miyamoto, "Hito no yōna dōbutsutachi: Gijinka dōbutsu manga no '*Norakuro*,'" in Ni'imi, *Norakuro de arimasu!*, 9. Some lists of the five races substitute Chinese for the Russians.

101. Skabelund, *Dogs*, 134–35, 152, 154–62, 165–67. Dog owners, especially children, were also encouraged to "donate" dogs suitable for the military to the war effort.

102. Max Dioniso, "Drawing on History: Tagawa Suihō and Early Japanese Manga Culture" (PhD diss., University of Pennsylvania, 2007), 96.

103. Tagawa, *Gunsō;* Skabelund, *Dogs*, 152.

104. Tatiana Linkhoeva, *Revolution Goes East: Imperial Japan and Soviet Communism* (Ithaca, NY: Cornell University Press, 2020), 58, 61, 63.

105. Ni'imi, *Norakuro de arimasu!*, 39.

106. Sabine Frühstück, *Playing War: Children and the Paradoxes of Modern Militarism in Japan* (Oakland: University of California Press, 2017), 86; Ni'imi, *Norakuro de arimasu!*, 41.

107. Young, *Japan's Total Empire*, 13.

108. Frühstück, *Playing War*, 46–56. War games were ubiquitous as Japanese children's play well into the 1960s.

109. Skabelund, *Dogs*, 154, 152.

110. Abe, *"Kodomo,"* 91–96.

111. Gregory J. Kasza, *The State and the Mass Media in Japan, 1918–1945* (Berkeley: University of California Press, 1988), 170–73.

112. Tagawa, *Norakuro sōkōgeki* (Tokyo: Kodansha, 1937), 5.

113. Ni'imi, *Norakuro de arimasu!*, 81–82.

114. Kajii, *Tore*, 83, 86.

115. Tagawa and Takamizawa, *Norakuro ichidaiki*, 154.

116. Tezuka, Ōshiro, and Matsumoto, "'Oh! Manga' 2," 215; Miyamoto, "Akahon," 24.

117. Tagawa and Takamizawa, *Norakuro ichidaiki*, 151–52; Young, *Japan's Total Empire*, 356–61; Ronald Suleski, "Northeast China Under Japanese Control: The Role of the Manchurian Youth Corps, 1934–1945," *Modern China* 7, no. 3 (1981): 353, 357–58. The peasants were also colonists on the land, having displaced indigenous groups during the late Qing era.

118. Ueda Toshiko, "Jibun no 'hagemashi manga' o kaitara, *Fuichin-san* ga umareta," in *Manga daihakubutsukan*, ed. Matsumoto Leiji and Hidaka Satoshi (Tokyo: Shogakukan Creative, 2004), 337; Sakamoto, "Memories," v.

119. Sakamoto, v.

120. Tagawa and Takamizawa, *Norakuro ichidaiki*, 152–53.

121. Ni'imi, *Norakuro de arimasu!*, 89.

122. Sakamoto, "How I Created Tank Tankuro," iv.

123. Tagawa, *Norakuro tankentai*, 160; Tagawa, *Norakuro zenshū*, 671–77.

124. Tagawa and Takamizawa, *Norakuro ichidaiki*, 155–56, 151.

125. Tagawa, *Norakuro zenshū*, 706.

126. Ozaki, "Norakuro no hanseiki," 43.

127. Tagawa and Takamizawa, *Norakuro ichidaiki*, 155–56.

128. Kajii, *Tore*, 123; Ni'imi, *Norakuro de arimasu!*, 86.

129. Tezuka, Ōshiro, and Matsumoto, "'Oh! Manga' 2," 209.

130. Tagawa and Takamizawa, *Norakuro ichidaiki*, 156–57.

131. Sakamoto, "Memories," v.

132. Tezuka, Ōshiro, and Matsumoto, "'Oh! Manga' 2," 209–14; Shimizu, *Manga zasshi hakubatsukan*, vol. 8, 170; Shimizu Isao, *Manga ni miru 1945-nen* (Tokyo: Yoshikawa Kōbunkan, 1995), 3, 59.

133. Kasza, *Mass Media in Japan*, 224.

134. Tezuka, Ōshiro, and Matsumoto, "'Oh! Manga' 2," 214.

CHAPTER FOUR: THE MANGA MEN

1. Haruhara Akihiko, "Introduction," in *Shinbun manga no me*, ed. Nihon Shinbun Hakubutsukan (Yokohama: Newspark, 2003), 3.

2. Shinozawa Misako, "The Birth of a Million Seller: Magazines as Media in the Meiji-Taishō Era," in *Million seller tanjō e! Meiji, Taishō no zasshi media*, ed. Insatsubutsukan (Tokyo: Tokyo Shoseki, 2008), 183.

3. Shimizu Isao, *Manga zasshi hakubutsukan* (Tokyo: National Diet Library, 1986–87; 12 vols.), vol. 11, 166.

4. Shimizu, vol. 9, 206–7.

5. Shimizu, vol. 9, 145–46, n.p.

6. The manga was adapted into a four-reel live-action movie starring Ōyama Kenji, with a script by Shimokawa, who also published a manga in *Kinema Junpō* promoting its release.

7. Shimizu Isao, *Manga tanjō: Taishō democracy kara no shuppatsu* (Tokyo: Yoshikawa, 1999), 143.

8. Shimizu, *Manga zasshi hakubutsukan*, vol. 12, 146.

9. Ronald Stewart, "Groundbreaking Women: Recovering the History of Forgotten Prewar Female Mangaka," paper presented at the Virtual Association for Asian Studies Conference, March 1, 2024.

10. Stewart, "Women."

11. Shimizu, *Manga zasshi hakubutsukan*, vol. 9, 146.

12. Shimizu, *Manga tanjō*, 162.

13. Shimizu, *Manga zasshi hakubutsukan*, vol. 9, n.p.

14. *The Manga Man*, January 1930, 2.

15. Eike Exner, *Comics and the Origins of Manga: A Revisionist History* (New Brunswick, NJ: Rutgers University Press, 2021), 153.

16. Exner, 153.

17. Shimizu, *Manga zasshi hakubutsukan*, vol. 10, n.p.

18. Ippei Seishiki, "Foreword," in Miyao Shigeo, *Miyao Shigeo no hon, vol. 11: Shigeo manga zukan 1* (Tokyo: Kanō Shobō, 1984), 1.

19. Shimizu, *Manga zasshi hakubutsukan*, vol. 11, 166; Stewart, "Women."

20. Kozawa Jō, "Shinmangaha Shūdan no hitotachi," *Gendaishi konwakai* 108 (2002): 14.

21. Shimizu, *Manga zasshi hakubutsukan*, vol. 10, n.p.

22. Ishiko Jun, *Nihon mangashi* (Tokyo: Shakai Shisōsha, 1988), 170.

23. Stewart, "Women."

24. Kozawa, "Shinmangaha shūdan," 13–14.

25. Shinmangaha shūdan, *Shinmangaha shūdan manga nenkan* (Yokohama: Bunza Shorin, 1933), 92–93, 95, 98–100.

26. Shimizu, *Manga zasshi hakubutsukan*, vol. 9, 211–12, 211.

27. Exner, *Comics*, 155.

28. Kajii Jun, *Tore, yochō no jū to pen: Senjika mangashi nōto* (Tokyo: Wise Shuppan, 1999), 144–46, 154–55.

29. Tatiana Linkhoeva, *Revolution Goes East: Imperial Japan and Soviet Communism* (Ithaca, NY: Cornell University Press, 2020), 154–57.

30. Kajii, *Tore*, 150–51.

31. Gennifer S. Weisenfeld, *MAVO: Japanese Artists and the Avant-Garde, 1905–1931* (Berkeley: University of California Press, 2002), 170.

32. Kajii, *Tore*, 155, 159. Three years before, Rakuten had retired from *Jiji* making 530 yen a month.

33. Linkhoeva, *Revolution*, 134.

34. See Andrew Gordon, *Labor and Imperial Democracy in Prewar Japan* (Berkeley: University of California Press, 1991).

35. Shimizu, *Manga tanjō*, 124, 152; "Arita Shigeshi," http://seimeisi.web.fc2.com/sigesi/sigesi.html (accessed November 9, 2023).

36. Weisenfeld, *MAVO*, 63–64.

37. Shimokawa acted in a play written by Yanase, in the role of "Worker F," in 1925. Weisenfeld, *MAVO*, 228.

38. Shimokawa Ōten, "Shinmanga, shinmangaka," *Bijutsu Shinron* 2, no. 8 (August 1927), 53–54.

39. Okamoto Tōki and Matsuyama Fumio, *Nihon proletarian bijutsushi* (Tokyo: Zōkeisha, 1967), 120–21.

40. Okamoto and Matsuyama, 120–21.

41. Okamoto and Matsuyama, 120–21.

42. Gregory J. Kasza, *The State and the Mass Media in Japan, 1918–1945* (Berkeley: University of California Press, 1988), 40, 42, 43.

43. Okamoto and Matsuyama, *Nihon proletarian*, 114, 119.

44. Okamoto and Matsuyama, *Nihon proletarian*, 132–35; Weisenfeld, *MAVO*, 253. Yanase most likely made contact with the Comintern's Far Eastern Bureau on one of these trips.

45. Shimizu, *Manga tanjō*, 150.

46. Shimizu, 147.

47. Okamoto and Matsuyama, *Nihon proletarian*, 160.

48. Ishiko, *Nihon mangashi*, 158; Okamoto and Matsuyama, *Nihon proletarian*, 142–47.

49. Okamoto and Matsuyama, *Nihon proletarian*, 116, 113–14.

50. Shimizu, *Manga zasshi hakubutsukan*, vol. 9, n.p., 205–7.

51. Okamoto and Matsuyama, *Nihon proletarian*, 148–49.

52. Weisenfeld, *MAVO*, 78, 253.

53. Mizushima Niō, "Nihon mangashiron," in *Manga kōza, vol. 3*, ed. Nihon Mangakkai (Tokyo: Kensetsusha, 1934), 6.

54. Kajii, *Tore*, 167, 170–71; Ishiko, *Nihon mangashi*, 159.

55. Kasza, *Mass Media in Japan*, 165.

56. Kasza, 188.

57. Weisenfeld, *MAVO*, 252.

58. Okamoto and Matsuyama, *Nihon proletarian*, 151, 149.

59. Quoted in Kajii, *Tore*, 169, 151.

60. Rei Okamoto Inouye, "Theorizing Manga: Nationalism and Discourse on the Role of Wartime Manga," *Mechademia* 4 (2009): 20–37, 21.

61. Nakamura Shirō, "Manga kanshō no takakusei," *Manga no Kuni* 4, no. 50 (June 1938), 11.

62. Shimizu Isao, "Nicchū sensō-ki no manga zasshi *Manga no Kuni*," https://www.kyotomm.jp/HP/about_syozo.html (accessed December 4, 2023); *Manga no Kuni* 3, no. 30 (July 1937); *Manga no Kuni* 3, no. 44 (December 1937); *Manga no Kuni* 4, no. 45 (January 1938). Ōta's daughter, animator Ōta Akemi (b. 1938), married Miyazaki Hayao, who eventually forced her to give up her career.

63. Ryan Holmberg, "Fukui Eiichi and the Judo Manga Revolution," in Fukui Eiichi, *Igaguri: Young Judo Master*, trans. Ryan Holmberg (Richmond, VA: Bubbles Zine Publications, 2024), xxviii.

64. Stewart, "Women."

65. *Manga no Kuni* 3, no. 30 (July 1937): 3.

66. *Karikare* 2, no. 1 (January 1939): 2.

67. Ishiko, *Nihon mangashi*, 157.

68. Quoted in Inouye, "Theorizing," 28.

69. Kasza, *Mass Media in Japan*, 221–24.

70. Kajii, *Tore*, 181.

71. Kajii, 183.

72. Kenneth J. Ruoff, *Imperial Japan at Its Zenith: The Wartime Celebration of the Empire's 2,600th Anniversary* (Ithaca, NY: Cornell University Press, 2010), 176.

73. Quoted in Kajii, *Tore*, 182, 183.

74. "Rakuten-sensei ōi ni kataru," *Manga*, August 1941, 19.

75. "Rakuten-sensei," 19–20.

76. "Rakuten-sensei," 20–21.

77. Kajii, *Tore*, 187–88.

78. "Rakuten-sensei," 21.

79. Komatsu Sakyō, "Taiken toshite no mangashi," in *Maboroshi no Komatsu Sakyō = Mori Minoru manga zenshū, vol. 4: Kaisetsuhen* (Tokyo: Shogakukan, 2002), 10.

80. Kajii, *Tore*, 190; Shimizu Isao, *Manga ni miru 1945-nen* (Tokyo: Yoshikawa Kōbunkan, 1995), 59.

81. Inouye, "Theorizing," 27–28.

82. Kajii, *Tore*, 189–90, 196; Inouye, "Theorizing," 31; Shimizu, *1945-nen*, 208.

83. Katō Etsurō, *Shinrinen manga no gihō* (Tokyo: Geijutsu Gakuin Shuppanbu, 1942), 67, 15.

84. Shimizu, *1945-nen*, 171.

85. Quoted in Kajii, *Tore*, 186.

86. Louise Young, *Japan's Total Empire: Manchuria and the Culture of Wartime Imperialism* (Berkeley: University of California Press, 1998), 68.

87. Tagawa Suihō and Takamizawa Junko, *Norakuro ichidaiki: Tagawa Suihō jijoden* (Tokyo: Kodansha, 1991), 105, 148–49.

88. Natsume Fusanosuke, "*Norakuro* to aratana mangashi," in *Kokkei to pathos: Tagawa Suihō "Norakuro" ichidaiki-ten*, ed. Machida Shimin Bunka Gakkan Kotobarando (Machida, Tokyo: Machida Shimin Bunka Gakkan Kotobarando, 2013), 4–5.

89. Ōtsuka Eiji, "An Unholy Alliance of Eisenstein and Disney: The Fascist Origins of Otaku Culture," trans. Thomas Lamarre, *Mechademia* 8 (2013), 255–57, 252, 258.

90. Hikari Hori, *Promiscuous Media: Film and Visual Culture in Imperial Japan, 1926–1945* (Ithaca, NY: Cornell University Press, 2017), 5.

91. Ishinomori Shōtarō, *Kizuna: Fushō no musuko kara fushō no musukotachi e* (Tokyo: NTT Shuppan, 1998), 63.

92. Miyamoto Hirohito, "Hito no yōna dōbutsutachi: Gijinka dōbutsu manga no '*Norakuro*,'" in *Norakuro de arimasu! Tagawa Suihō to kodomo manga no wonderland*, ed. Ni'imi Takuma (Kawasaki, Japan: Kawasaki City Museum, 2019), 11.

93. Hori, *Promiscuous Media*, 10–18.

94. Kajii, *Tore*, 194–96, 204–5.

95. Kajii, 99.

96. Komatsu, "Taiken," 10–11.

97. Komatsu, 7.

98. Tezuka Osamu, *Boku no manga jinsei* (Tokyo: Iwanami Shoten, 1997), 12.

99. Kajii, *Tore*, 194–95.

100. Inouye, "Theorizing," 34.

101. Tezuka Osamu, *Tezuka Osamu: Sōsaku nōto to shoki sakuhin* (Tokyo: Shogakukan Creative, 2013), "Fukusei Genga" supplement, n.p.

102. Tezuka, *Boku no manga jinsei*, 62.

103. Yokoyama Ryūichi, *Yokoyama Ryūichi: Waga yūgiteki jinsei* (Tokyo: Nihon Tosho Center, 1997), 93–95, 98–102, 110–11.

104. Tagawa and Takamizawa, *Norakuro ichidaiki*, 157–59.

105. Ni'imi Takuma, ed., *Norakuro de arimasu! Tagawa Suihō to kodomo manga no wonderland* (Kawasaki, Japan: Kawasaki City Museum, 2019), 92.

106. Frederik L. Schodt, "Henry (Yoshitaka) Kiyama," Stone Bridge Press, https://www.stonebridge.com/authors/henry-(yoshitaka)-kiyama (accessed March 29, 2025).

107. Yazaki Shigeshi et al., *Yokusan manga susume Yamato ikka* (Tokyo: Nihon Ezasshisha, 1942); Stewart, "Women."

108. Ueda Toshiko, "Jibun no 'Hagemashi manga' o kaitara, *Fuichin-san* ga umareta," in *Manga daihakubutsukan*, ed. Matsumoto Leiji and Hidaka Satoshi (Tokyo: Shogakukan Creative, 2004), 337.

109. Kajii, *Tore*, 116–18.

110. Gajō Sakamoto, "How I Created Tank Tankuro," in *Tank Tankuro: Prewar Works, 1934–1935*, trans. Maki Hakui and Shunsuke Nakazawa (Tokyo: Presspop, 2011), iv; Naoki Sakamoto, "Memories of My Father, Sakamoto Gajō," in Sakamoto, *Tank Tankuro*, v–vi.

111. Kajii, *Tore*, 190–91; Shimizu, *1945-nen*, 59.

112. Ni'imi, *Norakuro de arimasu!*, 84.

113. Matsumoto Leiji and Komatsu Sakyō, "*Kasei tanken* to Shōwa no manga," in *Kasei tanken*, 168–69, 180–81; Ono Kōsei, "Zenei artist toshite shuppatsu shita Tagawa Suihō to sono robot tachi," in Ni'imi, *Norakuro de arimasu!*, 110–11.

114. Shimizu Isao, *1945-nen* (Tokyo: Yoshikawa Kōbunkan, 1995), 3, 59. The January and October 1945 *Manga Nihon* issues are extant, but there was apparently one other issue between them, most likely in February. *Manga*'s final wartime issue is dated June/July 1945.

PART TWO CONCLUSION: EATING VEGETABLES, REREADING MANGA

1. *Manga Nihon*, October 1945, 7, 11.

2. Quoted in Edmund de Waal, *The Hare with Amber Eyes: A Family's Century of Art and Loss* (New York: Farrar, Straus and Giroux, 2010), chap. 35.

3. Tezuka Osamu, *Boku no manga jinsei* (Tokyo: Iwanami Shoten, 1997), 62–64; Tezuka Osamu, *Boku wa mangaka* (Tokyo: Kadokawa Shoten, 2000), 44. The details about understanding the surrender broadcast vary somewhat between the two memoirs.

4. Ueda Toshiko, "Sokoku wa narete," in *Boku no Manshū: Mangaka-tachi no haisen taiken*, ed. Chūgoku Hikiage Mangaka no Kai (Tokyo: Aki Shobō, 1995), 4.

5. Nagai Katsuichi, *Garo henshūchō: Watashi no sengo manga shuppanshi* (Tokyo: Chikuma Shobō, 1987), 95–100.

6. Ueda, "Sokoku," 14.

7. Miriam Silverberg, *Erotic Grotesque Nonsense: The Mass Culture of Japanese Modern Times* (Berkeley: University of California Press, 2006), 269.

8. Andrew Gordon, *Fabricating Consumers: The Sewing Machine in Modern Japan* (Berkeley: University of California Press, 2012), 120.

9. Kenneth J. Ruoff, *Imperial Japan at Its Zenith: The Wartime Celebration of the Empire's 2,600th Anniversary* (Ithaca, NY: Cornell University Press, 2010), 6–7, 113–15.

PART THREE OVERVIEW: NOWHERE TO GO BUT UP

1. See Miriam Kingsberg Kadia, *Moral Nation: Modern Japan and Narcotics in Global History* (Berkeley: University of California Press, 2013).

2. Shimizu Isao, *Manga ni miru 1945-nen* (Tokyo: Yoshikawa Kōbunkan, 1995), 171, 208, 248.

3. Miyamoto Hirohito, "Akahon manga," in *Mangagaku nyūmon*, ed. Natsume Fusanosuke and Takeuchi Osamu (Kyoto: Minerva Shobō, 2009), 26.

4. Natsume Fusanosuke, *Tezuka Osamu no bōken: Sengo manga no kamigami* (Tokyo: Shogakukan, 1998), 145–46, 156–57.

5. Tatsumi Yoshihiro, *Gekiga hyōryū* (Tokyo: Seirin Kōgeisha, 2008), vol. 1, 55–58.

CHAPTER FIVE: THE MANGA PULPS AND THE GOD OF MANGA

1. Ni'imi Takuma, ed., *Norakuro de arimasu! Tagawa Suihō to kodomo manga no wonderland* (Kawasaki, Japan: Kawasaki City Museum, 2019), 46.

2. Nakano Haruyuki, "*Shintakarajima* to Sakai Shichima," in *Shintakarajima dokuhon*, supplement to *Shintakarajima* by Tezuka Osamu and Sakai Shichima (Tokyo: Shogakukan Creative, 2009), 35.

3. Nakano, "*Shintakarajima*," 36–38; Takeuchi Osamu, "*Shintakarajima* no bōken," in *Shintakarajima dokuhon*, 16.

4. Nakano, "*Shintakarajima*," 38.

5. Ryan Holmberg, "The Heirs of Gottfredson: Osamu Tezuka," in Floyd Gottfredson, *Walt Disney's Mickey Mouse "Outwits the Phantom Blot,"* ed. David Gerstein and Gary Groth (Seattle: Fantagraphics Books, 2014), 280–81.

6. Nakano, "*Shintakarajima*," 38–43.

7. Takeuchi, "*Shintakarajima*," 27.

8. Komatsu Sakyō, "Manga to bungaku ni akekureta seishun," in *Maboroshi no Komatsu Sakyō = Mori Minoru manga zenshū, vol. 4: Kaisetsuhen* (Tokyo: Shogakukan, 2002), 72.

9. Nakano, "*Shintakarajima*," 29–30.

10. Tezuka Osamu, *Boku wa mangaka* (Tokyo: Kadokawa Shoten, 2000), 90.

11. Holmberg, "Heirs," 281–84.

12. Holmberg, "Heirs," 284–85. Tezuka completely redrew *Shintakarajima* for his collected works in 1986, and the original was not reissued in his lifetime.

13. Ni'imi, *Norakuro de arimasu!*, 98.

14. Fujiko Fujio A and Fujiko F. Fujio, *Futari de shōnen manga bakari kaitekita* (Tokyo: Nihon Tosho Center, 2010), 21–22.

15. Nagayama Kaoru, *Erotic Comics in Japan: An Introduction to Eromanga*, trans. Patrick W. Galbraith and Jessica Bauwens-Sugimoto (Amsterdam: Amsterdam University Press, 2021), 49.

16. Takeuchi, "*Shintakarajima*," 23.

17. Mori Seiji, "Commentary," in Tezuka Osamu and Sakai Shichima, *Shintakarajima original-han* (Tokyo: Kodansha, 2012), 198; Tatsumi Yoshihiro, *Gekiga hyōryū* (Tokyo: Seirin Kōgeisha, 2008), vol. 1, 281–82.

18. Takeuchi, "*Shintakarajima*," 19–20.

19. Nakano, "*Shintakarajima*," 44.

20. Tezuka Osamu, Ōshiro Noboru, and Matsumoto Leiji, "'Oh! Manga' 2: Sensō made" [1972], in Asai Tarō and Ōshiro Noboru, *Kasei tanken* (Tokyo: Tōdosha, 2003), 200.

21. Takeuchi, "*Shintakarajima*," 15.

22. Miyamoto Hirohito, "Akahon manga," in *Mangagaku nyūmon*, ed. Natsume Fusanosuke and Takeuchi Osamu (Kyoto: Minerva Shobō, 2009), 25; Nagai Katsuichi, *Garo henshūchō: Watashi no sengo manga shuppanshi* (Tokyo: Chikuma Shobō, 1987), 105–6.

23. Shimizu Isao, *'Manga Shōnen' to akahon manga: Sengo manga no tanjō* (Tokyo: Zoionsha, 1989), 74; Miyamoto, "Akahon," 25.

24. Shimizu, *Sengo manga*, 72–74.

25. Miyamoto, "Akahon," 25; Miyabe Sei'itsu, Kurosawa Tetsuya, Takeuchi Osamu, and Kajii Jun, *Mangakatachi no sensō bekkan shiryō* (Tokyo: Kinnohoshisha, 2013), 107.

26. *Nikkei*, "Komatsu Sakyō-san maboroshi no debut saku, Bei de hakken: Kyūsei sankō jidai no manga hon," June 14, 2014, https://www.nikkei.com/article/DGXNASDG1400L_U4A610C1CR0000/; Komatsu Sakyō and Saitō Takao, "Kaidan: Komatsu Sakyō vs. Saitō Takao: Shōwa nijū nendai manga tankōbon jijō," in Komatsu Sakyō, *Maboroshi no Komatsu Sakyō = Mori Minoru manga zenshū, vol. 4: Kaisetsuhen* (Tokyo: Shogakukan, 2002), 22, 25; Komatsu, "Manga to bungaku," 69.

27. Tezuka, *Boku wa mangaka*, 91.

28. Ryan Holmberg, "Osamu Tezuka and the First Story Manga," in Osamu Tezuka, *The Mysterious Underground Men*, ed. and trans. Ryan Holmberg (Brooklyn: PictureBox, 2013), viii, xi–xiv, xxxii, xxxvii.

29. Quoted in Nakano Haruyuki, *Tezuka Osamu no Takarazuka* (Tokyo: Chikuma Shobō, 1994), 192.

30. Shimizu, *Sengo manga*, 13. Misora and other real-life figures' appearance in akahon bears comparison with the form of fanfiction known as real-person fiction or RPF, which is controversial in anglophone fandom but mainstream in Korean and Thai BL fandoms.

31. Shimizu, 74, 78, 82.

32. Shimizu, 82.

33. Sharalyn Orbaugh, "'Kamishibai' and the Art of the Interval," *Mechademia* 7 (2012), 83.

34. Orbaugh, 87, 80. Contemporary kamishibai videos are available on YouTube.

35. Shimizu, *Sengo manga*, 83.

36. Orbaugh, "Kamishibai," 82; contemporary kamishibai theorist Imai Yone estimated that the prewar numbers were a 50 percent undercount (98).

37. Sawai Kōichi, "Tezuka no sodatta Osaka no sengo: Kamishibai, kashihon, akahon," in Tezuka Osamu and Ishinomori Shōtarō, *Tezuka Osamu × Ishinomori Shōtarō manga no chikara: Tokubetsuten* (Tokyo: NHK Promotion, 2013), 42.

38. Orbaugh, "Kamishibai," 78–79.

39. Ueda Toshiko, "Jibun no 'hagemashi manga' o kaitara, *Fuichin-san* ga umareta," in *Manga daihakubutsukan*, ed. Matsumoto Leiji and Hidaka Satoshi (Tokyo: Shogakukan Creative, 2004), 338.

40. Sawai, "Osaka," 43; Mura Nunoe, *Gegege no nyōbō: Jinsei wa . . . owari yokereba subete yoshi!!* (Tokyo: Jitsugyō no Nihonsha, 2011), 61.

41. Mura, *Gegege*, 61–63.

42. Orbaugh, "Kamishibai," 79; Yoshimi Shun'ya, "From Street Corner to Living Room: Domestication of TV Culture and National Time/Narrative," trans. Jodie Beck, *Mechademia* 9, no. 1 (2014), 128, 132.

43. Manga Shūdan, ed., *Manga Shōwashi: Manga Shūdan no 50-nen* (Tokyo: Kawade Shobo Shinsha, 1982), 7, 67.

44. Yokoyama Ryūichi, *Yokoyama Ryūichi: Waga yūgiteki jinsei* (Tokyo: Nihon Tosho Center, 1997), 119–20.

45. This paragraph draws on materials on display in the Hasegawa Machiko Museum in Setagaya, Tokyo, in August 2015.

46. Shimizu, *Sengo manga*, 115–16.

47. *Manga Shōnen*, no. 10 (October 1948), 2.

48. Tatsumi, *Gekiga*, vol. 1, 397.

49. Ronald Stewart, "Newspaper Comic Strips: Laughs in Four Panels," in Jaqueline Berndt, ed., *The Cambridge Companion to Manga and Anime* (Cambridge: Cambridge University Press, 2024), 35.

50. Stewart, "Comic Strips," 32; Shimizu Isao, "Giga, fūshiga, fūzokuga," in Natsume and Takeuchi, *Mangagaku*, 6–7; Yamaguchi Saeko, "4-koma manga," in Natsume and Takeuchi, *Mangagaku*, 14; Shimizu Isao, "Manga to shinbun," in Natsume and Takeuchi, *Mangagaku*, 64.

51. Stewart, "Comic Strips," 32, 36, 31.

52. *Kodomo Manga Times*, no. 92 (August 13, 1950), no. 103 (October 29, 1950), no. 129 (April 29, 1951). Many thanks to the National Diet Library staff for arranging my viewing of this newspaper in person.

53. Tatsumi, *Gekiga*, vol. 1, 33.

54. Fujiki Hideaki, "Implicating Readers: Tezuka's Early Seinen Manga," *Mechademia* 8 (2013), 200, 195.

55. Fujiki, 200.

56. Komatsu Sakyō, "Taiken toshite no mangashi," in *Maboroshi no Komatsu Sakyō = Mori Minoru manga zenshū, vol. 4: Kaisetsuhen* (Tokyo: Shogakukan, 2002), 14.

57. Ronald Stewart, "Groundbreaking Women: Recovering the History of Forgotten Prewar Female Mangaka," paper presented at the Virtual Association for Asian Studies Conference, March 1, 2024.

58. Matsumoto Masahiko, *Gekiga bakatachi!!* (Tokyo: Seirin Kōgeisha, 2009), 146, 173.

59. Tagawa and Takamizawa, Tagawa Suihō and Takamizawa Junko, *Norakuro ichidaiki: Tagawa Suihō jijoden* (Tokyo: Kodansha, 1991), 160–63.

60. Tatsumi, *Gekiga*, vol. 1, 75; Miyamoto Hirohito, "Wasureraretekita '*Norakuro*' no sengo," in *Norakuro sannintabi*, by Tagawa Suihō (Tokyo: Kyōiku Hyōronsha, 2021), n.p.

61. Ozaki Hotsuki, "Norakuro no hanseiki," in Tagawa Suihō, *Bokura no Norakuro: Norakuro 50-nen kinen album* (Tokyo: Kodansha, 1984), 46; Miyamoto, "Wasureraretekita," n.p.

62. Tagawa and Takamizawa, *Norakuro ichidaiki*, 147.

63. Tagawa, *Chinpin Norakuro-sō* (Tokyo: Kanda Shuppan, 1947), 5–6.

64. Nagai, *Garo*, 76.

65. *Shōnen Club*, May 1946, 56.

66. Katō Takeo, *"Manga Shōnen" monogatari: Henshūsha Katō Ken'ichi den* (Tokyo: Toshi Shuppan, 2002), 12, 126, 159.

67. Katō, 92, 101; Ryan Holmberg, "*Manga Shōnen:* Katō Ken'ichi and the Manga Boys," *Mechademia* 8 (2013), 177; Katō Ken'ichi, *Shōnen Kurabu jidai: Henshūchō no kaisō* (Tokyo: Kodansha, 1968), 117. At the end of his career, Katō reflected that the Tessetsusha's ethos probably influenced *Shōnen Kurabu* through him (117–18).

68. Katō Misako, "Chichi Ken'ichi to '*Manga Shōnen*,'" in Terada Hiroo, *"Manga Shōnen"-shi* (Fujisawa, Japan: Shōnan Shuppansha, 1981), 107–8; Ryan Holmberg, "Bat Kid: Inoue Kazuo and the Origins of Baseball Manga," in Inoue Kazuo, *Bat Kid*, trans. Ryan Holmberg (Richmond, VA: Bubbles Zine Publications, 2021), xix–xx, xxiii, xxv; Katō, *Henshūsha*, 26–29.

69. Terada, *"Manga Shōnen"-shi*, 11.

70. *Manga Shōnen* 1, no. 10 (October 1948), 26.

71. Katō, *Henshūsha*, 15–16.

72. *Manga Shōnen* 1, no. 10 (October 1948), 108, 110; Terada, *"Manga Shōnen"-shi*, 251; Holmberg, "Manga Boys," 183.

73. Katō, "Chichi," 109.

74. Ryan Holmberg, "Fukui Eiichi and the Judo Manga Revolution," in Fukui Eiichi, *Igaguri: Young Judo Master*, trans. Ryan Holmberg (Richmond, VA: Bubbles Zine Publications, 2024), xvii–xviii. Tezuka's 1947 meeting with Shimada "did not go well" (xviii).

75. Shimizu, *Sengo manga*, 54–55; Holmberg, "Bat Kid," xxvi.

76. Katō, *Henshūsha*, 18–20.

77. Shimizu, *Sengo manga*, 15, 27–29, 51–52.

78. Holmberg, "Bat Kid," xxxviii. Bat was named after Rakuten's disciple, mangaka Nagasaki Batten; Inoue and his siblings evacuated to Nagasaki's brother's house during the war (xvi).

79. Holmberg, xv.

80. Shimizu, *Sengo manga*, 153; *Manga Shōnen* 1, no. 10 (October 1948), 2; *Manga Shōnen* 1, no. 11 (November 1948).

81. Shimizu, *Sengo manga*, 93.

82. Holmberg, "Bat Kid," xli.

83. Shimizu, *Sengo manga*, 108–9.

84. Katō, "Chichi," 110.

85. Ishinomori Shōtarō, *Kizuna: Fushō no musuko kara fushō no musukotachi e* (Tokyo: NTT Shuppan, 1998), 44.

86. Terada, *"Manga Shōnen"-shi*, 135. In other words, #nohomo.

87. Yonezawa Yoshihiro, "*Manga Shōnen* kara Comiket e . . . ," in *Shōnen natsu man'ō* (zine) 16 (1995), 47.

88. Tezuka Osamu, "Katō Ken'ichi-shi to watashi," in Terada, *"Manga Shōnen"-shi*, 6.

89. Tezuka, *Boku wa mangaka*, 136–38.

90. Shimizu, *Sengo manga*, 121–23.

91. Holmberg, "Fukui Eiichi," xxix.

92. Tezuka, *Boku wa mangaka*, 88–90.

93. Natsume Fusanosuke, *Tezuka Osamu no bōken: Sengo manga no kamigami* (Tokyo: Shogakukan, 1998), 145–46.

94. Ishinomori, *Kizuna*, 71.

95. Futagami Hirokazu, "Manga to zasshi," in *Mangagaku nyūmon*, ed. Natsume Fusanosuke and Takeuchi Osamu (Kyoto: Minerva Shobō, 2009), 55.

96. Ishinomori, *Kizuna*, 70–72.

97. Gajō Sakamoto, "How I Created Tank Tankuro," in *Tank Tankuro: Prewar Works, 1934–1935*, trans. Maki Hakui and Shunsuke Nakazawa (Tokyo: Presspop, 2011), iii.

98. Nakashima Takashi, "*Com* to *Apple Core:* Gura-Com Kansai shibu tenmatsuki," *Biranji* 27 (March 2011), 114; Ryan Holmberg, "The Fukui Ei'ichi Incident and the Prehistory of Komaga-Gekiga," *The Comics Journal*, January 5, 2015, 3, https://www.tcj.com/the-fukui-eiichi-incident-and-the-prehistory-of-komaga-gekiga/.

99. Holmberg, 3, 5; Tezuka, *Boku wa mangaka*, 165. The vivid translation is Holmberg's.

100. Shimizu, *Sengo manga*, 123–25.

101. Ishinomori, *Kizuna*, 47.

102. Ishinomori, 72.

103. Holmberg, "Fukui Eiichi," xi–xiii, xvii.

104. Holmberg, xxix.

105. Holmberg, iii–iv; Tezuka, *Boku wa mangaka*, 133–34; Holmberg, "Fukui Ei'ichi Incident," 5.

106. Quoted in Holmberg, "Fukui Eiichi," xli, xxxviii–xxxix, lxxx.

107. Holmberg, lxvii, lxx.

108. Yonezawa Yoshihiro, "Shōwa 30-nen emonogatari no saishūshō," *Shōnen Natsu Man'ō* (zine) 19 (September 1995), 56–57.

109. TKS and Tezuka Productions, *Tokiwasō*, 41, 34.

110. TKS and Tezuka Productions, 34. Tagawa chose Nagata to continue the Norakuro manga after his death, along with twin brothers Yamane Ao'oni (b. 1935) and Akaoni (1935–2003).

111. Toshima-ku Kyōdo Shiryōkan [TKS] and Tezuka Productions, eds., *Tokiwasō no hero-tachi: Manga ni kaketa seishun: Toshima-ku hatsu manga bunka o ichidō ni shōkai* (Tokyo: Toshima-ku, 2009), 12.

112. TKS and Tezuka Productions, 12, 14.

113. Ishinomori, *Kizuna*, 58.

114. TKS and Tezuka Productions, *Tokiwasō*, 14, 41–42.

115. Fujiko Fujio A, *Ai . . . shiri someshi koro ni . . . vol. 1* (Tokyo: Shogakukan, 1997), 106, 89–90.

116. Fujiko, 16, 109–10.

117. Ishinomori, *Kizuna*, 59, 66, 76–81.

118. Yonezawa Yoshihiro and Shikijō Kyōtarō, *2Bdan gindama sensō no hibi: Shōwa 30-nendai—yume no shōnen ōkoku* (Tokyo: Shinpyōsha, 1982), 78–85.

119. Ishinomori, *Kizuna*, 70.

120. Ozaki Hotsuki, "Ke'ai de huizhen," in Ueda Toshiko, *Fuichin-san* (Tokyo: Mushi Pro Shōji, 1969), 217–18.

121. Ueda Toshiko, *Fuichin-san* (Tokyo: Shogakukan, 2015; 2 vols.).

122. Ozaki, "Ke'ai," 218.

123. Natsume, *Tezuka Osamu no bōken*, 145.

124. "Zadankai: Tanoshii quintet," *Himawari* 5, no. 10 (October 1951), 64–69.

CHAPTER SIX: MANGA FOR WHOM?

1. Naiki Toshio, "Maboroshi no sakunin to aeru yorokobi," in Komatsu Sakyō, *Maboroshi no Komatsu Sakyō = Mori Minoru manga zenshū, vol. 4: Kaisetsuhen* (Tokyo: Shogakukan, 2002), 122.

2. Kashihon manga kenkyūkai [KMK], *Kashihon manga returns* (Tokyo: Popurasha, 2006), 13–14.

3. Naiki, "Maboroshi," 123.

4. Nagai Katsuichi, *Garo henshūchō: Watashi no sengo manga shuppanshi* (Tokyo: Chikuma Shobō, 1987), 118.

5. Kajii Jun, "Introduction," in Zenkoku Kashihon Kumiai Rengōkai [ZKKR], *Zenkoku kashihon shinbun: Fukkokuban* (Tokyo: Fuji Shuppan, 2010), vol. 1, 1, 5.

6. Kure Tomofusa, "Kashihon manga, gekiga," in *Mangagaku nyūmon*, ed. Natsume Fusanosuke and Takeuchi Osamu (Kyoto: Minerva Shobō, 2009), 27; Yamakoshi Masatoshi, "Kashihonya," in Natsume and Takeuchi, *Mangagaku*, 34.

7. KMK, *Returns*, 14–15; Tatsumi Yoshihiro, *Gekiga hyōryū* (Tokyo: Seirin Kōgeisha, 2008), vol. 1, 9. In recent years, used bookstores have begun shrink-wrapping or otherwise sealing newly acquired popular manga to prevent tachiyomi.

8. *Manga no Kuni* 3, no. 44 (December 1937): 18.

9. Shimizu Isao, *'Manga Shōnen' to akahon manga: Sengo manga no tanjō* (Tokyo: Zoionsha, 1989), 10, 73; Nagai, *Garo*, 117.

10. KMK, *Returns*, 15.

11. Mura Nunoe, *Gegege no nyōbō: Jinsei wa . . . owari yokereba subete yoshi!!* (Tokyo: Jitsugyō no Nihonsha, 2011), 64–65, 85–86, 41. In 1956, as a rank newcomer, Ishinomori was making 1,000 yen per page in *Shōjo Club;* he did a kashihon manga in 1957 to buy a stereo, but estimated he lost at least 20,000 yen compared to what he would have earned serializing the story. Ishinomori Shōtarō, *Kizuna: Fushō no musuko kara fushō no musukotachi e* (Tokyo: NTT Shuppan, 1998), 70–71.

12. Nagai, *Garo*, 158–59.

13. KMK, *Returns*, 25–26, 20–21.

14. Ryan Holmberg, "Fukui Eiichi and the Judo Manga Revolution," in Fukui Eiichi, *Igaguri: Young Judo Master*, trans. Ryan Holmberg (Richmond, VA: Bubbles Zine Publications, 2024), xxxiii–iv.

15. ZKKR, *Zenkoku kashihon*, vol. 1, 4.

16. KMK, *Returns*, 16–17.

17. Nagai, *Garo*, 134, 136, 156–57.
18. ZKKR, *Zenkoku kashihon*, vol. 1, 27–28.
19. Nagai, *Garo*, 120–21.
20. Mura, *Gegege*, 122.
21. ZKKR, *Zenkoku kashihon*, vol. 2, 22, 48, 59, 66, 130–31.
22. ZKKR, vol. 2, 10–11.
23. ZKKR, vol. 1, 4.
24. Sharalyn Orbaugh, "'Kamishibai' and the Art of the Interval," *Mechademia* 7 (2012), 89.
25. Natsume Fusanosuke, *Tezuka Osamu no bōken: Sengo manga no kamigami* (Tokyo: Shogakukan, 1998), 122; Tatsumi, *Gekiga*, vol. 1, 340, 366–74, 416; Ishinomori, *Kizuna*, 62–63.
26. Matsumoto Masahiko, *Gekiga bakatachi!!* (Tokyo: Seirin Kōgeisha, 2009), 30.
27. Matsumoto, 202, 231.
28. Tatsumi, *Gekiga*, vol. 1, 406; KMK, *Returns*, 19–21.
29. Matsumoto Masahiko, "What Was Komaga?," in *The Man Next Door*, trans. Ryan Holmberg (London: Breakdown Press, 2014), n.p.
30. Quoted in Ryan Holmberg, "Proto-Gekiga: Matsumoto Masahiko's Komaga," *The Comics Journal*, October 22, 2014, 1, https://www.tcj.com/proto-gekiga-matsumoto-masahikos-komaga/.
31. Ryan Holmberg, "The Komaga Revolution," in Matsumoto, *Man Next Door*, n.p.
32. Kure, "Kashihon," 29; Tatsumi, *A Drifting Life*, trans. Taro Nettleton (Montréal: Drawn & Quarterly, 2009), 730.
33. Tatsumi, *Life*, 852–53, 730.
34. Nagayama Kaoru, *Erotic Comics in Japan: An Introduction to Eromanga*, trans. Patrick W. Galbraith and Jessica Bauwens-Sugimoto (Amsterdam: Amsterdam University Press, 2021), 53.
35. Natsume, *Tezuka Osamu no bōken*, 132, 156–57.
36. Ishinomori, *Kizuna*, 73.
37. Natsume, *Tezuka Osamu no bōken*, 158, 146–47.
38. KMK, *Returns*, 22.
39. Nagayama, *Introduction to Eromanga*, 54.
40. "Zadankai gekiga kaidō o shuppatsu suru," *Matenrō*, no. 1 (1959): 158–60.
41. Kure, "Kashihon," 32.
42. Natsume, *Tezuka Osamu no bōken*, 153–56.
43. Komatsu Sakyō and Saitō Takao, "Kaidan: Komatsu Sakyō vs. Saitō Takao: Shōwa nijū nendai manga tankōbon jijō," in Komatsu Sakyō, *Maboroshi no Komatsu Sakyō = Mori Minoru manga zenshū, vol. 4: Kaisetsuhen* (Tokyo: Shogakukan, 2002), 24.
44. Kure, "Kashihon," 28.
45. "Zadankai gekiga," 158–60.
46. "Zadankai gekiga," 158–60.

47. "Zadankai gekiga," 158–60.

48. *Musō*, no. 4 (1959): 179.

49. *Matenrō*, no. 1 (1959): 157.

50. *Matenrō*, no. 1 (1959): 33–37.

51. *Matenrō*, no. 2 (1959): 48.

52. *Matenrō*, no. 2 (1959): 55.

53. Kure, "Kashihon," 31–32.

54. Terada Hiroo, *"Manga Shōnen"-shi* (Fujisawa, Japan: Shōnan Shuppansha, 1981), 135. These contests were Tatsumi's idea.

55. Yonezawa Yoshihiro, "*Manga Shōnen* kara Comiket e . . . ," in *Shōnen natsu man'ō* (zine) 16 (1995), 48.

56. Ishinomori, *Kizuna*, 149.

57. Miyazaki Hayao, *Starting Point: 1979–1996*, trans. Beth Cary and Frederik L. Schodt (San Francisco: VIZ Media, 2009), 49–50, 436.

58. Tatsumi, *Life*, 730–817.

59. Kure, "Kashihon," 29.

60. Natsume, *Tezuka Osamu no bōken*, 295–96.

61. Quoted in Ishinomori, *Kizuna*, 73.

62. ZKKR, *Zenkoku kashihon*, vol. 2, 22, 143.

63. The anti-comics mania in the United States was stoked by psychologist Fredric Wertham and his book *Seduction of the Innocent* (1954); in Japan, it was a translation of journalist Albert E. Kahn's *The Game of Death: Effects of the Cold War on Our Children* (1953). Tezuka Osamu, *Boku wa mangaka* (Tokyo: Kadokawa Shoten, 2000), 188.

64. Miyamoto Hirohito, "Akahon manga," in *Mangagaku nyūmon*, ed. Natsume Fusanosuke and Takeuchi Osamu (Kyoto: Minerva Shobō, 2009), 26.

65. Jennifer S. Prough, *Straight from the Heart: Gender, Intimacy, and the Cultural Production of Shōjo Manga* (Honolulu: University of Hawai'i Press, 2011), 33.

66. Saitō Nobuhiko, "Hyōgen hisei to jiken," in Natsume and Takeuchi, *Mangagaku*, 153–54.

67. Takeuchi Osamu, *Sengo manga 50-nenshi* (Tokyo: Chikuma Shobō, 1995), 61–62.

68. Takeuchi, 64, 66.

69. Tagawa Suihō, *Chameken to Norakuro* (Tokyo: Saikensha, 1948), preface.

70. Terada, *"Manga Shōnen"-shi*, 250–52.

71. See David Hajdu, *The Ten-Cent Plague: The Great Comic Book Scare and How It Changed America* (New York: Farrar, Straus and Giroux, 2008).

72. Takeuchi, *Sengo*, 64; Tezuka, *Boku wa mangaka*, 187.

73. Tezuka, 187–89.

74. Kajii, "Introduction," 7.

75. Kure, "Kashihon," 32–33.

76. Tatsumi, *Life*, 815–16.

77. Takeuchi, *Sengo*, 64.

78. "Hirogaru akusho tsuihō undō," reprinted in *Manga Kenkyū* 3 (August 1995), 6.

79. Kajii, "Introduction," 7–8. By contrast, outlets of the contemporary used bookstore chain Book-Off do often have an age-segregated section of secondhand pornography.

80. KMKK, *Returns*, 26.

81. Shimotsuki Takanaka, ed., *COM 40-nenme no shūkangō* (Tokyo: Asahi Shinbun Shuppan, 2011), 128; Murakami Motoka, *Fuichin zaijian!* (Tokyo: Shogakukan, 2013–17; 10 vols.), vol. 7, 70–72, 102; Takeuchi, *Sengo*, 63.

82. Saitō, "Hyōgen," 154. Nagano was the last prefecture to adopt such an ordinance, in 2016.

83. Takeuchi, *Sengo*, 65; Tezuka, *Boku wa mangaka*, 189–91.

84. "Akusho tsuhō undō no nisshi," *Zushokan zasshi* 58, no. 7 (July 1964), 309.

85. Tezuka, *Boku wa mangaka*, 190–91.

86. Thomas Lamarre, *The Anime Ecology: A Genealogy of Television, Animation, and Game Media* (Minneapolis: University of Minnesota Press, 2018), 128–29.

87. Yonezawa Yoshihiro and Shikijō Kyōtarō, *2Bdan gindama sensō no hibi: Shōwa 30-nendai—yume no shōnen ōkoku* (Tokyo: Shinpyōsha, 1982), 80.

88. Quoted in Jayson Makoto Chun, *"A Nation of a Hundred Million Idiots"? A Social History of Japanese Television, 1953–1973* (New York: Routledge, 2007), 51.

89. Chun, *Japanese Television*, 53; Yoshimi Shun'ya, "Television and Nationalism: Historical Change in the National Domestic TV Formation of Postwar Japan," *European Journal of Cultural Studies* 6, no. 4 (2003): 463–65.

90. Yoshimi Shun'ya, "From Street Corner to Living Room: Domestication of TV Culture and National Time/Narrative," trans. Jodie Beck, *Mechademia* 9, no. 1 (2014), 128, 130–32.

91. Yoshimi, 132–33.

92. Chun, *Japanese Television*, 53.

93. Yoshimi, "Television and Nationalism," 466.

94. Yonezawa and Shikijō, *2Bdan*, 85; Yoshimi, "Domestication of TV," 133–34.

95. Chun, *Japanese Television*, 93.

96. Yoshimi, "Television and Nationalism," 476.

97. Yoshimi, "Domestication of TV," 136.

98. Yonezawa and Shikijō, *2Bdan*, 86, 81.

PART THREE CONCLUSION: POSTWAR PLATFORMS

1. Miyamoto Hirohito, "Manga to tankōbon," in *Mangagaku nyūmon*, ed. Natsume Fusanosuke and Takeuchi Osamu (Kyoto: Minerva Shobō, 2009), 69.

2. Marc Steinberg, "Genesis of the Platform Concept: From Japan's Platform Theory to Nintendo, iMode and Niconico Video," lecture at the University of California, Berkeley, March 10, 2016.

3. Marc Steinberg, *The Platform Economy: How Japan Transformed the Consumer Internet* (Minneapolis: University of Minnesota Press, 2019), 82.

4. Yonezawa Yoshihiro and Shikijō Kyōtarō, *2Bdan gindama sensō no hibi: Shōwa 30-nendai—yume no shōnen ōkoku* (Tokyo: Shinpyōsha, 1982), 106–7.

PART FOUR OVERVIEW: SHAMBLING TOWARD THE POSTMODERN

1. Andrew Gordon, *The Wages of Affluence: Labor and Management in Postwar Japan* (Cambridge, MA: Harvard University Press, 1998), 175.

2. Saitō Nobuhiko, "Shūkan shōnen mangashi, fūun gogo-nenshi," *Yuriika* 46, no. 3 (March 2014), 103.

3. Anne Allison, *Permitted and Prohibited Desires: Mothers, Comics, and Censorship in Japan* (Berkeley: University of California Press, 2000), xv.

4. Zenkoku Kashihon Kumiai Rengōkai, *Zenkoku kashihon shinbun: Fukkokuban* (Tokyo: Fuji Shuppan, 2010), vol. 2, 272.

5. Jaqueline Berndt, "Manga, Which Manga? Publication Formats, Genres, Users," in *Japanese Civilization in the 21st Century*, ed. Andrew Targowski, Juri Abe, and Hisanori Kato (New York: Nova Science Publishers, 2016), 124.

6. Marc Steinberg, *Anime's Media Mix: Franchising Toys and Characters in Japan* (Minneapolis: University of Minnesota Press, 2012), 10.

7. Jonathan Clements takes the minority view that Tezuka's anime business failings were an indicator that he was just ahead of his time. Jonathan Clements, "Tezuka's Anime Revolution in Context, *Mechademia* 8 (2013), 223–24.

8. Shimizu Isao, "Giga, fūshiga, fūzokuga," in *Mangagaku nyūmon*, ed. Natsume Fusanosuke and Takeuchi Osamu (Kyoto: Minerva Shobō, 2009), 6.

9. See Setsu Shigematsu, *Scream from the Shadows: The Women's Liberation Movement in Japan* (Minneapolis: University of Minnesota Press, 2012).

10. James Welker, *Transfiguring Women in Late Twentieth-Century Japan: Feminists, Lesbians, and Girls' Comics Artists and Fans* (Honolulu: University of Hawai'i Press, 2024), 4.

11. Nagayama Kaoru, *Erotic Comics in Japan: An Introduction to Eromanga*, trans. Patrick W. Galbraith and Jessica Bauwens-Sugimoto (Amsterdam: Amsterdam University Press, 2021), 60.

12. Yuriko Furuhata, "Searching for Japan's Bell Labs: Experiments in Computer Art," lecture at the University of California, Berkeley, March 10, 2016.

CHAPTER SEVEN: SEEKING ALTERNATIVES

1. Thomas Lamarre, *The Anime Machine: A Media Theory of Animation* (Minneapolis: University of Minnesota Press, 2009); Thomas Lamarre, *The Anime*

Ecology: A Genealogy of Television, Animation, and Game Media (Minneapolis: University of Minnesota Press, 2018); Ian Condry, *The Soul of Anime: Collaborative Creativity and Japan's Media Success Story* (Durham, NC: Duke University Press, 2013); Marc Steinberg, *Anime's Media Mix: Franchising Toys and Characters in Japan* (Minneapolis: University of Minnesota Press, 2012); Stevie Suan, *Anime's Identity: Performativity and Form Beyond Japan* (Minneapolis: University of Minnesota Press, 2021).

2. Jaqueline Berndt, "Anime in Academia: Representative Object, Media Form, and Japanese Studies," *Arts* 7, no. 4, 56 (2018): 6.

3. Jonathan Clements, *Anime: A History*, 2nd. ed (London: Bloomsbury and British Film Institute, 2023), 122–25, 129.

4. Tezuka Osamu, *Boku wa mangaka* (Tokyo: Kadokawa Shoten, 2000), 29–30.

5. Frederik L. Schodt, *Dreamland Japan: Writings on Modern Manga* (Berkeley, CA: Stonebridge Press, 1996), 238.

6. Clements, *Anime*, 158–60.

7. Clements, 160–61.

8. Ōtsuka Eiji, "Undō suru Tezuka Osamu: Kōei no jissen," in *Undō toshite no taishū bunka: Kyōdō, fan, bunka kōsaku*, ed. Ōtsuka Eiji (Tokyo: Suiseisha, 2021), 15. The *Momotarō* films also incorporated Disney influences via *Fantasia* (1940). Clements, *Anime*, 88.

9. Yamaguchi Yasuo, *Nihon no anime zenshi: Sekai o seishita Nihon anime no kiseki* (Tokyo: Ten Books, 2004), 69–75.

10. Jonathan Clements, "Tezuka's Anime Revolution in Context," *Mechademia* 8 (2013), 215–16.

11. Clements, *Anime*, 170–71.

12. Marc Steinberg, *Anime's Media Mix: Franchising Toys and Characters in Japan* (Minneapolis: University of Minnesota Press, 2012), 216–17, fn60.

13. Clements, "Revolution," 219–20.

14. Yamaguchi, *Nihon no anime*, 75.

15. Yamaguchi, 75.

16. Yonezawa Yoshihiro and Shikijō Kyōtarō, *2Bdan gindama sensō no hibi: Shōwa 30-nendai—yume no shōnen ōkoku* (Tokyo: Shinpyosha, 1982), 100.

17. Steinberg, *Media Mix*, 42.

18. Zenkoku Kashihon Kumiai Rengōkai [ZKKR], *Zenkoku kashihon shinbun: Fukkokuban* (Tokyo: Fuji Shuppan, 2010), vol. 2, 158–59, 183.

19. ZKKR, vol. 2, 143.

20. Deguchi Isao, "Akusho tsuihō undō no tenbō: Iwayuru 'akusho tsuihō' no dōki to mondaiten," *Gakkō Toshokan* 158 (December 1963): 12–13.

21. Kajii Jun, "Introduction," in ZKKR, *Zenkoku kashihon*, vol. 1, 9.

22. ZKKR, *Zenkoku kashihon*, vol. 2, 158.

23. ZKKR, vol. 2, 195.

24. ZKKR, vol. 2, 201, 228–29.

25. ZKKR, vol. 2, 243, 199, 253.

26. ZKKR, vol. 2, 180, 96, 104.

27. Yonezawa and Shikijō, *2Bdan*, 81.

28. ZKKR, *Zenkoku kashihon*, vol. 2, 197, 271.

29. ZKKR, vol. 2, 223.

30. Kashihon manga kenkyūkai [KMK], *Kashihon manga returns* (Tokyo: Popurasha, 2006), 28–30, 286.

31. KMK, 290, 310.

32. KMK, 272.

33. Sean Rhoads and Brooke McCorkle Okazaki, *Japan's Green Monsters: Environmental Commentary in Kaiju Cinema* (Jefferson, NC: McFarland, 2018),135–36.

34. ZKKR, *Zenkoku kashihon*, vol. 2, 311–12, 322.

35. Onoda Shō, "*Garo* and *COM:* The United Front Years," in Shirato Sanpei et al., *Garo COM manga meisakusen* (Tokyo: Kodansha, 2012), vol. 1, 284. Onoda Shō is a pen name of Asakawa Mitsuhiro (b. 1965), a former editor for Seirindō and Mandarake.

36. Quoted in Ryan Holmberg and Mitsuhiro Asakawa, "The Life and Art of Kuniko Tsurita," in Kuniko Tsurita, *The Sky Is Blue with a Single Cloud*, trans. Ryan Holmberg (Montréal: Drawn & Quarterly, 2020), viii.

37. Nagai Katsuichi, *Garo henshūchō: Watashi no sengo manga shuppanshi* (Tokyo: Chikuma Shobō, 1987), 16.

38. Ryan Holmberg, *Garo Manga: The First Decade, 1964–1973* (New York: Center for Book Arts, 2010), 6; Nagai, *Garo*, 28, 193.

39. *Garo*, no. 4 (December 1964), n.p.

40. Holmberg, *Garo*, 8, 10.

41. Nagai, *Garo*, 41, 44.

42. Holmberg, *Garo*, 6, 11; for the back issue advertisement, see, for example, *Garo*, no. 138 (February 1975), 210.

43. Nagai, *Garo*, 224.

44. Onoda, "*Garo* and *COM*," vol. 1, 284.

45. Nagai, *Garo*, 49–50, 199, 280–81, 215.

46. Akiyama Mitsuru, *COM no seishun: Shirarezaru Tezuka Osamu* (Tokyo: Heibonsha, 1990), 41.

47. Nagai, *Garo*, 238, 280–81.

48. Nagai, 197, 159; Mura Nunoe, *Gegege no nyōbō: Jinsei wa . . . owari yokereba subete yoshi!!* (Tokyo: Jitsugyō no Nihonsha, 2011), 136–37, 142–45. Kashihon manga paid so little that the tax office personnel couldn't believe two people were living on Mizuki's income. Mura, *Gegege*, 146.

49. Nagai, *Garo*, 209–10; Mura, *Gegege*, 159; Holmberg and Asakawa, "Tsurita," x–xi.

50. Holmberg and Asakawa, xix; Ryan Holmberg, "A Vogue for I Don't Get It: Hayashi Seiichi vs. Sasaki Maki, 1967–69," *The Comics Journal*, December 16, 2015.

51. Ueno Kōshi, "The First Age of *Garo:* Opening Up the *Garo* Age," in *The Wooden-Mortared Kingdom: Garo 20th Memorial Issue*, ed. Seirindō (Tokyo: Seirinsha, 1984), 570.

52. Ryan Holmberg, "Fujiwara Maki: The Art of Life with Tsuge Yoshiharu," in Maki Fujiwara, *My Picture Diary*, trans. Ryan Holmberg (Montréal: Drawn & Quarterly, 2023), 193–94.

53. Ryan Holmberg, "Anti-Manga: Sasaki Maki, Ishiko Junzō, and the Image," in *The Anti-Museum: An Anthology*, ed. Mathieu Copeland and Balthazar Lovay (Fribourg, Switzerland: Fri Art, 2017), 652.

54. Takeuchi Osamu, *Sengo manga 50-nenshi* (Tokyo: Chikuma Shobō, 1995), 153.

55. Kusunoki Shōhei, "Hatsugen," in Shirato Sanpei et al., *Garo COM manga meisakusen 2: 1968–1971* (Tokyo: Kodansha, 2012), 45.

56. Ono Kōsei, "*Garo* no jidai to sono eikyō," in *Garo to iu jidai: Sōkan 50-shūnen*, ed. Seirindō (Tokyo: Seirindō, 2014), 292.

57. Nagai, *Garo*, 194; Mura, *Gegege*, 142–44.

58. Ono, "*Garo*," 290.

59. Holmberg, *Garo*, 13, 15.

60. Holmberg and Asakawa, "Tsurita," xxv; Holmberg, "Anti-Manga," 650–52.

61. Holmberg, "Fujiwara," 195; Nagata Daisuke and Matsunaga Shintarō, "A New Labor Model for a New Era of Anime: A Case Study of Anime Production in the 1970s and 1980s," trans. Kendall Heitzman, *Mechademia* 16, no. 2 (2024): 65–66.

62. Ueno, "First Age," 572.

63. Nagayama Kaoru, *Erotic Comics in Japan: An Introduction to Eromanga*, trans. Patrick W. Galbraith and Jessica Bauwens-Sugimoto (Amsterdam: Amsterdam University Press, 2021), 69.

64. Nagayama, 55.

65. Ueno, "First Age," 571; Ryan Holmberg, "The Life and Art of Yamada Murasaki," in Yamada Murasaki, *Talk to My Back*, trans. Ryan Holmberg (Montréal: Drawn & Quarterly, 2022), xiii.

66. Holmberg and Asakawa, "Tsurita," vii.

67. Mangaseek Project, "Naka Keiko," Mangaseek, https://mangaseek.net/person/17151.html (accessed November 21, 2023).

68. Nagai, *Garo*, 309–10.

69. "Wooden Mortared Kingdom ni yosete," supplement to Seirindō, ed., *Wooden-Mortared Kingdom: Garo 20th Memorial Issue* (Tokyo: Seirindō, 1984), 12, 10.

70. Quoted in Holmberg, "Yamada," xiii, xxii.

71. Nagai, *Garo*, 311; Nagayama, *Introduction to Eromanga*, 55.

72. Nagai, *Garo*, 293–94, 215.

73. Natsume Fusanosuke, *Tezuka Osamu no bōken: Sengo manga no kamigami* (Tokyo: Shogakukan, 1998), 238, 249.

74. *COM*, no. 1 (January 1967), 202.

75. Shimotsuki Takanaka, ed., *COM 40-nenme no shūkangō* (Tokyo: Asahi Shinbun Shuppan, 2011), 122–24.

76. Shimotsuki, 122–24.

77. Holmberg and Asakawa, "Tsurita," vii.

78. Natsume, *Tezuka Osamu no bōken*, 239.

79. Ueno, "First Age," 573.

80. Akiyama, *COM no seishun*, 36–39.

81. Nakashima Takashi, "*Com* to *Apple Core:* Gura-Com Kansai shibu tenmatsuki," *Biranji* 27 (March 2011), 123.

82. Ishinomori Shōtarō, *Kizuna: Fushō no musuko kara fushō no musukotachi e* (Tokyo: NTT Shuppan, 1998), 147–48.

83. Shimotsuki, *COM 40-nenme*, 124, 129, 133.

84. Akiyama, *COM no seishun*, 38–39; Nagai, *Garo*, 238.

85. Akiyama, *COM no seishun*, 174–80, 144–45, 224.

86. Shimotsuki, *COM 40-nenme*, 128.

87. Shimotsuki, 138.

88. Yonezawa Yoshihiro, "*Manga Shōnen* kara Comiket e . . . ," in *Shōnen natsu man'ō* (zine) 16 (1995), 48–49.

89. Shimotsuki, *COM 40-nenme*, 139.

90. Nakashima, "*Com* to *Apple Core*," 122.

91. Shimotsuki, *COM 40-nenme*, 134–35.

92. Quoted in Holmberg, "Yamada," xv.

93. Quoted in Holmberg, "Yamada," xiii, xxxix, vii, xii–xiii.

94. Shimotsuki, *COM 40-nenme*, 132.

95. Akiyama, *COM no seishun*, 58–59.

96. Holmberg, "Yamada," xv–xvi, xl.

97. Yonezawa, "*Manga Shōnen*," 49.

98. Mori Seiichirō and AS, eds., *Manga dōjin no hanseiki: AS 50-nenten 1966–2016* (Kitakyushu, Japan: Kitakyushu Manga Museum, 2016), 9; Holmberg, "Yamada," xx.

99. *COM*, no. 2 (May 1967), 204.

100. *COM*, no. 3 (June 1967), 200, 204.

101. Holmberg, "Yamada," xxi.

102. *COM*, no. 3 (June 1967), 200–201.

103. Mori and AS, *Manga dōjin*, 2–4.

104. Mori and AS, 3–7.

105. Mori and AS, 6–7.

106. Comic Market Junbikai, *Comic Market 30's File: 1975–2005* (Tokyo: Comic Market Jūnbikai, 2005), 26.

107. Mori and AS, *Manga dōjin*, 10.

108. Nakashima, "*Com* to *Apple Core*," 127–29, 132.

109. Nakashima, 135, 133.

110. Comic Market Junbikai, *Comic Market 30's File*, 4, 7, 12–13.

111. Shimizu Isao, "Nicchū sensō-ki no manga zasshi *Manga no Kuni*," https://www.kyotomm.jp/HP/about_syozo.html (accessed December 4, 2023).

112. *COM*, no. 3 (June 1967): 203.

113. Shimotsuki, *COM 40-nenme*, 128.

114. Natsume, *Tezuka Osamu no bōken*, 202, 295.

115. *COM*, no. 12 (March 1968): 205.

116. Edward Fowler, *The Rhetoric of Confession:* Shishōsetsu *in Early Twentieth-Century Japanese Fiction* (Berkeley: University of California Press, 1988), 131.

117. *COM*, no. 2 (May 1967): 190.

118. Nihon Mangaka Kyōkai, ed., *Nihon Mangaka Kyōkai sōritsu 50-shūnen kinenshi* (Tokyo: Nihon Mangaka Kyōkai, 2015), iv–v.

119. *COM*, no. 2 (May 1967): 204.

120. ZKKR, *Zenkoku kashihon*, vol. 2, 137, 139. While researching this book, I heard a Crunchyroll VP express the exact same sentiments in March 2016.

121. Ishinomori, *Kizuna*, 65.

122. Mura, *Gegege*, 166–67.

123. Yamaguchi, *Nihon no anime*, 82–83, 117. For *Atomu* and metal toys, see Steinberg, *Media Mix*, chapter 3.

124. *COM*, no. 4 (July 1967), 70.

125. Fujiki Hideaki, "Implicating Readers: Tezuka's Early Seinen Manga," *Mechademia* 8 (2013), 208.

126. *COM*, no. 4 (July 1967), 70–73.

127. Okada Toshio, *Otakugaku nyūmon* (Tokyo: Shinchōsha, 2008), 285.

128. Takemiya Keiko, *Shōnen no na wa Gilbert* (Tokyo: Shogakukan, 2016), 27.

129. Fujiko Fujio A, *Ai . . . shiri someshi koro ni . . . vol. 1* (Tokyo: Shogakukan, 1997), 64.

130. Chin Teruko, "Ashisutanto," in *Mangagaku*, ed. Natsume Fusanosuke and Takeuchi Osamu (Kyoto: Minerva Shobō, 2009), 143.

131. Mura, *Gegege*, 79–80.

132. Chin, "Ashisutanto," 146.

133. Mura, *Gegege*, 140–45.

134. Murakami Motoka and Takemiya Keiko, "Murakami Motoka × Takemiya Keiko Talkshow," lecture at Kawasaki City Museum, Kawasaki, Japan, December 4, 2016.

CHAPTER EIGHT: THE EMERGENCE OF SEINEN MANGA AND THE SHŌJO REVOLUTION

1. Akiyama Mitsuru, *COM no seishun: Shirarezaru Tezuka Osamu* (Tokyo: Heibonsha, 1990), 134–36.

2. Shirato et al., *Garo COM manga meisakusen* (Tokyo: Kodansha, 2012), vol. 2, 2, 6.

3. Natsume Fusanosuke, *Tezuka Osamu no bōken: Sengo manga no kamigami* (Tokyo: Shogakukan, 1998), 245.

4. Nagai Katsuichi, *Garo henshūchō: Watashi no sengo manga shuppanshi* (Tokyo: Chikuma Shobō, 1987), 242–43.

5. Natsume, *Tezuka Osamu no bōken*, 247.

6. Fujiki Hideaki, "Implicating Readers: Tezuka's Early Seinen Manga," *Mechademia* 8 (2013), 202. From this point on, Tezuka adopted many gekiga elements in his later works.

7. Ryan Holmberg and Mitsuhiro Asakawa, "The Life and Art of Kuniko Tsurita," in Kuniko Tsurita, *The Sky Is Blue with a Single Cloud*, trans. Ryan Holmberg (Montréal: Drawn & Quarterly, 2020), xxv. Vin Packer was the lesbian writer Marijane Meaker (1927–2022); her pseudonym was misspelled "Paker."

8. *Big Comic*, no. 1 (April 1968): 312.

9. *Big Comic*, no. 3 (June 1968): 121, 181.

10. *Big Comic*, no. 2 (May 1968): 224.

11. Ronald Stewart, "Groundbreaking Women: Recovering the History of Forgotten Prewar Female Mangaka," paper presented at the Virtual Association for Asian Studies Conference, March 1, 2024.

12. Okada Toshio, *Otakugaku nyūmon* (Tokyo: Shinchōsha, 2008), 288.

13. Saitō Nobuhiko, "Shūkan shōnen mangashi, fūun gogo-nenshi," *Yuriika* 46, no. 3 (March 2014), 103.

14. Okada, *Otakugaku*, 288.

15. Saitō, "Shūkan shōnen mangashi," 102.

16. Natsume, *Tezuka Osamu no bōken*, 147.

17. Ozaki Hotsuki, ed., "Kore ga gekiga da!," *COM*, no. 2 (June 1967): 84–89.

18. Murakami Motoka and Takemiya Keiko, "Murakami Motoka × Takemiya Keiko Talkshow," lecture at Kawasaki City Museum, Kawasaki, Japan, December 4, 2016.

19. Okada, *Otakugaku*, 286; Natsume, *Tezuka Osamu no bōken*, 294.

20. Fujiki, "Implicating Readers," 199.

21. Nagayama Kaoru, *Erotic Comics in Japan: An Introduction to Eromanga*, trans. Patrick W. Galbraith and Jessica Bauwens-Sugimoto (Amsterdam: Amsterdam University Press, 2021), 58–59.

22. Patrick W. Galbraith, "Women Producing and Consuming Erotic Comics in Japan," paper presented at the Virtual Association for Asian Studies Conference, March 1, 2024.

23. Fujiki, "Implicating Readers," 199.

24. Nihon Mangaka Kyōkai, ed., *Nihon Mangaka Kyōkai sōritsu 50-shūnen kinenshi* (Tokyo: Nihon Mangaka Kyōkai, 2015), v; Shimizu Isao, "Giga, fūshiga, fūzokuga," in *Mangagaku nyūmon*, ed. Natsume Fusanosuke and Takeuchi Osamu (Kyoto: Minerva Shobō, 2009), 6.

25. Shimizu Isao, "Manga to shinbun," in Natsume and Takeuchi, *Mangagaku*, 65.

26. Ishiko Jun, *Nihon mangashi* (Tokyo: Shakai Shisōsha, 1988), 369; Tamura Hisako and Kurata Shin, "Watashi to manga: Tamura Hisako ga kotaru," *Bunka hyōron*, no. 208 (August 1978): 116–28.

27. Ishiko, *Nihon mangashi*, 368.

28. Nagayama, *Introduction to Eromanga*, 54.

29. Murakami Tomohiko, "Seinen manga toshite no shōjo manga," *Shisō no rigaku* 6 (1978), 55.

30. Murakami, 54.

31. Suzuki Maki, "'Manga-teki image no kakusan': 'Manga' to 'kōkoku' no kaikō o megutte," in *Dōin no media mix: "Sōsaku suru taishū" no senjika, sengo*, ed. Ōtsuka Eiji (Kyoto: Shibunkaku Shuppan, 2017), 115–16.

32. Deborah Shamoon, *Passionate Friendship: The Aesthetics of Girls' Culture in Japan* (Honolulu: University of Hawai'i Press, 2012), 85–89; James Welker, "A Brief History of *Shōnen'ai, Yaoi*, and Boys Love," in *Boys Love Manga and Beyond: History, Culture, and Community in Japan*, ed. Mark J. McLelland, Kazumi Nagaike, Katsuhiko Suganuma, and James Welker (Jackson: University Press of Mississippi, 2015), 43.

33. Tezuka Osamu, *Boku wa mangaka* (Tokyo: Kadokawa Shoten, 2000), 16.

34. Natsume, *Tezuka Osamu no bōken*, 114.

35. Leonie R. Stickland, *Gender Gymnastics: Performing and Consuming Japan's Takarazuka Revue* (Melbourne, Australia: Trans Pacific Press, 2007), 21–30.

36. Natsume, *Tezuka Osamu no bōken*, 115–16.

37. Nakano Haruyuki, *Tezuka Osamu no Takarazuka* (Tokyo: Chikuma Shobō, 1994), 189.

38. Hikari Hori, "Tezuka, Shōjo Manga, and Hagio Moto," *Mechademia* 8 (2013), 302.

39. Jennifer S. Prough, *Straight from the Heart: Gender, Intimacy, and the Cultural Production of Shōjo Manga* (Honolulu: University of Hawai'i Press, 2011), 36, 4.

40. *Nakayoshi*, September 1955, October 1955, and January 1965.

41. Prough, *Heart*, 64. Prough translates *furoku* as *supplements*.

42. Takemiya Keiko, *Shōnen no na wa Gilbert* (Tokyo: Shogakukan, 2016), 194–95.

43. Prough, *Heart*, 71.

44. Takemiya, *Gilbert*, 192–93.

45. Prough, *Heart*, 64–71.

46. Freebies and mail-order goods in *Juné* and *Be Love* in the late 1970s and early 1980s, for example, often featured Mickey Mouse and David Bowie.

47. Rachel Thorn, "Introduction" to Hagio Moto, *The Heart of Thomas*, trans. Rachel Thorn (Seattle: Fantagraphics, 2012).

48. Takemiya Keiko, *Shōjo manga no sekai: Genga dash 10-nen no kiseki* (Kyoto: Kyoto Seika Daigaku Kokusai Manga Kenkyū Center, 2011), 15, 72.

49. "Shōjo manga no genjitsu," ed. Ozaki Hotsuki, *COM*, no. 5 (August 1967): 70.

50. *COM*, no. 5 (August 1967): 70–71, 73, 74.

51. Takemiya, *Gilbert*, 83–87.

52. Quoted in Ryan Holmberg, "The Life and Art of Yamada Murasaki," in Yamada Murasaki, *Talk to My Back*, trans. Ryan Holmberg (Montréal: Drawn & Quarterly, 2022), xix.

53. Takemiya, *Gilbert*, 86–87, 95.

54. Fujimoto Yukari, *Watashi no ibasho wa doko ni aru no? Shōjo manga ga utsusu kokoro no katachi* (Tokyo: Gakuyō Shobō, 1998), 28–30.

55. This is Masuyama Norie's insight, reported in Takemiya, *Gilbert*, 94–95.

56. When he first saw Mizuno's manga, Tezuka thought she had to be a boy because the art was so good. Tezuka, *Boku wa mangaka*, 142.

57. Takemiya, *Gilbert*, 119–20; James Welker, *Transfiguring Women in Late Twentieth-Century Japan: Feminists, Lesbians, and Girls' Comics Artists and Fans* (Honolulu: University of Hawai'i Press, 2024), 166–67.

58. Chin Teruko, "Hana no 24-nen gumi," in Natsume and Takeuchi, eds., *Mangagaku*, 41.

59. Yonezawa Yoshihiro, ed., *Speech balloon ballad: Manga o meguru shōjotachi no bōken* (Tokyo: Kawade Shobō Shinsha, 1988), 123–24, 134, 142, 150–51.

60. Yonezawa Yoshihiro, "*Manga Shōnen* kara Comiket e . . . ," in *Shōnen natsu man'ō* (zine) 16 (1995), 46–47.

61. Yonezawa, *Speech balloon*, 127, 134–35, 47.

62. Hagio Moto, *Ichidokiri no Ōizumi no hanashi* (Tokyo: Kawade Shobō Shinsha, 2021), 21.

63. Takemiya, *Gilbert*, 16.

64. Holmberg, "Yamada," xii, xxxix.

65. Takemiya, *Gilbert*, 16.

66. Masuyama Norie, "Haikei, waga 'senyū' Takemiya Keiko-sama," in Takemiya Keiko, *Kaze to ki no uta* (Tokyo: Hakusensha, 1995), vol. 10, 313. Hagio used the same word to describe her meeting with Takemiya. Hagio, *Ōizumi*, 48.

67. Snarp, "Translation of a 2007 Interview with Keiko Takemiya," https://snarp.dreamwidth.org/279314.html (accessed April 9, 2017).

68. Takemiya, *Gilbert*, 172–84, 37. In her memoir, Hagio eschews any ambitions to change shōjo manga as a category.

69. Masuyama, "Haikei," 313–14.

70. Takemiya, *Gilbert*, 45–50; Hagio, *Ōizumi*, 39.

71. Takemiya, *Gilbert*, 54–55, 68–72; Hagio, *Ōizumi*, 122–28. For her part, Hagio paid assistants 2,000 to 3,000 yen per session.

72. Takemiya, *Gilbert*, 70–72; Hagio, *Ōizumi*, 305. Hagio liked SF before the Salon, but not the same subgenres as Masuyama and Satō.

73. Takemiya, *Gilbert*, 82, 100–101.

74. Takemiya, 73–74.

75. Takemiya, 75–78. Hagio's pay rate was 3,000 yen, which Yamamoto doubled to 6,000 yen after Kodansha asked her to return in 1974. Hagio then increased her assistants' pay rate. Hagio, *Ōizumi*, 235–36.

76. Nobuko Anan, "*The Rose of Versailles:* Women and Revolution in Girls' Manga and the Socialist Movement in Japan," *Journal of Popular Culture* 47, no. 1 (2014): 52.

77. Asahi Publishing, ed., *Shūkan Shōwa no. 22 (Shōwa 49-nen): Berubara boom, Mona Lisa-ten, Onoda Hiroo-shōi kikoku* (Tokyo: Asahi Publishing, 2009),

9; Nakagawa Yūsuke, "*Pō no ichizoku, Berusaiyu no bara:* Atarashii shōjo manga ga dōji tahatsu," October 22, 2019, https://web.archive.org/web/20191211103730/https://www.gentosha.jp/article/14064/.

78. Deborah Shamoon, "Revolutionary Romance: *The Rose of Versailles* and the Transformation of Shōjo Manga," *Mechademia* 2 (2007), 3.

79. Shamoon, *Passionate Friendship*, 120.

80. Setsu Shigematsu, *Scream from the Shadows: The Women's Liberation Movement in Japan* (Minneapolis: University of Minnesota Press, 2012), xvii; Welker, *Transfiguring*, 3–4; Oshiyama Michiko, *Shōjo manga gender hyōshōron: "Dansō no shōjo" no zōkei to identity* (Tokyo: Sairyūsha, 2007), 209.

81. Quoted in Anan, "*Rose of Versailles*," 51.

82. Fujimoto Yukari, "*Beruysaiyu no bara* to sono jidai," in Asahi Publishing, *Shūkan Shōwa no. 22*, 5.

83. Hagio, *Ōizumi*, 216.

84. Shamoon, "Revolutionary Romance," 11–12.

85. Oshiyama, *Shōjo manga gender*, 211–14.

86. Akiko Mizoguchi, "Akogare no Yoroppa," May 9, 2003, https://web.archive.org/web/20030509131032/http://natmi.coco.co.jp/AM/berubara.htm.

87. Asahi Publishing, *Shūkan Shōwa no. 22*, 9.

88. Takemiya, *Gilbert*, 40; Hagio, *Ōizumi*, 97.

89. Welker, "Brief History," 47.

90. Takemiya, *Gilbert*, 8–11.

91. Nagatani Kunio, *Nippon manga zasshi meikan* (Tokyo: Datahouse, 1995), 176.

92. Takemiya, *Gilbert*, 93.

93. Nagatani, *Nippon manga zasshi meikan*, 175.

94. Takemiya, *Gilbert*, 96–98.

95. Takemiya, 96–99.

96. Fujimoto Yukari, "Where Is My Place in the World? Early Shōjo Manga Portrayals of Lesbianism," trans. Lucy Fraser, *Mechademia* 9 (2014), 26–27; Yamagishi Ryōko, *Yamagishi Ryōko gashū terasu* (Tokyo: Kawade Shobō Shinsha, 2016), 151; Hagio, *Ōizumi*, 103.

97. James Welker, "Drawing Out Lesbians: Blurred Representations of Lesbian Desire in Shōjo Manga," in *Lesbian Voices: Canada and the World: Theory, Literature, Cinema*, ed. Subhash Chandra (New Delhi: Allied Publishers, 2006), 165.

98. Verena Maser, "Beautiful and Innocent: Female Same-Sex Intimacy in the Japanese Yuri Genre" (PhD diss., University of Trier, 2013), 51–61. *Playboy Comics Crazy* published lesploitation manga in 1968, but no one wants to put them into the lineage of yuri or GL manga. Holmberg and Asakawa, "Tsurita," xxv.

99. Hagio, *Ōizumi*, 66, 91.

100. Hagio Moto and Yoshimoto Taka'aki, "Jikohyōgen toshite no shōjo manga," *Yuriika* 13, no. 9 (1981), 90.

101. Hagio, *Ōizumi*, 93.

102. Suzuki, Shige (CJ), "Envisioning Alternative Communities Through a Popular Medium: Speculative Imagination in Hagio Moto's Girls' Comics," *International Journal of Comic Art* 13, no. 2 (Fall 2011): 59–60.

103. Nagatani, *Nippon manga zasshi meikan*, 175.

104. Edgar and Allan are fourteen because, thanks to the Vienna Boys' Choir, Hagio thought that fourteen was "the age of angels." Hagio, *Ōizumi*, 97. In 2018, with Hagio's permission, Ikeda connected *The Rose of Versailles* to *The Poe Clan* in the last chapter of the former's "new episodes," published in honor of *Margaret*'s fiftieth anniversary.

105. Takemiya, *Gilbert*, 139.

106. Prough, *Heart*, 49.

107. Hagio, *Ōizumi*, 216–31; Murakami Tomohiko, "Shōnengari," in Hagio Moto, *Hagio Moto sakuhinshū 9: Pō no ichizoku 4* (Tokyo: Shogakukan, 1978), 212–13.

108. Thorn, "Introduction," n.p.

109. Thorn, n.p.

110. Hagio, *Ōizumi*, 283; Welker, *Transfiguring*, 45, fn150.

111. Marc Steinberg, *Anime's Media Mix: Franchising Toys and Characters in Japan* (Minneapolis: University of Minnesota Press, 2012), 161. This insight draws on Gilles Deleuze.

112. Fujimoto, "*Beruysaiyu*," 4–5.

113. Asahi Publishing, *Shūkan Shōwa no. 22*, 9.

114. Stickland, *Gender Gymnastics*, 46.

115. Fujimoto, "*Berusaiyu*," 7. The sum is about 61.5 million yen in 2024 money; it was worth about $103,000 in U.S. dollars at the time, roughly $600,000 in 2024 dollars.

116. Kodansha, ed., *Nichiroku 20-seiki: 1970–1979, vol. 5: 1974—Berubara boom!* (Tokyo: Kodansha, 1997), 3.

117. Makiko Yamanashi, *A History of the Takarazuka Revue since 1914: Modernity, Girls' Culture, Japan Pop* (Leiden, The Netherlands: Global Oriental, 2012), 179.

118. Kodansha, *1974—Berubara boom!*, 3–4.

119. Stickland, *Gender Gymnastics*, 46.

120. Yamanashi, *Takarazuka Revue*, 88–89.

121. Steinberg, *Media Mix*, 152.

122. Stickland, *Gender Gymnastics*, 46.

123. Kodansha, *1974—Berubara boom!*, 3.

124. Yamanashi, *Takarazuka Revue*, 180.

125. Stickland, *Gender Gymnastics*, 162.

126. Stickland, 47.

127. Steinberg, *Media Mix*, 153.

128. Kodansha, *1974—Berubara boom!*, 4.

129. Murakami and Takemiya, "Talkshow."

PART FOUR CONCLUSION: TANKŌBON: THE MEANING OF A FORMAT

1. Miyamoto Hirohito, "Manga to tankōbon," in *Mangagaku nyūmon*, ed. Natsume Fusanosuke and Takeuchi Osamu (Kyoto: Minerva Shobō, 2009), 69.

2. Murakami Motoka and Takemiya Keiko, "Murakami Motoka × Takemiya Keiko Talkshow," lecture at Kawasaki City Museum, Kawasaki, Japan, December 4, 2016.

3. Yonezawa Yoshihiro, "Fukō to iu na no shiawase: *Shōnen King* no eikō to shūen," *Shōnen Natsu Man'ō* (zine) 18 (1995), 121.

4. Dalma Kálovics, "Manga Across Media: Style Adapting to Form in the 1950s and 1960s and in the Digital Age," *Mechademia* 12, no. 2 (2020), 109. Since 2005, tankōbon have comprised two-thirds of all print manga sales; this imbalance means that readers are less likely to be exposed to new manga via the magazines. Jaqueline Berndt, "Manga, Which Manga? Publication Formats, Genres, Users," in *Japanese Civilization in the 21st Century*, ed. Andrew Targowski, Juri Abe, and Hisanori Kato (New York: Nova Science Publishers, 2016), 126.

5. Jonathan Sterne, *MP3: The Meaning of a Format* (Durham, NC: Duke University Press, 2012), 11.

PART FIVE OVERVIEW: APPLAUDING THE DJ

1. Tessa Morris-Suzuki, *The Technological Transformation of Japan: From the Seventeenth to the Twenty-First Century* (Cambridge: Cambridge University Press, 1994), 210–11.

2. Manga Shūdan, ed., *Manga Shōwashi: Manga Shūdan no 50-nen* (Tokyo: Kawade Shobo Shinsha, 1982), 238–39.

3. Comic Market Junbikai, *Comic Market 30's File: 1975–2005* (Tokyo: Comiket, 2005), 26.

4. Patrick W. Galbraith, *Otaku and the Struggle for Imagination in Japan* (Durham, NC: Duke University Press, 2019), 31.

5. Nagayama Kaoru, *Erotic Comics in Japan: An Introduction to Eromanga*, trans. Patrick W. Galbraith and Jessica Bauwens-Sugimoto (Amsterdam: Amsterdam University Press, 2021), 106.

6. Galbraith, *Otaku*, 51.

7. Bessatsu Takarajima Henshūbu, ed., *Otaku no hon* (Tokyo: JICC Shuppankyoku, 1989), 3.

8. Okada Toshio, *Otakugaku nyūmon* (Tokyo: Shinchōsha, 2008), 298.

9. Jaqueline Berndt, "Manga in Transition: Subtly Receding from 'Popular Culture,'" in *Hokusai × Manga: Japanese Pop Culture since 1680*, ed. Sabine Schulze, Nora von Achenbach, and Simon Klingler (Munich: Hirmer, 2016), 235–36.

10. Jaqueline Berndt, "Manga, Which Manga? Publication Formats, Genres, Users," in *Japanese Civilization in the 21st Century*, ed. Andrew Targowski, Juri Abe, and Hisanori Kato (New York: Nova Science Publishers, 2016), 131.

11. Takeuchi Osamu, *Sengo manga 50-nenshi* (Tokyo: Chikuma Shobō, 1995), 154.

12. Azuma Hiroki, *Otaku: Japan's Database Animals*, trans. Jonathan E. Abel and Shion Kono (Minneapolis: University of Minnesota Press, 2009), 19 (emphasis in original).

13. The value of 10,000 yen in 1985 would be about 13,000 yen in 2024 money; at the time, it was worth about $73, or $213 in 2024 dollars. T-shirts at Uniqlo now retail for 1,500 yen or less.

CHAPTER NINE: SOMETHING POSTMODERN GOING ON

1. Comic Market Junbikai [CMJ], *Comic Market 30's File: 1975–2005* (Tokyo: Comiket, 2005), 26.

2. CMJ, *Comiket 20's: Comic Market 20-shūnen kinen shiryōshū* (Tokyo: Comic Market Junbikai, 1996), 24–26.

3. CMJ, *Comic Market 30's File*, 27.

4. Mori Seiichirō and AS, eds., *Manga dōjin no hanseiki: AS 50-nenten 1966–2016* (Kitakyushu, Japan: Kitakyushu Manga Museum, 2016), 11; Barbora and Arawi Keiichi, *Comitia-damashii: 40 years of manga and dōjinshi*, ed. Comitia Jikkō Iinkai (Tokyo: Film Art-sha, 2024), 28–29.

5. Patrick W. Galbraith, *Otaku and the Struggle for Imagination in Japan* (Durham, NC: Duke University Press, 2019), 26–28.

6. See Francesca Coppa, *Vidding: A History* (Ann Arbor: University of Michigan Press, 2022).

7. CMJ, *Comic Market 30's File*, 28.

8. Galbraith, *Otaku*, 27.

9. CMJ, *Comiket 20's*, 26.

10. CMJ, *Comic Market 30's File*, 29, 66.

11. CMJ, *Comic Market 30's File*, 29.

12. CMJ, *Comic Market-7 Report* (zine) (Tokyo: Comic Market Junbikai, 1978), 11–13.

13. CMJ, *Comiket Appeal 3* (zine) (Tokyo: Comic Market Junbikai, 1980): n.p.

14. This was the exact schedule of the dōjin event I attended at the same venue thirty-nine years later in December 2016.

15. CMJ, *Market-7 Report*, 11–13.

16. CMJ, *Comiket Appeal 3*, n.p.

17. CMJ, *Comiket Appeal 3*, n.p.

18. Barbora and Arawi, *Comitia-damashii*, 28–29

19. CMJ, *Comic Market Manual 1* (Tokyo: Comic Market Junbikai, 1982), 14–15. Official Comiket terminology now categorizes all three groups as

participants: "circle participants," "general participants," and "staff participants," respectively. These terms do not seem to have been standardized in this era.

20. Barbora and Arawi, *Comitia-damashii*, 29; Fan-Yi Lam, "Comic Market: How the World's Biggest Amateur Comic Fair Shaped Japanese Dōjinshi Culture," *Mechademia* 5 (2009), 236–37. From 1989 to 2015, a third Comiket was held once every five years or so, during the spring school holidays.

21. Barbora and Arawi, *Comitia-damashii*, 49.

22. CMJ, *Comic Market 30's File*, 66.

23. Quoted in Nagayama Kaoru, *Erotic Comics in Japan: An Introduction to Eromanga*, trans. Patrick W. Galbraith and Jessica Bauwens-Sugimoto (Amsterdam: Amsterdam University Press, 2021), 68 (emphasis in original).

24. Mori and AS, *Manga dōjin*, 11–12.

25. Takemiya Keiko, *Shōnen no na wa Gilbert* (Tokyo: Shogakukan, 2016), 37–38, 172–73, 183–84.

26. Takemiya Keiko, *Kaze to ki no uta* (Tokyo: Hakusensha, 1995; 10 vols.).

27. Takemiya, *Gilbert*, 220–21.

28. Ōgi Fusami, "Nihonshiki shōjo manga kara josei manga e," in *Josei manga kenkyū: Ōbei, Nihon, Ajia o tsunagu manga*, ed. Ōgi Fusami (Tokyo: Seikyusha, 2015), 31.

29. Takemiya, *Gilbert*, 224, 183–84.

30. Yamada Murasaki, "A Fondness for Corners: An Interview with Yamada Murasaki (1985)," in *Second Hand Love*, trans. Ryan Holmberg (Montréal: Drawn & Quarterly, 2024), viii.

31. Takemiya, *Kaze*, vol. 1, 8–11.

32. Patrick W. Galbraith, "Women Producing and Consuming Erotic Comics in Japan," paper presented at the Virtual Association for Asian Studies Conference, March 1, 2024.

33. Nagayama, *Introduction to Eromanga*, 72.

34. Frederik L. Schodt, *Dreamland Japan: Writings on Modern Manga* (Berkeley, CA: Stonebridge Press, 1996), 120.

35. James Welker, *Transfiguring Women in Late Twentieth-Century Japan: Feminists, Lesbians, and Girls' Comics Artists and Fans* (Honolulu: University of Hawai'i Press, 2024), 49.

36. *Comic Jun*, no. 1 (October 1978).

37. James Welker, "A Brief History of *Shōnen'ai, Yaoi*, and Boys Love," in *Boys Love Manga and Beyond: History, Culture, and Community in Japan*, ed. Mark J. McLelland, Kazumi Nagaike, Katsuhiko Suganuma, and James Welker (Jackson: University Press of Mississippi, 2015), 52, 88. *Tanbi* is *danmei* in Mandarin.

38. Itō Gō, *Manga wa kawaru: "Mangagatari" kara "mangaron" e* (Tokyo: Seidosha, 2007), 215–16.

39. Welker, *Transfiguring Women*, 51. *Sōsaku JUNE* (original June) was the Comiket term for original BL dōjinshi from 1987, changed to *Sōsaku (JUNE/BL)* only in 2012. Welker, *Transfiguring Women*, 87.

40. Sagawa Toshihiko, *June no jidai: BL no yoake mae* (Tokyo: Aki Shobō, 2024).

41. Sasaya Nanae et al., "Motto kimi no koto ga shiritai," *Comic Jun*, no. 2 (December 1978): 54; Takemiya, *Gilbert*, 40–41.

42. Sasaya et al., "Motto," 54.

43. Takemiya, *Gilbert*, 102.

44. Welker, *Transfiguring Women*, 140.

45. Deborah Shamoon, *Passionate Friendship: The Aesthetics of Girls' Culture in Japan* (Honolulu: University of Hawai'i Press, 2012), 104.

46. Thomas Baudinette, *Boys Love Media in Thailand: Celebrity, Fans, and Transnational Asian Queer Popular Culture* (London: Bloomsbury Academic, 2024), 34.

47. April S. Callis, "Homophobia, Heteronormativity, and Slash Fan Fiction," *Transformative Works and Cultures* 22 (September 2016).

48. Abigail De Kosnik, *Rogue Archives: Digital Cultural Memory and Media Fandom* (Cambridge, MA: MIT Press, 2016), 142.

49. Natsume Fusanosuke, "Parody," in *Mangagaku nyūmon*, ed. Natsume Fusanosuke and Takeuchi Osamu (Kyoto: Minerva Shobō, 2009), 213–14.

50. De Kosnik, *Rogue Archives*, 35; Nagayama, *Introduction to Eromanga*, 79.

51. Welker, "Brief History," 57.

52. De Kosnik, *Rogue Archives*, 147.

53. Akiko Mizoguchi, "Reading and Living *Yaoi:* Male-Male Fantasy Narratives as Women's Sexual Subculture in Japan" (PhD diss., University of Rochester, 2008), 9, 12–13, 16, 26. Ōe and her partner Ogawa Yoko were one of thirteen queer couples who sued the Japanese government for equal marriage rights on Valentine's Day 2019.

54. Thomas Baudinette, "Japanese Queer Popular Culture and the Production of Sexual Knowledge in the Philippines," in *Queer Southeast Asia* (London: Routledge, Taylor & Francis Group, 2023), 48–49; Thomas Baudinette, *Regimes of Desire: Young Gay Men, Media, and Masculinity in Tokyo* (Ann Arbor: University of Michigan Press, 2021), 108–13. Baudinette's young gay male informants in Tokyo, who expressed a range of opinions on BL manga, read it because it contains stories about gay men.

55. James Welker, "Lilies of the Margin: Beautiful Boys and Queer Female Identities in Japan," in *AsiaPacifiQueer: Rethinking Genders and Sexualities*, ed. Fran Martin, Peter A. Jackson, Mark McLelland, and Audrey Yue (Urbana: University of Illinois Press, 2008), 47, 49, 50–51.

56. Baudinette, "Sexual Knowledge," 52–56.

57. De Kosnik, *Rogue Archives*, 151.

58. Mizoguchi, "Reading and Living *Yaoi*," 43.

59. De Kosnik, *Rogue Archives*, 151.

60. David M. Halperin, *Saint Foucault: Towards a Gay Hagiography* (New York: Oxford University Press, 1995), 62 (emphasis original). Contemporary BL and media fans comprise all genders; "fudanshi" (rotten men) are becoming more visible in Japanese fan cultures.

61. Mizoguchi, "Reading and Living *Yaoi*," 289.

62. Henry Jenkins and Cynthia Jenkins, interview by Abigail De Kosnik, University of Iowa, August 14, 2012.

63. De Kosnik, *Rogue Archives*, 140.

64. Patrick W. Galbraith, "*Moe* Talk: Communication Among Female Fans of *Yaoi*," in McLelland et al., *Boys Love Manga and Beyond*, 157.

65. Galbraith, 155, 160–63.

66. James Welker, "From Vicarious Voyages to Jumbo Jets: Shōjo Manga Artists and Fans Head Abroad in the 1970s and 1980s," presentation at the National Conference of Popular Culture Association, Seattle, March 25, 2016.

67. Azuma Hiroki, *Otaku: Japan's Database Animals*, trans. Jonathan E. Abel and Shion Kono (Minneapolis: University of Minnesota Press, 2009), 27–28; obsession_inc, "Affirmational Fandom vs. Transformational Fandom," https://obsession-inc.dreamwidth.org/82589.html (accessed February 16, 2017).

68. Takemiya, *Gilbert*, 164–65.

69. Nagayama, *Introduction to Eromanga*, 72.

70. Asahi Publishing, ed., *Shūkan Shōwa no. 22 (Shōwa 49-nen): Berubara boom, Mona Lisa-ten, Onoda Hiroo-shōi kikoku* (Tokyo: Asahi Publishing, 2009), 9.

71. Hagio Moto and Yoshimoto Taka'aki, "Jikohyōgen toshite no shōjo manga," *Yuriika* 13, no. 9 (1981), 114.

72. Ōtsuka Eiji, *"Ribon" no furoku to otomechikku no jidai: Tasogaredoki ni mitsuketa mono* (Tokyo: Chikuma Shobo, 1995), 10–18, 22–23.

73. Nagayama, *Introduction to Eromanga*, 76.

74. Nishihara Mari, "Seijin manga," in Natsume and Takeuchi, *Mangagaku*, 46.

75. Takemiya Keiko, *Shōjo manga no sekai: Genga dash 10-nen no kiseki* (Kyoto: Kyoto Seika Daigaku Kokusai Manga Kenkyū Center, 2011), 77, 11.

76. *Be in Love* 1, no. 1 (November 1980): 238.

77. *Be Love* 3, no. 19 (December 1982): back cover.

78. *Be Love* 3, no. 19 (December 1982): 240; *Be Love* 3, no. 20 (December 1982): 240.

79. Nishihara, "Seijin manga," 46–47; Ryan Holmberg, "The Life and Art of Yamada Murasaki," in Yamada Murasaki, *Talk to My Back*, trans. Ryan Holmberg (Montréal: Drawn & Quarterly, 2022), viii.

80. Hayashi Sadae, "Ladies comic, for you," in *Shōjo zasshiron*, ed. Ōtsuka Eiji (Tokyo: Shoseki, 1991), 246–65, 284–85.

81. *Be in Love* 1, no. 1 (November 1980): 238. Many thanks to Caitlin Casiello for helping me clarify this point over Twitter.

82. *Be in Love* 1, no. 1: 238–39; *Be in Love* 1, no. 2 (December 1980): 238–39.

83. *Be in Love* 2, no. 1 (January 1981): 201.

CHAPTER TEN: LOST IN WONDERLAND

1. Okada Toshio, *Otakugaku nyūmon* (Tokyo: Shinchōsha, 2008), 289.

2. Nagayama Kaoru, *Erotic Comics in Japan: An Introduction to Eromanga*, trans. Patrick W. Galbraith and Jessica Bauwens-Sugimoto (Amsterdam: Amster-

dam University Press, 2021), 63; Saitō Nobuhiko, "Shūkan shōnen mangashi, fūun gogo-nenshi," *Yuriika* 46, no. 3 (March 2014), 103. Ōtsuka Eiji calls gekiga's absorption by mainstream magazines "depoliticization," but Shirato's manga notwithstanding, gekiga was not usually devoted to communicating an explicit ideology. Ōtsuka Eiji, "Otaku Culture as 'Conversion Literature,'" in *Debating Otaku in Contemporary Japan: Historical Perspectives and New Horizons*, ed. Patrick W. Galbraith, Björn-Ole Kamm, and Thiam Huat Kam (London: Bloomsbury Academic, 2015), xvii.

3. Azuma Hiroki and Itō Gō, "Rabukome to seishun no yukue: Adachi Mitsuru no keishikiteki senren, Takahashi Rumiko no tokuiten sonzai," *Yuriika* 46, no. 3 (March 2014): 117.

4. Saitō, "Shūkan shōnen mangashi," 103–4; Nagayama, *Introduction to Eromanga*, 63.

5. Okada, *Otakugaku*, 289–90.

6. Saitō, "Shūkan shōnen mangashi," 103–4.

7. Ryan Holmberg and Mitsuhiro Asakawa, "The Life and Art of Kuniko Tsurita," in Kuniko Tsurita, *The Sky Is Blue with a Single Cloud*, trans. Ryan Holmberg (Montréal: Drawn & Quarterly, 2020), xxxvi.

8. Saitō, "Shūkan shōnen mangashi," 104.

9. Okada, *Otakugaku*, 296, 298.

10. Saitō Tamaki, "Sunday to wa Takahashi Rumiko de aru," *Yuriika* 46, no. 3 (March 2014): 110.

11. Azuma and Itō, "Rabukome," 117.

12. Saitō, "Sunday," 111; Azuma and Itō, "Rabukome," 117–19.

13. Azuma and Itō, 117–18; Okada, *Otakugaku*, 298.

14. Azuma and Itō, "Rabukome," 119.

15. Azuma and Itō, 118.

16. Okada, *Otakugaku*, 300, 302.

17. Nagatani Kunio, *Nippon manga zasshi meikan* (Tokyo: Datahouse, 1995), 192.

18. Saitō, "Shūkan shōnen mangashi," 105.

19. Okada, *Otakugaku*, 291–92, 294, 302, 304.

20. Ryan Holmberg, "The Life and Art of Yamada Murasaki," in Yamada Murasaki, *Talk to My Back*, trans. Ryan Holmberg (Montréal: Drawn & Quarterly, 2022), viii.

21. Nagayama, *Introduction to Eromanga*, 73–75.

22. Kumota Haruko, "*Urusei Yatsura*-san," *Yuriika* 46, no. 3 (March 2014): 129.

23. Blanche Delaborde, "Hearing Manga," in *The Cambridge Companion to Manga and Anime*, ed. Jaqueline Berndt (Cambridge: Cambridge University Press, 2024), 91–92, 95.

24. Marc Steinberg, *Anime's Media Mix: Franchising Toys and Characters in Japan* (Minneapolis: University of Minnesota Press, 2012), 190.

25. Holmberg, "Yamada," xii.

26. Takayuki Tatsumi, "Mori Minoru's Day of Resurrection," trans. Christopher Bolton, *Mechademia* 1 (2006): 87–90. Komatsu's first akahon manga, *Kaijin*

skeleton hakushi, also features the sinking of the Japanese archipelago. *Nikkei*, "Komatsu Sakyō-san maboroshi no debut saku, Bei de hakken," June 14, 2014.

27. Renato Rivera Rusca, "Girls und Robots—Re-evaluating 'Genre' Demarcations in Anime," presentation at Anime Expo, Los Angeles, July 3, 2016.

28. Patrick W. Galbraith, "Real(ity) Problem: Otaku and the Politics of Imagination," lecture at Sophia University, Tokyo, July 22, 2015.

29. Murakami Tomohiko, "Seinen manga toshite no shōjo manga," *Shisō no rigaku* 6 (1978), 57–59. Viewing these developments as apostasy, Ōtsuka Eiji calls these media "tenkō literature." Ōtsuka, "Conversion Literature," xvii.

30. Renato Rivera Rusca, "1985: The End of the Anime Boom," presentation at Mechademia Tokyo, Aoyama Gakuin University, Tokyo, March 18, 2016; Yonezawa Yoshihiro, "Comiket's Progress Towards Its 20th Occurrence, 1975–1982," in *Comic Market Manual 1* (Tokyo: Comic Market Junbikai, 1982), 14.

31. Yonezawa, 1, 15.

32. Jonathan Clements, *Anime: A History*, 2nd ed. (London: Bloomsbury and the British Film Institute, 2023), 217, 224–25.

33. Sharon Kinsella, *Adult Manga: Culture and Power in Contemporary Japanese Society* (Honolulu: University of Hawaiʻi Press, 2000), 112; Fan-Yi Lam, "Comic Market: How the World's Biggest Amateur Comic Fair Shaped Japanese Dōjinshi Culture," *Mechademia* 5 (2009), 236.

34. Kimi Rito, *Hentai Manga! A Brief History of Pornographic Comics in Japan*, bilingual edition (zine) (Tokyo: Fractal Jigen, 2015), 4–5. My thanks to Kimi Rito for providing me a copy of this dōjinshi at Comiket 90, and to Patrick W. Galbraith for introducing us at the event.

35. Takekuma Kentarō, "Otaku no dai-ichi sedai no jiko bunseki: Akumade kojin-teki na tachina kara," in *Mōjō genron F-kai: Postmodern otaku sexuality*, ed. Azuma Hiroki (Tokyo: Seidōsha, 2003), 10.

36. Galbraith, *Otaku*, 28–32.

37. Ōtsuka Eiji, "An Unholy Alliance of Eisenstein and Disney: The Fascist Origins of Otaku Culture," trans. Thomas Lamarre, *Mechademia* 8 (2013), 251.

38. Ian Condry, "Love Revolution: Anime, Masculinity, and the Future," in *Recreating Japanese Men*, ed. Sabine Frühstück and Anne Walthall (Berkeley: University of California Press, 2011), 263.

39. Galbraith, *Otaku*, 55–62, 64.

40. Yamanaka Tomomi, "Birth of 'Otaku': Centring on Discourse Dynamics in *Manga Burikko*," in Galbraith, Kamm, and Kam, *Debating Otaku*, 35, 38–39.

41. Bessatsu Takarajima Henshūbu [BTH], ed., *Otaku no hon* (Tokyo: JICC Shuppankyoku, 1989), 3.

42. Galbraith, *Otaku*, 64–65.

43. BTH, *Otaku*, 3.

44. Yonezawa Yoshihiro, "Comiket: Sekai saidai no manga no saiten," in *Otaku no hon*, ed. Ishi'i Shinji (Tokyo: JICC Shuppankyoku, 1989), 88.

45. See Anne Allison, *Nightwork: Sexuality, Pleasure, and Corporate Masculinity in a Tokyo Hostess Club* (Chicago: University of Chicago Press, 1994).

46. Yamaguchi Yasuo, *Nihon no anime zenshi: Sekai wo seishita Nihon anime no kiseki* (Tokyo: Ten Books, 2004), 101.

47. Galbraith, *Otaku*, 10.

48. Galbraith, 21.

49. Nagayama, *Introduction to Eromanga*, 118, 121.

50. Quoted in Galbraith, *Otaku*, 22–25.

51. Nagayama, *Introduction to Eromanga*, 69.

52. Galbraith, *Otaku*, 28.

53. Nagayama, *Introduction to Eromanga*, 89–90, 108.

54. Galbraith, *Otaku*, 28–33.

55. Shimotsuki Takanaka, *Comic Market sōseiki* (Tokyo: Asahi Shinbun Shuppan, 2008), 179 (emphasis in original); Galbraith, *Otaku*, 33.

56. Galbraith, 34–36; Ōtsuka, *Otomechikku*, 10–11, 13, 16–18.

57. Galbraith, *Otaku*, 40–42.

58. Kimi, *Hentai!*, 7. The English translation is by Patrick W. Galbraith.

59. Nagayama, *Introduction to Eromanga*, 92, 94.

60. Galbraith, *Otaku*, 45, 44.

61. Nagayama, *Introduction to Eromanga*, 46.

62. Jessica Clement, "Topic: Video Game Industry - Statistics & Facts," Statista, November 6, 2024, https://www.statista.com/topics/868/video-games/#topicOverview.

63. Chris Kohler, *Power-Up: How Japanese Video Games Gave the World an Extra Life* (Mineola, NY: Dover, 2016), 37–41.

64. Quoted in Kohler, *Power-Up*, 24–28, 36.

65. Kohler, 47–48.

66. Alex Mateo, "Japanese Comic Market Grows to 675.9 Billion Yen," *Anime News Network*, February 28, 2022, https://www.animenewsnetwork.com/news/2022–02–28/japanese-comic-market-grows-to-675.9-billion-yen/.183095.

67. Shueisha, "Shūeisha shōshi," https://www.shueisha.co.jp/history/history.html (accessed July 31, 2024).

68. Shuppan Nenkan Henshūbu, ed., *Nenkan shuppan* (Tokyo: Shuppan News, 2001), 83.

69. Shuppan Nenkan Henshūbu, ed., *Zenshū sōgō mokuroku: 1990* (Tokyo: Shuppan News-sha, 1990), 123, 107.

70. Steinberg, *Media Mix*, 141 (emphasis in original).

71. Shuppan Nenkan Henshūbu, *1990*, 81.

72. Rivera Rusca, "1985."

73. Barbora and Arawi, *Comitia-damashii*, 26.

74. Nagayama, *Introduction to Eromanga*, 79.

75. Quoted in Barbora and Arawi, *Comitia-damashii*, 27–30.

76. Quoted in Barbora and Arawi, 34–36.

77. Barbora and Arawi, 45, 47; Nakamura Kimihiko, preface to *Comitia 30th Chronicle*, ed. Comitia Jikkō Iinkai (Tokyo: Comitia Jikkō Iinkai, 2014), vol. 1, n.p.

78. Barbora and Arawi, *Comitia-damashii*, 11–13.

79. Barbora and Arawi, 48–49; Comitia Jikkō Iinkai, "Comitia nitsuite," https://www.comitia.co.jp/html/about.html (accessed July 28, 2024).

80. Barbora and Arawi, *Comitia-damashii*, 45–46.

81. Nakamura, preface, n.p.

82. Nakamura Kimihiko, "Comitia History," in Comitia Jikkō Iinkai, *Comitia 30th Chronicle*, vol. 2, 642.

83. Barbora and Arawi, *Comitia-damashii*, 61–62.

84. Nakamura, "Comitia History," 629–31.

85. Bon Woo Koo, "Manga Editors and Their Artists," in Berndt, *Cambridge Companion to Manga and Anime*, 194.

86. Nagayama, *Introduction to Eromanga*, 78, 80; Saitō Nobuhiko, "Dōjinshi to sokubaikai," in *Mangagaku nyūmon*, ed. Natsume Fusanosuke and Takeuchi Osamu (Kyoto: Minerva Shobō, 2009), 223.

87. Jaqueline Berndt, "Manga in Transition: Subtly Receding from 'Popular Culture,'" in *Hokusai × Manga: Japanese Pop Culture since 1680*, ed. Sabine Schulze, Nora von Achenbach, and Simon Klingler (Munich: Hirmer, 2016), 234.

88. Shuppan Nenkan Henshūbu, *1990*, 65.

89. Shuppan News-sha, ed., *Shuppan databook: 1945nen—1991nen* (Tokyo: Shuppan News-sha, 1992), 107.

90. Nagayama, *Introduction to Eromanga*, 98–99.

91. Kinsella, *Adult*, 162–63.

92. Quoted in Holmberg, "Yamada," xxvi.

93. Koo, "Manga Editors," 190.

94. Nagayama, *Introduction to Eromanga*, 81.

95. Jaqueline Berndt, "Manga, Which Manga? Publication Formats, Genres, Users," in *Japanese Civilization in the 21st Century*, ed. Andrew Targowski, Juri Abe, and Hisanori Kato (New York: Nova Science Publishers, 2016), 128.

96. Kinsella, *Adult*, 202.

PART FIVE CONCLUSION: STILL PREOCCUPIED WITH 1989

1. Miyazaki Hayao, *Starting Point: 1979–1996*, trans. Beth Cary and Frederik L. Schodt (San Francisco: VIZ Media, 2009), 197.

2. Björn-Ole Kamm, "Opening the Black Box of the 1989 *Otaku* Discourse," in *Debating Otaku in Contemporary Japan: Historical Perspectives and New Horizons*, ed. Patrick W. Galbraith, Björn-Ole Kamm, and Thiam Huat Kam (London: Bloomsbury Academic, 2015), 64–65. Ironically, Ōtsuka and other manga and anime critics provided this term to the mainstream media by declaiming Miyazaki as *not* an exemplar of "otaku" culture.

3. Patrick W. Galbraith, *Otaku and the Struggle for Imagination in Japan* (Durham, NC: Duke University Press, 2019), 68.

4. Miyazaki was found guilty; he was hanged in June 2008 in what many saw as an official reaction to the Akihabara massacre just a week earlier. The

perpetrator of those murders—a very different kind of otaku crime—was executed in June 2022.

5. Natsume Fusanosuke, *Tezuka Osamu no bōken: Sengo manga no kamigami* (Tokyo: Shogakukan, 1998), 295.

6. Saitō Nobuhiko, "Dōjinshi to sokubaikai," in *Mangagaku nyūmon*, ed. Natsume Fusanosuke and Takeuchi Osamu (Kyoto: Minerva Shobō, 2009), 223.

7. Yonezawa Yoshihiro, "*Manga Shōnen* kara Comiket e . . . ," in *Shōnen natsu man'ō* (zine) 16 (1995), 46–47.

CONCLUSION: A DISTINCTIVE HISTORY

1. Ronald Stewart, "Newspaper Comic Strips: Laughs in Four Panels," in *The Cambridge Companion to Manga and Anime*, ed. Jaqueline Berndt (Cambridge: Cambridge University Press, 2024), 31–33, 37.

2. See Matsumoto Masahiko, *Gekiga bakatachi!!* (Tokyo: Seirin Kōgeisha, 2009).

3. Jaqueline Berndt, "Manga in Transition: Subtly Receding from 'Popular Culture,'" in *Hokusai × Manga: Japanese Pop Culture Since 1680*, ed. Sabine Schulze, Nora von Achenbach, and Simon Klingler (Munich: Hirmer, 2016), 235.

4. Berndt, 235; De Kosnik, *Archives*, 333–47.

5. Berndt, "Transition," 235.

6. Jaqueline Berndt, "Manga, Which Manga? Publication Formats, Genres, Users," in *Japanese Civilization in the 21st Century*, ed. Andrew Targowski, Juri Abe, and Hisanori Kato (New York: Nova Science Publishers, 2016), 125.

7. Dalma Kálovics, "Manga Across Media: Style Adapting to Form in the 1950s and 1960s and in the Digital Age," *Mechademia* 12, no. 2 (2020): 109, 111.

8. See Ramzi Fawaz, *The New Mutants: Superheroes and the Radical Imagination of American Comics* (New York: New York University Press, 2016).

9. Berndt, "Manga, Which Manga?," 126.

10. Alex Mateo, "Japanese Comic Market Grows to 675.9 Billion Yen," *Anime News Network*, February 28, 2022, https://www.animenewsnetwork.com/news/2022-02-28/japanese-comic-market-grows-to-675.9-billion-yen/.183095; Kálovics, "Manga Across Media," 109.

11. See Casey Brienza, *Manga in America: Transnational Book Publishing and the Domestication of Japanese Comics* (London: Bloomsbury Academic, 2017). In 2025, manga magazines are less ubiquitous in Japan, and used bookstores have begun to shrink as people buy fewer physical books.

12. See Thierry Groensteen, Musée de la bande dessinée, and CIBDI, *La Bande Dessinée: Son Histoire et Ses Maîtres* (Paris Angoulême: Skira Flammarion and Cité internationale de la bande dessinée et de l'image, 2009).

13. See Alex Leavitt and Andrea Horbinski, "Even a Monkey Can Understand Fan Activism: Political Speech, Artistic Expression, and a Public for the Japanese Dōjin Community," *Transformative Works and Cultures* 10 (June 2012).

14. Patrick W. Galbraith, "Manga Readerships, Imaginative Agency, and the 'Erotic Barrier,'" in Berndt, *Cambridge Companion to Manga and Anime*, 247–48.

15. Thomas Baudinette, *Boys Love Media in Thailand: Celebrity, Fans, and Transnational Asian Queer Popular Culture* (London: Bloomsbury Academic, 2024), 14–15, 31–32, 34; Thomas Baudinette, "Japanese Queer Popular Culture and the Production of Sexual Knowledge in the Philippines," in *Queer Southeast Asia* (London: Routledge, Taylor & Francis Group, 2023), 51, 61; Thomas Baudinette, "Boys Love Media in Thailand," presented at Citrus Con 2024, August 24, 2024. Taiwan and Thailand are the only Asian countries that have legalized gay marriage.

BIBLIOGRAPHY

PERIODICALS

All are published in Tokyo unless otherwise noted.

Be in Love/Be Love. Kodansha, 1980–present.

Big Comic. Shogakukan, 1968–present.

Bōken Katsugeki Bunko. Aka'akasha, 1948–50.

Shōnen Shōjo Bōken Ō/Bōken Ō. Akita Shoten, 1949–83.

COM. Tezuka Productions, 1967–71.

Comic Jun/Juné. Magazine Magazine, 1978–95.

Funny. Tezuka Productions, 1969–70, 1973.

Garo. Seirindō, 1964–2002.

Illustrated Monthly of the Box of Curios/The Weekly Box of Curios. Yokohama: E. V. Thorn & Son, 1892–1915.

The Japan Punch. Yokohama: n.p., 1862–87.

Jiji Manga/Manga to Shashin. Jiji Shinpōsha, 1921–32.

Karikare. Tokyo: Tokyo Manga Kenkyūkai, 1938–41.

Kodomo Manga Times. Kodomo Manga Times-sha, 1949–ca. 1951.

Kodomo Puck. Tokyosha, 1924.

Kokkei Shinbun. Ōsaka: Ōsaka Kokkei Shinbunsha, 1901–8.

Manga. Mangasha, 1941–50.

The Manga Man. Tokyo Manga Shinbunsha, 1929–31.

Manga no Kuni/Sashie Manga Kenkyū. Nihon Manga Kenkyūkai, 1935–41.

Manga Shōnen. Gakudosha, 1947–55.

Margaret. Shueisha, 1963–present.

Marumaru Chinbun. Chinbunkan, 1877–1907.

Matenrō. Togetsu Shobō, 1959–60.

Mimi. Kodansha, 1975–97.

Musansha Shinbun. Musansha Shinbunsha, 1925–27.

Musō. Togetsu Shobō, 1956–60.

Nakayoshi. Kodansha, 1955–present.

Omoshiro Book. Shueisha, 1949–59.
Osaka Puck/Manga Nippon/Manga to Yomimono. Osaka: Kibunkan et al., 1906–50.
Ribon. Shueisha, 1955–present.
Rōdō Nōmin Shinbun. Rōdō Nōmin Shinbunsha, 1927–31.
Shōjo Kurabu/Shōjo Club. Kodansha, 1923–62.
Shōnen Kurabu/Shōnen Club. Kodansha, 1914–62.
Shōnen Shōjo Tankai. Hakubunkan, 1920–39.
Shūkan Manga Times. Hobunsha, 1956–present.
Shūkan Shōnen Jump. Shueisha, 1968–present.
Shūkan Shōnen Magazine. Kodansha, 1959–present.
Shūkan Young Jump. Shueisha, 1979–present.
Tetsuwan Atomu Club. Tezuka Productions, 1964–67.
Tōbaé: Journal satirique. N.p., 1887–89.
Tokyo Puck. Yūrakusha, Tokyo Puck-sha et al., 1905–15, 1919–23, 1928–41, 1948.
Yomiuri Sunday Manga. Yomiuri Shinbunsha, 1930–31.
Yōnen Gahō. Hakubunkan, 1906–23.
Yōnen Kurabu/Yōnen Club. Kodansha, 1926–58.
Yōnen no Kuni. Shōnen no Kuni no Kai, 1900–2.
Yōnen no Tomo. Jitsugyo no Nihonsha, 1909–26.
Yōnen Sekai. Hakubunkan, 1900, 1911–23.
Yōnen Zasshi. Hakubunkan, 1891–94.

BOOKS, ARTICLES, FILMS, LECTURES, MANGA, AND DŌJINSHI

24 Hour Party People. Directed by Michael Winterbottom. 2002. Santa Monica, CA: MGM Home Entertainment, 2003.
Abe Noriko. *"Kodomo ga yoku naru Kōdansha no ehon" no kenkyū: Kaisetsu to saimoku database*. Tokyo: Kazama Shobō, 2011.
"Affirmational Fandom." Accessed February 19, 2017. https://fanlore.org/wiki/Affirmational_Fandom.
Akiyama Mitsuru. *COM no seishun: Shirarezaru Tezuka Osamu*. Tokyo: Heibonsha, 1990.
Allison, Anne. *Nightwork: Sexuality, Pleasure, and Corporate Masculinity in a Tokyo Hostess Club*. Chicago: University of Chicago Press, 1994.
———. *Permitted and Prohibited Desires: Mothers, Comics, and Censorship in Japan*. Berkeley: University of California Press, 2000.
Alt, Matt. *Pure Invention: How Japan's Pop Culture Conquered the World*. New York: Crown, 2020.
Anan, Nobuko. "*The Rose of Versailles:* Women and Revolution in Girls' Manga and the Socialist Movement in Japan." *Journal of Popular Culture* 47, no. 1 (2014): 41–63.

Annett, Sandra. *Anime Fan Communities: Transcultural Flows and Frictions.* New York: Palgrave Macmillan, 2014.

"Arita Shigeshi." Accessed November 9, 2023. http://seimeisi.web.fc2.com/sigesi/sigesi.html.

AS and Mori Sei'ichirō, eds. *Manga dōjin no hanseiki: AS 50-nenten 1966–2016.* Kitakyushu, Japan: Kitakyushu Manga Museum, 2016.

Asahi Publishing, ed. *Shūkan Shōwa no. 22 (Shōwa 49-nen): Berubara boom, Mona Lisa-ten, Onoda Hiroo-shōi kikoku.* Tokyo: Asahi Shinbun Shuppan, 2009.

Asai Tarō and Ōshiro Noboru. *Kasei tanken.* Tokyo: Tōdosha, 2003.

Azuma Hiroki. *Otaku: Japan's Database Animals.* Translated by Jonathan E. Abel and Shion Kono. Minneapolis: University of Minnesota Press, 2009.

Azuma Hiroki and Itō Gō. "Rabukome to seishun no yukue: Adachi Mitsuru no keishikiteki senren, Takahashi Rumiko no tokuiten sonzai." *Yuriika* 46, no. 3 (March 2014): 115–28.

Barbora and Arawi Keiichi. *Comitia-damashii: 40 Years of Manga and Dōjinshi.* Edited by Comitia Jikkō Iinkai. Tokyo: Film Art-sha, 2024.

Baudinette, Thomas. *Boys Love Media in Thailand: Celebrity, Fans, and Transnational Asian Queer Popular Culture.* London: Bloomsbury Academic, 2024.

———. "Boys Love Media in Thailand." Presented at Citrus Con 2024, August 24, 2024.

———. "Japanese Queer Popular Culture and the Production of Sexual Knowledge in the Philippines." In *Queer Southeast Asia*, 47–62. London: Routledge, Taylor & Francis Group, 2023.

———. *Regimes of Desire: Young Gay Men, Media, and Masculinity in Tokyo.* Ann Arbor: University of Michigan Press, 2021.

Berndt, Jaqueline. "Anime in Academia: Representative Object, Media Form, and Japanese Studies." *Arts* 7, no. 4 (2018): 10.3390/arts7040056.

———. "Introduction: Two Media Forms in Correlation." In *The Cambridge Companion to Manga and Anime*, edited by Jaqueline Berndt, 1–16. Cambridge: Cambridge University Press, 2024.

———. "Manga in Transition: Subtly Receding from 'Popular Culture.'" In *Hokusai × Manga: Japanese Pop Culture Since 1680*, edited by Sabine Schulze, Nora von Achenbach, and Simon Klingler, 230–37. Munich: Hirmer, 2016.

———. "Manga, Which Manga? Publication Formats, Genres, Users." In *Japanese Civilization in the 21st Century*, edited by Andrew Targowski, Juri Abe, and Hisanori Kato, 121–34. New York: Nova Science Publishers, 2016.

———. "Premodern Roots of Story-Manga?" In *The Cambridge Companion to Manga and Anime*, edited by Jaqueline Berndt, 19–30. Cambridge: Cambridge University Press, 2024.

Bessatsu Takarajima Henshūbu, ed. *Otaku no hon* (Tokyo: JICC Shuppankyoku, 1989).

Brienza, Casey. *Manga in America: Transnational Book Publishing and the Domestication of Japanese Comics.* London: Bloomsbury Academic, 2017.

Callis, April S. "Homophobia, Heteronormativity, and Slash Fan Fiction." *Transformative Works and Cultures* 22 (2016).

Chakuwiki. "Yūkannaru suihei no kaeuta." Accessed June 25, 2022. https://chakuwiki.org/wiki/勇敢なる水兵の替え歌.

Chin Teruko. "Ashisutanto." In *Mangagaku nyūmon*, edited by Natsume Fusanosuke and Takeuchi Osamu, 146. Kyoto: Minerva Shobō, 2009.

———. "Hana no 24-nen gumi." In *Mangagaku nyūmon*, edited by Natsume Fusanosuke and Takeuchi Osamu, 41. Kyoto: Minerva Shobō, 2009.

Chūjō Shōhei. "Gendai manga to *Shō-chan*." In Oda Shōsei and Kabashima Katsuichi, *Shō-chan no bōken*, 132–35. Tokyo: Shogakukan Creative, 2003.

Chun, Jayson Makoto. *"A Nation of a Hundred Million Idiots"? A Social History of Japanese Television, 1953–1973*. New York: Routledge, 2007.

Clement, Jessica. "Video Game Industry - Statistics & Facts." Statista, November 6, 2024. https://www.statista.com/topics/868/video-games/.

Clements, Jonathan. *Anime: A History*. 2nd ed. London: Bloomsbury and British Film Institute, 2023.

———. "Tezuka's Anime Revolution in Context." *Mechademia* 8 (2013): 214–26.

Comic Book Plus. "Puck 898 (UK Comic Books)," October 8, 1921. https://comicbookplus.com/?dlid=28592.

Comic Market Junbikai. *Comic Market 30's File: 1975–2005*. Tokyo: Comiket, 2005.

———. *Comic Market Manual 1* (zine). Tokyo: Comic Market Junbikai, 1982.

———. *Comic Market-7 Report* (zine). Tokyo: Comic Market Junbikai, 1978.

———. *Comiket 20's: Comic Market 20-shūnen kinen shiryōshū*. Tokyo: Comic Market Junbikai, 1996.

———. *Comiket Appeal 3* (zine). Tokyo: Comic Market Junbikai, 1980.

Comitia Jikkō Iinkai, ed. *Comitia 30th Chronicle*. Tokyo: Comitia Jikkō Iinkai, 2014. 3 vols.

———. "Comitia Nitsuite." Comitia. Accessed July 28, 2024. https://www.comitia.co.jp/html/about.html.

Condry, Ian. "Love Revolution: Anime, Masculinity, and the Future." In *Recreating Japanese Men*, edited by Sabine Frühstück and Anne Walthall, 262–83. Berkeley: University of California Press, 2011.

———. *The Soul of Anime: Collaborative Creativity and Japan's Media Success Story*. Durham, NC: Duke University Press, 2013.

Coppa, Francesca. *Vidding: A History*. Ann Arbor: University of Michigan Press, 2022.

De Kosnik, Abigail. *Rogue Archives: Digital Cultural Memory and Media Fandom*. Cambridge, MA: MIT Press, 2016.

De Waal, Edmund. *The Hare with Amber Eyes: A Family's Century of Art and Loss*. New York: Farrar, Straus and Giroux, 2010. Epub.

Deguchi Isao. "Akusho tsuihō undō no tenbō: Iwayuru 'akusho tsuihō' no dōki to mondaiten." *Gakkō Toshokan*, no. 158 (December 1963): 12–19.

Delaborde, Blanche. “Hearing Manga.” In *The Cambridge Companion to Manga and Anime*, edited by Jaqueline Berndt, 87–97. Cambridge: Cambridge University Press, 2024.

Dionisio, Max. “Drawing on History: Tagawa Suiho and Early Japanese Manga Culture.” PhD diss., University of Pennsylvania, 2007.

Dodd, Hannah E. “‘Welcome to the Sorority’: Second-Person Pronouns and the Diverse Readership of *Comic Yuri Hime*.” Paper presented at the Center for Japanese Studies Graduate Conference, University of California, Berkeley, April 8, 2017.

Duus, Peter. “‘Punch Pictures’—Localising Punch in Meiji Japan.” In *Asian Punches: A Transcultural Affair*, edited by Hans Harder and Barbara Mittler, 307–35. Berlin: Springer, 2013.

Exner, Eike. *Comics and the Origins of Manga: A Revisionist History*. New Brunswick, NJ: Rutgers University Press, 2021.

Fawaz, Ramzi. *The New Mutants: Superheroes and the Radical Imagination of American Comics*. New York: New York University Press, 2016.

Fowler, Edward. *The Rhetoric of Confession: Shishōsetsu in Early Twentieth-Century Japanese Fiction*. Berkeley: University of California Press, 1988.

Frühstück, Sabine. *Playing War: Children and the Paradoxes of Modern Militarism in Japan*. Oakland: University of California Press, 2017.

Fujiki Hideaki. “Implicating Readers: Tezuka’s Early Seinen Manga.” *Mechademia* 8 (2013): 195–212.

Fujiko Fujio A. *Ai . . . shiri someshi koro ni . . . vol. 1*. Tokyo: Shogakukan, 1997.

Fujiko Fujio A and Fujiko F. Fujio. *Futari de shōnen manga bakari kaitekita*. Tokyo: Nihon Tosho Center, 2010.

Fujimoto Yukari. “*Berusaiyu no bara* to sono jidai.” In *Shūkan Shōwa no. 22 (Shōwa 49-nen): Berubara boom, Mona Lisa-ten, Onoda Hiroo-shōi kikoku*, edited by Asahi Publishing. Tokyo: Asahi Shinbun Shuppan, 2009.

———. *Watashi no ibasho wa doko ni aru no? Shōjo manga ga utsusu kokoro no katachi*. Tokyo: Gakuyō Shobō, 1998.

———. “Where Is My Place in the World? Early Shōjo Manga Portrayals of Lesbianism.” Translated by Lucy Fraser. *Mechademia* 9 (2014): 25–42.

Furuhata, Yuriko. “Searching for Japan’s Bell Labs: Experiments in Computer Art.” Lecture at the University of California, Berkeley, March 10, 2016.

Futagami Hirokazu. “Manga to zasshi.” In *Mangagaku nyūmon*, edited by Natsume Fusanosuke and Takeuchi Osamu, 54–59. Kyoto: Minerva Shobō, 2009.

Galbraith, Patrick W. “Manga Readerships, Imaginative Agency, and the ‘Erotic Barrier.’” In *The Cambridge Companion to Manga and Anime*, edited by Jaqueline Berndt, 241–55. Cambridge: Cambridge University Press, 2024.

———. “*Moe* Talk: Communication among Female Fans of Yaoi.” In *Boys Love Manga and Beyond: History, Culture, and Community in Japan*, edited by Mark J. McLelland, Kazumi Nagaike, Katsuhiko Suganuma, and James Welker, 153–68. Jackson: University Press of Mississippi, 2015.

———. *Otaku and the Struggle for Imagination in Japan*. Durham, NC: Duke University Press, 2019.

———. "Real(ity) Problem: Otaku and the Politics of Imagination." Lecture at Sophia University, Tokyo, July 22, 2015.

———. "Women Producing and Consuming Erotic Comics in Japan." Paper presented at the Virtual Association for Asian Studies Conference, March 1, 2024.

Gerow, Aaron. *Visions of Japanese Modernity: Articulations of Cinema, Nation, and Spectatorship, 1895–1925*. Berkeley: University of California Press, 2010.

Gordon, Andrew. *Fabricating Consumers: The Sewing Machine in Modern Japan*. Berkeley: University of California Press, 2012.

———. *Labor and Imperial Democracy in Prewar Japan*. Berkeley: University of California Press, 1991.

———. *The Wages of Affluence: Labor and Management in Postwar Japan*. Cambridge, MA: Harvard University Press, 1998.

Groensteen, Thierry, Musée de la bande dessinée, and CIBDI. *La Bande Dessinée: Son Histoire et Ses Maîtres*. Paris Angoulême: Skira Flammarion and Cité internationale de la bande dessinée et de l'image, 2009.

Guinness World Records. "Longest-Running Anime TV Series." Accessed December 2, 2022. https://www.guinnessworldrecords.com/world-records/732770-longest-running-anime-tv-series.

Hagio Moto. *The Heart of Thomas*. Translated by Rachel Thorn. Seattle: Fantagraphics Books, 2012.

———. *Ichidokiri no Ōizumi no hanashi*. Tokyo: Kawade Shobō Shinsha, 2021.

———. *Tōma no shinzō*. Tokyo: Shogakukan, 1995.

Hagio Moto and Yoshimoto Taka'aki. "Jikohyōgen toshite no shōjo manga." *Yuriika* 13, no. 9 (1981): 82–119.

Hajdu, David. *The Ten-Cent Plague: The Great Comic-Book Scare and How It Changed America*. New York: Farrar, Straus and Giroux, 2008.

Halperin, David M. *Saint Foucault: Towards a Gay Hagiography*. New York: Oxford University Press, 1995.

Haruhara Akihiko. "Introduction." In *Shinbun manga no me: Hito seiji sekai*, edited by Nihon Shinbun Hakubutsukan, 3–9. Yokohama: Newspark, 2003.

Hasegawa Machiko. *Sazae-san*. Tokyo: Shimaisha, 1947.

Hayashi Sadae. "Ladies comic, for you." In *Shōjo zasshiron*, edited by Ōtsuka Eiji, 255–76. Tokyo: Shoseki, 1991.

Hemmann, Kathryn. *Manga Cultures and the Female Gaze*. Cham, Switzerland: Palgrave Macmillan, 2020.

Holmberg, Ryan. "Anti-Manga: Sasaki Maki, Ishiko Junzō, and the Image." In *The Anti-Museum: An Anthology*, edited by Mathieu Copeland and Balthazar Lovay, 650–66. Fribourg, Switzerland: Fri Art, 2017.

———. "Bat Kid: Inoue Kazuo and the Origins of Baseball Manga." In Inoue Kazuo, *Bat Kid*, iii–xlix. Translated by Ryan Holmberg. Richmond, VA: Bubbles Zine Publications, 2021.

———. "Fujiwara Maki: The Art of Life with Tsuge Yoshiharu." In Fujiwara Maki, *My Picture Diary*, 187–208. Translated by Ryan Holmberg. Montréal: Drawn & Quarterly, 2023.

———. "Fukui Eiichi and the Judo Manga Revolution." In Fukui Eiichi, *Igaguri: Young Judo Master*, ii-lxxv. Translated by Ryan Holmberg. Richmond, VA: Bubbles Zine Publications, 2024.
———. "The Fukui Ei'ichi Incident and the Prehistory of Komaga-Gekiga." *The Comics Journal*, January 5, 2015. https://www.tcj.com/the-fukui-eiichi-incident-and-the-prehistory-of-komaga-gekiga/.
———. *Garo Manga: The First Decade, 1964–1973*. New York: Center for Book Arts, 2010.
———. "The Heirs of Gottfredson: Osamu Tezuka." In Floyd Gottfredson, *Walt Disney's Mickey Mouse "Outwits the Phantom Blot."* Edited by David Gerstein and Gary Groth. Seattle: Fantagraphics Books, 2014.
———. "The Komaga Revolution." In *The Man Next Door*. Translated by Ryan Holmberg. London: Breakdown Press, 2014.
———. "The Life and Art of Yamada Murasaki." In Yamada Murasaki, *Talk to My Back*, vii–xli. Translated by Ryan Holmberg. Montréal: Drawn & Quarterly, 2022.
———. "*Manga Shōnen:* Katō Ken'ichi and the Manga Boys." *Mechademia* 8 (2013): 173–93.
———. "Osamu Tezuka and the First Story Manga." In Osamu Tezuka, *The Mysterious Underground Men*, viii–xliv. Edited and translated by Ryan Holmberg. Brooklyn, NY: PictureBox, 2013.
———. "Paper Megaphone: *Garo* Manga, 1964–1971." PhD diss., Yale University, 2007.
———. "Proto-Gekiga: Matsumoto Masahiko's Komaga." *The Comics Journal*, October 22, 2014. https://www.tcj.com/proto-gekiga-matsumoto-masahikos-komaga/.
———. "A Vogue for I Don't Get It: Hayashi Seiichi vs. Sasaki Maki, 1967–69." *The Comics Journal*, December 16, 2015. https://www.tcj.com/a-vogue-for-i-dont-get-it-hayashi-seiichi-vs-sasaki-maki-1967–69/.
Holmberg, Ryan, and Mitsuhiro Asakawa. "The Life and Art of Kuniko Tsurita." In Kuniko Tsurita, *The Sky Is Blue with a Single Cloud*, v–xli. Translated by Ryan Holmberg. Montréal: Drawn & Quarterly, 2020.
Hori, Hikari. *Promiscuous Media: Film and Visual Culture in Imperial Japan, 1926–1945*. Ithaca, NY: Cornell University Press, 2017.
———. "Tezuka, Shōjo Manga, and Hagio Moto." *Mechademia* 8 (2013): 299–312.
Hosokibara Seiki. *Nihon mangashi*. Tokyo: Yūzankaku, 1924.
Hotwagner, Sonja. "'*Punch*'s Heirs' between the (Battle) Lines: Satirical Journalism in the Age of the Russo-Japanese War of 1904–05." In *Asian Punches: A Transcultural Affair*, edited by Hans Harder and Barbara Mittler, 337–64. Berlin, Heidelberg: Springer Berlin Heidelberg, 2013.
Ikebe Hitoshi. *Sugu dekiru manga no kakikata*. Tokyo: Sūbundō Shoten, 1931.
Imaizumi Ippyō. *Ippyō zatsuwa*. Tokyo: Seishidō, 1901.
Imamura Taihei. "Japanese Cartoon Films." Translated by Thomas Lamarre. *Mechademia* 9 (2014): 107–24.

Inouye, Rei Okamoto. "Theorizing Manga: Nationalism and Discourse on the Role of Wartime Manga." *Mechademia* 4 (2009): 20–37.

Insatsubutsukan, ed. *Million seller e! Meiji, Taishō no zasshi media*. Tokyo: Tokyo Shoseki, 2008.

Ippei Seishiki. "Foreword." In Miyao Shigeo, *Miyao Shigeo no hon, vol. 11: Shigeo manga zukan 1*, 1–2. Tokyo: Kanō Shobō, 1984.

Ishii Hakutei. "Honchō mangashi." *Chūō Bijutsu* 4, no. 1 (January 1918): 139–42.

Ishiko Jun. *Nihon mangashi*. Tokyo: Shakai Shisōsha, 1988.

Ishinomori Shōtarō. *Kizuna: Fushō no musuko kara fushō no musukotachi e*. Tokyo: NTT Shuppan, 1998.

Itō Gō. *Manga wa kawaru: "Mangagatari" kara "mangaron" e*. Tokyo: Seidosha, 2007.

———. *Tezuka Is Dead: Hirakareta manga hyōgenron e*. Tokyo: NTT Shuppan, 2005.

Japan Cartoonists Association, ed. *Nihon Mangaka Kyōkai sōritsu 50-shūnen kinenshi*. Tokyo: Nihon Mangaka Kyōkai, 2015.

Jenkins, Henry. "Aca-Fandom and Beyond: John Edward Campbell, Lee Harrington, and Catherine Tossenberger (Part Two)," July 2011. http://henryjenkins.org/2011/07/aca-fandom_and_beyond_harringt_1.html.

Jenkins, Henry, and Cynthia Jenkins. Interview by Abigail De Kosnik, University of Iowa, August 14, 2012. Transcript.

Kajii Jun. *Tore, yōchō no jū to pen: Senjika mangashi nōto*. Tokyo: Wise Shuppan, 1999.

Kálovics, Dalma. "Manga Across Media: Style Adapting to Form in the 1950s and 1960s and in the Digital Age." *Mechademia* 12, no. 2 (2020): 102–23.

Kamm, Björn-Ole. "Opening the Black Box of the 1989 *Otaku* Discourse." In *Debating Otaku in Contemporary Japan: Historical Perspectives and New Horizons*, edited by Patrick W. Galbraith, Björn-Ole Kamm, and Thiam Huat Kam, 51–70. London: Bloomsbury Academic, 2015.

Kashihon Manga Kenkyūkai, ed. *Kashihon Manga Returns*. Tokyo: Popurasha, 2006.

Kasza, Gregory J. *The State and the Mass Media in Japan, 1918–1945*. Berkeley: University of California Press, 1988.

Katō Etsurō. *Shinrinen manga no gihō*. Tokyo: Geijutsu Gakuin Shuppanbu, 1942.

Katō Ken'ichi. *Shōnen Kurabu jidai: Henshūchō no kaisō*. Tokyo: Kodansha, 1968.

Katō Misako. "Chichi Ken'ichi to '*Manga Shōnen*.'" In Terada Hiroo, *"Manga Shōnen"-shi*, 107–10. Fujisawa, Japan: Shōnan Shuppansha, 1981.

Katō Takeo. *"Manga Shōnen" monogatari: Henshūsha Katō Ken'ichi den*. Tokyo: Toshi Shuppan, 2002.

Kern, Adam L. *Manga from the Floating World: Comicbook Culture and the Kibyōshi of Edo Japan*. 2nd ed. Cambridge, MA: Harvard University Asia Center, 2019.

Kimi Rito. *Hentai Manga! A Brief History of Pornographic Comics in Japan* (zine). Tokyo: Fractal Jigen, 2015.

Kinsella, Sharon. *Adult Manga: Culture and Power in Contemporary Japanese Society*. Honolulu: University of Hawai'i Press, 2000.

Kitazawa Rakuten. *Rakuten zenshū*. Tokyo: Atelier-sha, 1930. 9 vols.
Kiyama, Henry Yoshitaka. *The Four Immigrants Manga: A Japanese Experience in San Francisco, 1904–1924*. Translated by Frederik L. Schodt. Berkeley, California: Stone Bridge Press, 1999.
———. *Manga yonin shosei*. San Francisco: Kiyama Yoshitaka Gashitsu, 1931.
Kobayashi Hideo. "Manga." In *Shintei Kobayashi Hideo zenshū, vol. 12: Kangaeru hinto*. Edited by Ōoka Shōhei, Nakamura Mitsuo, and Etō Jun. Tokyo: Shinchōsha, 1978.
Kobayashi Kiyoshi and Kitazawa Rakuten. *Buta no heso: Manbun, manga*. Tokyo: Kōbunsha, 1928.
Kodansha, ed. *Nichiroku 20-seiki: 1970–1979, vol. 5: 1974—Berubara boom!* Tokyo: Kodansha, 1997. 10 vols.
Kohler, Chris. *Power-Up: How Japanese Video Games Gave the World an Extra Life*. Mineola, NY: Dover, 2016.
Komatsu Sakyō. "Manga to bungaku ni akekureta seishun." In Komatsu Sakyō, *Maboroshi no Komatsu Sakyō = Mori Minoru manga zenshū, vol. 4: Kaisetsuhen*, 68–73. Tokyo: Shogakukan, 2002.
———. "Taiken toshite no mangashi." In Komatsu Sakyō, *Maboroshi no Komatsu Sakyō = Mori Minoru manga zenshū, vol. 4: Kaisetsuhen*, 4–14. Tokyo: Shogakukan, 2002.
Komatsu Sakyō and Saitō Takao. "Kaidan: Komatsu Sakyō vs. Saitō Takao: Shōwa nijū nendai manga tankōbon jijō." In Komatsu Sakyō, *Maboroshi no Komatsu Sakyō = Mori Minoru manga zenshū, vol. 4: Kaisetsuhen*, 21–32. Tokyo: Shogakukan, 2002.
Koo, Bon Woo. "Manga Editors and Their Artists." In *The Cambridge Companion to Manga and Anime*, edited by Jaqueline Berndt, 187–98. Cambridge: Cambridge University Press, 2024.
Koyama-Richard, Brigitte. *One Thousand Years of Manga*. Paris: Flammarion, 2007.
Kozawa Jō. "Shinmangaha shūdan no hitotachi." *Gendaishi Konwakai* 108 (2002): 12–15.
Kumota Haruko. "*Urusei Yatsura*-san." *Yuriika* 46, no. 3 (March 2014): 129.
Kure Tomofusa. "Kashihon manga, gekiga." In *Mangagaku nyūmon*, edited by Natsume Fusanosuke and Takeuchi Osamu, 27–34. Kyoto: Minerva Shobō, 2009.
Kusunoki Shōhei. "Hatsugen." In Shirato Sanpei et al., *Garo COM manga meisakusen 2: 1968–1971*, 45. Tokyo: Kodansha, 2012.
Lam, Fan-Yi. "Comic Market: How the World's Biggest Amateur Comic Fair Shaped Japanese Dōjinshi Culture." *Mechademia* 5 (2010): 232–48.
Lamarre, Thomas. *The Anime Ecology: A Genealogy of Television, Animation, and Game Media*. Minneapolis: University of Minnesota Press, 2018.
———. *The Anime Machine: A Media Theory of Animation*. Minneapolis: University of Minnesota Press, 2009.
———. "Manga Empire: Comics and Companion Species." Lecture at Sophia University, Tokyo, April 27, 2015.

Leavitt, Alex, and Andrea Horbinski. "Even a Monkey Can Understand Fan Activism: Political Speech, Artistic Expression, and a Public for the Japanese Dōjin Community." *Transformative Works and Cultures* 10 (2012).

Linkhoeva, Tatiana. *Revolution Goes East: Imperial Japan and Soviet Communism.* Ithaca, NY: Cornell University Press, 2020.

Mack, Edward Thomas. *Manufacturing Modern Japanese Literature: Publishing, Prizes, and the Ascription of Literary Value.* Durham, NC: Duke University Press, 2010.

Manga Shūdan, ed. *Manga Shōwa-shi: Manga Shūdan no 50-nen.* Tokyo: Kawade Shobō Shinsha, 1982.

Mangaseek Project. "Naka Keiko." Mangaseek. Accessed December 3, 2023. https://mangaseek.net/person/17151.html.

Maser, Verena. "Beautiful and Innocent: Female Same-Sex Intimacy in the Japanese Yuri Genre." PhD diss., University of Trier, 2013.

Masuyama Norie. "Haikei, waga 'senyū' Takemiya Keiko-sama." In Takemiya Keiko, *Kaze to ki no uta, vol. 10,* 310–15. Tokyo: Hakusensha, 1995.

Matsumoto Leiji and Komatsu Sakyō. "*Kasei tanken* to Shōwa no manga." In Asai Tarō and Ōshiro Noboru, *Kasei tanken,* 168–81. Tokyo: Tōdosha, 2003.

Matsumoto Masahiko. *Gekiga bakatachi!!* Tokyo: Seirin Kōgeisha, 2009.

———. "What Was Komaga?" In *The Man Next Door.* Translated by Ryan Holmberg. London: Breakdown Press, 2014.

Mateo, Alex. "Japanese Comic Market Grows to 675.9 Billion Yen." *Anime News Network,* February 28, 2022. https://www.animenewsnetwork.com/news/2022-02-28/japanese-comic-market-grows-to-675.9-billion-yen/.183095.

McCloud, Scott. *Understanding Comics: The Invisible Art.* New York: HarperPerennial, 1994.

Mills, George. "The Scholarly Rebellion of the Early Baker Street Irregulars." *Transformative Works and Cultures* 23 (March 15, 2017).

Miyabe Sei'itsu, Kurosawa Tetsuya, Takeuchi Osamu, and Kajii Jun. *Mangakatachi no sensō bekkan shiryō.* Tokyo: Kinnohoshisha, 2013.

Miyake Okiko and Hideyuki Kōsokabe, eds. *Taishōki no ehon, ezasshi no kenkyū: Ichi shōnen no collection o tōshite.* Tokyo: Kanrin Shobō, 2009.

Miyamoto Hirohito. "Akahon manga." In *Mangagaku nyūmon,* edited by Natsume Fusanosuke and Takeuchi Osamu, 22–26. Kyoto: Minerva Shobō, 2009.

———. "Hito no yōna dōbutsutachi: Gijinka dōbutsu manga no '*Norakuro*.'" In *Norakuro de arimasu! Tagawa Suihō to kodomo manga no wonderland,* edited by Ni'imi Takuma, 6–12. Kawasaki, Japan: Kawasaki City Museum, 2019.

———. "Is This the First Manga?" Google Arts & Culture. Accessed November 2, 2023. https://artsandculture.google.com/story/is-this-the-first-manga/fQUBrahtnRoFKw.

———. "'Kōdansha no ehon' ni okeru 'kodomo ga yoku naru' manga no senren katei." *Manga Kenkyū* 10 (March 2007): 55–61.

———. "Manga to tankōbon." In *Mangagaku nyūmon,* edited by Natsume Fusanosuke and Takeuchi Osamu, 66–70. Kyoto: Minerva Shobō, 2009.

———. "'Ponchi-e' to 'manga,' sono shinbun no kakawari." In *Shinbun manga no me: Hito seiji sekai*, edited by Nihon Shinbun Hakubutsukan, 106–9. Yokohama: Newspark, 2003.

———. "'Ponchi' kara 'manga' e: journalism to 'bijutsu' no aida de hyōgen o migaku." In *Visual wide Meiji jidaikan*, edited by Masato Miyachi, 390–91. Tokyo: Shogakukan, 2005.

———. "Wasureraretekita '*Norakuro*' no sengo." In Tagawa Suihō, *Norakuro san-nintabi*. Tokyo: Kyōiku Hyōronsha, 2021.

Miyao Shigeo. *Manga no omatsuri*. Tokyo: Dai Nippon Yubenkai Kodansha, 1931.

———. *Miyao Shigeo no hon, vol. 11: Shigeo manga zukan 1*, 1–2. Tokyo: Kanō Shobō, 1984.

Miyazaki Hayao. *Starting Point: 1979–1996*. Translated by Beth Cary and Frederik L. Schodt. San Francisco: VIZ Media, 2009.

Mizoguchi, Akiko. "Akogare no Yoroppa," May 9, 2003. https://web.archive.org/web/20030509131032/http://natmi.coco.co.jp/AM/berubara.htm.

———. "Reading and Living *Yaoi:* Male-Male Fantasy Narratives as Women's Sexual Subculture in Japan." PhD diss., University of Rochester, 2008.

Mizushima Niō. "Nihon Mangashiron." In *Manga kōza, vol. 3*, edited by Nihon Mangakkai, 5–8. Tokyo: Kensetsusha, 1934.

Mori Seiji. "Commentary." In Tezuka Osamu and Sakai Shichima, *Shintakarajima original-han*, 198–99. Tokyo: Kodansha, 2012.

Morris-Suzuki, Tessa. *The Technological Transformation of Japan: From the Seventeenth to the Twenty-First Century*. Cambridge: Cambridge University Press, 1994.

Mura Nunoe. *Gegege no nyōbō: Jinsei wa . . . owari yokereba, subete yoshi!!* Tokyo: Jitsugyō no Nihonsha, 2011.

Murakami Motoka. *Fuichin zaijian!* Tokyo: Shogakukan, 2013–17. 10 vols.

Murakami Motoka and Takemiya Keiko. "Murakami Motoka × Takemiya Keiko Talkshow." Kawasaki City Museum, Kawasaki, Japan, December 4, 2016.

Murakami Tomohiko. "Seinen manga toshite no shōjo manga." *Shisō no rigaku* 6 (1978): 54–59.

———. "Shōnengari." In Hagio Moto, *Hagio Moto sakuhinshū 9: Pō no ichizoku 4*, 212–23. Tokyo: Shogakukan, 1978.

Nagai Katsuichi. *Garo henshūchō: Watashi no sengo manga shuppanshi*. Tokyo: Chikuma Shobō, 1987.

Nagamine Shigetoshi. "Magazines in Modern Japan and Their Readers." In *Million seller tanjō e! Meiji, Taishō zasshi media*, edited by Tokyo Printing Museum, 189–91. Tokyo: Tokyo Shōseki, 2008.

Nagata Daisuke and Matsunaga Shintarō. "A New Labor Model for a New Era of Anime: A Case Study of Anime Production in the 1970s and 1980s." Translated by Kendall Heitzman. *Mechademia* 16, no. 2 (2024): 51–72.

Nagatani Kunio. *Nippon manga zasshi meikan*. Tokyo: Datahouse, 1995.

Nagayama Kaoru. *Erotic Comics in Japan: An Introduction to Eromanga*. Translated by Patrick W. Galbraith and Jessica Bauwens-Sugimoto. Amsterdam: Amsterdam University Press, 2021.

Naiki Toshio. "Maboroshi no sakunin to aeru yorokobi." In Komatsu Sakyō, *Maboroshi no Komatsu Sakyō = Mori Minoru manga zenshū, vol. 4: Kaisetsuhen*, 120–24. Tokyo: Shogakukan, 2002.

Nakagawa Yūsuke. "*Poe no ichizoku, Berusaiyu no bara:* Atarashii shōjo manga ga dōji tahatsu," October 22, 2019. https://web.archive.org/web/20191211103730/https://www.gentosha.jp/article/14064/.

Nakamura Kimihiko. "Comitia History." In *Comitia 30th Chronicle 1*, edited by Comitia Jikkōiinkai, 624–31. Tokyo: Comitia Jikkōiinkai, 2014.

———. "Comitia History." In *Comitia 30th Chronicle 2*, edited by Comitia Jikkōiinkai, 642–48. Tokyo: Comitia Jikkōiinkai, 2014.

Nakano Haruyuki. *Nazo no mangaka Sakai Shichima den: "Shintakarajima" densetsu no hikari to kage*. Tokyo: Chikuma Shobō, 2007.

———. "*Shintakarajima* to Sakai Shichima." In *Shintakarajima dokuhon*, supplement to *Shintakarajima* by Tezuka Osamu and Sakai Shichima, 28–47. Tokyo: Shogakukan Creative, 2009.

———. *Tezuka Osamu no Takarazuka*. Tokyo: Chikuma Shobō, 1994.

Nakashima Takashi. "*Com* to *Apple Core:* Gura-Com Kansai shibu tenmatsuki." *Biranji* 27 (March 2011): 112–36.

Natsume Fusanosuke. "*Norakuro* to aratana mangashi." In *Kokkei to pathos: Tagawa Suihō "Norakuro" ichidaiki-ten*, edited by Machida Shimin Bunka Gakkan Kotobarando, 4–5. Machida, Tokyo: Machida Shimin Bunka Gakkan Kotobarando, 2013.

———. "Parody." In *Mangagaku nyūmon*, edited by Natsume Fusanosuke and Takeuchi Osamu, 211–14. Kyoto: Minerva Shobō, 2009.

———. *Tezuka Osamu no bōken: Sengo manga no kamigami*. Tokyo: Shogakukan, 1998.

Natsume Sōseki. "Okamoto Ippei no manga." In Okamoto Ippei, Natori Shunsen, and Nakada Katsunosuke, *Manga to yakubun*, 201–4. Tokyo: Kabushiki Kaisha Kokusho Kankōkai, 2019.

Nihon Shinbun Hakubutsukan, ed. *Shinbun manga no me: Hito seiji sekai*. Yokohama: Newspark, 2003.

Ni'imi Takuma, ed. *Norakuro de arimasu! Tagawa Suihō to kodomo manga no wonderland*. Kawasaki, Japan: Kawasaki City Museum, 2019.

Nishihara Mari. "Seijin manga." In *Mangagaku nyūmon*, edited by Natsume Fusanosuke and Takeuchi Osamu, 42–47. Kyoto: Minerva Shobō, 2009.

Noppe, Nele. "The Cultural Economy of Fanwork in Japan: Dōjinshi Exchange as a Hybrid Economy of Open Source Cultural Goods." PhD diss., Katholieke Universiteit Leuven, 2014. http://www.nelenoppe.net/dojinshi/Thesis.

Norakuro nitōhei. Directed by Murata Yasuji. 2 reels, 1933. http://animation.filmarchives.jp/works/view/11105.

obsession_inc. "Affirmational Fandom vs. Transformational Fandom." Accessed February 16, 2017. https://obsession-inc.dreamwidth.org/82589.html.
Oda Shōsei and Kabashima Katsuichi. *Shō-chan no bōken*. Tokyo: Shogakukan Creative, 2003.
Office for Emergency Management, War Relocation Authority, 3/18/1942–2/16/1944. "National Archives Photo No. 539490, 'Minidoka Relocation Center, Hunt, Idaho. Norakuro Band.,'" August 20, 1943. Records of the War Relocation Authority, Records Group 210, Central Photographic File of the War Relocation Authority. National Archives at College Park—Still Pictures, College Park, MD. Accessed November 27, 2015. https://catalog.archives.gov/id/539490.
Ōgi Fusami. "Nihonshiki shōjo manga kara josei manga e." In *Josei manga kenkyū: Ōbei, Nihon, Asia o tsunagu manga*, edited by Ōgi Fusami, 20–47. Tokyo: Seikyusha, 2015.
Ōhira Akira and Nihon Manga Kenkyūkai, eds. *Manga kenkyū shiryō kōza*. Tokyo: Nihon Manga Kenkyūkai, 1935. 4 vols.
Okada Toshio. *Otakugaku nyūmon*. Tokyo: Shinchōsha, 2008.
Okamoto Ippei. *Ippei zenshū*. Edited by Sugiura Yukio. Tokyo: Ōzorasha, 1990–91. 20 vols.
———. "Manga zassō." *Bijutsu Shinron* 2, no. 8 (August 1927): 42–46.
———. *Monomiyusan: Manga to Bun*. Tokyo: Isobe Kōyōdō, 1916.
———. *Shinmanga no kakikata*. Tokyo: Chūō Bijutsusha, 1928.
Okamoto Ippei, Natori Shunsen, and Nakada Katsunosuke. *Manga to yakubun*. Tokyo: Kabushiki Kaisha Kokusho Kankōkai, 2019.
Okamoto Tōki and Matsuyama Fumio. *Nihon proletarian bijutsushi*. Tokyo: Zōkeisha, 1967.
Ōkūsha, ed. *Gendai manga taikan bessatsu*. Supplement to *Gendai manga taikan*, edited by Shirota Shūichi. Tokyo: Ōkūsha, 2010. 10 vols.
Omiya-shi, ed. *Kitazawa Rakuten, Founder of the Modern Japanese Cartoon*. Omiya, Japan: Omiya City Planning Department International Culture Division, 1991.
Ono Kōsei. "*Garo* no jidai to sono eikyō." In *Garo to iu jidai: Sōkan 50-shūnen*, edited by Seirindō, 290–93. Tokyo: Seirindō, 2014.
———. "Ōbei no shinbun manga wa Nihon de dono yō ni ukeireraretaka." In *Shinbun manga no me: Hito seiji sekai*, edited by Nihon Shinbun Hakubutsukan, 118–21. Yokohama: Newspark, 2003.
———. "Zenei artist toshite shuppatsu shita Tagawa Suihō to sono robot tachi." In *Norakuro de arimasu! Tagawa Suihō to kodomo manga no wonderland*, edited by Ni'imi Takuma, 110–11. Kawasaki, Japan: Kawasaki City Museum, 2019.
Onoda Shō. "*Garo* and *COM:* The United Front Years." In Shirato Sanpei et al., *Garo COM manga meisakusen 1: 1964–1970*, 284–87. Tokyo: Kodansha, 2012.
Orbaugh, Sharalyn. "'Kamishibai' and the Art of the Interval." *Mechademia* 7 (2012): 78–100.
Oshiyama Michiko. *Shōjo manga gender hyōshōron: "Dansō no shōjo" no zōkei to identity*. Tokyo: Sairyūsha, 2007.

Ōtsuka Eiji. "Otaku Culture as 'Conversion Literature.'" In *Debating Otaku in Contemporary Japan: Historical Perspectives and New Horizons*, edited by Patrick W. Galbraith, Björn-Ole Kamm, and Thiam Huat Kam, xiii–xxix. London: Bloomsbury Academic, 2015.

———. *"Ribon" no furoku to otomechikku no jidai: Tasogaredoki ni mitsuketa mono.* Tokyo: Chikuma Shobō, 1995.

———. "Undō suru Tezuka Osamu: Kōei no jissen." In *Undō toshite no taishū bunka: Kyōdō, fan, bunka kōsaku*, edited by Ōtsuka Eiji, 11–33. Tokyo: Suiseisha, 2021.

———. "An Unholy Alliance of Eisenstein and Disney: The Fascist Origins of Otaku Culture." Translated by Thomas Lamarre. *Mechademia* 8 (2013): 251–77.

Ozaki Hotsuki. "Ke'ai de huizhen." In Ueda Toshiko, *Fuichin-san*, 217–18. Tokyo: Mushi Pro Shōji, 1969.

———, ed. "Kore ga gekiga da!" *COM*, no. 2 (June 1967): 84–89.

———. "Norakuro no hanseiki." In Tagawa Suihō, *Bokura no Norakuro: Norakuro 50-nen kinen album*, 42–45. Tokyo: Kodansha, 1984.

———, ed. "Shōjo manga no genjitsu." *COM*, no. 5 (August 1967): 70–74.

Patrick, Hugh T. "The Economic Muddle of the 1920's." In *Dilemmas of Growth in Prewar Japan*, edited by James William Morley and George M. Beckmann, 211–66. Princeton, NJ: Princeton University Press, 1971.

Prough, Jennifer S. *Straight from the Heart: Gender, Intimacy, and the Cultural Production of Shōjo Manga*. Honolulu: University of Hawai'i Press, 2011.

Rivera Rusca, Renato. "1985: The End of the Anime Boom." Presentation at Mechademia Tokyo, Aoyama Gakuin University, Tokyo, March 18, 2016.

———. "Girls und Robots—Re-evaluating 'Genre' Demarcations in Anime." Presentation at Anime Expo, Los Angeles, July 3, 2016.

Rhoads, Sean, and Brooke McCorkle Okazaki. *Japan's Green Monsters: Environmental Commentary in Kaiju Cinema*. Jefferson, NC: McFarland, 2018.

Roeder, Katherine. *Wide Awake in Slumberland: Fantasy, Mass Culture, and Modernism in the Art of Winsor McCay*. Jackson: University Press of Mississippi, 2014.

Ruoff, Kenneth J. *Imperial Japan at Its Zenith: The Wartime Celebration of the Empire's 2,600th Anniversary*. Ithaca, NY: Cornell University Press, 2010.

Sagawa Toshihiko. *June no jidai: BL no yoake mae*. Tokyo: Aki Shobō, 2024.

Saitō Nobuhiko. "Dōjinshi to sokubaikai." In *Mangagaku nyūmon*, edited by Natsume Fusanosuke and Takeuchi Osamu, 223–26. Kyoto: Minerva Shobō, 2009.

———. "Hyōgen hisei to jiken." In *Mangagaku nyūmon*, edited by Natsume Fusanosuke and Takeuchi Osamu, 152–57. Kyoto: Minerva Shobō, 2009.

———. "Shūkan shōnen mangashi, fūun gogo-nenshi." *Yuriika* 46, no. 3 (March 2014): 101–9.

Saitō Tamaki. "*Sunday* to wa Takahashi Rumiko de aru." *Yuriika* 46, no. 3 (March 2014): 110–14.

Sakamoto, Gajō. "How I Created Tank Tankuro." In Gajō Sakamoto, *Tank Tankuro: Prewar Works, 1934–1935*, ii–iv. Translated by Maki Hakui and Shunsuke Nakazawa. Tokyo: Presspop, 2011.

Sakamoto, Naoki. “Memories of My Father, Gajo Sakamoto.” In Gajō Sakamoto, *Tank Tankuro: Prewar Works, 1934–1935*, iv–vi. Translated by Maki Hakui and Shunsuke Nakazawa. Tokyo: Presspop, 2011.

Sakurai Shōichi. *Boku wa gekiga no shikakenin datta*. Tokyo: April Music, 1978.

Salter, Rebecca. *Japanese Popular Prints: From Votive Slips to Playing Cards*. Honolulu: University of Hawai‘i Press, 2006.

Sasaya Nanae, Nakajima Azusa, Takemiya Keiko, Lark, and Masuyama Norie. “Motto kimi no koto ga shiritai.” *Comic Jun*, no. 2 (December 1978): 52–56.

Sawai Kōichi. “Tezuka no sodatta Osaka no sengo: Kamishibai, kashihon, akahon.” In Tezuka Osamu and Ishinomori Shōtarō, *Tezuka Osamu × Ishinomori Shōtarō manga no chikara: Tokubetsuten*, 42–43. Tokyo: NHK Promotion, 2013.

Schodt, Frederik L. *Dreamland Japan: Writings on Modern Manga*. Berkeley, CA: Stone Bridge Press, 1996.

———. “Henry (Yoshitaka) Kiyama.” Stone Bridge Press. Accessed March 29, 2025. https://www.stonebridge.com/authors/henry-(yoshitaka)-kiyama.

———. *Manga! Manga! The World of Japanese Comics*. New York: Kodansha USA, 2012.

Seirindō, ed. *Wooden-Mortared Kingdom: Garo 20th Memorial Issue*. Tokyo: Seirindō, 1984.

Shamoon, Deborah. *Passionate Friendship: The Aesthetics of Girls’ Culture in Japan*. Honolulu: University of Hawai‘i Press, 2011.

———. “Revolutionary Romance: *The Rose of Versailles* and the Transformation of Shōjo Manga.” *Mechademia* 2 (2007): 3–17.

Shigematsu, Setsu. *Scream from the Shadows: The Women’s Liberation Movement in Japan*. Minneapolis: University of Minnesota Press, 2012.

Shimada Keizō. *Bōken Dankichi manga zenshū*. Edited by Katō Ken’ichi. Tokyo: Kodansha, 1967.

Shimizu Isao. “*Gendai manga taikan* zen 10-hen no motsu imi.” In *Gendai Manga Taikan Bessatsu*, edited by Ōzorasha Henshūbu, 6–16. Tokyo: Ōzorasha, 2010.

———. “Giga, fūshiga, fūzokuga.” In *Mangagaku nyūmon*, edited by Natsume Fusanosuke and Takeuchi Osamu, 2–7. Kyoto: Minerva Shobō, 2009.

———. *Manga ni miru 1945-nen*. Tokyo: Yoshikawa Kōbunkan, 1995.

. *“Manga Shōnen” to akahon manga: Sengo manga no tanjo*. Tokyo: Zoionsha, 1989.

———. *Manga tanjō: Taishō democracy kara no shuppatsu*. Tokyo: Yoshikawa Kōbunkan, 1999.

———. “Manga to shinbun.” In *Mangagaku nyūmon*, edited by Natsume Fusanosuke and Takeuchi Osamu, 60–65. Kyoto: Minerva Shobō, 2009.

———, ed. *Manga zasshi hakubutsukan*. Tokyo: Kokusho Kankōkai, 1986–87. 12 vols.

———. “Nicchū sensō-ki no manga zasshi *Manga no Kuni*.” Accessed December 4, 2023. https://www.kyotomm.jp/HP/about_syozo.html.

Shimokawa Ōten. “Shinmanga, shinmangaka.” *Bijutsu Shinron* 2, no. 8 (August 1927): 52–54.

Shimotsuki Takanaka, ed. *COM 40-nenme no shūkangō*. Tokyo: Asahi Shinbun Shuppan, 2011.

———. *Comic Market sōseiki*. Tokyo: Asahi Shinbun Shuppan, 2008.

Shinmangaha Shūdan, ed. *Shinmangaha Shūdan manga nenkan*. Yokohama: Bunza Shorin, 1933.

Shinozawa Misako. "The Birth of a Million Seller: Magazines as media in the Meiji-Taishō era." In *Million seller tanjō e! Meiji, Taishō zasshi media*, edited by Insatsubutsukan, 179–83. Tokyo: Tokyo Shoseki, 2008.

Shirato Sanpei, Tezuka Osamu, Mizuki Shigeru, Ishinomori Shōtarō, Tsuge Yoshiharu, Nagashima Shinji, Tatsumi Yoshihiro, Matsumoto Leiji, and Takita Yū. *Garo COM manga meisakusen*. Tokyo: Kodansha, 2012. 2 vols.

Shirota Shūichi, ed. *Gendai manga taikan*. Tokyo: Chūō bijutsusha, 1928. 10 vols.

———, ed. *Gendai manga taikan*. Tokyo: Ōkūsha, 2010. 10 vols.

Shueisha. "Shūeisha shōshi." Accessed July 31, 2024. https://www.shueisha.co.jp/history/history.html.

Shuppan Nenkan Henshūbu, ed. *Zenshū sōgō mokuroku: 1990*. Tokyo: Shuppan News-sha, 1990.

Shuppan News-sha, ed. *Shuppan databook: 1945-nen—1991-nen*. Tokyo: Shuppan News-sha, 1992.

Silverberg, Miriam. *Erotic Grotesque Nonsense: The Mass Culture of Japanese Modern Times*. Berkeley: University of California Press, 2006.

Skabelund, Aaron Herald. *Empire of Dogs: Canines, Japan, and the Making of the Modern Imperial World*. Ithaca, NY: Cornell University Press, 2011.

snarp. "Translation of a 2007 Interview with Keiko Takemiya." Accessed April 9, 2017. https://snarp.dreamwidth.org/279314.html.

Steinberg, Marc. *Anime's Media Mix: Franchising Toys and Characters in Japan*. Minneapolis: University of Minnesota Press, 2012.

———. "Genesis of the Platform Concept: From Japan's Platform Theory to Nintendo, iMode and Niconico Video." Lecture at the University of California, Berkeley, March 10, 2016.

———. "Otaku Consumption, Superflat Art and the Return to Edo." *Japan Forum* 16, no. 3 (2004): 449–71.

———. *The Platform Economy: How Japan Transformed the Consumer Internet*. Minneapolis: University of Minnesota Press, 2019.

Sterne, Jonathan. *MP3: The Meaning of a Format*. Durham, NC: Duke University Press, 2012.

Stewart, Ronald. "Groundbreaking Women: Recovering the History of Forgotten Prewar Female Mangaka." Paper presented at the Virtual Association for Asian Studies Conference, March 1, 2024.

———. "Manga as Schism: Kitazawa Rakuten's Resistance to 'Old-Fashioned' Japan." In *Manga's Cultural Crossroads*, edited by Jaqueline Berndt and Bettina Kümmerling-Meibauer, 39–61. London: Routledge, 2013.

———. "Newspaper Comic Strips: Laughs in Four Panels." In *The Cambridge Companion to Manga and Anime*, edited by Jaqueline Berndt, 31–43. Cambridge: Cambridge University Press, 2024.

Stickland, Leonie R. *Gender Gymnastics: Performing and Consuming Japan's Takarazuka Revue*. Melbourne, Australia: Trans Pacific Press, 2007.

Suan, Stevie. *Anime's Identity: Performativity and Form Beyond Japan*. Minneapolis: University of Minnesota Press, 2021.

Suleski, Ronald. "Northeast China Under Japanese Control: The Role of the Manchurian Youth Corps, 1934–1945." *Modern China* 7, no. 3 (1981): 351–77.

Sun Minqiao. "'*Jinzō ningen*' wa naze naku ka? Tagawa Suihō *Jinzō ningen* ni miru manga to avant-garde geijutsu no setten." In *Undō toshite no taishū bunka: Kyōdō, fan, bunka kōsaku*, edited by Ōtsuka Eiji, 131–47. Tokyo: Suiseisha, 2021.

Sunohara Fumihiro. "Mangaka e no shuppatsuten toshite no '*Manga to yakubun*' to Okamoto Ippei no sengo no hyōka." In Okamoto Ippei, Natori Shunsen, and Nakada Katsunosuke, *Manga to yakubun*, 215–33. Tokyo: Kabushiki Kaisha Kokusho Kankōkai, 2019.

Suzuki Maki. "'Manga-teki image no kakusan': 'Manga' to 'kōkoku' no kaikō o megutte." In *Dōin no media mix: "Sōsaku suru taishū" no senjika, sengo*, edited by Ōtsuka Eiji, 105–31. Kyoto: Shibunkaku Shuppan, 2017.

Suzuki, Shige (CJ). "Envisioning Alternative Communities Through a Popular Medium: Speculative Imagination in Hagio Moto's Girls' Comics." *International Journal of Comic Art* 13, no. 2 (Fall 2011): 57–74.

Suzuki, Shige, and Ronald Stewart. *Manga: A Critical Guide*. London: Bloomsbury Academic, 2023.

Tagawa Suihō. *Bokura no Norakuro: Norakuro 50-nen kinen album*. Tokyo: Kodansha, 1984.

———. *Chameken to Norakuro*. Tokyo: Saikensha, 1948.

———. *Chinpin Norakuro-sō*. Tokyo: Kanda Shuppan, 1947.

———. *Manga no kanzume*. Tokyo: Dai Nippon Yubenkai Kodansha, 1930.

———. *Norakuro gunsō*. Tokyo: Dai Nippon Yubenkai Kodansha, 1934.

———. *Norakuro jōtōhei*. Tokyo: Dai Nippon Yubenkai Kodansha, 1932.

———. *Norakuro sōchō*. Tokyo: Dai Nippon Yubenkai Kodansha, 1935.

———. *Norakuro sōkōgeki*. Tokyo: Dai Nippon Yubenkai Kodansha, 1937.

———. "Norakuro tanjōki." In *Manga Kenkyū* 2, 46–47. Tokyo: Nihon Jidō Manga Kenkyūkai, n.d. (ca. 1950s).

———. *Norakuro tankentai*. Tokyo: Dai Nippon Yubenkai Kodansha, 1939.

———. *Norakuro tosshintai: Manga book*. Tokyo: Dai Nippon Yubenkai Kodansha, 1933.

———. *Norakuro zenshū*. Tokyo: Kodansha, 1967.

Tagawa Suihō and Takamizawa Junko. *Norakuro ichidaiki: Tagawa Suihō jijoden*. Tokyo: Kodansha, 1991.

Takamizawa Junko. "Tagawa Suihō no kioku." In *Tsuitō Tagawa Suihō-ten: Norakuro to ayunda 90-nen*, edited by Machida Shiritsu Kokusai Hanga

Bijutsukan, 11–14. Machida, Tokyo: Machida Shiritsu Kokusai Hanga Bijutsukan, 1990.

Takayuki Tatsumi. "Mori Minoru's Day of Resurrection." Translated by Christopher Bolton. *Mechademia* 1 (2006): 87–90.

Takeda, Shuichiro. *The Beginner's Guide to Manga and Anime*. New York: Scholastic, 2024.

Takekuma Kentarō. "Otaku no dai-ichi sedai no jiko bunseki: Akumade kojin-teki na tachina kara." In *Mōjō genron F-kai: Postmodern otaku sexuality*, edited by Azuma Hiroki, 101–4. Tokyo: Seidōsha, 2003.

Takemiya Keiko. *Kaze to ki no uta*. Tokyo: Hakusensha, 1995. 10 vols.

———. *Shōjo manga no sekai: Genga dash 10-nen no kiseki*. Kyoto: Kyoto Seika Daigaku Kokusai Manga Kenkyū Center, 2011.

———. *Shōnen no na wa Gilbert*. Tokyo: Shogakukan, 2016.

Takeuchi Osamu. "Mangashi ni okeru *Shō-chan no bōken*." In *Shō-chan no bōken*, 136–38. Tokyo: Shogakukan Creative, 2003.

———. *Sengo manga 50-nenshi*. Tokyo: Chikuma Shobō, 1995.

———. "*Shintakarajima* no bōken." In *Shintakarajima dokuhon*, supplement to *Shintakarajima* by Tezuka Osamu and Sakai Shichima, 15–27. Tokyo: Shogakukan Creative, 2009.

Tamamura Yuka, Nemoto Hikaru, and Sato Yō. "Kami no kogeru nioi no naka ni: REFCY kami film no digital-ka to animation eiga no ikōki." *Kyōritsu Review* 51 (2023): 41–63.

Tamura Hisako and Kurata Shin. "Watashi to manga: Tamura Hisako ga kotaru." *Bunka hyōron*, no. 208 (August 1978): 116–28.

Tatsumi Yoshihiro. *A Drifting Life*. Translated by Taro Nettleton. Montréal: Drawn & Quarterly, 2009.

———. *Gekiga hyōryū*. Tokyo: Seirin Kōgeisha, 2008. 2 vols.

Terada Hiroo. *"Manga Shōnen"-shi*. Fujisawa, Japan: Shōnan Shuppansha, 1981.

Tezuka Osamu. *Boku no manga jinsei*. Tokyo: Iwanami Shoten, 1997.

———. *Boku wa mangaka*. Tokyo: Kadokawa Shoten, 2000.

———. "Katō Ken'ichi-shi to watashi." In Terada Hiroo, *"Manga Shōnen"-shi*, 6–8. Fujisawa, Japan: Shōnan Shuppansha, 1981.

———. "Norakuro no miryoku." In Tagawa Suihō, *Norakuro zenshū*, 802–5. Tokyo: Kodansha, 1967.

———. *Tezuka Osamu: Sōsaku nōto to shoki sakuhin*. Tokyo: Shogakukan Creative, 2013.

Tezuka Osamu, Matsumoto Leiji, and Ōshiro Noboru. "'Oh! Manga' 2: Sensō made." In Asai Tarō and Ōshiro Noboru, *Kasei tanken*, 200–15. Tokyo: Tōdosha, 2003.

Thorn, Rachel. "Introduction." In Hagio Moto, *The Heart of Thomas*, translated by Rachel Thorn. Seattle: Fantagraphics Books, 2012.

Toshima-ku Kyōdo Shiryōkan and Tezuka Productions, eds. *Tokiwasō no herotachi: Manga ni kaketa seishun: Toshima-ku hatsu manga bunka o ichidō ni shōkai*. Tokyo: Toshima-ku, 2009.

"Transformational Fandom." Accessed February 19, 2017. https://fanlore.org/wiki/Transformational_Fandom.
Tsuge Yoshiharu. *The Man Without Talent*. Translated by Ryan Holmberg. New York: The New York Review of Books, 2019.
Uchida Roan. "Manga Mandan." *Bijutsu Shinron* 2, no. 8 (August 1927): 38–41.
Ueda Shinji. "*The Rose of Versailles:* A Takarazuka Grand Romantic Play." In *The Columbia Anthology of Modern Japanese Drama*, edited by J. Thomas Rimer, Mitsuya Mōri, and M. Cody Poulton, translated by Keiko Kawasaki, 663–89. New York: Columbia University Press, 2014.
Ueda Toshiko. *Fuichin-san*. Tokyo: Shogakukan, 2015. 2 vols.
———. "Jibun no 'hagemashi manga' o kaitara, *Fuichin-san* ga umareta." In *Manga daihakubutsukan*, edited by Matsumoto Leiji and Hidaka Satoshi, 335–38. Tokyo: Shogakukan Creative, 2004.
———. "Sokoku wa narete." In *Boku no Manshū: Mangaka-tachi no haisen taiken*, edited by Chūgoku Hikiage Mangaka no Kai, 1–26. Tokyo: Aki Shobō, 1995.
Ueno Kōshi. "The First Age of *Garo:* Opening Up the *Garo* Age." In *Wooden-Mortared Kingdom: Garo 20th Memorial Issue*, edited by Seirindō, 569–73. Tokyo: Seirindō, 1984.
Weisenfeld, Gennifer S. *MAVO: Japanese Artists and the Avant-Garde, 1905–1931*. Berkeley: University of California Press, 2002.
Welker, James. "A Brief History of Shōnen'ai, Yaoi, and Boys Love." In *Boys Love Manga and Beyond: History, Culture, and Community in Japan*, edited by Mark J. McLelland, Kazumi Nagaike, Katsuhiko Suganuma, and James Welker, 42–75. Jackson: University Press of Mississippi, 2015.
———. "Drawing Out Lesbians: Blurred Representations of Lesbian Desire in Shōjo Manga." In *Lesbian Voices: Canada and the World: Theory, Literature, Cinema*, edited by Subhash Chandra, 156–84. New Delhi: Allied Publishers, 2006.
———. "From Vicarious Voyages to Jumbo Jets: Shōjo Manga Artists and Fans Head Abroad in the 1970s and 1980s." Presentation at the National Conference of the Popular Culture Association, Seattle, March 25, 2016.
———. "Lilies of the Margin: Beautiful Boys and Queer Female Identities in Japan." In *AsiaPacifiQueer: Rethinking Genders and Sexualities*, edited by Fran Martin, Peter A. Jackson, Mark McLelland, and Audrey Yue, 46–66. Urbana: University of Illinois Press, 2008.
———. *Transfiguring Women in Late Twentieth-Century Japan: Feminists, Lesbians, and Girls' Comics Artists and Fans*. Honolulu: University of Hawai'i Press, 2024.
World Economic Forum. "Global Gender Gap Report 2022." July 13, 2022. https://www.weforum.org/reports/global-gender-gap-report-2022.
Wu, Chinghsin. *Parallel Modernism: Koga Harue and Avant-Garde Art in Modern Japan*. Oakland: University of California Press, 2019.
Yamada Murasaki. "A Fondness for Corners: An Interview with Yamada Murasaki (1985)." In *Second Hand Love*, translated by Ryan Holmberg, v–xii. Montréal: Drawn & Quarterly, 2024.

Yamagishi Akane. "Seinen manga gannen." In Shirato Sanpei et al., *Garo COM manga meisakusen 2: 1968–1971*, 28. Tokyo: Kodansha, 2012.
Yamagishi Ryōko. *Yamagishi Ryōko gashū terasu*. Tokyo: Kawade Shobō Shinsha, 2016.
Yamaguchi Saeko. "4-koma manga." In *Mangagaku nyūmon*, edited by Natsume Fusanosuke and Takeuchi Osamu, 8–14. Kyoto: Minerva Shobō, 2009.
Yamaguchi Yasuo. *Nihon no anime zenshi: Sekai o seishita Nihon anime no kiseki*. Tokyo: Ten Books, 2004.
Yamakoshi Masatoshi. "Kashihonya." In *Mangagaku nyūmon*, edited by Natsume Fusanosuke and Takeuchi Osamu, 34. Kyoto: Minerva Shobō, 2009.
Yamamoto Kanae. "Gendai no kokkeiga oyobi fūshiga nitsuite." *Hōsun*, February 1907, 3–4.
Yamanaka Tomomi. "Birth of 'Otaku': Centring on Discourse Dynamics in *Manga Burikko*." In *Debating Otaku in Contemporary Japan: Historical Perspectives and New Horizons*, edited by Patrick W. Galbraith, Björn-Ole Kamm, and Thiam Huat Kam, 35–50. London: Bloomsbury Academic, 2015.
Yamanashi, Makiko. *A History of the Takarazuka Revue Since 1914: Modernity, Girls' Culture, Japan Pop*. Leiden, The Netherlands: Global Oriental, 2012.
Yanase Masamu. *Yanase Masamu zenshū*. Edited by Yanase Masamu Zenshū Kankō Iinkai. Kyoto: Sanninsha, 2013–19. 5 vols.
Yazaki Shigeshi, Matsushita Ichio, Yamamoto Ichirō, and Hasegawa Machiko. *Yokusan manga susume Yamato ikka*. Tokyo: Nihon Ezasshisha, 1942.
Yokoyama Ryūichi. *Yokoyama Ryūichi: Waga yūgiteki jinsei*. Tokyo: Nihon Tosho Center, 1997.
Yomota Inuhiko. *Nihon no manga e no kansha*. Tokyo: Ushio Shuppan, 2013.
Yonezawa Yoshihiro. "Comiket: Sekai saidai no manga no saiten," in *Otaku no hon*, edited by Ishi'i Shinji, 75–88 (Tokyo: JICC Shuppankyoku, 1989).
———. "Comiket's Progress Towards Its 20th Occurrence, 1975–1982." In Comic Market Junbikai, *Comic Market Manual 1*. Tokyo: Comic Market Junbikai, 1982.
———. "Fukō to iu na no shiawase: *Shōnen King* no eikō to shūen." *Shōnen Natsu Man'ō* (zine) 18 (1995): 120–23.
———. "*Manga Shōnen* kara Comiket e . . . ." *Shōnen Natsu Man'ō* (zine) 16 (1995): 46–49.
———. "Shōwa 30-nen emonogatari no saishūshō." *Shōnen Natsu Man'ō* (zine) 19 (September 1995): 54–57.
———, ed. *Speech balloon ballad: Manga o meguru shōjo-tachi no bōken*. Tokyo: Kawade Shobō Shinsha, 1988.
———. "Uchū o boku no te no hira ni: Uchū SF manga no nagare." *Shōnen Natsu Man'ō* (zine) 12 (1992): 38–41.
Yonezawa Yoshihiro and Shikijō Kyōtarō. *2Bdan gindama sensō no hibi: Shōwa 30-nendai—yume no shōnen ōkoku*. Tokyo: Shinpyōsha, 1982.
Yoshida Takashi and Mizuno Ryō. "Interview Lecture on *Record of Lodoss War*." University of Tokyo (Komaba campus), Tokyo, July 18, 2014.

Yoshimi Shun'ya. "From Street Corner to Living Room: Domestication of TV Culture and National Time/Narrative." Translated by Jodie Beck. *Mechademia* 9 (2014): 126–42.

———. "Television and Nationalism: Historical Change in the National Domestic TV Formation of Postwar Japan." *European Journal of Cultural Studies* 6, no. 4 (2003): 459–87.

Young, Louise. *Japan's Total Empire: Manchuria and the Culture of Wartime Imperialism.* Berkeley: University of California Press, 1998.

Zenkoku Kashihon Kumiai Rengōkai. *Zenkoku kashihon shinbun: Fukkokuban.* Edited by Kajii Jun. Tokyo: Fuji Shuppan, 2010. 2 vols.

INDEX

A, A' (1981–84 manga series) (Hagio Moto), 246
advertising: *Allan* (semi-professional periodical), 271; in *Be Love,* 277; characters from US comics in, 333n42; in *Juné,* 265; in kashihon newspaper for manga, 162, 195; manga characters in, 40, 83–84, 328n32; manga influence on, 188; in *Manga no Kuni,* 109; in *Manga Shōnen,* 140; in *Shōjo Kurabu,* 110
aesthetics: aesthetic eroticism, 239; camp aesthetic, 266; children's sense of, 174; of David Bowie, 266; of girls' culture, 225; of *Juné,* 266; *Ribon* aesthetic, 291; of shōjo manga, 225–226; tanbi aesthetic, 266
aidokusha (super-fans), 73, 225, 228
akahon manga: criticism of, 172, 178; decline of, 128, 157, 158, 159–160; defined, 319; gekiga and, 163, 169; kashihon manga as evolution of, 159–160; kashihonya and, 180, 181; *Kawaii Betty-san,* plate 7, 82; Komatsu Sakyō and, 284; Misora Hibari and, 303; popularity of, 80–85, 89, 128, 131–138, 149; spread of, 158; Tagawa Suihō and, 78, 81, 274, 308; Tezuka Osamu and, 117, 129, 149–151, 180; Tezuka Osamu's drawings for, 1; Watanabe Masako and, 276
Akamatsu Rinsaku, 30
Akatsuka Fujio, 132, 155, 156, 205, 213
Akihabara massacre, 370–371n4
Akihito, Emperor, 5, 84
Akimi Yoshida, 264
Akita Shoten (publisher), 149, 151, 152, 373
Akiyama Mitsuru, 199, 204, 207
Allan (semi-professional periodical): advertising in, 267; creation of, 310; open-submission model, 291; personal ads, 271; shōnen'ai manga in, 255
Ama-chan no nikkichō (Ama-chan's diary) (1946 four-panel manga) (Tezuka Osamu), 131
androgynous aesthetic, 237, 238, 266, 271
Andromeda Stories (1980–1982 manga) (Mitsuse and Takemiya), 285
anime: based on *Sazae-san,* 2; based on *Tetsuwan Atomu* (*Astro Boy*), 1, 310; Comiket cosplayers, 285–286; dōjin sphere and, 311; first television series, 1; gender and, 313; manga and, 314; *Namakura gatana* (The dull sword) (1917 animation) (Kōuchi Jun'ichi), 30; otaku of, 321; *Saru to kani* (Battle of a monkey and a crab) (1917 animation) (Kitayama Seitarō), 30; Shimokawa Ōten as pioneer of, 29; Tezuka Osamu as pioneer of, 191, 215. *See also specific animators*
anime media mix: cross-media adaptations, 310; dōjin sphere and, 311; video games in, 293. *See also* merchandising
animeppoi (anime-like), 289–290
aniparo (anime parody), 256, 270, 297
Aniwa Jun, 260, 297
anti-comics mania in U.S., 349n63

Aoike Yasuko, 233, 264
Apple Core (1972–75 dōjinshi), 210
AS (manga group), 207, 208–209, 210, 211, 212, 213, 259
Asahi Graph, 39, 40–41, 83, 99, 110, 113, 117, 119
Asahi Shinbun (periodical), 139–140; children's manga in, 39; comparisons to, 222; on kashihonya, 175–176; McManus and, 41; Okamoto Ippei at, 4, 14, 33, 34, 39, 53; *Sazae-san* (1946–74 manga) (Hasegawa), 2, 142; on story manga, 194; trainee mangaka, 110; Yazaki Takeko, 142
Asakawa Mitsuhiro (Onoda Shō), 353n35
Ashita no Joe (Tomorrow's Joe) (1968–73 boxing manga), 235, 280
Asia-Pacific War (Fifteen Years' War), 60, 61, 87, 114
Asō Yukata, 41
Asterix (character), 312
Atom (character), 332n23. See also *Tetsuwan Atomu* (*Astro Boy*) (1952–68 manga series) (Tezuka Osamu)
August scaries (publishing), 81, 334n74
Azuma Hideo, 254, 286, 290–291
Azuma Hiroki, 256, 274

bakumatsu period, 16, 22
ban bad books movement, 129–130, 174–176, 195, 314
Banana Fish (1985–94 shōnen'ai series) (Akimi Yoshida), 264
bandes dessinées (BD), 8–9, 27, 256, 311–312, 314
Bat-kun (Bat Kid) (1947–49 baseball manga) (Inoue Kazuo), 130, 147–148, 152, 345n78
Baudinette, Thomas, 269, 365n54, 372n15
Be in Love/Be Love (periodical), 276–279, 358n46, 373
BELNE, 299
Berndt, Jaqueline, 8, 190, 310, 329n70
BeruBara/Berusaiyu no bara (*The Rose of Versailles*) (1972–74 shōjo manga) (Ikeda Riyoko): anime media mix, 245; fans of, 236, 245; popularity of, 236, 238, 243, 275; success of, 245; Takarazuka stage version, 244–245. See also *The Rose of Versailles* (*Berusaiyu no bara*) (1972–74 shōjo manga) (Ikeda Riyoko)
Bessatsu Friend (periodical), 227
bessatsu furoku: competitions, 155; defined, 320; as marketing strategy, 228; pay rate increases for, 153–154; Tagawa Suihō and, 80–81; Tezuka Osamu and, 151
Bessatsu Margaret (periodical), 241, 290
Bessatsu Shōjo Comic (periodical), 259
Bessatsu Shōnen Magazine (periodical), 199
Big Comic (periodical), 218–220, 219*fig.*, 225, 277, 373
Bigot, Georges, 24
Bijutsu Shinron (periodical), 47, 56, 101
bishōjo manga, 254–255, 281, 286, 288–293, 305
bishōnen, 265, 266, 267
BL/boys' love manga: *Allan* (semi-professional periodical) and, 271; defined, 321; emergence of, 264, 288, 310, 321; expansion of, 315; gay men readers of, 365n54; gender of fans of, 269, 365n60; *Juné* (semi-professional periodical) and, 267, 271; *Kaze to ki no uta* (Song of the wind and trees) (1976–84 manga series), 263–264; Kumota Haruko, 283; lolicon dōjinshi, 291; shōnen'ai manga and, 238; *Sōsaku JUNE* (original June) term, 364n39; Takemiya Keiko and, 263–264, 265*fig. See also* shōnen'ai manga; yaoi manga
Bōken Dankichi (Adventure Dankichi) (1933–39 manga) (Shimada Keizō), 79*fig.*, 80, 86, 87–88, 89, 94, 114, 116, 147
Bōken Katsugeki Bunko (periodical), 373
book design: of *Norakuro* (1931–41 manga) (Tagawa Suihō), 78, 334n61; Shimokawa Ōten (Hekoten) on, 101; Tagawa Suihō and, 334n61; Yanase Masamu and, 334n61. *See also* format
The Book of Otaku (Otaku no hon), 255, 288
Bowie, David, 266, 358n46
Box of Curios (periodical), 2, 16, 24, 373
Boxer Rebellion, 25
Bringing Up Father (1913–2000 four-panel strip) (McManus), 41
Bubble economy, 5, 254, 256, 294, 320
Buta no heso (The pig's navel), 50

Captain Tsubasa (1981–88 manga), 270, 282, 295
caricatures: art style of, 34, 46, 66, 97, 104; British tradition of, 17; criticism of style of, 108–109, 111, 164; of Edo period, 52; manga referred to as, 13; in *Puck,* 26
cartoonists. *See* mangaka (manga creator)
cat ears (nekomimi) manga trope, 292
censorship: ban bad books movement, 129–130, 172, 174–176, 195, 314; Comics Code Authority, 172; consultation meetings, 90–92, 107; escalation after 1931, 87; Home Ministry media censorship, 88, 88–91; *The Japan Punch* and, 17; under New Order, 103, 106–108, 112; Nihon Jidōmangaka Kyōkai (Japan Children's Mangaka Association) and, 89; paper-rationing edict and, 89, 91, 91*fig.*, 92, 113; ponchi-e and, 3; under SCAP during Occupation, 138
Chame to Dekobō (Brown Eyes and Beetle-Brow/Playfulness and Mischief) (1902 manga) (Rakuten), 30, 66
Chameken to Norakuro (Chameken and Norakuro) (1948 manga) (Tagawa Suihō), 90, 173
Chaplin, Charlie, 41, 53, 67–68, 70, 71, 308
Chibikuro (1945 manga) (Tagawa Suihō), 131
children's manga: akahon manga boom, 80–85, 128, 135, 149; American animation and, 115–116, 128–129; anthologies and, 45; censorship, 88–89, 92; Children's Manga Research Group, 208, 210; commercialism and, 84; consumerism, 62, 88; conventions of, 164; criticism of, 62, 84; defined, 55; diversification of, 165; emergence of, 178; end of, 153–157, 216, 223; expansion of, 39, 308, 321; humor in, 156; *Manga Shōnen,* 149; merchandising, 73–79; nonsense manga and, 55; Okamoto Ippei and, 38; paper-rationing edict and, 116; popularity of, 2; readers' letters in, 326n57; reinvention of, 308–309; rise of, 64–67, 309; rise of militarism and, 42, 62, 86, 87, 114–115; *Shōnen Kurabu* (Boys' club) (periodical), 2; story manga and, 180; wartime restrictions on, 85–92. *See also* bessatsu furoku; Fukui Ei'ichi; *Jungle taitei* (Jungle emperor, *Kimba the White Lion*) (1950–1954 shōnen series) (Tezuka Osamu); Kitazawa Rakuten; kodomo manga (jidō); *Norakuro* (1931–41 manga) (Tagawa Suihō); Okamoto Ippei; shōjo manga; *Shōnen Kurabu* (Boys' club) (periodical); shōnen manga; Tagawa Suihō; Tezuka Osamu
China, 24, 28, 61, 86–87, 104, 108, 110, 315, 336n117
Chōjūgiga, 47
Chūjō Shōhei, 67
Chun, Jayson Makoto, 177–178
Clements, Jonathan, 190, 351n7
colonization: imperial colonies, 65, 86, 89, 90, 150, 156, 320; by Japan, 24–25; Japan's seizure of Germany's Asian colonies, 37; letters from imperial colonies, 73, 77; peasants as colonists, 336n117
COM (periodical): Akiyama Mitsuru and, 199, 207; alternative manga and, 187, 305; amateur manga submissions, 211–212; anti-manga activism and, 205; *Big Comic* and, 218; contests, 206; dōjinshi sphere and, 205–206, 207, 259, 275, 300; editorial freedom and, 217; end of, 205, 210, 211, 258; fandoms and, 205, 206, 310; on foreign manga, 256; Furukawa Masuzō and, 203; gender and, 202, 206; *Gura-Com* (Grand Companion) section, 207–211; Hagio Moto and, 233; influence of, 281; innovations of, 187–188, 200; Katō Misako and, 146; Masaki Mori and, 203–204; masukomii (mass communications) and, 215; Nakamura Kimihiko and, 298; Okada Fumiko and, 206; publication information, 373; readership of, 202, 205, 206, 208, 211–212; roundtable discussions, 204, 215–216, 222, 229–231; science fiction elements of, 284; *Shūkan Young Jump* and, 281; Takemiya Keiko and, 206, 239; Tezuka Osamu and, 186–187, 199, 203–205, 218, 246; Yamada Murasaki and, 202, 206, 207

COM Comics, 210
Comic Cuts (British periodical), 41
Comic Jun/June (periodical), 264–265, 373
Comic Life (British periodical), 41
comics: characters from US comics in ads, 333n42; comparisons to, 314; Euro-American comics, 4, 314, 330n3; fan communication through, 4; gender and, 313
Comics Code Authority, 172, 174, 314
Comiket (Comic Market): amateurs and, 296–302; *Apple Core* and, 210; creation of, 253–254; dōjin sphere and, 301, 304, 314; dōjinshi production and, 6–7, 319; as fan event, 309, 310; lolicon comics, 290–291; Meikyū and, 258–263; otaku at, 287; participant terminology, 363n19; science fiction and, 285–286; *Sōsaku JUNE* (original June) term, 364n39; spring school holiday events, 364n20
Comintern, 103, 338n44
Comitia, 256, 296–300, 301, 304, 319
commercialism, 75, 84, 90–91, 175, 177, 203, 214
compulsory education, 3, 19, 20, 76
Condry, Ian, 36, 287
constitutional monarchy, 20–21, 22
contests: *COM* contests, 206, 207; fan club contests, 273; *Jiji Manga* contests, 95; in kashihon anthologies, 202, 204; *Manga Shōnen* contests, 147–148; *Manga to Yomimono* contests, 141; mangaka and, 130, 164; in *Ribon*, 233; in *Shōjo Friend*, 233; Tatsumi Yoshihiro and, 141, 349n54; *Tokyo Puck* contests, 26. *See also* submissions
Cool Japan campaign, 314
cosplay, 228, 261, 272, 285, 297
Crime and Punishment (*Tsumi to batsu*) (1953 akahon adaptation) (Tezuka Osamu), 149–150
cute eroticism (kawaiiero), 290–291
cuteness (kawai-rashisa), 289–290
Cybele (dōjinshi anthology series), 254, 290

Dangokushisuke manyūki (Record of Dangokushisuke's pleasure trip) (Miyao Shigeo), 82
Daumier, Honoré, 19
DC Comics, 312–313
De Kosnik, Abigail, 269, 272, 273
Dekoboko Kurobē (Beetlebrow kid Kurobē) (1933–36 bessatsu furoku) (Tagawa Suihō), 81
democracy: after postwar constitution, 127; ban bad books movement and, 172–177; Democratic Party of Japan, 236; expansion of, 60; *Garo* as pro-democratic, 198; imperial democracy, 56, 101; Shimoda Ken'ichirō's support for, 106; transition to, 322
distribution: akahon manga and, 135; anime and, 190, 191; developments in, 31; distribution companies, 107; modernization of, 54; nontraditional outlets for, 128; Occupation inspections before, 144; outlets for akahon manga, 319; patterns of, 161; postwar networks of, 161, 180
dōjin (amateurs): first wave in 1930s, 62–63, 93, 109–110, 117, 130, 159, 207, 211; second wave in 1950s, 128–130, 142–143, 148, 157, 158–163, 169–172, 207, 236; third wave in 1970s-, 6–7, 187–189, 207. See also *COM* (periodical); fan clubs
dōjin goods, xvi, 83–84, 191, 228–229, 276, 319
dōjin magazines (dōjin zasshi), 212, 213, 319. *See also* zasshi (magazine); zines
dōjin media, 310, 319. *See also* video games
dōjin sphere, 7, 284, 295–296, 300–301, 304, 309–311, 314–315
dōjin zasshi. *See* dōjin zasshi (dōjin magazines)
dōjin zasshi (dōjin magazines), 213; WWII and, 211
dōjinshi (amateur publications): as alternative manga, 310; bishōjo comics, 286; *COM* and, 213; as coterie magazines, 274–275; influence on seinen manga, 310; AS (manga group), 209; relationship with professionals, 4–5; term usage, xvi, 211, 212, 319
dōjinshi circles: *COM* and, 206, 208, 210, 212, 213, 310; Comiket and, 260–262, 285; Comitia, 298, 299; events, 297–298;

fan clubs evolving into, 263; fanfiction/nijisōsaku, 297; increased competition among, 297; literary circles, 211; parody and, 270; regional circles, 298
Dōjinshi Grand Prix, 280
Donkey Kong (1980 video game) (Nintendo), 293–294
Dragon Ball (1984–85 manga), 282
Dragon Quest media mix, 295
Dream of the Rarebit Fiend (1904–11 comic strip) (McCay), 51

earthquakes: Great Kanto Earthquake (1923), 40–43, 44, 51, 52, 101, 307; Hanshin earthquake (1995), 320; Tōhoku earthquake (2011), 320
Edo period (1600–1867): culture of, 20, 319; defined, 319; education methods, 22; influences of, 25; Japanese traditions in, 15; kibyōshi (graphic fiction), 329n70; *manga* (term) usage, 4, 13, 26, 48, 323n1; nostalgia for, 15; print culture of, 3, 17; ukiyo-e (woodblock print) in, 322
education: Imperial Rescript on Education, 21–22; reforms in Meiji period, 20; school enrollment, 21–22
ehon (picture books): defined, 319; at Kodansha series, 83, 139
eiga manga (film manga), 29–30, 35–36, 74, 130, 132, 214
Eisenstein, Sergei, 115, 116, 137
Eji Sonta, 287
emonogatari: appeal of, 227; *Bōken Dankichi* as, 80; in children's magazines, 67, 70; comparisons to, 169; defined, 319; disappearance of, 154, 222; Fukui Ei'ichi and, 153; in *Manga Shōnen,* 145, 149; in *Nakayoshi,* 227; in *Shōnen Kurabu,* 67, 70; term usage, 89
ero gekiga style, 286
eromanga: bishōjo-style, 288–293; comparisons to, 220, 264; defined, 319; ero gekiga style, 286; influence of, 293; lolicon and, 290–292; *Manga Burikko* as, 291–292; moral panics and, 296; readership of, 281, 292–293; rise of, 188; Takahashi Rumiko and, 283; Tezuka Osamu on, 195
eroticism: in *Big Comic,* 219, 220; in BL/boys' love manga, 239; kawaiiero (cute eroticism), 290–291; in lolicon manga, 254; of Lum, 282; in *Manga,* 139; in seinen manga, 187, 220–221, 223; in *Shinyūkan* (New evening news) (periodical), 139; shōjo revolution creators and, 267–269; tanbi aesthetic and, 266; Tezuka Osamu on, 220–221
Euro-American comics: exposure to, 4; influence of, 15, 41, 307; manga history and, 314; movies and, 53; as nonsense manga, 307; parallel modernisms concept and, 330n3; publishing model for, 312–313; transnational connections, 8, 123
Exner, Eike, 42

fan clubs: *COM* and, 205; *Gura-Com* (Grand Companion) and, 207–211; mangaka and, 205. *See also* Akatsuka Fujio; Kaizuka Hiroshi; Tatsumi Yoshihiro; *specific mangaka fan clubs*
fan cultures: 1960s growth of, 187; gekiga and, 309; shōjo manga and, 310; Tezuka Osamu and, 310
fanfiction, 136, 213, 256, 269, 272, 274, 297, 310, 343n30
fans/fandoms: aidokusha (super-fans), 73, 225, 228; displacement of manga by, 311; fan circles, 206, 208; fan films, 4, 254; fan networks, 207, 210; fanboy/fangirl, xvi; fanworks, xvi; fanzine, xvi; Hagio Moto and, 242, 254, 259, 263, 273, 286; in postmodern period, 274; role in development and popularity of manga, 6, 309. *See also* Comiket; dōjinshi; Nihon Manga Taikai (ManTai)
Farewell Space Battleship Yamato (*Saraba uchū senkan Yamato: Ai no senshitachi*) (1978 anime film) (Matsumoto Leiji), 284
fascism: censorship by Homes Ministry, 88–91, 173; children's manga as target under, 85–92; debate over children's manga, 84–86, 113–116, 173; kokutai (national body) and, 99–100; military content in children's manga, 86–87, 88,

fascism *(continued)*
114–116; national policy manga, 108–116; Patriotic Youth Brigade, 89–90; Peace Preservation Laws and, 103, 106; proletarian arts movement and, 100–108, 109; propaganda production under, 89–91, 93, 112; in Shōwa period, 322; during wartime and Occupation, 59–63

Felix the Cat (cartoon character) (Messmer and Sullivan), 70, 71, 115, 308

Fifteen Years' War. *See* Asia-Pacific War (Fifteen Years' War)

film manga. *See* eiga manga (film manga)

Fire! (1969–71 manga series) (Mizuno Hideko), 231–232, 266

Fist of the North Star (Hokuto no ken) (1983–88 manga), 282

format: A4 format, 311; A5 format, 172; affordability, 248, 249, 312; akahon manga, 89, 128, 131, 135, 136, 158, 172; B4 format, plate 9, 26, 96; B5 format, 82, 140, 164, 172; B6 format, 131, 135, 140, 248, 319; B7 format, 135; B8 format, 135; *bandes dessinées* (BD), 311, 312; baseball analogy, 249; demographics and, 249, 313; digital format, 312; of fan films, 254; four-panel format, 38, 40–41, 42, 43–44, 66, 72, 107, 113, 140–141, 209, 294, 308; importance of, 7; innovations of, 4, 5; kabe shinbun format, 209; kamishibai format, 136; kashihon manga format, 157, 158–163, 164, 172, 309; magazine format, 30, 42, 55, 86, 141, 185, 186, 193; newspaper format, 19, 41–42, 55–56; one-volume story format, 193; popularity and, 315; portability, 248, 249, 312; publishers and, 7; questions of, 311–312; readers and, 7; shōsetsu manga, 39; tankōbon paperbacks, 74, 82–83, 247, 247–248; yonkoma format, 140. *See also* platforms

The Four Immigrants Manga (Manga yonin shosei) (1931 manga) (Kiyama "Henry" Yoshitaka), 54–55

Freedom and Popular Rights movement, 20–21, 21*fig.*

From Eroica with Love (*Eroica yori ai o komete*) (1979–2012 shōnen'ai series) (Aoike Yasuko), 264

fudanshi, 288, 319, 365n60

Fuichin (character), 142, 156–157

Fuichin-san (1957–62 manga) (Ueda Toshiko), 156, 217

Fujiko F. Fujio, 133, 154, 155

Fujiko Fujio A, 154, 155, 216

Fujiko Fujio (duo), 132, 133, 146, 148, 154

Fujimoto Yukari, 231, 237

Fujin Kurabu (Ladies' club) (periodical), 64, 81, 99

Fujin no Tomo (Lady's friend) (periodical), 81

Fujiwara period, 48, 49, 329n67

fujoshi, xvi, 272–273, 277, 288, 319

Fukui Ei'ichi, 129, 146, 151–154, 157

Fukuzawa Yukichi, 16, 21, 22, 24

Funny (periodical), 206, 241, 373

furoku (freebies): in 1960s manga, 1; defined, 320; in late 1970s, 358n46; as missing from pre-owned copies, 78; *Shōnen Kurabu* and, 79*fig.*; Tagawa Suihō and, 80; Tezuka Osamu and, 151; translation of, 358n41; in women's magazines, 81; *Yōnen Zasshi* (periodical), 326n57. *See also* bessatsu furoku

Fūshiga Kenkyūkai (Caricature Research Group), 108–109

Galbraith, Patrick W., 254–255, 273, 287, 288, 289–290, 291, 293

The Game of Death (Kahn), 349n63

Garo (periodical), 186, 187; as alternative manga, 187, 256, 304, 305; gekiga manga and, 200, 201; gender-based violence in, 201–202; influence of, 281; innovations of, 187; publication information, 373; shishōsetsu (I-novel) and, 212

Gegege no Kitarō (1968 anime adaptation) (Mizuki Shigeru), 137, 196

gekiga: in 1950s, 6, 129; 1960s and 1970s creators, 6, 309; action in, 167; ban bad books movement and, 129–130, 174, 174–175; *Big Comic* (periodical) and, 218, 219; *COM* (periodical) and, 203–207; defined, 320; dōjin second wave,

207; Fukui Ei'ichi and, 153–154; *Garo* (periodical) and, 200, 201; Gekiga Kōbō (Gekiga Workshop) group, 129, 165–166, 171; Hinomaru Bunko and, 143; Ichijō Yukari and, 232; Ikeda Riyoko and, 236; influence of, 224, 281, 286, 290; Ishikawa Fumiyasu, 166–167; K. Motomitsu, 166–167, 168, 171; kashihon and, 171; lolicon comics and, 290; Maki Miyako and, 276; manga as including, 208, 222; *Manga Burikko* and, 291; Matsumoto Masahiko and, 164–165; Nakajima Fumio and, 290; Ōtsuka Eiji and, 367n2; phenomena of, 168–172; philosophy of, 168; popularity of, 222, 223, 224, 280, 305, 309; proto-gekiga, 321; rejection of, 281, 290; Saito Takao and, 164, 171, 218, 222; Sakurai Shōichi, 165, 166, 167; Satō Masa'aki, 167, 168, 174–175; seinen manga and, 310; self-promotion, 212, 213; *Shōnen Jump* and, 256; *Shōnen Magazine* and, 200, 222; spread of, 158, 200; story manga and, 171, 180, 309; Tatsumi Yoshihiro and, 129, 163–166, 171–172, 200, 212; Tezuka Osamu and, 166, 167; Tsurita Kuniko and, 202; Yamamori Susumu, 168

Gekiga hyōryū (*A Drifting Life*, 1998–2006) (Tatsumi Yoshihiro), 174

Gekiga Kōbō (Gekiga Workshop) group, 129, 165–166, 170–171

gekigaka: disagreement among, 171; on gekigaka, 166–167; Hayao Miyazaki, 170; Ikeda Riyoko as, 236; influence of, 164; kashihon readership and, 166, 168; Matsumoto Masahiko as, 323n1; revolt against story manga, 309; submissions and, 169

Gekigakkai (Gekiga world) zine, 169, 170

Gellert, Hugo, 104

Gendai manga taikan (Contemporary manga survey), 44–49, 50, 52, 53, 55, 97

Gendai renzoku manga zenshū (Collected contemporary serial manga) (1935 anthology), 81, 116

gender issues: *Bat Kid* and, 147; children's manga and, 221, 320–321; Comiket and, 286; fan cultures and, 270–275; *Fuichin-san* and, 157; gender equality, 232, 237; gender roles, 179, 185, 221, 226, 227, 231, 237–238, 241, 288–290; gender-based violence, 201–202; gendered weeklies, 227; genre categories, 185, 186, 216; josei manga and, 275–279; male super-fans, 321; manga and, 246, 313; marketing strategies, 187; *Norakuro* and, 76; patriarchal gender expectations, 241–242; seinen as de-gendered, 187–188, 255, 300, 304, 310, 321; shōjo revolution, 247–248; *Shōnen Kurabu* and, 2, 76; *Yōnen Kurabu* and, 76. *See also* heterosexuality; homosexual representation; otaku; queerness; shōjo manga; shōnen manga; shōnen'ai manga

Genji picture scrolls, 329n63

girlness (shōjo-sei), 289–290

GL/girls' love manga, 360n98; defined, 322

Gōtō Shinpei, 29

Great Kanto Earthquake (1923), 40–43, 44, 51, 52, 101, 307, 322

Grosz, George, 104, 105

Gundam (1979–80 anime), 254, 285–286, 287

Gura-Com (Grand Companion) section, 207–211

Gura-Com Nihon, 210

Hachi no ki (manga show and zine) (AS), 210

Hagio Moto: assistants' pay, 359n71; *COM* and, 206, 233; Comiket and, 263, 286; debut, 233; on Edgar and Allan's age, 361n104; fans/fandoms and, 242, 254, 259, 263, 273, 286; *Garo* and, 202; *The Heart of Thomas*, 242; Ikeda Riyoko and, 237, 361n104; Kodansha and, 277, 359n75; *A, A'* (manga), 246; Masuyama Norie and, 233, 233–234, 238; on meeting with Takemiya, 359n66; "November Gymnasium," 259; Ōizumi Salon and, 234–235, 243; pay rate of, 359n75; *Pō no ichizoku* (*The Poe Clan*), 242–243, 248, 271, 361n104; popularity of, 242; readership of, 248, 285, 286; research for manga practices, 232; science fiction

Hagio Moto *(continued)*
books of, 285, 359n72; Shogakukan and, 277; shōjo manga and, 187, 254, 286, 359n68; shōnen'ai manga and, 241, 243; Shōwa 24 Group, 232, 233, 234, 242, 273; style of, 242; Takemiya Keiko and, 233–234, 238, 241, 359n66; Yamamoto Jun'ya and, 239, 242
Hakaba no Kitarō (Graveyard Kitarō, 1965–69 yōkai manga) (Mizuki Shigeru), 196, 217
"Hakase no chinsetsu" (The professor's novel idea) (1899 manga) (Imaizumi Ippyō), 23*fig.*
Hakubai-kai art society, 22
Halperin, David M., 272
hanji-e (rebus print) techniques, 18, 19–20
Happy Hooligan (1900–32), 41–42, 42, 43
Haruko-chan (1961 strip) (Yazaki Takeko), 142
Haruna Yuri, 245
Hasegawa Kazuo, 244
Hasegawa Machiko: anthologies and, 84; career of, 63, 142; debut, 225; as manga reader, 6, 130, 309; museum in Setagaya, Tokyo, 344n45; popularity of, 142, 163, 171; *Sazae-san* and, 2, 136, 139–140, 146; *Shōjo Kurabu* and, 139; Tagawa Suihō and, 2, 84, 118. See also *Sazae-san* (1946–1974 four-panel manga) (Hasegawa Machiko)
Hasegawa Mariko, 139–140
Hasegawa Nyozekan, plate 8, 95
Hayakawa (publisher), 285
The Heart of Thomas (shōjo manga) (Hagio Moto), 242, 248, 263, 279
Heisei period (1989–2019), 5, 9, 179, 320
Hekoten (Shimokawa Ōten). *See* Shimokawa Ōten (Hekoten)
Hello! Manga (periodical), 131
Hergé, 67, 312
heterosexuality: assumptions of, 270, 272; in Japanese society, 271; otaku and, 277; in *Ribon no kishi,* 227; in *The Rose of Versailles,* 238; in shōjo manga, 277; sidestepping social norms of, 241–242; unequal heterosexual relationships, 268. *See also* gender issues
Hi izuru tokoro no tenshi (Prince of the land of the rising sun) (1980–84 shōnen'ai series) (Yamagishi Ryōko), 264
Hi no tori (*Phoenix*) (manga series) (Tezuka Osamu), 149, 204, 205, 227, 284
High Treason Incident, 31–32, 35
Hinomaru Bunko (publisher), 135, 143, 164
Hinomaru Hatanosuke (1935–41 manga) (Nakajima Sakuo), 80
Hirohito, Emperor, 5, 303
Hokusai, 13, 44, 47, 48, 323n1
homogenization, 104, 162, 213
homophobia, 241, 243, 271, 272
homosexual representation: fan cultures and, 269; historical representations of, 266; platonic "dōseiai" media, 237–238; same-sex marriage, 271, 365n53, 372n17; sapphic relationships, 322; in shōnen'ai manga, 270–271; in *Thomas,* 242; in "Yuki to hoshi to tenshi to," 239. *See also* BL/boys' love manga; shōnen'ai manga; yaoi manga
Honda Kinkichirō, 19, 20, 21*fig.*
Hosokibara Seiki, 46, 47–48, 329n63, 329n67
humor writing (gibun), 19–20

Ichijō Yukari, 232, 233, 242, 264, 275
Igaguri-kun (1952–54/1954–60 judo manga) (Fukui Ei'ichi), 152–153, 163
Ikebe Hitoshi, 46
Ikeda Riyoko: on impact of *The Rose of Versailles,* 275; kashihon gekiga manga and, 236; on Oscar, 238; *The Poe Clan* connection, 361n104; readership of, 236–237; Shōwa 24 Group and, 187, 235–236. See also *The Rose of Versailles* (Ikeda Riyoko)
Imai Yone, 343n36
Imaizumi Ippyō: "Hakase no chinsetsu" (The professor's novel idea) (1899 manga), 23*fig.*; impact of, 55, 307; innovations of, 4, 22–23, 307; at *Jiji Shinpō* newspaper, 16, 24; manga term usage by, 2, 3, 4, 8, 14, 16, 25, 53; as pioneer of manga, 14; political manga of, 33

Imokawa Mukuzō genkanban no maki (Story of the concierge Imokawa Mukuzō) (Shimokawa Ōten), 29
"In the Sunroom" ("Sanrūmu nite") (Takemiya), 239–240, 240*fig.*
Inagaki Taruho, 239
Inoue Kazuo, 84, 130, 147–148, 345n78
I-novel (shishōsetsu), 212, 332n27
Ippei. *See* Okamoto Ippei
Ippyō. *See* Imaizumi Ippyō
Ishii Hakutei, 48
Ishinomori Shōtarō: Anpo protests and, 188; *Big Comic* and, 219–220; on cinematic-style techniques, 150, 152; *COM* and, 218; debut, 151–152; income, 347n11; influences on, 115; *Japan Inc.*, 301; *Jun*, 204, 205, 284; *Manga Shōnen* and, 148; *Shintakarajima* and, 132; shōjo manga and, 225; Tezuka Osamu and, 150, 166, 204, 215; Tokiwa-sō group and, 154–155, 171
Itō Aiko, 234
Itō Gō, 266, 281
Itō Kimio, 290

Japan Children's Manga Research Group, 210
The Japan Punch (periodical): importance of, 49; origins of, 17–18; political cartoons of, 24; ponchi-e (ponchi) and, 8, 19; publication information, 373; Wirgman and, 307
Jenkins, Henry, 272
jidō manga (kodomo), 156, 208, 320. *See also* kodomo manga (jidō)
Jiggs and Maggie (four-panel format), 41, 113
jiguchi-e (pun prints), 20
Jiji manga hibijutsu gahō (Timely manga unartistic illustrated news) (periodical), 25
Jiji Manga (periodical), 50; audiences of, 93; *Chame to Dekobō* (Brown Eyes and Beetle-Brow/Playfulness and Mischief) (1902 manga) (Rakuten), 30; covers, plate 4, plate 5, 50; as flip-flopper, 328n43; four-panel manga and, 40; name changes, 93–95; nonsense manga, 41–44; publication information, 373; Rakuten and, 37–38, 50, 66, 94, 95, 337n32; Sunday supplement, 24, 37
Jiji Shinpō (periodical), 2, 4, 16, 21–26, 32, 33, 37–38, 39, 141
Jinzō ningen (Artificial human) (1929 sci-fi manga) (Tagawa Suihō), 59, 68, 69
Jō Akiko, 234
josei manga, 202, 207, 246, 255, 275–279, 276, 300, 320, 321
Joshikai (Women's world) (periodical), 39
Jōtō Ponchi (High-class ponchi) (periodical), 48
Judy (1985–2008 magazine), 278
Jun (1967–71 manga) (Ishinomori Shōtarō), 204, 205, 284
June (semi-professional periodical): advertising in, 265; creation of, 255, 265–267, 271, 310; freebies in, 358n46; open-submission model, 291; publishing industry, 373; readership of, 271, 277; shōnen'ai manga and, 267–268
Jungle taitei (Jungle emperor, *Kimba the White Lion*) (1950–1954 shōnen series) (Tezuka Osamu), 149–150
Jungle taitei (Jungle emperor, *Kimba the White Lion*) (1965–67 anime) (Yamamoto), 195

Kabashima Katsuichi (Tōfūjin), 39, 40
Kage (Shadow) (1956–66 gekiga anthology), 161, 164
Kahn, Albert E., 349n63
Kai Yukiko, 234
Kaijin skeleton hakushi (1948 akahon) (Komatsu), plate 10, 135, 367n26
Kamakura period, 329n63
kamishibai: anime and, 186, 190, 191, 196, 244; contemporary videos of, 343n34; defined, 320; description of, 136–137, 138*fig.*; emonogatari and, 67, 319; end of, 155–156; gekiga and, 163, 200; Imai Yone on, 343n36; kashihonya and, 196; manga professionals and, 137–138; Norakuro and, 74; as resurrected media, 136; television and, 138, 156, 178, 186; as transwar continuities in manga and, 128; Ueda Toshiko and, 90; during wartime and Occupation, 137

Kanemochi kyōiku (Bringing up money-bags) (1930–31 strip) (Yanase Masamu), plate 8, 94–96, 104
kanji, 20, 144, 331n2
Kanno Sugako, 31–32
Kanokogi Takeshirō, 25
Kanto Massacre, 43
Karikare (Caricature) (periodical), 109, 110–111, 373
karōshi (death by overwork), 289
Karutobi Karusuke: Manga monogatari (Karutobi Karusuke: Manga story) (Miyao Shigeo), 66
Kasei tanken (Mars expedition) (1940 science manga) (Ōshiro Noboru and Asai Tarō), 119, 284
kashihon manga: anthologies, 205, 212; ban bad books movement and, 174–175; creators of, 159–160, 161, 217; as evolution of akahon, 159–160; Fukui Ei'ichi and, 153–154; gekiga and, 171, 200, 207, 309; gender and, 160, 161; Ishinomori and, 347n11; marketing, 160–161; outlets for, 320; payment level for, 353n48; spread of, 158–163. *See also* Kaneko Hisako; Mizuki Shigeru; Takizawa Michiko
kashihonya: anime and, 192–193; ban bad books movement and, 129–130, 172, 175–177, 179, 193, 194; contemporary manga and, 182; decline of, 197, 229, 236; decrease in, 371n11; defined, 320; fan meetups and, 195; gekiga and, 165; importance of, 232; kamishibai and, 196; manga publishers and, 193, 194; in postwar period, 180–181, 313; shōjo manga and, 195; spread of, 158–163; television and, 196
Katei Puck (Household Puck) (periodical), 32
Katō Etsuro, 93, 108–116, 120*fig.*, 127
Katō Ken'ichi, 84, 114, 144–146, 149, 151, 173, 345n67
Katō Yoshirō, 117, 139
The Katzenjammer Kids (comic strip) (Knerr), 24, 96
Kawabata Ryūshi, 30–31
Kawaii Betty-san (1934 akahon), plate 7, 82
kawai-rashisa (cuteness), 289–290
Kaze to ki no uta (Song of the wind and trees) (1976–84 manga series) (Takemiya Keiko), 263–265, 265*fig.*
Keaton, Buster, 71
Kern, Adam L., 13
kibyōshi (graphic fiction), 3, 329n70
kikanshi (in-house publication), 109, 110, 211–212
Kimi Rito, 292, 368n34
Kinema Comic (British periodical), 41
Kinema Junpō, 337n6
Kingu (King) (periodical), 64
Kinnikuman (*Ultimate Muscle*) (1979–87 manga), 282
Kitayama Seitarō, 30
Kitazawa Rakuten: at *Box of Curios*, plate 1, 16, 24; *Buta no heso* (The pig's navel), 50; collected works, 45; early career of, 23–30; forms used by, 38; *Gendai manga taikan* (Contemporary manga survey), 46, 47; impact of, 55; as innovator, 5–6, 44, 302, 307; Ippei and, 33–37, 38, 43; *Jiji Manga* and, 37–38, 66; at *Jiji Shinpō*, 2, 37, 38, 39, 66; Kondō's discussion with, 112–113; as later establishment figure, 6; manga term usage by, 4, 16, 37; modernity and, 50, 51–52; museum in Saitama, 317; Nihon Manga Hōkōkai (Japan Manga Public Duty Group) and, 116; on origin of manga, 49; as pioneer of manga, 14, 35–36, 98, 99; political manga of, 107; retirement from *Jiji*, 94, 95, 337n32; early cartoonist career, 2; students and assistants of, 36, 38, 80, 110, 217; Tokyo Mangakkai, 36; *Tokyo Puck* and, 4, 14, 25–30, 32, 33, 35, 53; topical satire of, 65–66; on women mangaka, 95
"Kitsune no men" (The fox's face) (1935 manga) (Hasegawa), 139
Kiyama "Henry" Yoshitaka, 54–55, 118
Kobayashi Hideo, 71, 143, 332n27
Kobayashi Ichizō, 226
Kobayashi Kiyochika, 20
Kōdan Kurabu (Conversation club) (periodical), 64
Kodansha: animators and, 152; animators move to, 152; *Be in Love/Be Love* (peri-

odical), 276–279; children's manga, 62, 64–67; comparisons to, 113, 239; Ehon series, 131, 139, 144–145, 319; *Fujin Kurabu* (periodical), 81; Hagio Moto and, 239, 359n75; Hasegawa Machiko and, 139; Katō Ken'ichi and, 144, 146–147, 151; during Occupation, 144; pay rate at, 199; sibling magazines of, 59–60, 64, 73, 146, 225; Tagawa Suihō and, 68, 69, 143, 308. See also *Norakuro* (1931–41 manga) (Tagawa Suihō); *Shōnen Kurabu*
kodomo manga (jidō): defined, 320–321; Okamoto Ippei and, 38–39. *See also* children's manga; jidō manga (kodomo); Tagawa Suihō
Kodomo Manga Times (periodical), 141, 373
Kodomo Puck (periodical), 39, 373
Kohler, Chris, 294
Kokkei Shinbun (Humorous news) (periodical), 23, 25, 30, 52, 373
Kōko Shinbun (The public news) (periodical), 17–18
Kokumin no Tomo (The people's friend) (periodical), 22
komaga style, 33–34, 164–165, 321
Komatsu Sakyō, 42, 65, 83, 113, 116, 135, 142, 219, 284
Kondō Hidezō, 96, 99–100, 111–112, 114, 116–118, 139, 142, 188, 201
Korea, 24–25, 28, 43, 86, 127, 178, 315, 343n30
Kosugi Misei (Hōan), 33
Kotera Kyūho, 131, 137
Kōtoku Shūsui, 19, 31–32
Kōuchi Jun'ichi, 30
Kumada Masahiro, 297–298
Kume Kōichi, 108, 109
Kumota Haruko, 283
Kurimoto Kaoru, 265, 267, 268, 273
Kyojin no hoshi (Star of the Giants) (1966–71 baseball manga), 280

La Voyage dans la Lune (A voyage to the moon) (1902 short film) (Méliès), 29
labor practices: assistant labor model, 216–217; collaboration, 216; editorial intervention, 216; kashihon publishers, 160–161
laughing/humor: as bodily practice, 328n53; children's manga humor, 156; humor writing (gibun), 19–20; *Kokkei Shinbun* (Humorous news) (periodical), 23, 25, 30, 52, 373; ponchi-e humor, 45–46; in verses, 333n51
lesploitation manga, 360n98
letters from readers, 326n57; *Be in Love/Be Love* (periodical), 276, 277, 278–279; *Big Comic* (periodical) and, 221; in children's magazines, 326n57; commercialism concerns in, 214; fan letters, 233, 234; fan organizations via, 208; on fan pages, 228; gekiga manga and, 169, 170; *Juné* and, 267, 271; on manga lending, 117; *Manga Shōnen* and, 146; from mothers of child readers, 84; Norakuro and, 73–77; perspectives of fans through, 6; protest letters, 229; *The Rose of Versailles* and, 237, 266; *Shōnen Kurabu* and, 225; *Shōnen Puck* and, 31; to Tezuka Osamu, 150. *See also* readers
literacy rates: in Edo period, 3, 17, 319; in Meiji period, 19
lithography, 23, 31
Little Nemo in Slumberland (cartoon) (McCay), 38, 72
lolicon manga, 254, 267, 286–292
Lolita complex, 286
Lost Decades, 5, 320. *See also* Heisei period (1989–2019)
Lum (character), 281, 282–283, 291
Lupin III: The Castle of Cagliostro (1979 animated film) (Miyazaki), 291
Lupin the Third (fan film), 261

Machi (kashihon anthology), 161, 169, 202, 204, 206, 212
magazines. *See* zasshi (magazines)
Mainichi Shōgakusei Shinbun (Daily elementary schooler news) (periodical), 83, 110, 177–178
Maki Miyako, 155, 232, 276
Manchurian Incident, 61, 75
manga: during Bubble economy, 294; displacement of, 311; evolution as key strength of, 6; expanding demographics of, 310; as modern phenomenon, 15;

manga *(continued)*
otaku of, 321; as platform for connection, 311; readership of mangaka, 6; transnational connections, 8–9. *See also specific genres of manga*
Manga (periodical), 139, 373
manga (term): in Edo period, 4, 13, 26, 48, 323n1; Imaizumi Ippyō on, 2, 3, 4, 8, 14, 16, 25, 44, 53; Kitazawa Rakuten on, 4, 16, 37; Matsumoto on, 323n1; Okamoto Ippei on, 4; origins of, 13, 44, 48, 323n1; in Shōwa period, 35
"Manga 53 Stations of the Tōkaidō Road," 44
Manga Burikko (Comic fake girl) (periodical), 287, 288, 291–293, 292*fig.*
manga creator. *See* mangaka (manga creator)
Manga Dokuhon (Manga reader) (periodical), 141
Manga History of Japan (*Manga Nihonshi*), 301
Manga jōsetsukan (Manga cinema) (Tagawa Suihō), 69
Manga kenkyū shiryō kōza (Manga research materials lectures), 48, 107
manga kisha (manga reporter), 14, 36, 99, 118, 321
Manga Kōrakkai (Rakuten's manga group), 37–38
Manga kōza, 49
Manga kyōshitsu (Manga classroom) (manga series), 148
manga magazines: in Japan, 371n11; platforms for, 313–314; publishing model for, 313; sugoroku game boards in, 326n49. *See also specific magazines*
manga manbun style: *Buta no heso* (The pig's navel), 50; defined, 321; development through, 54; image-plus-text pattern of, 66; Miyao Shigeo and, 65–66; Okamoto Ippei and, 4, 34–37, 34*fig.*, 40, 98, 101; Tagawa Suihō and, 72
Manga Mini Market/Manga Gallery and Market (MGM), 297, 298, 299
Manga Nihon (1945), 113, 119–121, 120*fig.*, 122, 340n114
Manga no kanzume (Canned manga) (Tagawa Suihō), 69, 71–72
Manga no Kuni/Sashie Manga Kenkyū (periodical): amateur manga submissions, 109–110, 211; dōjin first wave, 207; as dōjinshi, 211; publication information, 373; reader letters, 159
Manga no omatsuri (Manga festival) (Miyao Shigeo), 66
Manga Ō (Manga King) (periodical), 156, 286
Manga Shōnen (periodical): *Bat-kun* (Bat Kid), 147–148, 152, 345; bessatsu furoku and, 151; publication information, 373; reader contests, 148; Takita Yū and, 212; Takizawa Michiko and, 161
Manga Shūdan, 138–139
Manga Tarō (children's manga) (Miyao Shigeo), 39, 65, 82
Manga to Shashin (Manga and photographs) (periodical), 93–94, 95. See also *Jiji Manga/Manga to Shashin* (periodical)
Manga to yakubun (Manga and translations) (Ippei, Natori and Nakada), 34
Manga to Yomimono, 93, 141. See also *Jiji Manga/Manga to Shashin* (periodical)
mangaka (manga creator): defined, 321; kamishibai and, 320; term usage, xv, 26. *See also specific mangaka*
mangappoi (manga-like), 289–290
Mangasai (Manga festival) (periodical), 36
The Manga Man (periodical), plate 9, 94, 96, 97, 98, 99, 216, 373
The Man Who Fell to Earth (1976 film) (Roeg), 266
Margaret (periodical), 236, 361n104, 373. See also *The Rose of Versailles* (*Berusaiyu no bara*) (1972–74 shōjo manga) (Ikeda Riyoko)
Maru (periodical), 143
Maruchin (*Marumaru Chinbun*) (periodical): decline of, 33; Honda Kinkichirō cartoon, 21*fig.*; Okamoto Ippei on, 49; origins of, 18–19; popularity of, 20, 21; publication information, 373; ukiyo-e (woodblock print) in, 19
Marvel, 312–313

Masaki Mori, 203–205, 212
masukomii (mass communications), 215–216
Masuyama Norie: Hagio Moto and, 233, 241, 273; Inagaki Taruho and, 239; Ōizumi Salon and, 232, 234–235; science fiction and, 359n72; shōjo revolution and, 233–234; Shōwa 24 Group and, 233–234; Takemiya Keiko and, 233, 238, 241, 249, 263, 273
Matenrō (Skyscraper) (1959–60 anthology), 166, 167, 169, 170, 373
Matsumoto Katsuji, 225
Matsumoto Leiji, 132, 148, 155, 248, 284
Matsumoto Masahiko, 164–165, 321, 323n1
Matsuyama Fumio, 103, 104, 106, 107, 108–109, 127
MAVO movement, 59, 61–62, 68–69, 71, 94, 101, 106, 308
May (periodical), 278
McCay, Winsor, 38, 51, 72
McManus, George, 41, 328n34
Medama no chibi-chan (Big-eyed kid) (Tagawa Suihō), 68
Meiji period (1868–1912): akahon manga and, 81–82; defined, 321; *Gendai manga taikan* (anthology) and, 45; literacy rates, 19; manga at end of, 32; modernization in, 3; nishiki-e (brocade pictures) in, 322; pioneers of manga in, 14; pornography ban during, 322; publishers and, 31; social order in, 51; visual techniques in, 20
Meiji Restoration, 3, 15, 23, 43–44
Meikyū, 258–260, 267, 297
Méliès, Georges, 29
merchandising: Dankichi and, 80; Norakuro and, 59–60, 73–80; Shō-chan and, 331n12; *Tetsuwan Atomu* (*Astro Boy*), 191–192; Uniqlo, 363n13. *See also* anime media mix
Mickey Mouse (character), 71, 82, 115, 117, 123, 133, 147, 330n2, 358n46
militarism: children's manga and, 42, 62, 86–87, 88, 114–116; manga and, 59–63; Norakuro and, 72–73, 86. *See also* fascism
Mimi (periodical), 373
Misora Hibari, 136, 303, 343n30
Mitsuse Ryū, 285
Miyamoto Hirohito, 20, 33, 67, 147
Miyamoto Shigeru, 294
Miyao Shigeo: apprenticeship, 130; bessatsu furoku by, 81; employment for manga ads of, 328n32; *Manga Tarō* (1922 children's manga), 39, 65, 82; Nihon Mangakkai and, 97; nonsense manga and, 52; strips by, 96
Miyatake Gaikotsu, 19, 23
Miyazaki Hayao: first animated film, 291; gekiga and kashihon manga, 170; marriage of, 338n62; on Tezuka, 303
Miyazaki incident (1989), 303–304, 314, 321, 370n2, 370n4
Mizoguchi, Akiko, 238, 270, 272
Mizuki Shigeru: *Big Comic* and, 220; debut, 199; *Garo* and, 199–201, 218; *Gegege no Kitarō* (1968 anime adaptation), 137, 196; *Hakaba no Kitarō* (Graveyard Kitarō, 1965–69 yōkai manga), 196; income, 160, 199, 215, 353n48; kamishibai and, 137–138; Mura Nunoe and, 160, 216–217; Togetsu Shobō and, 162
Mizuno Hideko, 155, 225, 231, 233, 248, 266, 359n56
Modern Boy (mobo), 53, 68
Modern Girl (moga), 50, 51, 53
modernism: in 1930s, 123; dissatisfaction with, 15; Tagawa Suihō and, 72
modernization: in Meiji period, 3, 15, 24; in Taishō period, 322; Westernization and, 60
Momotarō: Umi no shinpei (*Momotarō: Sacred Sailors*) (1945 animated film) (Seo Mitsuyo), 152, 191, 352n8
Monthly Box of Curios (periodical). See *Box of Curios* (periodical)
Mōri Kazuo, 264
Mr. Dough and Mr. Dubb! (comics) (Opper), 41, 44
Mukuzō (character), 29
Mura Nunoe, 160, 216–217
Murakami Motoka, 217, 222, 248, 285
Murakami Tomohiko, 224–225, 285
Murayama Tomoyoshi, 69, 101, 104

Musansha Shinbun (periodical), 104, 373
Mushi Productions, 186, 190, 191, 204, 211, 230
music: in 1930s, 123; in children's manga, 70; DJ era analogy, 253; gekiga and, 167; as inspiration in 1970s, 266; *Norakuro* song, 74–76; *The Rose of Versailles* musical adaptation, 243–246
Musō (periodical), 168–169, 373
Muybridge, Eadweard, 27

Nagai Gō, 223
Nagai Katsuichi, 123, 134–135, 144, 160, 162, 197–199, 202–203, 218
Nagasaki Batten, 96, 345n78
Nagashima Shinji, 205, 212
Nagata Takemaru, 154, 346n110
Nagayama Kaoru, 275, 293, 301
Naiki Toshio, 158
Nakada Katsunosuke, 34, 327n5
Nakajima Azusa, 265
Nakajima Fumio, 290
Nakajima Sakuo, 80, 118
Nakamori Akio, 287
Nakamura Kimihiko, 297–299
Nakamura Manga Library, 82, 84, 89, 308
Nakamura Shoten, 82, 83, 89
Nakamura Yūjirō, 25
Nakashima Takashi, 210
Nakayoshi (periodical), 227–228, 233, 373
Nakayoshi Manga (Good friends) (Ōsaka Tokio), 131
Namakura gatana (The dull sword) (1917 animation) (Kōuchi Jun'ichi), 30, 326n53
Nankivell, Frank Arthur, 2, 16, 24
Nara period, 329n67
narrative manga, 78, 164, 169, 180, 218, 321. *See also* seinen manga
National United Kashihon Association (Zenkoku Kashihon Kumiai Rengōkai), 163, 172
Natori Shunsen, 34
Natsume Fusanosuke, 72, 114, 166, 203, 204, 212, 226, 304
Natsume Sōseki, 35, 47
Neo Shobō, 158–159
New Woman, 50
Newspaper Law of 1909, 31
Nicolas II, Tsar, 26
Nightow Yasuhiro, 299
Nihon Apache zoku (*The Japanese Apache*) (Komatsu Sakyō), 284
Nihon Jidōmangaka Kyōkai (Japan Children's Mangaka Association), 89
Nihon Keizai Shinbun (periodical), 80
Nihon Manga Hōkōkai, 116
Nihon Manga Kenkyūkai, 109–110, 373
Nihon Manga Kyōkai, 112
Nihon Manga Taikai (Mantai), 210, 211, 258–260, 310
Nihon Mangaka Renmei/Manren/Japan Cartoonists League, 101–102
Nihon Mangakkai, 36, 97
Nihon mangashi (History of Japanese manga) (Hosokibara Seiki), 46, 48, 329n63, 329n67
Ninja bugeichō (Book of ninja fighting arts) (1959–62 kashihon manga) (Shirato Sanpei), 161
Nintendo, 180–181, 293, 310
nishiki-e (brocade pictures), 322
Nomura Fumio, 19
Nonkina tōsan (Easygoing dad) (1923 four-panel manga) (Asō Yukata), 41
nonsense (nansensu) manga: foreign comics as, 307; Japanese modern times and, 40; Meiji period artists and, 55–56; Okamoto Ippei on, 308; Shinmangaha Shūdan (New Manga Faction Group) and, 100
Norakuro (1931–41 manga) (Tagawa Suihō): after Tagawa's death, 346n110; akahon manga and, 82, 274; banning of, 108; bessatsu furoku and, 80–81; book design of, 78, 334n61; children's literature purification policy and, 89; comparisons to, 72, 236; debut, 68–73; end of, 91, 94; fan club, 143; fan manga, 74, 84; format of, 78; furoku (freebies), 79; influence of, 5, 62, 82–83, 129; influences on, 71, 330n2, 332n27; in *Maru,* 143; military content in, 72–73, 86; pathos in, 71; popularity of, 2, 59–60, 69, 70, 80, 236, 274, 308, 309; readership of, 70, 73–74; scapegoating of, 85, 86, 114–115,

116; serialization of, 74, 143, 145; *Shōjo Kurabu* and, 91, 148; in *Shōnen Club,* 143; *Shōnen Kurabu* and, 78, 79, 81; support for empire in, 90–91, 100; tankōbon, 78, 80, 82, 83, 88, 133, 134*fig.*

Norakuro (character): about, 68; advertising, 78–79; akahon manga and, 81–82; appeal of, 70–71; *Chameken to Norakuro* (Chameken and Norakuro), 173; in *Chinpin Norakuro-sō,* 143; design of, 1, 70, 71; films with, 152; in final episodes, 143; *Manga Shōnen* and, 147; media mix, 75–78; merchandising, 74–75, 80; in military, 72–73, 86; popularity of, 71, 74, 77, 80; resignation of, 90; *Shōjo Kurabu* and, 225; son of, 131; tankōbon, 74

Norakuro films, 152

Norakuro jōtōhei (Private first class Norakuro) (Tagawa Suihō), 82

Norakuro tankōbon, 74, 78, 80, 82–83, 88, 133, 134*fig.*

Norakuro tosshintai (Norakuro charger squad) (1933 bessatsu furoku), 81

"November Gymnasium" (Hagio Moto), 241, 259

Occupation: akahon manga, 319; censorship during, 138; controls during, 1; effects on animation industry, 152; emergence of, 322; freedom of press under, 139; kamishibai during, 320; kashihonya during, 320

Oda Nobutsune (Oda Shōsei), 39

Ōe Chizuka, 271, 365n53

Ogata Katsuhiro, 291

Ogawa Jihei, plate 5, 38, 50, 101

Ogawa Tetsuo, 138–139

Ogawa Yoko, 365n53

Ōgi Fusami, 263–264

Ōizumi Salon, 232, 234–235, 238–241, 243, 265, 269, 277

Okada Fumiko, 206, 286

Okada Toshio, 222–223, 282

Okamoto Ippei: advertising, 40; at *Asahi Shinbun,* 4, 14, 33, 34, 39, 53; *Bijutsu shinron,* 56; collected manga of, 45; early career of, 33, 34, 302; eiga manga of, 35–36, 132; expansion of manga concept, 52, 53, 307; on foreign manga, 42; *Gendai manga taikan* (Contemporary manga survey), 46, 47, 55; impact of, 6, 14–15, 55; influence of, 33–37, 38; innovations of, 39; at *Jiji Shinpō,* 4; *Joshikai* (Women's world) and, 39; kodomo manga (jidō), 38–39; on manga, 43–44, 46, 48–49, 54, 56, 107; *The Manga Man* and, 96; manga manbun style, 4, 34–37, 40, 98, 101, 321; manga term usage by, 4; mangakkai concept, 97; Miyao Shigeo and, 130; nonsense manga and, 52, 55, 308; popularity of, 14, 65; Rakuten and, 4, 33; *Shinmanga no kakikata* (How to draw new manga), 48; shōsetsu manga, 39; social satire of, 65, 66; students and assistants of, 38, 80, 98, 99, 130

Okamoto Kanoko, 39, 50

Okamoto Tarō, 39

Okamoto Tōki, 104, 198

Omoshiro Book (periodical), 374

Onoda Shō (Asakawa Mitsuhiro), 353n35

OPEC oil embargo, 253–254

Opper, Frederick Burr, 41, 43

Orbaugh, Sharalyn, 137

Osaka Puck/Manga Nippon/Manga to Yomimono (periodical), 14, 17, 41, 52, 374

Ōsaka Tokio, 131

Osayo-san (manga) (Yazaki Takeko), 142

Ōshima Yumiko, 286, 292, 298

Ōshiro Noboru, 82–83, 91, 119

Ōta Akemi, 338n62

Ōta Kōji, 109, 110, 338n62

otaku: at Comiket, 286; consumption and, 289; crime and, 370n2, 370–371n4; science fiction media and, 285; term usage, xv, xvi, 255, 286–288, 321

Othering, 315

Otokoyamome no Gan-san (Bachelor Gan-san) (1932–33 manga) (Shimokawa Ōten), 94

otomechikku (girly) style, 275–276

Ōtomo Katsuhiro, 256

otona manga, 142, 143, 208, 223, 224, 321

Ōtsuka Eiji, 115–116, 276, 286, 291, 330n2, 367n2, 368n29, 370n2

Oyaji Kyōiku (Bringing up the old man) (comic strip), 41, 95, 328n34
Ōyama Kenji, 337n6

paper-rationing edict, 89, 91, 91*fig.*, 138
parody (paro), 270
Pax Tokugawa, 319
Perry, Matthew C., 16
Philippines, 315
Phoenix (*Hi no tori*) (manga series) (Tezuka Osamu), 149, 204, 205, 227, 284
picture puzzle (hanji-e) techniques, 19
Pip, Squeak, and Wilfred (British comic), 41
pirated manga, 41, 42, 55, 330n2
platforms: as elements of manga and comics, 313–314; kashihonya as, 136, 157, 158–163, 181; as mediator, 7; publishers and, 7; questions of, 311; readers and, 7. *See also* format
platonic "dōseiai" media, 237
Pō no ichizoku (*The Poe Clan* (1972–76/2016– manga) (Hagio Moto), 242–243, 248, 271, 361n104
politics: laughing as bodily practice and, 328n53; political cartoons, 23; political satire, 15, 20
ponchi-e (ponchi): beginnings of, 3; *Chōjūgiga* and, 47; defined, 321; as differentiated from manga, 27–28, 45–46, 55, 102; distancing from, 3, 8, 14, 15, 16, 22, 307; humor in, 45–46; *Jōtō Ponchi* (High-class ponchi), 48; Komatsu and, 117; *Marumaru Chinbun*'s use of, 18–19; obfuscatory practices of, 22, 23*fig.*; origins of, 8; Rakuten on, 25; satirical style of, 20; during Shōwa period, 35; during Taishō period, 35; term usage, 17–18, 26; use of words in, 20; visual strategies of, 20; widespread use of, 25, 32
pop culture, 3, 136, 186, 238, 276, 296, 315
pornography: ban bad books movement and, 174, 175–176, 195; ero in manga and, 50; eromanga and, 188, 220, 319; fujoshi and, 272; in Japanese comics, 188; *Juné*, 265; *May* (periodical), 278; nude gravures, 142; ukiyo-e (woodblock print) and, 322
postcard manga, 141
postmodern era: Comiket (Comic Market) and, 258–262; fan cultures and, 253–257, 269, 270–275; gender roles in, 289; manga genres and, 246; pop culture revolution and, 315; post-Bubble economy of, 320; postwar period and, 185–189; shōnen'ai manga and, 267–270; transition to, 189. See also *COM* (periodical); josei manga; queerness; shōnen'ai manga
postmodernity, 115, 315
precarity, 171, 320. *See also* Bubble economy
print culture, 3, 17. *See also* ukiyo-e (woodblock print)
proletarian arts movement, 5, 100–108
propaganda, 60–61, 89–91, 93, 112, 320
proto-gekiga manga, 321
Prough, Jennifer, 227, 242, 358n41
publishing industry: dōjinshi as alternative to, 4, 310; manga in Japanese market of, 5. *See also* censorship; dōjinshi (amateur publications); formats; platforms; readers; *specific companies; specific manga genres*
Puck (periodical), 2, 26, 30–31, 41
Puff (periodical), 297–298
pun prints (jiguchi-e), 20
Punch (periodical), 17, 19, 24, 25

Qing Empire, 22, 25, 336n117
queerness: BL manga and, 365n54; manga fan cultures and, 270–275; queer liberation, 189, 365n53, 372n15; shōjo revolution and, 188, 267–268, 310; in shōnen'ai manga, 270–275; world of 70s rock music and, 266

rakugo: comedy form of, 52, 59, 308; defined, 69; dialogue in, 65, 70; routines, 90; scriptwriting, 69, 308
Rakuten. *See* Kitazawa Rakuten
Rakuten Puck (periodical), 32
Ranpo, Edogawa, 50, 132
readers: bishōjo comics, 286, 292; capturing attention of, 36; catering to tastes of, 44, 130, 142–143; as collaborators, 236–237, 239; *COM* (periodical) and,

202, 205, 206, 208, 211–212; Comitia and, 299; competition for, 9, 280; empathy for interests and concerns of, 59; engagement of, 243; format availability and, 7; *Garo* (periodical) and, 197–200, 202; gekiga readership, 165–168, 169, 170, 171, 222, 281; gender and, 221, 222, 225, 230, 235, 255–256, 264, 268–269, 283, 313; government concern for, 62; increasing numbers of, 4, 94; josei manga, 276–279; *Jump* manga, 295; kashihon and, 196; kashihonya and, 128, 159, 162, 181, 193, 195; literacy levels of, 3; lolicon comics, 286, 290, 291; manga as comfort for, 45; *Manga Burikko* and, 287, 292; Manga Mini Market/MGM, 297; mangaka as, 6, 148; member profiles, 109; of newspapers, 19, 38; of nonsense manga, 42; Norakuro and, 70, 71, 73–78, 79, 88, 114, 143, 308; otaku readership, 282, 286–287; panel reading order and, 220; periodicals, 23; poaching of, 151; in postwar Japan, 175; queer readers, 270–275; reaching child readers, 81, 83–84, 84; reader-submitted art, 267; of *Ribon* (periodical), 275–276, 291; science fiction elements and, 283–284, 285; seinen manga and, 187, 218, 223, 224, 304, 310, 321; shared experience of manga between, 148; *Shintakarajima* and, 133; shōjo manga revolution and, 188, 229–230, 255, 321; shōnen manga and, 223, 270, 304; shōnen'ai manga and, 241, 267; social values of, 4; submission contests for, 95, 109, 141, 147–148, 169; surveys for, 188, 216, 228, 247, 282, 292; as sympathetic toward Gamu, 70; in Taishō period, 14; *Tank Tankurō* and, 80, 114; tankōbon paperbacks and, 248, 313, 362n4; *Terebi-kun* (TV kid), 217; touching the heart of, 136, 164–165; US reader organizations, 174; visual techniques and, 19, 20; during wartime and Occupation, 116–117, 129–130; young male readers of shōnen magazines, 157. *See also* letters from readers

real-person fiction (RPF), 343n30

rebus print (hanji-e) techniques, 19, 20

Reiwa period (2019-), 9, 275

Ribon (periodical), 227, 233, 241, 275–276, 291, 374

Ribon no kishi (Ribbon knight) (1953–56 shōjo manga) (Tezuka Osamu), 226–227, 228, 236

Ribonist (club), 275

Rōdō Nōmin Shinbun (periodical), 374

Roeder, Katherine, 51, 54

The Rose of Versailles (*Berusaiyu no bara*) (1972–74 shōjo manga) (Ikeda Riyoko): comparisons to, 238; impact of, 275; as inspiration in 1970s, 266; *The Poe Clan* connection, 361n104; pop culture revolution and, 238; popularity of, 243; sex scene in, 264; splash page for, plate 11, 236; as story manga, 242; synergy and, 244; Takarazuka musical adaptation, 243–245, 313; women audiences and, 237–238, 266, 275, 279, 313. See also *BeruBara* (*Berusaiyu no bara*) (*The Rose of Versailles*) (1972–74 shōjo manga) (Ikeda Riyoko)

roundtable discussions: ban bad books movement and, 175; *COM*-sponsored, 204, 215–216, 222, 229–231; gekigaka and, 166–168, 169, 171–172; kashihonya and, 194; manga fans' perspectives and, 6; with Rakuten, 112

RPF (real-person fiction), 343n30

Ruoff, Kenneth J., 60–61

Russo-Japanese War, 23, 25, 26, 33, 35

Sabu (Sub) (periodical), 265, 267

Sagawa Toshihiko, 265

Saint Seiya (1985–90 manga), 282

Saitō Ioe, 146

Saitō Takao, 146, 164, 167, 171, 218, 220, 222, 281

Sakai Shichima: *Hello! Manga,* 131; kamishibai and, 137; *Shintakarajima* (New Treasure Island) (1947 akahon manga), 129, 131–135, 342n12; Tezuka Osamu and, 130, 131–132

Sakamoto Gajō, 80, 85–86, 90, 91, 119, 151, 335n98

Sakata Yasuko, 234

Sakuragi Tetsurō, 265

Sakurai Shōichi, 148, 159, 160, 161, 165, 166, 167
same-sex relationships. *See* homosexual representation
sapphic relationships, 322. *See also* GL/girls' love manga; Yuri manga
Saru to kani (Battle of a monkey and a crab) (1917 animation) (Kitayama Seitarō), 30
Sasaya Nanaeko, 234, 265, 267
satirical cartoons: growing readership for, 23; ponchi-e (ponchi) term for, 321; Western concept of, 19
Satō Masa'aki, 167–168, 174–175, 179
Satō Shio, 234, 235, 359n72
Satonaka Machiko, 277
Sazae-san (1946–1974 four-panel manga) (Hasegawa Machiko), 2, 136, 139–140, 142, 146, 163, 166, 171
Science Fiction Bunko book series, 285
Seduction of the Innocent (Wertham), 349n63
seinen manga: *Big Comic* and, 218–221; defined, 321; as de-gendered, 300, 304, 310, 321; dōjinshi sphere and, 300–301; influence on shōnen manga, 223, 310; invention of, 187, 218; Maki Miyako and, 276; Murakami Motoka and, 222–223; Murakami Tomohiko on, 224–225; readership of, 278, 285; rise of, 223–224; science fiction and, 246, 255, 312; term usage, xvi; violence and sex in, 187–188, 202, 283, 292, 310; *Weekly Manga Times* and, 224; *Young Jump*, 280–281
Seirindō (publisher), 195, 197, 198, 199, 202, 203, 353n35
Seiyō zasshi (Occidental magazine) (periodical), 17
Senji Gahō (Wartime illustrated news) (periodical), 33
Senki (Battle flag) (periodical), 105*fig.*
Seo Mitsuyo, 152
Shaka Bontarō, 83
Shamoon, Deborah, 73, 236, 268
shiba-e (cartoons), 35
Shimada Keizō, 80, 81, 84, 110, 115, 146, 153, 345n74
Shimizu Isao, 13, 28, 32, 33, 50, 96, 106, 136–137, 147, 223, 318
Shimoda Ken'ichirō, 106
Shimokawa Ōten (Hekoten): live-action film adaptation script by, 337n6; on manga as art, 47; manga eiga (animated shorts), 29–30; on manga/ponchi distinction, 45; nonsense manga and, 55; *Otokoyamome no Gan-san* (Bachelor Gan-san), 94; pen name, 326n52; as pioneer of manga, 29; proletarian arts movement and, 101–102, 110; Yanase Masamu and, 101, 338n37; Yoshimoto Sanpei and, 83
Shimotsuki Takanaka, 259, 260, 262, 291, 297
Shinmanga no kakikata (How to draw new manga) (Okamoto Ippei), 48
Shinmangaha Shūdan (New Manga Faction Group), 6, 61, 83, 97–100, 118, 119, 138. *See also* Kondō Hidezō; Manga Shūdan; Sugiura Yukio; Yazaki Shigeshi; Yazaki Takeko; Yokoi Fukutarō; Yokoyama Ryūichi
Shinpen gessekai shinshi (New edition: The moony man) (1951 furoku manga) (Tezuka Osamu), 151
Shinshū Sakuranosuke (Sakuranosuke from Shinshū), 83
Shintakarajima (New Treasure Island) (1947 akahon manga) (Tezuka and Sakai), 129, 131–135
Shinyūkan (New evening news) (periodical), 139, 143
Shirato Sanpei, 161–162, 197–198, 199, 200, 202, 218, 367n2
Shirota Shūichi, 46
shishōsetsu (I-novel), 212, 332n27
Shō-chan no bōken (The adventures of Shō-chan) (1923 children's manga) (Tōfūjin and Oda Nobutsune), plate 6, 39, 41, 65–67, 331n12
Shogakukan (publisher): animators move to, 152; bessatsu furoku, 81; editors, 149, 175, 239; Hagio Moto and, 277; *Judy* (periodical), 278; kashihon manga and, 218; manga prizes, 205, 214; reader surveys, 228; series, 263, 283;

Takemiya Keiko and, 239, 263; tankōbon of series, 283
Shōjo Comic (periodical), 264
Shōjo Kurabu/Shōjo Club (periodical), 64–65, 80, 139, 347n11, 374
shōjo manga: B title classification as, 171; BL/boys' love manga and, 238–243; children's manga split into, 157, 185, 216, 221–225, 320–321; Comiket and, 259–265, 290–291; complaints about, 217; defined, 321; emergence of, 225–229; fans/fandoms, 261, 263, 290, 310; humor and, 155, 156; influence from, 268, 282; josei manga and, 207; kashihon manga and, 160, 171; kashihonya and, 195; mangaka, 6, 157, 187, 217, 282, 290–291, 299, 310; mature content, 195, 264; Murakami Motoka on, 217; protagonists in, 157, 231, 270; Takehisa Yumeji and, 39; tankōbon and, 247–249; term usage, xvi. See also *Margaret* (periodical); *The Rose of Versailles* (Ikeda Riyoko); Shōwa 24 Group; *specific mangaka*
shōjo revolution, 187–188, 229–232, 233, 254, 255, 263, 267–269, 285
shōjo-sei (girlness), 289–290
Shōkokumin (Little imperial subject) (periodical), 24
Shōkokumin Shinbun (periodical), 131–132
Shōnen Champion (periodical), 285
Shōnen Jump. See *Shūkan Shōnen Jump* (periodical)
Shōnen Kurabu/Shōnen Club (Boys' club) (periodical), 2, 59, 64–65, 67, 68, 70, 73, 76–77, 78, 79, 80, 81, 345n67, 374
Shōnen Magazine. See *Shūkan Shōnen Magazine* (periodical)
shōnen manga: complaints about, 217; defined, 321; influences on, 282; kodomo manga (jidō) split into, 320–321; seinen's influence on, 188, 310; term usage, xvi; A title classification as, 171
Shōnen Puck (periodical), 30–31
Shōnen Shōjo Bōken Ō/Bōken Ō (periodical), 373
Shōnen Shōjo Tankai (periodical), 374
Shōnen Sunday. See *Shūkan Shōnen Sunday* (periodical)
shōnen'ai manga: *Allan* and, 255, 310; BL/boys' love manga and, 238; defined, 321; emergence of, 269; Hagio Moto and, 241, 243; homosexual representation in, 270–271; *Juné* and, 255, 264–265, 267–268, 310; lolicon manga and, 291; post-modern era and, 267–270; queerness and, 270–275; readership of, 241, 267; sex scenes in, 264; in shōjo magazines, 264; Takemiya Keiko and, 243. *See also* BL/boys' love manga; yaoi manga
"Shōri no hi made" (Until the day of victory) (amateur manga) (Tezuka Osamu), 117
Shōsai Ikkei, 47, 329n62
shōsetsu (novel) manga, 39–40
Shōwa 24 Group, 187, 232, 235–236, 264, 265, 270, 273–275, 277, 278, 282, 292. *See also* Hagio Moto; Masuyama Norie; Takemiya Keiko; Yamagishi Ryōko
Shōwa period (1926–1989), 5, 35, 322
Shueisha (publisher), 241, 294, 373, 374. See also *The Rose of Versailles* (Ikeda)
Shufu no Tomo (Housewife's friend) (periodical), 81
Shūkan Manga Sunday (periodical), 141, 224
Shūkan Manga Times (periodical), 141, 224, 374
Shūkan Shōnen Jump (periodical), 256, 270, 280–281, 282, 294–295, 374
Shūkan Shōnen Magazine (periodical), 280, 281, 282, 374
Shūkan Shōnen Sunday (periodical), 280, 281, 282
Shūkan Young Jump (periodical), 281, 374
Silverberg, Miriam, 34, 40, 43, 47, 49, 68, 123, 328n53
Sino-Japanese War, 23, 24–25, 76
Skabelund, Aaron Herald, 60, 70–71, 87
slash fiction, 269–270, 270, 272, 273
Smurfs (characters), 312
Sōsaku JUNE (original June), 364n39
Space Battleship Yamato II (*Uchū senkan Yamato 2*) (1978–79 series) (Matsumoto Leiji), 254, 284
Space Battleship Yamato the Movie (1977 anime) (Matsumoto Leiji), 255, 284, 286, 297

Space Battleship Yamato (*Uchū senkan Yamato*) (1974–75 series) (Matsumoto Leiji), 254, 255, 284
speech bubbles, 27–28, 29, 38, 41, 42, 44, 70, 98, 242
Star Trek (1966–69 TV series), 269
Star Wars (1977 film) (Lucas), 254, 255, 284
Steinberg, Marc, 3, 13, 181, 186, 244, 295
Stewart, Ronald, 25, 28, 323n4
story manga: ban bad books movement and, 129–130, 194; children's manga and, 142–143, 150, 153, 154, 156, 309; decomposition in, 167; Fukui Ei'ichi and, 152–154; gekiga and, 163, 165, 166, 167, 169, 171, 180, 309; *Ribon no kishi* and, 226; rise of, 152, 165, 329n70; in shōjo, 242; Takeuchi Osamu on, 173; Tezuka Osamu and, 128–129, 135, 150–151, 152–153, 166, 181–182, 203, 308–309
street performance, 196, 320. *See also* kamishibai
submissions: *Allan,* 291; *Asahi Graph* and, 110; *COM,* 203, 206–207; evaluation of, 109; *Garo,* 197, 199; judging, 211; *Juné,* 265–266, 267, 291; *Mainichi Shinbun,* 110; *Manga no Kuni/Sashie Manga Kenkyū,* 109, 211; *Manga Shōnen,* 148, 204; *Musō,* 169. *See also* contests
Sugiura Shigeru, 84
Sugiura Yukio, 99–100, 112, 138, 139
Sun Minqiao, 69, 70
Sun Publishing, 264–265
Super Mario Bros. (1985 video game), 294
superhero genre, 65, 80, 215
supplements (furoku): defined, 320; for fan club, 94; as marketing strategy, 228, 276; Sunday supplements, 24, 37, 40–41, 93–96
surveys, 140, 188, 216, 228, 247, 270, 282, 292
Suzuki, Shige (CJ), 323n4
Suzuki Bunshirō, 40–41
Suzuki Katsumaru, 138
Suzuki Maki, 36
Suzuki Shin'ichi, 154–155
Swallowing the Earth (*Chikyū o nomu*) (1968–69 seinen series) (Tezuka Osamu), 219, 220–221
Tachihara Ayumi, 277
tachiyomi, 159, 347n7
Tagawa Suihō: akahon manga and, 81–82, 274; bessatsu furoku and, 80–81; book designs of, 334n61; Chibikuro (character), 131; death of, 5, 303, 346n110; debut, 308; fans of, 274; *Gendai renzoku manga zenshū* (Collected contemporary serial manga) (1935 anthology), 81; Hasegawa Machiko and, 2; Home Ministry meeting, 90–91, 108; influence of, 146, 308; *Jinzō ningen,* 69; Katō Ken'ichi and, 114, 173; Kobayashi on, 332n27; Manchukuo and, 89–90; manga debut of, 59; MAVO movement, 59, 68–69, 94, 308; *Medama no chibi-chan* (Big-eyed kid), 68; memorial hall, 334n65; Nagata Takemaru and, 346n110; *Norakuro jōtōhei,* 82; *Norakuro* tankōbon, 74, 78, 80, 82–83, 88, 133, 134*fig.*; Ōtsuka Eiji on, 330n2; popularity of, 2; rakugo scripts, 69, 308; robot manga and, 284; *Shinshū Sakuranosuke* (Sakuranosuke from Shinshū), 83; *Shinyūkan* (New evening news) (periodical), 139, 143; *Shōnen Club* and, 143; Shōwa Mangakkai and, 97, 146; students and assistants of, 84, 118, 154, 212; Tezuka on, 83, 332n23; three-panel layout of, 135; *Toppio* (1939–40 manga), 119. See also *Norakuro* (1931–41 manga) (Tagawa Suihō)
Taguchi Kyōjirō, 44–45
Taishō period (1912–1926): American popular culture in, 42; defined, 322; *Gendai manga taikan* (anthology) and, 45; literacy rates, 36; magazines on consignment, 31; manga during, 35; modernity in, 14, 34
Taiwan, 25, 28, 315, 372n17
Taiyō no kisetsu (*Season of the sun*) (1956 film), 162
Taiyōzoku manga, 162
Takahashi Macoto, 226
Takahashi Rumiko, 281, 282–283
Takahashi Yōichi, 270
Takamizawa Junko, 69
Takeda Kyōko, 277

Takehisa Yumeji, 39, 225
Takekuma Kentarō, 263, 286
Takemiya Keiko: BL/boys' love manga, 263–265; debut, 206, 239; on eroticism, 267–268; fans and, 254, 263, 273, 275, 286; *Funny* (periodical) and, 206; *Garo* and, 202; Hagio Moto and, 233–234, 238, 241, 359n66; *Juné* and, 265–266; *Kaze to ki no uta* (Song of the wind and trees) (1976–84 manga series), 263–265, 265*fig.*; *Manga Shōnen* and, 246; on manga styles, 242; Masuyama Norie and, 238, 249, 263, 273; Mitsuse Ryū, 285; Mizuno Hideko and, 232; Murakami Motoka and, 217; Ōizumi Salon and, 232, 234–235, 246; on reader surveys, 228; seinen manga and, 246, 300; shōjo manga and, 187, 230, 246; shōnen'ai manga, 243; Shōwa 24 Group and, 230–234; "In the Sunroom" ("Sanrūmu nite"), 239–240, 240*fig.*; *Tera e . . .* (*To Terra . . .*) (1977–80 sci-fi manga), 246, 285; Vienna Boys' Choir, 238; Yamamoto Jun'ya and, 235, 240
Takeuchi Osamu, 133, 172, 173
Takita Yū, 212
Takizawa Michiko, 148, 161
tanbi aesthetic, 266, 364n37
Tank Tankurō (1934–36 superhero manga) (Sakamoto Gajō), 65, 80, 85, 91, 114, 335n98
tankōbon: *COM* (periodical) and, 213; defined, 322; format of, 247–249, 312; fraction of all print manga sales as, 362n4; *Igaguri-kun,* 150; as income source, 163, 313; as industry advertisements, 187, 193; *Norakuro* tankōbon, 74, 78, 79, 80, 81, 82, 83, 88, 133, 134*fig.*; *Osayo-san* tankōbon, 134*fig.*; *Pō no ichizoku* tankōbon, 242; price increases, 193, 196; *Sazae-san,* 150; of Shogakukan series, 283; Tagawa Suihō and, 69; Tezuka Osamu and, 150; *Urusei Yatsura* tankōbon, 247–249
Tarasawa Michi, 234
Tatsumi Yoshihiro: ban bad books movement, 174; contests, 141, 148, 164, 169, 202, 349n54; evolution of style and, 212; fan clubs, 205; *Garo* and, 200, 212; Gekiga Kōbō (Gekiga Workshop) group, 129, 165–166, 171; gekiga manga and, 129, 163–165, 200, 320; *Kage* (Shadow, 1956–66), 164; kashihonya and, 159; "Kuro fubuki" (Black blizzard), 165; *Machi* and, 204; *Manga Shōnen* and, 148; meetups, 195; *Musō* and, 169; Osaka and, 161; popularity of, 171; on readership of gekiga, 169; *Shintakarajima* and, 132; Tsurita Kuniko and, 202
television, 138, 156, 177–179, 186, 196
Tempyō era, 329n67
Ten Billion Days and One Hundred Billion Nights (*Hyakuoku no hiru to sen'oku no yoru*) (Mitsuse Ryū), 285
Tenmei period (1781–89), 48
Terada Hiroo, 154
Tessetsusha (Steel and Snow Society), 145, 345n67
Tetsuwan Atomu (*Astro Boy*) (1952–68 manga series) (Tezuka Osamu), 1, 186, 190–192, 195, 215, 227
Tetsuwan Atomu (*Astro Boy*) (1963–66 anime series) (Tezuka Osamu), 186, 190–192, 204, 215, 310
Tetsuwan Atomu Club (periodical), 215, 374
Tetsuwan Atomu fan club, 205, 215
Tezuka Osamu: akahon manga drawings of, 1; on Atom (character), 332n23; ban bad books movement and, 174, 176; bessatsu furoku and, 151; *Big Comic* (periodical) and, 218, 220; business failings, 351n7; children's manga, 129, 147, 149; cinematic influence on, 164; *COM* (periodical), 186–187, 199, 203–207, 218, 246; *Crime and Punishment* (*Tsumi to batsu,* 1953), 149–150; death of, 5, 303; early career of, 130, 131–132; Fukui Ei'ichi and, 151, 152–153; *Garo* (periodical) and, 201; gekiga elements used by, 357n6; as God of Manga, 2, 5, 153; impact of, 5, 6, 59; influence of, 152–153, 154–155, 167, 169, 215; innovations of, 5, 128–129; Ishinomori Shōtarō and, 215; *Jungle taitei* (Jungle emperor, *Kimba the White Lion*) (1950–1954

Tezuka Osamu *(continued)*
shōnen series), 149–150; *Jungle taitei* (Jungle emperor, *Kimba the White Lion*) (1965–67 anime) (Yamamoto), 195; mandoku contributions, 142; on manga, 91, 117, 195; *Manga kyōshitsu* (Manga classroom), 148; *Manga Shōnen,* 149, 169; *Manga Shōnen* and, 246; meeting with Shimada, 345n74; on Mizuno, 359n56; Murakami Motoka and, 217; Mushi Productions, 190–191; *The Mysterious Underground Men* (*Chiteikoku no kaijin*) (1948 akahon manga), 135–136; Namiki House, 154, 155; popularity of, 5, 163, 171; screentones and, 154, 156; on seinen manga, 218, 220–221; *Shinpen gessekai shinshi* (New edition: The moony man) (1951 furoku manga), 151; *Shintakarajima* (New Treasure Island) (1947 akahon manga), 129, 131–135, 342n12; shōjo manga and, 225; "Shōri no hi made" (Until the day of victory) (amateur manga), 117; star system of, 334n72; story manga, 150–151, 165, 166, 167, 180, 181–182; students and assistants of, 212, 215; *Swallowing the Earth* (*Chikyū o nomu*) (1968–69 seinen series), 218, 220; Tagawa Suihō and, 83, 91; Tatsumi Yoshihiro and, 165; *Tetsuwan Atomu* (*Astro Boy*) (1952–68 manga series), 1, 186, 190–192, 195, 215; *Tetsuwan Atomu* (*Astro Boy*) (1963–66 anime series), 186, 190–192, 215; Tōei and, 190–191; Tokiwa-sō group, 154–155; during WWII, 117, 128, 170
Tezuka Osamu Cultural Award's Special Prize, 298
Thailand, 269, 315, 343n30, 372n17
three-panel horizontal manga style, 72, 78, 134, 135
Tintin (character), 67, 312
toba-e (cartoons), 35
Toba-e (periodical), 36
Tōbaé (periodical), 24, 374
Tōei Animation: Ishinomori Shōtarō and, 215; Tezuka Osamu and, 186, 190–191; Tsurita Kuniko and, 199
Tōfūjin (Kabashima Katsuichi), 39
Togetsu Shobō, 162, 373
Tōhō Labor Disputes, 152
Tōhoku earthquake (2011), 320
Tokiwa-sō group, 154–156, 171, 207, 216, 231, 234
Tokugawa shogunate, 3, 16, 307, 319
Tokyo Asahi (periodical), 67
Tokyo Maiyū Shinbun (periodical), 39
Tokyo Mangakkai (organization), 36, 44, 52, 97
Tokyo Nichinichi (periodical), 41, 115
Tokyo Olympics (1964), 1, 156, 193
Tokyo Print Workers' Association, 31
Tokyo Puck (periodical), 307; after earthquake, 52; debut of, 44; "Desertion of National Army" in, plate 3, 29; first issue cover, plate 2, 26–27; influence of, 30–32; manga and, 4; naming of, 25–26; publication information, 374; Rakuten and, 14, 53, 307; revival of, 37; speech bubbles, 42; success of, 26–30; sugoroku game boards in, 326n49; Yamamoto Kanae on, 48
Tōma no shinzō (*The Heart of Thomas*) (1974–75 shōnen'ai) (Hagio Moto), 241, 242–243, 248, 263, 279
Ton-chan (manga) (Yazaki Takeko), 142
Toppio (1939–40 manga) (Tagawa Suihō), 119
"Toshio no mita mono" (What Toshio saw) (1921 manga) (Okamoto Ippei and Okamoto Kanoko), 39
The Tramp (film character) (Chaplin), 41, 67–68, 70, 71, 308
Trigun (1995–97 manga), 299
Triple Disaster, 320
Tsuchiya Shinji, 297–298
Tsuge Yoshiharu, 199, 201, 212
Tsurita Kuniko, 199–202, 206, 281

Uchida Roan, 46
Ueda Shinji, 244
Ueda Toshiko: apprenticeship, 130; career of, 63, 118–119; as children's mangaka, 156–157; debut, 118; Fuichin (character), 142, 157; *Fuichin-san,* 156, 217; internship, 123; at NHK, 137; screen tones and, 156; Youth Brigade camp visits, 90

ukiyo-e (woodblock print): defined, 322; during Edo period, 3, 319; as fine art, 322; Hokusai and, 13, 44, 48, 323n1; *manga* (term) usage and, 26; on manga's roots in, 13–14, 15, 20; Rakuten's study of, 24; *Seiyō zasshi* and, 17; Shōsai Ikkei and, 47; style and methods of, 3, 19, 20; use of text on, 47
urbanites, 53, 101, 121, 322
Urusei Yatsura (Those annoying aliens) (1978–87 manga) (Takahashi Rumiko), 281, 282, 283, 291
used bookstores. *See* kashihonya (used bookstores)

video games: in anime media mix, 293–296; narrative structure in, 310; Nintendo, 180–181; otaku of, 321

Wada Shinji, 290
Watanabe Masako, 276
Weekly Manga Sunday. See *Shūkan Manga Sunday* (periodical)
Weekly Manga Times. See *Shūkan Manga Times* (periodical)
Weisenfeld, Gennifer S., 69, 108
Welker, James, 241, 266, 271, 324n6
Wertham, Fredric, 349n63
Wirgman, Charles, 8, 17, 18, 307
Wu, Chinghsin, 8, 54, 330n2

Yamada Mineko, 234
Yamada Murasaki, 202, 206–207, 210, 230, 264, 300–301
Yamagishi Ryōko, 232, 241, 264, 275, 290
Yamaguchi Masao, 71
Yamaguchi Yasuo, 191–192, 289
Yamakawa Sōji, 67
Yamamoto Jun'ya, 235, 239–240, 242
Yamamoto Kanae, 26, 48, 235, 359n75
Yamane Akaoni, 346n110
Yamane Ao'oni, 346n110
Yamato Waki, 232, 233
Yanagawa Shunsan, 17
Yanase Masamu: arrests, 106–107; Comintern and, 338n44; death of, 108; Fūshiga Kenkyūkai (Caricature Research Group), 108–109; Grosz and, 104, 105; Hasegawa Nyozekan and, 95; influence and popularity of, 104; *Kanemochi kyōiku,* plate 8, 94–96, 104; Katō Etsuro and, 113; MAVO movement and, 61–62, 101; political cartoons of, 95, 102*fig.*; proletarian arts movement and, 101–105, 107; in *Senki* (Battle flag), 105*fig.*; Shimokawa and, 101–102, 338n37; total book design philosophy of, 334n61
yaoi manga, 256, 270, 272, 295, 321. *See also* shōnen'ai manga
Yashiro Masako, 206, 241
Yashiro Sei'ichi, 71
Yazaki Shigeshi, 98, 118, 139, 142
Yazaki Takeko, 63, 97, 98, 118, 139, 142, 157, 224
Yokohama: in bakumatsu period, 16; *Box of Curios,* 373; Comiket 18 in, 262; foreigners residing in, 16–17; Great Kanto Earthquake and, 40; *The Japan Punch,* 8, 17–18; Rakuten in, 2, 24
Yokoi Fukutarō, 119, 136
Yokoo Tadanori, 148
Yokoyama Ryūichi, 99, 100, 117–118, 139
Yomiuri Shinbun (periodical), 14, 142, 159*fig.*, 173
Yomiuri Shōnen Shōjo Shinbun (periodical), 95
Yomiuri Sunday Manga (periodical), 94–96, 374
Yōnen Gahō (periodical), 374
Yōnen Kurabu/Yōnen Club (Children's club) (periodical), 64–65, 73, 76, 77, 79, 80, 84, 85, 91*fig.*, 374
yōnen manga, 320–321
Yōnen no Kuni (periodical), 374
Yōnen no Tomo (periodical), 374
Yōnen Sekai (periodical), 374
Yōnen Zasshi (periodical), 326n57, 374
Yonezawa Yoshihiro, 1, 7, 147, 148, 154, 179, 192, 194, 207, 210, 232, 258, 259, 260, 262, 285–286, 288, 290, 304
Young Jump. See *Shūkan Young Jump* (periodical)
Yukaina tankentai (Delightful expedition force) (Ōshiro Noboru), 82
Yūrakusha (publisher), 25, 374

yuri or GL ("girls' love") manga: defined, 322; origins of, 241; *Playboy Comics Crazy* manga and, 360n98; "Shiroi heya no futari" (The couple of the white room) (1971 manga) (Yamagishi Ryōko), 241. *See also* yaoi manga
"Yuri tsūshin" (Lily communication) column, 271

zasshi (magazine): exposure to new manga via, 362n4; *Manga zasshi hakubutsukan* series, 318; *Seiyō zasshi* (Occidental magazine), 17; term usage, 17; *Tokyo Puck* as kaiga zasshi (illustrated magazine), 26–27; *Yakyū Zasshi* (Baseball magazine), 147; *Yōnen Zasshi,* 326n57, 374. *See also* dōjin zasshi (dōjin magazines)
Zenkoku Kashihon Shinbun (periodical), 162, 175
zines: anime zines, 297; BL zines, 291; as dōjinshi, 4, 206, 211; lolicon dōjinshi, 291; manga fans' perspectives and, 6; manga zines, 206; oil embargo and, 254; term usage, xvi. *See also* dōjinshi (amateur publications); zasshi (magazine)

Founded in 1893,
UNIVERSITY OF CALIFORNIA PRESS
publishes bold, progressive books and journals on topics in the arts, humanities, social sciences, and natural sciences—with a focus on social justice issues—that inspire thought and action among readers worldwide.

The UC PRESS FOUNDATION
raises funds to uphold the press's vital role as an independent, nonprofit publisher, and receives philanthropic support from a wide range of individuals and institutions—and from committed readers like you. To learn more, visit ucpress.edu/supportus.